# Social choice, welfare, and ethics

This book presents an overview of recent developments in social choice theory and welfare economics, drawn from the proceedings of the eighth conference in the *International Symposia in Economic Theory and Econometrics,* under the general editorship of William Barnett.

The volume is divided into six parts, each exploring broad themes in social choice theory and welfare economics. The first is an overview of the short – yet intense – period of the subject's historical development. The second is a discussion of the ethical aspects of social choice, encompassing such issues as equal opportunity, individual rights, and population monotonicity. Parts three and four are devoted to algebraic and combinatorial aspects of social choice theory, including analyses of Arrow's theorem, consensus functions, and the role of geometry. Part five deals with the application of cooperative game theory to social choice. The final section is devoted to a study of aggregation with risk aversion to current and future variables, and the creation of an intertemporal framework to go beyond the usual static description of income distributions measured over a short period.

The conference from which these papers were drawn was the first conference of the newly organized Social Choice and Welfare Society, and attracted over 200 participants presenting 136 papers. This book collects 17 of the most important papers presented at that conference. The conference was held in Caen, France, on June 9–12, 1992. The Symposia in the series are sponsored by the IC² Institute at the University of Texas at Austin and are cosponsored by the RGK Foundation. This eighth conference was also cosponsored by the French Ministry of Education (now Ministry of the Universities and Research), the University of Caen, A.D.R.E.S., the City of Caen, and C.R.E.M.E.

International Symposia in Economic Theory and Econometrics

Editor
William A. Barnett, *Washington University in St. Louis*


*Other books in the series*

William A. Barnett and A. Ronald Gallant
*New approaches to modeling, specification selection, and econometric inference*

William A. Barnett and Kenneth J. Singleton
*New approaches to monetary economics*

William A. Barnett, Ernst R. Berndt, and Halbert White
*Dynamic econometric modeling*

William A. Barnett, John Geweke, and Karl Shell
*Economic complexity*

William A. Barnett, James Powell, and George E. Tauchen
*Nonparametric and semiparametric methods in econometrics and statistics*

William A. Barnett, Bernard Cornet, Claude D'Aspremont, Jean Gabszewicz, and Andreu Mas-Colell
*Equilibrium theory and applications*

William A. Barnett, Melvin J. Hinich, and Norman J. Schofield
*Political economy: Institutions, competition, and representation*

# Social choice, welfare, and ethics

Proceedings of the Eighth International Symposium
in Economic Theory and Econometrics

Edited by

WILLIAM A. BARNETT
*Washington University in St. Louis*

HERVÉ MOULIN
*Duke University*

MAURICE SALLES
*University of Caen*

NORMAN J. SCHOFIELD
*Washington University in St. Louis*

CAMBRIDGE
UNIVERSITY PRESS

CAMBRIDGE UNIVERSITY PRESS
Cambridge, New York, Melbourne, Madrid, Cape Town, Singapore, São Paulo

Cambridge University Press
The Edinburgh Building, Cambridge CB2 2RU, UK

Published in the United States of America by Cambridge University Press, New York

www.cambridge.org
Information on this title: www.cambridge.org/9780521443401

© Cambridge University Press 1995

First published 1995
This digitally printed first paperback version 2006

A catalogue record for this publication is available from the British Library

Library of Congress Cataloguing in Publication data
International Symposium in Economic Theory and Econometrics
(8th : 1993 : Caen, France)
Social choice, welfare, and ethics : proceedings of the eighth
International Symposium in Economic Theory and Econometrics
/ edited by William A. Barnett . . . [et al.].
p.    cm. – (International symposia in economic theory and
econometrics)
ISBN 0-521-44340-7
1. Social choice – Congresses.   2. Welfare economics – Congresses.
3. Economics – moral and ethical aspects – Congresses.   4. Social
choice – Econometric models – Congresses.   I. Barnett, William A.
II. Title.   III. Series.
HB846.8.I57   1993
302'.13 – dc20                                                     94-25322
                                                                          CIP

ISBN-13  978-0-521-44340-1 hardback
ISBN-10  0-521-44340-7 hardback

ISBN-13  978-0-521-02621-5 paperback
ISBN-10  0-521-02621-0 paperback

# Contents

v

# Series editor's preface

The contents of this volume comprise the proceedings of the conference, "Social Choice and Welfare," held at the University of Caen in Caen, France, on June 9-12, 1992. The conference was the first of the recently organized Social Choice and Welfare Society and attracted over 200 participants presenting 136 papers. This proceedings volume includes 17 of the most important papers presented at that conference. An introductory overview of the papers in the volume was contributed by Hervé Moulin, Maurice Salles, and Norman Schofield, who were among the four co-editors of the volume. Their introductory overview appears as the first paper in the volume, and includes their perspective regarding the conference papers and symposium topics as well as the history that led up to the conference and to the organization of the Social Choice and Welfare Society.

The volume is divided into six parts, corresponding to the six major topics of the conference. Part I of the volume consists of one paper dealing with historical aspects of social choice. Part II's topic is ethical aspects of social choice. Part III consists of two papers on algebraic and combinatorial aspects of social choice, while Part IV deals with geometric aspects of social choice. Part V brings together social choice and cooperative game theory, and Part VI contains two papers on other applications. An appendix lists the complete program of the conference, including the papers that are not included in this proceedings volume.

The conference that produced this proceedings volume is the eighth in a conference series entitled *International Symposia in Economic Theory and Econometrics*. The proceedings series is under the general editorship of William Barnett. Individual volumes in the series generally have co-editors, and the series has a permanent Board of Advisory Editors. The symposia in the series are sponsored by the $IC^2$ Institute at the University of Texas at Austin and are cosponsored by the RGK Foundation.[1]

[1] $IC^2$ stands for Innovation, Creativity, and Capital.

viii    **Preface**

The editors thankfully acknowledge the financial support of the IC$^2$ Institute at the University of Texas in Austin, the RGK Foundation, the French Ministry of Education (now Ministry of the Universities and Research), the University of Caen, A.D.R.E.S., the City of Caen, and C.R.E.M.E. I especially wish to thank Hervé Moulin, who pulled more than his fair share of the load in organizing the conference and editing the proceedings volume.

The first conference in this Cambridge series was co-organized by William Barnett and Ronald Gallant, who also co-edited the proceedings volume. That volume has appeared as the volume 30, October/November 1985 edition of the *Journal of Econometrics* and has been reprinted as a volume in this Cambridge University Press monograph series. The topic was "New Approaches to Modeling, Specification Selection, and Econometric Inference."

Beginning with the second symposium in the series, the proceedings of the symposia appear exclusively as volumes in this Cambridge University Press monograph series. The co-organizers of the second symposium and co-editors of its proceedings volume were William Barnett and Kenneth Singleton. The topic was "New Approaches to Monetary Economics." The co-organizers of the third symposium, "Dynamic Econometric Modeling," were William Barnett and Ernst Berndt; the co-editors of that proceedings volume were William Barnett, Ernst Berndt, and Halbert White. The co-organizers of the fourth symposium and co-editors of its proceedings volume, "Economic Complexity: Chaos, Sunspots, Bubbles, and Nonlinearity," were William Barnett, John Geweke, and Karl Shell. The co-organizers of the fifth symposium and co-editors of its proceedings volume, "Nonparametric and Semiparametric Methods in Econometrics and Statistics," were William Barnett, James Powell, and George Tauchen. The co-organizers and proceedings co-editors of the sixth symposium, "Equilibrium Theory and Applications," were William Barnett, Bernard Cornet, Claude d'Aspremont, Jean Gabszewicz, and Andreu Mas-Colell. The co-organizers of the seventh symposium, "Political Economy: Institutions, Competition, and Representation," were William Barnett, Melvin Hinich, Douglass North, Howard Rosenthal, and Norman Schofield. The co-editors of that proceedings volume were William Barnett, Melvin Hinich, and Norman Schofield.

The eighth symposium, which produced this proceedings volume, was part of a large-scale conference on "Social Choice, Welfare, and Ethics." That conference was held in Caen, France, on June 9–12, 1993. The organizers of the conference were Maurice Salles and Hervé Moulin, and the co-editors of the proceedings volume are William Barnett, Hervé Moulin, Maurice Salles, and Norman Schofield.

The ninth volume in the series will be the joint proceedings of a conference in Florence, Italy, on nonlinear dynamics in economics and the invited sessions of the annual meetings of the American Statistical Association in San Francisco. The co-editors will be William Barnett, Mark Salmon, and Alan Kirman.

The intention of the volumes in the proceedings series is to provide refereed journal-quality collections of research papers of unusual importance in areas of currently highly visible activity within the economics profession. Because of the refereeing requirements associated with the editing of the proceedings, the volumes in the series will not necessarily contain all of the papers presented at the corresponding symposia.

William A. Barnett
*Washington University in St. Louis*

# Contributors

Beth Allen
Department of Economics
University of Minnesota
and Research Department
Federal Reserve Bank of Minneapolis

William A. Barnett
Department of Economics
Washington University in St. Louis

Tilman Börgers
Department of Economics
University College London

Ezra Einy
Department of Economics
Ben-Gurion University of the Negev

Marc Fleurbaey
Département des Sciences Economiques
THEMA
Université de Cergy-Pontoise

William V. Gehrlein
Departments of Business
   Administration and Economics
University of Delaware

Peter J. Hammond
Department of Economics
Stanford University

Thierry Karcher
CREME
Université de Rennes I

Michel Le Breton
GREQAM
Institut Universitaire de France

Bruno Leclerc
Centre d'Analyse et de
   Mathématique Sociales
Université Paris I

Richard D. McKelvey
Division of Humanities and
   Social Sciences
California Institute of Technology

Iain McLean
Nuffield College
Oxford

Bernard Monjardet
Centre d'Analyse et de
   Mathématique Sociales
Université Paris I

Hervé Moulin
Department of Economics
Duke University

Patrick Moyes
CNRS and LARE
Université de Bordeaux I

Thomas R. Palfrey
Division of Humanities and
   Social Sciences
California Institute of Technology

Bezalel Peleg
Department of Mathematics
The Hebrew University

James Redekop
Department of Economics
University of Waterloo

Donald G. Saari
Departments of Mathematics
    and Economics
Northwestern University

Maurice Salles
CREMERC
Université de Caen

Norman J. Schofield
Center in Political Economy
Washington University in St. Louis

William Thomson
Department of Economics
University of Rochester

Craig A. Tovey
School of ISyE and
College of Computing
Georgia Institute of Technology

Alain Trannoy
THEMA
Université de Cergy-Pontoise

Shlomo Weber
Department of Economics
Southern Methodist University

# Introduction and overview

*Hervé Moulin, Maurice Salles, & Norman J. Schofield*

## 1    History of the Social Choice and Welfare Society

A conference on Social Choice and Welfare Economics was organized in Caen in 1980. From this first conference, it was already obvious that a specific feature of our subject, broadly conceived, was its interdisciplinarity. Its domain intersects economics of course, but also mathematics (not only discrete mathematics), political science, philosophy, management science, psychology, sociology, . . . . This observation is confirmed by the fact that the recent contributors to the subject are from these diverse disciplines.

The proceedings of the Caen conference, edited by Prasanta K. Pattanaik and Maurice Salles, eventually appeared under the title *Social Choice and Welfare* in 1983. This same year, the decision to publish a new journal with this title was taken. The first volume appeared in 1984. A number of conferences were organized after 1984, in particular in Brussels and Namur, in Marseilles (Luminy), and in Valencia – the last one specifically based upon the editorship of the journal, thanks to Salvador Barbera and the local organizer Antonio Villar. The idea of creating a scientific association was proposed at the Valencia conference, but several years elapsed before the project could be finalized in 1992. The first president (1992–93) of the new "Society for Social Choice and Welfare" was Kenneth J. Arrow and the second (1994–95) is Armatya K. Sen, two of the founding fathers of the modern rebirth of social choice. The objectives of the Society are essentially the sponsorship of the journal and the organization of meetings (open to everyone) and conferences. The meetings of the Society are in principle organized every other year.

## 2    The Caen conference, June 1992

The first meeting of the Social Choice and Welfare Society gathered over 200 participants presenting 136 papers. The complete program is detailed in the Appendix to this volume.

1

The papers were distributed along four broad themes. The first one was equity. This included two sessions on equality of opportunity and on equity as no-envy (see Appendix), two sessions on fair division, and three sessions on axiomatic cost and surplus sharing. Three more sessions discussed inequality measures and other indicators such as poverty indices and indices of social mobility.

The second theme was individual and collective choice. Two sessions explored the foundations of individual choice, and as many as ten sessions addressed collective choice. Half of these discussed the familiar normative issues: aggregation of preferences (two sessions), choice function and tournaments (one session), information pooling (one session), and the impact of individual rights on aggregation methods (one session). The other half was devoted to strategic implementation theory: two sessions on strategy-proofness, and three more on implementation under complete or incomplete information.

The third theme was political economy. In particular, topics included the normative properties of voting systems (two sessions), the strategic behavior of political actors in the geometric model of voting and other games (two sessions), some ethical aspects of the law (one session), and the provision of public goods (two sessions).

The fourth and last theme – markets and games – included one session on market equilibrium, two sessions on bargaining and other noncooperative games, two sessions on strategic cooperative games, one session on evolutionary models of cooperation, and one session on experiments.

## 3     Overview of this volume

This volume includes a selection of papers given during the Caen conference. All papers have been refereed according to the usual standards of scientific periodicals. We tried to classify the contributions according to some common feature. Though there is considerable overlap in the different groups, we classified the papers as follows: one paper concerns the history of the subject; three discuss the most fundamental ethical aspects; two have an obvious algebraic, order-theoretic, and combinatorial flavor; four consider some geometric structure, in particular on the set of alternatives; five papers linked in a very natural way social choice and cooperative games; and finally two were more concerned with applications. At this stage, we can already stress the importance of geometry and of cooperative games.

The unique historical paper by Iain McLean, the main contributor in this domain, covers a rather short period (less than 20 years) but an intense one during which several fundamental works were published. These works include Borda's and Condorcet's publications, in addition to the contributions of less well-known authors such as Lhuillier and Morales. McLean discusses these works in the light of the current literature of social choice.

The second part of this volume includes papers in which the ethical aspects of social choice are particularly developed. Marc Fleurbaey's contribution considers equal opportunity. In contrast with the traditional models of fair division, the existence of unequal claims on behalf of individuals – due to advantages or handicaps that are difficult to remove – are taken into account. The author's objective is to clarify the logical implications of any attempt at equalizing the opportunities made available to individuals. He shows that equal opportunity exists, but only under rather strong assumptions. Weakening the notion of equal opportunity itself unfortunately implies that some nice features of the equalizing procedure must be abandoned.

Peter Hammond reconsiders individual rights à la Sen and group rights à la Batra and Pattanaik. Gibbard provided an example showing the impossibility of granting rights to two different individuals over two binary issues each. Hammond argues that this kind of situation can be excluded by requiring individuals' preferences to be privately oriented. Mathematically, individual rights can generally be respected if and (except in some rare cases) only if they apply to independent components of a Cartesian product space of social states and each individual is indifferent to how others exercise their rights. Group rights could also be respected if they applied to the independent components of the different individuals in the group. Hammond also considers "libertarian" game forms in which individuals or groups have the power to determine any private issue over which they should have rights. In some sense, he shows that the game-form approach is not more general than the classical Sen approach: only exceptionally is it possible to respect all rights.

Population monotonicity is a requirement for solutions of decision rules which, in essence, states that the addition of individuals should affect the initially present individuals in the same direction. After presenting an abstract version of the principle, William Thomson studies a model of cost allocation and the classical problem of allocating a fixed bundle of divisible goods among agents with continuous, convex, and monotonic preferences. He also tackles economies with public goods and the case of single-peaked preferences. This paper surveys important contributions (many by Thomson and his associates), some of which are heretofore unpublished.

Part III of this book is devoted to some algebraic and combinatorial aspects of social choice theory. It was difficult to make a classification according to mathematical structures, and it may seem odd to use a mixture of philosophical, mathematical, or other criteria. As mentioned previously, however, the papers were classified according to their common features, not to some a priori design.

Arrow's theorem can be mathematically viewed as an algebraic (or, more precisely, an order-theoretic) result. The classical proof makes implicit use of three complete preorders over a three-alternative subset of the set of alternatives, which are similar to the rankings that give rise to the Condorcet paradox. A number of studies have calculated the frequency of this paradox under different assumptions, or the frequency of the existence of a Condorcet winner (Condorcet efficiency). The most classical of these assumptions is the so-called impartial culture assumption, under which every individual ranking is equally likely. William Gehrlein's paper is concerned with another assumption – namely, an assumption of social homogeneity, or the tendency of voters' preferences to be similar. By using Polya–Eggenberger probability models to describe distributions of the number of individuals having a specific ranking of alternatives, he shows that even relatively modest levels of social homogeneity produce high levels of Condorcet efficiency for almost all voting rules.

Bruno Leclerc and Bernard Monjardet analyze aggregation functions (which they call *consensus* functions) defined on the Cartesian product of a lattice, with values in this same lattice. They obtain several axiomatic characterizations of all consensus functions associated with simple games, and of subclasses of these functions such as oligarchic aggregation functions. They extend their results to lattices of valued (fuzzy) objects. An important merit of their paper is in showing how the use of lattice-theoretic structures unifies several approaches to the aggregation problem which apparently were quite different.

That geometry would pervade social choice theory became clear at the beginning of the 1980s, with the works of (among others) Chichilnisky, Heal, Greenberg, McKelvey, and Schofield building on the foundational contributions of Downs, Plott, and Kramer. It seems natural for economists (and political scientists) to assume the space of alternatives to be some subset of Euclidean space. What has become the standard framework of microeconomic theory – the Arrow–Debreu model of general equilibrium – describes the world of goods over which individual consumers have preferences to be a part of Euclidean space (or sometimes a more general space, either metric or topological, or a topological vector space) possibly endowed with some further structures. For public-goods economies, the sets of alternatives over which individual and social preferences are defined are identical. In the Arrow–Debreu framework, individual preferences in private-goods economies are defined over a subset of the Euclidean space of (say) $k$ dimensions if there are $k$ goods, whereas the normative concept of Pareto optimality is defined over the $n$-fold Cartesian product of Euclidean space if there are $n$ individuals. (Note that we are interested in choosing the "best" Walras allocations; i.e., the aggregation function must give rise to a set of best equilibrium allocations, and so goes beyond the theorems of classical welfare economics. In this sense social choice theory is the last part of general equilibrium theory, viz., the theory from which the "best" – according to normative criteria – Walras allocations could be selected.)

James Redekop's paper is a survey of the author's results heretofore obtained. Redekop and other contributors to Arrovian aggregation problems (within the usual economic domains) more or less restrict individual preferences according to the usual assumptions of microeconomic theory: we can impose monotonicity, convexity, homotheticity, . . . conditions over these preferences. In this case, do impossibility theorems remain true? The unfortunate answer given by Redekop is that, in economic environments, attempts to construct social welfare functions should proceed from the relaxation of some Arrow axiom other than the unrestricted domain condition.

Donald Saari's "geometry" is of a different kind; it can arise both from positional voting rules with so-called voting vectors and from the fraction of all voters having a specific ranking of the finite set of alternatives. The necessity of reasoning with rational numbers does not prevent us from using (sometimes quite advanced) mathematical techniques borrowed from analysis on manifolds, thanks to the denseness of the rational numbers in the set of real numbers. Saari demonstrates why inner consistency conditions, in particular the independence of irrelevant alternatives, lead to impossibility conclusions. He shows that independence (and other conditions) force the procedure to ignore the full dimensional aspects of some profiles of individual preferences: what arises, then, is a severe dimensional incompatibility between what the procedure can recognize and what the profile possesses. We must stress that Saari's contribution in this book is not too technical and can be read by anyone with a moderate knowledge of linear algebra.

In Norman Schofield's contribution, the set of alternatives is a smooth manifold of dimension $w$, a set that locally looks like the Euclidean space from a topological viewpoint and has a differential structure. First he reviews previous results showing that, depending on the dimension of the manifold, the choice of a voting rule is generically (i.e. almost always from a topological viewpoint, viz., for all open dense sets of profiles of smooth utility functions on the smooth manifold) empty and voting cycles are generically dense. Schofield then introduces a new solution concept called the "heart" (which will be difficult to translate in French, since *coeur* is already the French word for core and *noyau* is the French word for kernel or, sometimes, for core!). The heart imposes a local version of efficiency on the behavior of coalitions. Cycles may still exist but are restricted to the set of Pareto optimal alternatives. The heart may be non-empty under specific assumptions over the set of alternatives (in particular, if the smooth manifold is a compact, convex subspace of a finite-dimensional topological vector space). Other properties of the heart are described using the terminology of category theory (as used in algebraic topology). The author shows that the heart is an equilibrium notion that in some sense solves the social choice problem for an appropriate domain of preferences, in particular when preferences are Euclidean. Schofield considers also the heart in the case of an infinite set of voters, and outlines how the concept can be used in multiparty competition models.

Kramer showed that repeated proposals by competing vote-maximizing parties produce, for the Euclidean spatial models, sequences converging to a solution set called the "minmax" set. In his contribution, Craig Tovey studies the same kind of question for another solution set, the $\epsilon$-core. A point is in the $\epsilon$-core if no other point is more than $\epsilon$ closer to a simple majority of voters' ideal points. The real number $\epsilon$ is compared with the radius of the yolk. If $\epsilon$ is greater than the yolk radius, then the $\epsilon$-core is non-empty. If $\epsilon$ exceeds twice this radius, then there are no global intransitivities and a Condorcet voting process will reach the $\epsilon$-core in a number of steps which is a function of $\epsilon$, the yolk radius, and the distance from the starting point to the yolk center (for any number of voters and any finite dimension of the considered Euclidean space).

The links between social choice theory and game theory were already clear in the beginning of the 1950s. In his famous monograph, "Social Choice and Individual Values," Kenneth Arrow devoted several remarks to these links. The further development of these connections is exemplified by the tremendous number of contributions to the implementation literature following publications of (among others) Gibbard, Satterthwaite, Groves, et cetera. It is sometimes difficult to separate social choice theory from cooperative game theory, since a number of solution concepts (core, Shapley value, stability set, Gillies set, uncovered set) and basic structures (simple or voting games, Nakamura number, effectivity functions) belong to the two (?) subjects. This fundamental unity can be observed in recent books by Bezalel Peleg and Hervé Moulin in the Econometric Society monograph series. May we add that the death of cooperative game theory has perhaps been prematurely announced. (Some otherwise truly excellent books are entitled "Game Theory" without a single word on the concept of the core in cooperative game theory!)

In her contribution, Beth Allen deals precisely with the interface between cooperative and noncooperative game theory. She studies market games in which players may behave strategically within coalitions, where the information of coalitions need not be exogenously given. Modeling the extent of information sharing as the agents' strategic choice leads her to the definition of an underlying cooperative game with asymmetric information in terms of the payoffs that can be achieved via incentive compatible net trades. The incentive compatibility constraints can give rise to nonconvexities and to games that are not balanced; we can then obtain games with empty cores. Randomization can restore the existence of core allocations. If the concept of core is replaced by the concept of approximate core, it is proved that large replica economies with incentives always have a solution, and that the set of solutions contains allocations satisfying the equal treatment property.

Tilman Börgers reconsiders the implementation of social choice functions in strategies that are not strongly dominated or that survive iterated deletion of strongly dominated strategies. He assumes that the definition set of the choice functions includes unanimous profiles. He then shows that, in both types of implementation, only dictatorial social choice functions can be implemented. He uses a concept of strong dominance rather than the more common weak dominance. With strong dominance, individual $i$'s strategy $\bar{s}_i$ dominates $s_i$ if individual $i$ (strictly) prefers the outcome obtained from using strategy $\bar{s}_i$ to the outcome obtained from using strategy $s_i$, given that the other individuals' strategies are any other strategies (though of course each individual has the same strategy whether he uses $\bar{s}_i$ or $s_i$). Under weak dominance, $\bar{s}_i$ dominates $s_i$ if the outcome is at least as good for any strategies adopted by the other individuals and better for some of them. The use of strong dominance is justified and the results are compared with those based on weak dominance.

Ezra Einy and Bezalel Peleg offer a new definition of coalition-proof correlated equilibria. Deviations of coalitions are introduced only after their members are informed of the actions they should follow. This leads to "reduced games" with incomplete information. The authors define coalition-proof communication equilibria and informational efficiency. Coalition-proof communication equilibria are characterized for two-person Bayesian games. Analyzing the voting paradox, they prove that, for every choice of cardinal utilities for three players, the resulting game in strategic form has a coalition-proof communication equilibrium. Communication equilibria are then compared with coalition-proof Nash equilibria.

Michel Le Breton and Shlomo Weber consider an extension of a result (obtained by Greenberg and Weber) when the set of alternatives is a compact subset of the real line to the case where it is a multidimensional

8    Hervé Moulin, Maurice Salles, & Norman J. Schofield

Euclidean space. Greenberg and Weber introduced a new equilibrium concept in which each individual is free to join the coalition that adopts the alternative he likes best among those offered by the existing coalitions and in which each coalition is free to form. Le Breton and Weber impose specific requirements in the multidimensional setting. First, all individuals must have Euclidean preferences. Second, they consider models that can be represented by simple games. In this kind of approach, a society is *stable* if there is a partition of the set of individuals into two-person coalitions satisfying both free mobility and free entry. They define total stability and provide its characterization based upon distribution of individuals' bliss points.

Richard McKelvey and Thomas Palfrey investigate experimentally a two-person infinitely repeated game of incomplete information. Each player has private information on his type before the first game is played, and this is followed by an infinite sequence of identical simultaneous-move stage games. Payoffs in the game are given by the discounted sum of payoffs in all the stage games. In the stage game, each player chooses to give in or to hold out. Players privately know the cost of giving in, and each player receives a fixed benefit whenever at least one player gives in. The authors consider two questions: Does subject behavior approximate belief stationary equilibria? Is there evidence that subjects will converge to an equilibrium of the correct state? The authors conclude that subjects do not adopt symmetric belief stationary strategies for the holdout game. However, the behavior of experienced players is closer to the predicted symmetric belief stationary equilibria; that is, experience leads to more accurate inferences by subjects about the type of opponents they are facing.

The last part includes two papers. William Barnett studies aggregation with risk aversion to current and future variables. Aggregation is here understood to be aggregation over goods. The theory of aggregation over goods has been restricted heretofore mainly to the case of perfect certainty. The author derives the exact aggregation-theoretic monetary aggregate when consumers and firms are in a risky environment, and proves a theorem showing the potential usefulness of the aggregate in modeling and in policy. He identifies and imposes the conditions necessary for the existence of an exact monetary quantity aggregate to exist, and proves in an optimal control–theoretic framework that the resulting exact monetary aggregate can be used as an intermediate target of policy by the central bank. This result follows because the level of the exact theoretical monetary aggregate can be treated as a state variable in the solution of the consumer's or firm's intertemporal optimization problem. Barnett demonstrates that even if uncertainty exists regarding future prices and interest rates, the Divisia index's tracking ability – as a nonparametric approximation to the exact theoretical monetary aggregate – is not compromised by risk aversion, so long as the risk is relative only to the future stochastic process of interest rates or prices. However, he finds that the exact tracking theorem on the Divisia line integral does not apply when there is risk regarding current interest rates or prices. The degree to which the tracking ability of the Divisia index is degraded by contemporaneous risk is not currently known. Barnett also produces theoretical results regarding the connection between the Divisia monetary aggregate and the CE ("currency equivalent") index proposed by Rotemberg, Driscoll, and Poterba (1991).

Thierry Karcher, Patrick Moyes, and Alain Trannoy wish to go beyond the usual static description of income distributions measured over a short period, and do so by considering an intertemporal framework. Within this framework they retain stochastic dominance criteria by concentrating on a utilitarian social welfare function for which social welfare is the discounted sum of the expected utilities of income in each period. The authors consider three classes of utility functions and four classes of discount functions, and analyze the twelve possible stochastic dominance orderings that can then be obtained.

### REFERENCE

Rotemberg, Julio J., John C. Driscoll, and James M. Poterba (1991), "Money, Output, and Prices: Evidence from a New Monetary Aggregate," working paper, Department of Economics, Massachusetts Institute of Technology, Cambridge.

PART I

# Historical aspects of social choice

CHAPTER 1

# The first golden age of social choice, 1784–1803

*Iain McLean*

## 1    Introduction

It is well known that some of the post-1951 themes in social choice were anticipated by isolated and misunderstood scholars, notably Condorcet and Borda in the late eighteenth century and Nanson and Dodgson (Lewis Carroll) in the late nineteenth. Elsewhere (McLean and London 1990) we have shown that there was an earlier anticipation: Ramon Lull (c. 1235–1315) proposed the Condorcet procedure of pairwise comparison and what may be either the Borda or the Copeland aggregation procedure; Nicolas Cusanus (c. 1401–64) proposed the Borda count and defended it on the grounds that it took the fullest possible account of voters' preference orderings. This chapter attempts a survey of the work of Borda, Condorcet, and their contemporaries, with the aim of showing that this corpus was considerably more comprehensive than is generally realized in the English-speaking world; that it uses both the major (axiomatic) and the minor (probability calculus) modes of reasoning in use today; and that it deals with many of the same issues as the modern literature. It discusses cycles and what to do about them; the probability of intransitive social choice; grounds for choosing between the Borda winner and the Condorcet winner, where they differ; and manipulability. The writers of the "golden age" were all involved in devising voting rules for scientific academies or national assemblies, or both. In their writings, they propose procedures for real elections as well as speculating about the properties of ideal systems.

The works discussed in this chapter are listed in Table 1.

## 2    Borda and Condorcet's *Essai* of 1785

Borda's paper proposing the rank-order count – now always called the Borda method, although perhaps it should be called the Cusanus method –

This paper is based on research funded by the Nuffield Foundation.

Table 1. *Principal works*

| Work # | Author | Date | Title | Original-language version | English version |
|---|---|---|---|---|---|
| 1 | Borda, J-C de | 1784 | On Ballot Votes | | Grazia 1953; Sommerlad and McLean 1989 |
| 2 | [Condorcet, Marquis de] | 1784 | [Commentary on #1] | | Sommerlad and McLean 1989 |
| 3 | Condorcet | 1785 | Essay on the application of analysis . . . | Condorcet 1972 | Urken et al. forthcoming; Sommerlad and McLean 1989 |
| 4 | Condorcet | 1788 | Letters from a Freeman of New Haven to a Citizen of Virginia | Bernon 1986 | Sommerlad and McLean 1991 |
| 5 | Condorcet | 1788 | Essay on . . . Provincial Assemblies | Bernon 1986 | Sommerlad and McLean 1989 |
| 6 | Condorcet | 1789 | On the form of elections | Bernon 1986 | Sommerlad and McLean 1989 |
| 7 | Condorcet | 1793 | Survey of the principles underlying the draft Constitution | Arago and O'Connor 1847, vol. XII | Sommerlad and McLean 1989 |
| 8 | Condorcet | 1793/4 | On elections | Part Bernon 1986; part Crépel 1990 | Sommerlad and McLean 1989 |
| 9 | Lhuilier, S. | 1794 | An examination of the election method proposed in . . . France in 1793 . . . | Lhuilier 1976 | (Part) Sommerlad and McLean 1989 |
| 10 | Morales, J. I. | 1797 | Mathematical memoir on the calculation of opinion in elections | | McLean and Urken 1995 |
| 11 | Daunou, P. C. F. | 1803 | On elections by ballot | | Sommerlad and McLean 1991 |

*Note:* Where "Original-language version" is blank, the work has not re-appeared since its original printing.

was delivered orally to the French Academy of Science in 1770. The occasion was one of the Academy's periodic bouts of introspection and infighting over election procedures, which were its lifeblood. Elections reflected the tension between the Academy's wish to be a self-governing and self-reproducing intellectual elite and the wish of the King or the government to advance their nominees (Hahn 1971). The Academy commissioned, as was its normal practice, a report on Borda's paper, but none appears to have been made. Shortly afterward, on 30 June 1770, an election took place "selon la forme ordinaire,"[1] a formula which suggests that Borda's method was considered but rejected.

Borda was, in Condorcet's contemptuous description,

what they call "a good Academician", because he talks in Academy meetings, and likes nothing better than to waste his time drawing up prospectuses, examining machines etc, and especially because, realising he was eclipsed by other mathematicians, he abandoned mathematics for petty experiments (*la physicaille*). . . . Some of his papers display some talent, although nothing follows from them and nobody has ever spoken of them or ever will. (letter to Turgot 1775, in Henry 1883, pp. 214–15)

This reflects the contempt of the theoretical mathematician for the practical engineer. In 1767 Borda had conducted experiments on fluid resistance and had found that the formulas of Newton, Euler, and Johan Bernoulli all failed to match the results he obtained, so he derived a formula from his results – not a procedure calculated to impress Condorcet. Borda entered the Academy in 1756 and progressed up its grades to become a *pensionnaire* in the mathematics section in 1775. His work on ballistics drew him to the attention of Louis XV, who chose him to improve the scientific competence of the Navy. This took him away from Paris for long periods, including a period of service as a naval captain in the West Indies during the American War of Independence. He was captured by the English in 1782, and returned to France on parole, where he returned to his measurements; he "worked much and published little." In 1784 he was appointed principal of the royal School for [military] Engineers. A letter to the king urging his appointment describes him as "a mathematician who is both profound in theory and well versed in naval construction, who has learnt to apply scientific practice at sea." He kept his head down during the Revolution, which (unlike Condorcet) he survived. An orbituarist suggests that he tried unsuccessfully to save Condorcet's life during the Terror of 1793–94, but succeeded only in antagonizing the ruling Jacobins, who suppressed some of his work in return. The personnel records of his service in the navy include a letter from him expressing his "entire devotion to my country and my King" in March 1792, followed quickly by a series of payslips from the "French Republic, one and indivisible" from September

[1] This and (unless otherwise noted) all other references to the *procès-verbaux* of the Academy are due to Pierre Crépel, from a presentation made to the REHSEIS Seminar, Paris, March 1992.

1792 on. At the height of the Terror he was dismissed, but in April 1795 he was reinstated as principal and his arrears of salary paid. He died still in office.[2]

Borda probably played little or no role in having his 1770 paper published. Condorcet mentions it in the *Essai* of 1785, stating that he had heard of it orally but that it was not published until after the *Essai* was in press (*Essai*, Discours préliminaire, p. clxxix). This is misleading because it fails to reveal that it was Condorcet himself who published it. Condorcet had started thinking about applying probability theory to the evaluation of evidence in 1782 when, as secretary to the Academy of Sciences, he had to write the scientific obituary of Daniel Bernoulli (partly translated in Sommerlad and McLean 1989). This drew him to read and criticize Bernoulli's work on social applications of probability, and seems to have been the seed from which the vast *Essai* arose within three years. On 14 July 1784 Condorcet presented the *Essai* to the Academy, which appointed a committee that reported favorably on it on 17 July (! The *Essai* is 500 pages long). On 21 July a paper by Borda "on the probability of elections" [*sic*] was read to the Academy. It is not known whether this was the same as his paper of 1770. However, Condorcet immediately added Borda's paper to the contents of the Proceedings (*Histoire* and *Mémoires,* separately paginated but produced together) of the Academy for 178*1,* which he was then seeing through the press, with a commentary by himself. This gave the impression, intentionally or not, that Borda's paper was written in 1781, which has misled some modern writers. It implies that Condorcet immediately recognized Borda's method as an important challenge to his own. He remarks (Table 1, #2) that Borda's "observations on the drawbacks of the election method used almost everywhere [viz. plurality rule] are very important and totally original" but does not comment on the merits of the Borda method. In the *Essai* he limits himself to showing that the Borda method does not always choose the Condorcet winner; this follows immediately on a passage that Black (1958, pp. 177–8; cf. Condorcet [1785] 1972, pp. clxxvii–clxxix, 295–6) found impenetrably obscure. We shall argue here that the obscurity is penetrable and the passages were probably linked in Condorcet's mind. By 1788 he was to articulate the differences between his method and Borda's much more clearly.

The main arguments of Borda's paper and of the sections on social choice of Condorcet's *Essai* have been fairly familiar since the 1950s (Grazia 1953; Black 1958); we therefore summarize quickly, pausing on the

[2] The facts on Borda in this paragraph are from various sources collected in his *dossier individuel,* Archives de l'Académie des Sciences, Paris, and his *dossier,* Archives Nationales, Paris, call no. Marine C/7/37.

more recently cleared ground. Borda (Table 1, #1) opens by showing that the plurality winner of a three-candidate election may well be the absolute majority loser: this is implicitly to appeal to the Condorcet criterion that the winner in exhaustive pairwise comparisons ought to be chosen. He goes on to propose the general rank-order count, where each voter awards $a$ points for a last place and $b$ ($> 0$) for each interval above the last place. Ranks are summed, and the resulting vector of collective rankings provides a social ordering and a social choice. Borda uses an argument of equiprobability (or insufficient reason) to insist that $b$ must be the same for each interval and for each voter, referring to the "supposed equality between the voters" (i.e. anonymity, in May's 1952 terminology). He goes on to show that an exhaustive pairwise comparison of the candidates, with the scores for each candidate against the others being aggregated, is identical to a Borda count with $a = 0$ and $b = 1$. This identity is important for our interpretation of Condorcet's hidden reasoning. Borda finishes by establishing the necessary and sufficient condition to guarantee that the majority winner of a multicandidate election is actually the Borda winner. For an $m$-candidate election with $E$ voters, the minimum Borda count $y$ which guarantees that a candidate ranked first by a majority is the Borda winner is

$$y > E \cdot \frac{m-1}{m}.$$

Where the number of candidates equals or exceeds the number of electors ($m \geq E$), this reduces to $y > E - 1$. In other words, only a unanimity rule will guarantee that the majority winner is the Borda winner in elections where every voter is also a candidate. This was to cast an unexpected light on the notorious unanimity rule, the *liberum veto,* of the Polish Diet ("this surprising result justifies the way in which one of the Northern nations elects its kings" - #1; cf. also #2). Borda's reasoning was later to be paralleled independently by Morales (#10).

The main theme of Condorcet's *Essai* of 1785 is as given by its title; it concerns the probability that a majority of the independent observations of a number of imperfectly accurate observers are correct. Condorcet's basic jury theorem establishes that if $h$ observers are in the majority and $k$ are in the minority, the probability $\Pi$ that the majority decision is correct is given by

$$\Pi = \frac{v^{h-k}}{v^{h-k} + e^{h-k}},$$

where $v$ (for *vérité,* assumed $> 0.5$) is the probability that a juror is correct on any one judgment and $e$(*rreur* $= 1 - v$) the probability that this juror is mistaken. This function is increasing in both $v$ and $h-k$. Note that, as $h$ is the number of voters in the majority and $k$ is the number of voters in the minority, $h-k$ is the size of the majority.

We agree with Grofman and Feld (1988) that the jury theorem may be read as an axiomatization of Rousseau's General Will. There are few explicit references to Rousseau in Condorcet's work,[3] but the Rousseauvian phrase *volonté générale* and synonyms occur quite often in Condorcet. In 1785 Condorcet was not yet a democrat; in a letter accompanying a copy of the *Essai* presented to Frederick the Great of Prussia, Condorcet wrote:

the procedures for taking decisions cannot themselves guarantee the fulfilment of the necessary conditions, unless decisions are taken by very enlightened men. Hence we must conclude that the happiness of the people depends more on the enlightenment of their rulers than on the form of their political constitution. (Sommerlad and McLean 1991, p. 24)

No doubt we should expect that a letter to an enlightened despot would praise enlightened despotism, but this and other evidence suggests that until about 1791 Condorcet was more concerned to increase the trustworthiness of decisions by increasing $v$ than by setting a threshold for $h-k$. However, the two are complementary. The first drove Condorcet's work as an educational reformer (he was one of the originators of the French system of national education); the second drove his work on the design of constitutions.

## 3    Condorcet's choice and ordering rules

Black (1958, esp. p. 163) complained that "in the case of elections . . . the phrase 'the probability of the correctness of a voter's opinion' seems to be without definite meaning." Black continues (pp. 163–4): "[Condorcet's] real theory is a system of formal reasoning which is quite independent of the theory of probability. . . . [W]here he does introduce the theory of probability, he explicitly rejects its findings in favour of what he calls 'straightforward reasoning'." Black's first point is certainly correct; the second underestimates the extent to which probability and social choice remained entwined in Condorcet's mind. We cannot say that the social choice arguments are Condorcet's "real theory."

Three writers (Michaud 1985, Young 1988, and Monjardet 1990) have recently reconstructed Condorcet's intended general procedure for deriving

[3] But an interesting early one is in a letter to Turgot of 8 April 1770: "A state is lost, according to Rousseau, as soon as anyone believes that it is clever to be dispensed from obeying the laws" (Henry 1883, p. 8).

a social ordering from a set of individual orderings. The procedure is obscurely stated in the *Essai* (esp. pp. 119–26), and Condorcet's verbal and symbolic presentations do not match. The following paragraphs attempt to reconstruct Condorcet's argument.

Condorcet discovered a problem when he attempted to apply the jury theorem to cases with more than two alternatives. Condorcet requires each voter to rank the options. From the rank ordering, each voter's preferences over each pair of candidates can be inferred. The majority for each individual proposition of the form 'A is better than B' (or simply A > B) is calculated. With the majority size $h - k$ known for each proposition in the "system" of propositions – also called an "opinion" – the probability of the overall system is the product of the probabilities of each component proposition. One of Condorcet's own examples shows why this confronts him with a serious problem.

There are three candidates, A, B, and C, and the electors have ranked them as follows, where the number at the head of each column is the number of electors who have voted for that "system" or "opinion":

| 13 | 10 | 13 | 6 | 18 |
|----|----|----|---|----|
| A | A | B | B | C |
| C | B | C | A | B |
| B | C | A | C | A |

Candidate C is the Condorcet winner: C beats A and B by a margin of 31 to 29 in each case. "The system with plurality support" is CBA, which "embodies a vote in favour of C." Candidate B beats A by 37 to 23, and loses to C by 29 votes to 31. *But Condorcet's probabilistic formula does not necessarily choose C.* The probability that C is the best is the joint probability that 'C is better than B' and 'C is better than A' are true. From the formula

$$\Pi = \frac{v^{h-k}}{v^{h-k} + e^{h-k}}$$

we derive

$$\Pi(C) = \frac{v^2}{v^2 + e^2} \cdot \frac{v^2}{v^2 + e^2} = \frac{v^4}{v^4 + 2v^2 e^2 + e^4} \tag{1}$$

for the probability that C is the best. The probability that B is the best is the joint probability that 'B is better than C' and 'B is better than A' are true. This is given by

$$\Pi(B) = \frac{v^{14}}{v^{14} + e^{14}} \cdot \frac{e^2}{v^2 + e^2} = \frac{v^{14} e^2}{v^{16} + v^{14} e^2 + v^2 e^{14} + e^{16}}. \tag{2}$$

However, for values of $v$ not much greater than 0.5, (2) is greater than (1). Quite generally, as was shown first by Black (1958, pp. 169–71) and more fully by Young (1988, p. 1238), when $v$ is close to 0.5, the most probable candidate is the one who scores the largest total number of votes: in Condorcet's example, B is most probable, with $29 + 37 = 66$ votes as against C's $31 + 31 = 62$. But this is precisely the winner of the Borda count, in Borda's second interpretation, where a candidate's score represents the number of times he beats other candidates. When $v$ is close to 1, the most probable candidate is the one who wins his closest fight with the largest number of votes – in other words the Condorcet winner, if one exists.[4]

At this point Condorcet's argument takes a sharp turn. He points out that "Candidate A clearly does not have the preference" because he is a Condorcet loser. Therefore the choice is only between B and C; as C beats B, it would be perverse to choose B: "it seems that the results dictated by the calculus of probabilities contradict simple reason. . . . As soon as A is excluded, it is natural to prefer C to B" (*Essai,* p. lxv).

This is a momentous move. The case for excluding A is that A should be regarded as irrelevant to the comparison between B and C. So Condorcet's move already implied a principle of independence, nowadays labeled Sen's condition $\gamma$ of expansion consistency (Sen 1982, pp. 171–2). Condorcet's implicit argument is that as B is chosen in the set $\{B, C\}$, B should be preferred to C in the set $\{A, B, C\}$. Faced, as he felt, with a contradiction between the calculus of probabilities and "simple reason," Condorcet chose the latter, even though at the outset (*Essai,* p. ii) he had declared that "[a]lmost everywhere we shall find that our [probabilistic] results correspond to the dictates of the simplest reasoning." Young (1988, p. 1238) suggests that Condorcet "apparently realized" that his argument pointed to the Borda, not the Condorcet, rule for low $v$, and that his abrupt shift arises from his contempt for Borda.

If Condorcet had not made this shift, he would have been unable to deal with the discovery for which he is best known, that of cycles. Whenever there are more than two candidates or options, in Condorcet's language a "system" or "opinion" is made up from each of the pairwise "propositions" it contains. For three candidates, there are thus $2^3 = 8$ systems, disregarding ties. But there are only $3! = 6$ strong orderings of three candidates. Hence two of the eight possible systems are "contradictory." In

---

[4] Readers may be puzzled that Black, Young, and I – expounding on identical passages in Condorcet – each give different values in the equations. The reason is that Black, who uses the same formula as I do, takes the numbers from the equivalent passage in the main *Essai,* where they differ from those in the "Discours préliminaire"; while Young, who uses the same source as I do, uses a different (though algebraically equivalent) version of Condorcet's formula.

general, for $n$ candidates there are $2^{n(n-1)/2}$ systems, of which only $n!$ are noncontradictory. What are we to do if voting reveals a cycle? Condorcet deals first with the three-candidate case:

Now, imagine that the 3 propositions with plurality support form one of the 2 contradictory systems: if there is no need to elect someone immediately, then we should consider that no decision has been reached. If, however, an immediate decision is necessary, then we must take the results of the 2 most probable propositions. (*Essai*, p. lxvii)

"The results of the 2 most probable propositions" is an innocent-looking formula that has caused endless trouble. Condorcet does not mean "choose the candidate whose propositions have the highest combined probability," because that would take him straight back to Borda. Rather, he recommends excluding the candidate with the smallest plurality. While this gives a direct and intuitive resolution of three-candidate cycles, it does neither in the general case. His general ordering rule is given as follows (*Essai*, p. 126):

If, once each voter has given his opinion by indicating the order of merit he attributes to the candidates, we then compare them two by two, for each opinion we shall have $n(n-1)/2$ pairwise comparisons to consider separately. Taking the number of times that each is contained in the opinion of one of the $q$ voters, we shall obtain the number of votes for each proposition.

We shall form an opinion out of the $n(n-1)/2$ winning propositions. If this opinion is one of the $n . n-1 \ldots . 2$ possible ones, then we shall consider the candidate to whom this opinion gives the preference to be elected. If this opinion is one of the $2^{n(n-1)/2} - n . n-1 \ldots . 2$ impossible opinions, then we shall successively exclude from it the propositions with the lowest plurality, and adopt the opinion formed by those that remain.

Young (1988) shows that this can be made coherent by deleting from "then we shall successively" to the end, and substituting "then we shall successively reverse in it the set of propositions with the lowest combined plurality, and adopt the opinion formed by those that remain." This is Condorcet's ordering rule, which selects from the allowable strong orderings the maximum likelihood ordering given a set of paired comparisons that contains at least one cycle. It has been rediscovered many times since (see Michaud 1985 and especially Monjardet 1990) as a method of deriving the median ordering from a set of individual orderings.

Condorcet's *ordering* rule is thus securely re-established. Note, however, these two problems:

(i) if the ordering is to be interpreted in its original jury-theoretic way as "the one with the maximum likelihood of being correct," that likelihood will typically be low if only because the average likelihood of any strong ordering of $n$ objects can only be $1/n!$. This problem does not arise if the Condorcet ordering is simply interpreted as the median ordering. However,

(ii) the Condorcet ordering rule is NP-complete. Bartholdi, Tovey, and Trick (1989, p. 161) say of Lewis Carroll's rule, in words equally applicable to Condorcet's, "We think Lewis Carroll would have appreciated the idea that a candidate's mandate might have expired before it was ever recognised."

Where does this leave Condorcet's *choice* rule? – still ambiguous, because the choice rule consistent with the ordering rule ("select the candidate with the maximum likelihood of being the correct one") is not the same as the choice rule embodying the Condorcet criterion ("select the Condorcet winner if there is one"). We aim to show that Condorcet never resolved the tension between probability and social choice in his writings on elections during the last nine years of his life (Table 1, #4–#8).

## 4     Condorcet and an independence axiom

In both the "Discours préliminaire" of the 1785 *Essai* and the body of the *Essai* itself, Condorcet's demonstration that the Borda rule is not Condorcet efficient follows an extremely obscure passage in which Condorcet argues that, given that a voter has expressed the preferences (in Condorcet's notation) A > B, B > C, and A > C, there is no reason to argue that A > C is "more probable" than the other two opinions (*Essai,* pp. clxxv–clxxvii, 294–5; cf. Black 1958, pp. 177–8). We believe that in these passages, which differ between themselves, Condorcet is groping toward an axiom of independence of irrelevant alternatives, which he connected (although not yet explicitly) with his succeeding criticism of the Borda rule. In the Appendix to his *Essay on ... provincial assemblies* (work #5), Condorcet makes the connection explicit. He repeats from 1785 his example of a case where the Condorcet winner is not the Borda winner, as well as his demonstration that any ranking method must select B (Paul) unless it awarded a higher score for a second place than for a first (see Table 2).

The new argument in 1788 runs thus:

But how is it that Paul is not the clear winner when the only difference between himself and Peter is that Peter got 31 first places and 39 second, while Paul got 39 first and 31 second? Well, out of the 39 voters who put Peter second, 10 preferred him to Paul, whereas only one of the 31 voters who put Paul second preferred him to Peter. The points method confuses votes comparing Peter and Paul with those comparing either Peter or Paul to Jack and uses them to judge the relative merits of Peter and Paul. As long as it relies on irrelevant factors to form its judgements, it is bound to lead to error, and that is the real reason why this

Table 2. *Divergence of the Condorcet and Borda winners: Condorcet's example (1785, 1788)*

|  | Number of voters | | | | | |
|---|---|---|---|---|---|---|
|  | 30 | 1 | 29 | 10 | 10 | 1 |
| Favorite | A | A | B | B | C | C |
| Middle | B | C | A | C | A | B |
| Least-liked | C | B | C | A | B | A |

*Pairwise comparisons*
A > B (41/40)
A > C (60/21)
B > C (69/12)

*Borda count* ($a = 1$, $b = 1$)
A = 182
B = 190
C = 114

*Key:* A = "Peter"; B = "Paul"; C = "Jack".

method is defective for a great many voting patterns, regardless of the particular values assigned to each place. The conventional [plurality] method is flawed because it ignores elements which should be taken into account and the new one [Borda] because it takes into account elements which should be ignored.

This seems a plain statement of Arrow (or perhaps Nash) independence, which goes to the heart of the dispute between the Condorcet and Borda principles – in a way that is choice-theoretic, not probabilistic. As we have seen, when $v$ is not much greater than 0.5, the Borda rule is more likely to select the "correct" winner than is a search for the Condorcet winner, because Paul's total score counts for more than Peter's precarious and unreliable majority over Paul. However, in the 1788 *Essai,* Condorcet uncompromisingly judges other voting procedures by the Condorcet criterion, and boldly states that the Borda method "will always give the wrong result" in cases like that of Table 2.

## 5    Condorcet's practical proposals

Condorcet's work on social choice (1785–94) spans the most active constitution-making era in Western history until then, and the most active ever until 1989. Constitutions for the United States, Poland, and France were written, and Condorcet was connected with all three.

Work #4 is Condorcet's main attempt to influence the ratification of the U.S. Constitution. He believed that bicameralism was inferior to a qualified majority rule. He shared with the American Federalists a belief that a direct democracy would not produce good ("correct") decision making. In some respects his scheme resembled theirs: in particular, all his proposed constitutions for France involved the indirect election of executives, along the lines of the U.S. Constitutional provision for an electoral college. In *The Federalist* #68, Alexander Hamilton justifies the electoral college in Condorcetian terms: Electors to the Presidency are supposed to be people of superior wisdom who will therefore choose a better president than would the people if left to themselves. The people are entitled to elect electors, but not the president directly. In Condorcet's language, the electors have higher $v$ than the people at large, and therefore will more probably elect the correct president. (That this has not turned out to be the case may be due to the emergence in 1796 of electors pledged in advance to a particular candidate; almost no unpledged elector has ever been elected since then.)

However, Condorcet diverged sharply from the Federalists on bicameralism. "It is easy to see[5] (and this can be rigorously proved) that increasing the number of legislative bodies could never increase the probability of obtaining true decisions, and that this advantage can be obtained more simply and more certainly by requiring a fixed plurality in a single body" (#4, near the beginning of Letter 4). Here Condorcet is recommending setting a threshold level for $h-k$ such that the probability of coming to an incorrect decision is held acceptably low. However, these New Haven letters had almost no influence in the United States; few people read them at all, and of those who did, both James Madison and John Adams reacted with hostility (McLean and Urken 1992; Cappon 1959, p. 322).

The New Haven letters are the only text in which Condorcet proposes that elections should actually be conducted by a direct search for Condorcet winners. The extract that follows explains how each district assembly should select two of its own members to serve on the higher-tier legislature. The number of candidates should first be restricted to 20; thereafter,

each elector would form a list, ranking them in order of merit. We would then examine first whether a plurality declared one of the twenty candidates superior to each of the nineteen others, in which case he would be elected, and second, whether a plurality also declared some other candidate superior to the eighteen others, in which case he would be elected.

If no candidate is pronounced by a plurality to be superior to the nineteen others, then we would try to find a candidate declared by a plurality to be better

---

[5] A phrase which for Condorcet usually introduces something that is not in the least easy to see.

than eighteen of the others, and worse than just one, and we would elect these candidates in order, beginning with those for whom the total number of votes judging them better than one of the nineteen others was the greatest.

It is interesting that the second paragraph of this extract amounts to proposing the Copeland rule, with the Borda count as a tie breaker among the Copeland winners.[6] Condorcet then goes on to propose a sampling procedure in order to avoid having to count the 190 pairs on each of the 3000 ballots that would be submitted in his proposed districts. Both of these proposals disappear from Condorcet's later writings on voting: perhaps he realized that they fitted neither his probabilistic nor his choice-theoretic framework.

Condorcet took an active part in the French Revolution, tirelessly proposing voting schemes. The first of these (work #6), written in 1789, opens with an important distinction: "Elections which should in theory express a judgment in practice only express a will." The probabilistic (jury) theory of voting is applicable only to independent observers trying to form a judgment of an unknown fact, and not to the expression of preferences. Condorcet's admission here marks a step in separating his two theories, where he writes that a good choice procedure should secure "that the result of the election conforms with the will of the plurality of the voters" – an aim compatible with social choice theory but not with the calculus of probabilities. He goes on to admit that direct search for a Condorcet winner in a 20-candidate election would be "very time-consuming," and rejects the Copeland–Borda scheme mentioned in the previous paragraph. He then details an elaborate procedure which he clearly intended to be the best approximation to a Condorcet efficient one, although he still recommends using "the rigorous method" to begin with and his preferred method as a Condorcet completion scheme. Because it is complex and was abandoned in his later writings, we shall not discuss the procedure here.

In 1792, Condorcet was made the chairman of a committee to draw up a Constitution for France. His draft (#7) envisaged that for each election to fill $n$ places a mechanism would ensure that the number of candidates was restricted to exactly $3n$. (He discusses the case of fewer than $3n$ nominations, but only perfunctorily.) Each voter partitions the candidates into three lists of equal size: an "election column," a "supplementary column," and the remainder. Votes in the election column are counted, and if at least $n$ candidates each get a majority of the votes cast then they are elected, with the top $n$ being elected if more than $n$ each get a majority. If

---

[6] Or, depending on how one interprets the slightly odd phrase "judging them better than one of the nineteen others," ordering the members of the Copeland set in descending order of votes achieved against the one candidate who beat them.

the election cannot be completed in this way, votes in the supplementary column are brought in and counted equally with those in the election column; again, the top *n* of those who get over half of the votes are elected. If the election is completed from the votes in the election column, all those elected are "necessarily judged by the majority to be more worthy than the other candidates"; if the election has recourse to the supplementary column, "the candidates then elected will not have such strong majority support, but they will have more support than the remaining ones." Thus the intention of this scheme was to ensure that every elected candidate was a majority winner in some sense.

After the Jacobin coup d'état of 1 June 1793, Condorcet was out of power. His constitution was dumped in favor of one drawn up in great haste by Robespierre, who dropped all Condorcet's voting schemes. An outraged Condorcet published a pamphlet denouncing the Jacobin Constitution, for which he was proscribed and eventually outlawed. He hid in the house of a courageous Parisian landlady in the rue des Fossoyeurs (Gravediggers' Street).[7] In the spring of 1794 the National Convention decreed that not only any outlaw but also anybody found harboring one would be summarily guillotined without trial if discovered. In order to save his host's life, Condorcet escaped but was refused refuge in the house of some pre-Revolutionary friends. Condorcet was captured when he turned up, exhausted, in a village inn that happened to be run by a Jacobin informant,[8] and was found dead in prison two days later; by not revealing who he was, Condorcet may have saved the lives of his family and his landlady. He is the only person so far to have died for social choice.

Just before the Jacobin coup, Condorcet and some friends had founded a *Journal d'instruction sociale,* intended to keep the flag of enlightenment flying. It lasted only a month, during which it published part of Condorcet's last word on elections. Crépel (1990) has reconstructed the unpublished remainder from Condorcet's manuscripts, and the whole forms work #8. Condorcet was evidently not yet satisfied that he had found the ideal choice procedure: "I have far from exhausted the subject." He explains the existence of cycles, adding that "this only occurs in situations where it is certain that the majority has been mistaken at least once." This indicates that he was swinging back toward a probabilistic view of elections and away from the social choice view found in #5 and #6. He repeats that "there is only one way [viz. pairwise comparison and the Condorcet

[7] Now rue Servandoni, near the Eglise de St-Sulpice. The house is marked by a plaque.
[8] According to his daughter, Condorcet aroused suspicion because, when asked how many eggs he wanted in his omelette, he replied "a dozen," revealing his unfamiliarity with the cuisine of the working class. However, there is no record that she ever met his captors, so the story cannot be verified. For all this see Badinter and Badinter (1988).

ranking procedure] of obtaining a true decision" and that any practical substitute must come as close to this as possible. Here the printed text breaks off. The manuscript continuation is scrappy and inconclusive (not surprisingly, as the author was hiding in fear of his life). Only one firm conclusion can be drawn from its inconsistencies, false starts, deletions and reinstatements: Condorcet was not satisfied that he had solved the problem of social choice. Social choice and probabilistic arguments clash violently in this, his last word on elections.

## 6    Lhuilier, Morales, and Daunou

Simon Lhuilier (1750–1840) was from a French Protestant family that had emigrated to Geneva. A good mathematician, he had worked in Poland from 1777 to 1788 and had won a prize of the Berlin Academy of Science in 1786 for an essay on the theory of infinity. In 1794 he had only just returned to Geneva after a spell teaching at Tübingen, where (according to a biographer) he had gone in 1789 "fearing revolutionary disturbances" at home. He was professor of mathematics at the College of Geneva from 1795 to 1823, and was an active member of the legislative council, presumably until its suppression by Napoleon in 1798.

Lhuilier's "Examination" (#9; see also Monjardet 1976) revealed that Condorcet's procedure from #7 had been adopted in Geneva. Using an ingenious methodology of inferring unknown individual preference orderings from known aggregate totals of election-column and supplementary-column votes,[9] Lhuilier was able to show that the #7 procedure is not Condorcet efficient, and that it produces an arbitrary winner in the cyclical case. He also shows the nonmonotonicity, and hence the manipulability, of Condorcet's procedure. The note of triumph in Lhuilier's introduction is unmistakable:

I have no doubt whatsoever that when he saw the certainty of the principle on which my examination is based, and the necessary link between this principle and the results I have obtained, Condorcet would have rejected his own work.

Lhuilier had convicted Condorcet of the same failing as Condorcet had Borda in #5: of sometimes failing to select the Condorcet winner.

"Advocate Devégobre, a member of the national assembly," had suggested modifying Condorcet's method by weighting supplementary votes

---

[9] The 'Postscript' is particularly ingenious. Using the limited degrees of freedom present in Condorcet's system, Lhuilier lists exhaustively the possible permutations of individual preferences contained in a given vote outcome, and, assuming an impartial culture (i.e. that all orderings are equiprobable), calculates probability ratios for them. This is to start down the road not taken again until the 1960s, when analysts started to compute the probability of cycles given an impartial culture.

at one-half. This is of course to reinvent the Borda count. Lhuilier thought it was "very suitable for the case of three candidates, but . . . too arbitrary for elections in which a great many places are to be filled at once" because the information from strong orderings of many candidates is unreliable for candidates far down a voter's preference ordering.

The most disappointing part of Lhuilier's paper concerns his positive proposal, which ultimately relied on plurality votes if too few candidates received an overall majority. It is inconceivable that a writer of Lhuilier's sophistication was unaware of the drawbacks of this procedure. It is possible (although there is no direct textual evidence) that Lhuilier had observed the dynamic consequences of adopting Condorcet's practical method, and had appreciated that the number of candidates is partly a function of the choice rule and that plurality tends to reduce the number of candidates; see Riker (1982, p. 113) for such an argument.

J. I. Morales (circa 1790–1810) was a Spanish mathematician whose eye was caught by a newspaper report that the Institut de France (the Academy of Sciences and the other academies, reconstituted after the Terror in 1795) had adopted the Borda rule for its internal elections. By his own admission unaware of any literature on the subject, Morales thought through a justification of the Borda method (#10), which he sent to the Institute in 1797. His arguments are sometimes parallel to Borda's, particularly in calculating how large a qualified majority is needed to ensure that a majority winner is also a Borda winner. He drew a sharp distinction between elections of people and votes on propositions, arguing that the Borda procedure was appropriate for the first but binary procedures were appropriate for the second.

P. C. F. Daunou (1761–1840) was a historian and literary critic who had both political and intellectual associations with Condorcet in the early 1790s. Like Condorcet, Daunou was expelled from the National Convention after the Jacobin coup in 1793 and imprisoned for some months. However, he survived and gained prominent political offices after the fall of the Jacobins on the 10 Thermidor an III (July 1794). He was responsible for having Condorcet's *Esquisse* ("Outline for a history of the progress of the human mind") – which had been written in hiding in the rue des Fossoyeurs – published at public expense in 1795. He was also a prime mover in the refoundation of the academies as the Institut de France, and he was on the committee that drafted its constitution. This constitution instituted the Borda rule in 1796, the event which had caught Morales's eye. However, the Borda rule was abandoned following what is said to have been Napoleon's only intervention in the affairs of the Institut. One reason for abandoning it was its susceptibility to manipulation ("My election method is only for honest men" said Borda when this was pointed out).[10] Daunou's paper (#11) was written when a consensus was growing for replacing the Borda method by one in which candidates for a vacancy in one of the academies must obtain an absolute majority of the votes, with the place remaining unfilled if no candidate did so. In spite of Daunou's opposition, this system did indeed supplant the Borda count in 1804.

Daunou's review is very sophisticated. Broadly speaking, he sides with Condorcet and against Borda, although he was probably the author of the Borda scheme in the constitution of the Institute. His attack on the Borda count opens by showing that a voting system cannot measure the degrees of intensity of preference sincerely held by the voters. Therefore, rank orderings (as in the Borda count) cannot be held to be measures of intensity. The thrust of this is toward reasserting the independence of irrelevant alternatives. Borda (and Laplace – for whom see Black 1958, pp. 181–2) wish to claim that if, say, A is 6 places ahead of B on one ballot and B is one place ahead of A on another, then this is some evidence that A is socially preferred to B. This claim is denied by Condorcet, Daunou, and all those who believe that a choice system should respect independence.

Daunou goes on to analyze existing and proposed procedures. He gives plurality and runoff methods very short shrift: "I do not consider it necessary to prove" their defects, but discuss them "only because we constantly resort" to them. He rejects Condorcet's supplementary list scheme on the same grounds as had Lhuilier, though without reference to him. He points out that qualified majority schemes can be minority veto schemes. He confirms that the Borda count had been "abused" in the Institute by voters' "deliberately ranking [their favorite's] most dangerous opponents last." Like Condorcet, he points out that the Borda count violates (Nash) independence and expansion consistency (Sen's condition $\gamma$):

But how can the intervention of another candidate alter or reverse the relationship established by the voters between . . . two candidates? . . . [as if to] say "if the choice is between just A and B, then we categorically prefer A, but if it is between A, B, and also C, then we consider that B beats not only C, but A as well."

Discussing Borda's proof that only a unanimity rule would guarantee that a majority winner was also the Borda winner, Daunou argues that this should have caused Borda to re-evaluate a method which had such a perverse implication: "we must judge the method by the maxim, and not the maxim by the method." He continues boldly by attacking "Citizen Laplace . . . this wise teacher," who had justified the Borda count from a more explicit axiom of equiprobability than Borda's (cf. Black 1958, pp. 181–2). Laplace's justification produces a geometrical, not arithmetical,

---

[10] The original source for this much-quoted remark is *Eloge de Borda* by S. F. Lacroix, in *dossier Borda,* Archives de l'Académie des Sciences, Paris.

progression of numbers, and there can be no reason to regard this progression as a measure of the unmeasurable "true" intervals between candidates in voters' minds. The only merit Daunou now sees in the Borda count is that the Borda loser cannot be the Condorcet winner, as he demonstrates. Next, Daunou makes clear what was only reintroduced into social choice by the papers of Michaud (1985), Young (1988), and Monjardet (1990): namely, that Condorcet's ordering procedure is one of choosing the "most probable" system, which does not lead to the same result as ranking the candidates in order of their aggregate votes in pairwise comparisons (i.e. Borda's second method). He concludes by warning the Institute (vainly, as it turned out) against reverting to runoff majoritarian methods of election.

## 7     Discussion

We have shown that many issues in the current literature of social choice were aired between 1770 and 1803. Both in modes of reasoning and in substantive concerns, the literature reviewed here seems remarkably modern. For instance, Condorcet (when in social choice mode) takes it as axiomatic that the majority winner should be chosen and that the choice from a set of options should be independent of irrelevant alternatives; he then proves that the Borda count violates both axioms, although the first was implicit in Borda's own statement of the problem. Daunou – initially a proponent of the Borda rule – came to share this opinion, using the same form of reasoning to attack Borda, Morales, and Laplace: the last attack a remarkably bold one, in that a writer and administrator of purely literary background was taking on a colleague already recognized as one of the greatest mathematicians of his day. Lhuilier turns this axiomatic method against Condorcet himself by proving that his own practical procedure does not satisfy his axioms. These authors were well aware of the manipulability of the Borda count and sought a nonmanipulable system. Condorcet's practical procedures were diverse; though he was satisfied by none of them, it is of interest that at one point he proposed the Copeland rule supplemented by a tie-breaking Borda count.

Black (1958) was largely, but not wholly, correct in depicting Condorcet's probabilism as an obstacle to the development of social choice. But the probabilistic theory of voting has merits which are only now being recovered. The jury theorem is a perfectly valid piece of reasoning that can be applied both to normative political theory (axiomatizing Rousseau's General Will) and to the analysis of voting situations that meet its preconditions. An example of the latter would be setting rules for the majority required before (say) a number of computer systems could close down machinery that some of them report to be malfunctioning. Here is an application where, with a known $v$, it is easy to calculate the threshold value of $h - k$ to achieve the desired balance between avoiding a false positive and a false negative. (For a current review see Berg 1992.) Another use of probability was exploited by Lhuilier (and to some extent by Laplace and Daunou): calculating the probability of the possible profiles in a set of orderings, given an assumption that any ordering of a pair is as likely as any other (what is now labeled an "impartial culture").

Why then was this work lost to sight? The immediate reason is that neither politicians nor mathematicians understood it. Although Condorcet intervened in the writing of the American and French Constitutions, and the Polish Constitution of 1791 was written by friends and admirers of his (for which see Marchione 1983; Libiszowska 1991), our study of the documents in all three cases has failed to reveal that anybody except Lhuilier understood Condorcet's arguments. Among mathematicians, understanding of social choice died out with Condorcet's pupil S. F. Lacroix (1765–1843), whose grasp of social choice was never secure. Although his *Elementary Treatise on the Calculus of Probabilities* went through many editions as a standard text, nobody followed up his brief and confusing references to social choice. As to probability, the jury theorem was discussed by Poisson and Cournot with minimal reference to Condorcet, and the idea of even investigating the "probability" of a judgment was rejected as absurd by every intervening generation of mathematicians until our own. (For Lacroix, Cournot, and Poisson see Sommerlad and McLean 1991, part V).

But this is merely to redescribe, not explain. The *mathematics* of social choice is not difficulty; it seems that the difficulty for Condorcet – as for his predecessors Lull and Cusanus and his successors Nanson and Dodgson – lay in persuading colleagues that there was a phenomenon which required explanation. It is striking that there is evidence that Lull, Cusanus, Condorcet, Dodgson, and Nanson were each regarded as a lonely thinker and a difficult-to-follow teacher. (Lull revealed in his autobiography that nobody understood him when he lectured at the University of Paris. Cusanus wrote bad Latin, by his own admission. Condorcet's attempts to teach were embarrassing failures. Dodgson was a prickly eccentric, none of whose colleagues shared his mathematical interests. Nanson was uninterested in teaching and was reproved by a Royal Commission for the poor state of mathematics teaching at the University of Melbourne.) Perhaps there is a lesson for us even today: It is as important to communicate with the outside world as with one another.

## REFERENCES

Arago, M. F., and A. Condorcet O'Connor, eds. (1847), *Oeuvres de Condorcet,* 12 vols. Paris: Firmin-Didot.

Badinter, E., and R. Badinter (1988), *Condorcet (1743–1794): un intellectuel en politique.* Paris: Fayard.

Bartholdi, J., III, C. A. Tovey, and M. A. Trick (1989), "Voting Schemes for which It Can Be Difficult to Tell Who Won the Election," *Social Choice and Welfare* 6: 157–66.

Berg, S. (1992), "Condorcet's Jury Theorem: Dependency among Jurors," paper presented at the June 1992 meeting of the Society for Social Choice and Welfare (Caen, France).

Bernon, O. de, ed. (1986), *Condorcet: sur les élections et autres textes.* Paris: Fayard.

Black, D. (1958), *The Theory of Committees and Elections.* Cambridge: Cambridge University Press.

Borda, J-C de (1784), "Mémoire sur les élections par scrutin," *Mémoires de l'Academie Royale des sciences année 1781,* pp. 657–65.

Cappon, L. J., ed. (1959), *The Adams–Jefferson Letters: The Complete Correspondence between Thomas Jefferson and Abigail and John Adams.* Chapel Hill: University of North Carolina Press.

[Condorcet, M. J. A. N., marquis de] (1784), "Sur les élections par scrutin," *Histoire de l'Académie Royale des sciences année 1781,* pp. 31–4.

Condorcet, M. J. A. N., marquis de ([1785] 1972), *Essai sur l'application de l'analyse à la probabilité des décisions rendues à la pluralité des voix.* New York: Chelsea (orig. Paris: Imprimerie Royale).

Crépel, P. (1990), "Le dernier mot de Condorcet sur les élections," *Mathématiques, Informatique et Sciences Humaines* 111: 7–43.

Grazia, A. de (1953), "Mathematical Derivation of an Election System," *Isis* 44: 42–51.

Grofman, B., and S. Feld (1988), "Rousseau's General Will: A Condorcetian Perspective," *American Political Science Review* 82: 567–76.

Hahn, R. (1971), *The Anatomy of a Scientific Institution: The Paris Academy of Sciences, 1666–1803.* Berkeley: University of California Press.

Henry, C., ed. (1883), *Correspondance inédite de Condorcet et de Turgot 1770–9.* Paris: Charavay.

Lhuilier, S. ([1794] 1976), "Examen du mode d'élection proposé à la Convention Nationale de France en février 1783, et adopté à Genève," *Mathématiques et Sciences Humaines* 54: 7–24 (orig. Geneva: Comité Legislatif).

Libiszowska, Z. (1991), "England–Poland during the 18th Century," in *The Polish Road to Democracy: the Constitution of May 3, 1791* (exhibition in the Polish Cultural Institute in London, April 18–June 18, 1991). Warsaw: Seym, pp. 7–20.

McLean, I., and J. London (1990), "The Borda and Condorcet Principles: Three Medieval Applications," *Social Choice and Welfare* 7: 99–108.

McLean, I., and A. B. Urken (1992), "Did Jefferson or Madison Understand Condorcet's Theory of Social Choice?" *Public Choice* 73: 445–57.

ed. and trans. (1995), *Classics of Social Choice.* Ann Arbor: University of Michigan Press.

Marchione, M., ed. and trans. (1983), *Philip Mazzei: Selected Writings and Correspondence,* 3 vols. Prato: Edizioni del Palazzo.

May, K. O. (1952), "A Set of Independent Necessary and Sufficient Conditions for Simple Majority Decision," *Econometrica* 20: 680-4.

Michaud, P. (1985), "Hommage à Condorcet: version intégrale pour le bicentenaire de l'Essai de Condorcet," étude F.094, Centre Scientifique IBM, Paris.

Monjardet, B. (1976), "Lhuilier contre Condorcet, au pays des paradoxes," *Mathétiques et Sciences Humaines* 54: 33-43.

(1990), "Sur diverses formes de la 'Règle de Condorcet' d'agrégation des préférences," *Mathématiques, Informatique et Sciences Humaines* 111: 61-71.

Morales, J. I. (1797), *Memoria matemática sobre el cálculo de la opinion en las elecciones.* Madrid: Imprenta Real.

Riker, W. H. (1982), *Liberalism against Populism.* San Francisco: Freeman.

Sen, A. K. (1982), *Choice, Welfare, and Measurement.* Oxford: Blackwell.

Sommerlad, F., and I. McLean, eds. and trans. (1989), "The political theory of Condorcet," working paper 1/89, Social Studies Faculty Centre, Oxford University (available from Department of Politics, University of Warwick, Coventry CV4 7AL, UK).

eds. and trans. (1991), "The political theory of Condorcet II," working paper 1/1991, Social Studies Faculty Centre, Oxford University (available from Department of Politics, University of Warwick, Coventry CV4 7AL, UK).

Urken, A. B., et al., eds. and trans. (forthcoming), *Condorcet's Essai.* New Haven, CT: Yale University Press.

Young, H. P. (1988), "Condorcet's Theory of Voting," *American Political Science Review* 82: 1231-44.

PART II

# Ethical aspects of social choice

CHAPTER 2

# The requisites of equal opportunity

*Marc Fleurbaey*


## 1    Introduction

The ideal of equal opportunity has received renewed attention in recent papers (Arneson 1989, Cohen 1989, Roemer 1993). A former wave of interest was initiated by Dworkin (1981), followed by Roemer (1985, 1986, 1987) and Varian (1985). The specificity of these works, in contrast with the traditional models of fair division, is that they acknowledge the existence of unequal claims on behalf of the individuals, owing to advantages or handicaps that cannot be easily altered or removed. The first wave (Dworkin–Roemer–Varian) focused on that point, coining the phrase "equality of resources" to designate the idea that some equalizing mechanism should be applied to the comprehensive bundles of external and internal resources of the members of society, one that would imply some compensation of internal handicaps by additional external allowances. However, no compelling mechanism emerged from the literature, and it was unclear how far equality of resources could remain from equality of welfare (for a survey of this literature, see Van Parijs 1990). The second wave (Arneson–Cohen–Roemer) tends to emphasize that individuals bear some responsibility for their personal characteristics, so that the equalizing procedure must be conceived of as partial. The phrase "equal opportunity" emerges from this renewed approach, suggesting indeed that it is up to the individual to seize the opportunities offered by society.

The aim of this paper is to clarify the logical implications of any attempt at equalizing the opportunities made available to individuals. Precise candidate definitions of equal opportunity are given in the next sections. The paper shows that equal opportunity is non-empty under rather strong separability conditions, which are unlikely to be satisfied except in rather special cases. On the other hand, to circumvent this problem by weakening

This paper has benefitted from comments by J. Roemer and discussions with M. Quinzii.

the requisites of equal opportunity implies that some desirable features of the equalizing procedure must be abandoned.

The framework is as follows. Equal opportunity involves four dimensions: (1) the outcome or performance that the individuals strive for; (2) the effort or ambition (or whatever), which is under their responsibility and does not elicit compensation; (3) the handicaps or advantages that individuals happen to be endowed with; and (4) the external resources that society provides in order to implement equal opportunity. In some circumstances – as when the external resources are of the same nature as the handicaps – the last two dimensions may collapse into one but this is quite rare. For brevity, in the sequel $O(r_i, h_i, w_i)$ will denote the outcome obtained by individual $i$, where $O$ is the outcome function (the same for everybody), $r_i$ the external resources received by $i$, $h_i$ the handicap that falls on $i$, and $w_i$ the "will" exerted by $i$. This latter term is chosen here to convey the ambiguity of designating both Dworkinian "ambitions" and the "will power" of the Arneson–Cohen–Roemer approach. All these notations and names should not obscure the fact that the analysis is very general, and that the distinction between $h$ and $w$ can be of any sort provided $h$ is to be compensated and $w$ is to be rewarded (or at least not compensated). The outcome $O$ can similarly be of any kind (welfare, success, exams, career, power, etc.).

## 2     Strong equal opportunity

In the general framework just described, an allocation of resources $(r_1, ..., r_n)$ among the $n$ individuals of society will be said to *equalize opportunities* if the expressions $O(r_i, h_i, \cdot)$ for $i = 1, ..., n$, each viewed as a function of $w_i$, are the same for all individuals. In other words, considering that only $w_i$ is under the responsibility of individual $i$ ($r_i$ is allotted by a social agency, and $h_i$ by Nature), the value of individual outcome she can reach for any selection of $w_i$ is the same as for any other individual.

This definition may be justified if one makes the simplifying assumption that individuals all have the same kind of access to a given set of possible wills $W$. It is then not necessary to describe exactly the kind of access (difficulty, knowledge, ability, strength of character required, etc.) that individuals have to the various wills of $W$. This assumption also makes sense if the parameter $h$ is meant to capture all of the undue factors that may influence individual behavior. Differential access to $W$ would indeed mean that $w$ is not entirely equally freely chosen by each individual.[1]

---

[1] This definition of equal opportunity seems to correspond to Arneson's. See Fleurbaey (1994b).

Equal opportunity, thus defined, will make sense only if it is non-empty under general circumstances; in particular, it should not be non-empty only for a narrow range of aggregate resources to be distributed to the individuals. The following proposition shows that if equal opportunity is feasible for any amount of aggregate resources (with possibly a positive lower bound), then a separability condition is satisfied by the function $O$. For simplicity's sake, the external resource $r$ is assumed to be 1-dimensional (e.g. income). Let $H = \{h_1, ..., h_n\}$.

**Assumption 2.1.** $O$ is a mapping from $\mathbb{R}_+ \times H \times W$ to $\mathbb{R}$, and is continuous increasing in its first argument.

**Assumption 2.2.**

$$\forall i, j \in \{1, ..., n\}, \quad \forall w \in W, \quad \forall r \in \mathbb{R}_+, \quad \exists r' \in \mathbb{R}_+ : O(r', h_i, w) > O(r, h_j, w).$$

Assumption 2.2 means that no handicap is so overwhelming that no amount of resources $r$ can alleviate its impact on the outcome $O$. It is indeed trivial that if the handicaps are too strong, equal opportunity may be impossible to achieve. This difficulty is well known and easily dealt with (e.g., replace equality with maxmin), and it is not the focus of this paper. What is shown here is that, even when this difficulty is assumed away, severe problems remain – problems that are less obvious and less simply handled.

**Definition 2.1.** Equal opportunity is non-empty for the aggregate resource $\Omega$ if there exists an allocation $(r_1, ..., r_n)$ and a function $\hat{\theta}: W \to \mathbb{R}$ such that $\sum_i r_i = \Omega$ and, for all $i$, $O(r_i, h_i, \cdot) = \hat{\theta}$.

**Theorem 2.1.** *Assume that there exists $\underline{r}$ such that equal opportunity is non-empty for any $\Omega \geq \underline{r}$. Then, under Assumptions 2.1 and 2.2, there exist functions $\underline{\theta}: W \to \mathbb{R}$, $\nu: \mathbb{R}_+ \times H \to \mathbb{R}$, and $\mu: \mathbb{R} \times W \to \mathbb{R}$ such that*

$$\forall (r, h, w) \in \mathbb{R}_+ \times H \times W, \quad O(r, h, w) \geq \underline{\theta}(w) \Rightarrow O(r, h, w) = \mu(\nu(r, h), w).$$

*Proof:* Let Assumptions 2.1 and 2.2 hold, and assume non-emptiness of equal opportunity for $\Omega \geq \underline{r}$.

*Fact 1:* Under equal opportunity, $\Omega' > \Omega$ if and only if for all $i$, $r_i' > r_i$.

Sufficiency is obvious. For necessity, assume that – on the contrary – $\Omega' > \Omega$ and the conclusion is false. Then there exist $i, j$ such that $r_i' > r_i$ and $r_j' \leq r_j$. But $O(r_i, h_i, \cdot) = O(r_j, h_j, \cdot)$. Hence $O(r_i', h_i, \cdot) > O(r_j', h_j, \cdot)$, in contradiction with equal opportunity.

A similar argument shows that $\Omega' \geq \Omega$ if and only if for all $i$, $r_i' \geq r_i$, implying the uniqueness of the equal opportunity allocation $(r_1, ..., r_n)$ for a given $\Omega$. Moreover, equal opportunity implies:

$$\forall i, j, \quad h_i = h_j \Rightarrow r_i = r_j;$$

$$\forall i, j, \quad w_i = w_j \Rightarrow O(r_i, h_i, w_i) = O(r_j, h_j, w_j).$$

One can thus define functions $\gamma(\Omega, h)$ and $\theta(\Omega, w)$, by $\gamma(\Omega, h_i) = r_i$ and $\theta(\Omega, w) = O(r_i, h_i, w)$, where $r_i$ is what $i$ receives under equal opportunity when the aggregate resource is $\Omega$. By fact 1, both are increasing in $\Omega$.

*Fact 2:* $\theta(\Omega, w)$ is continuous in $\Omega$, for all $w$ in $W$.

Let a sequence $\Omega^k$ converge to $\Omega$, with (say) $\Omega^k < \Omega$. Assume there are $\alpha$ and $w$ such that for all $k$, $\theta(\Omega^k, w) \leq \alpha < \theta(\Omega, w)$. Since $O$ is continuous in its first argument, this implies that for any $i$ there is an $\alpha_i'$ such that for all $k$, $\gamma(\Omega^k, h_i) \leq \alpha_i' < \gamma(\Omega, h_i)$. Then $\Omega^k = \sum_i \gamma(\Omega^k, h_i) \leq \sum_i \alpha_i' < \sum_i \gamma(\Omega, h_i) = \Omega$, a contradiction.

*Fact 3:* For any $r \in \mathbb{R}_+$, $h \in H$, and $w \in W$, there exists an $\Omega$ such that $\theta(\Omega, w) \geq O(r, h, w)$.

Otherwise, there exist $(r, h, w)$ such that, for all $\Omega$, $\theta(\Omega, w) < O(r, h, w)$. Hence, for all $\Omega$, $\gamma(\Omega, h) < r$. Because of Assumption 2.2, there exists $M > r$ such that for all $i$, $O(M, h_i, w) > O(r, h, w)$. When $\Omega = nM$, the agent with handicap $h$ receives $\gamma(\Omega, h) < r < M$. As a consequence, there is necessarily an $i$ who receives more than $M$, that is, such that $\gamma(nM, h_i) > M > r > \gamma(nM, h)$. Hence

$$O(M, h_i, w) < O(\gamma(nM, h_i), h_i, w) = O(\gamma(nM, h), h, w) < O(r, h, w),$$

in contradiction with equal opportunity.

*Fact 4:* Let $\underline{\theta}(w) = \theta(\underline{r}, w)$. Choose any $r, r', h, h', w, w'$ in the relevant sets. One has:

$$\underline{\theta}(w) \leq O(r, h, w) \leq O(r', h', w) \Leftrightarrow \underline{\theta}(w') \leq O(r, h, w') \leq O(r', h', w').$$

Indeed, if $\underline{\theta}(w) \leq O(r, h, w) \leq O(r', h', w)$, by fact 3 there is $\Omega_0$ such that $\theta(\Omega_0, w) \geq O(r, h, w)$. By continuity (fact 2), there is $\Omega_1 \geq \underline{r}$ such that $\theta(\Omega_1, w) = O(r, h, w)$. Thus $\gamma(\Omega_1, h) = r$ and, owing to the previous inequality, $\gamma(\Omega_1, h') \leq r'$. These statements imply that $\underline{\theta}(w') \leq \theta(\Omega_1, w') = O(r, h, w') = O(\gamma(\Omega_1, h'), h', w') \leq O(r', h', w')$. This proves the implication, and the converse is true by symmetry.

To complete the proof, choose any $w_0$ and define the functions $\nu$ and $\mu$ as follows:

$$\nu(r, h) = O(r, h, w_0);$$

$$\mu(t, w) = O(r, h, w) \quad \text{whenever } \nu(r, h) = t.$$

If $O(r, h, w) \geq \underline{\theta}(w)$ then $\mu$ is well-defined. Indeed this implies that $O(r, h, w_0) \geq \underline{\theta}(w_0)$, and if $\nu(r', h') = t$ then $O(r, h, w_0) = O(r', h', w_0)$, which implies (by fact 4) that $O(r, h, w) = O(r', h', w)$. Hence $O(r, h, w) \geq \underline{\theta}(w)$ implies $O(r, h, w) = \mu(\nu(r, h), w)$. $\qquad\square$

One could easily show that $\mu$ and $\nu$ are both continuous in their first argument. When the problem under consideration is such that $O(\cdot, \cdot, w)$ is a utility function defined over $\mathbb{R}_+ \times H$, with the argument $w$ characterizing the individuals' personal utility parameters, the separability condition obtained previously simply means that individuals have preference pre-orderings over pairs $(r, h)$ which are independent of $w$:

$$\forall r, r', h, h', w, w', \quad O(r, h, w) \geq O(r', h', w) \Leftrightarrow \nu(r, h) \geq \nu(r', h')$$
$$\Leftrightarrow O(r, h, w') \geq O(r', h', w').$$

If this is the case then individuals always have the same preferences, whatever their different choices of $w$.

Notice that the theorem applies without any modification to the case when the individual wills are already known and we require equal opportunity only with respect to these actual wills, that is, with $W = \{w_1, \dots, w_n\}$.

When the separability condition is satisfied, equal opportunity is implemented by equalizing $\nu(r, h)$ between the individuals. The function $\nu$ provides a way to aggregate external resources and internal handicaps, and unambiguously defines a Dworkinian "extended" bundle of resources.

This result simply points to a particular condition. Whether this condition is likely to be verified or not is an empirical question that cannot be fully addressed here. There is a particular class of cases which is very favorable in this respect – namely, when the resource $r$ and the handicap $h$ have the same nature and are additive. Think of the weight of competitors in a race: it is very easy to load the lighter ones with weights so as to equalize the total weight $\nu = r + h$. Another example is the compensation of inherited wealth inequalities through money transfers.

But outside this particular class, it is quite difficult to imagine general reasons why the required separability is likely to hold. Consider for instance the case of schooling, and assume one seeks to neutralize the social background of pupils and to reveal their effort and talent. The separability condition implies that if, for normally talented and hardworking pupils, two training methods – the first applied to workers' children and the second to executives' children – give the same opportunities to both categories, then this should hold for any level of effort and talent. If, on the contrary, effort and talent tend to mitigate the impact of a low social background, then – with the same pair of programs – gifted and hardworking workers' children will do better than similarly gifted executives' children, whereas the reverse will be observed for lazy, untalented children. The opposite is also possible; that is, effort and talent may very well increase the advantage of a well-off background. At any rate, the separability condition turns out to be a very special configuration in such a context, and therefore appears highly implausible.

## 3     Weak equal opportunity

One feature which makes the above concept of equal opportunity quite demanding is that it somehow requires the allocation of resources $r$ to be selected ex ante, that is, before the individuals choose their will. A less demanding version of the concept would be satisfied if ex post (once the individual wills are known) one can find an allocation that compensates for handicaps and also rewards effort or "good" will. Although the former version implies separability of the outcome function, it might be the case that a large class of "will" configurations enables the social planner to implement the latter, ex post version even without a separable function.

For more precision, assume that $r$, $h$, and $w$ can all be represented by real numbers, and that $O$ is increasing in the three arguments. *Weak equal opportunity* would only require that, for given distributions of handicaps and will levels in the population, $r_i$ should be inversely related to $h_i$ ("Adequate Compensation") and $O(r_i, h_i, w_i)$ should be positively related to $w_i$ ("Adequate Reward").

**Definition 3.1.**   Consider an economy with $n$ agents, each characterized by $(h_i, w_i)$. The allocation $r = (r_1, \ldots, r_n)$ satisfies *Adequate Compensation* if

$$\forall i, j, \quad h_i \geq h_j \Leftrightarrow r_i \leq r_j;$$

it satisfies *Adequate Reward* if

$$\forall i, j, \quad w_i \geq w_j \Leftrightarrow O(r_i, h_i, w_i) \geq O(r_j, h_j, w_j).$$

It is obvious that these two properties, in this particular context, are entailed by the strong version of equal opportunity discussed in the previous section. Adequate Compensation requires that the allocation of resources should not deepen the original inequalities between the individuals, whereas Adequate Reward prevents the outcome from not reflecting the differential effort levels. The strong version of equal opportunity ensured that the *size* of the differential handicaps or wills was reflected in the size of the differential resources or outcomes. This weaker version only ensures that the *signs* are correctly accounted for.

Table 1

| Pupils | $h$    | $w$ |
|--------|--------|-----|
| Ann    | −4.00  | 3.5 |
| Bob    | −3.50  | 2.0 |
| Chris  | +1.25  | 1.5 |
| Dave   | +1.50  | 4.0 |

Unfortunately, unless the outcome function is separable, the two properties are generally incompatible. Consider the following example. Let $O$ denote school results, $r$ the amount of educational resources, $h$ the children's social background, $w$ their effort (talent is dropped for brevity). Assume $O(r, h, w) = r + h/w + w$. For $h < w^2$, $O$ is increasing in its three arguments. But a high effort not only directly enhances the school results, but also helps reduce the impact of a poor social background. Four pupils are in the class, and their social background and observed effort are displayed in Table 1.

For this example, a quick computation shows the following property:

$$r_A \geq r_B \geq r_C \geq r_D \;\Rightarrow\; O_B < O_C \text{ or } O_A > O_D.$$

In other words, if one wants to give more educational resources to the poorer pupils, then either Chris will do better than Bob or Ann will do better than Dave, even though Chris and Ann are lazier. Conversely, if one makes sure that the lazy pupils do not overtake those who work harder, a poorer pupil will receive fewer resources than a richer one, a quite unappealing situation.

It is easy to see that such an example may be found with any nonseparable outcome function, which proves the general incompatibility of Adequate Compensation and Adequate Reward and provides the following theorem. Let $D$ be a subset of $\mathbb{R} \times \mathbb{R}$, int $D$ its interior, $H = \{h \in \mathbb{R}: \exists w \in \mathbb{R}, (h, w) \in \text{int } D\}$, and $W = \{w \in \mathbb{R}: \exists h \in \mathbb{R}, (h, w) \in \text{int } D\}$. Let an *economy* be a set of agents, a set of pairs $(h, w)$, and a function from the former to the latter assigning a pair $(h, w)$ to each agent.

**Definition 3.2.** $\Gamma$ is the set of economies with a finite number of agents such that, for any agent $i$, $(h_i, w_i) \in D$.

**Definition 3.3.** Given an economy in $\Gamma$ (with $n$ agents), weak equal opportunity is non-empty for the per-capita resource $\bar{r}$ if there exists an allocation $r = (r_1, ..., r_n)$ such that $(1/n) \sum_i r_i = \bar{r}$ and $r$ satisfies Adequate Compensation and Adequate Reward.

**Assumption 3.1.** $O$ is a mapping from $\mathbb{R}_+ \times D$ to $\mathbb{R}$, continuous in $r$, and increasing in its three arguments.

**Assumption 3.2.** For all $h, h', w$ such that $(h, w) \in D$ and $(h', w) \in D$,

$$\forall r \in \mathbb{R}_+, \; \exists r' \in \mathbb{R}_+ : O(r', h', w) > O(r, h, w).$$

**Assumption 3.3.** $D$ is compact and is the closure of an open connected set.

**Theorem 3.1.** *Assume that there exists $\underline{r}$ such that, for any economy in $\Gamma$, weak equal opportunity is non-empty for any per-capita resource $\bar{r} \geq \underline{r}$. Then, under Assumptions 3.1–3.3, there exist functions $\underline{\theta}: W \to \mathbb{R}$, $\nu: \mathbb{R}_+ \times H \to \mathbb{R}$, and $\mu: \mathbb{R} \times W \to \mathbb{R}$ such that:*

$$\forall (r, h, w) \in \mathbb{R}_+ \times \text{int } D, \quad O(r, h, w) \geq \underline{\theta}(w) \; \Rightarrow \; O(r, h, w) = \mu(\nu(r, h), w).$$

*Proof:* See the Appendix.

It may be noticed that one needs economies with at least four agents to prove this theorem: whereas strong equal opportunity implies separability even with two individuals, weak equal opportunity begins running into trouble for $n \geq 4$. Still, one can find many cases with significant numbers of individuals in which weak equal opportunity is non-empty. This raises the question of the general degree of feasibility of weak equal opportunity. The answer is that the separability condition becomes more and more necessary as the size of the population increases. A moment of reflection will convince the reader that separability is entailed by weak equal opportunity in the case of a continuum of individuals (i.e., with characteristics $h$ and $w$ varying continuously on a support). Indeed, with a continuum of agents weak equal opportunity is almost equivalent to strong equal opportunity: if $(h, w)$, $(h, w')$, $(h', w)$, and $(h', w')$ belong to the support then there exist individuals with these characteristics, so weak equal opportunity implies $O(r, h, w) = O(r', h', w)$ and $O(r, h, w') = O(r', h', w')$.

It remains to show that the continuum case is indeed the limit of what happens in large but finite populations. This is the purpose of the next theorem, which states that the separability condition is already entailed by weak equal opportunity in a discrete countable population.

Consider a countable population of agents indexed by $i = 1, 2, \ldots$. Each agent $i$ is characterized by a pair $(h_i, w_i)$ in $\mathbb{R}^2$. Let the closure of $P = \{(h_i, w_i): i \geq 1\}$ be denoted by $D$. Let $H$ and $W$ be as defined previously.

**Definition 3.4.** Weak equal opportunity is non-empty for the per-capita resource $\bar{r}$ if there exists an allocation $r = (r_i)_{i \geq 1}$ such that

$$\lim_{n \to \infty}(1/n) \sum_{i=1}^{n} r_i = \bar{r}$$

and $r$ satisfies both Adequate Compensation and Adequate Reward.

**Assumption 3.4.** $O$ is a mapping from $\mathbb{R}_+ \times D$ to $\mathbb{R}$, continuous increasing in its three arguments.

**Assumption 3.5.** For all $h, h', w, w'$ such that $(h, w) \in D$ and $(h', w') \in D$,

$$\forall r \in \mathbb{R}_+, \ \exists r' \in \mathbb{R}_+ : O(r', h', w') > O(r, h, w).$$

**Assumption 3.6.** $\mathrm{int}\, D$ is a connected set. Moreover, if $c_n = |\{i: i \leq n, (h_i, w_i) \in \mathrm{int}\, D\}|$ then $\lim_{n \to \infty}(c_n/n) = 1$.

The second part of Assumption 3.6 simply means that those agents $i$ for whom $(h_i, w_i)$ belongs to the boundary of $D$ form a negligible part of the population.

**Theorem 3.2.** *Assume that, in this economy, there exists $\underline{r}$ such that weak equal opportunity is non-empty for any per-capita resource $\bar{r} \geq \underline{r}$. Then, under Assumptions 3.4–3.6, there exist functions $\underline{\theta}: W \to \mathbb{R}$, $\nu: \mathbb{R}_+ \times H \to \mathbb{R}$, and $\mu: \mathbb{R} \times W \to \mathbb{R}$, such that:*

$$\forall (r, h, w) \in \mathbb{R}_+ \times \mathrm{int}\, D, \quad O(r, h, w) \geq \underline{\theta}(w) \ \Rightarrow \ O(r, h, w) = \mu(\nu(r, h), w).$$

*Proof:* See the Appendix.

## 4 Weakening again

The conclusion of the previous section is clear: If one wants a generally non-empty solution, at least one of the two twin properties of weak equal opportunity must be dropped. Whether, after doing so, one can still relate the resulting solutions to the ideal of equal opportunity is questionable, but in any case three families of solutions can be derived from such a move. The first one abandons the positive relationship between effort and outcome, the second one drops the negative relationship between handicap and resource, and the third one simultaneously weakens both requirements. A comprehensive (but surely not exhaustive) study of these solutions is given in Fleurbaey (1994a,c). Here only two of them will be briefly presented, because these are the solutions which, in the equal-opportunity framework, achieve general existence with the minimal cost in terms of ethical properties. Their duality is also of some interest, and appears clearly in the present context. Before defining these solutions, some refinements of the framework are needed. We retain Assumptions 3.1 and 3.2 throughout this section, and assume that for the domain $\Gamma$ (Definition 3.2) there is a reference handicap $\tilde{h}$ and a reference will $\tilde{w}$ that are defined a priori, with $(\tilde{h}, \tilde{w})$ in $D$. A *solution* is a correspondence which, for any economy in $\Gamma$ and any aggregate resource $\Omega$, selects a subset of feasible allocations; an allocation is *feasible* if $\sum_i r_i = \Omega$.

**Definition 4.1.** An allocation $r = (r_1, \ldots, r_n)$ satisfies *Bipolar Compensation* if

$$\forall i, j, \quad h_i \leq \tilde{h} \leq h_j \;\Rightarrow\; r_i \geq r_j;$$

it satisfies *Bipolar Reward* if

$$\forall i, j, \quad w_i \geq \tilde{w} \geq w_j \;\Rightarrow\; O(r_i, h_i, w_i) \geq O(r_j, h_j, w_j).$$

In other words, the reference handicap $\tilde{h}$ splits the population into the handicapped and the gifted (or poor and rich), and Bipolar Compensation guarantees that the allocation provides the former with more resources than the latter, but does not preclude perverse situations within the two classes. Similarly, the reference will $\tilde{w}$ splits the population into lazy and hardworking individuals, and Bipolar Reward ensures that the latter will do better than the former, but can offer no such guarantee within each class.

The first solution to be described here belongs to the first of the families just listed, and can be derived from Roemer (1993). I propose to name it Conditional Equality, because it selects an allocation that would ensure equal outcome if all agents had the will $\tilde{w}$.

**Definition 4.2.** The *Conditional Equality* solution selects the feasible allocation $r = (r_1, \ldots, r_n)$ such that

$$\forall i, j, \quad O(r_i, h_i, \tilde{w}) = O(r_j, h_j, \tilde{w}).$$

This solution is indeed single-valued in the current framework. It satisfies Adequate Compensation, but only Bipolar Reward. In terms of preferences (i.e., viewing $O(\cdot, \cdot, w)$ as a utility function), any agent whose will is $\tilde{w}$ is indifferent with respect to everybody else's extended resources $(r, h)$.

The second solution, which appears as a dual of the previous one, is the Egalitarian Equivalent solution of Pazner and Schmeidler (1978).

**Definition 4.3.** The *Egalitarian Equivalent* solution selects the feasible allocation $r = (r_1, ..., r_n)$ such that

$$\exists \tilde{r} : \forall i,\ O(r_i, h_i, w_i) = O(\tilde{r}, \tilde{h}, w_i).$$

This solution is also single-valued in the current framework. It satisfies Adequate Reward, but only Bipolar Compensation. With this solution, every individual $i$ obtains the same outcome as would any agent with the handicap $\tilde{h}$ and the same will $w_i$. In the language of preferences, this allocation is such that everybody is indifferent with respect to the representative agent's bundle of extended resources.

These two criteria solve the existence problem, as the next theorem shows. More precise notation is required. An economy will be denoted $\xi = (n; h; w)$, with $n$ the number of agents, $h = (h_1, ..., h_n)$ their handicaps, and $w = (w_1, ..., w_n)$ their wills. A solution is a correspondence $F$ with argument $(\xi; \Omega) = (n; h; w; \Omega)$ such that $F(\xi; \Omega)$ is a subset of feasible allocations.

Under Assumption 3.2, for any economy $\xi = (n; h; w)$ and any agent $i \le n$, one can define the function $\gamma_{\xi, i}$ by

$$\gamma_{\xi, i}(r) = \begin{cases} 0 & \text{if } O(0, h_i, w_i) \ge O(r, \tilde{h}, w_i), \\ r' & \text{if } O(r', h_i, w_i) = O(r, \tilde{h}, w_i). \end{cases}$$

Under Assumption 3.1, $\gamma_{\xi, i}$ is continuous and nondecreasing over $\mathbb{R}_+$. Let $f_\xi : \mathbb{R}_+ \to \mathbb{R}_+$ be defined by $f_\xi(r) = \sum_{i=1}^{n} \gamma_{\xi, i}(r)$. It is easily checked that, under Assumption 3.2, $f_\xi(\mathbb{R}_+) \cap \mathbb{R}_{++} \ne \emptyset$. Moreover, $f_\xi$ is increasing over $\{r \in \mathbb{R}_+ : f_\xi(r) > 0\}$. Therefore, one can define the function $g_\xi$: $f_\xi(\mathbb{R}_+) \cap \mathbb{R}_{++} \to \mathbb{R}_+$ by $g_\xi(\Omega) = f_\xi^{-1}$. In words, $g_\xi(\Omega)$ is the value of $\tilde{r}$ such that, with the aggregate resource $\Omega$, one can find a feasible allocation $r = (r_1, ..., r_n)$ such that for all $i$, either $r_i = 0$ and $O(0, h_i, w_i) \ge O(r, \tilde{h}, w_i)$ or $r_i > 0$ and $O(r_i, h_i, w_i) = O(r, \tilde{h}, w_i)$.

**Definition 4.4.**

$\Gamma_1 = \{(n; h; w; \Omega): (n; h; w) \in \Gamma \text{ and } \forall i, j, O(\Omega/n, h_i, \tilde{w}) \ge O(0, h_j, \tilde{w})\};$

$\Gamma_2 = \{(n; h; w; \Omega): (n; h; w) \in \Gamma \text{ and } \forall i, O(g_\xi(\Omega), \tilde{h}, w_i) \ge O(0, h_i, w_i)\}.$

**Theorem 4.1.** *The Conditional Equality solution is non-empty on the domain $\Gamma_1$, and the Egalitarian Equivalent solution is non-empty on $\Gamma_2$.*

The proof is standard, and is omitted for brevity.

The final result of this section is a dual characterization of these two solutions, based on the properties of compensation and reward. If $x = (x_1, \ldots, x_n)$ and $I \subset \{1, \ldots, n\}$, let $x_I$ denote the collection of $x_i$ such that $i \in I$.

**Definition 4.5.**   Consider an economy $(n; h; w)$, a resource $\bar{r}$, a subset $I \subset \{1, \ldots, n\}$, and the subeconomy $(|I|; h_I; w_I)$. The solution $F$ is *consistent* if

$$\forall r \in F(n; h; w; \bar{r}), \quad r_I \in F(|I|; h_I; w_I; \textstyle\sum_{i \in I} r_i).$$

**Theorem 4.2.**   *On the domain $\Gamma_1$, the Conditional Equality solution is the only single-valued consistent solution satisfying Adequate Compensation and Bipolar Reward. On the domain $\Gamma_2$, the Egalitarian Equivalent solution is the only single-valued consistent solution satisfying Bipolar Compensation and Adequate Reward.*

*Proof:*   Let $F$ be the solution under consideration.

(1) For Conditional Equality, let $(\xi; \Omega) \in \Gamma_1$ with $\xi = (n; h; w) \in \Gamma$, and let $r = (r_1, \ldots, r_n) = F(\xi; \Omega)$. Consider $\xi' = (2n; h, h; w')$, where $w_i' = w_i$ for $i \le n$ and $w_i' = \bar{w}$ for $i > n$. Obviously $\xi' \in \Gamma$. Moreover, $(\xi'; 2\Omega) \in \Gamma_1$ because

$$\forall i, j \in \{1, \ldots, 2n\}, \quad O(2\Omega/2n, h_i, \bar{w}) = O(\Omega/n, h_i, \bar{w}) \ge O(0, h_j, \bar{w}).$$

Therefore there exists $r' = (r_1', \ldots, r_{2n}') = F(\xi'; 2\Omega)$. Since $h_i = h_{i+n}$ for all $i \le n$, by Adequate Compensation one has $r_i' = r_{i+n}'$. As a consequence there is an $r'' = (r_1'', \ldots, r_n'')$ such that $r' = (r'', r'')$ and $\sum_{i=1}^{n} r_i'' = 2\Omega/2 = \Omega$. By consistency, retaining the first $n$ agents of $\xi$ one obtains $r'' = F(\xi; \Omega) = r$. Since $w_i = w_j = \bar{w}$, for all $i, j > n$, by Bipolar Reward one has

$$\forall i, j > n, \quad O(r_i', h_i, \bar{w}) = O(r_j', h_j, \bar{w}).$$

Recall that $r_i' = r_{i-n}$ and $r_j' = r_{j-n}$. Then,

$$\forall i, j \le n, \quad O(r_i, h_i, \bar{w}) = O(r_j, h_j, \bar{w}).$$

That is, $r$ satisfies the definition of Conditional Equality. Conversely, Conditional Equality satisfies the three properties stated in the theorem, and is single-valued under the current assumptions.

(2) For Egalitarian Equivalence, let $(\xi; \Omega) \in \Gamma_2$ with $\xi = (n; h; w) \in \Gamma$, and let $r = (r_1, \ldots, r_n) = F(\xi; \Omega)$. Consider $\xi' = (2n; h'; w, w)$, where $h_i' = h_i$ for $i \le n$ and $h_i' = \tilde{h}$ for $i > n$. Obviously, $\xi' \in \Gamma$. Examine $f_{\xi'}$. For $i \le n$, $\gamma_{\xi', i} = \gamma_{\xi, i}$; for $i > n$, $\gamma_{\xi', i}(x) = x$. As a consequence, $f_{\xi'}(x) = \sum_i \gamma_{\xi, i}(x) + nx = f_{\xi}(x) + nx$.

Let $\Omega' = \Omega + ng_\xi(\Omega)$. Since $\Omega = f_\xi \circ g_\xi(\Omega)$, one has $\Omega' = f_{\xi'} \circ g_\xi(\Omega)$ and so $g_{\xi'}(\Omega') = g_\xi(\Omega)$. As a result, it is easily checked that $(\xi'; \Omega') \in \Gamma_2$. Let $r' = (r_1', \ldots, r_{2n}') = F(\xi'; \Omega')$. As $h_i = h_j = \bar{h}$ for all $i, j > n$, by Bipolar Compensation there is an $\bar{r}$ such that $r_i' = r_j' = \bar{r}$. By Adequate Reward one has,

$$\forall i \leq n, \quad O(r_i', h_i, w_i) = O(\bar{r}, \bar{h}, w_{i+n}) = O(\bar{r}, \bar{h}, w_i).$$

Thus, for all $i \leq n$, $\gamma_{\xi, i}(\bar{r}) = r_i'$. Hence $f_\xi(\bar{r}) = \sum_{i=1}^n r_i'$ and $\bar{r} = g_\xi(\sum_{i=1}^n r_i')$. Similarly, $f_{\xi'}(\bar{r}) = \sum_{i=1}^n r_i' + n\bar{r} = \Omega'$ and thus $\bar{r} = g_{\xi'}(\Omega')$. Recall that $g_{\xi'}(\Omega') = g_\xi(\Omega)$. Therefore $g_\xi(\sum_{i=1}^n r_i') = g_\xi(\Omega)$, and so (since $g_\xi$ is increasing) $\Omega = \sum_{i=1}^n r_i'$.

By consistency, $(r_1', \ldots, r_n') = F(\xi; \Omega) = r$. This implies that

$$\forall i \leq n, \quad O(r_i, h_i, w_i) = O(\bar{r}, \bar{h}, w_i),$$

which is the definition of Egalitarian Equivalence. Conversely, Egalitarian Equivalence satisfies the three properties and is single-valued under the current assumptions.                                                    □

This last theorem shows that, although the pairs {Adequate Compensation, Bipolar Reward} and {Bipolar Compensation, Adequate Reward} are mutually compatible, they considerably reduce the range of acceptable solutions. Under consistency and uniqueness, only one solution remains in each case. As a result, Theorem 4.2 proves that, under consistency and uniqueness, it is impossible to combine with Adequate Compensation (resp. Adequate Reward) a stronger property than Bipolar Reward (resp. Bipolar Compensation).

This result also emphasizes the prominence of the Conditional Equality and Egalitarian Equivalent solutions. Both satisfy not only consistency, as stated in the theorem, but also Population Monotonicity (every agent suffers when new agents join the population) and Resource Monotonicity (every agent benefits when the aggregate resource $\bar{r}$ increases).[2] These three properties have now become classical ethical requirements in the literature of fair division. Besides, a specific advantage of Conditional Equality is that the allocation $r$ can be made ex ante (i.e., before the agents have chosen their wills), which is closer to the spirit of equal opportunity (cf. Section 2).

## 5    Concluding remarks

The purpose of this paper is to point out some of the stringent requisites of the ethical principle of equal opportunity. There is no claim of exhaustivity in what has been done here, and other difficulties and pitfalls can

---

[2] See Fleurbaey (1994c).

50      Marc Fleurbaey

of course be encountered on more sociological or philosophical grounds
(see Fleurbaey 1994b). Even in the field of economic theory, the question
of implementation has yet to be dealt with. But there is already a trade-off
between first-best existence and the degree of satisfaction of the equal-
opportunity principle, and this paper focuses on this trade-off.

Such a trade-off originates in a more general framework than equal
opportunity. It arises whenever one undertakes the project of equalizing
more than the external resources but less than the final outcomes (see
Fleurbaey 1994a for an examination). The consistency of such a project
with the general configuration of a nonseparable outcome function may
appear questionable, and this problem seems to have been overlooked by
the literature that advocates equality of (extended) resources, equality of
opportunity, or equality of access to advantage.

### Appendix

*Proof of Theorem 3.1:*   Under Assumption 3.3, all pairs $(h, w)$ and $(h', w')$
of int $D$, $(h, w) \neq (h', w')$, are "joined" in the following sense: There exist
$n$ and $(h_k, w_k)_{1 \leq k \leq n} \subset \text{int } D$ such that all $(h_k, w_k)$ are different, and:

$$(h_1, w_1) = (h, w) \quad \text{and} \quad (h_n, w_n) = (h', w');$$

$$\forall k < n, \quad h_k = h_{k+1} \text{ or } w_k = w_{k+1}.$$

Let $(h_k, w_k)_{1 \leq k \leq n}$ be called an $f$ *path* joining $(h, w)$ and $(h', w')$. Given
$r \geq 0$, an $f$ path is said to be *clear* for $r$ if there exists $(r_k)_{1 \leq k \leq n}$ such that
$r_1 = r$ and, for any $k < n$:

$$h_k = h_{k+1} \Rightarrow r_k = r_{k+1};$$

$$w_k = w_{k+1} \Rightarrow O(r_k, h_k, w_k) = O(r_{k+1}, h_{k+1}, w_{k+1}).$$

Consider $(h, w) \in \text{int } D$. Assume that for any $M$, there is an $r > M$,
$(h', w') \in \text{int } D$, a joining $f$ path clear for $r$, and a related $(r_k)_{1 \leq k \leq n}$ such
that $r_k < \underline{r}$ for some $k$. However, for a given $f$ path, $(r_k)_{1 \leq k \leq n}$ is an
unbounded increasing function of $r$. Since moreover $D$ is compact and $O$
is continuous, it is clear that the above assumption is impossible. Therefore an $L$ exists such that for any $r > L$, any $(h', w') \in \text{int } D$, and any joining $f$ path clear for $r$, the related $(r_k)_{1 \leq k \leq n}$ is such that $r_k \geq \underline{r}$ for all $k$.

Similar reasoning shows that there also exists an $L$ such that, for any
$r > L$ and any $(h', w') \in \text{int } D$, all joining $f$ paths are clear for $r$ and the
related $(r_k)_{1 \leq k \leq n}$ are such that $r_k \geq \underline{r}$ for all $k$. Notice that for $(h, w)$ and
$(h'', w)$ one can choose $L$ and $L''$ such that $O(L, h, w) = O(L'', h'', w)$. By
such a consistent choice of $L$, one can define a function $\theta$ by $\theta(w) =
O(L, h, w)$. Choose a particular $(h_0, w_0)$ in int $D$.

Take any $(r, h, w)$ in $\mathbb{R}_+ \times \operatorname{int} D$ such that $O(r, h, w) \geq \underline{\theta}(w)$. Consider two joining $f$ paths from $(h, w)$ to $(h_0, w_0)$, $(h_k, w_k)_{1 \leq k \leq n}$ and $(h'_k, w'_k)_{1 \leq k \leq m}$, and the related $(r_k)_{1 \leq k \leq n}$ and $(r'_k)_{1 \leq k \leq m}$. Consider the $(n + m - 2)$-agent economy characterized by the handicaps and wills $(h, w)$, $(h_k, w_k)_{2 \leq k \leq n-1}$, $(h'_k, w'_k)_{2 \leq k \leq m-1}$, and $(h_0, w_0)$. Finally, take the per-capita resource $\bar{r}^* = [r + \sum_{i=2}^{n-1} r_i + \sum_{i=2}^{m-1} r'_i + r_n]/(n + m - 2)$; $\bar{r}^* \geq \underline{r}$ because $r$ and any $r_i$ or $r'_i$ are each greater than $\underline{r}$. Therefore weak equal opportunity is non-empty in this economy. It is easy to see that the resulting allocation can only be $(r, (r_k)_{2 \leq k \leq n-1}, (r'_k)_{2 \leq k \leq m-1}, r_n)$. This implies $r_n = r'_m$, since $h_n = h'_m = h_0$. In conclusion, for any $(r, h, w)$ such that $O(r, h, w) \geq \underline{\theta}(w)$, this method provides a unique $r_0$ for $(h_0, w_0)$. Moreover, such a $r_0$ is obviously independent of $w$. One can then define a function $\nu$ by $\nu(r, h) = O(r_0, h_0, w_0)$, where $r_0$ is derived from $(r, h)$ in this way.

Assume there exist $(r', h')$ such that $(h', w) \in \operatorname{int} D$, $O(r', h', w) \geq \underline{\theta}(w)$, and $\nu(r', h') = \nu(r, h)$. This equality means that any joining $f$ path from $(r, h, w)$ or $(r', h', w)$ to $(h_0, w_0)$ will yield the same $r_0$, using the method just described. Let $(h'_k, w'_k)_{1 \leq k \leq n}$ be an $f$ path joining $(h', w)$ to $(h_0, w_0)$; $[(h, w), (h'_k, w'_k)_{1 \leq k \leq n}]$ is then an $f$ path joining $(h, w)$ to $(h_0, w_0)$. Necessarily, a related $(r'_k)_{1 \leq k \leq n+1}$ will be such that $r'_1 = r$, $r'_2 = r'$, and $O(r'_1, h, w) = O(r'_2, h', w)$. Hence $O(r, h, w) = O(r', h', w)$. One can then define a function $\mu$ by $\mu(t, w) = O(r, h, w)$ whenever $\nu(r, h) = t$, if $(h, w) \in D$ and $O(r, h, w) \geq \underline{\theta}(w)$. $\qquad \square$

*Proof of Theorem 3.2:* Let $r^* = (r_i)_{i \geq 1}$ be a weak equal opportunity allocation for $\bar{r}$. Consider any sequence $(h_k, w_k)_{k \geq 1} \subset P$ such that

$$\lim_{k \to \infty} (h_k, w_k) = (h, w) \in \operatorname{int} D.$$

Let $(r_k)_{k \geq 1}$ be the related sequence (derived from $r^*$). Assume that $(r_k)_{k \geq 1}$ is unbounded, and consider any agent $i$. Let $B_\epsilon(h, w)$ denote the ball of center $(h, w)$ and radius $\epsilon$ for the Euclidean metric. Due to Assumption 3.5, one has:

$$\forall \epsilon, \ \exists (h_k, w_k) \in B_\epsilon(h, w): r_k > r_i \text{ and } O(r_k, h_k, w_k) > O(r_i, h_i, w_i).$$

By weak equal opportunity, this implies:

$$\forall \epsilon, \ \exists (h_k, w_k) \in B_\epsilon(h, w): h_k < h_i \text{ and } w_k > w_i.$$

Hence $h \leq h_i$ and $w \geq w_i$. But this would be true for any $i$, which contradicts $(h, w) \in \operatorname{int} D$. Therefore the sequence $(r_k)_{k \geq 1}$ is bounded.

Choose any $(h, w) \in \operatorname{int} D$. For $\epsilon > 0$, define:

$$V_\epsilon^1(h, w) = B_\epsilon(h, w) \cap \{(x, y) \in D: (x, y) \geq (h, w)\};$$

$$V_\epsilon^2(h, w) = B_\epsilon(h, w) \cap \{(x, y) \in D: (x, y) \leq (h, w)\}.$$

There exist sequences $(h_k^1, w_k^1)_{k \geq 1}$ and $(h_k^2, w_k^2)_{k \geq 1}$ such that, for all $k$, $(h_k^1, w_k^1) \in P \cap V_{1/k}^1(h, w)$ and $(h_k^2, w_k^2) \in P \cap V_{1/k}^2(h, w)$. Let $(r_k^1)_{k \geq 1}$ and $(r_k^2)_{k \geq 1}$ be the related sequences (derived from $r^*$). By the preceding argument, they are bounded. Let $r^1$ and $r^2$ be limits of convergent subsequences. By weak equal opportunity, $r_k^1 \leq r_k^2$ for all $k$, and thus $r^1 \leq r^2$. But one also has $O(r_k^1, h_k^1, w_k^1) \geq O(r_k^2, h_k^2, w_k^2)$ for all $k$. Hence, by continuity, $O(r^1, h, w) \geq O(r^2, h, w)$, which implies $r^1 \geq r^2$. Therefore $r^1 = r^2$. In conclusion, for any $(h, w)$ in int $D$, one can derive a unique $r$ from $r^*$ in this way. This defines a function $\gamma$, with $\gamma(h, w; r^*)$ taking this value of $r$.

Let $h, w_1, w_2$ be such that $(h, w_1) \in$ int $D$ and $(h, w_2) \in$ int $D$. For any $(\sigma, \tau)$ in $\{1, 2\}^2$, choose a sequence $(h_k^{\sigma\tau}, w_k^{\sigma\tau})_{k \geq 1}$ in $P \cap V_{1/k}^\sigma(h, w_\tau)$. As before, one can take related sequences $(r_k^{\sigma\tau})_{k \geq 1}$ and limits of convergent subsequences $r^{\sigma\tau}$. By the previous argument, $r^{11} = r^{21} = \gamma(h, w_1; r^*)$ and $r^{12} = r^{22} = \gamma(h, w_2; r^*)$. But since $h^{22} \leq h^{11}$ and $h^{21} \leq h^{12}$, by weak equal opportunity $r^{22} \geq r^{11}$ and $r^{21} \geq r^{12}$. Hence $\gamma(h, w_1; r^*) = \gamma(h, w_2; r^*)$. The function $\gamma$ is independent of $w$, and therefore it will be denoted $\gamma(h; r^*)$ from now on.

Let $h_1, h_2, w$ be such that $(h_1, w) \in$ int $D$ and $(h_2, w) \in$ int $D$. By the same method as before, one shows that $O(\gamma(h_1; r^*), h_1, w) = O(\gamma(h_2; r^*), h_2, w)$. One can thus define a function $\theta$ by $\theta(w; r^*) = O(\gamma(h; r^*), h, w)$ for any $h$ such that $(h, w) \in$ int $D$.

Let $\bar{r}' > \bar{r}$, and let $r'$ and $r$ be respective weak equal opportunity allocations. Assume there is an $h$ in $H$ such that $\gamma(h; r') \leq \gamma(h; r)$. Since int $D$ is connected, necessarily there are $h_1, h_2, w$ such that $(h_1, w) \in$ int $D$, $(h_2, w) \in$ int $D$, and:

$$\gamma(h_1; r') \leq \gamma(h_1; r) \quad \text{and} \quad \gamma(h_2; r') > \gamma(h_2; r).$$

But this contradicts $O(\gamma(h_1; x), h_1, w) = O(\gamma(h_2; x), h_2, w)$ for $x = \bar{r}, \bar{r}'$. Therefore, for any $h$ in $H$, $\gamma(h; r') > \gamma(h; r)$.

A similar argument would show that $\bar{r}' \geq \bar{r}$ entails $\gamma(h; r') \geq \gamma(h; r)$ for any $h$. One can thus redefine the functions $\gamma$ and $\theta$ so as to make them depend on the per-capita resource $\bar{r}$ instead of the allocation $r^*$. One has $\theta(w; \bar{r}) = O(\gamma(h; \bar{r}), h, w)$ for any $h$ such that $(h, w) \in$ int $D$. Both functions are increasing in $\bar{r}$.

The function $\gamma$ is continuous in $\bar{r}$ for any $h$ in $H$. Here is a sketch of the argument proving this statement. When $\bar{r}$ increases, a jump by $\gamma$ can only be positive on $H$ (because $\gamma$ is increasing). The resource $\bar{r}$ cannot be a discontinuity point for all $\gamma(h; \cdot)$ with $h \in H$, because by Assumption 3.6 this would require a jump of the per-capita resource itself. Now, assume that $\bar{r}$ *is* a discontinuity point for all $\gamma(h; \cdot)$ with $h \in H_0 \subset H$. This implies that – for all $h \in H_0$, $h' \in H \setminus H_0$, and $w, w' \in W$ such that $(h, w) \in$ int $D$ and $(h', w') \in$ int $D$ – one has $h < h'$ and $w > w'$. But this is incompatible with the connectedness of int $D$.

Assume there exist $(r, h, w)$ such that $(h, w) \in \text{int} \, D$ and, for all $\bar{r}$, $\theta(w; \bar{r}) < O(r, h, w)$. Thus $\gamma(h; \bar{r}) < r$ for all $\bar{r}$. In view of Assumption 3.5, this implies that $\gamma(h'; \cdot)$ is bounded for any $h'$ such that there is $w'$ with $(h', w') \in \text{int} \, D$ and $(h, w') \in \text{int} \, D$. But because $\text{int} \, D$ is connected, the set of such $h$s is $H$ itself. The boundedness of $\gamma(h; \cdot)$ for all $h$ in $H$ contradicts Assumption 3.6, and so

$$\forall (r, h, w) \in \mathbb{R}_+ \times \text{int} \, D, \; \exists \bar{r} : \theta(w; \bar{r}) \geq O(r, h, w).$$

Let $\underline{\theta}$ be defined by $\underline{\theta}(w) = \theta(w; \underline{r})$. Let $(r, h, w) \in \mathbb{R}_+ \times \text{int} \, D$ be such that $O(r, h, w) \geq \underline{\theta}(w)$. By continuity and unboundedness of $\gamma$, there is an $\bar{r}$ such that $\gamma(h; \bar{r}) = r$; hence $\theta(w; \bar{r}) = O(r, h, w)$. Choose $(h_0, w_0)$ in $\text{int} \, D$ and let the function $\nu$ be defined by $\nu(r, h) = O(\gamma(h_0; \bar{r}), h_0, w_0)$, where $\bar{r}$ is derived from $\gamma(h; \bar{r}) = r$.

Take any $(r', h')$ such that $(h', w) \in \text{int} \, D$, $O(r', h', w) \geq \underline{\theta}(w)$, and $\nu(r', h') = \nu(r, h)$. This equality means that $\gamma(h_0; \bar{r}') = \gamma(h_0; \bar{r})$, where $\gamma(h'; \bar{r}') = r'$; hence $\bar{r}' = \bar{r}$. As a consequence, $\theta(w; \bar{r}) = O(r, h, w) = O(r', h', w)$. One can therefore define a function $\mu$ by $\mu(t, w) = O(r, h, w)$ for any $(r, h, w)$ such that $(h, w) \in \text{int} \, D$, $O(r, h, w) \geq \underline{\theta}(w)$, and $\nu(r, h) = t$. $\qquad \Box$

## REFERENCES

Arneson, R. J. (1989), "Equality and Equal Opportunity for Welfare," *Philosophical Studies* 56: 77–93.

Cohen, G. A. (1989), "On the Currency of Egalitarian Justice," *Ethics* 99: 906–44.

Dworkin, R. (1981), "What Is Equality? Part 2: Equality of Resources," *Philosophy and Public Affairs* 10: 283–345.

Fleurbaey, M. (1994a), "On Fair Compensation," *Theory and Decision* 36: 277–307.

(1994b), "Equal Opportunity or Equal Social Outcome?" *Economics and Philosophy* (to appear).

(1994c), "Three Solutions for the Compensation Problem," *Journal of Economic Theory* (to appear).

Pazner, E., and D. Schmeidler (1978), "Egalitarian-Equivalent Allocations: A New Concept of Economic Equity," *Quarterly Journal of Economics* 92: 671–87.

Roemer, J. E. (1985), "Equality of Talent," *Economics and Philosophy* 1: 151–87.

(1986), "Equality of Resources Implies Equality of Welfare," *Quarterly Journal of Economics* 101: 751–84.

(1987), "Egalitarianism, Responsibility, and Information," *Economics and Philosophy* 3: 215–44.

(1993), "A Pragmatic Theory of Responsibility for the Egalitarian Planner," *Philosophy and Public Affairs* 22: 146–66.

Van Parijs, Ph. (1990), "Equal Endowments as Undominated Diversity," *Recherches Economiques de Louvain* 56: 327–55.

Varian, H. (1985), "Dworkin on Equality of Resources," *Economics and Philosophy* 1: 110–25.

CHAPTER 3

# Social choice of individual and group rights

*Peter J. Hammond*

## 1    Introduction

It is more than twenty years since Amartya Sen set out to incorporate respect for individual rights in social choice theory. Though dictatorship is generally undesirable, there are certain private matters over which it is probably desirable for individuals' preferences to be decisive in the Arrow social welfare function that determines social preferences. Sen's decisiveness approach was soon extended to group rights by Batra and Pattanaik (1972) in their discussion of "federalism." In the case of individual rights, this approach is what Riley (1989) called "formulation A." Section 2 explains what it means for a social choice rule to respect both individual and group rights.

Sen (1970a,b) showed how it was generally impossible to grant even just two individuals rights over a single issue each without generating a Pareto inefficient outcome. He provided an example in which individuals have certain rights to create externalities, so that exercising those rights leads to Pareto inefficiency. Gibbard (1974) had another example showing how it could be impossible to grant rights to two different individuals over two binary issues each. For instance, suppose there are two people, the first of whom wants to wear the same color clothing as the second while the second wants to wear a different color from the first. Then there is no feasible choice of colors that respects both individuals' rights to choose what color clothing to wear.

Section 3 argues that this kind of example can be excluded by restricting individuals' preferences to be *privately oriented,* as in Hammond (1982).[1]

July 1993 revision of a paper presented to the first meeting of the Society for Social Choice and Welfare, at Caen in June 1992, and then revised in August 1992.
[1]  Similar restrictions on preferences have also been considered by Bernholz (1974), Gibbard (1974), Blau (1975), Farrell (1976), Breyer (1977), Ferejohn (1978), Suzumura (1978), Gaertner and Krüger (1981), and Riley (1990), among others.

That is, each individual should be indifferent over any issue that some other individual or group has the right to decide. Really, this amounts to assuming that when any individual or group exercises its rights, this never creates externalities for any other individuals or groups. It is then easy to prove that restricting preferences to be privately oriented is sufficient to ensure that *any* social choice rule can be strictly Paretian only if it respects not just individual rights, as in Coughlin (1986), but group rights as well. In particular, there is no longer any conflict between different individual and group rights, nor between rights and the Pareto principle. Of course, Sen's and Gibbard's original examples, together with many others of interest, involve preferences that are not privately oriented.

The rest of Section 3 goes on to present necessary conditions for it to be true that, given any pair of social states, there always exist privately oriented preferences allowing somebody to express a strict preference over this pair. In fact, the effective rights of different individuals, including also those of the groups to which they belong, must be *independent,* meaning that they involve disjoint components of a Cartesian product set of social states, as in the formulation due to Bernholz (1974) and Gibbard (1974).

Many libertarians and others wanting to emphasize the value of freedom have objected to this social choice formulation of rights. They claim that society should not have any preference over personal issues, which should be settled by individual rather than social choice. This view underlies Nozick's (1974) influential work, and has been forcefully expressed by numerous other writers, including Barry (1985). It suggests that, if an individual $i$ or a group $G$ has a right to choose $x$ over $y$, then the social system must provide that individual or group with some way of ensuring that $y$ never comes about when $x$ is feasible.

Since the work of Sugden (1978, 1985a,b, 1986), followed by Seidl (1986) and Gaertner, Pattanaik, and Suzumura (1992), it has become common to model this approach to rights by means of a game form.[2] A "libertarian" game form is one in which individuals or groups are given the power to determine any private issue over which they should have rights. This version of rights is what Riley (1989) called "formulation B." In Section 4 it is shown that any social choice rule that selects among the

---

[2] Gärdenfors (1981) has often been credited with using game forms to model rights. In fact, he modeled a right as giving an individual or group the power to confine the social outcome within a specified set of outcomes. His model of rights therefore resembles the "effectiveness functions" considered by Rosenthal (1972), Moulin and Peleg (1982), Moulin (1983), Peleg (1984), and Kolpin (1988). Gärdenfors did also consider strategic games in which individuals and groups could choose to exercise or waive each of their rights; cf. Gibbard (1974). These are very particular game forms, however. Also, the approach derives a game form from rights, rather than using a game form to represent rights.

relevant "strong equilibria" of the game form must respect rights. Conversely, under the assumptions of Section 3, there exists a game form (with complete information) implementing a strictly Pareto efficient outcome that must also respect rights – but the game form is generally not libertarian. In this sense, the game-form approach seems to be no more general than the classical Sen approach.

In my view, however, neither of these two approaches treats rights satisfactorily. Both treat rights as absolutes, never to be violated. Or at least they follow Rawls (1971) in giving rights absolute priority over outcomes in a lexical social preference ordering. Yet the results of Section 3 show how rarely is it possible to respect all individual and group rights. Also, if individuals prefer good outcomes to the chance to exercise all their rights, and if exercising some of these rights would lead to bad outcomes, why should all their rights predominate? As Gibbard (1982, p. 604) states, "liberty is a matter of norms." This suggests that, along with social states in the usual sense, both individual and group rights should themselves become the object of both individual preference and social choice. So one needs to consider a space of *rights-inclusive social states*.

Section 5 discusses three different versions of this formulation, leading up to a new way of including rights in the social state. This follows Pattanaik and Suzumura (1992) in considering the entire game form, not just equilibrium strategies or the outcomes these strategies lead to. But since it is *outcomes* and the opportunities to change those outcomes that seem to matter, I will suggest that one should represent game forms by their induced *rights structures*. These simply specify what opportunities to change the outcome of the game form are enjoyed by each individual and each group.

Section 6 contains a summary and some concluding remarks.

## 2 Rights-respecting social choice

### 2.1 *Preferences and social choice*

Suppose that there is a fixed *underlying set* $X$ of social states, as well as a fixed finite set of individuals $N$ with variable *preference orderings* $R_i$ ($i \in N$), which are complete and transitive binary relations defined on $X$. Let $P_i$ and $I_i$ ($i \in N$) denote the corresponding *strict preference* and *indifference* relations, respectively; these must also be transitive.

Write $R^N$ for the typical *preference profile* $\langle R_i \rangle_{i \in N}$ of individual preference orderings. Then, for each such profile $R^N$ and each non-empty $G \subset N$, let $P_G(R^N)$ and $P_G^*(R^N)$ denote the corresponding *strict* and *strongly strict group preference relations* defined for all pairs $a, b \in X$ by

58     Peter J. Hammond

$$a P_G(R^N) b \Leftrightarrow \forall i \in G : a P_i b;$$

$$a P_G^*(R^N) b \Leftrightarrow \{[\forall i \in G : a R_i b] \ \& \ [\exists h \in G : a P_h b]\}.$$

Because each individual's preference relation is transitive, so are the relations $P_G(R^N)$ and $P_G^*(R^N)$. In particular, the *weak* and the *strict Pareto dominance relations* $P_N(R^N)$ and $P_N^*(R^N)$ are both transitive.

Let $\mathcal{F}(X)$ denote the set of all non-empty finite subsets of $X$. A *social choice rule* (or SCR) is a mapping $C(\cdot, \cdot) : \mathcal{F}(X) \times \mathcal{P}^N \to \mathcal{F}(X)$ that determines, for every *feasible set* $A \in \mathcal{F}(X)$ and every preference profile $R^N$ in a (restricted) *domain* $\mathcal{P}^N$, a non-empty *choice set* $C(A, R^N) \subset A$. Given the SCR $C$ and the preference profile $R^N \in \mathcal{P}^N$, define the corresponding *revealed strict preference relation* $P^C(R^N)$ so that

$$a P^C(R^N) b \Leftrightarrow [\forall A \in \mathcal{F}(X) : a \in A \Rightarrow b \notin C(A, R^N)].$$

In particular, $a P^C(R^N) b$ implies that $b \notin C(\{a, b\}, R^N)$, but the same condition imposes restrictions on choice from larger sets $A \supset \{a, b\}$ as well. Because $C(A, R^N)$ must be non-empty whenever $A$ is non-empty and finite, it is easy to see that the relation $P^C(R^N)$ must be *acyclic* – that is, there can be no *cycle* $c^0, c^1, c^2, \ldots, c^n$ with $c^0 = c^n$ and $c^k P^C(R^N) c^{k-1}$ for $k = 1, \ldots, n$.

Say that the SCR $C$ is *strictly Paretian* provided that $a P^C(R^N) b$ whenever $a, b \in X$ and $R^N \in \mathcal{P}^N$ satisfy $a P_N^*(R^N) b$. In this case, for every feasible set $A \in \mathcal{F}(X)$, the SCR $C$ will always select some of the (strictly) Pareto efficient social states in $A$. Recall that Sen's (1970a) *strict Pareto extension rule* is defined as the SCR $C^{\mathrm{Par}}(\cdot, \cdot)$ which, for every feasible set $A \in \mathcal{F}(X)$ and every $R^N \in \mathcal{P}^N$, has

$$C^{\mathrm{Par}}(A, R^N) = \{a \in A \mid b P_N^*(R^N) a \Rightarrow b \notin A\}.$$

In other words, $C^{\mathrm{Par}}(A, R^N)$ consists of those members of $A$ that are strictly Pareto efficient given the preference profile $R^N$. Evidently a general SCR $C$ is strictly Paretian if and only if $\emptyset \neq C(A, R^N) \subset C^{\mathrm{Par}}(A, R^N)$ throughout the domain $\mathcal{F}(X) \times \mathcal{P}^N$. Note especially that, because $P_N^*(R^N)$ is transitive and so acyclic, one has $C^{\mathrm{Par}}(A, R^N) \neq \emptyset$ throughout $\mathcal{F}(X) \times \mathcal{P}^N$. This implies that there is a strictly Paretian SCR; in fact, there must be many unless the preference domain $\mathcal{P}^N$ is very restricted.

Given any pair $a, b \in X$, the (non-empty) group $G \subset N$ is said to be *decisive for a over b* if, whenever the profile $R^N$ is such that $a P_G(R^N) b$, then $a P^C(R^N) b$. This definition implies, of course, that $\{a\} = C(\{a, b\}, R^N)$ when $a P_G(R^N) b$; thus, if $G$ is decisive for $a$ over $b$, then $a$ is the only possible social choice from the pair $\{a, b\}$ when all members of the group $G$ strictly prefer $a$ to $b$. In case $G$ is decisive for $b$ over $a$ as well as for $a$ over $b$, say that $G$ is *decisive over* $\{a, b\}$.

## 2.2    Rights

Sen, together with Batra and Pattanaik, regarded the rights of each individual and of each group $G \subset N$ as being represented by a (possibly
empty) collection $D_G \subset X \times X$ of ordered pairs over which $G$ is supposed
to be decisive. Of course, this set $D_G$ can be regarded as the graph of a
binary preference relation; this being so, $D_G$ can be called a *rights relation* without undue confusion. It will be assumed that $D_G$ is irreflexive in
the sense that there is no $x \in X$ with $x D_G x$.

Let $\mathcal{G}$ denote the collection of groups $G$ having nontrivial rights relations $D_G$. In other work it is often assumed that only individuals have
rights, so that $\mathcal{G} = \{\{i\} \mid i \in N\}$. But no such assumption will be needed
here – groups may have rights, and some or all individuals may have no
rights. Often $D_i$ instead of $D_{\{i\}}$ will be used to indicate individual $i$'s rights
relation.

As Sen (1992) is right (and also has the right) to remind us, the purpose
of his original work was to demonstrate how the Pareto principle could
easily conflict with even such a minimal form of liberalism as that requiring there to be at least two pairs of social states $\{x_i, y_i\}, \{x_j, y_j\}$ (possibly
overlapping, as in his example concerning which of two rather perverse
individuals is to read one particular copy of D. H. Lawrence's novel *Lady
Chatterley's Lover*) and two individuals $i, j \in N$ who are granted the right
to be decisive for $x_i$ over $y_i$ and for $x_j$ over $y_j$, respectively. Nevertheless,
it is still a powerful and much used model of rights for a broader class of
problems.

In what follows, it will be assumed that a particular *rights profile* $D^{\mathcal{G}}$
of irreflexive rights relations $\langle D_G \rangle_{G \in \mathcal{G}}$ has been specified for some set
$\mathcal{G} \subset 2^N$ of groups (and individuals) with rights. Though minimal rights
relations need not satisfy this extra property, the results of Section 3 will
require each rights relation $D_G$ to be *symmetric* in the sense that $x D_G y$
if and only if $y D_G x$. Note that, if $G'$ is a proper subset of $G$, then $G$
will be decisive over $\{x, y\}$ whenever $G'$ is. However, in order to avoid
redundancy it will be assumed that, if $x D_G y$, then there is no proper
subset $G'$ of $G$ for which $x D_{G'} y$. In other words, I shall consider only
*minimal* decisive groups as having rights. Thus, one should regard $D_G$ as
indicating what extra rights $G$ has in addition to those of all its proper
subgroups.

Finally, say that the SCR $C: \mathcal{F}(X) \times \mathcal{P}^N \to \mathcal{F}(X)$ *respects the rights
profile* $D^{\mathcal{G}}$ if, whenever $a, b \in X$ with $a D_G b$ and $a P_G(R^N) b$, then
$a P^C(R^N) b$. In other words, whenever $a, b \in X$ with $a D_G b$, group $G$
should be decisive over $\{a, b\}$.

## 3      Independent rights

### 3.1      *Privately oriented preferences*

Given the rights profile $D^\mathcal{G} = \langle D_G \rangle_{G \in \mathcal{G}}$ together with any individual $i \in N$, let $E_i$ denote the corresponding *no-rights* relation defined on $X$ so that

$$a E_i b \Leftrightarrow \exists G \in \mathcal{G} : [i \notin G \ \& \ a D_G b].$$

The interest of this relation is that, if $a E_i b$, then it is generally impossible to allow $i$ to have a right between $x$ and $y$ without contradicting some other individual's or group's right over the same pair. For obviously, if $a D_G b$ and also $b D_{G'} a$ for some disjoint pair of groups $G, G'$, then it is impossible to respect both groups' rights whenever their members' preferences are strictly opposed, with $a P_G(R^N) b$ and also $b P_{G'}(R^N) a$.

Let $\mathcal{R}(X)$ denote the set of all logically possible preference orderings defined on the set $X$. Let

$$\mathcal{R}_i(X, D^\mathcal{G}) := \{R \in \mathcal{R}(X) \mid a E_i b \ \Rightarrow \ a I_i b\}$$

denote the set of *privately oriented* preference orderings for individual $i$ relative to the rights profile $D^\mathcal{G}$ – namely, the set of those orderings on $X$ that express indifference over any pair for which some group excluding $i$ has a right. The Sen and Gibbard paradoxes arise from preferences that are not privately oriented in this way. Note how the definition extends that of Hammond (1982) not only by allowing group as well as individual rights, but also by not requiring $X$ to be a Cartesian product space. Shortly, however, the need for such a product space will be demonstrated, under a weak additional condition on the domain of allowable preferences. Let $\mathcal{R}^N(X, D^\mathcal{G}) := \prod_{i \in N} \mathcal{R}_i(X, D^\mathcal{G})$ denote the set of all possible privately oriented preference profiles (or POPPs).

The following result shows how the Sen and Gibbard paradoxes can indeed be avoided by limiting the preference domain to POPPs; there is no need for any more severe restrictions on individuals' preferences. Actually, as Coughlin (1986) has noticed, Pareto efficiency even *requires* respect for individual rights in this case; now it will be shown that group rights must be respected as well.

**Theorem 1.**   *Suppose that, for the given rights profile $D^\mathcal{G}$, the domain $\mathcal{P}^N$ of allowable preference profiles $R^N$ is restricted to POPPs so that $\mathcal{P}^N \subset \mathcal{R}^N(X, D^\mathcal{G})$. Then the social choice rule $C(A, R^N)$ on the domain $\mathcal{F}(X) \times \mathcal{P}^N$ satisfies the strict Pareto rule only if it respects both individual and group rights.*

*Proof:* Suppose that the social states $a, b \in X$ and the group $G \in \mathcal{G}$ are such that $a\, D_G\, b$. Suppose too that the POPP $R^N \in \mathcal{R}^N(X, D^{\mathcal{G}})$ satisfies $a\, P_G(R^N)\, b$. Since $R^N$ is a POPP, it follows that $a\, I_i\, b$ for all $i \in N \setminus G$, and so $a\, P_N^*(R^N)\, b$. If the SCR $C$ is strictly Paretian, therefore, it must be true that $a\, P^C(R^N)\, b$, proving that $G$ is decisive for $a$ over $b$. Hence all rights are respected by any strictly Paretian SCR.                                    $\square$

Since a Pareto efficient SCR certainly exists, Theorem 1 assures us that when preferences are privately oriented, then all rights can be respected; indeed, they must be, by any strictly Paretian SCR. Nor need the strict Pareto criterion then be violated in respecting individual and group rights.

The converse of Theorem 1 would state that respecting individual and group rights is sufficient for Pareto efficient social choice. This is true for individual rights alone under the extra assumptions imposed by Coughlin (1986), but is not true generally; see Section 3.3.

## 3.2    *Necessity of independent rights*

Suppose that $a, b$ are two different social states in $X$. Then it seems reasonable that there should be a preference profile $R^N$ in the domain $\mathcal{P}^N$ for which at least one individual $i \in N$ has a preference ordering with $a$ and $b$ not indifferent. Moreover, this should be true even when preference profiles are restricted to POPPs in $\mathcal{R}^N(X, D^{\mathcal{G}})$. Call this the *rich private domain assumption*. It will now be shown that this assumption has the important implication that the underlying set $X$ has a Cartesian product structure such as that originally considered by Bernholz (1974) and Gibbard (1974).

Indeed, say that the rights profile $D^{\mathcal{G}} = \langle D_G \rangle_{G \in \mathcal{G}}$ is *weakly independent* if $X$ is equivalent to a subset of some Cartesian product set $X^N := \prod_{i \in N} X_i$ with the property that, for each $G \subset N$, and for each pair $a = \langle a_i \rangle_{i \in N}$ and $b = \langle b_i \rangle_{i \in N} \in X$, one has $a\, D_G\, b$ only if $a_i = b_i$ for all $i \in N \setminus G$ (cf. Hammond 1982). Thus $X$ can be regarded as a subset of a product space with a separate component $X_i$ for each individual $i \in N$, such that groups (including those with single individuals) have rights only to issues affecting just their members' components of the product space. Similarly, say that $D^{\mathcal{G}}$ is *strongly independent* if it is weakly independent and if the component spaces $X_i$ ($i \in N$) also have the property that

$$a\, D_G\, b \Leftrightarrow G = \{i \in N \mid a_i \neq b_i\}.$$

It might seem at first that these two definitions of independent rights exclude the possibility that the underlying set of social states takes the form of a Cartesian product $Z = \prod_{G \in \mathcal{G}_{\geq 2}} Z_G \times \prod_{i \in N} Z_i$ where, for any $G$ in the set $\mathcal{G}_{\geq 2}$ of groups in $\mathcal{G}$ having at least two members, $Z_G$ consists of public or club good vectors shared by all the members of group $G$, while each $Z_i$ consists of $i$'s private good consumption vectors. In fact, however, it is possible to construct a separate copy $Z_{Gi}$ of the space $Z_G$ whenever $G \in \mathcal{G}_{\geq 2}$, and then to let $X_i := \prod_{i \in G \in \mathcal{G}_{\geq 2}} Z_{Gi} \times Z_i$ for each $i \in N$. This allows $X$ to be defined as the subset of $X^N := \prod_{i \in N} X_i$ whose elements take the form $x^N = \langle (\langle z_{Gi} \rangle_{i \in G \in \mathcal{G}_{\geq 2}}, z_i) \rangle_{i \in N}$ with a common $z_G \in Z_G$ for which $z_{Gi} = z_G$ (all $i \in G \in \mathcal{G}_{\geq 2}$); that is, each such $z_{Gi}$ is just a personalized copy of $z_G$. Of course, this is equivalent to the device used by Foley (1970) and Milleron (1972) to describe allocations with public goods, with Lindahl prices as the prices of personalized public goods.

**Lemma 2.**   *Suppose that the set $\mathfrak{R}^N(X, D^{\mathcal{G}})$ of POPPs satisfies the rich private domain assumption. Then rights are weakly independent. Moreover, the component spaces $X_i$ ($i \in N$) for which $X \subset \prod_{i \in N} X_i$ have the property that $a\, I_i\, b$ whenever $a, b \in X$, $i \in N$, $a_i = b_i$, and $R^N \in \mathfrak{R}^N(X, D^{\mathcal{G}})$.*

*Proof:*   For each $i \in N$, let $E_i$ denote $i$'s no-rights relation, which can be thought of as $\bigcup_{i \notin G \in \mathcal{G}} D_G$. Let $E_i^*$ denote the *transitive completion* of $E_i$ – that is, the relation defined so that $a\, E_i^*\, b$ if and only if there is a finite chain $c^0, c^1, c^2, ..., c^m \in X$ with $c^0 = a$ and $c^m = b$ such that $c^{k-1} E_i c^k$ for $k = 1, ..., m$. Evidently $E_i^*$ is reflexive, symmetric, and transitive, so it is an equivalence relation.

For each $i \in N$, let $Q_i := X/E_i^*$ denote the quotient set whose members are the $E_i^*$ equivalence classes in $X$. For each $x \in X$, let $[x]_i \in Q_i$ denote the unique $E_i^*$ equivalence class having $x$ as a member.

Now suppose that $i \in N$ and $[a]_i = [b]_i$. By definition, it must then be true that $a\, E_i^*\, b$. Suppose too that $R^N$ is any POPP in $\mathfrak{R}^N(X, D^{\mathcal{G}})$. Then, since $x E_i y \Rightarrow x I_i y$, and since the indifference relation $I_i$ is transitive, it must be true that $a\, I_i\, b$.

Next, suppose that $a, b \in X$ are such that $[a]_i = [b]_i$ for all $i \in N$. Then, for any POPP $R^N \in \mathfrak{R}^N(X, D^{\mathcal{G}})$, the previous paragraph shows that $a\, I_i\, b$ (all $i \in N$). So the rich private domain assumption implies that $a = b$.

It follows that there is a one-to-one mapping $x \mapsto \langle [x]_i \rangle_{i \in N}$ from $X$ into the Cartesian product $Q^N := \prod_{i \in N} Q_i$ of the quotient spaces. Hence we can identify $X$ with the range

$$Q := \{ \langle q_i \rangle_{i \in N} \in Q^N \mid \exists x \in X : q_i = [x]_i \text{ (all } i \in N) \} \subset Q^N$$

of this one-to-one mapping. Thus, there is a one-to-one correspondence $\rho : X \to Q$ with $\rho(x) := \langle [x]_i \rangle_{i \in N}$ for all $x \in X$. After identifying $X$ with $Q$, we can go on to regard $X$ as a subset of $\prod_{i \in N} X_i$, where each $X_i$ is just a relabeling of $Q_i$. Then each $x \in X$ can be expressed as $\langle x_i \rangle_{i \in N}$, where $x_i \in X_i$ is really just shorthand for $[x]_i \in Q_i$. Hereafter, the condensed notation $x_i$ will be used throughout. By the result of the next-to-last preceding paragraph, it follows that $a\,I_i\,b$ whenever $a, b \in X$, $i \in N$, $a_i = b_i$, and $R^N \in \mathfrak{R}^N(X, D^{\mathcal{G}})$.

Finally, suppose that $a\,D_G\,b$ for some pair $a, b \in X$ with $a \neq b$. Then, for all $i \in N \setminus G$, one has $a\,E_i\,b$ and so $a_i = b_i$. This completes the proof of weak independence.                                                                                     $\square$

Though simple, Lemma 2 has powerful implications. There is a clear sense in which exercising rights creates no externalities precisely when there is a POPP. Lemma 2 states that one can have a POPP *without* forcing everybody always to be indifferent between some pair of social states if and only if the underlying set is a subset of a Cartesian product set in a way that makes rights weakly independent.

Even under the rich private domain assumption, it is not generally true that rights must be strongly independent. Nevertheless, it is possible to replace the original rights profile $D^{\mathcal{G}}$ with the new strongly independent rights profile $\hat{D}^{2^N} = \langle \hat{D}_G \rangle_{G \subset N}$ having the following four properties:[3]

(1) the domains of all POPPs relative to the two different rights profiles are equal;

(2) whenever $a\,D_G\,b$ then, though it may not be true that $a\,\hat{D}_G\,b$, there is nevertheless some subset $G'$ of $G$ for which $a\,\hat{D}_{G'}\,b$;

(3) any SCR that respects the new rights profile $\hat{D}^{2^N}$ will also respect $D^{\mathcal{G}}$;

(4) any SCR that is strongly Paretian on some domain of POPPs will respect the new rights profile $\hat{D}^{2^N}$ (as well as $D^{\mathcal{G}}$).

Thus $\hat{D}^{2^N}$ is virtually an extension of $D^{\mathcal{G}}$ because of properties (2) and (3). Yet, because of properties (1) and (4), the Sen and Gibbard paradoxes are avoided for the same domain of POPPs. Indeed, we have the following.

**Theorem 3.** *Suppose that the set $\mathfrak{R}^N(X, D^{\mathcal{G}})$ of POPPs satisfies the rich private domain assumption. Then $X$ is equivalent to a subset of $\prod_{i \in N} X_i$ such that, for the strongly independent rights profile $\hat{D}^{2^N}$ defined on that subset by*

$$a\,\hat{D}_G\,b \leftrightarrow G = \{i \in N \mid a_i \neq b_i\} \ (\text{all } G \subset N),$$

*the properties* (1)–(4) *are satisfied.*

---

[3] Really, I should print $\hat{D}^{2^N \setminus \{\emptyset\}}$ instead of $\hat{D}^{2^N}$. But the empty group will be given a vacuous rights relation anyway.

*Proof:* The four properties are verified in turn as follows.

(1a) Suppose that $R^N$ is any POPP in $\Re^N(X, D^G)$. For any $i \in N$ and $a, b \in X$, suppose that $a\hat{D}_G b$ for some $G \ni i$. Then $a_i = b_i$ and so, by Lemma 2, $a I_i b$. Hence the restrictions for $R^N \in \Re^N(X, \hat{D}^{2^N})$ are all satisfied.

(1b) Conversely, for any $i \in N$ and $a, b \in X$, suppose that $a D_G b$ for some $G \ni i$. Then $a E_i b$ and so, by the construction used in the proof of Lemma 2, $a_i = b_i$. This implies that $a\hat{D}_{G'} b$ for some $G' \ni i$. Thus, for any $R^N \in \Re^N(X, \hat{D}^{2^N})$, it follows that $a I_i b$. Hence the restrictions for $R^N \in \Re^N(X, D^G)$ are all satisfied by any $R^N \in \Re^N(X, \hat{D}^{2^N})$.

(2) Suppose that $a, b \in X$ is any pair satisfying $a D_G b$. By Lemma 2, $a_i = b_i$ for all $i \in N \setminus G$; also $a \neq b$, because $D_G$ is assumed to be irreflexive. Hence there is a non-empty $G' \subset G$ for which $a_i \neq b_i$ if and only if $i \in G'$, so $a\hat{D}_{G'} b$ for this subset $G'$.

(3) Suppose that $C$ is an SCR that respects $\hat{D}^{2^N}$. Let $a, b \in X$ be any pair of social states and $G \subset N$ any group for which both $a D_G b$ and $a P_G(R^N) b$. Then $a P_{G'}(R^N) b$ for every $G' \subset G$. But by (2) there exists a $G' \subset G$ for which $a\hat{D}_{G'} b$. Since $C$ respects $\hat{D}^{2^N}$, it follows that $a P^C(R^N) b$. This proves that $C$ respects $D^G$.

(4) Suppose that $a, b \in X$ is any pair satisfying $a\hat{D}_G b$ for the group $G \subset N$. By definition of $\hat{D}_G$, it must be true that $a_i = b_i$ if and only if $i \in N \setminus G$. Because of Lemma 2, for any POPP $R^N$ in $\Re^N(X, \hat{D}^{2^N})$ or in the identical set $\Re^N(X, D^G)$, it must be true that $a I_i b$ for all $i \in N \setminus G$. Hence, whenever $a P_G(R^N) b$ is also true then $a P_N^*(R^N) b$, implying that $a P^C(R^N) b$ for any strictly Paretian SCR $C$ defined on a domain of POPPs (as in the proof of Theorem 1). Therefore any such $C$ respects the rights profile $\hat{D}^{2^N}$. □

## 3.3     *A counterexample*

Under the same assumptions as Theorem 1, and for the special case when there are only individual rights and $X$ is a Cartesian product space with one component for each individual, Coughlin (1986) also proved that any rights-respecting SCR that corresponds to a binary social preference relation must be Paretian. As remarked in Section 3.1, this is the natural converse to Theorem 1. There is no such general result when there are also group rights to respect, however, as can be seen from the following modification of an example considered by Gibbard (1974, p. 398) and Gärdenfors (1981).[4] Suppose that there are three individuals, $N = \{A, E, J\}$, *where A denotes Angelina, E Edwin, and J the (male) judge.* Suppose too that $X = \prod_{\emptyset \neq G \subset N} X_G$, where

---

[4] Readers who are not already familiar with the Gilbert and Sullivan operettas may care to see *Trial by Jury* for what seems to be the original story.

$$X_G = \begin{cases} \{0_G, 1_G\} & \text{if } G \in \{\{A, E\}, \{A, J\}\}, \\ \{\bar{x}_G\} & \text{otherwise.} \end{cases}$$

Here $1_G$ represents the couple $G$ getting married, while $0_G$ represents them not doing so. Also, $\bar{x}_G$ denotes a dummy option for groups $G \notin \{\{A, E\}, \{A, J\}\}$, representing the absence of rights for these other groups (and individuals) on their own.

Write the four possible social states in the obvious summary form $0, e, j, b$, where 0 indicates that Angelina marries nobody, $e$ that she marries Edwin, $j$ that she marries the judge, and $b$ that she marries both Edwin and the judge. Though $b$ may well be excluded from the (legally) feasible set, it is in the underlying set because that set must always be a Cartesian product. Incidentally, this illustrates how restrictive is Riley's (1989) assumption that the feasible set is always an entire Cartesian product set – though actually, in the plausible case where the judge is much older than both Angelina and Edwin, $b$ could be interpreted as Angelina marrying the judge first, and then marrying Edwin a few years later when the judge has died!

Assume that each potential couple $\{A, E\}, \{A, J\}$ has the group right to decide whether or not to get married. Then, to be strongly independent, the two nontrivial rights relations $D_{AE}$ and $D_{AJ}$ must respectively satisfy:

$$0 D_{AE} e, \quad e D_{AE} 0; \quad j D_{AE} b, \quad b D_{AE} j;$$
$$0 D_{AJ} j, \quad j D_{AJ} 0; \quad b D_{AJ} e, \quad e D_{AJ} b.$$

Note that this configuration gives each couple the right to marry, even if Angelina also marries the other man.

Suppose that the three individuals' basic preference orderings $R_i$ ($i \in \{A, E, J\}$) satisfy $b P_A j P_A e P_A 0$, while $0 P_E e$ and $j P_J 0$. Edwin and the judge's preferences can then be extended in a unique (though somewhat perverse) manner to a POPP satisfying $j I_E 0 P_E e I_E b$ and $b I_J j P_J 0 I_J e$, with each man indifferent to the externality that arises when Angelina marries the other.

According to the definition given in Section 2.2, when individuals have this POPP, respecting the joint rights of Angelina and the judge requires that:

(i)   $b P e$ because $b P_A e$, $b P_J e$, and $b D_{AJ} e$;
(ii)  $j P 0$ because $j P_A 0$, $j P_J 0$, and $j D_{AJ} 0$.

On the other hand, because of the conflicting preferences $e P_A 0$ and $0 P_E e$, as well as $b P_A j$ and $j P_E b$, it follows that any social preferences over the two pairs $\{0, e\}$ and $\{j, b\}$ will respect the joint rights of Angelina and Edwin, as specified by the rights relations $0 D_{AE} e$, $e D_{AE} 0$, $j D_{AE} b$, and

$b D_{AE} j$. Finally, no individual or couple has rights over either of the pairs $\{0, b\}$ and $\{j, e\}$, so that any social preferences over these pairs are consistent with respect for rights. Accordingly, the social preference relation defined by $b P e P j P 0$ respects each couple's rights. Yet the particular social preference $e P j$ clearly violates even the weak Pareto principle, since all three individuals prefer $j$ to $e$.

Though this example is somewhat contrived, it does show how Pareto efficiency is not ensured by respecting group rights, even for the case when preferences are privately oriented and rights are strongly independent. The converse to Theorem 1 is therefore not true in general.

## 4    Power in game forms

### 4.1    *Libertarian game forms*

Suppose that for every feasible set $A \in \mathcal{F}(X)$ there is a corresponding *game form* $\Gamma_A = (S_A^N, g_A)$, with individual *strategy sets* $S_{iA}$ ($i \in N$) and an *outcome function* $g_A(\cdot): S_A^N \to A$ whose domain is the Cartesian set $S_A^N :=$ $\prod_{i \in N} S_{iA}$. Thus, a unique *outcome* $g_A(s^N) \in A$ is specified for each *strategy profile* $s^N = (s_i)_{i \in N} \in S_A^N$.

In the following, for any group $G \in \mathcal{G}$, let $S_A^G$ denote the Cartesian product set $\prod_{i \in G} S_{iA}$ of strategy profiles for the members of the group $G$, with typical member $s^G$; let $S_A^{N \setminus G}$ denote the set $\prod_{i \in N \setminus G} S_{iA}$ of strategy profiles for the members of the complementary group $N \setminus G$, with typical member $s^{N \setminus G}$.

Given the rights profile $D^{\mathcal{G}}$, say that the game form $\Gamma_A = (S_A^N, g_A)$ is *libertarian* provided that, if $a D_G b$ for some $G \in \mathcal{G}$ and $a, b \in A$, while $\bar{s}^N \in S_A^N$ and $b = g_A(\bar{s}^N)$, then there exists some $s^G \in S_A^G$ for which $a = g_A(s^G, \bar{s}^{N \setminus G})$. Thus, whenever $G \in \mathcal{G}$ and $a D_G b$, the group $G$ must have the power to change the outcome from $b = g_A(\bar{s}^G, \bar{s}^{N \setminus G})$ to $a = g_A(s^G, \bar{s}^{N \setminus G})$, no matter what strategies $\bar{s}^{N \setminus G} \in S_A^{N \setminus G}$ may be chosen by individuals outside the group.

Relative to any preference profile $R^N$, the strategy profile $\bar{s}^N \in S_A^N$ is said to be a $\mathcal{G}$-*strong equilibrium* for the game form $(S_A^N, g_A)$ if there is no group $G \in \mathcal{G}$ with an alternative strategy profile $s^G \in S_A^G$ for which $g_A(s^G, \bar{s}^{N \setminus G}) P_G(R^N) g_A(\bar{s}^N)$. Thus $\bar{s}^G$ must be an efficient response to $\bar{s}^{N \setminus G}$ for every group $G \in \mathcal{G}$. For each preference profile $R^N$, denote by $E_{\mathcal{G}}(\Gamma_A, R^N)$ the corresponding set of $\mathcal{G}$-strong equilibria of the game form $\Gamma_A = (S_A^N, g_A)$; this set is a (possibly empty) subset of $S_A^N$.

**Theorem 4.** *Let $D^{\mathcal{G}}$ be a given rights profile on $X$. Suppose that the libertarian game form $\Gamma_A = (S_A^N, g_A)$ has the property that the $\mathcal{G}$-strong* *equilibrium set $E_{\mathcal{G}}(\Gamma_A, R^N)$ is non-empty for all feasible sets $A \in \mathcal{F}(X)$ and all preference profiles $R^N$ in the restricted domain $\mathcal{P}^N$. Then any SCR satisfying $\emptyset \neq C(A, R^N) \subset g_A(E_{\mathcal{G}}(\Gamma_A, R^N))$ everywhere in the domain $\mathcal{F}(X) \times \mathcal{P}^N$ must respect rights.*

*Proof:* Suppose that some such SCR $C(\cdot, \cdot)$ did not respect rights. Then there would exist a feasible set $A \in \mathcal{F}(X)$, a profile $R^N \in \mathcal{P}^N$, a group $G \in \mathcal{G}$, and social states $a, b \in A$ such that $a D_G b$ and $a P_G(R^N) b$ yet $b \in C(A, R^N) \subset g_A(E_{\mathcal{G}}(\Gamma_A, R^N))$. Hence there would be a $\mathcal{G}$-strong equilibrium $\bar{s}^N \in E_{\mathcal{G}}(\Gamma_A, R^N) \subset S_A^N$ such that $b = g_A(\bar{s}^N)$.

Because the game form $\Gamma_A$ is libertarian and $a D_G b$, there must exist some group strategy profile $s^G \in S_A^G$ for which $a = g_A(s^G, \bar{s}^{N \setminus G})$. Because $a P_G(R^N) b$, the strategy $\bar{s}^G$ could not then be an efficient response for group $G$ to $\bar{s}^{N \setminus G}$ after all, and so $\bar{s}^N$ could not be a $\mathcal{G}$-strong equilibrium – a contradiction. It has therefore been proved (by contradiction) that the SCR $C(\cdot, \cdot)$ must respect the rights profile $D^{\mathcal{G}}$. $\qquad \square$

Theorem 4 states that rights-respecting SCRs are no less general than libertarian game forms *for the same given configuration of rights*. Note that there was no need even to assume any restrictions such as privately oriented preference profiles or independent rights, though the theorem is in danger of being vacuous without such restrictions.

## 4.2    An implementation

The following result shows how, under the rich private domain assumption used in Section 3, it is possible to construct a game form that will implement in strong equilibrium any given strictly Pareto efficient outcome. Moreover, every Nash equilibrium will yield an outcome which every individual finds indifferent to that given outcome. By Theorem 1, the resulting choice of outcome must respect both individual and group rights.

**Theorem 5.** *Suppose that the set $\mathcal{R}^N(X, D^{\mathcal{G}})$ of POPPs satisfies the rich private domain assumption so that, by Lemma 2, $X$ is equivalent to a subset of the product space $\prod_{i \in N} X_i$ with the properties that $a I_i b$ whenever $a_i = b_i$ and that $a D_G b$ implies $a_j = b_j$ for all $j \in N \setminus G$. Then, for every feasible set $A \in \mathcal{F}(X)$, every POPP $R^N \in \mathcal{R}^N(x, D^{\mathcal{G}})$, and any $\bar{x} \in A$ that is strictly Pareto efficient given $R^N$, there exists a game form $\Gamma_A$ with strategy sets $S_{iA} = X_i$ $(i \in N)$ and outcome function*

$$g_A(s^N) := \begin{cases} s^N & \text{if } s^N \in A, \\ \bar{x} & \text{if } s^N \notin A, \end{cases}$$

*such that there is one strong equilibrium with $\bar{s}^N = \bar{x}$, and all Nash equilibria $\hat{s}^N$ of $\Gamma_A$ satisfy $g_A(\hat{s}^N) I_i \bar{x}$ (all $i \in N$).*

*Proof:* First, let $\bar{s}_i = \bar{x}_i$ (all $i \in N$). Now, given any non-empty $G \subset N$, let $s^G \in S_A^G$ and $a \in A$ be such that $a = g_A(s^G, \bar{s}^{N\backslash G}) \neq \bar{x}$. Then it must be true that $a = (s^G, \bar{x}^{N\backslash G}) \in A$. Hence $a I_i \bar{x}$ for all $i \in N\backslash G$. But then $a P_G(R^N) \bar{x}$ would imply that $a P_N^*(R^N) \bar{x}$, contradicting the hypothesis that $\bar{x}$ is strictly Pareto efficient in $A$. This confirms that $\bar{x}^N$ is a strong equilibrium.

Second, let $\hat{s}^N$ be any other Nash equilibrium. Then, because $i$ could choose $\bar{x}_i \in S_{iA}$ instead, one must have $g_A(\hat{s}^N) R_i g_A(\bar{x}_i, \hat{s}^{N\backslash\{i\}})$ for all $i \in N$. But by definition of the outcome function $g_A(\cdot)$, it must be true that $g_A(\bar{x}_i, \hat{s}^{N\backslash\{i\}})$ is equal to $\bar{x}$ or to $(\bar{x}_i, \hat{s}^{N\backslash\{i\}})$. In either case $g_A(\bar{x}_i, \hat{s}^{N\backslash\{i\}}) I_i \bar{x}$. Since $R_i$ is transitive, it follows that $g_A(\hat{s}^N) R_i \bar{x}$ for all $i \in N$. But $\bar{x}$ is strictly Pareto efficient, and so $g_A(\hat{s}^N) I_i \bar{x}$ for all $i \in N$. □

Note that the game form $\Gamma_A$ need not be libertarian, however. For suppose that $a \in X$ and $G \subset N$ are such that $a D_G \bar{x}$. But now, if $s^N \notin A$ and so $g_A(s^N) = \bar{x}$, it is generally not true that $G$ can change the outcome from $\bar{x}$ to $a$ by finding an $\bar{s}^G \in S_A^G$ for which $g_A(\bar{s}^G, s^{N\backslash G}) = a$. In fact, this would require not only that group $G$ choose $\bar{s}^G = a^G$ but also the coincidence that $s^{N\backslash G} = a^{N\backslash G} = \bar{x}^{N\backslash G}$, even though $g_A(s^N) = \bar{x}$ for every $s^N$ such that $s^N \in A$. For instance, if $A = \{0, e, j\}$ and $\bar{x} = j$ in the example of Section 3.3, there is no way that the game form $\Gamma_A$ just constructed allows Angelina and Edwin to change the outcome to $e$ while the judge continues to choose the strategy of marrying Angelina.

This absence of libertarianism makes Theorem 5 weaker than the corresponding result in Riley (1989). The difference arises because here the outcome function $g_A(s^N)$ must be well-defined for all $s^N \in \prod_{i \in N} X_i$ even when $A$ is a proper subset of this product space, and even when $A$ is not itself a product space. In the special case when $A = \prod_{i \in N} A_i$, one could take $\tilde{S}_{iA} = A_i$ (all $i \in N$) and use the alternative outcome function $\tilde{g}_A(s^N) := s^N$ for all $s^N \in S_A^N$. This yields an alternative libertarian game form $\tilde{\Gamma}_A$ with a set of strong equilibria that coincides with the set of all strictly Pareto efficient social states – that is,

$$g_A(E_G(\tilde{\Gamma}_A, R^N)) = C^{\text{Par}}(A, R^N)$$

for every preference profile $R^N$.

### 4.3    Direct game forms

Of particular interest in Section 5.2 will be the special case of *direct game forms,* in which all individuals' strategies coincide with their respective preference orderings. Thus, as in the direct mechanisms that occur in the literature on incentive compatibility, it is as though the game form were being played by having individuals report their preferences directly, after which the outcome function selects the appropriate social state for the reported profile of preferences. Apart from this analogy, direct game forms would also seem appropriate for normative judgments concerning a social system, since they tell us precisely how the social state reflects individuals' preferences.

Of course, restricting oneself to such direct game forms places a potentially serious limitation on just which SCRs can be implemented. Indeed, it was by allowing a weak form of implementation – through indirect game forms or mechanisms such as those considered by Maskin (1979, 1985) – that Riley (1989) was able to demonstrate exact equivalence between formulations A and B, that is, between the rights-respecting social choice approach and his version of the libertarian game-form approach. Of course, Riley also restricted attention to binary SCRs, individual rather than group rights, and feasible sets in the Cartesian product form $A = \prod_{i \in N} A_i$. An indirect game form was also used in Section 4.2 to prove the closely related Theorem 5.

Indirect game forms are crucial here, however. Indeed, given the negative results for fully Pareto efficient dominant strategy mechanisms such as those surveyed by Dasgupta, Hammond, and Maskin (1979) or Groves and Ledyard (1987), it is clear that direct game forms cannot implement as many SCRs as indirect game forms do. For suppose it were possible to construct a direct game form for which truthfulness was always a $\mathcal{G}$-strong equilibrium, no matter what the privately oriented preference profile may be. Then, arguing as in Dasgupta et al. (1979), for each group $G \in \mathcal{G}$, no matter what privately oriented preferences are being reported by the individuals who are not members of $G$ among the set of all possible reports of privately oriented preferences, truthfulness would always be an optimal strategy for each individual in $G$, as well as an efficient strategy for group $G$ and all its subgroups. In fact, truthfulness would therefore always be a "$\mathcal{G}$-dominant strategy equilibrium," in an obvious sense, contradicting the negative results just cited.

Yet indirect game forms have their own serious problems. Their equilibrium outcomes are generally sensitive to players' beliefs about each other and about how the game form will be played, as pointed out in the discussions of implementation via Bayesian or Nash equilibrium in Ledyard (1978, 1986), Dasgupta et al. (1979), and Hammond (1990, 1994). Furthermore, indirect game forms typically implement only *extended* social choice rules that can be expressed as $C(A, R^N, \theta^N)$, where $\theta^N = (\theta_i)_{i \in N}$ is a profile of types that are sufficient to determine each individual's actions and beliefs in the game form.

## 5      Rights-inclusive social states

### 5.1      *Motivation*

As mentioned in Section 1, I now want to call into question the way in which past discussions of rights have usually described the social states themselves. As a reason for doing so, note that it is impossible to tell whether a political system is a meaningful democracy unless one knows not only the social states or outcomes that emerge from the system but also how well those outcomes reflect individual preferences and values. This illustrates the rather obvious point, which Sugden (1978, 1981, 1986) has also made in a rather different way, that a social choice rule cannot really be judged only on the basis of the social outcomes it generates; it is important to know as well how these outcomes depend on individual preferences. This, of course, takes us to the kind of direct game form introduced in Section 4.3. It is true that such game forms can be classified as libertarian or not, according to the definition given in Section 4.1. Yet this treats respect for rights as an absolute standard, to be satisfied entirely. There is no room for compromise, and no way of discussing how serious is the extent of any rights violations. Moreover, we live in a world that confronts us with many unfortunate issues where trade-offs between different kinds of rights for different individuals seem unavoidable, so the lack of a framework for discussing how to make the necessary compromises is disturbing.

An alternative formulation seems rather obvious. Following Pattanaik and Suzumura (1992), we should consider rights themselves as part of the social state; in other words, we should have *rights-inclusive social states*. Then, along with social outcomes, rights assignments will become objects of preference according to some higher-order individual preference relations. Rights assignments will also become objects of social choice according to some higher-order social choice rule. In this new approach, respect for rights and liberty becomes a relative concept. Some social choice rules will unambiguously show more respect for rights than others do because they choose both more extensive rights assignments and social outcomes that heed rights better. But there may be no social choice rule at all that respects rights fully.

This, then, is another way to formulate the issue of how (much) to respect rights. The urgent question to be considered next is how to model an assignment of rights before incorporating it in the social state. Note that Pattanaik and Suzumura (1992) chose to model rights as general game forms. Yet this suffers from the disadvantage of paying too much attention to the strategies themselves (and their labels) but not enough to the outcomes resulting from those strategies. After all, it is not clear why one profile of strategy sets should be preferred to another unless the two profiles are likely to give rise to different social outcomes, or at least to different opportunities for individuals and groups to obtain preferred outcomes by exercising their rights. Accordingly, the rest of this section will consider two other ways of modeling rights.

## 5.2    Rights as direct game forms

Recall that direct game forms were defined in Section 4.3 as mappings directly from individual preference profiles to social outcomes. Modeling rights as direct game forms differs from the framework used by Pattanaik and Suzumura (1992), who allow complete general game forms, rather than only direct game forms, to be objects of individual preference and of social choice. Nevertheless, it seems only natural at first that the social choice rule should involve choosing a non-empty set of direct game forms.

For one thing – just as in the theory of mechanism design – given any game form and any set of behavior rules mapping individual preference profiles into equilibrium strategies, there is an equivalent direct game form mapping individual preference profiles into social outcomes. Direct game forms are also an obvious object of individual preference if we admit that individuals may be unsure of their own preferences, especially with regard to future outcomes, and that they may also value flexibility for its own sake. Once again there is an analogy with the literature on incentive compatibility, which teaches us to consider direct mechanisms in their entirety in order to see how well an economic system performs. In both cases, moreover, there is yet a further analogy with the Arrow–Debreu theory of resource allocation under uncertainty, with its suggestion that allocations of all possible state-contingent commodities should be considered. Indeed, if one thinks of individuals' preferences as uncertain or as at least private information, then "state-contingent social outcomes" are the obvious counterparts in social choice theory.

The difficulty with such direct game forms, however, is that they rely excessively on reaching an equilibrium in order to know how the social outcome depends on individual preferences. To see this, consider the "matching shirts" example, originally due to Gibbard (1974), which was briefly mentioned in Section 1. This same example also figures prominently in the recent interchange between Gaertner et al. (1992), Pattanaik and Suzumura (1990), and Sen (1992). Recall that it is really just a version of the well known two-person zero-sum game of "matching pennies," but played with shirts of two different colors – for example, white and blue. There are two players: one is a conformist who wants to match; the other is a nonconformist who wants to be different. It seems natural to give each individual the right to choose what color shirt to wear. Yet then none of the four different possible allocations of two shirt colors to two individuals respects both individuals' rights. Nor does the game have a Nash equilibrium in pure strategies.

Thus, there is no good way to construct a direct game form that specifies what color shirt each individual will wear in the case when their preferences take this form. Nevertheless, there is a clear sense in which, no matter what color shirt each individual chooses to wear, they each exercise their right to wear what they choose. Of course, one player will want to change shirts after observing what color the other is wearing, and may even claim that his rights have been violated. But this is a spurious claim. It is true that this player has made a choice which is regretted later; this may be because of inappropriate expectations or miscalculation, among many other possible reasons. Yet, as Pattanaik and Suzumura (1990) are right to emphasize, players can make mistakes in playing a game form without necessarily having their rights violated. Indeed, the rights of individuals and groups clearly would be violated if they were to be prevented from ever making any mistake! For this reason, therefore, I have come to understand that rights are not adequately modeled by direct game forms.

## 5.3    Rights relations induced by game forms

Fortunately, there is another way of inferring which individual and group rights (to control the social outcome) emerge from the structure of the game form. Indeed, given the feasible set $A$, let $\Gamma_A = (S_A^N, g_A)$ be a game form as defined in Section 4.1. Then the *individual rights structure* induced by $\Gamma_A$ consists of the profile $D^N = \langle D_i \rangle_{i \in N}$ of individual rights relations defined so that, for all $i \in N$ and all pairs $a, b \in A$, one has $a D_i b$ if and only if, whenever there exists $s^N \in S_A^N$ for which $g_A(s^N) = b$, there also exists some other $\bar{s}_i \in S_{iA}$ for which $g_A(\bar{s}_i, s^{N \setminus \{i\}}) = a$. In other words, $a D_i b$ requires that individual $i$ alone always has the power to change the outcome $b$ into the outcome $a$, no matter what fixed strategies $s^{N \setminus \{i\}}$ are chosen by the other individuals. Note that, if the individual rights relations really were these $D_i$ ($i \in N$), then $\Gamma_A$ would be individually libertarian.

Now suppose that $a D_i b$ and $a P_i b$ yet, because of a mistake by $i$ or for some other reason, $b$ is still the social outcome that results from the game form. Even so, it is illegitimate for $i$ to claim any rights violation, because $i$ could have altered the outcome to $a$ instead. Disappointed expectations and mistaken free choices are different from violations of personal rights.

A similar construction is possible for group rights, building recursively from the induced individual rights structures defined above. Indeed, the *group rights structure* induced by $g_A(\cdot)$ consists of the profile $\langle D_G \rangle_{G \subset N}$ of rights relations defined so that, for all non-empty $G \subset N$ and all $a, b \in A$, one has $a\,D_G\,b$ if and only if there is no proper subset $H$ of $G$ for which $a\,D_H\,b$ and also, whenever there exists $s^N \in S_A^N$ for which $g_A(s^N) = b$, there also exists $\bar{s}^G \in S_A^G$ for which $g_A(\bar{s}^G, s^{N\backslash G}) = a$. In other words, $a\,D_G\,b$ requires that: (i) group $G$ always has the power to change the outcome $b$ into the outcome $a$ on its own, no matter what strategies individuals outside the group choose; (ii) no proper subset of $G$ has this same power to change $b$ into $a$. Note that this definition does *not* presume that individuals and groups always exercise their rights in order to maximize their preferences.

Thus every game form induces a rights structure in a natural way. These rights structures describe what power individuals and groups have to change the social outcome. Each game form is libertarian with respect to its induced rights structure, and it is these rights structures that I believe should be incorporated in the description of each social state.

## 6 Summary and concluding remarks

Section 3 investigated the inevitable limits to the individual and group rights that can be respected, especially if there is to be no conflict with the Pareto criterion. It was suggested that it is natural to consider *privately oriented preference profiles,* for which Theorem 1 says that all such conflicts disappear. However, if the domain of such preference profiles is rich enough to allow that, given any pair of different social states, at least one individual can express a strict preference over that pair, then the underlying set of social states can be given a product structure such that individuals (and groups) effectively have independent rights over their own (members') components of the product space.

Thereafter, Section 4 set out the relationship between the rights-respecting social choice and libertarian game form formulations of rights. In particular, Theorem 4 tells us that selecting social states from the appropriate strong equilibrium outcomes of a libertarian game form always generates a rights-respecting social choice rule. On the other hand, some rights-respecting social choice rules cannot be implemented by means of a libertarian game form. Thus, when the two approaches differ, it must always be the rights-respecting or decisive social choice approach that is somewhat more general. It bears repeating, however, that Riley (1989) was able to obtain exact equivalence by restricting attention to feasible sets in the form of Cartesian products.

74     Peter J. Hammond

The characterization results of Sections 3 and 4 are essentially negative, showing how unlikely it is that all individual and group rights can be respected. Generally, therefore, a choice must be made of which rights to satisfy and which to violate. Accordingly, Section 5 contained three different suggestions for incorporating rights within the description of each social state. It was argued that the rights relations induced by a game form may be the most appropriate way of respecting those rights.

Finally, I should say that I am uncomfortably aware of the ultimate endnote in Sen (1992). This warns us that:

While the process through which a state of affairs is reached can be brought into the characterization of that social state (and this adds substantially to the domain of the social-choice formulations of liberty), the implicit nature of this presentation can be sometimes rather unhelpful.

This note refers to a fuller discussion in Sen's 1991 Arrow Lectures on "freedom and social choice," which I have so far not had the opportunity of seeing. Nor was I able to hear the lectures as they were delivered, so I am presently unable to say whether I agree or disagree. In fact, though, the specification of an induced rights structure says virtually nothing about "the process through which" the social state finally emerges, and so I remain unsure whether the point I wish to make is really being addressed at all.

Nevertheless, I take heart from some other words of Sen's:

While there is some obvious advantage in seeing liberty as control, it is a mistake to see it *only* as control. The simpler social choice characterizations catch one aspect of liberty well (to wit: whether people are getting what they *would have chosen* if they had control), but miss another (to wit: who actually controlled the decision). But the view of liberty as control misses the former important aspect altogether even though it catches the latter. A more satisfactory theory of liberty in particular and rights in general would try to capture both aspects . . . . (1985, pp. 231-2)

Including in the description of each social state the rights structure induced by a game form does indeed "try to capture both aspects" of liberty. Future work will determine how successful this attempt will be.

### Acknowledgments

The results in Section 3 owe their origins to work that was excluded from Hammond (1982) because it remained seriously incomplete, but to which I had promised to return. In addition, I owe much to Peter Coughlin and Jonathan Riley, whose writings prompted me to begin work on some later results presented here.

I am also grateful to Wulf Gaertner, Prasanta Pattanaik, and Kotaro Suzumura, for it was as a result of the very clear presentation of their (1992) joint paper to the previous "Social Choice and Welfare" conference in Valencia that the idea for the formulation of Section 5.2 started to take shape, which turned out to be similar to that incorporated in Pattanaik and Suzumura (1992). The later formulation of Section 5.3 was then inspired by Prasanta Pattanaik's "Economic Theory" seminar at Stanford in February, 1992, together with the extended discussion which occurred at that seminar – involving Kenneth Arrow and Patrick Suppes, among others.

Also, apart from the obvious debt that all who work in this area owe to Amartya Sen, it took some of his recent unpublished work to convince me that the issue really is still worth discussing. I have also benefited from useful conversations with Susan Snyder while she has been working on closely related matters. Finally, the constructive criticisms of an anonymous referee are gratefully acknowledged. None of these acknowledged here is responsible for any deficiencies in this paper.

## REFERENCES

Barry, B. (1985), "Lady Chatterley's Lover and Doctor Fischer's Bomb Party: Liberalism, Pareto Optimality, and the Problem of Objectionable Preferences," in J. Elster and A. Hylland (eds.), *Foundations of Social Choice Theory.* Cambridge: Cambridge University Press, pp. 11-43.

Batra, R. N., and P. K. Pattanaik (1972), "On Some Suggestions for Having Non-Binary Social Choice Functions," *Theory and Decision* 3: 1-11.

Bernholz, P. (1974), "Is a Paretian Liberal Really Impossible?" *Public Choice* 20: 99-107.

Blau, J. H. (1975), "Liberal Values and Independence," *Review of Economic Studies* 42: 395-401.

Breyer, F. (1977), "The Liberal Paradox, Decisiveness over Issues, and Domain Restrictions," *Zeitschrift für Nationalökonomie* 37: 45-60.

Cohen, L. J., J. Łoś, H. Pfeiffer, and K.-P. Podewski, eds. (1982), *Logic, Methodology and the Philosophy of Science,* vol. VI. Amsterdam: North-Holland.

Coughlin, P. J. (1986), "Rights and the Private Pareto Principle," *Economica* 53: 303-20.

Dasgupta, P. S., P. J. Hammond, and E. S. Maskin (1979), "The Implementation of Social Choice Rules: Some General Results on Incentive Compatibility," *Review of Economic Studies* 46: 185-216.

Farrell, M. J. (1976), "Liberalism in the Theory of Social Choice," *Review of Economic Studies* 43: 3-10.

Ferejohn, J. A. (1978), "The Distribution of Rights in Society," in H. W. Gottinger and W. Leinfellner (eds.), *Decision Theory and Social Ethics: Issues in Social Choice.* Dordrecht: Reidel, pp. 119-31.

Foley, D. K. (1970), "Lindahl's Solution and the Core of an Economy with Public Goods," *Econometrica* 38: 66-72.

76     Peter J. Hammond

Gaertner, W., and L. Krüger (1981), "Self-Supporting Preferences and Individual Rights: The Possibility of Paretian Libertarianism," *Economica* 48: 17–28.
Gaertner, W., P. K. Pattanaik, and K. Suzumura (1992), "Individual Rights Revisited," *Economica* 59: 161–77.
Gärdenfors, P. (1981), "Rights, Games and Social Choice," *Noûs* 15: 341–56.
Gibbard, A. (1974), "A Pareto-Consistent Libertarian Claim," *Journal of Economic Theory* 7: 388–410.
(1982), "Rights and the Theory of Social Choice," in Cohen et al. (1982), pp. 595–605.
Groves, T., and J. O. Ledyard (1987), "Incentive Compatibility since 1972," in T. Groves, R. Radner, and S. Reiter (eds.), *Information, Incentives and Economic Mechanisms: Essays in Honor of Leonid Hurwicz*. Minneapolis: University of Minnesota Press, pp. 48–111.
Hammond, P. J. (1982), "Liberalism, Independent Rights and the Pareto Principle," in Cohen et al. (1982), pp. 607–20.
(1990), "Incentives and Allocation Mechanisms," in R. van der Ploeg (ed.), *Advanced Lectures in Quantitative Economics*. New York: Academic Press, pp. 213–48.
(1994), "A Revelation Principle for (Boundedly) Bayesian Rationalizable Strategies," in R. P. Gilles and P. H. M. Ruys (eds.), *Imperfections and Behavior in Economic Organizations*. Boston: Kluwer, pp. 39–70.
Kolpin, V. W. (1988), "A Note on Tight Extensive Game Forms," *International Journal of Game Theory* 17: 187–91.
Ledyard, J. O. (1978), "Incentive Compatibility and Incomplete Information," *Journal of Economic Theory* 18: 171–89.
(1986), "The Scope of the Hypothesis of Bayesian Equilibrium," *Journal of Economic Theory* 39: 59–82.
Maskin, E. (1979), "Implementation and Strong Nash Equilibrium," in J.-J. Laffont (ed.), *Aggregation and Revelation of Preferences*. Amsterdam: North-Holland, pp. 433–9.
(1985), "The Theory of Implementation in Nash Equilibrium: A Survey," in L. Hurwicz, D. Schmeidler, and H. Sonnenschein (eds.), *Social Goals and Social Organization*. Cambridge: Cambridge University Press, pp. 173–204.
Milleron, J.-C. (1972), "Theory of Value with Public Goods: A Survey Article," *Journal of Economic Theory* 5: 419–77.
Moulin, H. (1983), *The Strategy of Social Choice*. Amsterdam: North-Holland.
Moulin, H., and B. Peleg (1982), "Cores of Effectivity Functions and Implementation Theory," *Journal of Mathematical Economics* 10: 115–45.
Nozick, R. (1974), *Anarchy, State and Utopia*. New York: Basic Books.
Pattanaik, P. K., and K. Suzumura (1990), "Professor Sen on Minimal Liberty," discussion paper no. 231, Institute of Economic Research, Hitotsubashi University.
(1992), "Individual Rights and Social Evaluations: A Conceptual Framework," paper presented at the June 1992 meeting of the Society for Social Choice and Welfare (Caen, France).
Peleg, B. (1984), *Game Theoretic Analysis of Voting in Committees*. Cambridge: Cambridge University Press.
Rawls, J. (1971), *A Theory of Justice*. Cambridge, MA: Harvard University Press.
Riley, J. (1989), "Rights to Liberty in Purely Private Matters, Part I," *Economics and Philosophy* 5: 121–66.

(1990), "Rights to Liberty in Purely Private Matters, Part II," *Economics and Philosophy* 6: 27–64.

Rosenthal, R. W. (1972), "Cooperative Games in Effectiveness Form," *Journal of Economic Theory* 5: 88–101.

Seidl, C. (1986), "The Impossibility of Nondictatorial Tolerance," *Journal of Economics* (Suppl. 5) 46: 211–25.

Sen, A. K. (1970a), *Collective Choice and Social Welfare*. San Francisco: Holden Day.

(1970b), "The Impossibility of a Paretian Liberal," *Journal of Political Economy* 78: 152–7 (reprinted in Sen 1982).

(1982), *Choice, Welfare and Measurement*. Oxford: Basil Blackwell.

(1985), "Foundations of Social Choice Theory: An Epilogue," in J. Elster and A. Hylland (eds.), *Foundations of Social Choice Theory*. Cambridge: Cambridge University Press, pp. 213–38.

(1992), "Minimal Liberty," *Economica* 59: 139–59.

Sugden, R. (1978), "Social Choice and Individual Liberty," in M. J. Artis and A. R. Nobay (eds.), *Contemporary Economic Analysis*. London: Croom Helm.

(1981), *The Political Economy of Public Choice*. Oxford: Martin Robertson.

(1985a), "Why Be Consistent?" *Economica* 52: 167–84.

(1985b), "Liberty, Preference and Choice," *Economics and Philosophy* 1: 213–29.

(1986), *The Economics of Rights, Co-operation and Welfare*. Oxford: Basil Blackwell.

Suzumura, K. (1978), "On the Consistency of Libertarian Claims," *Review of Economic Studies* 45: 329–42.

CHAPTER 4

# Population monotonic allocation rules

*William Thomson*

## 1 Introduction

In the recent developments that have occurred in axiomatic analysis, several requirements have been formulated that are designed to ensure the good behavior of decision rules, or solutions, when the number of individuals involved varies. Among these requirements, the principle of population monotonicity has been playing an increasingly important role. It is the objective of this paper to present this principle, to survey the various applications that have been made of it, and to provide a guide for future research.

Like several of the principles that have been considered in normative studies of solutions, population monotonicity expresses the solidarity of agents as their circumstances change; in this case, what changes is how many agents there are. Here is a statement of the principle for the canonical problem of fairly dividing a vector of resources among agents who possess equal rights with respect to those resources, a problem that has inspired the principle's introduction: Consider, for instance, the division of an estate among several heirs. After the division is performed by applying some solution, a new claimant appears whose rights on a share of the estate are recognized to have equal validity; hence, the estate must be redivided. We say that the solution is population monotonic if none of the heirs originally present gains as a result of this new claimant's arrival. Equivalently, if some of the heirs relinquish their rights then none of the remaining heirs loses.

Our starting point in this survey will be the following more abstract form of the requirement: When additional agents arrive, and the profile

Support from NSF under grant SES 9212557 and the very helpful comments of Sang-Young Sonn, Yves Sprumont, Koichi Tadenuma, and an anonymous referee are gratefully acknowledged. Thanks also to Tarık Kara, my LaTeX coach.

of welfare levels chosen by the solution for the initial group remains feasible only by "ignoring the newcomers," then none of the agents initially present gains. Conversely, the departure of some of the agents, if it permits a Pareto improvement for the remaining agents, is indeed accompanied by such an improvement.

We first apply the principle to two standard models of game theory – bargaining problems and coalitional form games – and, after examining a somewhat more concrete model of cost allocation, we turn to the classical problem of fairly allocating a bundle of infinitely divisible goods. Then we examine several special classes of problems of allocation of goods: economies with public goods; economies with indivisible goods; and finally economies with single-peaked preferences, both in the private-good and the public-good case.

As we shall see, much remains to be done. Ideally, we would like to know how restrictive the condition is by completely describing the class of solutions satisfying it, together of course with standard conditions. Such characterizations are available for only a few models. Population monotonic solutions have been identified for a number of other models, but we are still far from fully understanding the implications of the property.

We conclude by outlining the various components that a systematic analysis of population monotonicity on a given domain should comprise. Such an analysis should identify the most natural form of the property for the domain; find out if the main solutions for the domain satisfy the property; describe the class of solutions satisfying it, together with standard properties; clarify the extent to which the requirement is compatible with other properties of interest; and, when solutions exist that do satisfy population monotonicity, formulate criteria permitting evaluation of how well these solutions perform the job – if all agents lose, how "evenly" are the losses distributed across them? On the other hand, when the property is too restrictive one must be satisfied with weaker versions of it. The tasks then are to formulate weakenings that retain as wide a range of applicability as possible; to identify subdomains of interest on which the main property can still be met; and to formulate criteria permitting evaluation of how frequently solutions fail to satisfy the property.

Such a program was pursued by Thomson (1983a,b,c, 1984a,b, 1987a), Thomson and Lensberg (1983), and Chun and Thomson (1988, 1989, 1992) in the context of abstract bargaining problems. Recent studies by Chun (1986), Alkan (1994), Sprumont (1990), Moulin (1990a, 1992a), Thomson (1991), and others will permit us in the final section of this survey to reformulate, in more precise terms and by reference to some specific models, a number of components of the program.

## 2 Population monotonicity: a general formulation

In most axiomatic studies, the number of agents is held fixed. Here we allow it to vary, and require of solutions that they provide recommendations for economies of all admissible cardinalities. The axiom of population monotonicity is meant to help us relate the recommendations made by solutions as the number of agents varies.

The formulation given previously for the problem of fair division is the one that has been adopted in most applications, since typically – and here we deliberately use vague language so as to obtain a statement that is meaningful for as wide a range of models as possible – the arrival of newcomers is indeed a "burden" on the agents initially present. It implies a restriction of their opportunities in the sense that the list of welfare levels initially selected for them is feasible only by ignoring the newcomers, although they should of course not be ignored.

In some situations of interest, however, the arrival of the newcomers permits a "sufficient" expansion of opportunities, by which we mean that the list of welfare levels initially selected is now Pareto dominated by the list of welfare levels attained at a decision under which the rights of all agents, including those of the newcomers, are fully acknowledged. Here, the requirement will be that none of the agents initially present be made to lose.

In a third class of models, the arrival of newcomers may or may not be beneficial, depending on their characteristics. Here, the natural formulation of the property is that all agents initially present be affected in the same direction by this arrival: either none of them loses or none of them gains (Chun 1986).

We believe that an essential part of what is generally (although often implicitly) understood by the phrase "economic justice" is that agents be affected in the same direction as their circumstances change, provided no one bears any special responsibility for these changes. Changes in circumstances might be increases or decreases in the quantities of the goods available for consumption or of the inputs to be used in production; improvements in technology or fluctuations in climate; or, as we consider here, variations in the population. In this latter case, we can imagine actual changes due to immigration or emigration, epidemics, or births. However, the changes may be hypothetical: we often evaluate decision rules in terms of what they would recommend in situations other than the one we actually face. Some of the changes just listed could of course be due to some particular action that some agents may have taken. But here, eschewing issues of incentives and responsibilities, we will limit ourselves to those situations where changes occur independently of the will of the agents whose welfare levels are to be chosen.

It is particularly illuminating to test rules by having some agents *leave* the scene. In this case, two possibilities arise: (1) A decision has already been made, and a commitment to certain payoffs for the departing agents must be honored. In most models, efficiency – together with the requirements that all remaining agents be affected in the same direction by this departure – implies that the remaining agents also end up with the same payoffs. This gives us a form of the "consistency" condition, which has been the object of a considerable literature in the last few years.[1] (2) Alternatively, in situations where it is natural to assume that agents relinquish their rights when they leave, we obtain the requirement imposed on the rule that is being studied here.

Population monotonicity is an ordinal requirement, that is, it depends only on agents' preferences. Its application does not rely on the social planner's ability to measure, let alone compare and (even less) equate, sacrifices or gains. But it is conceptually compatible with the use of such operations, and in any case, if so desired – we will see several examples of this – population monotonicity can be applied in models specified in utility space. In such models the principle can be complemented with additional requirements based on cardinal information.

In order to deal with a variable number of agents, we need a sufficiently general formulation. We assume that there is an infinite number of potential agents, indexed by the positive integers $\mathbb{N}$, but we only consider problems involving finite groups. Let $\mathcal{Q}$ be the class of all finite subsets of $\mathbb{N}$, with generic elements $Q, Q', \ldots$ . A *solution* is a correspondence which associates with every problem in the class that the group $Q$ may face, where $Q \in \mathcal{Q}$, a set of outcomes in the feasible set of that problem, each of which being interpreted as a recommendation for that problem. (If we assumed the set of potential agents to be finite, the statements of most of the characterization results would have to be weakened.) Our generic notation for a solution is the letter $\varphi$.

When we apply population monotonicity to a solution correspondence, we require that the rule be able to compare *all* of the allocations chosen in the initial economy to *all* of the allocations chosen in any larger economy. We could imagine weaker statements allowing the comparison of at least one allocation from each set, or one allocation from one set to all of the allocations from the other set. In the case of single-valued solutions, all of these conditions are of course equivalent.

We are now ready to turn to applications of the principle.

---

[1] This connection is made by Chun (1985) in the context of rights problems. See Thomson (1993) for a survey of the literature devoted to the analysis of consistency. We will encounter the condition on several other occasions below.

# 3     Bargaining problems

Bargaining problems are decision problems specified as subsets of utility space that satisfy certain regularity conditions. A familiar concrete application of this abstract model is to the distribution of goods when consumers are equipped with utility functions satisfying appropriate assumptions; then the subset in question is the image in utility space of the set of feasible allocations. If utility information is available then any allocation problem can be so represented, but it is important to emphasize that when the analysis of a class of allocation problems is limited to their representations in utility space, information about their concrete structure is ignored – information that in some situations might be quite relevant. Later on, we will explore the implications of population monotonicity in concretely specified economic models. Also, we should note that not all allocation problems give rise to feasible sets satisfying the assumptions that have been imposed in the study of bargaining problems.

## 3.1    *Population monotonic solutions*

A group of agents $Q \in \mathcal{Q}$ can attain any of the points of a *feasible set* $S$, a subset of their utility space $\mathbb{R}^Q$, by unanimously agreeing on it.[2] Failing to reach an agreement yields a particular outcome $d \in S$, the *disagreement point*. A *bargaining problem* is a pair $(S, d) \in 2^{\mathbb{R}^Q} \times \mathbb{R}^Q$. We make the standard assumptions that $S$ is convex and compact, and that there exists at least one point of $S$ that strictly dominates $d$. We also assume that $S$ is *d-comprehensive:* If a point $x$ is feasible, then any point $y$ such that $d \leq y \leq x$ is also feasible. This mild assumption is imposed to guarantee that the solutions we consider always select outcomes that are at least weakly Pareto optimal.[3] In order to simplify the exposition, and with no loss of generality (since the requirement that solutions be invariant with respect to changes in the origin of the utility scales is used in all of the literature reviewed), we assume $d = 0$ and write $S$ instead of $(S, 0)$. Finally, we assume that all points of $S$ dominate $d$. For each $Q \in \mathcal{Q}$, let $\Sigma^Q$ be the class of all problems satisfying all of the assumptions just listed. A *solution* is a function that, for every $Q \in \mathcal{Q}$, associates with every $S \in \Sigma^Q$ a unique alternative in $S$. Depending upon the context, this alternative is interpreted as the recommendation that an impartial arbitrator would make, or as a prediction as to which alternative the agents would select

---

[2] By the notation $\mathbb{R}^Q$ we designate the Cartesian product of $|Q|$ copies of $\mathbb{R}$, indexed by the members of $Q$.

[3] A formal definition will be given shortly.

on their own. The Nash (1950) solution chooses the feasible alternative at which the product of utility gains from the disagreement point is maximal.

Consider the two-person problem $S$, involving agents 1 and 2, which is represented in Figure 1 in the coordinate subspace relative to them. Solve the problem by applying the Nash solution, and then imagine that an additional agent (agent 3) comes in. In this context, there is a natural way of specifying the resulting three-person problem $T$ so that the arrival of the new agent can be described as a burden on the initial group: require that its intersection with the coordinate subspace pertaining to the initial group (i.e., the set of alternatives at which the new agent receives his coordinate of the disagreement point, here 0) be the initial problem $S$. Note that, if the problem is derived from the distribution of private goods, then this is exactly what happens. Now, it is easy to specify $S$ and $T$ so that the projection $N_{\{1,2\}}(T)$, of $N(T)$, the Nash solution outcome of $T$, onto the two-dimensional subspace in which $S$ lies is not dominated by $N(S)$, the Nash solution outcome of $S$. Any such example reveals that the Nash solution does not satisfy population monotonicity, which on this domain takes the following form.

**Population monotonicity for bargaining problems.**  For all $Q, Q' \in \mathcal{Q}$ with $Q \subset Q'$ and for all $T \in \Sigma^{Q'}$, $\varphi_Q(T) \leq \varphi(T_Q)$, where $\varphi_Q(T)$ and $T_Q$ are the projections of $\varphi(T)$ and $T$, respectively, onto the coordinate subspace relative to $Q$.

On the other hand, consider the solution introduced by Kalai and Smorodinsky (1975): this solution picks the maximal feasible alternative proportional to the *ideal point,* the point whose $i$th coordinate is equal to the maximal feasible utility for agent $i$. That this solution is population monotonic is illustrated in Figure 1(b). Indeed, the projection of the ideal point of the three-person problem $T$ (this is the point marked $a(T)$) onto the two-dimensional space in which $S$ lies coincides with the ideal point of $S$ (the point marked $a(S)$), so that the projection $K_{\{1,2\}}(T)$ of $K(T)$ onto that subspace is collinear with $K(S)$; the fact that $K(S)$ dominates $K_{\{1,2\}}(T)$, coordinate by coordinate, follows from the comprehensiveness of $T$.

The *egalitarian* solution (Kalai 1977), which selects the maximal feasible point of equal coordinates, is another population monotonic solution. In fact, so is any member of the following family of monotone path solutions. A *monotone path* in $\mathbb{R}_+^Q$ is the graph of a continuous function $f: \mathbb{R} \to \mathbb{R}_+^Q$, each component of which is increasing, such that $f(0) = 0$ and $\|f(\lambda)\| \to \infty$ as $\lambda \to \infty$. A *monotone path solution* on $\Sigma^Q$ is a solution

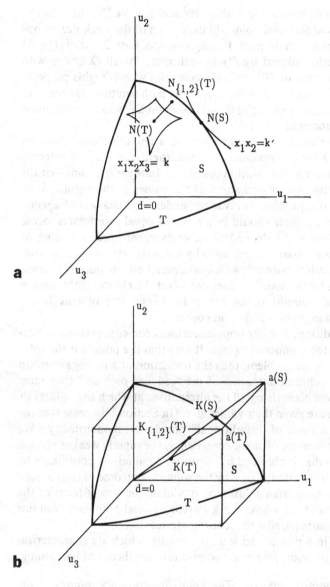

Figure 1. Population monotonicity in bargaining theory. (a) The Nash solution is not population monotonic since agent 2 receives less in the two-person problem $S$ than in the three-person problem $T$ that results from the arrival of agent 3. (b) The Kalai–Smorodinsky solution is population monotonic: neither agent 1 nor agent 2 gains upon the arrival of agent 3.

such that, for some monotone path in $\mathbb{R}_+^Q$ and any $S \in \Sigma^Q$, the solution outcome of $S$ is the maximal point of intersection of the weak Pareto optimal boundary of $S$ with the path. Finally, consider a list $G = \{G^Q \mid Q \in \mathcal{Q}\}$ of monotone paths indexed by $Q \in \mathcal{Q}$ such that, for all $Q, Q' \in \mathcal{Q}$ with $Q \subset Q'$, the projection of $G^{Q'}$ onto $\mathbb{R}^Q$ coincides with $G^Q$ (this property of projections is crucial). Then the monotone path solution *relative to G* is the solution that, for each $Q \in \mathcal{Q}$, coincides on $\Sigma^Q$ with the monotone path solution associated with $G^Q$.

To present the results we need to impose a few other conditions on solutions. *Weak Pareto optimality* states that there is no feasible outcome that all agents prefer to the solution outcome. *Anonymity* means that the solution is invariant under exchanges of the names of the agents. *Symmetry* says that if a problem is invariant under all exchanges of agents, then the solution outcome should be a point of equal coordinates. *Scale invariance* requires any independent agent-by-agent linear rescaling of the utility functions to be accompanied by a similar rescaling of the solution outcome. Under *contraction independence*,[4] elimination of alternatives not chosen by the solution does not affect the choice, if this choice is still feasible. *Continuity* states that small changes in problems do not produce large changes in solution outcomes.

The final condition, just like population monotonicity, pertains to possible changes in the number of agents. It says that if a point $x$ is the solution outcome of some problem, then the restriction of $x$ to any subgroup of agents is the solution outcomes of the "reduced problem" they face: this is the problem comprising all the alternatives at which the utilities of the other agents are given their values at $x$. (In Section 1 we presented the requirement as a form of "conditional" population monotonicity.) We will use, under the name of *weak consistency*, the slightly weaker version of the condition that is obtained by requiring domination, coordinate by coordinate, of the restriction of $x$ by the solution outcome of the reduced problem.[5] (The egalitarian solution may violate the strong form of the condition for problems whose weak Pareto optimal boundary contains nondegenerate parts parallel to a coordinate subspace.)

We are now in a position to state the results, which are characterizations of two of the most important solutions in the theory of bargaining.

**Theorem 1** (Thomson 1983a). *The Kalai–Smorodinsky solution is the only solution satisfying weak Pareto optimality, anonymity, scale invariance, continuity, and population monotonicity.*

[4] This condition is more commonly known as *independence of irrelevant alternatives*.

[5] As this condition is somewhat less transparent than the others, we give it in full: For all $Q, Q' \in \mathcal{Q}$ with $Q \subset Q'$ and for all $T \in \Sigma^{Q'}$, we have $\varphi(r_Q^x(T)) \geq x_Q$, where $x = \varphi(T)$ and $r_Q^x(T) = \{y \in \mathbb{R}_+^Q \mid (y, x_{Q' \setminus Q}) \in T\}$.

**Theorem 2** (Thomson 1983b). *The egalitarian solution is the only solution satisfying weak Pareto optimality, symmetry, contraction independence, continuity, and population monotonicity.*[6]

**Theorem 3** (Thomson 1984b). *The egalitarian solution is the only solution satisfying weak Pareto optimality, anonymity, continuity, population monotonicity, and weak consistency.*

It is worth noting that the egalitarian solution – as do all other monotone path solutions – satisfies an even stronger monotonicity condition: The arrival of any group of agents, no matter how it influences the shape of the feasible set, affects all agents initially present in the same direction. This is certainly not true for the Kalai–Smorodinsky solution.

Chun and Thomson (1992) consider the class of problems obtained by specifying, in addition to the data needed to define a bargaining problem, a "claims point" representing prior claims that the agents may start with. The conjunction of these claims results in an infeasible point, but the claims are made in good faith or represent commitments that cannot be jointly met, so a "good" solution should take them into account. Chun and Thomson provide characterizations of the solution that selects the maximal point on the segment connecting the disagreement point to the claims point. One of these characterizations is based on the natural form of population monotonicity for that domain.

## 3.2   Guarantee structures

Although population monotonicity is designed to ensure that when additional agents arrive, none of the agents initially present gain, it would be unfortunate if the burden fell disproportionately on some of them. If a solution satisfies weak Pareto optimality and population monotonicity, the arrival of new agents must hurt each of the agents initially present. If all of them are negatively affected, it is natural next to want them to be affected in a quantitatively similar way. In the context of bargaining, losses can be easily measured and compared by means of the cardinal information conveyed by the utility functions. Here, we propose to use this information to evaluate how well solutions distribute the burden (due to the arrival of newcomers) across the agents initially present, and to compare them on that basis.

---

[6] Variants of this theorem are given in Thomson (1984a), where it is shown that if weak Pareto optimality is dropped then a certain family of "truncated egalitarian" solutions obtains. Also, a characterization of the monotone path solutions obtains if anonymity is dropped.

88    **William Thomson**

Given $Q, Q' \in \mathfrak{Q}$ with $Q \subseteq Q'$, let $S \in \Sigma^Q$ and $T \in \Sigma^{Q'}$ be such that $S = T_Q$. Given $i \in Q$, the proportional loss incurred by agent $i$ upon the arrival of the group $Q' \backslash Q$ is equal to 1 minus the ratio $\varphi_i(T)/\varphi_i(S)$. Now, calculate the smallest value taken by this quantity as $S$ and $T$ vary subject to the conditions stated previously. Let this value be denoted by $\alpha$. Seen positively, $\alpha$ can be interpreted as a "guarantee" offered by the solution to agent $i \in Q$ that, as the group enlarges from $Q$ to $Q'$, $i$'s final utility will be at least $\alpha$ times $i$'s initial utility. When a solution $\varphi$ is anonymous, this guarantee depends only on the cardinalities of $Q$ and $Q'$ and can be written as $\alpha_\varphi^{qq'}$, where $q = |Q|$ and $q' = |Q'|$. The collection of all the numbers $\alpha_\varphi^{qq'}$ for $q, q' \in \mathbb{N}$, $q' > q$, is the *guarantee structure* of $\varphi$. This notion can be used to obtain a partial ordering on the space of solutions. Solutions that offer greater guarantees are of course more desirable. One would perhaps not expect to find maximal elements in the space of solutions, and therefore the following result may be surprising.

**Theorem 4** (Thomson and Lensberg 1983). *The guarantee structure of the Kalai-Smorodinsky solution is greater than the guarantee structure of any weakly Pareto optimal and anonymous solution.*

Naturally, offering high guarantees to individuals might be costly to the groups to which they belong. In order to understand the trade-offs between protection of individuals and protection of groups, we define the *collective* guarantee structure of a solution by considering, for each pair $S, T$ as specified before, the arithmetic average of the proportional losses incurred by the members of the initial group upon the arrival of additional agents, and again calculating the smallest value taken by this ratio (of course, the geometric average or some other measure could be considered). Now we find that the Nash solution performs better than any weakly Pareto optimal and anonymous solution (in particular, better than the Kalai-Smorodinsky solution; see Thomson 1983c).

Instead of focusing on how much agents may lose, one could alternatively focus on how much they may gain, and rank solutions on the basis of the extent to which they allow such gains. Here too, the Kalai-Smorodinsky solution performs better than any weakly Pareto optimal and anonymous solution when individuals are examined, but it is the Nash solution that performs the best in that class when groups are examined (Thomson 1987b).

Finally, we could compare how any two initially present agents fare, using the ratio of their relative losses, and look for solutions where this ratio is as close to unity as possible. Here, the Kalai-Smorodinsky solution performs better than any weakly Pareto optimal, anonymous, and scale invariant solution, whereas the egalitarian solution performs better than any weakly Pareto optimal, anonymous, and contraction independent solution (Chun and Thomson 1989).

## 4    Games in coalitional form

The next class of problems that we will examine is richer than the class of bargaining problems because their specification involves a description of the opportunities available to each group, or "coalition," of agents. Two subclasses of such problems are usually considered. In a "transferable utility" game, what a coalition can achieve is given as a single number; in a "nontransferable utility" game, it is given as a subset of utility space. As an example, consider an economy in which agents can form productive units. The productivity of each subgroup depends on the complementarities between the skills of the agents composing it. It is measured by the output that they can jointly produce, or the value of this output at some given prices. Another standard application of this model is to cost allocation, where each coalition is characterized by the cost of providing a certain service to its members when it is isolated from the rest of the economy.

### 4.1    *The transferable utility case*

We start with the class of *transferable utility* (TU) games. There is a group $Q \in \mathbb{Q}$ of agents whose members may gather in *coalitions*.[7] What each coalition can achieve on its own is its *worth*. A *game in coalitional form* is a vector $v \in \mathbb{R}^{2^{|Q|}-1}$, the worth of each coalition being one of the coordinates of $v$. Let $v(S)$ denote the worth of coalition $S$. Restrictions may be imposed on $v$, making the game monotonic (if $S \supset T$ then $v(S) \geq v(T)$) or superadditive (the worth of a coalition is greater than the sum of the worths of the coalitions comprising a partition, no matter what that partition is). For all $Q \in \mathbb{Q}$, let $\mathcal{G}^Q$ be a class of admissible games for the group $Q$.

#### 4.1.1    *Population monotonic solutions*
We would like to reward agents as a function of the worths of the various coalitions. A *solution* is a correspondence that associates with every $v \in \mathcal{G}^Q$, $Q \in \mathbb{Q}$, a non-empty set of vectors $x \in \mathbb{R}^Q$ such that $\sum_{i \in Q} x_i \leq v(Q)$. The $i$th coordinate of such a vector represents one of the possible payments to agent $i \in Q$ for being involved in the game. Already in this model we must allow for multivaluedness; even though some interesting single-valued solutions exist, many others are multivalued.

---

[7] A coalition is a non-empty subset of $Q$.

A well-known solution is the *core:* given $Q \in \mathbb{Q}$ and $v \in \mathcal{G}^Q$, it recommends any payoff vector $x \in \mathbb{R}^Q$ such that $\sum_{i \in Q} x_i = v(Q)$ and that for no $S \subset Q$ is $v(S) > \sum_{i \in S} x_i$. Another important solution is the *Shapley value* (Shapley 1953); it recommends, for each $i \in Q$, the payoff $x_i = \sum_{S \subset Q, S \ni i} k_S(v(S) - v(S \setminus \{i\}))$, where $k_S = [(|S|-1)! (|Q|-|S|)!]/|Q|!$. Finally, evaluate the "dissatisfaction" of coalition $S$ at $x \in \mathbb{R}^Q$ by the number $v(S) - \sum_{i \in S} x_i$. Then the *nucleolus* (Schmeidler 1969) selects the allocation $x \in \mathbb{R}^Q$ with $\sum_{i \in Q} x_i = v(Q)$ at which the dissatisfactions of coalitions are minimized in a lexicographic way in the set $\{x' \in \mathbb{R}^n \mid x_i' \geq v(\{i\})$ for all $i \in N$, and $\sum_{i \in Q} x_i' = v(N)\}$, starting with the most dissatisfied coalition.

In the study of coalitional form games, most investigators have limited their attention to situations where the arrival of new agents is beneficial to the agents originally present. A central issue in the literature is identifying when these benefits are sufficient to make all of these agents gain. We will refer to the requirement that all agents do gain from the arrival of the newcomers as population monotonicity$_+$. Letting the newcomers in is of course the socially efficient choice, so the property helps to engender compatibility of individual and social interests. Given $Q' \in \mathbb{Q}$, $v \in \mathcal{G}^{Q'}$, and $Q \subseteq Q'$, let $v_Q \in \mathcal{G}^Q$ be defined by $v_Q = (v(S))_{S \subseteq Q}$.

**Population monotonicity$_+$ for coalitional form games.**  *For all $Q, Q' \in \mathbb{Q}$ with $Q \subset Q'$ and for all $v \in \mathcal{G}^{Q'}$, $\varphi_i(v) \geq \varphi_i(v_Q)$ for all $i \in Q$.*

As we shall see, in order to obtain the property it is necessary to limit oneself to classes of games with a non-empty core; however, much more is needed. An important class of games admitting population monotonic$_+$ solutions is the class of convex games – that is, games $v$ such that for all $S, S' \subseteq Q$, $v(S \cup S') + v(S \cap S') \geq v(S) + v(S')$. For such games the returns to cooperation increase quite rapidly with the size of coalitions. Conversely, on the class of concave games (games for which the inequality just written is reversed), population monotonicity can be met. This result is based on an observation due to Ichiishi (1988) that in a concave game, given any fixed order of the players, the population monotonicity inequalities are met by the payoff vectors obtained as follows: each player $i$ is paid an amount equal to $i$'s contribution to the coalition made up of the preceding players in the ordering.

**Proposition 1** (Sprumont 1990; Rosenthal 1990).  *On the class of concave games, the Shapley value is a population monotonic solution; on the class of convex games, it is a population monotonic$_+$ solution.*

Sprumont identifies another interesting class of games admitting population monotonic$_+$ solutions, and for that class he exhibits a population monotonic$_+$ solution that bears a certain relationship to the Shapley value: it is the class of games for which, given any two coalitions $S$ and $T$ with $S \subset T$, the *average* contribution of the members of $S$ to the worth of $S$ is less than the comparable quantity for $T$.

Next, we present results obtained for three special classes of games. Sönmez (1993) shows that the nucleolus is not population monotonic$_+$ on the class of convex games, and that neither are the solutions known as the "separable cost remaining benefit" (Moulin 1988) and the $\tau$ value (Tijs 1981). He also studies a class of games that are exemplified by the well-known "airport problem" (Littlechild 1974; Littlechild and Owen 1973): each agent is characterized by a number, which can be interpreted as the cost of a public project (the length of the runway) when provided at the appropriate level. The corresponding cost for each coalition is the greatest cost associated with any of its members. The main result is that, on this subclass of the class of convex games, the nucleolus is a population monotonic$_+$ solution. (On the other hand, the separable cost remaining benefit solution and the $\tau$ value continue to fail the test.)

Rosenthal (1990) considers a class of "flow games" on graphs in which players control edges. To each edge is associated a number interpreted as the value that is created by transport along this edge. The worth of a coalition is defined to be the maximal flow along the subgraph consisting of the edges controlled by the members of the coalition. He shows that for this class the Shapley value is not population monotonic$_+$, but he identifies characteristics of the new agents for which the payoffs attributed to the agents initially present – by both the Shapley value and a certain selection from the core – satisfy the inequalities required by the property. Then, a "conditional" form of the requirement is met.

Grafe, Iñarra, and Zarzuelo (1992) analyze the simple class of games defined as follows: For each $i \in \mathbb{N}$, there is a coefficient $\beta_i \in \mathbb{R}_+$ that can be interpreted as a measure of agent $i$'s "usefulness"; there is also an increasing function $r: \mathbb{N} \to \mathbb{R}$ indicating the productivities of groups as a function of their sizes. These data are combined so as to give the worth of each coalition $S$ by the formula $(\sum_{i \in S} \beta_i) r(|S|)$. Grafe et al. also consider the special case when $r(|S|)$ takes the form $|S|^\sigma$ for $\sigma \in [0, 1]$; they study the population monotonicity$_+$ of the Shapley value and of the nucleolus on this class of games. The results are negative. However, the rule that divides the worth of the grand coalition proportionally to the coefficients $\beta_i$ clearly does have the property.

### 4.1.2 *Population monotonic payoff configurations*

Instead of searching for population monotonic$_+$ solutions, we now limit ourselves to the less ambitious task of searching, game by game, for population monotonic$_+$ payoff configurations. Given $Q \in \mathbb{Q}$ and $v \in \mathbb{G}^Q$, a *payoff configuration* for $v$ (Hart 1985) is a list $(x^S)_{S \subseteq Q}$ where, for each $S \subseteq Q$, $x^S \in \mathbb{R}^S$ and $\sum_{i \in S} x_i^S = v(S)$. A payoff configuration provides a recommendation for each coalition $S$, should it form, on the division of its worth $v(S)$ among its members; this recommendation may depend on the components of $v$ pertaining to coalitions that are not subsets of $S$.

**Population monotonic$_+$ payoff configuration.** Given $Q \in \mathcal{Q}$ and $v \in \mathcal{G}^Q$, the payoff configuration for $v$, denoted $(x^S)_{S \subseteq Q}$, is population monotonic$_+$ if, for all $S, S' \subseteq Q$ with $S \subset S'$ and for all $i \in S$, $x_i^S \le x_i^{S'}$.[8]

To better understand the relationship between the concept of a population monotonic$_+$ *solution* on some domain and that of a population monotonic$_+$ *payoff configuration* for a game, note first that if a game and all of its subgames belong to a domain on which there exists a population monotonic$_+$ solution then, of course, the game has a population monotonic$_+$ payoff configuration; simply apply the solution to the game and its subgames. On the other hand, a domain of games each of which has a population monotonic$_+$ payoff configuration does not necessarily admit of a population monotonic$_+$ solution. To see this, consider the domain consisting of the following two three-person games $v$ and $w$ and their subgames: $Q = \{1, 2, 3\}$, $v(i) = 0$ for all $i$, $v(23) = 0$, $v(S) = 1$ for all other $S \subseteq Q$, $w(i) = 0$ for all $i$, $w(13) = 0$, and $w(S) = 1$ for all other $S \subseteq Q$. The game $v$ has a unique population monotonic$_+$ payoff configuration at which all players always get 0, excepting player 1, who gets 1 in the subgames $v_{\{1,2\}}$, $v_{\{1,3\}}$, and $v$ itself; a similar statement holds for $w$, where it is player 2 who gets the nonzero payoffs. Since the subgames of $v$ and $w$ relative to players 1 and 2 are the same, we obtain a contradiction.[9]

Obtaining population monotonic$_+$ payoff configurations requires that restrictions be imposed on the game. As a preparation for the main result on this issue, first note that any such game has a non-empty core. Indeed, let $(x^S)_{S \subseteq Q}$ be a payoff configuration for $v$. Given $S \subseteq Q$, if $x_i^Q \ge x_i^S$ for all $i \in S$ then $\sum_{i \in S} x_i^Q \ge \sum_{i \in S} x_i^S = v(S)$, so that $S$ cannot improve upon $x_Q$. A similar inequality can be established for any pair $S, S'$ with $S \subseteq S'$ (and not just pairs where $S' = Q$), so that the cores of all subgames of $v$ are non-empty as well.[10] If $|Q| = 3$ then this condition turns out to be sufficient, but if $|Q| > 3$ it is not, as shown by the following example.

**Example** (Sprumont 1990).  Let $Q = \{1, 2, 3, 4\}$. Each of players 1 and 2 owns a left glove. Each of players 3 and 4 a right glove. A pair of

---

[8] Note that the set of population monotonic$_+$ payoff configurations is convex.

[9] I am grateful to Y. Sprumont for providing me with this example.

[10] This is the condition known as "total balancedness."

gloves has value 1. A single glove has value 0. This situation can be described by the following game:

$v(i) = 0$ for all $i \in Q$;
$v(12) = v(34) = 0$, $v(13) = v(14) = v(23) = v(24) = 1$;
$v(ijk) = 1$ for all $i, j, k \in Q$;
$v(Q) = 2$.

The core of each three-person subgame of $v$ is a single point, at which the "odd man out" gets 1 and the others get 0. Since each player is involved in a three-person game with a payoff of 1, for the configuration $(x^S)_{S \subseteq Q}$ to be population monotonic$_+$ for $v$ we need $x_i^Q \geq 1$ for all $i \in Q$ – but this is impossible, since $v(Q) = 2$. The cores of the two-person subgames (and, of course, of each one-person subgame) are also non-empty. Sprumont generalizes this example to show that no assignment game having at least two buyers and two sellers such that every buyer–seller pair derives some benefit from trade has a population monotonic$_+$ payoff configuration.

To state the main result of this section, which is a characterization of the class of games admitting population monotonic$_+$ payoff configurations, we need a few additional definitions: The game $v \in \mathcal{G}^Q$ is *simple* if $v(S) = 0$ or 1 for all $S \subseteq Q$; *monotonic* if, for all $S, S' \subseteq Q$ with $S \subset S'$, $v(S) \leq v(S')$; and *additive* if there is an $a \in \mathbb{R}$ such that $v(S) = a|S|$ for all $S \in \mathcal{S}$. Finally, player $i \in Q$ is a *veto player* in $v \in \mathcal{G}^Q$ if, for all $S$ such that $i \notin S$, $v(S) = 0$.

**Theorem 5** (Sprumont 1990). *A game has a population monotonic$_+$ payoff configuration if and only if it is the sum of an additive game and a positive linear combination of monotonic simple games with veto players.*[11]

Moulin (1990a) investigates the existence of population monotonic$_+$ payoff configurations satisfying certain individual upper bounds. In the economic application motivating his work, the bound relative to a given agent $i$ is defined to be the maximal payoff $i$ would obtain under the assumption that all other agents had the same preferences as $i$'s, and under the requirements of efficiency and equal treatment of equals.[12] Formally (returning to our abstract model), given $Q \in \mathcal{Q}$ and $v \in \mathcal{G}^Q$, an *aspiration* for $v$ (Bennett 1983) is a vector $y \in \mathbb{R}^Q$ such that $\sum_{i \in S} y_i^S \geq v(S)$ for all $S \subseteq Q$. Similarly, an *aspiration configuration* for $v$ is a list $(y^S)_{S \subseteq Q}$ such that, for all $S \subseteq Q$, $y^S$ is an aspiration for $v(S)$. The configuration is population

---

[11] Sonn (1990) shows that by solving a simple linear program one can determine whether or not a game can be decomposed as stated in the theorem.

[12] We will come back to this bound, defined by reference to economies composed of identical agents.

monotonic$_+$ if, for all $i \in Q$ and for all $S, S' \subset Q$ with $i \in S \subseteq S' \subseteq Q$, we have $y_i^S \le y_i^{S'}$.

**Proposition 2** (Moulin 1990a). *Let $Q \in \mathbb{Q}$ and let $v \in \mathcal{G}^Q$ be a convex game. Let $(y^S)_{S \subseteq Q}$ be a population monotonic$_+$ aspiration configuration such that, for all $i \in Q$ and for all $S, S' \subseteq Q$ with $i \in S \cap S'$ and $|S| = |S'|$, $y_i^S = y_i^{S'}$. Then $v$ has a population monotonic$_+$ payoff configuration bounded above by $y$.*

Moulin shows that the result does not necessarily hold if the uniformity assumption (the condition that $y_i^S = y_i^{S'}$ for all $i \in Q$ and for all $S, S' \subseteq Q$ with $i \in S \cap S'$ and $|S| = |S'|$) is not made. But in his application of the result to economies with public goods, if aspirations are defined as here – by reference to economies made up of agents with identical preferences – then the uniformity assumption does hold. (See Section 8 for additional results on public goods economies.)

### 4.2    The nontransferable utility case

Consider now a richer model, where what each coalition $S \subseteq Q$ can achieve is given as a subset $V(S)$ of the utility space $\mathbb{R}^S$ pertaining to that coalition. Each $V(S)$ is of course required to satisfy certain regularity conditions. These games are called *nontransferable utility* (NTU) games. For each $Q \in \mathbb{Q}$, let $\mathcal{K}^Q$ be a class of admissible NTU games involving the group $Q$; then a solution associates with every $V \in \mathcal{K}^Q$ a non-empty subset of $V(Q)$.

In this model, we are even further from a full understanding of the implications of population monotonicity$_+$. However, a result is available which concerns a special subclass that has recently been the object of some attention. This is the class of *hyperplane* games $V \in \mathcal{K}^Q$, that is, games where $V(S)$ is a hyperplane for all $S \subseteq Q$. (A TU game can be represented as a hyperplane game in which the normals to the hyperplanes are vectors of 1s.) Maschler and Owen (1989), who introduced this class of games, proposed for it an extension of the Shapley value that is defined as follows. Given $Q \in \mathbb{Q}$, $v \in \mathcal{K}^Q$, and an ordering $\{i_1, i_2, \ldots, i_{|Q|}\}$ of the players, consider the payoff vector $x$ obtained by giving: (1) to agent $i_1$ the most that he can get on his own, $x_{i_1} = \max\{x \in V(i_1)\}$; (2) to agent $i_2$ the most that $i_2$ can get in $V(i_1 i_2)$ subject to agent $i_1$ getting $x_{i_1}, \ldots$; (k) to agent $i_k$ the most that $i_k$ can get in $V(i_1 i_2 \ldots i_k)$ subject to each of the preceding agents $i_l$ getting $x_{i_l}, \ldots$. Finally, the *Maschler–Owen solution* of the game is the average of the payoff vectors so obtained when all orders are equally likely. We will consider the subclass of hyperplane games satisfying a certain property of "strong cardinal convexity" (Sharkey 1981) which ensures that the feasible sets expand sufficiently as the number of agents enlarges. Now we have the following positive result.

**Proposition 3** (Rosenthal, 1990b). *On the class of strongly convex hyperplane games, the Maschler–Owen solution is population monotonic$_+$.*

Concerning the existence, for each given game, of population monotonic$_+$ payoff configurations, we can only report that the counterpart of Proposition 1 that one might have hoped for does not hold: there do exist ordinally convex games (Peleg 1986) for which the payoff configuration that consists of the marginal contributions vectors are *not* population monotonic.

## 5    Quasilinear cost allocation problems

We now turn to a family of somewhat more concrete decision problems. Imagine a society that must select one among a finite number of projects; with each project is associated a certain level of utility for each agent and a certain cost. Which project should be selected and how should its cost be allocated among the agents? This class of problems differs from the classes examined so far in that information is retained on the manner in which utility levels are generated. However, no particular structure is imposed on the physical nature of the options available. In the sections to follow, we will keep on record a complete description of the physical features of the alternatives comprised by the feasible set.

Formally, let $A$ be a finite set of public projects. A *quasilinear cost allocation problem* is a pair $((u_i)_{i \in Q}, C) = (u_Q, C) \in \mathbb{R}^{|A|Q} \times \mathbb{R}^{|A|}$. Here, $C$ is the *cost vector* and each coordinate of $C$ is the cost of the corresponding project. In addition, there is a private good called "money" that can be used for compensation. The preferences of agents $i \in Q$, defined over the product $A \times \mathbb{R}$, admit a quasilinear numerical representation $u_i$: given the project $a \in A$ and given agent $i$'s holdings of money $m_i \in \mathbb{R}$, $i$'s utility is $u_{ia} + m_i$. For each $Q \in Q$, let $\mathfrak{M}^Q$ be the class of these problems; then a solution is a function that associates with every $Q \in Q$ and every $(u_Q, C) \in \mathfrak{M}^Q$ a vector $x \in \mathbb{R}^Q$ such that $\sum_{i \in Q} x_i \leq \max_{a \in A}(\sum_{i \in Q} u_{ia} - C_a)$. A family of examples are obtained by first selecting the project for which the difference between the sum of utilities and the cost is the highest, and then choosing contributions so that all agents receive an equal share of the surplus over some reference level generated in this way.

Chun (1986) proposed for this model the condition that all agents be affected in the same direction by the arrival of additional agents, which is indeed the appropriate form of the principle of population monotonicity for this model. This is the first time in this survey that we find it necessary to use this condition.

**Weak population monotonicity for quasilinear cost allocation problems.**
For all $Q, Q' \in \mathbb{Q}$ with $Q \subset Q'$, all $(u_{Q'}, C) \in \mathfrak{M}^{Q'}$, and all $z \in \varphi(u_Q, C)$ and $z' \in \varphi(u_{Q'}, C)$, either $z_i \geq z_i'$ for all $i \in Q$ or $z_i \leq z_i'$ for all $i \in Q$.

Chun searched for solutions satisfying the following additional requirements (formulated by Moulin 1985a,b in his extensive analysis of this class of problems). *Pareto optimality* requires the decision to maximize net aggregate benefit, *anonymity* that the solution be invariant under exchanges of the names of agents. *Independence of the zero of the utility functions* states that the solution is invariant under the addition of an arbitrary constant to the agents' utilities, while *independence of the zero of the cost function* means that an increase in the cost function, uniform across all alternatives, is distributed evenly among the agents. Under *cost monotonicity*, an increase in the cost function is borne by all agents.

The following theorems give a very complete picture of the implications of weak population monotonicity in this model. Essentially, all admissible solutions can be described as "egalitarian," as they consist in dividing equally a surplus over some vector of reference utility levels; the solutions differ in the way that reference levels are computed. Let $e$ be the vector of all 1s in $\mathbb{R}^{|A|}$.

**Theorem 6** (Chun 1986). *A solution $\varphi$ satisfies Pareto optimality, anonymity, the two independence axioms, and weak population monotonicity if and only if there is a function $g: [\mathbb{R}^A]^2 \to \mathbb{R}$ satisfying*

   (i)   $g(x + \alpha e, z) = g(x, z) + \alpha$ *for all $x, z \in \mathbb{R}^A$ and for all $\alpha \in \mathbb{R}$,*
   (ii)  $g(0, z) = 0$ *for all $z \in \mathbb{R}^A$,*
   (iii) $g(x, z + \alpha e) = g(x, z)$ *for all $x, z \in \mathbb{R}^A$ and for all $\alpha \in \mathbb{R}$,*

*and such that for all $Q \in \mathbb{Q}$, all $i \in Q$, and all $(u_Q, C) \in \mathfrak{M}^Q$,*

$$\varphi_i(u_Q, C) = (1/|Q|) \max_{a \in A} \{\Sigma_{i \in Q} u_{ia} - C_a\}$$
$$+ (1/|Q|)\{(|Q| - 1)g(u_i, C) - \Sigma_{j \in Q \setminus \{i\}} g(u_j, C)\}$$

**Theorem 7** (Chun 1986). *A solution $\varphi$ satisfies the five axioms of Theorem 6 and also cost monotonicity if and only if there is a function $\bar{g}: \mathbb{R}^A \to \mathbb{R}$ satisfying*

   (i)   $\bar{g}(z + \alpha e) = \bar{g}(x) + \alpha$ *for all $x \in \mathbb{R}^A$ and for all $\alpha \in \mathbb{R}$,*
   (ii)  $\bar{g}(0) = 0$,

*and such that for all $Q \in \mathcal{Q}$, all $i \in Q$, and all $(u_Q, C) \in \mathfrak{M}^Q$,*

$$\varphi_i(u_Q, C) = (1/|Q|) \max_{a \in A} \{\Sigma_{i \in Q} u_{ia} - C_a\}$$
$$+ (1/|Q|)\{(|Q| - 1)\tilde{g}(u_i) - \Sigma_{j \in Q \setminus \{i\}} \tilde{g}(u_j)\}.$$

Alternatively, an axiom of *consistency* (informally described in Section 2) can be used in Theorem 7 instead of cost monotonicity. Additional characterizations are offered in Chun (1986). The requirements that no agent be able to gain by disposing of utility, and that the solution provide a minimal reference utility to each individual, place further restrictions on the $g$ functions. These restrictions can be completely described.

# 6    Fair allocation in economies with private goods

We now apply the idea of population monotonicity to one of the most commonly studied problems, that of allocating a fixed bundle of goods among a group of agents with equal rights on these goods.

## 6.1    *Population monotonicity for the classical problem of fair division*

The model is as follows. There are $l \in \mathbb{N}$ goods and a group $Q \in \mathcal{Q}$ of agents; for each $i \in Q$, $R_i$ is agent $i$'s continuous, convex, and monotone preference relation defined over $\mathbb{R}^l_+$; $I_i$ designates the indifference relation associated with $R_i$. Let $\mathcal{R}_{cl}$ be the class of all such "classical" preference relations. Also needed is $\Omega \in \mathbb{R}^l_+$, the *social endowment*. A *problem of fair division* is a pair $((R_i)_{i \in Q}, \Omega) \in \mathcal{R}^Q_{cl} \times \mathbb{R}^l_+$, or simply $(R_Q, \Omega)$. This formulation is to be distinguished from formulations in which each agent is entitled to a particular "individual" share of the social endowment (this formulation will be discussed shortly). Here, we assume instead that agents are collectively entitled to the resources $\Omega$. For each $Q \in \mathcal{Q}$, let $\mathcal{E}^Q$ be a class of admissible economies involving the group $Q$. A solution is a correspondence that associates with every $Q \in \mathcal{Q}$ and every $(R_Q, \Omega) \in \mathcal{E}^Q$ a non-empty subset of the set of feasible allocations of $(R_Q, \Omega)$: $Z(e) = \{z \in \mathbb{R}^{l|Q|}_+ \mid \Sigma_{i \in Q} z_i \leq \Omega\}$. We have already discussed (in Section 1) the condition of population monotonicity for this model, and we will not give a formal statement since it is straightforward.

A simple example of a population monotonic solution is the one that always chooses equal division: $z_i = \Omega/|Q|$ for all $i \in Q$. Of course, this solution suffers from the major drawback of not being efficient. To obtain efficiency, give the entire social endowment to the agent with the lowest

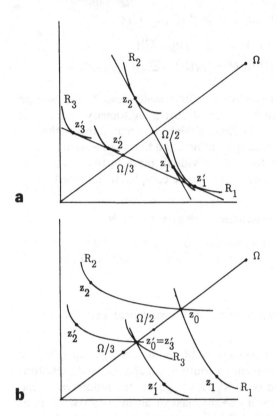

Figure 2. Population monotonicity in exchange economies. (a) The Walrasian solution operated from equal division is not population monotonic. (b) The egalitarian solution, defined by requiring all agents to be indifferent between their consumptions and the same-scale multiple of the social endowment, is population monotonic.

index in $Q$ and nothing to the others. This population monotonic solution is efficient, but quite unappealing from the distributional viewpoint.

The suggestion is often made to solve problems of fair division by operating the Walrasian mechanism from equal division. Is the solution so defined population monotonic? The example of Figure 2(a), which is taken from Chichilnisky and Thomson (1987), shows that it is not. In the two-person economy consisting of agents 1 and 2 where the vector $\Omega \in \mathbb{R}^2_+$ must be divided, such a solution leads to the allocation $(z_1, z_2)$. After the arrival of agent 3, it leads to the allocation $(z_1', z_2', z_3')$. Since agent 1 prefers $z_1'$ to $z_1$, population monotonicity fails. We add that the example can be specified with homothetic preferences; this assumption often has regularizing implications (together with the assumption of equal endowments, it implies uniqueness and stability of the Walrasian equilibrium), but it does not prevent the undesirable possibility that the presence of one more claimant benefits one of the original agents. Quasilinearity of preferences would not help, either.

The following theorem provides additional information about the circumstances in which violations occur. It relates the likelihood of population monotonicity being violated by the Walrasian solution operated from equal division to the likelihood of the solution being subject to the "transfer problem" – a problem that has been the object of a considerable amount of attention in the international trade literature. A solution is said to be subject to the (strong form of the) transfer problem if transferring part of agent 1's endowment (say) to agent 2 ultimately benefits agent 1 and hurts agent 2.

**Proposition 4** (Jones 1987). *Consider the class of economies with homothetic preferences. In the absence of substitution effects, the Walrasian solution from equal division is subject to the transfer paradox if and only if it violates population monotonicity. In the presence of substitution effects, the Walrasian solution may violate population monotonicity even in situations where no transfer paradox would occur.*

For a positive result, we have the *egalitarian* solution (Pazner and Schmeidler 1978), which is defined by selecting the efficient allocation(s) at which utilities are equal, using the utility representations obtained by calibrating along the ray through the aggregate bundle. Figure 2(b) illustrates the fact that this solution is population monotonic: in the two-person economy $(R_1, R_2, \Omega)$, the efficient allocation $(z_1, z_2)$ is egalitarian because there exists $z_0$ proportional to $\Omega$ such that both agents are indifferent between their consumptions and $z_0$. In the enlarged three-person economy $(R_1, R_2, R_3, \Omega)$, the efficient allocation $(z_1', z_2', z_3')$ is egalitarian with a reference bundle $z_0'$ that can only be lower than $z_0$ on the ray through $\Omega$. Therefore, both agent 1 and agent 2 lose upon the arrival of agent 3.

This solution is only one example in a large family of population monotonic solutions defined as follows (Thomson 1987b). Let $\mathfrak{B}$ be a family of choice sets $\{B(\lambda) \subseteq \mathbb{R}_+^l \mid \lambda \in \mathbb{R}_+\}$ with the following properties.

(i)   $B(\lambda)$ is closed for all $\lambda \in \mathbb{R}_+$.
(ii)  $B(0) = \{0\}$.
(iii) $B(\cdot)$ is upper semicontinuous.
(iv)  $B(\cdot)$ is monotonic: $B(\lambda) \subseteq B(\lambda')$ whenever $\lambda \leq \lambda'$.
(v)   $B(\cdot)$ is unbounded: for all $r \in \mathbb{R}_+$, there exists $\lambda$ such that
      $r(1, ..., 1) \in B(\lambda)$.

Now, for each strictly monotone preference relation $R_i \in \mathbb{R}_{cl}$, let $u_i$ be a continuous numerical representation of $R_i$. Given an economy $e = (R_Q, \Omega) \in \mathbb{R}_{cl}^Q \times \mathbb{R}_+^l$ in which preferences are strictly monotone, let $\varphi_\mathbb{R}(e)$ be the set of efficient allocations $z$ of $e$ such that for some $\lambda \in \mathbb{R}_+$ and for all $i \in Q$, $z_i I_i z_i^*$ where $z_i^* R_i z_i'$ for all $z_i' \in B(\lambda)$. It is easy to see that any such *equal-opportunity equivalent solution* $\varphi_\mathbb{R}$ is population monotonic. The following proposition is a straightforward generalization of an observation made in Thomson (1987b).

**Proposition 5.**  *On the domain of classical economies in which preferences are strictly monotone, the equal-opportunity equivalent solutions are population monotonic selections from the Pareto solution.*

These solutions are directly inspired by the monotone path solutions of bargaining theory (Section 3). Here, the monotone path is obtained by tracing out the image in utility space of the list of maximizers $(z_i^*)_{i \in Q}$ in $B(\lambda)$ of the preference relations $(R_i)_{i \in Q}$ as $\lambda$ varies. Under our assumptions on preferences, the image of the feasible set is comprehensive (Section 3.1). For $\lambda = 0$, a point in the feasible set is obtained; by the unboundedness of $B(\cdot)$, for $\lambda$ large enough, a point outside of the feasible set results. That the solutions are well-defined follows from these observations. Proving that they are population monotonic is straightforward.

Examples of interesting families satisfying these conditions are the following:

$B(\lambda) = \{x \in \mathbb{R}^l \mid 0 \le x \le \lambda \Omega\}$ (note that the solution associated with this family is the egalitarian solution defined previously);

$B(\lambda) = \{x \in \mathbb{R}^l \mid 0 \le x \le d\}$ for some $d \in \mathbb{R}_+^l$;

$B(\lambda) = \{z \in \mathbb{R}_+^l \mid pz \le \lambda\}$ for fixed $p \in \Delta^{l-1}$.

As already noted, we are not interested only in population monotonicity. We certainly want our allocation rule to be efficient, that is, to be a subsolution of the Pareto solution; but we also want it to satisfy some distributional requirements. The distributional requirements that have played the main role in the literature are embodied in the following solutions. The *no-envy* solution (Foley 1967) selects the set of feasible allocations $z$ such that $z_j P_i z_i$ for *no* pair $\{i, j\} \subseteq Q$; at such an allocation, no agent would want to exchange bundles with anyone else. The *individual rationality from equal division* solution selects the set of feasible allocations that all agents prefer to equal division. The *egalitarian equivalence* solution (Pazner and Schmeidler 1978) selects the set of feasible allocations $z$ such that, for some $z_0 \in \mathbb{R}_+^l$ and for all $i \in Q$, $z_0 I_i z_i$.

The egalitarian solution, a selection from both the individual rationality from equal division solution and the egalitarian equivalence solution, is population monotonic. On the other hand, the Walrasian solution from equal division is a selection from both the no-envy solution and the individual rationality from equal division solution but, as we saw earlier, it is not population monotonic.

Is there any population monotonic selection from the no-envy and Pareto solution? The next theorem states that the answer is No. We should point out, however, that its proof relies on having access to economies with a large number of agents (a continuum), and this leaves open the question of whether the impossibility holds for the small-number case. (All of the other negative results reviewed here are proved by means of examples with a small number of agents.)

**Theorem 8** (Moulin 1990c).   *There is no population monotonic selection from the no-envy and Pareto solution.*

In order to better understand the strength of population monotonicity, the following result is useful: A solution satisfying both consistency (see Section 2 for a general statement of this property and Section 3 for an application to bargaining) and resource monotonicity (any increase in the resources to be divided benefits everyone) automatically satisfies population monotonicity (Fleurbaey 1992c, 1993; Chun 1985 establishes this fact for bankruptcy problems). Consequently, as Fleurbaey (1992) notes, in exchange economies satisfying the familiar gross substitutability assumption and in which all goods are normal, the Walrasian rule from equal division is a single-valued population monotonic solution. This is because under those assumptions it is single-valued, as is well known; it is also resource monotonic (this follows from Polterovich and Spivak 1983, as noted in Moulin and Thomson 1988). Finally, this solution satisfies consistency (Thomson 1988).

## 6.2   *A generalized notion of population monotonicity*

If the commodity to divide is a "bad" then the counterpart of population monotonicity is that all agents benefit from the arrival of additional agents, the requirement that we considered for coalitional form games under the name of population monotonicity$_+$. Moulin (1990d) points out that for a quasilinear domain (Section 6.5) the egalitarian solution of Pazner and Schmeidler (1978) is a population monotonic$_+$ selection from the individual rationality from equal division and Pareto solution. On the negative side, it remains true that there exists no population monotonic$_+$ selection from the no-envy and Pareto solution (Moulin 1990d).

It can be argued that it is really when we have efficiency in mind that in the classical problem of fair division we require that none of the agents initially present gains upon the arrival of additional claimants, and in the model with bads that none of them loses. If we desire to keep efficiency considerations separate from fairness considerations, weak population monotonicity should be used instead. In the classical case, and when efficiency is imposed, weak population monotonicity reduces to population monotonicity; in the case of bads, it reduces to population monotonicity$_+$. Another advantage of using weak population monotonicity is that it is better adapted to nonclassical models. We have already seen its relevance in the analysis of quasilinear cost allocation problems. Here are several other illustrations for general resource allocation problems. First, suppose that the mere presence of additional agents positively affects the agents initially present. Then it might be possible to make the latter better-off in spite of the fact that resources have not changed. More generally, an agent's welfare may depend on the consumptions of others (and not just on the agent's own consumption), and here too – if these external effects are positive and strong enough – it may be possible to make all agents initially present gain when new agents come in.

Or suppose that it is not aggregate resources that are constant but rather resources per capita. Then, depending upon the preferences, one may well be able to make all agents initially present gain when new agents come in.

The case of the division of a good when preferences are single-peaked will be discussed in Section 10. Here we note only that this case is a mixture of the classical one and the case of bads: the situation is sometimes like the classical one, and the arrival of additional agents is bad news, but sometimes the arrival of additional agents is good news. In this model, the appropriate requirement is weak population monotonicity.

## 6.3    Economies with individualized endowments

A further generalization would allow agents to be differentially endowed with the various goods. Here, too, the most that one can legitimately require is weak population monotonicity.

Formally, an economy is now a pair $(R_Q, \omega_Q)$, where $Q \in \mathcal{Q}$, $R_Q$ is (as before) a profile of preference relations, and $\omega_Q$ is a profile of endowments: $\omega_Q = (\omega_i)_{i \in Q} \in \mathbb{R}^{\ell}_+$. Let $\mathcal{F}^Q$ be the class of all such economies. Solutions are defined on the union of all $\mathcal{F}^Q$ for $Q \in \mathcal{Q}$.

That the Walrasian solution does not satisfy the property can be proved by a simple modification of Figure 2(a). An example of a weakly population monotonic solution is the solution that picks any allocation such that all agents are indifferent between their net trade and a reference trade proportional to some multiple of a fixed vector. This solution is the natural counterpart for economies in which individual endowments are specified,

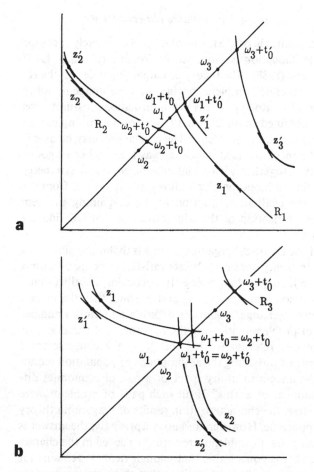

a

b

Figure 3. The $d$-egalitarian trade solution is weakly population monotonic. (a) In the example depicted here, both agents 1 and 2 gain upon the arrival of agent 3. (b) In this example, both agents 1 and 2 lose upon the arrival of agent 3.

of the solution we considered earlier under the name of "egalitarian." For a formal definition, let $d \in \mathbb{R}^l_+$. Given $Q \in \mathcal{Q}$ and $e = (R_Q, \omega_Q) \in \mathcal{F}^Q$, the $d$-egalitarian trade solution picks the efficient allocations $z$ of $e$ such that there is a $\lambda > 0$ with, for all $i \in Q$, $z_i I_i (\omega_i + \lambda d)$. It is well-defined when preferences are strictly monotonic. Figure 3 illustrates the fact that the solution is weakly population monotonic and that indeed both cases may occur: upon the arrival of new agents, all agents initially present may gain (Figure 3(a)) or they may all lose (Figure 3(b)).

6.4    *Bargaining solutions used as resource allocation rules*

The relevance of bargaining theory to the resolution of concretely specified problems of resource allocation is discussed by Roemer (1986a,b, 1988) and Chun and Thomson (1988). The theory of bargaining relies on the requirement that two "concrete" problems having the same image in utility space be treated the same. Roemer spells out informational assumptions under which results obtained in the abstract theory of bargaining can be rewritten for concrete economic problems. The crucial property he uses is designed to relate the recommended allocations as the number of goods varies. This property – together with standard efficiency and symmetry conditions and population monotonicity – allows him to derive, from the characterization of the egalitarian solution to the bargaining problem (Theorem 2), a characterization of the counterpart of that solution for the economic domain.

The advantage of the abstract bargaining model is that many situations can be represented in utility space as objects satisfying the assumptions typically made in the theory of bargaining. In particular, if utility functions are continuous, monotone increasing, and concave, then the images in utility space of two exchange economies differing only in the number of agents are pairs of problems satisfying the hypotheses of the axiom of population monotonicity relevant to that theory. Is the converse true? Given a pair of problems satisfying the assumptions of population monotonicity, are they the images in utility space of a pair of economies differing only in the number of agents? If all such pairs of problems were possible then, of course, the characterization results of bargaining theory would be directly applicable. However, and not surprisingly, the answer is No. However, not all pairs of problems are actually needed in the characterization proofs, and it is conceivable that enough richness remains for these characterizations to hold. It is intuitive that this richness depends on the number of goods. The question is then whether some bounds on the number of commodities can be identified that help predict whether the property can be met. The answer is Yes, as we explain next.

Chun and Thomson (1988) show that, in the one-commodity case, the Nash solution is population monotonic (recall that the Nash solution does not have this property on the general domain). The proof is simple: Let each agent $i \in \mathbb{N}$ be equipped with a concave utility function $u_i \colon \mathbb{R}_+ \to \mathbb{R}$. Allocating $\Omega$ units of the unique good among the members of a group $Q \in \mathbb{Q}$ according to the Nash solution means finding $(x_i)_{i \in Q} \in \mathbb{R}_+^Q$ that maximizes the product $\prod_{i \in Q} u_i(x_i')$ with respect to $(x_i')_{i \in Q} \in \mathbb{R}_+^Q$, subject to the condition $\sum_{i \in Q} x_i' = \Omega$. Assuming for simplicity that all utilities are differentiable, this exercise is solved by equating the ratios $u_i'(x_i)/u_i(x_i)$

across all agents. But since each ratio is a decreasing function of its argument, it follows that increasing the number of agents can only increase the common value of the ratios solving this exercise, which results in a smaller consumption for all agents initially present.

However, it turns out that as soon as there are two goods, the class of admissible problems is sufficiently rich to produce the same behavior as on arbitrary problems. The next proposition summarizes these results.

**Proposition 6** (Chun and Thomson 1988). *In the one-commodity case, the Nash solution (used as a resource allocation rule) is population monotonic; for any greater number of commodities, it is not.*

Note that any solution defined by maximizing a sum $\sum_{i \in Q} f_i(x_i)$ – subject to the condition $\sum_{i \in Q} x_i = \Omega$ where, for each $i \in N$, $f_i$ is continuous, monotone increasing, and concave – also is population monotonic.

### 6.5 Solutions to games in coalitional form used as resource allocation rules

Recall that on the class of TU concave coalitional form games the Shapley value is population monotonic (Section 4). This result can be applied to economies that can be represented as concave games. What are those economies?

A TU economy is one in which agents can be described in terms of utility functions, where utility is transferable from any agent to any other agent at a one-to-one ratio. This is mathematically equivalent to adding an "accounting" good such that each agent's preferences can be represented by a function that is separable additive in the accounting good (on the one hand) and (on the other hand) some function of the other goods, and is linear in the accounting good. If this formulation is adopted, the social endowment of the accounting good is of course equal to zero. Alternatively, and in fact more generally, we can assume that this special good is an actual good, without necessarily requiring its social endowment to be equal to zero. We will adopt this formulation and refer to the good as "money." In summary, we say that agent $i$'s preferences are *quasilinear* if they admit a numerical representation that is separable additive in money (on the one hand) and all other goods (on the other hand) and linear in money: $u_i(x_i, y_i) = x_i + v_i(y_i)$, where $x_i \in \mathbb{R}$ is agent $i$'s consumption of money and $y_i \in \mathbb{R}_+^{l-1}$ is the vector of $i$'s consumption of the other goods. It is standard to assume that $x_i$ is unconstrained in sign and unbounded below. These assumptions are usually imposed for mathematical convenience, but they are of particular significance for our problem. For each $Q \in \mathbb{Q}$, let $\mathcal{E}_{ql}^Q$ be the class of quasilinear economies. Since the social endowment of money may be negative, there is of course no reason to require population monotonicity, and in these cases we will limit ourselves to the search for weakly population monotonic solutions.

On the domain of quasilinear economies with an endowment of money equal to zero, the Walrasian solution from equal division is still not population monotonic. In fact, the property cannot be met even if no distributional requirements are imposed, as stated in the next theorem.

**Theorem 9** (Moulin 1992b). *On the domain of quasilinear economies in which the social endowment of money is zero, and even if the functions $v_i$ are concave, there is no population monotonic selection from the Pareto solution.*

However, the counterpart of the egalitarian solution of Pazner and Schmeidler (1978) (see Section 6.1), which is obtained by requiring the reference bundle to be proportional to the social endowment vector, is obviously weakly population monotonic. This solution is a selection from the individual rationality from equal division and Pareto solution. Another weakly population monotonic solution is obtained by choosing allocations at which the surplus measured in terms of money is divided equally (Moulin 1992b). This solution satisfies only a weaker condition of individual rationality, one that requires each agent $i$'s utility level – evaluated in terms of the quasilinear function representing $i$'s preferences normalized so that the utility of the zero bundle is equal to zero – to be at least as large as $i$'s utility, divided by the number of agents, from consuming the social endowment.

Population monotonic solutions do exist if preferences are appropriately restricted. Given $Q \in \mathbb{Q}$ and $e = (R_Q, \Omega) \in \mathcal{E}_{ql}^Q$, where $R_i$ is represented by the function $(x_i, y_i) \in \mathbb{R} \times \mathbb{R}_+^{l-1} \to x_i + v_i(y_i)$, consider the coalitional form game $w_e = (w_e(S))_{S \subseteq Q} \in \mathcal{G}^{|Q|}$ defined by:

$$w_e(S) = \max\{\textstyle\sum_{i \in S}(x_i + v_i(y_i)) \mid \sum_{i \in S}(x_i, y_i) = \Omega\}.$$

This is the *stand-alone* game associated with the economy. Finally, let $Sh^*(e)$ be the set of allocations $z = (x_i, y_i)_{i \in Q} \in Z(e)$ such that, for all $i \in Q$, $x_i + v_i(y_i) = Sh_i(w_e)$, the $i$th coordinate of the payoff vector chosen by the Shapley value for the game $w_e$.

To specify a useful restriction on the domain, first say that two goods $j$ and $k$ are *substitutes* for the function $v_i \colon \mathbb{R}^l \to \mathbb{R}$ if, for all $y_i \in \mathbb{R}_+^l$ and for all $a, b \in \mathbb{R}_+$,

$$v_i(y_i + be^k) - v_i(y_i) \geq v_i(y_i + ae^j + be^k) - v_i(y_i + ae^j),$$

where $e^j$ denotes the $j$th unit vector. This means that the marginal benefit of an additional unit of good $k$ decreases as the consumption of good

$j$ increases. Writing the condition for $j = k$ means that the function $v_i$ is concave in $y_j$. Also, a function $v_i$ satisfies *substitutability* if any two goods are substitutes in $v_i$. We now have the following proposition.

**Proposition 7** (Moulin 1992b). *On the domain of quasilinear economies in which the social endowment of money is any positive number and such that, for each $S \subseteq Q$, the function $w_e(S)$ (defined previously) satisfies substitutability, the Shapley value Sh\* (used as a resource allocation rule) is population monotonic.*

Note that, on this domain, the Shapley value satisfies only the weak individual rationality condition described in the first paragraph following Theorem 9. However, the stronger condition of individual rationality from equal division can be met, together with population monotonicity. Moulin (1990b) has proposed a constructive algorithm that produces such a solution.[13]

If there is only one good in addition to money, the hypothesis of substitutability is equivalent to concavity of the function $v_i$. Moulin gives other examples of application of Proposition 7. For instance, the result holds if there are only two goods in addition to money and if each function $v_i$ is concave and submodular over $\mathbb{R}^2_+$. It also applies in the $l$-good case if each function $v_i$ is twice continuously differentiable in the interior of $\mathbb{R}^l_+$, strictly concave, exhibits gross substitutability, and has an infinite marginal utility of each good at zero.

Finally, we note that on the domain of public good economies (Section 8), the associated stand-alone game is convex without the imposition of additional assumptions on preferences beyond quasilinearity. The Shapley value is then a population monotonic$_+$ solution (Moulin 1990a).

## 7 Fair allocation in economies with production

Generalizing even further, we turn next to economies with production. We first augment the description of an economy by a production set, interpreted as being jointly owned by everyone. To complete the specification of the model, we have several choices. One is to add a social endowment of a vector of goods that can be used as inputs or distributed for private consumption. The other (and more interesting) choice is to endow each agent with some amount of "time": time also can be used as an input or consumed as a private good in the form of leisure, but it is not transferable across agents. We will make this second choice, which

---

[13] A disadvantage of the solution is that, in contrast with the Shapley value, it does not respond well to changes in resources.

raises a number of interesting issues. An economy is thus a list $(R_Q, \omega_Q, Y)$, where $(R_Q, \omega_Q)$ are as in the specification of economies with individual endowments and $Y \subseteq \mathbb{R}^l$ is a *production set.* Let $\mathcal{P}^Q$ be the class of all economies so specified, where $Q \in \mathcal{Q}$; then a solution is a mapping, defined on the union of all such $\mathcal{P}^Q$, that selects for each economy a non-empty subset of its feasible set.

Here, too, depending upon the nature of the technology and depending on agents' endowments, the arrival of new agents might be good news or bad news for the agents initially present. Consequently, we will use population monotonicity, as well as population monotonicity$_+$ and weak population monotonicity.

It is easy to see that the equal-opportunity equivalent solutions $\varphi_\mathcal{B}$ associated with monotonic families $\mathcal{B}$ of choice sets (as described in Section 6.1) are still well-defined here. They continue to be population monotonic when production sets are convex, and they are weakly population monotonic in general.

Moulin (1988, 1990c,d) studies the *free-access upper bound,* the considerably weaker form taken by population monotonicity when the small group contains only one agent. The one-person components of all efficient solutions agree, so that instead of pertaining to the comparison of the recommendations made by a solution for two economies of different sizes, the axiom essentially reduces to a one-economy axiom ( just as individual rationality from equal division in the exchange case). Therefore, the following negative result – in which the no-envy requirement should be understood to apply to trades, since agents may be differentially endowed – is all the more disappointing: On the class of one-input, one-output economies with concave production functions, there is no subsolution of the no-envy (for trades) and Pareto solution satisfying the free-access upper bound (Moulin 1990c). However, when the no-envy requirement is dropped, not only the free-access upper bound but also population monotonicity itself can be met, in particular by the *constant returns-to-scale equivalent solution,* defined as follows: Given $e = (R_Q, \omega_Q, Y)$, this solution selects any $z \in Z(e)$ such that, for some reference constant returns-to-scale technology and for all $i \in Q$, $z_i I_i z_i^*$, where $z_i^*$ maximizes $R_i$ under the assumption that agent $i$ has access to that reference technology.

**Proposition 8** (Moulin 1990c). *On the class of one-input, one-output production economies with concave production functions, the constant returns-to-scale equivalent solution is population monotonic.*[14]

---

[14] It is, in fact, the only selection from the Pareto solution satisfying technological monotonicity and the free-access upper bound.

In the case of quasilinear economies in which the social endowment of money is equal to zero, Moulin (1990c) notes the existence of a selection from the Pareto solution satisfying population monotonicity and the *identical preferences upper bound:* no agent $i$ is better off than at the allocation that would be chosen if all others had preferences identical to $i$'s, under the requirements of efficiency and equal treatment of equals.

In economies with increasing returns-to-scale technologies, there is no selection from the Pareto solution satisfying no-envy (for trades) and the requirement that all agents prefer what they receive to the best they could achieve if given free access to the technology – a requirement which, in view of our earlier terminology, it is natural to call the *free-access lower bound* (Moulin 1990d). This requirement is a special case of population monotonicity$_+$. However, the constant returns-to-scale equivalent solution is a population monotonic$_+$ selection from the Pareto solution (Moulin 1990c).

On the domain of economies such that the marginal rate of substitution between the input and the output increases along each ray in the commodity space, the "proportional benefit" solution (Roemer and Silvestre 1993) – which selects the efficient allocation such that all consumptions are proportional to each other – is single-valued and population monotonic (Fleurbaey 1992c). Fleurbaey (1992c) gives some insight about the shape of those newcomers' preferences likely to cause various solutions, in particular the equal-income Walrasian solution, to violate population monotonicity.

## 8 Fair allocation in economies with public goods

We next consider economies with public goods. Here, too, the implications of population monotonicity are not well understood. For the case of general preferences, a brief discussion appears in Thomson (1987c), where it is observed that certain egalitarian solutions possess the property. We also have the following positive result.

**Proposition 9** (Moulin 1992a). *The selection from the egalitarian equivalent and Pareto solution, obtained by requiring the reference bundle to be proportional to the unit vector corresponding to the public good, is population monotonic$_+$.*

We have already noted that on the class of quasilinear economies in which the social endowment of money is zero, the Shapley value – used as a resource allocation rule and applied to the stand-alone game associated with each economy – is a population monotonic selection from the Pareto solution (Section 6.5; Moulin 1990a). On that domain, and applying the concept of population monotonic payoff configurations of cooperative games (Section 6.5), Moulin (1990a) also shows the existence of what could be called *population monotonic$_+$ allocation configurations*. The component allocations are selected from the Pareto solution and meet the identical preferences upper bound.

Consider now the following model of an economy with a public "bad": there is one private good, produced according to a technology with an input consumed at the same level by all agents (think of a productive activity that creates pollution). Moulin (1990d) notes that for such a model, the selection from the egalitarian equivalent and Pareto solution, obtained by requiring the reference bundle to be proportional to the unit vector corresponding to the public good, is population monotonic$_+$. Also, a selection from the Pareto solution satisfying population monotonicity$_+$ and the identical preferences upper bound can be defined as follows: Given a parameter $\lambda \in \mathbb{R}_+$, determine for each $i$ the highest welfare that $i$ could obtain subject to the condition that $x_i$ units of the input would yield $f(\lambda x_i)$ units of the output, where $f$ is the production function. Then select the efficient allocation such that, for some $\lambda$, each agent $i$'s welfare is equal to $i$'s welfare at the solution of this maximization exercise (Moulin 1990c).

## 9     Fair allocation in economies with indivisible goods

We now turn to the problem of allocating jobs and salaries among workers with equal seniorities and qualifications. The jobs are not identical, and the workers' preferences for the various job–salary packages differ. Each job is to be assigned to only one worker, and the sum of the salaries is not to exceed a certain budget. How should the job–salary packages be defined and assigned?

The formal model is as follows. There is a group $Q \in \mathbb{Q}$ of agents and a collection $A$ of *objects*. An amount $\Omega \in \mathbb{R}_+$ of an infinitely divisible good, called *money*, is also available for distribution. Each agent $i \in Q$ has a preference relation $R_i$ defined over the space $A \times \mathbb{R}$. It is continuous and strictly monotonic in its second argument and, for all $\alpha, \beta \in A$ and for all $m \in \mathbb{R}$, there is $m' \in \mathbb{R}$ such that $(\beta, m') I_i (\alpha, m)$. Let $\mathfrak{R}_{ind}$ be the class of all such preference relations. Each agent should receive one and only one object. An allocation is a pair $z = (\sigma, m)$ of a function $\sigma : Q \to A$ specifying which object each agent receives, and a vector $m \in \mathbb{R}^A$ such that $\sum_{\alpha \in A} m_\alpha = \Omega$ specifying how much money is associated with each object. The bundle received by agent $i \in Q$ at $z$ is $(\sigma(i), m_{\sigma(i)})$. A *problem of fair allocation with indivisible goods* is a triple $(R_Q, A, \Omega) \in \mathfrak{R}_{ind}^Q \times A \times \mathbb{R}_+$,

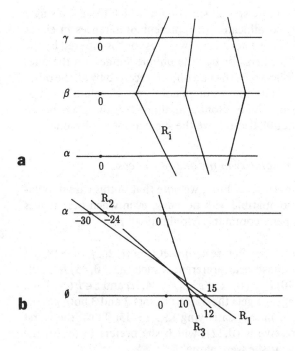

Figure 4. The allocation of indivisible objects when monetary compensations are feasible. (a) Representation of preferences. (b) Upon the arrival of agents 1 and 2, agent 3 may gain.

where $Q \in \mathcal{Q}$. Let $\mathcal{I}^Q$ be the class of these problems; then a solution is a correspondence that associates with every $Q \in \mathcal{Q}$ and every $e = (R_Q, A, \Omega) \in \mathcal{I}^Q$ a non-empty subset of the feasible set of $e$.

In Figure 4, along each of the axes (indexed by the jobs) is measured the salary that is associated with the corresponding job. To keep track of which job-salary combinations an agent finds indifferent to each other, we connect them by an "indifference curve." A few sample indifference curves are indicated for agent $i$. As in the previous section, we look for selections from the no-envy solution. The notion of an envy-free allocation applies to this situation just as well; under our assumptions, envy-free allocations exist. In fact, there is usually a continuum of them and here, too, a natural question is how to make selections from this continuum.

A special case of the model just described is when the objects are all identical. For instance, consider the allocation of jobs on an assembly line when there are more workers than jobs, all extra workers being allocated the "null" object (denoted $\emptyset$), which corresponds to unemployment.

Finally, we have the even more special situation in which there is a single object and some money to allocate. To represent preferences in either one of these two situations, we need only two axes: one is indexed by the object received by the "winners" or by "the unique winner" in the one-object case; the other is indexed by the null object, received by all the other agents – the "losers." For multiple winners not to envy each other, they should receive the same amount of money. Similarly, for the losers not to envy each other, they should also receive the same amount of money.

### 9.1    *Population monotonicity in the one-object case*

We start with the one-object case. First, we note that in this case population monotonicity is incompatible with no-envy, even when preferences are quasilinear (Alkan, pers. commun.; Moulin 1990b).

**Example** (Moulin 1990c).    See Figure 4(b). Let $Q = \{1, 2, 3\}$, $A = \{\emptyset, \alpha\}$, and $\Omega = 0$. Agents have quasilinear preferences such that $(\emptyset, 45) I_1 (\alpha, 0)$, $(\emptyset, 36) I_2 (\alpha, 0)$, and $(\emptyset, 10) I_3 (\alpha, 0)$. Let $e = (R_Q, A, \Omega)$ and $z \in F(e)$. Then efficiency requires that agent 1 gets the object; agents 2 and 3 both get the null object and $t$ units of money satisfying $12 \leq t \leq 15$. Thus, the worst bundle agent 3 could receive is $(\emptyset, 12)$, which she prefers to $(\alpha, 0)$, the bundle she would receive if she were alone.

In the example, agent 3 is better off at any envy-free allocation of the three-person economy than if she were alone, so that a violation of the counterpart of the free-access upper bound introduced earlier (see Section 7) is unavoidable if no-envy is insisted upon.

However, since here consumption spaces are unbounded below, it may be unnatural to require agents to lose when new agents come in. This is because the model is essentially equivalent to a production model. Receiving the object is similar to being given a chance to produce "utility" by using the object. When new agents come in with "good" production functions, they may be able to use the object very productively, and it may be possible to make the agents originally present benefit. In order to deal with this case, and with the case where the new agent has a poor production function, we return to the condition of weak population monotonicity.

Consider the solution $\varphi^*$ that systematically selects the envy-free allocation least favorable to the winner, as illustrated in Figure 5. At this allocation, the winner's indifference curve through his bundle passes through the losers' common bundle. It is easy to see that this solution is weakly population monotonic.

The solution $\varphi^*$ is a selection from the egalitarian equivalence solution introduced in Section 6.1. (It is because there is only one object that

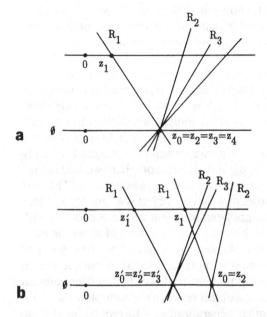

Figure 5. A weakly population monotonic selection from the no-envy solution in the one-object case. (a) Definition of the solution: It picks the allocation that is the worst for the winner in the set of envy-free allocations, so that all indifference curves pass through a common "reference bundle." (b) Its weak population monotonicity: As the number of agents changes, the reference bundle moves to the left or to the right. In the example, the reference bundle moves from $z_0$ to $z_0'$ upon the arrival of agent 3.

egalitarian equivalence is compatible with no-envy.[15]) Moreover, a characterization of the solution can be obtained on the basis of weak population monotonicity. To formally state the result, we need the following very mild condition of *neutrality:* If an allocation – obtained by exchanges of bundles from an allocation chosen by the solution – leaves unaffected the welfare of each agent, then it is also chosen by the solution. We will also use the condition of *translation invariance,* which states that if all the preference maps are translated by some amount $t \in \mathbb{R}$, and if the social endowment of money is changed by $t$ times the number of agents, then the recommended bundle for each agent is obtained from his old one by increasing its money component by the amount $t$.

---

[15] In general, the two distributional requirements of no-envy and egalitarian equivalence are incompatible (Thomson 1990).

**Theorem 10** (Tadenuma and Thomson 1993). *In the one-object case, the solution $\varphi^*$ is the only weakly population monotonic, neutral, and translation invariant selection from the no-envy solution.*

In economies with indivisible goods, there is no meaning to "equal division," but a particularly useful distributional requirement is obtained by insisting that each agent $i$ be made at least as well off as at the only envy-free allocation that would exist in an economy in which all agents had the same preference as $i$'s; this is the identical preferences lower bound encountered earlier. In the two-person case, meeting this bound is actually the same condition as no-envy, but if there are more than two agents then the identical preferences lower bound is weaker than no-envy. The next few results pertain to economies in which the object is a "good": an agent would always need to be compensated to give it up. In economies with quasilinear preferences in which the social endowment of money is zero, Moulin (1990b) shows that the Shapley value applied to the associated stand-alone game is a population monotonic selection from the Pareto solution that meets the identical preferences lower bound (this solution differs from $\varphi^*$). A generalization of this result to the multiple-object case appears in Section 9.2. Another generalization – to economies that do not satisfy quasilinearity and in which the social endowment of money is any positive number – is given by Bevia (1992), who constructs an extension of this solution having these same properties.

### 9.2    *Population monotonicity in the multiple-object case*

In the multiple-object case, the selection from the egalitarian equivalence and Pareto solution obtained by requiring the reference bundle to contain a fixed object is weakly population monotonic, but is no longer guaranteed to be a selection from the no-envy solution (Thomson 1990). In fact, if no-envy is insisted upon then we have the following impossibility, which holds even on the quasilinear domain.

**Theorem 11** (Tadenuma and Thomson 1992). *In the multiple-object case, there is no weakly population monotonic selection from the no-envy solution.*

The following positive result is available, however.

**Proposition 10** (Moulin 1992b). *In the multiple-object case, if preferences are quasilinear and the social endowment of money is equal to zero, then the Shapley value applied to the stand-alone game associated with* *each economy* (see Section 6.5) *is a population monotonic selection from the Pareto solution.*[16]

Finally, consider the more general case where each agent can be assigned several objects. A general analysis of this case has been carried out by Bevia (1993).

**Proposition 11** (Bevia 1993). *Consider the multiple-object case, where each agent can be assigned several objects. Then, even if preferences are quasilinear and the social endowment of money is zero, there is no population monotonic selection from the Pareto solution. However, if preferences are quasilinear and satisfy the counterpart of the substitutability assumption of Section 6.5, and if the social endowment of money is nonnegative, then the Shapley value applied to the stand-alone game associated with each economy is a population monotonic selection from the Pareto solution.*

### 9.3 Locally extendable allocations

Theorem 11 shows that weak population monotonicity is a very strong requirement in the present context, so it is natural to investigate the possibility of satisfying weaker requirements. Alkan's (1994) contribution is along those lines. He asks the following question: For each given economy, is there *some* allocation such that the arrival of another agent can be made to affect all agents initially present in the same direction, and such that the departure of an agent can be made to affect all remaining agents in the same direction?

**Locally extendable allocation.** Let $\varphi$ be a solution. Let $Q \in \mathcal{Q}$, $e = (R_Q, A, \Omega) \in \mathcal{I}^Q$, and $z \in \varphi(e)$. Let $m_M$ be the maximal amount of money received by anyone at $z$. The solution $\varphi$ permits the *local upper extendability* of $z$ if, for any $i \in Q$, there exists $z' \in \varphi(R_{Q \setminus \{i\}}, A, \Omega)$ such that: (i) $z'_j P_j z_j$ for all $j \in Q \setminus \{i\}$ if $m_M > 0$; (ii) $z'_j I_j z_j$ for all $j \in Q \setminus \{i\}$ if $m_M = 0$; and (iii) $z_j P_j z'_j$ for all $j \in Q \setminus \{i\}$ otherwise. The solution $\varphi$ permits the *local lower extendability* of $z$ if, for all $i \notin Q$, there exists $z' \in \varphi(R_{Q \cup \{i\}}, A, \Omega)$ such that: (i) $z_j R_j z'_j$ for all $j \in Q$ if $z_j P_j (\emptyset, 0)$ for all $j \in Q$; (ii) $z'_j I_j z_j$ for all $j \in Q$ if $z_j I_j (\emptyset, 0)$ for all $j \in Q$; and (iii) $z'_j R_j z_j$ for all $j \in Q$ otherwise.

It turns out that the no-envy solution $F$ permits only limited local extendability. The allocations that can be so extended are defined as follows.

---

[16] This result should be compared to Proposition 7 (Section 6.5).

Given $e = (R_Q, A, \Omega)$ and $z \in \varphi(e)$, define the *welfare* of agent $i \in Q$ at $z$ to be the amount of money which by itself would constitute a bundle that the agent finds indifferent to $z_i$. We say that $z$ is a *maxmin welfare allocation* of $F(e)$ if the agent with the lowest welfare at $z$ has the highest possible welfare in $F(e)$; we say that $z$ is a *minmax money allocation* of $F(e)$ if the maximal amount of money received by anyone at $z$ is the smallest among all allocations in $F(e)$.

**Theorem 12** (Alkan 1989).   *The no-envy solution permits the local upper extendability of the minmax money allocation and the local lower extendability of the maxmin welfare allocation; it permits the local upper extendability of the minmax money allocation only.*

Alkan also shows that local lower extendability is an easier requirement to meet than local upper extendability. Indeed, there are economies in which the no-envy solution permits the local lower extendability of all its allocations.

Fleurbaey (1993) considers a version of this model in which the indivisible goods are interpreted as nontransferable talents or handicaps, and establishes the population monotonicity of several solutions.

## 10     Fair division in private goods economies with single-peaked preferences

Examples abound of activities that one enjoys up to a point but with any time spent on it beyond that point decreasing one's overall satisfaction; in many cases, there may well be a point beyond which one wishes that one would not have started at all. Consider such an activity to be divided up among the members of a team, and assume that the activity must be completed.[17] How should this division be done?

Formally, there is a group $Q \in \mathbb{Q}$ of agents among whom to allocate $\Omega > 0$ units of an infinitely divisible commodity. For each $i \in Q$, $R_i$ is agent $i$'s continuous and single-peaked preference relation defined over $\mathbb{R}_+$ – that is, there is a number $p(R_i) \in \mathbb{R}_+$ such that, for all $x_i, x_i' \in \mathbb{R}_+$, if $x_i' < x_i \leq p(R_i)$ or $p(R_i) \leq x_i < x_i'$ then $x_i P_i x_i'$. Let $\mathfrak{R}_{sp}$ be the class of all such preference relations. A *problem of fair division with single-peaked preferences* is a pair $(R_Q, \Omega) \in \mathfrak{R}_{sp}^Q \times \mathbb{R}_+$. For each $Q \in \mathbb{Q}$, let $\mathbb{S}^Q$ be the class of all problems involving the group $Q$; then a solution associates with every $Q \in \mathbb{Q}$ and every $(R_Q, \Omega) \in \mathbb{S}^Q$ a non-empty subset of the set of feasible allocations of $(R_Q, \Omega)$, $\{z \in \mathbb{R}_+^Q \mid \Sigma_{i \in Q} z_i = \Omega\}$. Note that feasibility

---

[17] Another situation with an identical mathematical representation is rationing in a two-goods economy.

is defined with an equality sign, reflecting the fact that the commodity is not freely disposable. The axiomatic analysis of this class of problems was initiated by Sprumont (1991).

Efficiency is easily understood. If the amount to divide is larger than the sum of the preferred amounts – we will say there is "too much" of the commodity – then efficiency requires that each agent consume more than she would prefer; if the opposite holds – we will say there is "not enough" – then efficiency requires that each agent consume less than she would prefer. Fairness, in addition to efficiency, is one of our objectives. We will consider the same distributional requirements as in Section 6, no-envy and individual rationality from equal division. Just as in classical economies, there is a continuum of efficient allocations satisfying these distributional requirements, so once again the question of selection arises.

An appealing selection is the "uniform" rule, introduced in the fixed-price literature and recently characterized by Sprumont (1991) on the basis of incentive considerations. It is defined as follows. Let $Q \in \mathbb{Q}$ and $(R_Q, \Omega) \in \mathbb{S}^Q$. Then $x \in \mathbb{R}^Q_+$ is the *uniform allocation* of $(R_Q, \Omega)$ if: (i) when $\Omega \le \sum_{i \in Q} p(R_i)$ there is a $\lambda \in \mathbb{R}_+$ such that, for all $i \in Q$, $x_i = \min\{p(R_i), \lambda\}$; and (ii) when $\sum_{i \in Q} p(R_i) \le \Omega$ there is a $\lambda \in \mathbb{R}_+$ such that, for all $i \in Q$, $x_i = \max\{p(R_i), \lambda\}$. In each case, $\lambda$ is chosen so as to ensure feasibility. It is easy to see that the uniform rule selects efficient allocations that are both envy-free and individually rational from equal division. The rule is illustrated in Figure 6 for each of the two cases.

In this model, the arrival of additional agents may be either good news (in cases when there is too much of the good to begin with) or bad news, and the natural property to consider is weak population monotonicity. Unfortunately, the property is quite demanding. For instance, the equal division rule does not satisfy it. To see this, let $Q = \{1, 2\}$ and $\Omega = 6$; then equal division is $(3, 3)$. Now let $Q' = \{1, 2, 3\}$; here, equal division is $(2, 2, 2)$. If $p(R_1) = 2$ and $p(R_2) = 3$, $(3, 3)$ is worse for agent 1 and better for agent 2 than $(2, 2, 2)$. If in addition $p(R_3) = 2$, then the allocations $(3, 3)$ and $(2, 2, 2)$ are the uniform allocations of the economies $(R_Q, \Omega)$ and $(R_{Q'}, \Omega)$, so the example shows that the uniform rule is not weakly population monotonic, either.

These negative results extend much further, as stated in the next proposition. We will use the requirement of *symmetry:* identical agents are to be treated identically.

**Theorem 13** (Thomson 1991). *There is no weakly population monotonic selection from the no-envy solution, nor from the individually rational solution from equal division. Also, there is no weakly population monotonic and symmetric solution that depends only on preferred consumptions.*

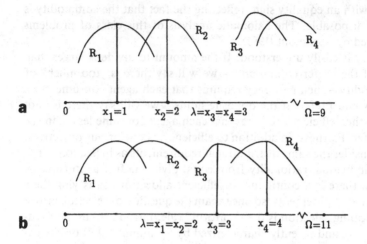

Figure 6. The uniform rule illustrated for $Q = \{1, 2, 3\}$. (a) The case $\Omega \leq \sum_{i \in Q} p(R_i)$: each agent whose preferred consumption is smaller than $\lambda$ gets preferred consumption; each of the others gets $\lambda$. (b) The case $\sum_{i \in Q}(R_i) \leq \Omega$: each agent whose preferred consumption is greater than $\lambda$ gets her preferred consumption; each of the others gets $\lambda$.

These are disappointing results. Note in particular that they obtain even though efficiency is not required. However, if the distributional requirements of no-envy and individual rationality from equal division are dropped then anonymous and weakly population monotonic selections from the Pareto solution can be found on large subdomains of the primary domain. For example, certain solutions based on equating "sacrifices," as measured by the size of upper contour sets, satisfy the property. These "egalitarian" solutions do provide appealing ways of solving the problem.

Moreover, upon close examination of the proofs of the negative results stated in Theorem 13, one discovers that they involve comparing economies where initially there is too much of the commodity and, after the arrival of the new agents, there is not enough of it (or conversely). This naturally suggests limiting one's attention to situations in which changes in the population are not so disruptive, that is, situations in which there is too much before and after, or there is not enough before and after, the arrival of new agents.

**One-sided population monotonicity.** For all $Q, Q' \in \mathbb{Q}$ with $Q' \subset Q$ and for all $(R_Q, \Omega) \in \mathbb{S}^Q$, if $\sum_{i \in Q'} p(R_i) \leq \Omega$ or if $\sum_{i \in Q} p(R_i) \geq \Omega$ then

$$\varphi_i(R_Q, \Omega) R_i \varphi_i(R_{Q'}, \Omega) \quad \text{for all } i \in Q.$$

The property retains a wide range of relevance and is fortunately satisfied by a number of interesting solutions, including the uniform rule, the proportional rule (which allocates the commodity in proportion to the preferred amounts), and others. However, among these, the uniform rule is close to being the only one to satisfy the no-envy requirement. This is stated in the next theorem, which also makes use of the requirement of *replication invariance:* If an allocation is chosen for some economy then, for any order of replication, the replica allocation is chosen for the replica economy. This is a weak requirement, and is satisfied by most of the solutions that have been proposed for this model.

For this next result, we impose on preferences the requirement that there be a finite consumption indifferent to the zero consumption.

**Theorem 14** (Thomson 1991). *The uniform rule is the only replication invariant and one-sided population monotonic selection from the no-envy and Pareto solution.*

## 11 Public decision in economies with single-peaked preferences

The public-good version of the model discussed in the previous section is examined by Ching and Thomson (1993). In brief, there is an interval $[0, \Omega]$ of possible levels of a public good, and all potential agents have single-peaked preferences over this interval. A solution associates with each profile of preferences a single level of the public good.

It is easy to check that the following solutions, indexed by the parameter $a \in [0, \Omega]$, are population monotonic: Given some profile of preferences, select the level $a$ if it is efficient (i.e., if it is between the smallest and the largest preferred levels in the profile of preferences); if not, select the preferred level in the profile the closest to $a$ (note that the parameter $a$ is required to be the same for all cardinalities). These solutions constitute a subfamily of a family introduced by Moulin (1984) and characterized by him on the basis of strategy-proofness. Let $C_a$ be the solution associated with the parameter $a$.

**Theorem 15** (Ching and Thomson 1993). *The solutions $\{C_a \mid a \in [0, \Omega]\}$ are the only population monotonic selections from the Pareto solution.*

Since here the only good present is a public good and the feasible set does not change as the number of agents enlarges (this model should be compared with the model of Section 8), there is no means of compensating an agent for any change in the chosen level that the arrival of newcomers might cause. As a result, population monotonic is quite a strong condition.

## 12    Conclusion

Although the principle of population monotonicity is well understood in some of the models in which it has been investigated, not much is known about its implications in a number of other important contexts. It is usually easy to find out whether a given solution does or does not satisfy the property. However, when it comes to characterizing the class of well-behaved solutions that satisfy the property, relatively little has been accomplished. We hope that this review will stimulate the search for answers to the numerous questions that are still open. To help in this work, we offer the following guidelines for the analysis of population monotonicity (or its variants, population monotonicity$_+$ and weak population monotonicity) in a given model.

*Identify population monotonic solutions.* In particular, determine if the most widely used solutions for the model satisfy the property.

(A) If such solutions do exist, characterize all of them. Of course, the class of population monotonic solutions might be large, so a characterization may only be possible if the solutions are also required to satisfy minimal requirements of efficiency and distribution.

(B) Study the compatibility of the property with other properties of interest.

(C) Formulate criteria that would help evaluate how well the various population monotonic solutions perform, and compare them on that basis. Obtaining population monotonicity is only the first step. In a second step, one may want to ensure that sacrifices (or gains) not only be in the same direction but also be distributed "evenly" (see the notion of guarantee structure used in bargaining theory).

*Identify domain restrictions.* If population monotonic solutions do *not* exist on the primary domain of interest, identify interesting domain restrictions that would help recover existence. For example, quasilinearity of preferences has been a useful restriction in the study of exchange economies and in the case of indivisible goods; in the latter case, so has allowing only one object. In production economies, allowing only two goods has been a useful assumption.

(A) Formulate weaker monotonicity requirements; for example:

   (i)   Conditions involving a given problem and all of its subproblems, instead of a general class of problems (see the notion of a population monotonic payoff configuration used in the context of coalitional form games).

(ii) Conditions involving only unit changes in the population (see the notion of local upper or lower extendability introduced in economies with indivisible goods).

(iii) Conditions based on comparing what each agent gets in some problem to the average of what that agent gets in the subproblems.[18]

(iv) Conditions based on specifying an order in which new agents arrive. When the space of characteristics is endowed with an order structure, limiting one's attention to situations where agents' arrivals are in agreement with that order might be of some interest.

(v) Finally, special features of the model might be relevant in formulating conditions restricting the applicability of the condition (as we saw on the single-peaked domain).

(B) Formulate criteria that would help evaluate how far from population monotonic a given solution may be. If some agents gain when they should lose, taking the maximal (or average) gain they might incur could provide the basis for comparisons of solutions.

### REFERENCES

Alkan, A. (1994), "Monotonicity and Fair Assignments," *Journal of Economic Theory* (to appear).

Bennett, E. (1983), "The Aspiration Approach to Predicting Coalition Formation and Payoff Distribution in Sidepayment Games," *International Journal of Game Theory* 12: 1–28.

Bevia, C. (1992), "Equal Split Guarantee Solution in Economies with Indivisible Goods. Consistency and Population Monotonicity," mimeo, Department of Economics, University of Alicante, Spain.

(1993), "Fair Allocation in a General Model with Indivisible Goods," mimeo, Department of Economics, University of Alicante, Spain.

Chichilnisky, G., and W. Thomson (1987), "The Walrasian Mechanism from Equal Division Is Not Monotonic with Respect to Variations in the Number of Agents," *Journal of Public Economics* 32: 119–24.

Ching, S., and W. Thomson (1993), "Population-monotonic Solutions in Public Good Economies with Single-peaked Preferences," *Social Choice and Welfare* (to appear).

Chun, Y. (1985), unpublished notes, Department of Economics, University of Rochester, New York.

(1986), "The Solidarity Axiom for Quasi-linear Social Choice Problems," *Social Choice and Welfare* 3: 297–320.

Chun, Y., and W. Thomson (1988), "Monotonicity Properties of Bargaining Solutions When Applied to Economies," *Mathematical Social Sciences* 15: 11–27.

---

[18] This approach is similar to the way Maschler and Owen suggested weakening the condition of consistency.

(1989), "Bargaining Solutions and Relative Guarantees," *Mathematical Social Sciences* 17: 285–95.

(1992), "Bargaining Problems with Claims," *Mathematical Social Sciences* 24: 19–33.

Fleurbaey, M. (1992), "Preference Responsibility and Monotonicity in Fair Division," Mimeo, INSEE, Paris.

(1993), "Three Solutions for the Compensation Problem," *Journal of Economic Theory* (to appear).

Foley, D. (1987), "Resource Allocation and the Public Sector," *Yale Economic Essays* 7: 45–98.

Grafe, F., E. Iñarra, and J. M. Zarzuelo (1992), "On Externality Games," discussion paper no. 102, SEEDS.

Hart, S. (1985), "An Axiomatization of Harsanyi's Nontransferable Utility Solution," *Econometrica* 53: 1295–1313.

Ichiishi, T. (1988), "The Cooperative Nature of the Firm," mimeo, Department of Economics, Ohio State University, Columbus.

Jones, R. (1987), "The Population Monotonicity Property and the Transfer Paradox," *Journal of Public Economics* 32: 125–32.

Kalai, E. (1977), "Proportional Solution to Bargaining Problems: Interpersonal Utility Comparisons," *Econometrica* 45: 1023–30.

Kalai, E., and M. Smorodinsky (1975), "Other Solutions to Nash's Bargaining Problem," *Econometrica* 43: 513–18.

Littlechild, S. C. (1974), "A Simple Expression for the Nucleolus in a Special Case," *International Journal of Game Theory* 3: 21–9.

Littlechild, S. C., and G. Owen (1973), "A Simple Expression for the Shapley Value for a Special Case," *Management Science* 20: 370–2.

Maschler, M., and G. Owen (1989), "The Consistent Shapley Value for Hyperplane Games," *International Journal of Game Theory* 18: 389–406.

Moulin, H. (1984), "Generalized Condorcet-Winners for Single-peaked and Single-plateau Preferences," *Social Choice and Welfare* 1: 127–47.

(1985a), "The Separability Axiom and Equal Sharing Methods," *Journal of Economic Theory* 36: 120–48.

(1985b), "Egalitarianism and Utilitarianism in Quasi-linear Bargaining," *Econometrica* 53: 49–67.

(1988), *Axioms of Cooperative Decision-making.* Cambridge: Cambridge University Press.

(1990a), "Cores and Large Cores When Population Varies," *International Journal of Game Theory* 19: 219–52.

(1990b), "Joint Ownership of a Convex Technology: Comparisons of Three Solutions," *Review of Economic Studies* 57: 439–52.

(1990c), "Fair Division under Joint Ownership: Recent Results and Open Questions," *Social Choice and Welfare* 7: 149–70.

(1990d), "Interpreting Common Ownership," *Recherches Economiques de Louvain* 56: 303–26.

(1992a), "All Sorry to Disagree: A General Principle for the Provision of Nonrival Goods," *Scandinavian Journal of Economics* 94: 37–51.

(1992b), "An Application of the Shapley Value to Fair Division with Money," *Econometrica* 60: 1331–49.

Moulin, H., and W. Thomson (1988), "Can Everyone Benefit from Growth? Two Difficulties," *Journal of Mathematical Economics* 17: 339–45.

Nash, J. F. (1950), "The Bargaining Problem," *Econometrica* 18: 155-62.
Pazner, E., and D. Schmeidler (1978), "Egalitarian Equivalent Allocations: A New Concept of Economic Equity," *Quarterly Journal of Economics* 92: 671-87.
Polterovich, V., and V. Spivak (1983), "Gross Substitutability of Point-to-Set Correspondences," *Journal of Mathematical Economics* 92: 117-40.
Roemer, J. (1986a), "The Mismarriage of Bargaining Theory and Distributive Justice," *Ethics* 97: 88-110.
  (1986b), "Equality of Resources Implies Equality of Welfare," *Quarterly Journal of Economics* 101: 751-84.
  (1988), "Axiomatic Bargaining Theory on Economic Environments," *Journal of Economic Theory* 45: 1-31.
Roemer, J., and J. Silvestre (1993), "The Proportional Solution for Economies with Both Private and Public Ownership," *Journal of Economic Theory* 59: 426-44.
Rosenthal, E. (1990), "Monotonicity of the Core and Value in Dynamic Cooperative Games," *International Journal of Game Theory* 19: 45-57.
Schmeidler, D. (1969), "The Nucleolus of a Characteristic Function Game," *SIAM Journal of Applied Mathematics* 17: 1163-70.
Shapley, L. (1953), "A Value for *n*-person Games," in H. Kuhn and A. W. Tucker (eds.), *Contributions to the Theory of Games II* (Annals of Mathematics Studies, vol. 28). Princeton, NJ: Princeton University Press, pp. 307-17.
Sharkey, W. (1981), "Convex Games without Side-payments," *International Journal of Game Theory* 10: 101-6.
Sönmez, T. (1993), "Population-monotonicity of the Nucleolus on a Class of Public Good Problems," mimeo, Department of Economics, University of Rochester, New York.
Sonn, S. (1990), "A Note on Sprumont's Characterization," mimeo, Department of Economics, University of Rochester, New York.
Sprumont, Y. (1990), "Population-monotonic Allocation Schemes for Cooperative Games with Transferable Utility," *Games and Economic Behavior* 2: 378-94.
  (1991), "The Division Problem with Single-peaked Preferences: A Characterization of the Uniform Allocation Rule," *Econometrica* 59: 509-19.
Tadenuma, K., and W. Thomson (1992), "Solutions to the Problem of Fair Allocation in Economies with Indivisible Goods," mimeo, Department of Economics, University of Rochester, New York (to appear in *Theory and Decision*).
  (1993), "The Fair Allocation of an Indivisible Good When Monetary Compensations Are Possible," *Mathematical Social Sciences* 25: 117-32.
Thomson, W. (1983a), "The Fair Division of a Fixed Supply among a Growing Population," *Mathematics of Operations Research* 8: 319-26.
  (1983b), "Problems of Fair Division and the Egalitarian Solution," *Journal of Economic Theory* 31: 211-26.
  (1983c), "Collective Guarantee Structures," *Economics Letters* 11: 63-8.
  (1984a), "Truncated Egalitarian Solutions," *Social Choice and Welfare* 1: 25-32.
  (1984b), "Monotonicity, Stability and Egalitarianism," *Mathematical Social Sciences* 4: 15-28.
  (1987a), "Individual and Collective Opportunities," *International Journal of Game Theory* 16: 245-52.

(1987b), "Monotonic Allocation Rules," mimeo, Department of Economics, University of Rochester, New York (revised August 1993).

(1987c), "Monotonic Allocation Rules in Economies with Public Goods," mimeo, Department of Economics, University of Rochester, New York (revised August 1993).

(1988), "A Study of Choice Correspondences in Economies with a Variable Number of Agents," *Journal of Economic Theory* 46: 237–54.

(1990), "On the Non-existence of Envy-free and Egalitarian-Equivalent Allocations in Economies with Indivisibilities," *Economics Letters* 34: 227–9.

(1991), "Population-monotonic Solutions to the Problem of Fair Division When Preferences are Single-peaked," discussion paper, Department of Economics, University of Rochester, New York (revised June 1992; to appear in *Economic Theory*).

(1993), "Consistent Allocation Rules," mimeo, University of Rochester, New York.

Thomson, W., and T. Lensberg (1983), "Guarantee Structures for Problems of Fair Division," *Mathematical Social Sciences* 4: 205–18.

Tijs, S. (1981), "Bounds for the Core and the $\tau$-value," in O. Moeschlin and E. Pallaschke (eds.), *Game Theory and Mathematical Economics*. Amsterdam: North-Holland, pp. 123–32.

# PART III

# Algebraic and combinatorial aspects of social choice

CHAPTER 5

# Condorcet efficiency and social homogeneity

*William V. Gehrlein*

## 1 Introduction

We wish to consider elections in which there are three candidates $\{A, B, C\}$. Voters are assumed to have complete linear preference rankings (no indifference) on candidates; they are also assumed to vote in accordance with these preferences. The possible preference rankings on three candidates are given as:

$A > B > C : n_1,$

$A > C > B : n_2,$

$B > A > C : n_3,$

$C > A > B : n_4,$

$B > C > A : n_5,$

$C > B > A : n_6.$

Here, $A > B$ denotes that $A$ is preferred to $B$, and $n_i$ denotes the number of voters with the associated preference ranking on candidates, with $\sum_{i=1}^{6} n_i = n$. The number of voters, $n$, is assumed to be odd throughout.

A candidate is the Condorcet winner if able to defeat each other candidate by simple majority rule under pairwise comparison. Thus, $A$ is the Condorcet winner if $A$ beats $B$ by majority rule, with $n_1 + n_2 + n_4 > n_3 + n_5 + n_6$, and $A$ beats $C$ by majority rule with $n_1 + n_2 + n_3 > n_4 + n_5 + n_6$. It is well known that a Condorcet winner does not necessarily exist (Condorcet 1785), but the Condorcet criterion suggests that the Condorcet winner should be selected whenever there is one. A number of recent studies have called for the use of the Condorcet criterion in evaluating election procedures. See, for example, Felsenthal and Machover (1992) and Sommerlad and McLean (1989). This brings renewed interest to evaluating the propensity of various voting rules to meet the Condorcet criterion.

127

128     William V. Gehrlein

The Condorcet efficiency of a voting rule refers to the propensity of that rule to elect the Condorcet winner, given that there is a Condorcet winner. Condorcet efficiency is technically defined as the conditional probability that a voting rule elects the Condorcet winner, given that a Condorcet winner exists. Impetus for examining Condorcet efficiency was provided by Tideman (1992), who used results from actual elections to show that it is quite likely that a Condorcet winner will exist in an election. This is particularly true for elections with smaller numbers of candidates and large electorates. The current study is concerned with evaluating the Condorcet efficiency of simple election procedures. Of particular interest is the impact that social homogeneity, or the tendency of voters' preferences to be similar, has on the Condorcet efficiency of voting rules. Earlier work by Fishburn (1973) and others has suggested that increased homogeneity should lead to increased Condorcet efficiency. The current study shows that this relationship is valid over a range of voting procedures by expanding earlier work of Berg (1985a,b) and Gehrlein and Berg (1992), who used Pólya–Eggenberger (hereafter, PE) probability models to describe distributions of $n_i$s to represent voters' preferences. Results show that even relatively modest levels of social homogeneity produce high levels of Condorcet efficiency for almost all voting rules.

## 2     Condorcet winner probabilities

Many different studies have been conducted to develop representations for the probability that a Condorcet winner exists, given various assumptions about how likely it is that different combinations of $n_i$s result to represent voters' preferences. A survey of this research was given in Gehrlein (1983).

Gehrlein and Berg (1992) presented a generalized representation for the probability that a Condorcet winner exists under a PE probability model for the selection of $n_i$s. Pólya–Eggenberger models define a family of discrete multivariate probability distributions that can be described as a simple urn experiment. Consider an urn with six balls of different colors. For this example, each color represents one of the complete preference rankings on three alternatives, as just described. Balls are then drawn one at a time, and after each draw the ball plus $\alpha$ balls of the same color as the last ball drawn are put back into the urn. The probability of drawing $n_i$ balls of each color $i$ for $i = 1, 2, ..., 6$ after $n$ successive draws is $p(n_1, n_2, ..., n_6)$, with (Johnson and Kotz 1977)

$$p(n_1, n_2, ..., n_6) = \frac{n!}{6^{(n,\alpha)}} \prod_{i=1}^{6} \frac{1^{(n_i,\alpha)}}{n_i!}, \tag{1}$$

where $k^{(x,\alpha)}$ is the generalized ascending factorial with $k^{(x,\alpha)} = k(k+\alpha)\cdots$ $(k+\alpha(x-1))$, for $x = 0, 1, \ldots, n$ and $k^{(0,\alpha)} = k^{(1,\alpha)} = k$.

A representation for the probability $P^{\alpha}(n)$ that a Condorcet winner exists for $n$ voters on three alternatives, with $n_i$s generated by a PE model with parameter $\alpha$, was given by Gehrlein and Berg (1992) as

$$P^{\alpha}(n) = \frac{3n!}{6^{(n,\alpha)}} \sum\nolimits^1 \prod_{i=1}^{6} \frac{1^{(n_i,\alpha)}}{n_i!}, \qquad (2)$$

where $\sum^1$ is a five-summation function with summation indices consistent with

$$0 \le n_6 \le \frac{n-1}{2},$$

$$0 \le n_5 \le \frac{n-1}{2} - n_6,$$

$$0 \le n_4 \le \frac{n-1}{2} - n_6 - n_5,$$

$$0 \le n_3 \le \frac{n-1}{2} - n_6 - n_5,$$

$$0 \le n_2 \le \frac{n-1}{2} - n_6 - n_5 - n_4 - n_3,$$

and $n_1 = n - n_6 - n_5 - n_4 - n_3 - n_2$. Computed values of $P^{\alpha}(n)$ are shown in Table 1 for each $n = 3, 5, 7, 9, 11, 25$ with each $\alpha = 0, 1, 2, 3, 4, 5, 10, 15, 20, 25$. Consistent with the observations in Berg (1985a), $P^{\alpha}(n)$ decreases in $n$ for given $\alpha$ and increases in $\alpha$ for given $n$.

Two special cases of these PE models in (2) have been considered in detail in the literature. When $\alpha = 0$, $p(n_1, n_2, \ldots, n_6)$ reduces to the simple multinomial case with equal probabilities for selecting any particular preference ranking for a given voter. This has been referred to as the "impartial culture" condition (IC) in the literature. A number of representations of $P^0(n)$ have been developed (see Gehrlein 1983), with the most computationally tractable representation being given in Gehrlein and Fishburn (1976a) as

$$P^0(n) = 3^{-n+1} \sum\nolimits^2 \frac{n!}{n_{56}! \, n_4! \, n_3! \, n_{12}!} 2^{-n_3 - n_4}. \qquad (3)$$

Here, $n_{56} = n_5 + n_6$, $n_{12} = n_1 + n_2$, and $\sum^2$ is a three-summation function with summation indices consistent with

Table 1. $P^\alpha(n)$, the probability that a Condorcet
winner exists for n voters on three candidates for
PE probabilities with parameter $\alpha$

| $\alpha$ | $n$ | | | | | |
|---|---|---|---|---|---|---|
| | 3 | 5 | 7 | 9 | 11 | 25 |
| 0 | .9444 | .9306 | .9250 | .9220 | .9202 | .9157 |
| 1 | .9643 | .9524 | .9470 | .9441 | .9423 | .9387 |
| 2 | .9750 | .9665 | .9626 | .9604 | .9590 | .9561 |
| 3 | .9815 | .9753 | .9724 | .9708 | .9698 | .9675 |
| 4 | .9857 | .9811 | .9789 | .9776 | .9769 | .9750 |
| 5 | .9886 | .9850 | .9833 | .9824 | .9817 | .9803 |
| 10 | .9952 | .9838 | .9931 | .9927 | .9925 | .9919 |
| 15 | .9974 | .9966 | .9963 | .9961 | .9959 | .9956 |
| 20 | .9983 | .9979 | .9977 | .9975 | .9975 | .9973 |
| 25 | .9988 | .9985 | .9984 | .9983 | .9983 | .9981 |

$$0 \le n_{56} \le \frac{n-1}{2},$$

$$0 \le n_4 \le \frac{n-1}{2} - n_{56},$$

$$0 \le n_3 \le \frac{n-1}{2} - n_{56},$$

and $n_{12} = n - n_{56} - n_4 - n_3$. Guilbaud (1952) developed a representation
for the limiting case in voters $P^0(\infty)$ under IC as

$$P^0(\infty) = \frac{3}{4} + \frac{3}{2\pi} \sin^{-1}\left(\frac{1}{3}\right) \approx .91226. \tag{4}$$

The special case of the PE model in (2) with $\alpha = 1$ reduces to the situation where all specific combinations of $n_i$'s are equally likely to be observed. This has been referred to as the "impartial anonymous culture" condition (IAC) in the literature (Berg 1985a,b; Berg and Bjurulf 1983; Berg and Lepelley 1990; Gehrlein 1981a, 1982, 1990a,b, 1991; Kuga and Nagatani 1974; Lepelley 1986, 1989; Lepelley and Mbih 1987).

Gehrlein and Fishburn (1976b) develop a closed-form representation for $P^1(n)$ under IAC as

$$P^1(n) = \frac{15(n+3)^2}{16(n+2)(n+4)}. \tag{5}$$

## 3          Condorcet winners and social homogeneity

Social homogeneity refers to the propensity of voters to have similar preferences. The special case of IC represents the least homogeneous situation, while the case in which all voters have identical preferences represents the most homogeneous situation. Intuition suggests that an increase in social homogeneity would tend to correspond to an increased likelihood that a Condorcet winner exists. It is well known (Abrams 1976) that an increase in homogeneity does not necessarily correspond to an increase in the likelihood that a Condorcet winner exists. However, we might still expect a general overall tendency for this to occur. Research investigating the link between social homogeneity and the likelihood of a Condorcet winner has been conducted by Abrams (1976), Berg (1985a,b), Fishburn and Gehrlein (1980), Gehrlein (1986), and Kuga and Nagatani (1974). The work of Berg and Bjurulf (1983) and Berg (1985a,b) directly applies PE models to the study of this relationship.

Pólya–Eggenberger probability models are used as basic dependence or contagion models. As $\alpha$ becomes large, there will be a relatively high likelihood that the second ball drawn will be the same color as the first ball drawn. In the context of our specific example of voters' preferences, this is equivalent to the notion that preferences of randomly selected voters would tend to be more consistent with each other over the population of voters. Thus, increasing $\alpha$ would tend to reflect an increase in social homogeneity.

Fishburn (1973) first suggested that Kendall's coefficient of concordance (Kendall and Smith 1939) should be used as a measure of social homogeneity. Gehrlein (1987) performed a comparative analysis of many different measures of social homogeneity. Results suggested that Kendall's coefficient tends to outperform all other measures of social homogeneity in studies related to Condorcet efficiency. A link between Condorcet efficiency and Kendall's coefficient is also suggested by Sommerlad and McLean (1989). As a result, we shall use Kendall's coefficient as a measure of social homogeneity, and we are therefore interested in the relationship of Kendall's coefficient of concordance to the parameter $\alpha$ in PE probability models. Kendall's coefficient of concordance, $W$, is obtained in the following fashion for the preference rankings in our example:

$$W = \frac{1}{2n^2} \sum_{i=1}^{3} S_i^2,$$

where

$$S_1 = -n_1 - n_2 + n_5 + n_6,$$
$$S_2 = -n_3 - n_5 + n_2 + n_4,$$
$$S_3 = -n_4 - n_6 + n_1 + n_3.$$

Table 2. $W^\alpha(n)$, *the conditional expected value of Kendall's coefficient of concordance, given that a Condorcet winner exists, for n voters on three candidates for PE probabilities with parameter* $\alpha$

| $\alpha$ | $n$ 3 | 5 | 7 | 9 | 11 | 25 |
|---|---|---|---|---|---|---|
| 0 | .3529 | .2139 | .1534 | .1195 | .0979 | .0432 |
| 1 | .4444 | .3290 | .2789 | .2508 | .2329 | .1873 |
| 2 | .5128 | .4130 | .3699 | .3458 | .3304 | .2914 |
| 3 | .5660 | .4778 | .4398 | .4186 | .4051 | .3708 |
| 4 | .6087 | .5295 | .4954 | .4764 | .4643 | .4337 |
| 5 | .6437 | .5718 | .5408 | .5236 | .5127 | .4850 |
| 10 | .7536 | .7042 | .6830 | .6712 | .6637 | .6447 |
| 15 | .8117 | .7739 | .7578 | .7488 | .7430 | .7286 |
| 20 | .8476 | .8171 | .8040 | .7967 | .7921 | .7804 |
| 25 | .8720 | .8463 | .8354 | .8293 | .8254 | .8156 |

The coefficient $W$ has a value of 1 for the case of perfect social homogeneity with $n_i = n$ for some $1 \le i \le 6$, while $W = 0$ for perfect heterogeneity with $n_i = n/6$ for all $1 \le i \le 6$.

The conditional expected value of $W$ over all possible profiles with $n$ voters in which there is a Condorcet winner, and where profiles are obtained by a PE model, was denoted by $W^\alpha(n)$ in Gehrlein and Berg (1992) and given as

$$W^\alpha(n) = \frac{3n!}{2n^2 6^{(n,\alpha)}} \left\{ \Sigma^1 \left[ \left\{ \sum_{i=1}^{3} S_i^2 \right\} \prod_{i=1}^{6} \frac{1^{(n_i,\alpha)}}{n_i!} \right] \right\} \bigg/ P^\alpha(n). \qquad (6)$$

Table 2 shows computed values of $W^\alpha(n)$ for each $n = 3, 5, 7, 9, 11, 25$ with each $\alpha = 0, 1, 2, 3, 4, 5, 10, 15, 20, 25$. As would be expected, $W^\alpha(n)$ increases as $\alpha$ increases for any given $n$ and decreases as $n$ increases for any given $\alpha$.

A comparison of $P^\alpha(n)$ values from Table 1 and $W^\alpha(n)$ values from Table 2 shows a very distinct relationship between social homogeneity, as measured by Kendall's coefficient of concordance, and the likelihood that a Condorcet winner exists. These observations hold on the basis of expected-value calculations. But, as pointed out before, there are specific situations where combinations of $n_i$s with greater social homogeneity yield a lower likelihood of there being a Condorcet winner.

4    Condorcet efficiency and social homogeneity

Condorcet efficiency of a voting rule has been defined as the conditional probability that the voting rule selects the Condorcet winner in an election, given that a Condorcet winner exists. A number of simulation studies that evaluate Condorcet efficiency of simple voting rules were summarized in Fishburn and Gehrlein (1982). Gehrlein (1981b) determined the most Condorcet efficient simple voting rules for a large number of voters under IC. Gehrlein (1982) developed closed-form representations, like the representation in (5), for Condorcet efficiency of some simple voting rules under IAC.

Intuition suggests that an increase in social homogeneity would tend to lead to an increase in Condorcet efficiency. For example, if all voters have the same preference ranking on candidates then we have perfect social homogeneity, a Condorcet winner (the most preferred candidate) will exist, and almost any reasonable voting rule will select that candidate. Gehrlein (1986) and Berg (1985b) have partially examined this general relationship. Our interest here is to more fully examine the relationship between social homogeneity and Condorcet efficiency on an expected-value basis by using PE models. We shall examine four different types of voting rules in this study: single-stage constant scoring rules, single-stage weighted scoring rules, two-stage constant scoring rules, and lottery rules.

Let $E[\alpha, \mathrm{VR}]$ denote the Condorcet efficiency of a voting rule VR under a PE model. It follows directly from the logic that led to the development of (2) from Gehrlein and Berg (1992) that

$$E[\alpha, \mathrm{VR}] = \frac{3n!}{6^{(n,\alpha)}} \left[ \sum{}^{1} \delta(\mathrm{VR}) \prod_{i=1}^{6} \frac{1^{(n_i, \alpha)}}{n_i!} \right] \Big/ P^{\alpha}(n), \qquad (7)$$

where

$$\delta(\mathrm{VR}) = \begin{cases} 1 & \text{if VR strictly selects the Condorcet candidate} \\ & (A) \text{ as the winner of the election,} \\ 0 & \text{otherwise.} \end{cases}$$

By having VR strictly select the Condorcet candidate, we mean that the candidate is never involved in a tie with other candidates at any step of the election process. Thus, $E(\alpha, \mathrm{VR})$ evaluates the propensity of VR to select the Condorcet winner in a clear-cut fashion, where the Condorcet winner could not possibly be eliminated by any tie-breaking procedure at any step of the election process.

## 4.1    *Single-stage constant scoring rules*

Single-stage constant scoring rules (SSC) select the winner of an election in a single-step procedure. The use of an SSC does not require voters to report rankings on their preferences, but simply requires them to report some fixed number $k$ of their most preferred candidates. Let SSC$(k, n)$ denote the SSC in which each of $n$ voters report their $k$ most preferred candidates. The winner is determined as the candidate receiving the most total votes. SSC$(1, n)$ is the commonly used plurality rule in which each voter reports their most preferred candidate. All voters are assumed to vote according to their true preferences throughout this study. For the three-candidate case, SSC$(2, n)$ is the negative plurality rule, which is equivalent to having each voter vote against their least preferred candidate.

Previous research in evaluating representations of $E[\alpha, \text{SSC}(1, n)]$ and $E[\alpha, \text{SSC}(2, n)]$ has produced several results. Gehrlein (1981b) showed that, for IC,

$$E[0, \text{SSC}(1, \infty)] = E[0, \text{SSC}(2, \infty)].  \tag{8}$$

Gehrlein and Fishburn (1978) gave results that lead to a representation for the Condorcet efficiency of SSC$(1, \infty)$ under IC as

$$E[0, \text{SSC}(1, \infty)]$$

$$= \left\{ \frac{1}{4} + \frac{3}{4\pi^2} \left[ \left\{ \cos^{-1}\left( -\sqrt{\frac{2}{3}} \right) \right\}^2 - \frac{1}{4} \left\{ \pi - \sin^{-1}\left( \frac{1}{3} \right) \right\}^2 \right] \right.$$

$$\left. + \frac{3}{4\pi} \sin^{-1}\left( \sqrt{\frac{1}{6}} \right) + \frac{9}{8\pi^2} \int_0^{1/3} \frac{\sin^{-1}[\gamma/(1+2\gamma)]}{\sqrt{(1-\gamma^2)}} \, d\gamma \right\} \Big/ P^0(\infty).  \tag{9}$$

The expected value $E[0, \text{SSC}(1, \infty)]$ must be evaluated by quadrature, which ultimately leads to a value of $E[0, \text{SSC}(1, \infty)] = .757200$. Paris (1975) and Satterthwaite (1972) developed earlier estimates of $E[0, \text{SSC}(1, \infty)]$ by appealing to nonrigorous techniques.

Gehrlein (1982) considered the case of IAC to develop the representations

$$E[1, \text{SSC}(1, n)] = \frac{119n^4 + 1348n^3 + 5486n^2 + 10812n + 10395}{135(n+1)(n+3)^2(n+5)},$$

$$E[1, \text{SSC}(2, n)] = \frac{68n^3 + 501n^2 + 834n - 315}{108(n+1)(n+3)(n+5)},  \tag{10}$$

where $n$ is an odd multiple of 3.

Computed values of $E[\alpha, \text{SSC}(1, n)]$ and $E[\alpha, \text{SSC}(2, n)]$ are shown respectively in Tables 3 and 4 for each $n = 3, 5, 7, 9, 11, 25$ with each $\alpha =$

Table 3. $E[\alpha, \text{SSC}(1, n)]$, *the Condorcet efficiency of plurality rule for n voters on three candidates for PE probabilities with parameter* $\alpha$

|          | n      |        |        |        |        |        |
|----------|--------|--------|--------|--------|--------|--------|
| $\alpha$ | 3      | 5      | 7      | 9      | 11     | 25     |
| 0        | .8235  | .6766  | .7372  | .7447  | .7076  | .7365  |
| 1        | .8889  | .8250  | .8480  | .8508  | .8440  | .8630  |
| 2        | .9231  | .8868  | .8996  | .9007  | .8976  | .9081  |
| 3        | .9434  | .9198  | .9281  | .9286  | .9267  | .9333  |
| 4        | .9565  | .9399  | .9457  | .9460  | .9446  | .9492  |
| 5        | .9655  | .9531  | .9574  | .9576  | .9566  | .9599  |
| 10       | .9855  | .9810  | .9826  | .9826  | .9822  | .9833  |
| 15       | .9920  | .9897  | .9905  | .9905  | .9903  | .9908  |
| 20       | .9950  | .9936  | .9940  | .9940  | .9939  | .9942  |
| 25       | .9965  | .9956  | .9959  | .9959  | .9958  | .9960  |

Table 4. $E[\alpha, \text{SSC}(2, n)]$, *the Condorcet efficiency of negative plurality rule for n voters on three candidates for PE probabilities with parameter* $\alpha$

|          | n      |        |        |        |        |        |
|----------|--------|--------|--------|--------|--------|--------|
| $\alpha$ | 3      | 5      | 7      | 9      | 11     | 25     |
| 0        | .5294  | .5473  | .5346  | .6084  | .6142  | .6515  |
| 1        | .4444  | .4750  | .5040  | .5365  | .5525  | .5902  |
| 2        | .3846  | .4296  | .4674  | .4941  | .5119  | .5521  |
| 3        | .3396  | .3924  | .4330  | .4588  | .4774  | .5524  |
| 4        | .3043  | .3607  | .4018  | .4274  | .4464  | .4958  |
| 5        | .2759  | .3334  | .3740  | .3993  | .4184  | .4711  |
| 10       | .1884  | .2402  | .2745  | .2968  | .3141  | .3701  |
| 15       | .1432  | .1870  | .2155  | .2346  | .2494  | .3008  |
| 20       | .1156  | .1530  | .1770  | .1935  | .2063  | .2523  |
| 25       | .0969  | .1293  | .1501  | .1645  | .1757  | .2169  |

$0, 1, 2, 3, 4, 5, 10, 15, 20, 25$. The computed values in Tables 3 and 4 are consistent with appropriate values given in Gehrlein and Fishburn (1972) and Gehrlein (1982).

Given the PE probability model as $\alpha \to \infty$, all voters will have identical preferences. It follows directly that $E[\infty, \text{SSC}(1, n)] = 1$. With the definition of Condorcet efficiency requiring a strict winner, it also follows directly that $E[\infty, \text{SSC}(2, n)] = 0$.

Results from Tables 3 and 4 indicate that $\text{SSC}(1, n)$ consistently outperforms $\text{SSC}(2, n)$, based on Condorcet efficiency. In comparing Table 2 to Table 3, we see that relatively large (greater than about 90%) values of Condorcet efficiency can be obtained by plurality rule with relatively low levels of social homogeneity, as measured by Kendall's coefficient of concordance (with $\alpha \geq 2$).

### 4.2    *Single-stage weighted scoring rules*

Single-stage weighted scoring rules (SSW) select the winner in an election in a single-step procedure, as with SSC. However, SSW voting requires voters to rank candidates, so that different weights are given to candidates depending on where they appear in the voter's preference ranking. For three candidates, let $\text{SSW}(\lambda, n)$ denote the SSW that gives one point to a voter's most preferred candidate, some positive $\lambda$ points for the second most preferred, and zero points for the least preferred candidate. The winner is selected as the candidate receiving the greatest total number of points from the voters. By definition, $\text{SSW}(0, n)$ is equivalent to $\text{SSC}(1, n)$ and $\text{SSW}(1, n)$ is equivalent to $\text{SSC}(2, n)$, and neither of these two particular cases actually requires voters to report a ranking of preferences on candidates.

Gehrlein and Fishburn (1978) showed that

$$E[0, \text{SSW}(\lambda, \infty)] = E[0, \text{SSW}(1 - \lambda, \infty)], \tag{11}$$

and that $E[0, \text{SSW}(\lambda, \infty)]$ was maximized at $\lambda = \frac{1}{2}$ with

$$E\left[0, \text{SSW}\left(\frac{1}{2}, \infty\right)\right]$$
$$= \left\{ \frac{3}{2} - \frac{3}{2\pi}\left[\cos^{-1}\left(\sqrt{\frac{8}{9}}\right) + \cos^{-1}\left(\sqrt{\frac{2}{9}}\right)\right]\right\} \Big/ P^0(\infty), \tag{12}$$

which is evaluated as $E[0, \text{SSW}(\frac{1}{2}, \infty)] = .901189$.

The efficiency $E[0, \text{SSW}(\lambda, n)]$ is maximized at $\lambda = \frac{1}{2}$ only when $n \to \infty$. Gehrlein and Fishburn (1978) gave the range of $\lambda$ values to maximize $E[0, \text{SSW}(\lambda, n)]$ for small $n$, showing that there are very small differences between the maximum possible Condorcet efficiencies and the Condorcet efficiency obtained with $\lambda = \frac{1}{2}$. As in our discussion concerning the Condorcet efficiency of SSC, $E[\infty, \text{SSW}(\lambda, n)] = 1$ for all $0 \leq \lambda < 1$. The special case of $\lambda = \frac{1}{2}$ is the SSW referred to as *Borda rule*.

Gehrlein (1992) showed that

Table 5. $E[\alpha, \text{SSW}(\frac{1}{2}, n)]$, the Condorcet efficiency of
Borda rule for n voters on three candidates for PE
probabilities with parameter $\alpha$

| $\alpha$ | n |  |  |  |  |  |
|---|---|---|---|---|---|---|
|  | 3 | 5 | 7 | 9 | 11 | 25 |
| 0 | .9118 | .8839 | .8743 | .8711 | .8703 | .8746 |
| 1 | .8889 | .8750 | .8800 | .8825 | .8848 | .8965 |
| 2 | .8846 | .8845 | .8964 | .8959 | .8982 | .9091 |
| 3 | .8868 | .8959 | .9105 | .9063 | .9093 | .9191 |
| 4 | .8913 | .9062 | .9216 | .9147 | .9184 | .9273 |
| 5 | .8966 | .9151 | .9305 | .9217 | .9259 | .9341 |
| 10 | .9203 | .9431 | .9560 | .9444 | .9498 | .9556 |
| 15 | .9363 | .9575 | .9679 | .9569 | .9622 | .9666 |
| 20 | .9472 | .9661 | .9748 | .9649 | .9697 | .9733 |
| 25 | .9550 | .9718 | .9793 | .9703 | .9747 | .9778 |

$$E\left[1, \text{SSW}\left(\frac{1}{2}, \infty\right)\right] = \frac{41}{45}. \tag{13}$$

Borda rule has been shown to have a number of unique positive qualities
among SSW (Fishburn and Gehrlein 1976; Saari 1990, 1991). Thus, we restrict our examination of SSW to Borda rule in this study. Table 5 gives
computed values of $E[\alpha, \text{SSW}(\frac{1}{2}, n)]$ for each $n = 3, 5, 7, 9, 11, 25$ with each
$\alpha = 0, 1, 2, 3, 4, 5, 10, 15, 20, 25$.

A comparison of the results in Tables 3 and 5 shows some interesting
results. In particular, Borda rule shows significantly greater Condorcet
efficiency than plurality rule for $\alpha = 0, 1$. However, for $\alpha \geq 2$, plurality
rule tends to have marginally greater Condorcet efficiency than Borda rule.
This result is somewhat surprising because SSW requires more information from voters, in the form of preference rankings on candidates, than
does SSC. The requirement of additional information from voters might
also generate reduced voter participation in the form of abstentions. Gehrlein and Fishburn (1979) examined this relationship between Condorcet
efficiency and abstention rate, under IC, for both SSC and SSW.

### 4.3 Two-stage constant scoring rules

Two-stage voting procedures with three candidates select the winner by
going through a two-step process. In the first step, some criterion is used

to eliminate the least preferred candidate. The remaining two candidates are then retained in the second stage, where the winner is determined by majority rule. Two-stage constant scoring rules (TSC) use a constant scoring rule, as used in SSC, to eliminate the loser in the first stage. Let TSC($k, n$) denote the TSC in which $n$ voters vote for their $k$ most preferred candidates in the first stage. The candidate receiving the fewest votes is then eliminated from consideration in the second stage. Rule TSC($1, n$) is referred to as plurality elimination, and TSC($2, n$) is referred to as negative plurality elimination.

We do not consider two-stage weighted scoring rules (TSW) in this study. Any particular TSW($\lambda, n$) uses a weighted scoring rule, as used in SSW($\lambda, n$), to determine the least preferred candidate for elimination. It is easy to show for three-candidate elections that $E[\alpha, \text{TSC}(k, n)] \geq E[\alpha, \text{SSC}(k, n)]$ and that $E[\alpha, \text{TSW}(\lambda, n)] \geq E[\alpha, \text{SSW}(\lambda, n)]$. Fishburn and Gehrlein (1976) extended the work of Smith (1973) to show that if Borda rule is used in the first stage to eliminate the candidate with the smallest point score, then the winner at the end of the second stage must be the Condorcet winner, given that one exists. Thus, the most Condorcet efficient TSW is known to be Borda elimination, TSW($\frac{1}{2}, n$), with a Condorcet efficiency equal to 1.

Gehrlein (1993) considered the limiting case of voters under IC to show that

$$E[0, \text{TSC}(1, \infty)] = E[0, \text{TSC}(2, \infty)] \tag{14}$$

and

$$E[0, \text{TSC}(1, \infty)]$$

$$= \left\{ -1 - \frac{3}{4\pi^2} \left[ \sin^{-1}\left(\sqrt{\frac{1}{3}}\right) \right]^2 + \frac{3}{16\pi^2} \left[ 3\pi + \sin^{-1}\left(\frac{1}{3}\right) \right]^2 \right.$$

$$\left. + \frac{3}{4\pi} \sin^{-1}\left(\sqrt{\frac{1}{6}}\right) - \frac{9}{8\pi^2} \int_0^{1/3} \frac{\sin^{-1}[\gamma/(1+2\gamma)]}{\sqrt{(1-\gamma^2)}} \, d\gamma \right\} \bigg/ P^0(\infty). \tag{15}$$

After evaluation by quadrature, we find $E[0, \text{TSC}(1, \infty)] = .962902$. Gehrlein (1982) examined IAC to develop the representations

$$E[1, \text{TSC}(1, n)] = \frac{523n^4 + 6191n^3 + 25117n^2 + 40749n + 22140}{540(n+1)(n+3)^2(n+5)},$$

$$\tag{16}$$

$$E[1, \text{TSC}(2, n)] = \frac{131n^4 + 1542n^3 + 6144n^2 + 9018n + 3645}{135(n+1)(n+3)^2(n+5)},$$

where $n$ is an odd multiple of 3. As in previous cases, $E[\infty, \text{TSC}(1, n)] = E[\infty, \text{TSC}(2, n)] = 1$.

Table 6. $E[\alpha, \text{TSC}(1, n)]$, *the Condorcet efficiency of two-stage voting rule with plurality elimination for n voters on three candidates for PE probabilities with parameter* $\alpha$

|          | n     |       |       |       |       |       |
|----------|-------|-------|-------|-------|-------|-------|
| $\alpha$ | 3     | 5     | 7     | 9     | 11    | 25    |
| 0        | .8235 | .9751 | .9189 | .9139 | .9549 | .9412 |
| 1        | .8889 | .9750 | .9440 | .9524 | .9606 | .9624 |
| 2        | .9231 | .9792 | .9591 | .9663 | .9692 | .9714 |
| 3        | .9434 | .9831 | .9688 | .9745 | .9757 | .9775 |
| 4        | .9565 | .9862 | .9754 | .9799 | .9805 | .9819 |
| 5        | .9655 | .9886 | .9802 | .9837 | .9840 | .9851 |
| 10       | .9855 | .9947 | .9913 | .9928 | .9927 | .9931 |
| 15       | .9920 | .9970 | .9951 | .9959 | .9958 | .9961 |
| 20       | .9950 | .9980 | .9969 | .9974 | .9973 | .9974 |
| 25       | .9965 | .9986 | .9978 | .9982 | .9981 | .9982 |

Table 7. $E[\alpha, \text{TSC}(2, n)]$, *the Condorcet efficiency of two-stage voting rule with negative plurality elimination for n voters on three candidates for PE probabilities with parameter* $\alpha$

|          | n     |       |       |       |       |       |
|----------|-------|-------|-------|-------|-------|-------|
| $\alpha$ | 3     | 5     | 7     | 9     | 11    | 25    |
| 0        | .8235 | .9005 | .9546 | .9110 | .9253 | .9513 |
| 1        | .8889 | .9250 | .9520 | .9429 | .9490 | .9627 |
| 2        | .9231 | .9446 | .9608 | .9570 | .9608 | .9701 |
| 3        | .9434 | .9578 | .9687 | .9665 | .9691 | .9758 |
| 4        | .9565 | .9669 | .9747 | .9733 | .9752 | .9801 |
| 5        | .9655 | .9734 | .9793 | .9783 | .9796 | .9835 |
| 10       | .9855 | .9884 | .9906 | .9902 | .9907 | .9922 |
| 15       | .9920 | .9936 | .9947 | .9945 | .9948 | .9955 |
| 20       | .9950 | .9959 | .9966 | .9965 | .9966 | .9971 |
| 25       | .9965 | .9972 | .9976 | .9976 | .9977 | .9980 |

Tables 6 and 7 (respectively) show computed values of $E[\alpha, \text{TSC}(1, n)]$ and $E[\alpha, \text{TSC}(2, n)]$ for each $n = 3, 5, 7, 9, 11, 25$ with each $\alpha = 0, 1, 2, 3, 4, 5, 10, 15, 20, 25$. A comparison of $E[\alpha, \text{TSC}(1, n)]$ and $E[\alpha, \text{TSC}(2, n)]$ values shows that $\text{TSC}(1, n)$ consistently out-performs $\text{TSC}(2, n)$ on the

140    William V. Gehrlein

basis of Condorcet efficiency for all $\alpha \geq 2$. For $\alpha \leq 2$, TSC$(1, n)$ generally out-performs TSC$(2, n)$. We find $E[\alpha, \text{TSC}(1, n)]$ to be significantly greater than $E[\alpha, \text{SSC}(1, n)]$, particularly for $\alpha \leq 3$. Even for very low values of social homogeneity, we find $E[\alpha, \text{TSC}(1, n)] > .91$ for all $n > 3$. In comparing the results of Tables 5 and 6, we find that TSC$(1, n)$ outperforms SSW$(\frac{1}{2}, n)$ in all situations.

### 4.4    Pairwise proportional lottery rule

Lottery rules are based on the notion that the winner of an election should ultimately be based on a random selection procedure. In this random selection, the likelihood that a candidate is elected is based on the number of votes received from the voters in an initial election. Procedures of this type were suggested by Coleman (1973). Fishburn and Gehrlein (1977) examined properties of these lottery rules for elections on two alternatives. More recently, Mueller (1989) and Gehrlein (1991) extended this notion to more than two alternatives to consider a series of pairwise elections. Let $p(a, b)$ denote the probability that $a$ will be selected over $b$ under a pairwise proportional lottery rule (PPL). Then $p(a, b) = (n_1 + n_2 + n_4)/n$ and $p(a, c) = (n_1 + n_2 + n_3)/n$. Let PPL$(n)$ define an election procedure where the winner is determined by finding the alternative that defeats all other candidates by pairwise elections with PPL.

Gehrlein and Berg (1992) show that

$$E[0, \text{PPL}(\infty)] = \tfrac{1}{4}. \tag{17}$$

Results from Gehrlein (1990a) lead to

$$E[1, \text{PPL}(n)] = \frac{47n^4 + 354n^3 + 787n^2 + 450n + 42}{105n^2(n+3)^2}. \tag{18}$$

Following earlier arguments, it follows that $E[\infty, \text{PPL}(n)] = 1$.

Computed values of $E[\alpha, \text{PPL}(n)]$ from Gehrlein and Berg (1992) are shown in Table 8 for each $n = 3, 5, 7, 9, 11, 25$ with each $\alpha = 0, 1, 2, 3, 4, 5, 10, 15, 20, 25$. The $E[\alpha, \text{PPL}(n)]$ values from Table 8 clearly show that PPL$(n)$ is dominated by all other voting rules considered in this study (excluding negative plurality) on the basis of Condorcet efficiency.

## 5    Conclusion

The use of PE models to determine the Condorcet efficiency of some simple voting models on three-candidate elections leads to some decisive conclusions. Plurality, Borda rule, and plurality elimination all display relatively high Condorcet efficiency for relatively modest levels of social

Table 8.  $E[\alpha, \mathrm{PPL}(n)]$, *the Condorcet efficiency of pairwise proportional lottery rule alternatives for PE probabilities with parameter* $\alpha$

|  | n | | | | | |
|---|---|---|---|---|---|---|
| $\alpha$ | 3 | 5 | 7 | 9 | 11 | 25 |
| 0 | .5882 | .4945 | .4493 | .4218 | .4029 | .3463 |
| 1 | .6420 | .5690 | .5365 | .5179 | .5058 | .4741 |
| 2 | .6838 | .6224 | .5959 | .5811 | .5716 | .5474 |
| 3 | .7170 | .6635 | .6408 | .6282 | .6202 | .6001 |
| 4 | .7440 | .6963 | .6763 | .6653 | .6583 | .6409 |
| 5 | .7663 | .7233 | .7053 | .6955 | .6893 | .6738 |
| 10 | .8374 | .8082 | .7961 | .7896 | .7854 | .7752 |
| 15 | .8753 | .8531 | .8440 | .8391 | .8360 | .8283 |
| 20 | .8989 | .8810 | .8737 | .8697 | .8672 | .8610 |
| 25 | .9150 | .9000 | .8939 | .8905 | .8884 | .8833 |

homogeneity, as measured by Kendall's coefficient of concordance. Borda rule requires the ranking of candidates, but it produces significantly greater Condorcet efficiency than plurality for low levels of social homogeneity. For relatively modest levels of social homogeneity, corresponding to $\alpha \geq 2$ in a PE model, plurality rule consistently out-performs Borda rule. When a two-stage constant scoring rule is used, the voting procedure becomes more complicated than plurality or Borda rule. However, plurality elimination clearly dominates both plurality and Borda rule, in terms of Condorcet efficiency, at all levels of social homogeneity. The pairwise proportional lottery rule is generally inferior to plurality, Borda, and plurality elimination, based on Condorcet efficiency.

## REFERENCES

Abrams, R. (1976), "The Voter's Paradox and the Homogeneity of Individual Preference Orders," *Public Choice* 26: 19–27.
Berg, S. (1985a), "Paradox of Voting under an Urn Model: The Effect of Homogeneity," *Public Choice* 47: 377–87.
    (1985b), "A Note on Plurality Distortion in Large Committees," *European Journal of Political Economy* 1: 271–84.
Berg, S., and B. Bjurulf (1983), "A Note on the Paradox of Voting: Anonymous Preference Profiles and May's Formula," *Public Choice* 40: 307–16.
Berg, S., and D. Lepelley (1990), "Voting Cycles, Plurality Rule and Strategic Manipulation," *Annals of Operations Research* 23: 247–56.
Coleman, J. S. (1973), *Mathematics of Collective Action*. Chicago: Aldine Press.

Condorcet, Marquis de (1785), *Essai sur l'application de l'analyse à la probabilité des décisions rendues à la pluralité de voix*. Paris: Imprimerie Royale.

Felsenthal D. S., and M. Machover (1992), "After Two Centuries: Should Condorcet's Voting Procedure Be Implemented?" paper presented at the March 1992 meeting of the Public Choice Society (New Orleans).

Fishburn, P. C. (1973), "Voter Concordance, Simple Majority, and Group Decision Methods," *Behavioral Science* 18: 364-76.

Fishburn, P. C., and W. V. Gehrlein (1976), "Borda's Rule, Positional Voting, and Condorcet's Simple Majority Principle," *Public Choice* 28: 79-88.

    (1977), "Towards a Theory of Elections with Probabilistic Voting," *Econometrica* 45: 1907-23.

    (1980), "Social Homogeneity and Condorcet's Paradox," *Public Choice* 35: 403-20.

    (1982), "Majority Efficiencies for Simple Voting Procedures: Summary and Interpretation," *Theory and Decision* 14: 141-53.

Gehrlein, W. V. (1981a), "The Expected Probability of Condorcet's Paradox," *Economics Letters* 7: 33-7.

    (1981b), "Single Stage Election Procedures for Large Electorates," *Journal of Mathematical Economics* 8: 263-75.

    (1982), "Condorcet Efficiency and Constant Scoring Rules," *Mathematical Social Sciences* 2: 123-30.

    (1983), "Condorcet's Paradox," *Theory and Decision* 15: 161-97.

    (1986), "Weighted Scoring Rules, the Impartial Culture Condition, and Homogeneity," *Quality and Quantity* 20: 85-107.

    (1987), "A Comparative Analysis of Measures of Social Homogeneity," *Quality and Quantity* 21: 219-31.

    (1990a), "The Expected Likelihood of Transitivity of Preference," *Psychometrika* 55: 695-706.

    (1990b), "The Expected Likelihood of Transitivity for a Probabilistic Chooser," *Annals of Operations Research* 23: 235-46.

    (1991), "Coincidence Probabilities for Simple Majority and Proportional Lottery Rules," *Economics Letters* 35: 349-53.

    (1992), "Condorcet Efficiency of Simple Voting Rules for Large Electorates," *Economics Letters* 40: 61-6.

    (1993), "Condorcet Efficiency of Two Stage Constant Scoring Rules," *Quality and Quantity* 27: 95-101.

Gehrlein, W. V., and S. Berg (1992), "The Effect of Social Homogeneity on Coincidence Probabilities for Pairwise Proportional Lottery and Simple Majority Rules," *Social Choice and Welfare* 9: 361-72.

Gehrlein, W. V., and P. C. Fishburn (1972), "Coincidence Probabilities for Simple Majority and Positional Voting Rules," *Social Science Research* 7: 272-83.

    (1976a), "The Probability of the Paradox of Voting: A Computable Solution," *Journal of Economic Theory* 13: 14-25.

    (1976b), "Condorcet's Paradox and Anonymous Preference Profiles," *Public Choice* 26: 1-18.

    (1978), "Probabilities of Election Outcomes for Large Electorates," *Journal of Economic Theory* 19: 38-49.

    (1979), "The Effects of Abstentions on Voting Procedures in Three-Candidate Elections," *Behavioral Science* 24: 346-54.

Guilbaud, G. T. (1952), "Les theories de l'interet general et le probleme logique de l'aggregation," *Economie Appliquee* 5: 501-84.

Johnson, N. L., and S. Kotz (1977), *Urn Models and Their Application*. New York: Wiley.

Kendall, M. G., and B. B. Smith (1939), "The Problem of *m* Rankings," *Annals of Mathematical Statistics* 10: 275-87.

Kuga, K., and H. Nagatani (1974), "Voter Antagonism and the Paradox of Voting," *Econometrica* 42: 1045-67.

Lepelley, D. (1986), "Some Results on the Probability of Electing the Condorcet Loser," paper presented at the April 1986 meeting of the European Public Choice Society (Noordwijkerhout, The Netherlands).

(1989), "Contribution à l'analyse des procédures de décision collective," unpublished doctoral dissertation, Université de Caen, France.

Lepelley, D., and B. Mbih (1987), "The Proportion of Coallitionally Unstable Situations under Majority Rule," *Economics Letters* 25: 311-16.

Mueller, D. (1989), "Probabilistic Majority Rule," *Kyklos* 42: 151-70.

Paris, D. C. (1975), "Plurality Distortion and Majority Rules," *Behavioral Science* 20: 125-33.

Saari, D. G. (1990), "The Borda Dictionary," *Social Choice and Welfare* 7: 279-317.

(1991), "Relationship Admitting Families of Candidates," *Social Choice and Welfare* 8: 21-50.

Satterthwaite, M. (1972), "Coalition Constructing Voting Procedures," paper presented at the May 1972 meeting of the Public Choice Society (Pittsburgh).

Smith, J. H. (1973), "Aggregation of Preferences with Variable Electorate," *Public Choice* 28: 79-88.

Sommerlad, F., and I. McLean (1989), "The Political Theory of Condorcet," working paper, Social Studies Faculty Center, University of Oxford.

Tideman, N. (1992), "Collective Decision and Voting: Cycles," paper presented at the March 1992 meeting of the Public Choice Society (New Orleans).

# CHAPTER 6

# Latticial theory of consensus

*Bruno Leclerc & Bernard Monjardet*

## 1    Introduction

Since Arrow's theorem (1951-57), many "Arrowian" results have been obtained in various fields (social choice, paired comparisons methods, cluster analysis, data analysis, etc.). The general aggregation problem met in
these fields is to "aggregate" any $n$-tuple of objects into a unique object –
for example, to aggregate $n$ relations of preferences into a relation of
preference, or $n$ choice functions into a choice function. We recall in Section 2 several Arrowian results; all can be seen as axiomatic characterizations of classes of consensus (aggregation) functions. It then can be
noticed that many of these "concrete" results are similar, while some of
them are different; a more abstract theory is the appropriate means of
accounting for these similarities and differences. In Section 3, we present
the foundations of a latticial theory, where we study consensus functions
defined on a lattice $L$, that is, functions $F: L^n \to L$. These functions are
especially the *federation consensus functions* associated with the families
$\mathcal{F}$ of subsets of $N = \{1, ..., n\}$, called *federations* (or *simple games*). We
obtain several axiomatic characterizations of all the federation consensus
functions, in some cases, or of significant subclasses of such functions,
including the *meet* (or *join*) *projection consensus functions,* in the other
cases. These characterizations depend on the structural properties of the
considered lattice, and especially on the properties of a binary relation $\beta$
of *dependence* defined on the set $J$ of the join- (or meet-) irreducible elements of $L$. (For instance, in the case of the aggregation of relations of
preferences, the join-irreducible elements are the ordered pairs of compared objects and the dependence relation is related with the *transitive
closure* operation on relations.) Hence, the properties of the dependence
relation – especially its type of *connexity* – are the key to the understanding of many of the concrete results just mentioned. In Section 4, we apply

146    Bruno Leclerc & Bernard Monjardet

and extend this theory to the case of *valued objects* such as fuzzy preferences, after first giving a precise formalization of valued objects as mappings of a lattice of objects into a lattice of values satisfying certain properties. Hence the set of all the valued objects is a lattice and we can use
our general theory; in fact, more specific results are obtained by using
more specific axioms. We end this paper by pointing out some generalizations and topics of research.

The proofs of the results given in this paper can be found in Monjardet
(1990) and Leclerc (1991).

## 2    Some examples of axiomatic results in consensus problems

We illustrate the axiomatic approach for consensus problems by recalling
seven results, four in the field of social choice theory and three in the field
of cluster analysis. We shall use the following definition. A *federation* (or
*simple game*) on a set $N$ is a family $\mathfrak{F}$ of subsets of $N$ satisfying the monotonicity property: $[A \in \mathfrak{F}, B \supseteq A] \Rightarrow [B \in \mathfrak{F}]$.

A (partial) order on a set $X$ is a reflexive, antisymmetric, and transitive relation on $X$; we denote it by $o$. By *profile* we mean an $n$-tuple
$\Pi = (o_1, ..., o_i, ..., o_n)$ of $n$ orders on $X$ – that is, a mapping of a set $N =
\{1, ..., i, ..., n\}$ (the "individuals") into the set $\mathcal{O}$ of all the orders on $X$. A
*consensus function* on $\mathcal{O}$ is a mapping $F$ from $\mathcal{O}^n$ into $\mathcal{O}$; it associates an
order with each profile $\Pi$ of $n$ orders. Set $o = F(\Pi)$ and $o' = F(\Pi')$.

A consensus function $F$ is said to be *binary* if, for all $\Pi, \Pi' \in \mathcal{O}^n$ and
for all ordered pairs $(x, y)$ in $X^2$,

$$[\{i \in N : (x, y) \in o_i\} = \{i \in N : (x, y) \in o_i'\}] \Rightarrow [(x, y) \in o \Leftrightarrow (x, y) \in o']$$

This axiom is close to (but stronger than) the classical "independence of
irrelevant alternatives" property, which states that the restriction of $o$ to
the subset $\{x, y\}$ depends only on the restrictions of the $o_i$'s to this subset.

The function $F$ is *Paretian* if, for every $\Pi \in \mathcal{O}^n$ and for all $(x, y)$ in $X^2$,

$$[\forall i \in N, (x, y) \in o_i] \Rightarrow [(x, y) \in o].$$

Then one has the following result of Brown (1975) and Barthélemy (1982).

*A function $F$ is binary and Paretian if and only if there exists a subset $M$
of $N$ such that, for every $\Pi$ in $\mathcal{O}^n$, $o = \bigcap\{o_i, i \in M\}$.*

A *choice function* on a set $X$ is a mapping $c$ from the set $2^X$ of all the
subsets of $X$ into $2^X$ satisfying the condition $c(A) \subseteq A$ for every $A \subseteq X$
(we do not assume here the usual condition $c(A) \neq \emptyset$). A choice function
$c$ satisfies the *heritage* (or *Chernoff*) property if $A \subseteq B$ implies $A \cap c(B) \subseteq
c(A)$; it satisfies the *concordance* property if $c(A) \cap c(B) \subseteq c(A \cup B)$. We

denote by $\mathcal{C}$ a set of choice functions on $X$ and by $\mathcal{C}^n$ the set of all the profiles $\Pi = (c_1, \ldots, c_i, \ldots, c_n)$ of $n$ choice functions belonging to $\mathcal{C}$. A *consensus function* on $\mathcal{C}$ is a mapping $F$ from $\mathcal{C}^n$ into $\mathcal{C}$; we set $c = F(\Pi)$ and $c' = F(\Pi')$.

A consensus function $F$ is *local* if, for all $\Pi, \Pi' \in \mathcal{C}^n$ and for every $A \subseteq X$ and every $x$ in $A$,

$$[\{i \in N : x \in c_i(A)\} = \{i \in N : x \in c'_i(A)\}] \Rightarrow [x \in c(A) \Leftrightarrow x \in c'(A)].$$

The function $F$ is *neutral monotonic* if, for all $\Pi, \Pi' \in \mathcal{C}^n$ and for every $A \subseteq X$ and every $x, y$ in $A$,

$$[\{i \in N : x \in c_i(A)\} \subseteq \{i \in N : y \in c'_i(A)\}] \Rightarrow [x \in c(A) \Rightarrow y \in c'(A)].$$

A function $F$ is *Paretian* if, for every $\Pi \in \mathcal{C}^n$ and for every $A \subseteq X$ and every $x$ in $A$,

$$[\forall i \in N, x \in c_i(A)] \Rightarrow [x \in c(A)].$$

Then one has the following results of Aizerman and Aleskerov (1986).

*Let $F$ be a consensus function on a set $\mathcal{C}$ of choice functions.*

(1) *If $\mathcal{C}$ is the class of the choice functions satisfying the heritage property, then $F$ is neutral monotonic and Paretian if and only if there exists a federation $\mathcal{F}$ on $N$ such that, for every $\Pi$ in $\mathcal{C}^n$,*

$$c(A) = \bigcup_{M \in \mathcal{F}} [\bigcap_{i \in M} c_i(A)].$$

(2) *If $\mathcal{C}$ is the class of choice functions satisfying the heritage and the concordance properties, then $F$ is neutral monotonic and Paretian if and only if there exists a subset $M$ of $N$ such that, for every $\Pi$ in $\mathcal{C}^n$,*

$$c(A) = \bigcap \{c_i(A), i \in M\}.$$

It is worth noting that in this example the same axioms on the consensus function $F$ characterize either a restricted class of (so-called oligarchic) functions or a much broader class of (so-called federation) functions. An oligarchic function is a federation function since it is obtained by associating with a subset $M$ of $N$ the filter of all the subsets of $N$ containing $M$. Other examples of this second situation can be found in Monjardet (1978) and Mirkin (1981).

A *valued* (or *fuzzy*) preorder on a set $X$ is a mapping $p$, from the set $X^2$ of all the ordered pairs of elements of $X$ into the real interval $[0, 1]$, satisfying the following two properties: for every $x$ in $X$, $p(x, x) = 1$; for all $x, y, z$ in $X$, $p(x, z) \geq \min[p(x, y), p(y, z)]$. (Equivalently, for every $\lambda$ in $[0, 1]$, the *threshold relation* $R(\lambda) = \{(x, y) : p(x, y) \geq \lambda\}$ is a preorder.)

We denote by $\mathcal{V}$ the set of all valued preorders on $X$ and by $\mathcal{V}^n$ the set of all profiles $\Pi = (p_1, ..., p_i, ..., p_n)$ of $n$ valued preorders. A *consensus function* on $\mathcal{V}$ is a mapping $F$ from $\mathcal{V}^n$ into $\mathcal{V}$; we set $p = F(\Pi)$ and $p' = F(\Pi')$.

A consensus function $F$ is *binary* if, for all $\Pi, \Pi' \in \mathcal{V}^n$ and for all $x, y$ in $X$,

$$[\forall i \in N, \ p_i(x,y) = p_i'(x,y)] \Rightarrow [p(x,y) = p'(x,y)].$$

A consensus function $F$ is *Paretian* if, for every $P \in \mathcal{V}^n$ and for every $(x, y)$ in $X^2$ and every $\lambda$ in $[0, 1]$,

$$[\forall i \in N, \ \lambda \le p_i(x,y)] \Rightarrow [\lambda \le p(x,y)].$$

A mapping $\phi$ from $[0, 1]$ into $[0, 1]$ is said to be *extensive* if $\lambda \le \phi(\lambda)$ and *isotone* if $\lambda \le \lambda'$ implies $\phi(\lambda) \le \phi(\lambda')$. One then has the following result of Leclerc (1984).

*Let $F$ be a consensus function on the set $\mathcal{V}$ of all the valued preorders on $X$. Then $F$ is binary and Paretian if and only if there exist $n$ extensive and isotone mappings $\phi_i$ from $[0, 1]$ into $[0, 1]$ such that, for every $\Pi$ in $\mathcal{V}^n$,*

$$p(x,y) = \min[\phi_i \circ p_i(x,y), \ i \in N].$$

We now consider two classical consensus problems in cluster analysis: first, the consensus of partitions. We denote by $\mathcal{P}$ the set of all partitions of a set $X$ and by $\mathcal{P}^n$ the set of all profiles $\Pi = (\pi_1, ..., \pi_i, ..., \pi_n)$ of $n$ partitions. A *consensus function* on $\mathcal{P}$ is a mapping $F$ from $\mathcal{P}^n$ into $\mathcal{P}$; we set $\pi = F(\Pi)$ and $\pi' = F(\Pi')$. If $\pi$ is a partition then $x\pi y$ means that $x$ and $y$ are in a same class of $\pi$.

A consensus function $F$ is *binary* if, for all $\Pi, \Pi' \in \mathcal{P}^n$ and for all $x, y$ in $X$,

$$[\{i \in N: x\pi_i y\} = \{i \in N: x\pi_i' y\}] \Rightarrow [x\pi y \Leftrightarrow x\pi' y].$$

A consensus function $F$ is *co-binary* if, for all $\Pi, \Pi' \in \mathcal{P}^n$ and for every $A \subseteq X$,

$[\{i \in N: A$ is a union of classes of $\pi_i\}$

$= \{i \in N: A$ is a union of classes of $\pi_i'\}]$

$\Rightarrow [A$ is a union of classes of $\pi \Leftrightarrow A$ is a union of classes of $\pi']$.

We denote by $\pi_X$ (resp. $\pi_\Delta$) the partition with a single class (resp. the partition where each element constitutes a class). A consensus function $F$ on $\mathcal{P}$ is $\pi_X$-*idempotent* (resp. $\pi_\Delta$-*idempotent*) if $F(\pi_X, ..., \pi_X, ..., \pi_X) = \pi_X$ (resp. $F(\pi_\Delta, ..., \pi_\Delta, ..., \pi_\Delta) = \pi_\Delta$). One then has the following Mirkin (1975) and Leclerc (1984) result (see also Fishburn and Rubinstein 1986):

*A function F is binary and $\pi_X$-idempotent if and only if there exists a subset M of N such that, for every $\Pi$ in $\wp^n$, $\pi = \wedge\{\pi_i, i \in M\}$;*

as well as the Neumann and Norton result (1986):

*A function F is co-binary and $\pi_\Delta$-idempotent if and only if there exists a subset M of N such that, for every $\Pi$ in $\wp^n$, $\pi = \vee\{\pi_i, i \in M\}$.*

Here, $\wedge$ and $\vee$ denote (respectively) the meet and the join of partitions.

We consider now the consensus of ultrametrics. An *ultrametric* on a set $X$ is a mapping $u$ from the set $X^{[2]}$ of all the unordered pairs $xy$ of distinct elements of $X$ into the set $\mathbb{R}^+$, satisfying the following property: for all distinct $x, y, z$ in $X$, $u(xz) \leq \max[u(xy), u(yz)]$; equivalently, for every $\lambda$ in $\mathbb{R}^+$, the threshold relation $R(\lambda) = \{(x, y) : x = y$ or $u(xy) \leq \lambda\}$ is an equivalence relation. We denote by $\mathfrak{U}$ the set of all ultrametrics on $X$ and by $\mathfrak{U}^n$ the set of all profiles $\Pi = (u_1, \ldots, u_i, \ldots, u_n)$ of $n$ ultrametrics. A *consensus function* on $\mathfrak{U}$ is a mapping $F$ from $\mathfrak{U}^n$ into $\mathfrak{U}$; we set $u = F(\Pi)$ and $u' = F(\Pi')$.

A consensus function $F$ is *binary* if, for all $\Pi, \Pi' \in \mathfrak{U}^n$ and for all $xy$ in $X^{[2]}$,

$$[\forall i \in N, u_i(xy) = u_i'(xy)] \Rightarrow [u(xy) = u'(xy)].$$

A consensus function $F$ is *co-Paretian* if, for every $\Pi \in \mathfrak{U}^n$ and for every $xy$ in $X^{[2]}$ and every $\lambda$ in $\mathbb{R}^+$,

$$[\forall i \in N, u_i(xy) \leq \lambda] \Rightarrow [u(xy) \leq \lambda].$$

A mapping $\phi$ from $\mathbb{R}^+$ into $\mathbb{R}^+$ is said to be *reductive* if $\lambda \geq \phi(\lambda)$ for every $\lambda \in \mathbb{R}^+$ and *isotone* if $\lambda \leq \lambda'$ implies $\phi(\lambda) \leq \phi(\lambda')$. Then one has the following result of Leclerc (1984).

*Let F be a consensus function on the set $\mathfrak{U}$ of all the ultrametrics on X. Then F is binary and co-Paretian if and only if there exist n reductive and isotone mappings $\phi_i$ from $\mathbb{R}^+$ into $\mathbb{R}^+$ such that, for every $\Pi$ in $\mathfrak{U}^n$,*

$$u(xy) = \max[\phi_i \circ u_i(xy), i \in N].$$

Several observations have been made in Barthélemy, Leclerc, and Monjardet (1986) in the classification cases. Indeed, these observations can be made more generally for many axiomatic results and especially for the seven similar results of this section. First, in all these cases, the set of "objects" to be aggregated is endowed with a natural partial order. For the sets of choice functions, valued preorders, and ultrametrics, this partial order is simply the *pointwise* order between mappings: $f \leq g$ if $f(x) \leq g(x)$ for every $x$. For the set of partitions, it is the well-known *refinement* order: $\pi \leq \pi'$ if every class of the partition $\pi$ is contained in a class of the partition $\pi'$. In other terms, for all $x, y$ in $X$, $x \pi y$ implies $x \pi' y$. Moreover, endowed with these partial orders, the sets $(\mathcal{C}, \mathcal{V}, \mathcal{P}, \mathcal{U})$ are *lattices;* $\mathcal{O}$ is only a semilattice, but can be transformed into a lattice by adding the universal relation $X^2$. In these sets, a subset $S$ has always a greatest lower bound, called its *meet* and denoted by $\bigwedge S$, and a least upper bound, called its *join* and denoted by $\bigvee S$. For instance, in the lattice of all the choice functions satisfying the heritage property, the join (resp. the meet) of the choice functions $c$ and $c'$ is given by $(c \vee c')(A) = c(A) \cup c'(A)$ (resp. $(c \wedge c')(A) = c(A) \cap c'(A)$) for every $A \subseteq X$.

A consequence of this (finite) latticial structure is the existence of "elementary" objects, the so-called *join-irreducible* elements of the lattice – that is, the elements that cannot be obtained as the join of other elements; there exist also, dually, *meet-irreducible* elements. For instance, in the lattice of all the choice functions satisfying the heritage property, the join-irreducible elements are the choice functions denoted by $c_x$ and defined by $c_x(A) = \{x\}$ if $A = \{x\}$ and $c_x(A) = \emptyset$ otherwise. In the lattice of all the partitions, the join-irreducible elements are the partitions, denoted by $\pi_{xy}$, where each element is the unique one in its class except for $x$ and $y$ forming a class, while the meet-irreducible elements are the partitions, denoted by $\pi_{AB}$, with only two classes $A$ and $B$ (the so-called bipartitions). In a finite lattice, each element (object) can be obtained as a join of join-irreducible elements or, dually, as a meet of meet-irreducible elements.

A second observation is that an "ordinal form" can be given to all the axioms used in the previous results; they express, with only partial order, the latticial operations and the join- or meet-irreducible elements. For instance, the Pareto axiom for valued preorders can be written $\bigwedge p_i \leq F(\Pi)$, the co-Pareto axiom for ultrametrics can be written $\bigvee u_i \geq F(\Pi)$, and the binary and co-binary axioms for partitions can be respectively written:

$$[\{i \in N : \pi_{xy} \leq \pi_i\} = \{i \in N : \pi_{xy} \leq \pi_i'\}] \Rightarrow [\pi_{xy} \leq \pi \Leftrightarrow \pi_{xy} \leq \pi'];$$

$$[\{i \in N : \pi_{AB} \geq \pi_i\} = \{i \in N : \pi_{AB} \geq \pi_i'\}] \Rightarrow [\pi_{AB} \geq \pi \Leftrightarrow \pi_{AB} \geq \pi'].$$

A third observation is that all the classes of consensus functions characterized in the previous results have "latticial expressions": they are *generalized latticial polynomials,* obtained by first transforming the given elements by isotone mappings (that can be identity mappings) and then taking the joins of the meets of some subsets of these transformed elements. In some cases (orders, partitions), the class of consensus functions characterized by the axioms is only, in the language of social choice theory, the class of oligarchic or co-oligarchic consensus functions – that is, in the language of lattice theory, the class of meet or join projections.

## 3 The axiomatic latticial theory of consensus

The aim of an abstract axiomatic theory of consensus is to derive general results allowing one to obtain old or new "concrete" results as special cases and, especially, to account for the resemblances and differences observed in these results. The previous observations show that lattice theory can provide such an abstract theory. What does this mean? We consider the objects to be aggregated as the elements of an abstract lattice $L$; a consensus function on $L$ is a mapping $F$ from $L^n$ into $L$ that associates an element $x = F(\Pi)$ of $L$ with each $n$-tuple $\Pi = (x_1, ..., x_i, ..., x_n)$ of elements of $L$. The theory relates two kinds of definitions for a consensus function $F$: axiomatic definitions on the one hand, and, on the other hand, constructive definitions where $F$ is obtained from the latticial operations $\wedge$ and $\vee$. More precisely, we obtain theorems axiomatically characterizing some classes of latticial consensus functions *according to the structural properties of the lattices on which they are defined* (for the definitions on lattices not recalled here, see e.g. Barbut and Monjardet 1970 or Birkhoff 1967).

We first give the most important latticial axioms for a consensus function $F$ used in this theory. The set of all the join-irreducible elements of the lattice $L$ is denoted by $J$; for $\Pi = (x_1, ..., x_i, ..., x_n) \in L^n$ and $j \in J$ we set $N_j(\Pi) = \{i \in N: j \le x_i\}$. A consensus function $F$ on $L$ is *decisive* (D) if, for every $j \in J$ and for all $\Pi, \Pi' \in L^n$,

$$[N_j(\Pi) = N_j(\Pi')] \Rightarrow [j \le F(\Pi) \Leftrightarrow j \le F(\Pi')].$$

A consensus function $F$ on $L$ is *neutral monotonic* (NM) if, for all $j, j' \in J$ and for all $\Pi, \Pi' \in L^n$,

$$[N_j(\Pi) \subseteq N_{j'}(\Pi')] \Rightarrow [j \le F(\Pi) \Rightarrow j' \le F(\Pi')].$$

A consensus function $F$ is *Paretian* (P) if, for every $\Pi \in L^n$,

$$\wedge\{x_i, i \in N\} \le F(\Pi).$$

It is clear that such axioms are the abstract forms of the Arrowian axioms used in the results of Section 2. We can also use classical ordinal or algebraic axioms, as in the following definitions. A consensus function $F$ is *idempotent* if, for every $x$ in $L$, $F(x, ..., x, ..., x) = x$. A consensus function $F$ is *isotone* if, for all $\Pi, \Pi' \in L^n$,

$$[\forall i \in N, x_i \le x_i'] \Rightarrow [F(\Pi) \le F(\Pi')].$$

A consensus function $F$ is a $\wedge$-*morphism* (resp. a $\vee$-*morphism*) if, for all $\Pi, \Pi' \in L^n$,

$$F(\Pi \wedge \Pi') = F(\Pi) \wedge F(\Pi') \quad (\text{resp. } F(\Pi \vee \Pi') = F(\Pi) \vee F(\Pi')),$$

where the $n$-tuple $\Pi \wedge \Pi'$ is given by

$$\Pi \wedge \Pi' = (x_1 \wedge x_1', \ldots, x_i \wedge x_i', \ldots, x_n \wedge x_n')$$

and similarly for $\Pi \vee \Pi'$.

Now it is assumed that the lattice $L$ has a greatest element, denoted $1_L$, and a least element, denoted $0_L$ (any lattice may be completed with such elements, if they are not already present). We define two classes of latticial consensus functions. Recall that a *federation* on $N = \{1, \ldots, n\}$ is a family $\mathcal{F}$ of subsets of $N$ satisfying $[A \in \mathcal{F}, \ B \supseteq A] \Rightarrow [B \in \mathcal{F}]$. A consensus function $F_{\mathcal{F}}$ on $L$ may be associated with each federation $\mathcal{F}$ on $N$ by $F(\Pi) = \bigvee_{A \in \mathcal{F}} (\bigwedge_{i \in A} x_i)$ for each $\Pi$ in $L^n$. A *federation consensus function* is a consensus function $F$ on $L$ obtained in this way – that is, for which there exists a federation $\mathcal{F}$ such that, for each $\Pi$ in $L^n$,

$$F(\Pi) = \bigvee_{A \in \mathcal{F}} (\bigwedge_{i \in A} x_i).$$

A *generalized federation consensus function* is a consensus function $F$ for which there exists a federation $\mathcal{F}$ and $n$ isotone mappings (scaling functions) $\psi_i$ from $L$ into $L$ such that, for each $\Pi$ in $L^n$,

$$F(\Pi) = \bigvee_{A \in \mathcal{F}} (\bigwedge_{i \in A} \psi_i(x_i)).$$

A consensus function $F(x_1, \ldots, x_i, \ldots, x_n) = \bigwedge\{\psi_i(x_i), \ i \in M\}$, obtained by taking as $\mathcal{F}$ the federation formed by all subsets of $N$ containing a given subset $M$, is called a *generalized meet projection*. Notice that $M$ can be taken equal to $N$ without loss of generality: Define $\psi^1$ as the mapping from $L$ into $L$ such that $\psi^1(x) = 1_L$ for any $x \in L$, and set $\psi_i = \psi^1$ for any $i \notin M$ in the previous definition. The generalized meet projection is now written as $F(\Pi) = \bigwedge\{\psi_i(x_i), \ i \in N\}$.

A special case of a generalized meet projection consensus function is obtained when $\psi_i$ is the identity mapping on $L$ ($\psi_i(x_i) = x_i$) if $i$ belongs to $M$ and when $\psi_i = \psi^1$ ($\psi_i(x_i) = 1$) otherwise; $F$ is then a *meet projection* consensus function (called also an *oligarchic* consensus function): $F(x_1, \ldots, x_i, \ldots, x_n) = \bigwedge\{x_i, \ i \in M\}$. In particular, $F(x_1, \ldots, x_i, \ldots, x_n) = x_i$ is a *projection* when $|M| = 1$, and $F(x_1, \ldots, x_i, \ldots, x_n) = \bigwedge\{x_i, \ i \in N\}$ is the *Pareto* (or *unanimity*) consensus function when $M = N$. Dually, the *generalized join projection* consensus functions, associated with the federation formed by all subsets of $N$ containing any element of a given subset $M$, are given by $F(x_1, \ldots, x_i, \ldots, x_n) = \bigvee\{\psi_i(x_i), \ i \in M\}$. They include the *join projection* consensus functions: $F(x_1, \ldots, x_i, \ldots, x_n) = \bigvee\{x_i, \ i \in M\}$.

When $n = 2p+1$, $\mathcal{F} = \{A \subseteq N : |A| \geq p+1\}$, and all the $\psi_i$ are the identity mapping, one obtains the so-called *median consensus function*:

$$F_{(p+1)}(\Pi) = \bigvee_{|A| \geq p+1} (\bigwedge_{i \in A} x_i).$$

Let $F^1$ and $F^0$ be the constant consensus functions that map all the profiles into, (respectively) the greatest element $1_L$ and the least element

$0_L$ of $L$. With the classical equalities $\bigwedge \emptyset = 1_L$ and $\bigvee \emptyset = 0_L$ (which require that $L$ be a complete lattice, a condition satisfied by all finite lattices and by the most usual infinite ones), they are special instances of federation consensus functions. The federation corresponding to $F^1$ is the family $\mathcal{P}(N)$ of all subsets of $N$, whereas the federation corresponding to $F^0$ is the empty family.

The results obtained for axiomatic latticial consensus theory depend on the structural properties of the involved lattices and, especially, on the properties of a *dependence relation* $\beta$ defined on the set $J$ of all the join-irreducible elements of $L$. For $j$ and $j'$ in $J$:

$$j \beta j' \Leftrightarrow j \neq j' \text{ and } \exists x \in L \mid j, j' \not\leq x \ \& \ j < j' \vee x.$$

Notice that this relation $\beta$ contains the order relation between the join-irreducible elements (if $j < j'$ then $j < j' \vee 0_L!$). It can be shown that the relation $\beta$ equals the order relation between the join-irreducible elements of $L$ if and only if $L$ is a *distributive lattice*.

The relation $\beta$ defines an oriented graph on the set $J$ of all the join-irreducible elements of $L$. The lattice $L$ is said to be $\beta$-*strong* if this graph is strongly connected. One can now give the general results of the latticial axiomatic consensus theory.

**Theorem 1.**  *Let $L$ be a finite lattice and $F$: $L^n \to L$ a consensus function.*

(1)  *If $L$ is distributive, then $F$ is a federation consensus function if and only if it is neutral monotonic.*

(2)  *If $L$ is not distributive, then $F$ is a meet projection (oligarchic) consensus function if and only if it is neutral monotonic and it is not equal to $F^0$ or $F^1$.*

(3)  *If $L$ is $\beta$-strong, then $F$ is a meet projection (oligarchic) consensus function if and only if it is decisive and Paretian.*

There is a dual theorem using dual axioms and a dual dependence relation defined on the set of all the meet-irreducible elements of $L$; it leads, in particular, to a characterization of the join projection (co-oligarchic) consensus functions. The results on partial orders, choice functions, and partitions recalled in Section 2 are all special cases of Theorem 1, or of its dual theorem:

> the Brown and Barthélemy result on orders, and the Mirkin and Leclerc and Neumann and Norton results on partitions, are obtained as special cases of the third part of Theorem 1;
>
> the Aizerman and Aleskerov results on choice functions are obtained as special cases of the first part (when only the heritage

property is required) and of the second part (when the concordance property is added).

All these results characterize classes of federation consensus functions.
Some classes of generalized federation consensus functions are characterized in the next section.

## 4    The consensus of valued objects

We shall use a classical model for a valued (or fuzzy) object (see e.g.
Achache 1988 or Negoita 1981). It needs two lattices: the (finite) lattice $L$
of the considered objects (for instance, $L$ could be the lattice of all the
preorders on $X$, of all the partitions, etc.) and the lattice $V$ of values. The
latter may be not finite, but it is convenient to assume that it is complete
(any subset of $V$ has a meet and a join); moreover, it is assumed that $V$
has join-irreducible elements that cannot be obtained as the join of a
*finite* set of other elements, and that every element of $V$ is the join of a
finite number of join-irreducible ones. These assumptions are not too
restrictive since, for instance, $V$ can be $\{0,1\}$, $[0,1]$, $\mathbb{R}^+$ (completed with
an infinite element), $(\mathbb{R}^+)^k$, et cetera. We denote by $J_L$ (resp. $J_V$) the set
of all join-irreducible elements of $L$ (resp. of all join-irreducible elements
of $V$). We first give two equivalent definitions of a valued object; we then
point out a significant equivalent concept.

A *valued object* is a mapping $v: J_L \to V$ satisfying one of the following
two equivalent properties:

(1)   For every $j \in J_L$ and $I \subseteq J_L$, $j \le \bigvee I$ implies $v(j) \ge \bigwedge\{v(i): i \in I\}$.
(2)   For every $\lambda \in V$, there exists $x \in L$ such that $\{j \in J_L: v(j) \ge \lambda\} =$
$\{j \in J_L: j \le x\}$.

It is an easy exercise to see that if $L$ is (for instance) the lattice of all the
transitive relations on $X$, with $V$ the real interval $[0,1]$, then: property (1)
is equivalent to the property

"for all $x, y, z$ in $X$, $p(x, z) \ge \min[p(x, y), p(y, z)]$"

(the classical maxmin transitivity of fuzzy set theory; see e.g. Dubois
and Prade, 1980); and property (2) is equivalent to the property "for
every $\lambda$ in $[0, 1]$, the threshold set $R(\lambda) = \{(x, y): p(x, y) \ge \lambda\}$ is a transitive relation." Then, by adding the convenient property $p(x, x) = 1$, the
valued preorders of Section 2 are again obtained.

Let $v: J_L \to V$ be a valued object. The domain of the mapping $v$ can
extend to $L$ by setting:

$$\forall x \in L, \quad v(x) = \bigwedge\{v(j): j \ge x\}.$$

Then it may be shown that this extended mapping $v$ is a *Galois mapping* between the lattices $L$ and $V$; that is, it satisfies the following two properties:

$$v(0_L) = 1_V \quad \text{and} \quad \forall(x, y) \in L, \ v(x \wedge y) = v(x) \vee v(y)$$

or, equivalently, the property:

$$\forall \lambda \in V, \quad \exists y \in L \mid \{z \in L : v(z) \geq \lambda\} = \{z \in L : z \leq y\}.$$

Conversely, if $v$ is a Galois mapping between the lattices $L$ and $V$, its restriction to the set $J_L$ defines a mapping $v$ satisfying properties (1) and (2); that is, $v$ is then a valued object.

The extension and restriction mappings just defined are two inverse bijections between the set of all the valued objects $v: J_L \to V$ and the set of all the Galois mappings $v: L \to V$. Moreover, when these two sets of mappings are endowed with the pointwise order, these two bijections are two inverse-order isomorphisms. The ordered set of all the Galois mappings $v: L \to V$ has been well studied (see especially Shmuely 1974). This set is a lattice, usually denoted by $L \otimes V$; we shall denote by $\mathcal{V}$ the isomorphic lattice of all the valued objects $v$.

In order to apply our general theory to consensus functions on $\mathcal{V}$, we need to identify the set of join-irreducible elements and the dependence relation $\beta$ on this lattice. We first define, for every $j$ in $J_L$ and every $\lambda$ in $V$, a valued object denoted by $j\lambda$:

$$\forall j' \in J_L, \quad j\lambda(j') = \begin{cases} \lambda & \text{if } j' \leq j, \\ 0 & \text{otherwise.} \end{cases}$$

We then have the following two results.

(i)   *The set $J_{\mathcal{V}}$ of the join-irreducible elements of $\mathcal{V}$ is given by*

$$J_{\mathcal{V}} = \{j\lambda : j \in J_L, \lambda \in J_V\}$$

(ii)  *For all $j, j' \in J_L$ and $\lambda, \lambda' \in J_V$, $j\lambda \, \beta \, j'\lambda'$ if and only if $j \beta j'$ and $\lambda \beta \lambda'$.*

The set $J_{\mathcal{V}}$ is thus order-isomorphic to the product of $J_L$ and $J_V$, while the relation $\beta$ on $J_{\mathcal{V}}$ is also the product of those of $J_L$ and $J_V$. This last property allows us to show that if the lattices $L$ and $V$ are both distributive (resp. $\beta$-strong) then the lattice $\mathcal{V}$ also is distributive (resp. $\beta$-strong).

Now the set $J_{\mathcal{V}}$ of all join-irreducible elements of $\mathcal{V}$ is known, with the further observation that $j\lambda \leq v$ is equivalent to $\lambda \leq v(j)$. Setting $F(\Pi) = v$, $F(\Pi') = v'$, and $N_{j,\lambda}(v_1, ..., v_i, ..., v_n) = \{i \in N : \lambda \leq v_i(j)\}$, the three main axioms for consensus functions $F$ on the lattice $\mathcal{V}$ may be formulated as follows. For all $\Pi, \Pi' \in \mathcal{V}^n$, $j, j' \in J_L$, and $\lambda, \lambda' \in J_V$,

(D)   $[N_{j,\lambda}(\Pi) = N_{j,\lambda}(\Pi')] \Rightarrow [\lambda \le v(j) \Leftrightarrow \lambda \le v'(j)]$,

(NM)  $[N_{j,\lambda}(\Pi) \subseteq N_{j',\lambda'}(\Pi')] \Rightarrow [\lambda \le v(j) \Rightarrow \lambda' \le v'(j)]$,

(P)   $\bigwedge\{v_i, i \in N\} \le F(\Pi)$.

Then, using the previous results, we can state our second theorem.

**Theorem 2.**  *Let $\mathcal{V}$ be a lattice of valued objects $v: J_L \to V$, and let $F$: $\mathcal{V}^n \to \mathcal{V}$ be a consensus function.*

(1)  *If $L$ and $V$ are distributive, then $F$ is a federation consensus function if and only if it is neutral monotonic.*

(2)  *If $L$ and $V$ are $\beta$-strong, then $F$ is a meet-projection (oligarchic) consensus function if and only if it is decisive and Paretian.*

(3)  *In all other cases, $F$ is a meet-projection (oligarchic) consensus function if and only if it is neutral monotonic and it is not equal to $F^0$ or $F^1$.*

These results use the general axioms on $F$ that bear on the join-irreducible elements of the lattice $\mathcal{V}$ of valued objects. But more specific and natural axioms for the consensus functions of valued objects may be considered. Indeed, the consensus valued object $v = F(v_1, ..., v_i, ..., v_n)$ is given either by its values $v(j)$ on the elementary objects $j \in J_L$, or by its threshold sets $J(v, \lambda) = \{j \in J_L: v(j) \ge \lambda\}$; this leads us to consider (respectively) axioms on elementary objects and threshold axioms, as follows: For all $\Pi, \Pi' \in \mathcal{V}^n$ and $j, j' \in J_L$,

($J_L$-D)   $[\forall i \in N, v_i(j) = v_i'(j)] \Rightarrow [v(j) = v'(j)]$,

($J_L$-NM)  $[\forall i \in N, v_i(j) \le v_i'(j')] \Rightarrow [v(j) \le v'(j')]$;

for all $\Pi, \Pi' \in \mathcal{V}^n$ and $\lambda, \lambda' \in J_V$,

($J_V$-D)   $[\forall i \in N, J(v_i, \lambda) = J(v_i', \lambda)] \Rightarrow [J(v, \lambda) = J(v', \lambda)]$,

($J_V$-NM)  $[\forall i \in N, J(v_i, \lambda) \subseteq J(v_i', \lambda')] \Rightarrow [J(v, \lambda) \subseteq J(v', \lambda')]$.

It is worth noting that the ($J_L$-D) axiom (or some variant of it, sometimes weaker) is the most frequently encountered one in the literature on the aggregation of fuzzy preferences; see (among others) Leclerc ( 1984), Barrett, Pattanaik, and Salles (1986), and Dutta (1987).

The general axioms are decomposable into the four axioms just listed. Indeed, for a consensus function $F$ on $\mathcal{V}$, one has the equivalences

(D) $\Leftrightarrow$ ($J_L$-D) + ($J_V$-D)   and   (NM) $\Leftrightarrow$ ($J_L$-D) + ($J_V$-NM),

which make it clear that, say, condition ($J_L$-D) is weaker than (D), and so on.

Since Theorem 2 uses the general axioms, one may ask what happens when only some of the simpler axioms are considered. There is an answer when $L$ is $\beta$-strong, where it may be shown that (1) every consensus function $F$ on $\mathcal{V}$ satisfying $(J_L\text{-D})$ and (P) satisfies also $(J_L\text{-NM})$; and (2) every consensus function $F$ on $\mathcal{V}$ satisfying $(J_L\text{-NM})$ is an $\wedge$-morphism. From this, one obtains the following two generalizations of the Leclerc (1984) results. Here, a mapping $\phi: V \to V$ is said to be *admissible* if the composition mapping $\phi \circ v$ belongs to $\mathcal{V}$ whenever $v$ does. The class of admissible functions depends on $L$ and, of course, on $V$; indeed, these functions are the isotone ones when $L$ is distributive and the meet homomorphisms (then isotone again) otherwise.

**Theorem 3.** *Let $\mathcal{V}$ be a lattice of valued objects $v: J_L \to V$, where $L$ is a $\beta$-strong lattice, and let $F: \mathcal{V}^n \to \mathcal{V}$ be a consensus function.*

  (1) *There exist $n$ admissible and extensive mappings $\phi_i$ from $V$ into $V$ such that, for every $\Pi$ in $\mathcal{V}^n$, $F(\Pi) = \wedge\{\phi_i \circ v_i, i \in N\}$ if and only if $F$ is $J_L$-decisive and Paretian.*

  (2) *There exists an isotone mapping from $J_V$ into $2^N$ associating a subset $M(\lambda)$ of $N$ with every $\lambda$ in $J_V$ such that, for every $\gamma$ in $V$, $J(v, \gamma) = \cap\{J(v_i, \gamma), i \in M(\gamma)\}$ if and only if $F$ is $J_L$-decisive, $J_V$-decisive, and Paretian.*

The consensus function obtained in (1) is a generalized meet projection, as defined in Section 3. Let $\phi$ be an admissible function, and set $\psi(v) = \phi \circ v$ for all $v \in \mathcal{V}$. Since $\phi$ is isotone, $v \le v'$ implies $\psi(v) = \phi \circ v \le \psi(v') = \phi \circ v'$ and hence the mapping $\psi$ associated with $\phi$ is isotone; here, the maps $\phi_i$ may be seen as scale transforms on $L$. In (2), the hypotheses seem to be close to those of Theorem 1(3). In fact, they are weaker because $V$ (and so $\mathcal{V}$) is not assumed to be $\beta$-strong. The consensus functions then characterized might be called "threshold oligarchic" consensus functions; for every $\gamma$ in $V$, the $n$-tuple of threshold sets $J(v_i, \gamma)$ is aggregated into the unique threshold set $J(v, \gamma)$ by means of an oligarchic procedure. Although the oligarchies $M(\gamma)$ depend on the threshold level $\gamma$, they can be made constant by adding an axiom of neutrality.

## 5   Conclusion

The axiomatic approach to aggregation problems has led, since the first Arrow result of 1951, to a large literature with many important results. The main reason for developing an abstract mathematical approach is to bring some unification and structure to (at least) a part of this literature.

This is done here with Theorems 1 and 3, which account for many specific Arrowian results previously published in the literature (further examples may be added to those recalled in Section 2; see e.g. Monjardet 1990). But other axiomatic abstract approaches have been developed, especially by Barthélemy and Janowitz (1991) and Rubinstein and Fishburn (1986). In the former it is assumed, as here, that the objects belong to a latticial structure and the join-irreducible representation of the objects is again used. But the system of axioms is different, since the aim is to obtain an abstract theory for the median rule, or for more general quota rules; recall that the median rule generalizes the majority rule (see e.g. Barthélemy and Monjardet 1981, 1988) and can lead to several consensus objects. The Rubinstein and Fishburn approach is based on linear algebra and, more precisely, on the use of a vector space on a finite field; we intend in the future to compare the linear and latticial approaches; they may not be as far apart as one might think. (After all, although not often pointed out, several classical results on a vector space $S$ are indeed results on the associated lattice of all the subspaces of $S$.)

We end with mention of several directions for further research.

1: Consequences of weakening the hypotheses on the ordered set $L$. When it is assumed only that $L$ is a semilattice, the answer – at least in the case of unvalued objects – is given in Monjardet (1990): Theorem 1 remains valid, under slight changes, with an appropriate definition of the distributivity. From another point of view, assume that the range of the consensus function $F$ is restricted to a subset of a semilattice $L$ which is not stable for the meet operation. Then the projection function (the "dictatorial" rule) may be obtained as the only available meet projection (for concrete cases see Barthélemy 1982 or Leclerc 1984). A general dictatorial result may be derived in this way from Theorem 1.

2: Study of the $\beta$ relation, which plays a major role in our results, perhaps leading to interesting developments in lattice theory. Indeed, Hicheri (1992) has already shown that it is related to a classical projectivity relation between the join- and meet-irreducibles of the lattice; he has also proved some properties of $\beta$ in upper locally distributive lattices.

3: Characterization of the generalized federation consensus functions. Those appearing in Section 4 (Theorem 3) are of a very special type. The problem remains open for the functions defined in Section 3, which appear to be relevant extensions of the classical lattice polynomials; their characterization should use axioms weaker than the Arrowian ones, which are often considered as too strong in the literature.

*Added in proof:* Recent results in the first of these research directions have been obtained by G. D. Crown, M. F. Janowitz, and R. C. Powers

(1993, *Mathematical Social Sciences* 25: 231-50) and by B. Monjardet (unpublished manuscript).

REFERENCES

Achache, A. (1988), "How to Fuzzify a Closure Space," *Journal of Mathematical Analysis and Applications* 130: 538-44.
Aizerman, M. A., and F. T. Aleskerov (1986), "Voting Operators in the Space of Choice Functions," *Mathematical Social Sciences* 11: 201-42.
Arrow, K. J. (1951), *Social Choice and Individual Values*. New York: Wiley.
Barbut, M., and B. Monjardet (1970), *Ordre et classification, algèbre et combinatoire*. Paris: Hachette.
Barrett, C. R., P. K. Pattanaik, and M. Salles (1986), "On the Structure of Fuzzy Social Welfare Functions," *Fuzzy Sets and Systems* 19: 1-10.
Barthélemy, J. P. (1982), "Arrow's Theorem: Unusual Domain and Extended Codomain," *Mathematical Social Sciences* 3: 79-89.
Barthélemy, J. P., and M. F. Janowitz (1991), "A Formal Theory of Consensus," *SIAM Journal of Discrete Mathematics* 4: 305-22.
Barthélemy, J. P., B. Leclerc, and B. Monjardet (1986), "On the Use of Ordered Sets in Problems of Comparison and Consensus of Classifications," *Journal of Classification* 3: 187-224.
Barthélemy, J. P., and B. Monjardet (1981), "The Median Procedure in Cluster Analysis and Social Choice Theory," *Mathematical Social Sciences* 1: 235-68.
(1988), "The Median Procedure in Data Analysis: New Results and Open Problems," in H. H. Bock (ed.), *Classification and Related Methods of Data Analysis*. Amsterdam: North-Holland, pp. 309-16.
Birkhoff, G. (1967), *Lattice Theory*, 3rd ed. Providence, RI: American Mathematical Society.
Brown, D. J. (1975), "Aggregation of Preferences," *Quarterly Journal of Economics* 89: 456-69.
Dubois, D., and H. Prade (1980), *Fuzzy Sets and Systems: Theory and Applications*. New York: Academic Press.
Dutta, B. (1987), "Fuzzy Preferences and Social Choice," *Mathematical Social Sciences* 13: 215-29.
Fishburn, P. C., and A. Rubinstein (1986), "Aggregation of Equivalence Relations," *Journal of Classification* 3: 61-5.
Hicheri, S. (1992), "Relation de dépendance entre sup-irréductibles d'un treillis," *Mémoire de Diplôme d'Etudes Approfondies*, Université Paris V.
Leclerc, B. (1984), "Efficient and Binary Consensus Functions on Transitively Valued Relations," *Mathematical Social Sciences* 8: 45-61.
(1991), "Aggregation of Fuzzy Preferences: A Theoretic Arrow-like Approach," *Fuzzy Sets and Systems* 43: 291-309.
Mirkin, B. G. (1975), "On the Problem of Reconciling Partitions, in *Quantitative Sociology, International Perspectives on Mathematical and Statistical Modelling*. New York: Academic Press, pp. 441-9.
(1981), "Federations and Transitive Group Choice," *Mathematical Social Sciences* 2: 35-8.
Monjardet, B. (1978), "An Axiomatic Theory of Tournament Aggregation," *Mathematics of Operations Research* 3: 334-51.

(1990), "Arrowian Characterizations of Latticial Federation Consensus Functions," *Mathematical Social Sciences* 20: 51–71.

Negoita, C. V. (1981), *Fuzzy Systems,* Tunbridge Wells, Great Britain, Abacus Press.

Neumann, D. A., and V. T. Norton, Jr. (1986), "On Lattice Consensus Methods," *Journal of Classification* 3: 225–55.

Rubinstein, A., and P. C. Fishburn (1986), "Algebraic Aggregation Theory," *Journal of Economic Theory* 38: 63–77.

Shmuely, Z. (1974), "The Structure of Galois Connections," *Pacific Journal of Mathematics* 54: 209–25.

PART IV

# Geometric aspects of social choice

CHAPTER 7

# Arrow theorems in economic environments

*James Redekop*

## 1    Introduction

The celebrated impossibility theorem of Arrow [1] shows the inconsistency of a set of axioms for a social welfare function $f$ that maps profiles of individual preferences into social preferences on a set of alternatives $X$. One of these axioms is that $f$ must be defined on all profiles in the *unrestricted* domain $P(X)^N$, where $P(X)$ is the set of all preference orderings on $X$ and $N$ is the set (or number) of individuals in the society. This assumption diminishes the theorem's importance for economics because, in any economic model, both the set $X$ and the preferences individuals have on $X$ will be restricted by reasonable structural assumptions. For example, if $X = \mathbb{R}_+^m$ and points $x \in X$ denote vectors of public goods, then it is reasonable to assume that individuals' preferences are monotonic. In such a situation, Arrow's theorem does not rule out the possibility that some social welfare function $f$ has the domain $P_M(X)^N$, where $P_M(X)$ denotes the set of monotonic preferences on $X$ and where $f$ satisfies all the rest of the Arrow axioms. Given a set $X$ and a set of profiles $D \subseteq P(X)^N$, we call $D$ *Arrow-consistent* if such an $f$ exists and *Arrow-inconsistent* otherwise. In these terms, Arrow's theorem states that if $X$ has at least three elements then the unrestricted domain $D = P(X)^N$ is Arrow-inconsistent.

The literature on Arrow-consistent domains of preferences actually pre-dates Arrow [1], since it includes Black's analysis [2] of single-peaked preferences. The study of economic domains of preferences, with a view to establishing their Arrow consistency or inconsistency, begins with Blau's consistency result [3] for the private goods model. Other authors – notably Border [4], Bordes and Le Breton [6], Campbell [9, and articles cited therein], Kalai, Muller, and Satterthwaite [15], and Maskin [20] – have found Arrow inconsistency to be prevalent in economic environments with public or private goods. For recent surveys, see Donaldson and Weymark [12] or Le Breton and Weymark [18].

163

In this paper we state theorems, appearing in [24; 25; 26; 28], regarding the Arrow inconsistency of a large number of domains that arise in economic models. We begin with the cases of public goods and private goods with continuous monotonic preferences which are also selfish in the case of private goods, and then specialize and generalize in several ways. The generalizations include models with both public and private goods, and models in which the alternatives are stochastic or dynamic or both. The specializations are to smaller sets of preferences, via the imposition of economic assumptions such as convexity, homotheticity, or even identity of tastes in the case of private goods; parametric assumptions on utility functions; and various axiomatically derived functional forms for preference functionals in the case of stochastic alternatives. We also consider domains consisting of arbitrarily small subsets of these economic domains. This allows for the possibility that – in addition to properties of individuals' preferences such as convexity, log linearity, or expected utility – the social planner has some more specific information. This information may be that an individual's preference lies in some open set of preferences; or perhaps the planner has estimated an individual's Cobb–Douglas preference parameter vector to lie in some small open subset of the unit simplex.

Subject to some mild regularity conditions, in all of these economic environments the domains that naturally arise are Arrow-inconsistent. Worse, the inconsistency persists even for arbitrarily small open subsets of these domains. Thus, neither economic assumptions nor additional information on individuals' preferences can yield an Arrow-consistent domain of preference profiles. The conclusion is that, in economic environments, attempts to construct social welfare functions should proceed from the relaxation of some Arrow axiom other than the unrestricted domain condition.

## 2     The Arrow axioms and the local approach

Throughout this paper we let $X$ denote the set of alternatives and $N$ the (finite) set of individuals; $B(X)$ denotes the set of binary relations on $X$ and $P(X) \subseteq B(X)$ contains those relations which are complete and transitive, that is, preferences on $X$. For $p \in P(X)$, $\hat{p}$ and $\bar{p}$ denote strict preference and indifference, respectively. If $D \neq \emptyset$ and $D \subseteq P(X)^N$, then any $f: D \to B(X)$ is a *social welfare function* (SWF). An SWF $f$ is defined to satisfy:

(1)   CT if, for all $(p_1, ..., p_N) \in D$, $f(p_1, ..., p_N)$ is complete and transitive;

(2)   WP (weak Pareto) if, for all $(p_1, ..., p_N) \in D$ and for all $x, y \in X$,

$$[x \, \hat{p}_i \, y \ \forall i \in N] \Rightarrow x \, \hat{f}(p_1, ..., p_N) \, y; \tag{2.1}$$

(3)   IIA (independence of irrelevant alternatives) if, for all $x, y \in X$
and for all $(p_1, \ldots, p_N)$ and $(q_1, \ldots, q_N)$ in $D$,

$$[x \, p_i \, y \Leftrightarrow x \, q_i \, y \; \forall i \in N] \Rightarrow [x \, f(p_1, \ldots, p_N) \, y \Leftrightarrow x \, f(q_1, \ldots, q_N) \, y]; \qquad (2.2)$$

(4)   ND (nondictatorship) if there exists no $i \in N$ such that, for all
$x, y \in X$ and for all $(p_1, \ldots, p_N) \in D$,

$$[x \, \hat{p}_i \, y] \Rightarrow [x \, \hat{f}(p_1, \ldots, p_N) \, y]. \qquad (2.3)$$

We call these four conditions the *Arrow axioms*, omitting the unrestricted domain axiom $D = P(X)^N$ since it does not hold in any of our economic environments. A domain $D$ is *Arrow-consistent* if some SWF $f: D \to B(X)$ satisfies CT, WP, IIA, and ND; otherwise, $D$ is *Arrow-inconsistent*. Clearly a domain $D$ is Arrow-inconsistent if and only if one can show that, if $f: D \to P(X)$ satisfies WP and IIA, then $f$ is dictatorial in the sense that for some $i \in N$, (2.3) holds for all $x, y \in X$ and all $(p_1, \ldots, p_N) \in D$.

A simple but powerful method of proving the Arrow-inconsistency of domains was devised by Kalai, Muller, and Satterthwaite ([15], henceforth KMS) and is called the *local approach*. One begins by identifying *free triples* of alternatives $\{x, y, z\}$, meaning that any profile of preferences on $\{x, y, z\}$ is the restriction to $\{x, y, z\}$ of some profile in $D$. If $f: D \to P(X)$ satisfies WP and IIA, then Arrow's theorem implies the existence of a *dictator* on the triple; and if two free triples intersect in a pair of elements, then the dictators on those triples must be the same individual. The same reasoning applies to chains of free triples that overlap in pairs of elements; they must each have the same dictator. Thus if every pair of alternatives (on which individuals can disagree in preference) belongs to a free triple connected by such a chain to some common free triple, then there must be a dictator on every such pair. Domains for which this line of reasoning works are called *saturating*. In [15], KMS showed that a saturating domain is Arrow-inconsistent and that, in the public goods model, the domain of profiles of continuous, strictly monotonic, and convex preferences is saturating. Bordes and Le Breton [6] have extended the notion of a saturating domain to other types of Arrow-inconsistent domains that include those arising in some standard economic models.

In economic environments, a weaker, strict version of this method is sufficient to prove impossibility results. Say that $\{x, y, z\}$ is a *strictly* free triple if any profile of strict preferences on $\{x, y, z\}$ is the restriction to $\{x, y, z\}$ of some profile in $D$; write $\hat{F}_D(x, y, z)$ to denote that this is true. (Note that this is a weaker condition on $D$ and $\{x, y, z\}$ than requiring $\{x, y, z\}$ to be a free triple.) Given $f: D \to P(X)$, let $\hat{D}_i(a, b)$ denote that:

If $a\,\hat{p}_i\,b$ and if, $\forall j \in N$, either $a\,\hat{p}_j\,b$ or $b\,\hat{p}_j\,a$,

then $a\,\hat{f}(p_1, \ldots, p_N)\,b$.                                    (2.4)

In this case we say that $i \in N$ is *strictly decisive* for $a$ over $b$.

**Proposition 2.1.**   *If* $f: D \to P(X)$ *satisfies WP and IIA and* $\hat{F}_D(x, y, z)$, *then there is an* $i \in N$ *such that* $\hat{D}_i(a, b)$ *for all* $\{a, b\} \subseteq \{x, y, z\}$.

One can prove the proposition using strict versions of the usual group contraction and field expansion lemmas (see Sen [30]). Overlapping chains of free triples also have a natural analog in this strict local approach. If $(w, x)$ and $(y, z)$ are distinct pairs of distinct elements, then we write $\hat{C}_D((w, x), (y, z))$ to denote the existence of a finite sequence $u_1, u_2, \ldots, u_K$ such that

$$u_1 = w, \quad u_2 = x, \quad u_{K-1} = y, \quad u_K = z,    \qquad (2.5)$$

and

$$\hat{F}_D(u_k, u_{k+1}, u_{k+2}) \quad \text{for all } k, \ 1 \le k \le K-2. \qquad (2.6)$$

The foregoing saturating domain argument adapts easily to prove the next proposition.

**Proposition 2.2.**   *Let* $f: D \to P(X)$ *be a function that satisfies WP and IIA. If* $\hat{C}_D((w, x), (y, z))$, *then there is an* $i \in N$ *such that* $\hat{D}_i(w, x)$ *and* $\hat{D}_i(y, z)$.

Propositions 2.1 and 2.2 are the only fully general results used in proving the theorems of this paper. The rest of the proofs are more environment-specific and can be broken up into the following steps, which refer to the *product domain* case $D = E^N$ with $E$ an open set of preferences.

*Step 1:*   Assume that some $f: D \to P(X)$ satisfies WP and IIA.

*Step 2:*   Fix $p \in E$ and $x \in X$. Find a class of pairs $\{y, z\}$ for which $\hat{F}(x, y, z)$ holds.

Typically, if $x\,\bar{p}\,y\,\bar{p}\,z$ then $p$ can be perturbed arbitrarily slightly so as to get a preference $q$ satisfying $x\,\hat{q}\,y\,\hat{q}\,z$ or any other strict ordering of $\{x, y, z\}$. Because $E$ is open, we can choose $q$ to lie in $E$ also. Thus the class of pairs in step 2 can usually be taken as the set of all pairs $\{y, z\}$ in the same $p$-indifference class as $x$.

*Step 3:*   There exist an individual $i(p, x) \in N$ and an open set $U(p, x)$ containing the $p$-indifference class containing $x$, such that $\hat{D}_{i(p, x)}(a, b)$ holds whenever $a, b \in U(p, x)$ and $a\,\hat{p}\,b$.

If the usual case holds in the preceding step 3, the proof of this step is a straightforward application of Propositions 2.1 and 2.2.

*Step 4:* $i(p, x)$ does not depend on $x$. Hence we can write this function as $i(p)$.

In economic environments, we can usually write the set of alternatives as a continuously indexed union of $p$-indifference classes (think of an indifference map in $\mathbb{R}^2$). The result is that the sets $U(p, x)$ in step 3 overlap a lot and, where they intersect, the function $i(p, x)$ cannot vary with $x$ because the intersection will contain strictly free pairs. The index $x$ of the union varies over a connected set, so if $i(p, x)$ cannot vary locally with $x$ then it cannot vary at all with $x$.

*Step 5:* $i(p)$ does not depend on $p$. That is, there is a *local dictator* $i \in N$ such that: For all $x \in X$ and $p \in E$, there is an open set $U(p, x)$ such that $\hat{D}_i(a, b)$ holds whenever $a, b \in U(p, x)$ and $a\,\hat{p}\,b$.

If $i$ varied with $p$ then, because of the product assumption, we could arrange a profile of preferences and pair of alternatives $a, b$ for which both $a\,\hat{f}\,b$ and $b\,\hat{f}\,a$ would have to occur, violating CT.

*Step 6:* A local dictator is a global dictator.

Proof of step 6 is greatly aided by the following *continuous climb property* of preferences $p$: Whenever $x\,\hat{p}\,y$, there is a continuous function $\gamma: [0,1] \to X$ such that $\gamma(0) = y$, $\gamma(1) = x$, and $\gamma(s)\,\hat{p}\,\gamma(t)$ for all $s > t$. The property holds in all the environments studied here and proves step 6 as follows: Let $i$ be a local dictator, let $p_i = p \in E$, and let $x\,\hat{p}_i\,y$. We can then choose $0 = t_0 < t_1 < \cdots < t_n = 1$ with the $t_k$s close enough together so that the local dictator enforces each of $\gamma(t_{k+1})\,\hat{f}\,\gamma(t_k)$. Then $x\,\hat{f}\,y$ follows from transitivity.

Clearly, if the reasoning in steps 1–6 all applies, then we have a proof of an impossibility theorem. Complications arise when we must deal with points not in the interior of the alternative set, nonproduct domains, or weaker topological assumptions on the domain ("near openness" rather than openness – see (3.3)ff). Furthermore, the peculiarities of each environment require different types of reasoning in proving the steps, especially steps 2 and 3. For these reasons, there is no general theorem from which the results of the next sections follow.

## 3    Public goods economies

In this section, points in $X = \mathbb{R}^m_+$ denote vectors of public goods that the society will consume, and preferences will always be assumed to lie in

$$P_{MC}(X) = \{p \in P(X) \mid p \text{ is continuous, and } x > y \Rightarrow x\,\hat{p}\,y\}. \tag{3.1}$$

Also, we assume throughout this section that $m \geq 2$. The natural topology on $P_{MC}(X)$ is Kannai's [16], which is fine enough to make sets of the form

$$Q(x, y) = \{p \in P_{MC}(X) \mid x \, \hat{p} \, y\} \qquad (3.2)$$

open. Indeed, these sets can be taken as a sub-base for this topology (see [27]). In any topological space, a set is *somewhere dense* if its closure contains a non-empty open set and *nowhere dense* otherwise. Thus, nowhere dense sets are in a sense topologically negligible; but a better interpretation is that a nowhere dense set must be somehow *contrived* or sensitive to perturbation. Theorems 3.1–3.4 appear in [24].

**Theorem 3.1.** *Let $E \subseteq P_{MC}(X)$ be somewhere dense, and let $D = E^N$. Then $D$ is Arrow-inconsistent.*

One rationale for considering proper subsets of $P_{MC}(X)^N$ as potential domains for an SWF is that perhaps the planner has prior information on individuals' preferences. Since individuals may be different, this information may likewise be different for different individuals. Thus it is desirable, wherever possible, to avoid the common domain assumption $D = E^N$. The next three results avoid this assumption in different ways.

First, if $X$ is any subset of $\mathbb{R}^m$ then $X$ inherits both the relation $>$ and the usual topology, so the definition of $P_{MC}(X)$ still makes sense. Second, define

$$P_{SC}(X) = \{p \in P_{MC}(X) \mid x \geq y, \text{ and } x \neq y \Rightarrow x \, \hat{p} \, y\}, \qquad (3.3)$$

the set of *strictly* monotonic continuous preferences on $X \subseteq \mathbb{R}^m$. And third, given a topological space $Y$, say that $E \subseteq Y$ is *near-open* if $\bar{E} = \bar{O}$ for some open set $O \subseteq Y$. Note that a non-empty near-open set must be somewhere dense.

**Theorem 3.2.** *Let $X = \mathbb{R}^m_{++}$, and let $D \subseteq P_{MC}(X)^N$ be somewhere dense in the product topology. Then $D$ is Arrow-inconsistent.*

**Theorem 3.3.** *Let $X = \mathbb{R}^m_+$, and let $D \subseteq P_{SC}(X)^N$ be somewhere dense. Then $D$ is Arrow-inconsistent.*

**Theorem 3.4.** *Let $X = \mathbb{R}^m_+$, and let $D \subseteq P_{MC}(X)^N$ be near-open and non-empty. Then $D$ is Arrow-inconsistent.*

We now consider the possibility of adding the economic assumptions of convexity or homotheticity (or both) to the assumptions of continuity and monotonicity. Unfortunately, the proofs depend on the common domain assumption $D = E^N$; it is currently an open question under what topological or other general conditions a domain of the form $D = E_1 \times \cdots \times E_N$ is Arrow-consistent in this setting. Also, we state the results to follow using preferences that are strictly monotonic and convex, and assume that the domains are near-open. In general, preferences satisfying strict assumptions are dense in the sets of preferences satisfying weak versions of the same assumptions; for example, a weakly monotonic preference can be arbitrarily well approximated by a strictly monotonic preference. Also, near-openness (or, indeed, openness) of the domain is well motivated by the interpretation that proper subsets of a set of admissible preferences represent information that the planner may have on individuals' preferences. Hence the strictness and near-openness assumptions are relatively innocuous compared to the common domain assumption.

Let $X = \mathbb{R}^m_+$, and define

$$P_1 = \{ p \in P_{SC}(X) \mid p \text{ is strictly convex} \}, \tag{3.4}$$

$$P_2 = \{ p \in P_{SC}(X) \mid p \text{ is homothetic} \}, \tag{3.5}$$

$$P_3 = P_1 \cap P_2. \tag{3.6}$$

**Theorem 3.5** (see [25, thm. 3.1]). *Let $E$ be any non-empty near-open subset of $P_1$, $P_2$, or $P_3$. Then $D = E^N$ is Arrow-inconsistent.*

Finally, we consider the possibility of making further assumptions on preferences, of the sort usually postulated by econometricians. That is, we parameterize utility functions representing preferences, and assume some functional-form flexibility and parameter uncertainty in place of the assumption that the domain is somewhere dense. It can happen that the parameterization forces preferences to be convex or homothetic or both, so the domains analyzed next can be topologically negligible subsets of $P_3$ even without parameter restrictions. For example, the set of Cobb-Douglas preferences is a trivially small subset of $P_3$ even if the parameter vector is allowed to vary over its entire admissible range. But if $m \geq 3$ and this vector is allowed to vary only in an arbitrarily small open subset of that range, then the resulting domain of preference profiles is Arrow-inconsistent.

In order to study parametric domains of preferences, we let $B \subseteq \mathbb{R}^k$ denote a set of admissible parameter vectors, and let $V: \mathbb{R}^m_+ \times B \to \mathbb{R}$ represent a family of preferences $\{ p(\beta) \}$ whereby

$$x \, p(\beta) \, y \Leftrightarrow V(x, \beta) \geq V(y, \beta). \tag{3.7}$$

For instance,

$$V(x, \beta) = \prod_{i=1}^{m} x_i^{\beta_i}, \qquad B = \mathbb{R}_+^m, \qquad (3.8)$$

could represent the Cobb–Douglas preferences in the previous paragraph. (This parameterization over-indexes the implied set of preferences, and $V$ is not smooth on the boundary of $X$ in general, but (3.8) still illustrates and emphasizes that we are viewing $V$ as a function of both its arguments.) Assume that, for every $x \in \mathbb{R}_{++}^m$, the gradient of $V$ with respect to $x$ exists in $\mathbb{R}_{++}^m$; define the normalized gradient function

$$V_1(x, \beta)_j = \frac{\partial}{\partial x_j} V(x, \beta) \bigg/ \sum_1^m \frac{\partial}{\partial x_j} V(x, \beta), \qquad (3.9)$$

which then maps $\mathbb{R}_{++}^m \times B$ into the unit simplex in $\mathbb{R}_+^m$. Finally, given $E \subseteq B$, consider a domain of the form

$$D(E) = \{ p(\beta) \mid \beta \in E \}^N. \qquad (3.10)$$

**Theorem 3.6** (see [26, prop. 3.3]).  *Let $m \geq 3$, and suppose $V$ and $E$ are such that, for all $x \in \mathbb{R}_+^m$, the set*

$$\{ V_1(x, \beta) \mid \beta \in E \} \qquad (3.11)$$

*has the same closure as some open subset $O(x)$ of the unit simplex. Then $D(E)$ is Arrow-inconsistent.*

As a special case, consider the KMS [15] linear preferences model, where $B$ is the unit simplex in $\mathbb{R}_+^m$, $m \geq 3$, and

$$V(x, \beta) = x \cdot \beta, \qquad (3.12)$$

$$E = B. \qquad (3.13)$$

Here the domain $D(E)$ is the set of all monotonic linear preferences on $\mathbb{R}_+^m$ and, as the authors show, this domain is Arrow-inconsistent. However, according to the theorem we can replace $B$ by any open subset $E$ of the simplex and obtain the same result, for in this case the set in (3.11) is identically $E$. Yet if $m = 2$ then this domain is Arrow-consistent! See KMS [15] or Nitzan [21].

In general, if the set (3.11) is identically the unit simplex, then econometricians say that the parametric family of preferences is a *first-order approximation* to an arbitrary smooth monotonic utility function. For any such $U$ and any $x$, there is a member of the parametric family whose normalized gradient at $x$ is the same as that of $U$. (If the unnormalized gradient is at all important then it too can be matched by introducing a multiplicative scale parameter in the specification of $V$.) This degree of richness in the parametric family is certainly a minimal condition to impose on a parameterization, so the Arrow-inconsistent domains of Theorem 3.6 include arbitrarily small subsets of domains that are themselves only minimally rich.

A generalization of the condition in (3.11) enables the analysis of parametric domains that are not necessarily monotonic or do not necessarily approximate all gradients, even in a neighborhood of a point. The condition imposes restrictions on the rank of the matrix function $V_{x\beta}(x, \beta)$ whose $ij$ entry is

$$[V_{x\beta}(x, \beta)]_{ij} = \frac{\partial^2}{\partial x_i \partial \beta_j} V(x, \beta), \tag{3.14}$$

and ensures that the gradient at $x$ can vary in a 3-dimensional manifold as $\beta$ varies in $B$. The degree of richness in this parameterization is enough to guarantee the existence of strictly free triples near $x$; and these free triples, together with the continuous climb property of Section 2, are sufficient to imply the Arrow-inconsistency of the domain.

**Example 3.1.** Let $X = \mathbb{R}^m = B$, and define

$$V(x, \beta) = -(x - \beta) \cdot (x - \beta) \tag{3.15}$$

so that $\beta$ indexes the set of Euclidean preferences on $X$ with *bliss points* $\beta$. If $E$ has the same closure as an open subset of $\mathbb{R}^m$ and if $m \geq 3$, then $D(E)$ is Arrow-inconsistent. More generally, if the closure of $E$ is diffeomorphic to a set $F$ in $\mathbb{R}^k$ ($k \geq 3$), and if $F$ has the same closure as an open set in $\mathbb{R}^k$ then $D(E)$ is Arrow-inconsistent. The case of $E = \mathbb{R}^m$ ($m \geq 2$) is studied in Border [5] and Bordes and Le Breton [7], where the resulting domains are shown to be Arrow-inconsistent. However, if $m \geq 3$, then even arbitrarily small subsets of these domains are also Arrow-inconsistent.

## 4    Private goods economies

In this section we would like to take the set of alternatives to be $X = (\mathbb{R}_+^l)^N$, where $l \geq 2$ is the number of goods in the economy, and where an alternative $x = (x_1, \ldots, x_N)$ indicates that individual $i \in N$ receives the vector $x_i \in \mathbb{R}_+^l$ of private goods. An example due to Blau [3] shows that all the domains we shall now discuss are Arrow-consistent, although the example SWF is acquitted on a technicality of the charge of dictatorship. With $N = 2$, the example is constructed as follows.

Let

$$A_{12} = \{(x_1, x_2) \in X \mid x_1 \neq 0, \ x_2 \neq 0\},$$
$$A_1 = \{(x_1, x_2) \in X \mid x_1 \neq 0, \ x_2 = 0\},$$
$$A_2 = \{(x_1, x_2) \in X \mid x_2 \neq 0, \ x_1 = 0\}, \tag{4.1}$$
$$A_0 = \{0\},$$

and let $D$ be the set of profiles of strictly monotonic, continuous, *selfish* preferences on $X$. That is, $(p_1, p_2) \in D$ if there are preferences $q_1, q_2 \in P_{SC}(\mathbb{R}^l_+)$ such that

$$x \, p_i \, y \Leftrightarrow x_i \, q_i \, y_i. \tag{4.2}$$

Define $f: D \to P(X)$ by

$$f(p_1, p_2) \mid A_{12} = p_1 \mid A_{12}, \qquad f(p_1, p_2) \mid A_1 = p_1 \mid A_1,$$
$$f(p_1, p_2) \mid A_2 = p_2 \mid A_2, \qquad A_{12} \, \hat{f} \, A_2 \, \hat{f} \, A_1 \, \hat{f} \, A_0. \tag{4.3}$$

Then $f$ satisfies WP and IIA and hence shows that $D$ is Arrow-consistent. But, according to the first specification in (4.3), individual 1 has dictatorial powers that are only trivially different from those of a full dictator; 1 fails to be a dictator only because $f$ ranks $A_2$ above $A_1$. Recognizing this possibility, Border [4] analyzed the set of alternatives $X = (\mathbb{R}^l_{++})^N$ and found that the domain $D$ just described is Arrow-inconsistent when restricted to this new set of alternatives. Similarly, in this paper we let

$$X = (\mathbb{R}^l_+ - 0)^N, \tag{4.4}$$

and state our theorems regarding the Arrow-inconsistency of domains of selfish preferences restricted to this set. In general, we may take any $N$ Arrow-inconsistent domains of the last section and derive the product domain in which $i$'s preference on $\mathbb{R}^l_+$ belongs to $E_i \subseteq P_j$. We then write

$$D_s(E_1, ..., E_N) = \{(p_1, ..., p_N) \mid \forall i, \ \exists q_i \in E_i \text{ such that } x \, p_i \, y \Leftrightarrow x_i \, q_i \, y_i\} \tag{4.5}$$

to denote the profiles of selfish preferences in which $p_i$ ignores commodity vectors other than the $i$th, and ranks alternatives in $X$ the same way $q_i \in E_i$ ranks the $i$th commodity vectors.

For compactness of notation, define

$$P_0 = P_{SC}(\mathbb{R}^l_+), \tag{4.6}$$

and recall the notation in (3.4)-(3.6) for $P_1$, $P_2$, and $P_3$, which were the sets of strictly convex and/or homothetic monotonic preferences on $\mathbb{R}^l_+$. Now let $0 \leq j \leq 3$.

**Theorem 4.1** [25, thm. 4.1]. *Let $l \geq 2$ and let $E_i \subseteq P_j$ be non-empty and near-open subsets of $P_j$ for all $i \in N$. Then $D_S(E_1, \ldots, E_N)$ is Arrow-inconsistent.*

In private-goods economies, the set of alternatives is so rich in strictly free triples that much more severely restricted domains can be proven to be Arrow-inconsistent. Such richness arises because we can vary the commodity vectors independently for different individuals; this explains why we can dispense with the common domain assumption in Theorem 4.1, and hints at why the next theorem might be true. If $E$ is a set of preferences on $\mathbb{R}_+^l$, then let

$$D_S^=(E) = \{(p_1, \ldots, p_N) \mid \exists q \in E \text{ such that } \forall i, \, x \, p_i \, y \Leftrightarrow x_i \, q \, y_i\} \tag{4.7}$$

be the set of profiles of selfish preferences on $X$, where individuals have *identical tastes* corresponding to some preference in $E$. Again, let $0 \leq j \leq 3$.

**Theorem 4.2** [25, thm. 4.2]. *Let $l \geq 2$ and let $E \subseteq P_j$ be non-empty and near-open. Then $D_S^=(E)$ is Arrow-inconsistent.*

Of course, the domains of Theorem 4.2 are unreasonably restrictive because of the identity-of-tastes assumption. But these results still serve to illustrate the strength of the Arrow axioms, indeed *because* of that restrictiveness.

Finally, consider parametric domains of preferences of the sort introduced in Section 3.

**Theorem 4.3** [26, prop. 4.1]. *Let $l \geq 3$ and suppose that $V$ and $E_i$ satisfy the hypotheses of Theorem 3.6 for all $i \in N$. Then $D_s(E_1, \ldots, E_N)$ is Arrow-inconsistent.*

For the domains of this section, one might wish to consider the set of alternatives

$$X = (\mathbb{R}_+^l)^N \tag{4.8}$$

rather than $(\mathbb{R}_+^l - 0)^N$. In this case the domains $D$ are essentially Arrow-inconsistent in the sense that, if $f: D \to P(X)$ satisfies WP and IIA, then for some $i \in N$ we have

$$x \, \hat{p}_i \, y \Rightarrow x \, \hat{f}(p_1, \ldots, p_N) \, y \quad \forall (p_1, \ldots, p_N) \in D, \, \forall x, y \in X, \tag{4.9}$$

except, perhaps, when some $x_j = 0$.

## 5     Mixed Economies

We now study the model of Ritz [29] and Bordes and Le Breton [7], where the set of alternatives contains vectors both of public and of private goods. For the same reasons as in Section 4, we specify this set as

$$X = \mathbb{R}_+^m \times (\mathbb{R}_+^l - 0)^N, \tag{5.1}$$

and write $x \in X$ as

$$x = (x_0, x_1, ..., x_N) \tag{5.2}$$

to denote that $x_0 \in \mathbb{R}_+^m$ is the vector of public goods and $x_i \in \mathbb{R}_+^l$ is the nonzero vector of private goods allocated to the $i$th individual. We shall reconsider all of the preferences in the sets $P_0, ..., P_3$ (see (3.4)-(3.6) and (4.6)) as preferences on $\mathbb{R}_+^{m+l}$, and form domains from subsets of these analogously to (4.5). We shall also consider the assumption of separability of public and private goods, analogously to the treatment of convexity and homotheticity given in Section 3. By *separability* of $p \in P_{SC}(\mathbb{R}_+^{m+l})$ we mean that there exist preferences $q \in P_{SC}(\mathbb{R}^m)$ and $r \in P_{SC}(\mathbb{R}_+^l)$ such that, for all $w, x \in \mathbb{R}^m$ and all $y, z \in \mathbb{R}_+^l$,

$$(w, y)\, p\, (w, z) \Leftrightarrow (x, y)\, p\, (x, z) \Leftrightarrow y\, r\, z \tag{5.3}$$

and

$$(w, y)\, p\, (x, y) \Leftrightarrow (w, z)\, p\, (x, z) \Leftrightarrow w\, q\, x. \tag{5.4}$$

This happens if and only if there are continuous strictly monotonic functions $U: \mathbb{R}_+^2 \to \mathbb{R}_+$, $V: \mathbb{R}_+^m \to \mathbb{R}_+$, and $W: \mathbb{R}_+^l \to \mathbb{R}_+$ such that

$$(w, y)\, p\, (x, z) \Leftrightarrow U(V(w), W(y)) \geq U(V(x), W(z)). \tag{5.5}$$

Now let

$$P_4 = \{\, p \in P_0 \mid p \text{ is separable}\}, \tag{5.6}$$

$$P_5 = P_4 \cap P_1, \tag{5.7}$$

$$P_6 = P_4 \cap P_2, \tag{5.8}$$

$$P_7 = P_4 \cap P_3. \tag{5.9}$$

For $E_i \subseteq P_0$, define

$$D(E_1, ..., E_N) = \{(p_1, ..., p_N) \mid \forall i, \exists q_i \in E_i \text{ such that:}$$
$$\forall x, y \in X\ x\, p_i\, y \Leftrightarrow (x_0, x_i)\, q_i\, (y_0, y_i)\}, \tag{5.10}$$

and let $0 \leq j \leq 7$.

**Theorem 5** [28, thms. 3.9–3.16]. *Let $l \geq 2$ and let $E_1, \ldots, E_N$ be non-empty near-open subsets of $P_j$. Then $D(E_1, \ldots, E_N)$ is Arrow-inconsistent.*

As in Section 4, if we let the set of alternatives be

$$X = \mathbb{R}_+^{m + lN} \tag{5.11}$$

rather than (5.1), and if $D$ is any domain of the form given in the preceding theorems, then the following version of Arrow's theorem holds: If $f: D \to P(X)$ satisfies WP and IIA then, for some $i \in N$, we have

$$x \hat{p}_i y \Rightarrow x \hat{f}(p_1, \ldots, p_N) y \quad \forall (p_1, \ldots, p_N) \in D \tag{5.12}$$

for all $x, y \in X$ except, perhaps, when $(x_0, x_j) = 0$ for some $j \in N$.

## 6 Stochastic alternatives

We now consider an environment studied by Le Breton and Trannoy [17] – namely, the set of alternatives consisting of all distribution functions on some interval $J = [a, b]$. We let

$$X = \mathfrak{D}(J)$$
$$= \{F: J \to [0, 1] \mid F \text{ is nondecreasing and right-continuous, } F(b) = 1\},$$
$$\tag{6.1}$$

and interpret $F \in X$ as either the probability distribution of some public good $x \in J$ or as the cross-sectional distribution of some good such as wealth in a population. In the first case we assume that individuals $i \in N$ all agree that $x$ is in fact a good, so that under either interpretation of $X$ it is reasonable to assume that individuals' preferences all agree with first-order stochastic dominance. Thus if $F, G \in X$,

$$F(t) \leq G(t) \quad \text{for all } t \in J,$$
$$F(t) < G(t) \quad \text{for some } t \in J. \tag{6.2}$$

We will then write $F > G$ and assume that

$$\forall (p_1, \ldots, p_N), \quad F > G \Rightarrow F \hat{p}_i G \ \forall i \in N. \tag{6.3}$$

We also endow $X$ with the usual topology of weak convergence, in which $F_n \to F$ if and only if

$$\int g \, dF_n \to \int g \, dF \tag{6.4}$$

for all bounded continuous $g: J \to \mathbb{R}$; we assume that all individuals' preferences are continuous in this topology. The topological space $X$ is compact and metrizable, so if we denote by $P_C(X)$ the set of preferences on $X$ that are continuous in this topology, then the Kannai [16] topology on $P_C(X)$ exists (see [28]). In what follows we use the Kannai topology to define open sets, closures, and so on. If we let $P_{MC}(X)$ denote the set of preferences in $P_C(X)$ that agree with stochastic dominance as in (6.3), then one can show that the Kannai topology on $P_{MC}(X)$ coincides with the topology of closed convergence on this set.

We shall treat the set $P_{MC}(X)$ of preferences on $X$ in the same way that we analyzed the set $P_0$ in Section 3. That is, we will impose various economic assumptions on preferences in addition to monotonicity and continuity, and state theorems regarding the Arrow inconsistency of product domains formed from subsets of the resulting sets of preferences. There is a substantial literature, beginning with von Neumann and Morgenstern [31], in which authors have stated axioms of preference for stochastic alternatives and characterized the implied restrictions by providing general functional forms for value functions representing the preferences. In this section we will work directly with these functional forms; for example we define the subset $P_{EU}$ of expected utility preferences in $P_{MC}(X)$ by

$$P_{EU} = \{p \in P_{MC}(X) \mid \text{there exists a continuous strictly monotonic } u: J \to \mathbb{R}$$
$$\text{such that } \forall F, G \in X, \ F \, p \, G \Leftrightarrow \int u \, dF \geq \int u \, dG\}$$

$$(6.5)$$

without giving an axiomatic discussion of the preferences in this set. We define several other families of preferences similarly, by giving formulas for value functions $V_p(F)$ that represent typical elements of the families. Thus, for $p \in P_{EU}$ we have $V_p(F) = \int u \, dF$.

**Definitions.**

$$P_{GQ} = \{p \in P_{MC}(C) \mid V_p(F) = \int uw \, dF / \int w \, dF,$$
$$\text{where } u: J \to \mathbb{R} \text{ is continuous and increasing and}$$
$$\text{where } w: J \to \mathbb{R}_+ \text{ is continuous}\}, \qquad (6.6)$$

the set of *generalized quasilinear mean* preferences (see Chew [10]).

$$P_{AU} = \{p \in P_{MC}(X) \mid V_p(F) = \int u \, d(f(1-F)),$$
$$\text{where } u \text{ and } f \text{ are continuous and increasing and}$$
$$\text{where } f(0) = 0 \text{ and } f(1) = 1\}, \qquad (6.7)$$

the set of *anticipated utility* preferences (see Quiggin [22]).

$$P_{TM} = \{p \in P_{MC}(X) \mid V_p(F) = \int u \, dF / \int w \, dF,$$
$$\text{where } u \text{ is continuous and increasing and}$$
$$\text{where } w \text{ is continuous and positive}\}, \qquad (6.8)$$

the set of *transitive measurable utility* preferences (see Fishburn [14]).

$P_{\text{IL}} = \{p \in P_{\text{MC}}(X) \mid v = V_p(F) \text{ solves } \int u(x, v)\, dF(x) = v,$

where $u: J \times [0, 1] \to \mathbb{R}$ is continuous and increasing

in $x \in J$ and continuous and decreasing in $v \in [0, 1]\}$,

(6.9)

the set of *implicit linear utility* preferences (see Dekel [11]).

$P_{\text{DL}} = \{p \in P_{\text{MC}}(X) \mid V_p(F) = \int f(1 - F(x))\, dx, \text{ where}$

$f: [0, 1] \to \mathbb{R} \text{ is continuous and decreasing}\},$   (6.10)

the set of *dual linear* preferences (see Yaari [32]).

For $1 \le j \le 6$, we have the following theorem.

**Theorem 6** [28, thms. 4.1–4.6]. *Let $X = \mathfrak{D}(J)$ and let $P$ be any of the sets of preferences in* (6.5)–(6.10). *If $E \subseteq P$ is non-empty and near-open, then $D = E^N$ is Arrow-inconsistent. In the EU case, $P$ may be taken to include only risk-averse preferences.*

In these theorems, the topology on each $P$ should be understood to be the topology of closed convergence on $P_{\text{MC}}(X)$ relative to $P$.

In economic terms, we can think of the social choice problem in this environment as that of a committee of share holders in some corporation, all of whom agree that (stochastically) higher returns are better but may disagree in their attitudes toward risk. The disagreement may arise because shareholders may have unequal shares or unequal levels of certain wealth, and the functional forms here allow for risk preferences to change with wealth. Another interpretation could be that the individuals are behind a "veil of ignorance" in the sense of Rawls [23], and must express their preferences on the set $X$ of wealth distributions prior to realizing their own wealth as a random element $x \in J$ drawn according to $F \in X$. However, none of the analysis here applies if we assume further, as Rawls did, that individuals are perfectly risk-averse in the sense that they evaluate distributions $F$ according to

$$V_p(F) = \inf\left\{ y \mid \int_{x < y} dF(x) = 0 \right\}.$$   (6.11)

In this case of unanimity, of course, the unique SWF satisfying WP will also rank distributions according to the welfare of the ex post worst-off individual. But the Rawlsian interpretation is rather loose because we have assumed at the outset that the society is finite, whereas the interpretation of $F$ is that there exists an atomless set of individuals, the proportion of whom receiving wealth of at most $x$ is $F(x)$.

A final motivation for a stochastic public goods model is that we wish to consider stochastic alternatives in richer environments, especially the dynamic and stochastic setting of Section 8. In that framework we will use the preferences of this section as building blocks in constructing preferences on alternatives in which the infinite future is uncertain.

## 7     Infinite-horizon models

In this section we take the set of alternatives $Y$ to be

$$Y = \{(x_0, x_1, \dots) \mid x_t \in X \; \forall t\} = X^\infty, \tag{7.1}$$

where $X$ is any of the atemporal sets of alternatives in Sections 3–5. We endow $Y$ with the product topology and order this set by $>$, where

$$x > y \quad \text{if} \quad \begin{cases} x_t \geq y_t \text{ for all } t, \\ x_t > y_t \text{ for some } t. \end{cases} \tag{7.2}$$

We assume that individuals' preferences are continuous in this topology and agree with the partial ordering $>$. Letting $P_{\mathrm{MC}}(Y)$ denote the set of all such preferences, we treat $P_{\mathrm{MC}}(Y)$ in the same way as we analyzed $P_0$ and $P_{\mathrm{MC}}(X)$ in Sections 3–6; that is, we impose additional economic assumptions on preferences and state theorems regarding the Arrow-inconsistency of various product domains formed from subsets of $P_{\mathrm{MC}}(Y)$. We specialize immediately to the case where preferences are aggregative in the sense of Lucas and Stokey [19]. Such preferences have utility representations defined implicitly by the equation

$$U(x) = W(u(x_0), U(_1x)), \tag{7.3}$$

where $_1x$ is the sequence $(x_1, x_2, \dots) \in Y$, $u: X \to \mathbb{R}$ represents an *atemporal* preference in $P_{\mathrm{MC}}(X)$, and $W: \mathbb{R}^2 \to \mathbb{R}$ reflects the *intertemporal* aspects of the preference on $Y$.

We wish to construct domains of profiles of preferences on $Y$ that allow for some diversity of preference. This presents technical problems: for example, ordinally equivalent atemporal utilities $u$ may generate ordinally different aggregative preferences via (7.3), and different $u$s or $W$s may even generate different subsets of $Y$ on which the function $U$ is well-defined by (7.3). In order to minimize these difficulties and focus instead on the social welfare–theoretic issues, we restrict the sets of alternatives, utilities, and aggregators as follows:

$$X = \mathbb{R}^m_+ \quad \text{or} \quad (\mathbb{R}^l_+ - 0)^N \quad \text{or} \quad \mathbb{R}^m_+ \times (\mathbb{R}^l_+ - 0)^N, \tag{7.4}$$

$$\bar{X} = \mathbb{R}^{lN}_+ \quad \text{or} \quad \mathbb{R}^m_+ \times \mathbb{R}^{lN}_+, \tag{7.5}$$

$$Y = \{x \in X^{\infty} \,|\, \exists b \text{ s.t. } \|x_t\| \le b \; \forall t\}, \tag{7.6}$$

$$\bar{Y} = \{x \in \bar{X}^{\infty} \,|\, \exists b \text{ s.t. } \|x_t\| \le b \; \forall t\}, \tag{7.7}$$

$$\mathcal{U}_j = \{u \colon \bar{X} \to \mathbb{R} \,|\, u(0) = 0, \; u \text{ is continuous,}$$
$$\text{bounded, and represents a preference in } P_j\} \tag{7.8}$$

$$\mathcal{W} = \{W \colon \mathbb{R}_+^2 \to \mathbb{R} \,|\, W(0,0) = 0; \; W \text{ is continuous,}$$
$$\text{monotonic, and concave; and } \exists \beta \in (0,1) \text{ s.t.}$$
$$|W(u,y) - W(u,y')| \le \beta |y - y'| \; \forall (u,y,y') \ge 0\}. \tag{7.9}$$

Here we distinguish between $X$ and $\bar{X}$ and between $Y$ and $\bar{Y}$ for the same reasons as in Sections 4 and 5. We wish to have utilities well-defined on $\bar{X}$ and $\bar{Y}$ but will state our theorems with reference to the set $Y$. Also, in (7.8) we refer to the sets $P_j$ of (3.4)–(3.6), (4.6), and (5.6)–(5.9), so that $0 \le j \le 7$; but not all of these sets apply to all of the $X$s in (7.4)–(7.5) because the separability assumption of Section 5 refers only to the mixed-goods case. The boundedness conditions in (7.6)–(7.7) make the following summary of facts easy to prove by the usual contraction mapping arguments (see Boyd [8] or Lucas and Stokey [11]).

**Lemma 7.1.** *Let $W \in \mathcal{W}$ and $u \in \mathcal{U}_j$. Then there is a unique monotonic continuous $U \colon \bar{Y} \to \mathbb{R}$ satisfying (7.3) for all $x \in \bar{Y}$. Moreover, if $U_0(x) = W(u(x_0), y)$ and $U_n(x) = W(u(x_0), U_{n-1}(_1 x))$ then $\lim_n U_n(x) = U(x)$ for all $x \in \bar{Y}$ and $y \ge 0$.*

We now introduce a topology on the $\mathcal{U}_j$, defined by the metric

$$d(u, u') = \sup_{x \in \bar{X}} |u(x) - u'(x)|, \tag{7.10}$$

and we immediately point out that $u$ and $u'$ may be ordinally equivalent but different, according to (7.10). In case this is perceived as a problem, we introduce the sets of normalized utilities

$$N(\mathcal{U}_j) = \{u \in \mathcal{U}_j \,|\, u(t1) = t \; \forall t \ge 0\}, \tag{7.11}$$

restrict $d$ to (7.11), and hence obtain open sets of atemporal preferences rather than atemporal utilities. Next, for a fixed aggregator $W \in \mathcal{W}$ and a set of utilities $A \subseteq \mathcal{U}_j$ or $N(\mathcal{U}_j)$, define the set of preferences

$$P(W, A) = \{p \in P_{\mathrm{MC}}(\bar{Y}) \,|\, \exists u \in A \text{ such that } x \, p \, y \Leftrightarrow U(x) \ge U(y),$$
$$\text{where } u, W, \text{ and } U \text{ satisfy (7.3)}\}. \tag{7.12}$$

We are now ready to construct some domains of preferences and to state theorems regarding their Arrow-consistency. The next four results appear as Theorems 5.1 and 5.2 in [28].

**Theorem 7.1.**   *Let $M \geq 2$ and $X = \mathbb{R}_+^m$, and let $Y$ be given by (7.6); let $0 \leq j \leq 3$, let $W \in \mathcal{W}$, and let $A \subseteq \mathcal{U}_j$ or $N(\mathcal{U}_j)$ be non-empty and near-open. If $E_i = P(W_i, A_i)$ then $D(E_1, ..., E_N)$ is Arrow-inconsistent.*

**Theorem 7.2.**   *Let $l \geq 2$ and $X = (\mathbb{R}_+^l - 0)^N$, and let $Y$ be given by (7.6); let $0 \leq j \leq 3$, let $W_i \in \mathcal{W}$ for $i \in N$, and let $A_i \subseteq \mathcal{U}_j$ or $N(\mathcal{U}_j)$ be non-empty and near-open. If $E_i = P(W_i, A_i)$ then $D(E_1, ..., E_N)$ is Arrow-inconsistent.*

**Theorem 7.3.**   *Let $l \geq 2$ and $X = \mathbb{R}_+^m \times (\mathbb{R}_+^l - 0)^N$, and let $Y$ be given by (7.6); let $0 \leq j \leq 7$, let $W_i \in \mathcal{W}$ for $i \in N$, and let $A_i \subseteq \mathcal{U}_j$ or $N(\mathcal{U}_j)$ be non-empty and near-open. If $E_i = P(W_i, A_i)$ then $D(E_1, ..., E_N)$ is Arrow-inconsistent.*

In Theorems 7.1–7.3 the domains allow for some diversity of atemporal preferences and utilities, but the intertemporal preferences implicit in each individual's aggregator are taken as fixed. As one would expect, allowing for additional diversity of preference by admitting larger sets of aggregators $W$ will not introduce Arrow-consistency where it did not exist before. We can allow for this additional diversity by metrizing $\mathcal{W}$ with the metric

$$\delta(W, W') = \sup_{u, U \geq 0} |W(u, U) - W'(u, U)| \qquad (7.13)$$

and then considering *sets* $\Omega \subseteq \mathcal{W}$ of aggregators in constructing our domains. We summarize the analogs of Theorems 7.1–7.3 in a single statement as follows.

**Theorem 7.4.**   *In any of Theorems 7.1–7.3 replace $W$ or $W_i$ by any subsets $\Omega$ or $\Omega_i$ of $\mathcal{W}$ which are connected in the topology derived from (7.13). Then the resulting domains are Arrow-inconsistent.*

## 8    Dynamic and stochastic environments

We now extend the results of the infinite-horizon models of Section 7 to allow for uncertainty in the stream of future consumption vectors. We do so with some trepidation because the existence theory for value functionals on our space of objects of preference seems to be limited, at the moment, to the case of a single good and to certain parametric classes of functionals; whereas we would like to consider models with several goods and reasonably rich families of functionals describing the atemporal preferences, patience, risk attitudes, and intertemporal substitution propensities of the individuals. In what follows we shall consider many sets of preferences, some of which may well be empty! However, for our purposes the addition of uncertainty to the environment does not matter very much because there are enough strictly free triples in the set of *deterministic* sequences to generate dictatorship on that subset of alternatives and hence on the rest of the space.

The results of this section are notationally quite painful, so here is a verbal summary: Begin with any of the sets of atemporal and nonstochastic alternatives of Sections 3-5. Create a set of dynamic and stochastic alternatives by forming the infinite product of the atemporal alternative set, and then allowing the future stream of goods vectors to be random. Perform similar operations on any of the Arrow-inconsistent domains of Sections 3-5; that is, extend individuals' atemporal preferences to the dynamic and stochastic alternative set by introducing both aggregators and certainty equivalents. The result will be an Arrow-inconsistent set of preference profiles. The rest of the section is just a more careful statement of this summary, so the reader may well prefer to skip directly to Section 9.

We take the sets of pure outcomes to be the same as in Section 7 – namely,

$$\bar{Y} = \bar{X}^\infty, \qquad \bar{X} = \mathbb{R}_+^m \text{ or } \mathbb{R}_+^{lN} \text{ or } \mathbb{R}_+^{m+lN} \qquad (8.1)$$

However, the set of alternatives is now a set of $\bar{Z}$ satisfying:

$$\bar{Z} \text{ is homothetic to } \bar{X} \times P(\bar{Z}), \qquad (8.2)$$

where for any metric space $S$ the set $P(S)$ denotes the set of probability measures defined on the Borel subsets of $S$. Epstein and Zin [13] have shown how to identify such a set $\bar{Z}$ with a subset of $\bar{Z}_0 \times \bar{Z}_1 \times \cdots \times \bar{Z}_t \times \cdots$, where $\bar{Z}_t$ is the set of measures on $\bar{Y}$ for which all uncertainty is resolved at or before time $t$. Hence $\bar{Y}$ can be identified with $\bar{Z}_0$ and we can begin our specification of individuals' preferences by assuming that, on this set, alternatives are ranked as in Section 7. That is, there exist $u_i$, $W_i$, and $U_i$ such that, for all $x, y \in \bar{Z}_0$,

$$x \, p \, y \Leftrightarrow U_i(x_0, \delta(_1 x)) \geq U_i(y_0, \delta(_1 y)) \qquad (8.3)$$

where

$$U_i(x_0, \delta(_1 x)) = W_i((u_i(x_0), U_i(x_1, \delta(_2 x))), \qquad (8.4)$$

analogously to (7.3). Here $\delta(x) \in P(\bar{Z})$ denotes the probability measure with probability 1 concentrated on $x \in \bar{Y}$. To extend these preferences to pairs of stochastic alternatives, we assume that each individual has a *certainty equivalent functional*

$$\mu_i : \mathfrak{D}(u_i(\bar{X})) \to \mathbb{R}; \qquad (8.5)$$

that is, a function continuous in the weak convergence topology on $\mathfrak{D}(J)$ which agrees with first-order stochastic dominance, and for which

$$\mu_i(\delta(u)) = u \quad \forall u \in J. \tag{8.6}$$

Any of the value functionals in Section 6 generates a certainty equivalent functional according to

$$\mu(F) = \{u \mid V_p(\delta(u)) = V_p(F)\}$$
$$= \{u \mid \delta(u) \, \bar{p} \, F\}. \tag{8.7}$$

We can now attempt to define value functionals on all of $\bar{Z}$ by the recursive relation

$$U_i(x_0, m_1) = W_i(u_i(x_0), \mu_i(\tilde{U}_i(\tilde{x}_1, \tilde{m}_2))). \tag{8.8}$$

Here $m_1$ is a probability measure on $\bar{Z}$ and hence generates a random element $\tilde{x}_1 \in \bar{X}$ and a random measure $\tilde{m}_2$, also in $P(\bar{Z})$. Hence tomorrow's utility is random, and is converted by $\mu_i$ to a certainty equivalent level of utility, completing the recursive definition of $U_i$. The function $U_i$ is derived from $u_i$, $W_i$, and $\mu_i$ as the fixed point of the transformation $T(U_i)$ defined by (8.8). Such a fixed point is known to exist in the special cases described in Epstein and Zin [13], and may or may not exist in more general situations. When it does exist, we write $P(u, W, \mu)$ to denote the resulting preference in $P(\bar{Z})$, and denote the family of preferences

$$P(A, \Omega, M) = \{P(u, W, \mu) \mid u \in A, \ W \in \Omega, \ \mu \in M\}, \tag{8.9}$$

where $A \subseteq \mathcal{U}_j$, $\Omega \subseteq \mathcal{W}$ as in Section 7, and $M$ is any set of certainty equivalent functionals. We now summarize a large number of results in a single statement, as we did in Theorem 7.4. Theorem 8.1 refers to the set $Z$ obtained from $\bar{Z}$ by eliminating all alternatives in which any individual receives – with probability 1 – a zero allocation of private goods for every time period, and so is only trivially different from an impossibility result concerning the whole set $\bar{Z}$. We take any domain $D(E_1, ..., E_N)$ of preferences on $\bar{Y}$ covered by Theorem 7.4, and extend these sets of preferences on $\bar{Y}$ to sets of preferences on $\bar{Z}$ by allowing certainty equivalent functionals $\mu_i$ to lie in non-empty sets $M_i$ for which $U_i$ is always well-defined by (8.3)–(8.8). In the public-goods model $\bar{X} = \mathbb{R}_+^m$, we assume $m \geq 2$, $A_i = A \subseteq \mathcal{U}_j$ or $N(\mathcal{U}_j)$ for some common $A$, $0 \leq j \leq 3$, $\Omega_i = \Omega \subseteq \mathcal{W}$ for some common connected set of aggregators $\Omega$, and $M_i = M$ for some common set $M$ of certainty equivalent functionals. In the private- or mixed-goods models with $\bar{X} = \mathbb{R}_+^{Nl}$ or $\bar{X} = \mathbb{R}_+^{m+Nl}$, we require $l \geq 2$ and the same conditions as before on the $A_i, \Omega_i, M_i$, except that these can now be different for different individuals.

**Theorem 8.1.**   *Construct as just described the sets of preferences $E_i = P(A_i, \Omega_i, M_i)$ on $\bar{Z}$, and restrict these preferences to $Z$. Then*

$$D = D(E_1, \ldots, E_N)$$

*is Arrow-inconsistent.*

This rather vaguely worded result is the content of Section 6 in [28].

## 9 Conclusion

If $D$ is Arrow-consistent, then we can denote by $f_D$ some SWF with domain $D$ which satisfies WP, CT, ND, and IIA; if $D' \subseteq D$, then a natural candidate SWF with domain $D'$ is simply $f_D|_{D'} = f_{D'}$. This restricted SWF will inherit three of the four Arrow properties from $f_D$, and can fail to satisfy ND only if the shrinkage from $D$ to $D'$ systematically eliminates profiles for which some individual is *not* decisive on some pairs of alternatives. Therefore, except in contrived circumstances (see KMS [15] for an example), *smaller domains are more likely to be Arrow-consistent.* Given this observation, the results of this paper are quite surprising because the domains studied here are arbitrarily small and yet remain Arrow-inconsistent. This smallness arises because we allow for a wide variety of economic assumptions to be made on preferences, including some that are quite restrictive; and because we allow for further restrictions on preferences – restrictions of the form that would arise if the social planner had arbitrarily large finite amounts of information on individuals' preferences (i.e., the preferences lie in finite intersections of sets of the form in (3.2)). The sets of alternatives and the restrictions imposed on preferences arise naturally in economics; the regularity assumptions of near-openness, product domains, and the elimination of zero allocations of private goods are all reasonable; and the common domain assumption, required here for the pure public-goods models, can be relaxed as soon as there are private goods in the economy. With purely public goods and a small common domain of preferences, dictatorship of an individual is not necessarily a grossly inequitable arrangement; the smaller the common domain, the less anyone cares who this dictator is. But with at least one private good, dictatorship of an individual leads to grossly inequitable choice sets from any standard feasible set of allocations, since the dictator can confiscate all the private goods and, if the feasible set permits, reduce the public-goods vector in order to increase his own allocation of private goods. Hence our conclusion is that, in any reasonably rich economic model with any reasonably diverse set of admissible preference profiles, the Arrow axioms other than nondictatorship cannot be satisfied by any reasonable SWF. Therefore, in such situations social welfare functions should be allowed to violate at least one Arrow axiom other than – that is, in addition to – the unrestricted domain condition.

REFERENCES

[1]  Arrow, K. J. (1963), *Social Choice and Individual Values,* 2nd ed. New York: Wiley.
[2]  Black, D. (1948), "On the Rationale of Group Decision-Making," *Journal of Political Economy* 56: 23–34.
[3]  Blau, J. H. (1957), "The Existence of Social Welfare Functions," *Econometrica* 25: 302–13.
[4]  Border, K. (1983), "Social Welfare Functions for Economic Environments with and without the Pareto Principle," *Journal of Economic Theory* 29: 205–16.
[5]  Border, K. (1984), "An Impossibility Theorem for Spatial Models," *Public Choice* 43: 293–300.
[6]  Bordes, G., and M. Le Breton (1989), "Arrovian Theorems with Private Alternatives Domains and Selfish Individuals," *Journal of Economic Theory* 47: 257–81.
[7]  Bordes, G., and M. Le Breton (1990), "Arrovian Theorems for Economic Domains: The Case Where There Are Simultaneously Private and Public Goods," *Social Choice and Welfare* 7: 1–17.
[8]  Boyd, J. H. (1990), "Recursive Utility and the Ramsey Problem," *Journal of Economic Theory* 50: 326–45.
[9]  Campbell, D. E. (1992), *Equity, Efficiency, and Social Choice.* Oxford: Oxford University Press.
[10]  Chew, S. H. (1983), "A Generalization of the Quasilinear Mean with Applications to the Measurement of Income Inequality and Decision Theory Resolving the Allais Paradox," *Econometrica* 51: 1065–92.
[11]  Dekel, E. (1986), "Axiomatic Characterization of Preferences Under Uncertainty," *Journal of Economic Theory* 40: 304–18.
[12]  Donaldson, D., and J. A. Weymark (1988), "Social Choice in Economic Environments," *Journal of Economic Theory* 46: 291–308.
[13]  Epstein, L., and S. Zin (1989), "Substitution, Risk Aversion, and the Temporal Behaviour of Consumption and Asset Returns: A Theoretical Framework," *Econometrica* 57: 937–69.
[14]  Fishburn, P. (1983), "Transitive Measurable Utility," *Journal of Economic Theory* 31: 293–317.
[15]  Kalai, E., E. Muller, and M. Satterthwaite (1979), "Social Welfare Functions When Preferences Are Convex, Strictly Monotonic, and Continuous," *Public Choice* 34: 87–97.
[16]  Kannai, Y. (1970), "Continuity Properties of the Core of a Market," *Econometrica* 38: 791–816.
[17]  Le Breton, M., and A. Trannoy (1987), "Measures of Inequality as an Aggregation of Individual Preferences about Income Distribution: The Arrovian Case," *Journal of Economic Theory* 41: 248–65.
[18]  Le Breton, M., and J. A. Weymark (1992), "An Introduction to Arrovian Social Welfare Functions on Economic and Political Domains," discussion paper no. 91-28, Department of Economics, University of British Columbia, Vancouver.
[19]  Lucas, R., and N. Stokey (1984), "Optimal Growth with Many Consumers," *Journal of Economic Theory* 32: 139–71.

[20] Maskin, E. (1976), "Social Welfare Functions for Economics," mimeo, Department of Economics, Harvard University, Cambridge, MA.
[21] Nitzan, S. (1976), "On Linear and Lexicographic Orders, Majority Rule and Equilibrium," *International Economic Review* 17: 213-26.
[22] Quiggin, J. (1982), "A Theory of Anticipated Utility," *Journal of Economic Behavior and Organization* 3: 323-43.
[23] Rawls, J. ( 1971), *A Theory of Justice.* Cambridge, MA: Harvard University Press.
[24] Redekop, J. (1991), "Social Welfare Functions on Restricted Economic Domains," *Journal of Economic Theory* 53: 396-427.
[25] Redekop, J. (1993a), "Arrow-Inconsistent Economic Domains," *Social Choice and Welfare* 10: 107-26.
[26] Redekop, J. (1993b), "Social Welfare Functions on Parametric Domains," *Social Choice and Welfare* 10: 127-48.
[27] Redekop, J. (1993c), "The Questionnarie Topology on some Spaces of Economic Preferences," *Journal of Mathematical Economics* 22: 479-94.
[28] Redekop, J., "Arrow Theorems in Mixed Goods, Dynamic and Stochastic Environments," *Social Choice and Welfare* (to appear).
[29] Ritz, Z. (1985), "Restricted Domains, Arrow Social Welfare Functions, and Noncorruptible and Nonmanipulable Social Choice Correspondences: The Case of Private and Public Alternatives," *Journal of Economic Theory* 35: 1-18.
[30] Sen, A. K. (1970), *Collective Choice and Social Welfare.* San Francisco: Holden-Day.
[31] Von Neumann, J., and O. Morgenstern (1947), *Theory of Games and Economic Behavior,* 2nd ed. Princeton, NJ: Princeton University Press.
[32] Yaari, M. (1987), "The Dual Theory of Choice under Risk," *Econometrica* 55: 95-115.

CHAPTER 8

# Inner consistency or not inner consistency: A reformulation is the answer

*Donald G. Saari*

## 1    Introduction

The enormous attraction of social choice derives, in part, from its many conclusions that defy intuition, expectations, or even common sense. Although it seems perfectly reasonable to expect "rational decisions" from an organization of rational people, this need not happen. Here, the definition of rationality is inherited from the expected transitive actions of a person. For example, if a person prefers apple to pumpkin pie, then, when offered a choice among apple, pumpkin, and blueberry pie, we don't expect pumpkin to be selected. We might anticipate a similar inner consistency to hold for an organization. If a group prefers $c_1$ over $c_2$ with a majority vote then we don't expect $c_2$ to be selected from $\{c_1, c_2, c_3\}$; and yet, this can happen.[1] So, paraphrasing Prof. Higgins of *My Fair Lady* fame, the issue is to understand "Why can't an organization be more like a person!"

The study of inner consistency for group decision making has developed into a major research issue since it was carefully articulated in Arrow's impossibility theorem (Arrow 1951) with his axiom of independence of irrelevant alternatives (IIA). Because Arrow proved that no procedure can satisfy IIA along with some other innocuous, desirable assumptions, the ultimate goal is to find appropriate inner consistency conditions that do admit reasonable procedures. As Sen (1992) correctly cautions, in this search, inner consistency conditions must not be artificially imposed; they

This article is based on my presentation at the first meeting of the Social Choice and Welfare Society (Caen, France) 10 June 1992. Most of this article was written in May 1992, while I visited the Institutet for Framtidsstudier (Stockholm, Sweden); my thanks to my host, Ake Andersson, for his many courtesies during my stay. This research was supported, in part, by NSF grant IRI 9103180.

[1] If two voters have the ranking $c_1 > c_3 > c_2$, two have $c_3 > c_1 > c_2$, and three have $c_2 > c_3 > c_1$, then $c_1$ beats $c_2$ by $4:3$ and the plurality ranking is $c_2 > c_1 \sim c_3$ with the tally $3:2:2$.

188    Donald G. Saari

must be natural to the problem being modeled. I add a different word of warning; inner consistency conditions must be natural to the "geometry" of decision making (i.e., the informational structure) if we want acceptable possibility assertions.

The purpose of this essay is to explain why the inner consistency requirements need to be reformulated to achieve compatibility between inner consistency and existence. I then describe how to do this. There are four parts to the discussion.

1. I review why certain kinds of inner consistency conditions form an important and natural part of decision analysis.

2. I explain why the standard inner consistency conditions lead to impossibility theorems. As shown, the problem is an informational one; the traditional conditions prove to be unable to cope with the higher-dimensional nature of certain profiles. A similar argument explains why the procedures admitted by "possibility theorems" tend to be so stilted that few, if anyone, would promote their acceptance. For expositional purposes, I compare the inner consistency problem with the difficulties experienced by a resident from Abbott's *Flatland* (1952) who is trying to "see" a 3-dimensional object.

3. Once we know why the traditional inner consistency conditions cause impossible situations, the requirements can be reformulated to admit reasonable procedures. One of the three types of reformulations described here is related to the strategies a *Flatland* citizen must adopt to interpret higher-dimensional objects.

4. To show that similar consistency issues arise with other aggregation procedures, I describe conclusions from economics and statistics.

## 2    Why inner consistency?

A strong argument demonstrating the need for inner consistency requirements comes from the way we use and abuse decision and election outcomes. For instance, suppose a university department having a single open tenured position ranks the candidates as $c_1 > c_2 > \cdots > c_n$. If the top-ranked candidate, $c_1$, is unavailable, it is natural to turn to the runner-up, $c_2$. This appears to require the tacit inner consistency assumption that the group's ranking of $\{c_2, c_3, ..., c_n\}$ is the inherited $c_2 > c_3 > \cdots > c_n$. Is it? As an alternative scenario, suppose the bottom-ranked candidate, $c_n$, drops out of consideration. Her departure changes the set of candidates, so do we need a new departmental election? I know of no department, even those including well-known experts in choice theory, that would do so. Instead, they would proceed with the inner consistency assumption that $c_1$ remains top-ranked. But is she?

A second need for inner consistency conditions is to help select a procedure from among the wealth of available methods. The selection difficulty already arises with positional voting. Recall that a positional method is defined by a voting vector $\mathbf{w}^n = (w_1, w_2, \ldots, w_n = 0)$, $w_i \geq w_{i+1}$, $w_1 > 0$, where $w_j$ points are assigned to a voter's $j$th ranked candidate. The ranking of the candidates is determined by the number of points assigned to each of them where "more is better." In this manner, the voting vectors $(1, 0, 0)$ and $(2, 1, 0)$ define, respectively, the plurality vote and the Borda Count (BC).

Even though there are an infinity of choices of voting vectors, we might wonder whether it matters which $\mathbf{w}^n$ is used. It does. With three candidates, there are profiles where different rankings emerge when different positional voting vectors are used. And I don't mean minor differences, but rather rankings that directly contradict each other![2] In fact, there are profiles where – simply by changing the voting method – *seven* different rankings emerge.[3]

While it is disturbing to learn that seven different election outcomes can arise with a single three-candidate profile, this statement fails to adequately indicate the severity of the problem. For example, with just 10 candidates, there are profiles for which varying the choice of the voting method generates over 84 *million* different election rankings (Saari 1992a). The profile representing the voters' views remains fixed, but, by changing the way we decide, radically contradictory conclusions emerge. So, which of these millions of widely conflicting election outcomes best characterizes the voters' true intentions? Clearly, the choice of a procedure matters! Thus, we need to establish criteria for finding the "optimal" method.

Conditions characterizing such an optimal procedure can and should be controversial. On the other hand, it is easier to reach a consensus about the properties we want a choice procedure to avoid. For instance, common sense dictates that if the group's outcomes are the rankings $c_1 > c_2 > c_3$, $c_1 > c_2 > c_4$, $c_1 > c_3 > c_4$, and $c_2 > c_3 > c_4$ for the four triplets of four candidates, then the reversed ranking $c_4 > c_3 > c_2 > c_1$ fails to accurately represent their true views.[4] Thus, in order to limit our search to minimally acceptable procedures, we need help from inner consistency.

---

[2] The seemingly nondescript profile where 6 voters have the ranking $c_1 > c_3 > c_2$, 5 have $c_2 > c_3 > c_1$, and 4 have $c_3 > c_2 > c_1$ has the plurality ranking of $c_1 > c_2 > c_3$ and the reversed Borda ranking of $c_3 > c_2 > c_1$.

[3] Four of the rankings are strict and three involve a tie between two candidates. One such profile is described in note 2. A geometric prescription for finding the voting vectors is in Saari (1992a, 1994).

[4] This set of rankings can occur with almost all positional methods! See Section 4 or Saari (1989).

The problem is to find a realistic set of these conditions. A surprising fact is that, even with "weak" conditions where the goal is merely to avoid "bad" outcomes, the Borda Count often emerges as the only possible reasonable procedure.

## 3    What causes the impossibility conclusions?

Forty years of modern social choice theory have proved that the standard kinds of inner consistency conditions are useless, because they lead either to impossibility conclusions or to procedures that are not compatible with standard views of a democracy. These negative assertions are both profound and, often, difficult to prove. Consequently, it is surprising that the basic cause for these conclusions admits of an elementary explanation. Indeed, the central idea comes from the high-school algebra lesson showing that with $m$ equations and $n$ unknowns, $n \geq m$, we should expect an $(n-m)$-dimensional space of solutions. Solutions always exist if the $m$ equations are independent.

I illustrate the use of this algebraic fact in choice theory by explaining cycles. First, assign labels to the six ways of linearly ranking the three candidates $\{c_1, c_2, c_3\}$ according to the following table.

| Type | Ranking | Type | Ranking |
|------|---------|------|---------|
| 1 | $c_1 > c_2 > c_3$ | 4 | $c_3 > c_2 > c_1$ |
| 2 | $c_1 > c_3 > c_2$ | 5 | $c_2 > c_3 > c_1$ |
| 3 | $c_3 > c_1 > c_2$ | 6 | $c_2 > c_1 > c_3$ |

If $x_j \geq 0$, $j = 1, \ldots, 6$, denotes the fraction of all voters that are of the $j$th type, where $\mathbf{x} = (x_1, x_2, \ldots, x_6)$ is the profile, then the $\{c_1, c_2\}$ election outcome is

$$F_{c_1, c_2}(\mathbf{x}) = x_1 + x_2 + x_3 - (x_4 + x_5 + x_6) = q_{1,2},$$

where $c_1$ wins if $q_{1,2} > 0$ and $c_2$ wins if $q_{1,2} < 0$. The election outcome is determined, then, by computing $F_{c_1, c_2}(\mathbf{x}) = q_{1,2}$ and checking the sign of $q_{1,2}$. By determining who would vote for whom, the election outcome for all three pairs is

$$F_{c_1, c_2}(\mathbf{x}) = x_1 + x_2 + x_3 - x_4 - x_5 - x_6 = q_{1,2},$$
$$F_{c_2, c_3}(\mathbf{x}) = x_1 - x_2 - x_3 - x_4 + x_5 + x_6 = q_{2,3}, \qquad (1)$$
$$F_{c_3, c_1}(\mathbf{x}) = -x_1 - x_2 + x_3 + x_4 + x_5 - x_6 = q_{3,1},$$

where $c_i$ wins if $q_{i,j} > 0$ and $c_j$ wins if $q_{i,j} < 0$.

Accompanying the three equations in six unknowns is a fourth equation; the constraint equation $\sum_{j=1}^{6} x_j = 1$, requiring the sum of the fraction to equal unity. These $m = 4$ equations are independent and there are

$n = 6$ unknowns; hence, for any $\mathbf{q} = (q_{1,2}, q_{2,3}, q_{3,1})$, the system (1) admits a $6 - 4 = 2$-dimensional linear space of solutions.[5] Because the ordinal rankings are determined by the signs of the $q_{i,j}$s, and because there are no restrictions on these signs, "anything can happen." For instance, a cycle emerges if the $q_{i,j}$s are chosen to have the same sign. Thus, the traditional Condorcet cycle – defined by the profile where the voters are evenly split among the types $c_1 > c_2 > c_3$, $c_2 > c_3 > c_1$, and $c_3 > c_1 > c_2$ – is just one of an infinite number of solutions that defines a cycle where all of the $q_{i,j}$s are positive.

## 3.1    Dimensional properties of profiles

The rank (independence) condition for pairwise voting endows certain profiles with higher-dimensional properties. These properties are determined by the "different directions" defined by the level sets of the $F_{c_i, c_j}$ functions in the space of profiles.[6] Thus, if a profile is moved (i.e. modified) so that it remains on the same level set for each equation,[7] the values of the functions remain fixed. The process I use is only slightly more ambitious; a profile is moved so that it remains in the level sets for three of the four equations; namely, the values of three equations remain fixed and only the fourth changes. (This motion is equivalent to solving a series of problems where the values for three equations remain fixed and the fourth varies; solutions always exist because the equations are independent.)

To use this directional dynamic to create a cycle, start at a profile $\mathbf{x}_1$ and check the sign of $q_{1,2}$; suppose it is positive. The goal is to modify $\mathbf{x}_1$ so as to obtain a profile where $q_{2,3} > 0$, $q_{3,1} > 0$. To start, change $\mathbf{x}_1$ in a direction along the appropriate $F_{c_i, c_j}$ level sets so that only the $q_{2,3}$ value varies; keep changing until, at profile $\mathbf{x}_2$, $q_{2,3}$ is positive. Next, move from profile $\mathbf{x}_2$ in a direction so that only the $q_{3,1}$ value changes; keep moving until $q_{3,1}$ has a positive value. By construction, the final profile $\mathbf{x}_3$ defines a cycle.

The geometric description[8] of moving from $\mathbf{x}_1 \to \mathbf{x}_2 \to \mathbf{x}_3$, by changing directions (dictated by the level sets of the appropriate $F_{c_i, c_j}$ functions) in

---

[5]   A technical condition remains. To show there are solutions where all of the $x_j$s are nonnegative, start with the solution $(\frac{1}{6}, \frac{1}{6}, \ldots, \frac{1}{6})$ for the tie outcomes given by $\mathbf{q} = (0, 0, 0)$. By continuity, if the $q_{i,j}$ terms are sufficiently small in value, then solutions with positive components exist.

[6]   The fact that the level sets do not coincide, and so define different directions, is equivalent to the rank condition.

[7]   There is a 2-dimensional space of solutions, so this can be done in two dimensions.

[8]   Mathematically, the different level sets are leaves of a foliation. The change in profiles is a rough way to capture both the dimension of the foliation and the integrability conditions. Integrability would involve using another path to go from $\mathbf{x}_1$ to $\mathbf{x}_3$ and then comparing results.

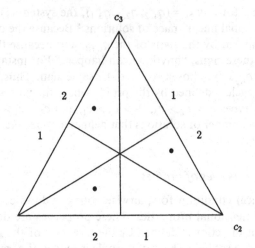

Figure 1. Condorcet triplet. The dots in the figure provide a geometric representation for the Condorcet triplet. For instance, the dot in the lower left-hand corner is in the ranking region for $c_1 > c_2 > c_3$, the one on the right-hand side represents $c_2 > c_3 > c_1$, and the last one corresponds to $c_3 > c_1 > c_2$.

a space of profiles, suggests that cycles can be identified with profiles that have higher-dimensional properties. This is correct, and to further illustrate this important point with a more intuitive argument, I provide a geometric interpretation for the Condorcet triplet.

Let each vertex of the equilateral triangle in Figure 1 be identified with a candidate. The ordinal ranking of a point in the triangle is determined by its distance to each vertex where, as in love, "closer is much better." In this manner, the six small, open, triangular regions correspond to the six linear rankings of the candidates. For instance, the region with a dot in the lower left-hand corner is closest to the $c_1$ vertex, next closest to the $c_2$ vertex, and farthest from $c_3$, so it represents the ranking $c_1 > c_2 > c_3$.

On a line, points can be separated only by an angle of 0° or 180°, but not 120°. Hence, the simplest 2-dimensional symmetrical figure that cannot be drawn on a line is each pair of three points separated by an angle of 120°. Such a configuration is given by the three dots in the figure, where the vertex of the angles is the barycentric point corresponding to $c_1 \sim c_2 \sim c_3$. Observe that the rankings associated with these three points define the Condorcet triplet. In other words, geometrically, the Condorcet triplet corresponds to the simplest 2-dimensional symmetrical configuration that cannot be faithfully represented in a 1-dimensional space.

The Condorcet profile has each alternative top-, second-, and bottom-ranked once, so no candidate has an advantage over another. Therefore, the appropriate group ranking is $c_1 \sim c_2 \sim c_3$. An immediate by-product of the 2-dimensional symmetry of the profile is that the tie ranking is the only possible outcome for a *neutral* welfare function – for example, a positional voting method. This tie outcome, however, severely disagrees with the cyclic pairwise rankings.

The reason the 2-dimensional Condorcet profile causes problems with pairwise elections is that *a pairwise election is a 1-dimensional process*. To support this assertion, notice that the tally between $c_i$ and $c_j$ is determined by the number of dots on each side of the bisecting dividing line. (As this line is equidistant from the $c_i$ and $c_j$ vertices, it is the set of points with the relative ranking $c_i \sim c_j$.) Equivalently, project the dots to the $c_i$-$c_j$ edge of the triangle, and then count how many projected dots are on each side of the midpoint of the edge. In the figure, the tally for each pair is specified near the appropriate edge. As the process just involves counting points on a line, it is clearly a 1-dimensional procedure.

What arises, then, is a severe dimensional incompatibility between what the procedure can recognize and what the profile possesses. Namely, a pairwise vote processes only a restricted portion of the 2-dimensional nature of the Condorcet triplet. When vital information about the voters' beliefs is ignored, we must expect incompatibility between the pairwise votes and the ranking of all three alternatives. Nevertheless, the almost circular and 2-dimensional symmetry of the Condorcet profile must manifest itself in some manner, and so it does – as a cycle.[9] The key observation, then, is this: *It is the ignored information that accounts for the incompatibility between the cyclic pairwise rankings and the ranking of all three alternatives.*

To see what information is lost, observe that, when $\{c_1, c_2\}$ is considered with the Condorcet profile, two voters have the ranking $c_1 > c_2$ and one voter has the ranking $c_2 > c_1$. However, as soon as there is an available third candidate, we obtain refined information about the *intensity* of these rankings. For instance, the single voter with the relative ranking $c_2 > c_1$ prefers $c_2$ so much more than $c_1$ that $c_3$ is used to separate them to arrive at $c_2 > c_3 > c_1$. On the other hand, the two voters with the ranking $c_1 > c_2$ are not as intense; the $c_1 > c_2$ ranking is kept intact with $c_3$ available because the alternative candidate is ranked either above or below the pair. Thus, when other alternatives are available, at least two types of information can be extracted about a voter's ranking of a pair: (1) the

---

[9] A similar explanation accounts for the differences between election rankings of the $\binom{n}{k}$ sets of $k$ candidates and the set of all $n$ candidates. The inconsistencies are caused by the higher-dimensional properties of profiles.

relative ranking, and (2) the intensity of this ranking. Most positional voting methods use both types of information; a pairwise majority vote ignores the intensity portion of the information set. Indeed, a pairwise cycle always indicates that the profile has a 2-dimensional symmetry component (Saari 1994), so *cycles arise only because a certain type of available information is not being used.*

Another way to think about the intensity condition is in terms of conditional probability. The probability of an event $A$ can change with the existence of another event $B$; in general, $P(A) \neq P(A \mid B)$. Similarly, we should expect changes in a ranking $c_1 > c_2$ when accompanied by the existence of alternative $c_3$. Therefore, the weak and strong intensity label can be loosely identified as a way to designate $P(c_1 > c_2 \mid c_3)$ when $c_3$ is a viable alternative.

Finally, in Saari (1994) it is argued that losing the intensity information corresponds to dropping the critical assumption that the voters have transitive preferences! If this critical assumption is ignored, we must expect all sorts of problems (such as cycles) to emerge.

## 3.2    *An extension of Arrow's theorem*

An extension of the "rank" conditions just described explains the difficulties caused by the inner consistency conditions of choice theory. In particular, with only technical modifications, the same $x_1 \to x_2 \to x_3$ profile-change argument (a weak form of the rank conditions) explains and extends Arrow's theorem.

To outline the ideas, suppose there exists a social welfare function $F$. Arrow's IIA condition requires the relative ranking of a pair of candidates to be determined by the voters' relative ranking of the same pair. In other words, to determine $F$'s relative ranking of $\{c_i, c_j\}$, we need only know each voter's relative ranking of the pair. Consequently, as true for the pairwise vote, *IIA forces us to ignore all information concerning the intensity of this comparison.* (As suggested previously, this also forces us to ignore Arrow's critical assumption that the voters have transitive preferences!) To exploit this fact, observe that the $\{c_i, c_j\}$ relative ranking of $F$ implicitly defines a function $F_{c_i, c_j}$. To be specific: For a profile $\mathbf{p}$, $F_{c_i, c_j}(\mathbf{p})$ is the $\{c_i, c_j\}$ relative ranking determined by $F(\mathbf{p})$. In this manner, the combination of IIA and the existence of $F$ defines the three functions $(F_{c_1, c_2}, F_{c_2, c_3}, F_{c_3, c_1})$.

By using only restricted information, the IIA condition allows profiles to be modified so that the ranking defined by one of the (implicitly defined) $F_{c_i, c_j}$ functions can change while the other two remain fixed. To indicate why this is so, suppose that only a voter with the relative rankings of $c_2 > c_3$ and $c_2 > c_1$ changes $\{c_1, c_3\}$ rankings (between $c_2 > c_1 > c_3$ and $c_2 > c_3 > c_1$). Then, according to IIA, only the $F_{c_3, c_1}$ outcome can vary; the $F_{c_1, c_2}$ and $F_{c_2, c_3}$ outcomes remain fixed. Thus, the IIA condition requires the level sets of the $\{F_{c_i, c_j}\}$ functions to define different directions in the profile space; that is, it forces a type of "independence of equations" condition to be satisfied. In turn, the independence indicates that a $x_1 \rightarrow x_2 \rightarrow x_3$ profile-change argument can be used to prove Arrow's theorem.[10] By adding appropriate conditions, this is the case.

The only role played by the remaining axioms is to ensure that the rank condition is satisfied. For instance, for a system of $m$ equations to have rank $j$, we need at least $j$ nonconstant equations. The $x_1 \rightarrow x_2 \rightarrow x_3$ profile-change argument requires rank 2, so we need at least two of the implicitly defined equations, $\{F_{c_i, c_j}\}$, to be nonconstant. This is the first imposed condition (which replaces the Pareto requirement). "Involvement" requires *the image set of at least two of the $F_{c_i, c_j}$ functions to contain at least two different rankings.* In practical terms, such involvement requires that for each of two pairs $\{c_i, c_j\}$, two outcomes of $F$ can be found with different relative rankings of the pair. (The term "involvement" reflects the fact that with two pairs, three candidates are listed and so all three candidates are "involved.") This condition is so weak that it is satisfied even by an $F$ which admits only the two outcomes $c_1 > c_2 > c_3$ and $c_3 > c_2 > c_1$. (For each pair $\{c_i, c_j\}$, one outcome has the relative ranking $c_i > c_j$ while the other has the relative ranking $c_j > c_i$.) It is obvious that involvement includes the traditional Pareto and unanimity assumptions as special cases; indeed, involvement trivially includes any condition that forces the image of $F$ to include at least one strict ranking and its reversal. Consequently, involvement holds even if the traditional Pareto condition is relaxed to hold only for one strict ranking and its reversal!

"Involvement" captures the $m$-equations aspect from algebra; now we turn to the $n$ unknowns. The number of unknowns cannot be less than the rank, so we need conditions that ensure there are at least two unknowns. But the "unknowns" are each voter's preferences, so the sole purpose of the remaining conditions is to ensure that at least two voters' preferences are involved. These conditions are:

(a) *two or more voters; and*
(b) *universality of domain.*

From a mathematical perspective, these conditions are minimal for a rank condition – an impossibility theorem – to hold. Indeed, these conditions, which are weaker than those used by Arrow or Wilson (1972),

---

[10] Thus we have a set-theoretic formulation of level sets from a foliation defined by the assumed existence of a welfare function.

are sufficient to obtain the sharpest possible impossibility theorem (Saari 1991).[11] The combinatorics proving the following theorem describe the $x_1 \rightarrow x_2 \rightarrow x_3$ profile change needed to create a profile with a nontransitive ranking. (From this mathematical perspective, the role of the "decisive" or "swing" voters described in the literature is to identify the points of directional changes of the profiles.)

**Theorem (Saari 1991).** *For $n = 3$ alternatives and a finite number of voters, the only procedures satisfying universality of domain, IIA, and involvement are dictatorships or antidictatorships.*

With $n > 3$ alternatives, there are many more (i.e. $\binom{n}{2}$) implicitly defined equations, so the involvement condition needs to be strengthened to "involve" more than just three candidates. A condition that is much stronger than necessary (yet weaker than any in the literature) is to require that each $F_{c_i, c_j}$ be nonconstant. Again, this exceptionally weak condition is satisfied by any welfare function with a strict ranking (say, $c_1 > c_2 > \cdots > c_n$) and its reversal ($c_n > \cdots > c_2 > c_1$) as outcomes. Again, this means that the traditional Pareto condition is far too strong; we can get away with much less.

This discussion leads to an information-theoretic interpretation for Arrow's theorem. The key fact is that IIA restricts what type of information can be used about each pair; the relative ranking is permitted, but not the intensity of the pairwise ranking. Thus, we arrive at a new interpretation: Arrow's theorem asserts that the ignored information is vital; *it is impossible to construct a procedure that systematically discards these data.* Stated in another way, if a procedure can use only 1-dimensional information (thanks to IIA) then it must be lower-dimensional in nature (e.g., it must be a procedure based on a single unknown, $n = 1$; this corresponds to a dictator or antidictator). Observe that this informational perspective toward Arrow's theorem provides a far more benign explanation than some of the draconian interpretations found in the literature.

## 3.3    Other inner consistency conditions

A similar informational interpretation explains why other inner consistency conditions – or requirements imposed on the rankings of a subset

---

[11] The word "sharpest" comes from the fact that by weakening any condition, there are ways to avoid the full rank. A possibility theorem occurs because such avoidance of the rank conditions can be used to define choice or welfare functions (see Saari 1991). Consequently, these conditions characterize the frontier between possibility and impossibility conclusions for the traditional inner consistency conditions.

of alternatives such as required by Sen's (1970) Pareto liberal or certain interpersonal relationships – either lead to impossibility assertions or admit procedures that severely restrict voter participation. The approach for proving the theorems is the same: use a combination of the consistency condition and the assumed existence of a choice or welfare function $F$ to define a set of functions $\{F_S\}$; the implicitly defined function $F_S$ specifies the ranking of the subset $S$. Traditionally, $F_S$ is related to $F$'s relative ranking of the candidates in $S$. A typical inner consistency condition is to require the $F_S$ outcome to be based on voters' relative rankings of candidates in $S$ (although this condition forces the "intensity" information to be ignored). This *projection* type of inner consistency, where the projection (restriction) to the relative rankings of $S$ is denoted by $\Pi_S$, can be represented as

$$\{\text{Profile space, all candidates}\} \xrightarrow{\ F\ } \{\text{Outcomes}\}$$

$$\downarrow \Pi_S \qquad\qquad\qquad\qquad \downarrow \Pi_S$$

$$\{\text{Relative profiles for } S\} \xrightarrow{\ F_S\ } \{\text{Outcomes for } S\}.$$

Indeed, in light of this "$m$ equation and $n$ unknown" approach, we must treat any axiom that restricts the outcomes of a subset of candidates $S$ as implicitly defining a function $F_S$. All that remains is to impose natural conditions on the implicitly defined functions so that a $x_1 \rightarrow x_2 \rightarrow x_3$ type of argument holds. With this mathematical perspective, the distinction between externally imposed conditions and inner consistency conditions becomes blurred. And even though all this is described in terms of a social welfare function, it works equally well with functionals.

With the implicitly defined $F_S$ functions, negative assertions are obtained by imposing appropriate, innocuous assumptions to guarantee that the rank conditions are satisfied. As before, these conditions can be much weaker than the usual axioms found in choice theory. Our approach is to use the "$m$ equations in $n$ unknowns" guidelines to impose axioms ensuring that the $F_S$ functions have an appropriate image set ($m$ equations) and that enough voters ($n$ unknowns) are participating. This approach offers considerable flexibility. Furthermore, modifications are obtained by relaxing the restrictions on the rank conditions. In this manner, results involving acyclicity, quasitransitivity, and so on (see e.g. Mas-Colell and Sonnenschein 1972; Brown 1975; Hansson 1976; Blau and Deb 1977; and Kelly 1978, among others) can be recaptured and significantly extended.

Again, the information-theoretic lesson about the negative assertions is that, whenever there exist more candidates than in $S$, we know (a) how each voter ranks the candidates in $S$, and (b) the various degrees of intensity of this ranking. The critical point is that inner consistency conditions force the procedure to ignore the intensity information. Consequently, an interpretation of the resulting negative theorems is that the ignored information is vital – such information must be retained.

While much of this discussion is in terms of intensity, the real message concerns the dimensional aspects of the information. Indeed, the real message is that any assumption to show that the implicitly defined functions have full rank (whether it be Pareto conditions, involvement, etc.) leads to the same kind of conclusion. This can be further illustrated with Sen's impossibility theorem. Here, terms such as "inner consistency" and "intensity" don't convey the correct tone. When discussing an individual's rights over purely personal matters, "intensity of information" almost suggests a compromise of these rights. Although the terms need to be changed, the dimensional description and conclusions remain. After all, the mere assertion that only I have the right to order $c_1$ and $c_2$ *explicitly* defines $F_{c_1, c_2}$; if all of the implicitly and explicitly defined equations admit a $x_1 \to x_2 \to x_3$ kind of scenario then an impossibility conclusion results, showing that these rights are in conflict with one another.

### 3.4    Possibility theorems and useless procedures

Of course, there are combinations of consistency conditions and profile restrictions leading to possibility theorems (see e.g. Gibbard, Hylland, and Weymark 1987; Kalai and Muller 1977; Saari 1991). However, the kinds of procedures that emerge usually are not acceptable for decision making. To understand why this is so, consider the plight of a *Flatland* artist charged with depicting a 3-dimensional object. Being limited to 2-dimensional sketches, the best she can do is to carefully position several 2-dimensional drawings so that the ordering represents the missing dimension. A sequence of drawings, for example, could represent the order of cross sections of the object. (This strategy is used to understand the fourth dimension, where the "ordering" of the cross sections is made into a film; see the fascinating work of Banchoff 1984.)

Now consider the choice procedures admitted by "possibility theorems." The trade-off in the design of profile restrictions is either to impose sufficiently severe restrictions (such as Black's single-peakedness) to eliminate the troublesome higher-dimensional profiles,[12] or to find a procedure to accommodate the higher-dimensional aspects of the remaining profiles. In the latter case, the inner consistency requirements still require the mechanism to depend on only partial information about the profiles. Thus, this mechanism design problem (with the constraint of using only lower-dimensional information) is related to the difficulties facing the

---

[12] Thus, profile restrictions are ways to reduce the number $n$ of unknowns.

*Flatland* artist. Also, the solutions for both problems are related; this is why the admitted choice procedures often require an ordered series of lower-dimensional methods – for example, a sequential dictatorship, or procedures where a dictator (a 1-dimensional procedure) reigns unless his preferences are of a certain type and then the relative ranking of a particular pair is decided by a majority vote (another 1-dimensional process) (Gibbard et al. 1987; Saari 1991), et cetera. Again, the lesson is that if a procedure must use lower-dimensional information then it must assume a lower-dimensional nature.

In summary, there are informational reasons why standard inner consistency conditions lead to impossibility situations or to unacceptable procedures. As demonstrated by the "rank" proof, the consistency conditions – by requiring vital higher-dimensional aspects of information to be ignored – permit the rankings of the parts of an outcome to be computed independently of the rankings for the other parts. Consequently, by ignoring the information that allows the outcomes of the parts to be coordinated, it is impossible to achieve a consistent whole. The lesson from the negative conclusions of these theorems, then, is that this ignored information is vital: it must be incorporated in the mechanism design process.

### 3.5    *An inner consistency problem from economics*

The importance of inner consistency issues extends beyond social choice; similar concerns arise in almost any other area that uses aggregation methods. This includes many of the procedures used in statistics, economics, and other fields. For the same informational and dimensional reasons, we must expect serious problems to arise. This can be seen with the standard supply-and-demand explanation of how prices adjust to an equilibrium.

In economics, as in voting, the 1-dimensional situation[13] provides no serious difficulties. However, once the dimension of the preference space grows by adding alternatives (equivalent to increasing the values of $m$, $n$, and $n-m$), problems arise. A dramatic illustration is the theorem of Sonnenschein (1973), Mantel (1974), and Debreu (1974; reprinted 1983), which asserts that with two or more commodities, "anything can happen" with the aggregate excess demand function. The mathematical reason for their conclusion is that the dimensional aspects of the information overwhelm the processing capabilities of the price mechanism. An important consequence of the so-called SMD theorem is that *the dynamics of the market place need not force prices to a Walrasian equilibrium*. Indeed, for similar informational reasons, it is impossible to design a finite procedure based on market pressures that always converges to an equilibrium

---

[13] This imposes a limit of two candidates for voting and one commodity for economics.

200     Donald G. Saari

(Saari 1985). Mathematically, the source of the convergence problem is that vital information about the excess demand is ignored. Thus, there is an informational, mathematical relationship between Arrow's theorem and the convergence difficulty.

The actual problems with the supply-and-demand aggregation model are much more severe. To illustrate, recall the several techniques from economics that use an inner consistency assumption about the aggregate excess demand. This includes consumer surplus (where part of the goal is to use the excess demand from each good to re-create aspects of the excess demand for the full economy), macro methods (where data for only a subset of all commodities are collected and then used to explain how the full economy fares), and even revealed preference (where if the excess demand from the full economy is known, then it is suspected that this explains the behavior of subeconomies). All of these approaches seem to require tacit inner consistency assumptions reminiscent of those used in the example about departmental rankings for the sole tenured position. What we need to know, then, is whether the assumed inner consistency holds for the excess demand function. For instance, in a simple pure exchange setting, this means we must characterize the relationship among the different excess demand functions that are created by withholding various goods from the market. The answer is that there are none: For $n$ commodities, the excess demand functions for the $2^n - (n+1)$ different subsets of two or more commodities need not be related in any manner, so indeed anything can happen (see Saari 1992b). In other words, the negative conclusions from choice theory become even more extreme in economics.

4     Reformulations of inner consistency

The informational reasons for the impossibility theorems can be exploited to formulate resolutions. In what follows, three different approaches to circumvent the difficulties are described. The first approach reformulates the IIA conditions to include the missing information. The second approach retains the restricted information of the traditional inner consistency conditions, but changes what we can expect from them. The third approach relaxes the terms of agreement of the inner consistency conditions. With all three approaches, the Borda Count often emerges as the only procedure that satisfies the new conditions.

4.1     A reformulation of IIA

The information-theoretic interpretation of Arrow's theorem shows that we cannot and must not ignore certain vital aspects of the information about the profiles. If we do, the heavy penalty is the nonexistence of any procedure that does what we want it to do. The obvious remedy is to change the inner consistency conditions so that they do include vital aspects of the previously ignored data. The following definition is one way to do so.

**Definition.** The *binary intensity IIA* condition for $n \geq 3$ candidates requires the relative ranking of each pair to be determined by each voter's relative ranking of the pair, and the intensity of this ranking to be determined by how many other candidates (but not their identities) are ranked between them.

By replacing the traditional IIA condition with the binary intensity IIA condition, the proof of Arrow's theorem fails. To see why, recall that I illustrated the key argument for the "level set" approach by showing that a voter can keep the relative rankings of $c_2 > c_3$ and $c_2 > c_1$ fixed while varying the $\{c_1, c_3\}$ ranking. However, using added information that (say) $c_2$ is intensely preferred to $c_3$, it becomes impossible to change the $\{c_1, c_3\}$ rankings; this is because the intensity information fixes the ranking as $c_2 > c_3 > c_1$. This rigidity forces the $x_1 \rightarrow x_2 \rightarrow x_3$ profile-change argument to collapse. Consequently, a possibility theorem should emerge.

**Theorem 1.** *For $n \geq 3$ candidates, there exist nondictatorial procedures satisfying unanimity, universal domain, and the binary intensity IIA condition.*

In order to motivate the intensity IIA condition, observe that there are good reasons why we should doubt the reliability of the pairwise rankings[14] when they are used to choose from among $n \geq 3$ candidates. After all, if a procedure systematically ignores important available information, then we should question its outcomes. So, for an alternative pairwise ranking method consider the *intensity-of-comparison* approach (Saari 1994) for $n = 3$ candidates, which modifies the pairwise majority vote in the following manner. In a pairwise majority vote between $\{c_i, c_j\}$, one point is assigned to the candidate a voter prefers, and zero points to the other candidate. In the intensity-of-comparison procedure there is but one difference: if a voter intensely prefers one candidate to another, then that candidate is given two points. To see the impact of this procedure, observe that all three intensity-of-comparison pairwise rankings for the Condorcet triplet

---

[14] We should likewise doubt associated procedures such as an agenda, a Condorcet winner, et cetera.

202     Donald G. Saari

are ties, as they should be when all three alternatives are available.[15] By using this intensity approach, which incorporates both types of information, we have the following special case of Theorem 1.

**Theorem 2.** *For n = 3, the intensity-of-comparison pairwise rankings always agree with the Borda rankings. For n ≥ 3, the Borda count is the only positional voting method that always satisfies Theorem 1 with the binary intensity IIA condition.*

In other words, the BC satisfies Theorem 1. Although these theorems resolve the troublesome issue raised by Arrow's theorem, the proof is trivial. The existence follows immediately from comparing the intensity of comparison approach with the BC (see also Section 4.2.2). For the uniqueness assertion, see Saari (1989), where it is shown that the BC is the only positional method whose outcomes must be related to the pairwise rankings. Indeed, Theorem 1 is close to serving as an axiomatic representation for the BC.[16] If the binary intensity IIA condition is modified to emphasize subsets of candidates other than pairs, other positional voting methods are admitted (see Section 4.2.3). However, if the intensity IIA condition is extended to all subsets of two or more candidates, then the BC is the only admissible positional method.

It remains to address Sen's concern whether this inner consistency condition is "natural." Here I use the two motivating examples of Section 2. As indicated by Theorem 2, these conditions clearly assist in the selection of a decision process. (Compare this with the traditional inner consistency conditions that offer no assistance whatsoever.) As for situations captured by the example concerning tenure (where candidates are removed), it is easy to argue that the integrity of the department's original ranking *is* preserved when candidates are eliminated from further consideration. After all, each voter's original ranking was determined when all *n* candidates were available, so this ranking captures the intensity of voter

---

[15] But, as K. Saari notes, there is a cost. When used with two candidates, the standard pairwise vote is immune from manipulation whereas the intensity approach can be manipulated. Part of the reason is that, to avoid being manipulated, a procedure needs to restrict a voter's options to a single dimension. This can be done by using behavioral assumptions, profile restrictions, or whatever. By including the intensity information, the single-dimensional aspect is lost. What we see is a trade-off between a procedure avoiding manipulation and providing outcomes that are reasonable. Compare this with the usual approach, which, unfortunately, appears to place almost all weight on the manipulation issue to the exclusion of matters involving outcome integrity.

[16] By adding conditions such as anonymity, neutrality, and a couple of others, the conditions of Theorem 2 do characterize the BC; see Saari (1990b).

preferences for the rankings of the different subsets of candidates. However, as Theorem 2 and the comment following show, this argument has validity if and only if the positional voting ranking is determined by the Borda Count.

## 4.2    A reformulation with standard information

The intensity IIA condition may suffice for situations where candidates are removed from an original list, but it is inappropriate for settings where candidates are added. In the former case, the rankings of subsets use the intensity comparisons based on alternatives that are available and truly being considered. In the latter case, we don't know who the viable alternatives are, so the intensity information is unavailable. Therefore, we need to understand how to use inner consistency conditions based on the traditional kind of restricted information.

To motivate this more complicated problem, observe that the difficulties generated by traditional inner consistency conditions can be compared with the frustrations of an art critic from *Flatland* trying to judge a sculpture. The myopic, dimensional limitations of the *Flatland* critic frustrate her attempts to "see" a 3-dimensional sculpture; all she can observe are the projected shadows. But, if she is clever, she can better understand the object by combining information about the projections taken from different perspectives. Of course, a faithful representation of the sculpture with all of its subtleties and nuances may be impossible – after all, vital information has been lost. On the other hand, she can obtain some reliable (albeit limited) insight and understanding of the sculpture.

A similar resolution applies to choice theory. When we try to use the standard inner consistency conditions, we end up sharing the dimensional frustrations of a *Flatland* citizen. The problem is that we must use the restrictive, lower-dimensional information to analyze a higher-dimensional object. So, instead of rigidly requiring total acceptance of the information coming from each single projection, perhaps we should combine the accumulated information gained from different perspectives. Namely, the inner consistency conditions should be based on the combination of the rankings of several subsets of candidates, rather than just a single subset. I show how this can be done.

### 4.2.1    Lower rank conditions
If impossibility results are obtained via full rank conditions, then possibility theorems must be associated with lower rank situations. The ideas are illustrated with positional voting methods. With $n \geq 3$ candidates, there

are $2^n - (n+1)$ subsets of two or more candidates. List them as $S_1, S_2, ...,$ $S_{2^n-(n+1)}$. For each subset, assign a positional voting method to tally the ballots; this list defines the *system voting vector*

$$W^n = (w^1, w^2, ..., w^{2^n-(n+1)})$$

where $w^j$ is the voting vector used with the subset of candidates $S_j$, $j = 1, ..., 2^n - (n+1)$. With $n$ candidates, there are $n!$ linear rankings, so there are $n!$ voter types. Following the lead of the discussion of cycles, if $x_i$ represents the fraction of all voters of the $i$th type, $i = 1, ..., n!$, then there is an algebraic equation representing each candidate's tally for each subset of candidates. (The coefficients are determined by the assigned positional voting method.)

The equations describing the election tallies and the constraint equation $\sum_{i=1}^{n!} x_i = 1$ define a system of $m$ equations in $n!$ unknowns where $n! \geq m$ (equality occurs if and only if $n = 2, 3$). Thus we must expect, in general, the maximal rank condition to be satisfied; it is, and so for most positional election procedures, "anything can happen."

**Theorem** (Saari 1989, 1990b). *With the exception of an algebraic set $\alpha^n$, the system voting vector $W^n$ admits a full rank for the system of equations. Thus, for each of the $2^n - (n+1)$ subsets of candidates, choose any ranking of the candidates. There then exists a profile such that, for each subset of candidates, the selected ranking is the sincere election ranking.*

Thus, there exists a profile such that the plurality ranking of the $n$ candidates is $c_1 > c_2 > \cdots > c_n$ while the plurality ranking of each subset of candidates is the appropriate restriction of the reversed ranking $c_n > c_{n-1} > \cdots > c_1$. (This example illustrates why the inner consistency conditions assumed by many departments, as described in the tenure example of Section 2, are false – at least if the candidates are plurality ranked.) It can also be that the ranking of all pairs of candidates is based on the natural restriction of $c_1 > c_2 > \cdots > c_n$, the plurality ranking of all triplets is based on $c_2 > c_3 > \cdots > c_n > c_1$, the plurality rankings of all sets of four candidates is based on $c_3 > c_4 > \cdots > c_n > c_1 > c_2$, and so forth.

### 4.2.2  Inner consistency of positional voting
The critical set $\alpha^n$ identifies all system voting vectors that offer relief from all possible election paradoxes. Therefore, $\alpha^n$ contains all of the positional voting procedures that allow some sort of an inner consistency relationship. The insight gained about these relationships leads to a reformulation of more abstract inner consistency conditions.

To characterize the system vectors in $\alpha^n$, help comes again from elementary algebra. If a system of $m$ equations in $n \geq m$ unknowns fails to have the full rank $m$, it is because at least one of the equations is a linear combination of the others. This statement can be unscrambled to prove that *the only way a system voting vector $W^n$ admits inner consistency relationships is if the voting vector $w^k$ for $S_k$ is a linear expression of the voting vectors assigned to particular subsets of candidates from $S_k$.* While precise statements are left to the references (Saari 1992c, 1993), what follows indicates the types of inner consistency conditions that are feasible.

In order to see what can happen, start with the pairwise majority vote and $n = 3$ candidates. A voter with the ranking $c_1 > c_2 > c_3$ assigns points to the candidates in the following manner.

|             | $\{c_1\}$ | $\{c_2\}$ | $\{c_3\}$ |
|-------------|-----------|-----------|-----------|
| $\{c_1, c_2\}$ | 1         | 0         |           |
| $\{c_1, c_3\}$ | 1         |           | 0         |
| $\{c_2, c_3\}$ |           | 1         | 0         |
| Totals      | 2         | 1         | 0         |

Observe that the totals define the Borda vector $(2, 1, 0)$. Consequently, by using the Borda Count (BC), this voter provides each candidate the same number of points as in the three pairwise elections. (Notice that with $(2, 1, 0)$, the differential of points assigned to candidates in a pair agree with those used in the intensity-of-comparison approach.) The same relationship occurs for any value of $n$, so this dependency on $(1, 0)$ will be denoted by $w^n((1, 0)) = (n - 1, n - 2, ..., 0)$.

A common scalar multiple (unity) of $(1, 0)$ is used for each subset of candidates in the summation of the preceding table and so, because of neutrality, the point assignment assertion holds for any strict ranking of the candidates. Thus, a voter with the ranking of (say) $c_3 > c_1 > c_2$ assigns each candidate – via the BC – the same number of points as with the three pairwise elections. Therefore, by knowing the tallies for the pairwise elections, we can find the Borda outcome by adding the tallies; as done in the following table.

|             | $\{c_1\}$ | $\{c_2\}$ | $\{c_3\}$ |
|-------------|-----------|-----------|-----------|
| $\{c_1, c_2\}$ | 16        | 14        |           |
| $\{c_1, c_3\}$ | 17        |           | 13        |
| $\{c_2, c_3\}$ |           | 21        | 9         |
| Borda       | 33        | 35        | 22        |

This summation relationship means, then, that the algebraic equations for each candidate's BC tally is the sum of the algebraic equations for the candidate's pairwise tallies. These equations are linearly related, so we must expect lower rank conditions to prevail. With the lower rank, the "anything can happen" assertion is replaced with election relationships forcing certain inner consistency conditions to be satisfied.

Similarly, in more abstract settings, impossibility theorems are avoided with lower rank conditions for the implicitly defined set of equations. Traditional inner consistency conditions assume a "trickle down" philosophy, as indicated by the projection diagram. But, as dramatically demonstrated by the impossibility theorems, the information that trickles down is insufficient to be of any practical use. Consequently, we should emphasize what happens with the subsets of candidates and build up from this base. That is, we should use the procedures assigned to specified subsets of candidates to devise a procedure for the set of all candidates; in this manner, inner consistency conditions can be satisfied. Namely, if the designated subsets are $S_1, S_2, ..., S_\beta$ and if a procedure for the set of all candidates can be represented as a composite function

$$F = F(F_{S_1}, F_{S_2}, ..., F_{S_\beta}), \tag{2}$$

then we can expect consistency conditions to emerge.

### 4.2.3 *Realistic inner consistency conditions*
The kinds of inner consistency relationships admitted by the summation representation for the BC are relatively easy to derive. For instance, a Condorcet winner ($c_1$ in the above table) receives over half of the vote in each of her pairwise contests. She is involved in two of the three pairwise elections, so she must receive over $1/3$ (over $1/n$ for $n$-candidate elections) of all points cast over all pairwise elections. This $1/3$ lower bound endows her with more than the average number of BC points, so she is protected from being BC bottom-ranked; however, as the preceding table shows, she need not be BC top-ranked.[17] Similarly, a Condorcet loser ($c_3$ in the table) must receive less than $1/3$ of all votes cast (in general, less than $1/n$), so she cannot be BC top-ranked and she must be ranked below the Condorcet winner. Incidentally, for $n = 3$ candidates, the BC is the only positional method that admits any of these election relationships. In

---

[17] It is not uncommon for experts in choice theory to view the difference in rankings to be a flaw of the Borda Count. Recall, however, that the Condorcet winner is determined by using only limited information about the profile. In this way it is possible to argue (Saari 1994) that, in fact, the disagreement in the rankings underscores a serious weakness of the Condorcet winner.

general, if some sort of inner consistency between the pairs and the set of all $n$ candidates is needed, only the BC can comply; *no other* system vectors satisfy any pairwise ordinal inner consistency condition (Saari 1990b). The BC properties indicate a realistic type of inner consistency conditions. They may not be as strong or restrictive as desired, but they indicate what is possible. The trade-off is between using more stringent consistency conditions but ending up with stilted procedures (at best), or adopting the more realistic conditions offered here and being rewarded with the existence of realistic procedures. In other words, in designing inner consistency conditions that permit reasonable possibility assertions, we have the same limitations as our *Flatland* art critic. In both cases, the lower-dimensional information cannot faithfully reconstruct a higher-dimensional object, so a realistic approach is to do what is possible.

These conditions extend to more abstract settings. For instance, the main tool used in the derivation of the BC properties was the monotonicity of the summation process. Therefore, if $F$ in equation (2) has appropriate monotonic properties, then it probably satisfies relationships similar to those for the BC. Following is a partial list of the kinds of conditions that can be used both with positional voting and more abstract settings.

1. If a candidate is top-ranked in all $k$-candidate subsets, then she cannot be bottom-ranked in the full set of $n > k$ candidates.
2. If all elections of $k$ candidates end in a complete tie, then so does the election of all $n$ candidates.
3. If a candidate is bottom-ranked in all $k$-candidate subsets, then she cannot be top-ranked in the full set of $n > k$ candidates.

Inner consistency conditions of the type just listed lead to existence assertions (Saari 1990b, 1992c, 1993) with reasonable procedures other than the BC.[18] Moreover, there are an infinite number of positional voting methods that join the BC in admitting the more general (i.e., $k > 2$) setting. (However, the BC admits more election relationships – it satisfies a wider variety of inner consistency conditions – than any other positional voting method; see Saari 1990b.) To see how other procedures may be constructed, suppose $k = 3$ and $n = 4$. The following table describes how a voter with the ranking $c_1 > c_2 > c_3 > c_4$ assigns points to each candidate over the four sets of triplets using the voting vector $\mathbf{w}^3 = (w_1, w_2, 0)$.

---

[18] For example, Black's (1958) procedure chooses the Condorcet winner when one exists; otherwise it selects the BC top-ranked candidate. Thus, this procedure satisfies this kind of inner consistency condition.

|  | $\{c_1\}$ | $\{c_2\}$ | $\{c_3\}$ | $\{c_4\}$ |
|---|---|---|---|---|
| $\{c_1,c_2,c_3\}$ | $w_1$ | $w_2$ | 0 | |
| $\{c_1,c_2,c_4\}$ | $w_1$ | $w_2$ | | 0 |
| $\{c_1,c_3,c_4\}$ | $w_1$ | | $w_2$ | 0 |
| $\{c_2,c_3,c_4\}$ | | $w_1$ | $w_2$ | 0 |
| Totals | $3w_1$ | $w_1+2w_2$ | $2w_2$ | 0 |

From this table and neutrality, we should suspect that if

$$\mathbf{w}^4(\mathbf{w}^3) = (3w_1, w_1+2w_2, 2w_2, 0)$$

is used with the four-candidate set, then there exist election relationships among the triplets and the set of all four candidates. These relationships do exist: they are the inner consistency conditions listed before the preceding paragraph. This is because the tally for the $\mathbf{w}^4(\mathbf{w}^3)$ election is obtained by adding up the tallies for the four three-candidate elections. For instance, if $(1,0,0)$ (the plurality election) is used with the three-candidate elections, leading to the following table, then the totals give each candidate's tally in the set of four candidates when tallied with $\mathbf{w}^4((1,0,0)) = (3,1,0,0)$.

|  | $\{c_1\}$ | $\{c_2\}$ | $\{c_3\}$ | $\{c_4\}$ |
|---|---|---|---|---|
| $\{c_1,c_2,c_3\}$ | 14 | 13 | 12 | |
| $\{c_1,c_2,c_4\}$ | 14 | 13 | | 12 |
| $\{c_1,c_3,c_4\}$ | 14 | | 13 | 12 |
| $\{c_2,c_3,c_4\}$ | | 20 | 19 | 0 |
| Totals | 42 | 46 | 44 | 24 |

Thus, if a candidate is top-ranked in all triplets ($c_1$ in the preceding table), she cannot be bottom-ranked in the four-candidate set (she is ranked next-to-bottom in the table). Likewise, a candidate who is bottom-ranked in all triplets cannot be top-ranked in the set of all candidates. For different values of $k$ and $n$, a similar relationship occurs. (However, there can be surprises; there are choices of voting vectors where a Condorcet loser can have an advantage over a Condorcet winner. See Saari 1992c for details.)

There are other inner consistency conditions that allow existence, but they tend to have the same flavor. Instead of being able to assert who wins when a particular candidate is top-ranked in certain subsets of candidates, the best we can do is state what horrible fate she avoids. But, if we must ignore the intensity information, this kind of condition is the best we can and should expect.

Returning to Sen's concern of whether these inner consistency conditions are natural, observe that they provide guidance in selecting a decision procedure; again, the BC comes out on top. Next, consider those situations characterized by the tenure example. Remember, the motivation for these inner consistency conditions is the case where a candidate is added to a list, not removed from it. Now, if a new candidate becomes available, a department may or may not need to hold another election. In practical terms, the department would be inclined to hold an election only if the new candidate is top-ranked when compared with other candidates or with several subsets of other candidates. In other words, if the listed inner consistency conditions are satisfied, we might expect the need for a new departmental ranking. It now is trivial to collect these observations as a theorem.

## 4.3    Relaxed standards of acceptance

To motivate a third approach, consider the departmental election if the initial ranking is $c_1 > c_2 > \cdots > c_n$ and $c_n$ withdraws. One reason we don't hold another election is our expectation that $c_1$ *probably* remains top-ranked. This suggests that the absolute inner consistency condition could be replaced with a probabilistic one. Namely, instead of the requirement "if $c_1 > c_2 > c_3 > \cdots > c_n$, then it must be that $c_2 > c_3 > \cdots > c_n$," we can require this outcome to be "likely." This changes the emphasis – from a futile search for an absolute projection condition – to a "next best, but possible" search for the procedure maximizing the probability that the specified inner consistency condition holds. Here there is a wide choice of possible solutions; in fact, different answers can emerge when different assumptions are made about the probability distributions of profiles (see Saari 1990a).

Although a reformulation of inner consistency was not the motivation of the following authors, important work in this direction has been done for positional voting methods. In particular, for $n = 3$ candidates, see the seminal work of Fishburn and Gehrlein (1982). For a more encompassing contribution that allows more general choices of probability distributions and considers all $n \geq 3$ candidates, see Van Newenhizen's paper (1992). The thrust of these results is that over the space of all profiles and with a neutral probability distribution, the BC maximizes the *likelihood* that the traditional inner consistency conditions are satisfied.

Upon reflection, the conclusion must be expected. The BC is the sum of the outcomes of the pairwise elections, so its ranking must closely reflect these pairwise conclusions. For similar reasons, a related probability statement holds for inner consistency conditions relating the outcome of a

$w^n(w^k)$ election of $n$ candidates and the $\binom{n}{k}$ elections of $k$-candidate subsets tallied with $w^k$. However, the answer comparing more general classes of choice procedures (such as runoffs, etc.) remains open.

## 4.4     Statistics

As a related inner consistency example from another area, consider those nonparametric methods from statistics that rank alternatives. As an example, suppose we are to rank three steel firms based on the quality of samples of their products. Among the many available techniques, one of the better known procedures is the Kruskal–Wallis test (see almost any textbook on probability and statistics). Now, if one firm withdraws from the comparison, the data remaining from the first two firms are used to rank the pair. The inner consistency condition here concerns understanding how the ranking of the two firms relates to their relative ranking among all three firms.

For the same informational reasons that plague choice theory, it turns out that no procedure always renders a faithful comparison. In fact, as Haunsperger (1992) shows by considering the inner consistency requirements, the Kruskal–Wallis test has many more problems and difficulties than previously suspected. This result suggests that statistical ranking procedures should be compared in terms of the inner consistency conditions they satisfy. By doing so, as also shown by Haunsperger, the optimal method is the Kruskal–Wallis test; it satisfies all of the inner consistency conditions that other procedures satisfy as well as a wide variety of others.

## 5     Summary

Traditional inner consistency conditions force a procedure to ignore important aspects of the available information. Viewed from this perspective, it is not surprising that impossibility theorems emerge. However, these defects can be remedied by creating inner consistency conditions of the type that admit possibility theorems, and/or by considering the likelihood that inner consistency conditions are satisfied. It is interesting that the Borda Count is the one procedure that tends to satisfy all the new classes of inner consistency conditions.

### REFERENCES

Abbott, E. A. (1952), *Flatland; A Romance of Many Dimensions,* 6th ed. New York: Dover.

Arrow, K. J. (1951), *Social Choice and Individual Values.* New York: Wiley (second edition, 1963).

Banchoff, T. (1984), "Differential Geometry and Computer Graphics," in W. Jager, J. Moser, and R. Remmert (eds.), *Perspectives in Mathematics*. Boston: Birkhäuser, pp. 43–60.

Black, D. (1958), *The Theory of Committees and Elections*. Cambridge: Cambridge University Press.

Blau, J. H., and R. Deb (1977), "Social Decision Functions and Veto," *Econometrica* 45: 871-9.

Brown, D. J. (1975), "Aggregation of Preferences," *Quarterly Journal of Economics* 89: 456-69.

Debreu, G. (1983), *Mathematical Economics. Twenty Papers of Gerard Debreu*. Cambridge: Cambridge University Press.

Fishburn, P., and W. Gehrlein (1982), "Borda's Rule, Positional Voting, and Condorcet's Simple Majority Principle," *Public Choice* 28: 79-88.

Gibbard, A., A. Hylland, and J. A. Weymark (1987), "Arrow's Theorem with a Fixed Feasible Alternative," *Social Choice and Welfare* 4: 105-15.

Hansson, B. (1976), "The Existence of Group Preferences," *Public Choice* 28: 89-98.

Haunsperger, D. (1992), "Dictionaries of Paradoxes for Statistical Tests on *k* Samples, *Journal of the American Statistical Association* 87: 149-55.

Kalai, E., and E. Muller (1977), "Characterization of Domains Admitting Nondictatorial Social Welfare Functions and Nonmanipulable Voting Procedures," *Journal of Economic Theory* 16: 457-69.

Kelly, J. (1978), *Arrow Impossibility Theorems*. New York: Academic Press.

Mantel, R. (1974), "On the Characterization of the Aggregate Excess Demand," *Journal of Economic Theory* 7: 348-53.

Mas-Colell, A., and H. Sonnenschein (1972), "General Possibility Theorem for Group Decisions," *Review of Economics Studies* 39: 185-92.

Saari, D. G. (1985), "Iterative Price Mechanisms," *Econometrica* 53: 1117-33.

  (1989), "A Dictionary for Voting Paradoxes," *Journal of Economic Theory* 48: 443-75.

  (1990a), "Susceptibility to Manipulation," *Public Choice* 64: 21-41.

  (1990b), "The Borda Dictionary," *Social Choice and Welfare* 7: 279-317.

  (1991), "Calculus and Extensions of Arrow's Theorem," *Journal of Mathematical Economics* 20: 271-306.

  (1992a), "Millions of Rankings from a Single Profile," *Social Choice and Welfare* 9: 277-306.

  (1992b), "Aggregate Excess Demand Function and Other Aggregation Processes," *Economic Theory* 2: 359-88.

  (1992c), "Symmetry Extensions of Neutrality. I. Advantage to the Condorcet Loser," *Social Choice and Welfare* 9: 307-36.

  (1993), "Symmetry Extensions of Neutrality. II. Partial Ordering of Dictionaries," *Social Choice and Welfare* 10: 301-34.

  (1994), *Geometry of Voting*. New York: Springer.

Sen, A. (1970), "The Impossibility of a Paretian Liberal," *Journal of Political Economy* 72: 152-7.

  (1992), "Internal Consistency and Social Choice, Version 2," Mimeo notes prepared for the June 1992 meeting of the Social Choice and Welfare Society (Caen, France).

Sonnenschein, H. (1973), "Do Walras' Identity and Continuity Characterize the Class of Community Excess Demand Functions," *Journal of Economic Theory* 6: 345-54.

Van Newenhizen, J. (1992), "The Borda Method Is Most Likely to Respect the Condorcet Principle," *Economic Theory* 2: 69-83.

Wilson, R. (1972), "Social Choice Theory without the Pareto Principle," *Journal of Economic Theory* 5: 478-86.

CHAPTER 9

# Existence of a smooth social choice functor

*Norman J. Schofield*

## 1    Introduction

The fundamental problem in social choice concerns the existence of a welfare function $\sigma$ that maps a profile $P = (P_1, \ldots, P_n)$ of preferences for the society $N$ to a social preference $\sigma(P)$, and which preserves certain normative and efficiency properties. In recent years there has been much examination of the structure of voting rules when the preferences are defined on some policy space $W$, usually assumed to be a compact convex subset of Euclidean space $\mathbb{R}^w$. In such a context it is known that any voting rule $\mathfrak{D}$ without vetoers will generally be badly behaved. In particular, the choice for the social preference, $\sigma_{\mathfrak{D}}(P)$, will "nearly always" be empty and voting cycles will go "almost everywhere." Such a social preference will violate the natural efficiency property that social outcomes belong to the Pareto set.

These instability results have been based on genericity arguments using the topological structure of the space of smooth utility functions. If we denote the space of smooth utility profiles on the space $W$ by $U(W)^N$, then a property $\Psi$ of $\sigma_{\mathfrak{D}}$ is called *generic* if and only if (hereafter "iff") it is true of an open dense set of profiles within the space $U(W)^N$. Section 2 of this paper reviews previous results showing that two properties of a voting rule $\sigma_{\mathfrak{D}}$ are generically true. Depending on the dimension of the space, the choice of $\sigma_{\mathfrak{D}}$ is generically empty and $\sigma_{\mathfrak{D}}$ voting cycles are generically dense. In this section, four propositions based on earlier work are presented without proof. A classification theorem on the generic properties of a smooth voting rule is also presented. In Section 3 an equilibrium notion known as the *heart* $\mathcal{H}_{\mathfrak{D}}$ of the voting rule $\mathfrak{D}$ is defined. The heart is a correspondence $\mathcal{H}_{\mathfrak{D}}$ from $U(W)^N$ to $W$. Essentially $\mathcal{H}_{\mathfrak{D}}$ imposes a local

With thanks to David Austen-Smith, Jeffrey Banks, Michel Le Breton, Craig Tovey, and an anonymous referee. This chapter is based on work supported by NSF grant SES-88-20845.

version of efficiency on the behavior of coalitions. Although cycles may still be possible, they are restricted to the Pareto set (at least when the underlying preferences satisfy a weak convexity property). The definitions are quite general and are valid for $W$ a smooth manifold. There is an obstruction, defined in terms of the Euler characteristic of $W$, for the non-emptiness of $\mathfrak{IC}_{\mathfrak{D}}$. Call $W$ a *Fan manifold* iff $\mathfrak{IC}_{\mathfrak{D}}(u)$ is non-empty for any smooth profile $u \in U(W)^N$. In particular, if $W$ is a compact and convex subspace of a finite-dimensional topological vector space then it is a Fan manifold, and in this case is called a Fan space. We also show that $\mathfrak{IC}_{\mathfrak{D}}$ is "lower hemicontinuous" on a (topological) subspace $X(W)^N$ of $U(W)^N$. Here $X(W)^N$ comprises all smooth, locally stable, utility profiles. For example, if each utility function $u_i$ is "single-peaked" in the sense that it has a unique critical point that is nondegenerate and a global maximum, then the profile belongs to $X(W)^N$.

Section 4 develops the notion of a heart of a social choice rule. Instead of defining $\mathfrak{IC}_{\mathfrak{D}}(u)$ for a utility profile, it is shown that $\mathfrak{IC}_{\mathfrak{D}}(h)$ can be defined for a preference profile $h$. In particular if $u, u'$ are two smooth utility profiles whose individual components are locally stable and which define (in an appropriate sense) the same preference profile, then $\mathfrak{IC}_{\mathfrak{D}}(u) = \mathfrak{IC}_{\mathfrak{D}}(u')$. In other words, we may define $h$ to be the equivalence class $[u] = [u']$ and write $\mathfrak{IC}_{\mathfrak{D}}(h) = \mathfrak{IC}_{\mathfrak{D}}(u)$, et cetera. We say that $\mathfrak{IC}_{\mathfrak{D}}$ *factors through* a space $\mathfrak{I}(W)^N$ of smooth locally stable preference profiles. With this domain, $\mathfrak{IC}_{\mathfrak{D}}$ is again shown to be lower hemicontinuous. We use the terminology of categories, functors, and commutative diagrams (Spanier 1966). Thus if $\mathfrak{IC}_{\mathfrak{D}}: U(W)^N \to 2(W)$ is a correspondence for each Fan manifold $W$ (where $2(W)$ is the power set of $W$)), then we say $\mathfrak{IC}_{\mathfrak{D}}$ has a *factorization* through $\mathfrak{I}(W)^N$ iff there is a commutative diagram as shown in Diagram 1. Here $h^N$ takes a utility profile $u$ to a preference profile $h^N(u)$ and $\mathfrak{IC}_{\mathfrak{D}}(u) = \mathfrak{IC}_{\mathfrak{D}}(h^N(u))$. $\mathfrak{IC}_{\mathfrak{D}}$ is a functor, and the object $\{U(W)^N: W$ is a manifold$\}$ is a category.

The fundamental goal of Section 4 can be expressed in the following way. Consider an arbitrary welfare function $\sigma$ satisfying appropriate normative conditions. The heart $\mathfrak{IC}_{\sigma}$ defined by $\sigma$ will be a correspondence from $\mathfrak{I}(W)^N$ to $W$, which under general conditions will be non-empty, Paretian, and lower hemicontinuous. If $\mathfrak{IC}_{\sigma}$ admits a continuous selection $g_{\sigma}$, then there is a social choice *function* $g_{\sigma}: \mathfrak{I}(W)^N \to W$ which has desirable continuity and Pareto properties. We may say that the heart is a general equilibrium notion that in some sense solves the social choice problem for an appropriate domain of preferences.

Section 5 examines this possibility when preferences are Euclidean. That is, each individual $i$ has a unique bliss point $x_i$; preferences are defined in terms of the distance from $x_i$. With this restriction we may identify a

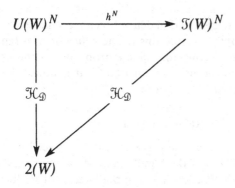

Diagram 1

preference profile with a vector $(x_1, ..., x_n) \in W^N$ of bliss points. In this case $\mathcal{K}_\mathfrak{D}: W^N \to 2(W)$ is again non-empty, Paretian, and lower hemicontinuous (with respect to the Euclidean topology on $W^N$).

Section 6 considers the case of an infinite electorate (with Euclidean preferences) distributed by a density function $f$ on a Fan space $W$. It is known from earlier work that if $W$ is the closed ball $B$ and if $f$ is spherically symmetric around the center of $B$, then the choice under "plurality" rule is non-empty (Arrow 1969). More generally, Schofield and Tovey (1992) have shown that if $f$ is weakly symmetric in some sense and if samples of size $n$ are independently obtained from $f$, then the probability of existence of a plurality-rule equilibrium approaches 1 as $n$ approaches infinity. In the case where the plurality-rule equilibrium is empty, the *yolk* (McKelvey 1986) has been proposed as a useful geometric indicator of the structure of the voting rule. In particular, the yolk belongs to an equilibrium set called the *uncovered set*. In an example discussed in Section 6, the heart is defined by three envelope curves that are tangential to the yolk boundary. This suggests that there is an intimate geometric relationship between the yolk and the heart.

Finally, Section 7 briefly outlines how the concept of the heart may be used to model multiparty competition. (See Schofield 1993a,b for a further elaboration.) The basic idea is that parties transmit messages to an electorate and that these determine the policy options and post-election party strengths. If political negotiations are determined by a continuous selection from the heart, then there may exist a (mixed strategy) Nash equilibrium in the choice of party messages. Recently Schofield and Parks (1993) have shown the existence of pure strategy Nash equilibria in a simplified version of this model.

The concept of the heart gives a formal solution to the existence of a continuous, Paretian social choice function defined on a reasonable class of preference profiles. Attempts to apply this to the behavior of a representative democracy require solving formidable problems for the existence of Nash equilibria and incentive compatibility. It is hoped that these questions can be addressed in later work.

## 2    Choice and cycle set of a preference field

Let $W$ be a smooth manifold of dimension $w = \dim(W)$, and let $TW$ be the tangent bundle with $\Pi: TW \to W$ the bundle map. At a point $x \in W$, $\Pi^{-1}(x)$ is the tangent space, $T_x W$, at $x$. If $x$ is in the interior of $W$, then $T_x W$ is isomorphic to $\mathbb{R}^w$. For a boundary point $x \in \partial W$, $T_x W$ is isomorphic to a closed half-space of $\mathbb{R}^w$. We shall simply write $T_x W \simeq \mathbb{R}^w$, noting how boundary points are treated. A point in $\Pi^{-1}(x)$ is called a *tangent vector* at $x$. The tangent bundle is locally trivial in the sense that, for a neighborhood $V$ of $x$, $\Pi^{-1}(V) \simeq V \times \mathbb{R}^w$. If $u: W \to \mathbb{R}$ is a smooth function then the differential $du(x)$ of $u$ at $x$ is a linear function $du(x): \Pi^{-1}(x) \to \mathbb{R}$. If $W \subset \mathbb{R}^w$ then $du$ is a continuous function $du: W \to L(\mathbb{R}^w, \mathbb{R})$, where $L(\mathbb{R}^w, \mathbb{R})$ is the space of linear functions from $\mathbb{R}^w$ to $\mathbb{R}$. Then $du(x)$ is the Jacobian at $x$. For $W$ a smooth manifold, a local coordinate system on a neighborhood $V$ of $x$ gives a representation $du: V \to L(\mathbb{R}^w, \mathbb{R})$. The class of all smooth functions $\{u: W \to \mathbb{R}\}$ can be given the Whitney topology: loosely speaking, if $u_a$ lies in a neighborhood of $u_b$ then values of $u_a, u_b$ are everywhere close, as are all differentials of $u_a, u_b$ (see Hirsch 1976 for details). If $N = \{1, \ldots, n\}$ is a society, then a smooth function $u = (u_1, \ldots, u_n): W \to \mathbb{R}^n$ representing the preferences of $V$ on $W$ is called a *smooth n-profile*. The class of smooth $n$-profiles with the Whitney topology is written $U(W)^N$.

In social choice theory it is usual to consider social welfare functions that map from the class of preference profiles, rather than utility profiles, to a social preference or set of social states. There are some theoretical difficulties in the appropriate definition of the quotient map from $U(W)^N$ to the class of preference profiles $P(W)^N$ for $N$ on $W$. For example, we can define the quotient map $q^N: U(W)^N \to P(W)^N$ by $q^N(u_1, \ldots, u_n) = (q(u_1), \ldots, q(u_n))$, where $q(u_i)$ is the equivalence class of $u_i$ given by $q(u_i) = q(u_i')$, iff for all $x \in W$,

$$\{y: u_i(y) > u_i(x)\} = \{y: u_i'(y) > u_i'(x)\}.$$

Then the fundamental social choice problem would be the existence of a social welfare function

$$U(W)^N \xrightarrow{q^N} P(W)^N \xrightarrow{E_a} 2(W),$$

where $2(W)$ is the class of subsets of $W$ and $E_\sigma(P_1, \ldots, P_n)$ is the choice set of "optimal" or unbeaten alternatives in $W$. Does there exist a $\sigma$ which is continuous in some sense, and which satisfies other optimality or efficiency properties? It is difficult to put a topology on $P(W)^N$ that is "natural" with respect to the Whitney topology on utility. The problem in particular is that the Whitney topology is a fine topology, whereas the usual topologies on $P(W)^N$ are coarser than the quotient topology induced on $P(W)^N$ by $q^N$ (see Le Breton 1987).

In this paper we deal with this problem by constructing a space of preference fields, rather than preferences, by an operation which is natural with respect to a quotient map.

**Definition 1.**

1. A *vector field* $X$ is a smooth function $X: W \to TW$ such that, for any $x \in W$ where $X$ is defined, $X(x) \in \Pi^{-1}(x)$.

2. A *preference field* $H$ is a correspondence $H: W \to TW$. That is, $H$ has domain, $\text{dom}(H) \subset W$, and $H(x)$ is defined and $H(x) \subset \Pi^{-1}(x)$ at each $x \in \text{dom}(H)$. Moreover,

   (a) $H(x)$ is a cone in $\Pi^{-1}(x)$ in the sense that, if $v \in H(x)$ for some tangent vector $v \in \Pi^{-1}(x)$, then $\lambda v \in H(x)$ for all $\lambda > 0$;
   (b) $0 \notin H(x)$.

3. A vector field $X$ is *integral* for a preference field $H$ on an open set $V \subset W$ iff $X(x) \in H(x)$ for all $x \in V$. (Note that $X(x) \neq 0$ for all $x \in V$.)

4. A preference field $H$ is *continuous* iff, for each $x \in \text{dom}(H)$ with $H(x) \neq \emptyset$, then for each $v \in H(x)$ there exists a neighborhood $V(x)$ of $x$ and a vector field $X$, integral for $H$ on $V(x)$, with $X(x) = v$.

5. A preference field $H$ is *S-continuous* iff $H$ is continuous and, for each $x \in \text{dom}(H)$,

   (a) $H(x)$ is open in $\Pi^{-1}(x)$;
   (b) if $v \in H(x)$ and $X(x) = v$ for some vector field $X$, then there exists a neighborhood $V(x)$ of $x$ with $X$ integral for $H$ on $V(x)$.

6. A preference field $H$ is *half-open* iff, for each $x \in \text{dom}(H)$ with $H(x) \neq \emptyset$, then there exists a linear function $f: \Pi^{-1}(x) \to \mathbb{R}$ such that $f(v) > 0$ for all $v \in H(x)$.

7. An *integral curve* for a preference field $H$ at a point $x$, in the interior of $W$, is a smooth curve $c: (-1, 1) \to W$ such that $c(0) = x$ and the derivative $[c](x')$ of $c$ at each point $x' = c(t)$ belongs to $H(x')$. For $x$ on the boundary $\partial W$, the curve $c$ has domain $[0, 1)$.

8. A *local preference relation* $\rho$ on $W$ is a binary relation on $W$ such that $y \rho x$ iff there is a smooth curve $c: (-1, 1) \to W$ such that $x = c(0)$ and

$y = \lim_{t \to 1} c(t)$ and $c(t) \rho c(t')$ whenever $-1 < t' < t < 1$. (Again, the domain of $c$ must be changed to $[0, 1)$ if $x$ is a boundary point.)

9. The *local preference relation* $\rho(H)$ induced by a preference field $H$ is a binary relation on $W$ defined as follows: $y \rho(H) x$ iff there exists an integral curve $c$ for $H$ from $x = c(0)$ to the point $y = \lim_{t \to 1} c(t)$. The image of $c$ is simply called a *preference path* from $x$ to $y$.

10. Let $C(W)$, $S(W)$, and $L(W)$ represent (respectively) the classes of continuous and $S$-continuous preference fields and local preference relations on $W$. For a society $N$, we use the notation $C(W)^N$, $S(W)^N$, and $L(W)^N$ for classes of profiles of preference fields and local preference relations.

Clearly $S(W) \subset C(W)$, so $S(W)^N \subset C(W)^N$. Moreover, the transformation from a preference field $H$ to the local preference relation $\rho(H)$ defines the maps $\rho: C(W) \to L(W)$ and $\rho^N: C(W)^N \to L(W)^N$. Note from the definition that if $H(x) = \emptyset$ for some specific $x$, then $y \rho(H) x$ for no $y \in W$. In general social choice problems, the set

$$E(P) = \{x \in W: y P x \text{ for no } y\}$$

is usually called the *core,* or choice set, associated with the social preference relation $P$. If we identify $P$ with its correspondence $P: W \to 2(W)$ then $E(P) = \{x \in W: P(x) = \emptyset\}$. For a preference field $H$, the analog is the *choice set* $E(H)$.

**Definition 2.** If $H$ is a preference field on $W$, then the *choice* of $H$ on $W$ is

$$E(H) = \{x \in \text{dom}(H) \subset W: H(x) = \emptyset\}.$$

Also, the *choice* of $\rho(H)$ on $W$ is

$$E(\rho(H)) = \{x \in \text{dom}(H) \subset W: y \rho(H) x \text{ for no } y \in W\}.$$

Note that if $H$ is continuous then $E(H) = E(\rho(H))$. Our general concern is with the nature of the choice correspondences $E: S(W) \to 2(W)$ and $E: L(W) \to 2(W)$. Under some conditions on $H$ or $W$, existence of $E(H)$ can be guaranteed. The most important condition concerns the dual of $H$. Given a preference field $H$, define the dual field in the following way: For each $x \in W$, let $[H(x)]^*$ be the family of linear functions $\{f: \Pi^{-1}(x) \to \mathbb{R}\}$ such that $f(v) > 0$ for all $v \in H(x)$. Since $L(\mathbb{R}^w, \mathbb{R})$ is isomorphic to $\mathbb{R}^w$, $[H(x)^*]$ can be identified with a cone $H^*(x)$ in $\Pi^{-1}(x)$. Now define the dual field of $H$ by $H^*(x) = [H(x)]^*$, and define $\text{dom}(H^*)$, the domain of $H^*$, to be $W \setminus E(H)$ in order to avoid dealing with the interpretation of the dual of the empty set. This gives a preference field $H^*: W \to TW$, called the *dual* of $H$. Note that $H$ is half-open iff $H^*(x) = \emptyset$ for no $x \in W$. Thus $E(H^*) = \emptyset$ iff $H$ is half-open. A generalization of the theorem of Fan (1961) and Bergstrom (1975, 1992) on the existence of choice sets can be expressed in terms of the duality implicit in the following definition.

**Definition 3.**

(i)  $W$ is a *Fan manifold* iff $W$ is a smooth compact manifold such that, for any $H \in C(W)$, $E(H) \cup E(H^*) \neq \emptyset$.

(ii) $W$ is a *Fan space* iff $W$ is a compact convex subset of $\mathbb{R}^w$ with smooth boundary.

In Schofield (1984a, thm. 1) it was shown that if $W$ is an affine manifold (of dimension $w$) which is compact and convex, and if $E(H^*) = \emptyset$, then $H$ can be used to construct a correspondence $\tilde{H}: W \to 2(W)$ that satisfies the convexity and continuity properties required of the Fan–Bergstrom theorem. This guarantees the existence of a choice $E(\tilde{H})$ of $\tilde{H}$ that coincides with the choice $E(H)$. Thus a Fan space is also a Fan manifold. Moreover, Schofield (1984a, thm. 2) generalized this result to show that any smooth compact manifold with nonzero Euler characteristic is a Fan manifold. For example, any even-dimensional sphere is a Fan manifold. In contrast, on odd-dimensional spheres it is possible to find a preference field $H$ with $E(H^*) = \emptyset$ yet $E(H) = \emptyset$. Since the class of Fan manifolds includes the class of compact sets usually taken to be the domain of social choice and equilibrium theory, this suggests that the *dual choice set* $E(H) \cup E(H^*)$ is an appropriate "equilibrium" model. Unfortunately, analysis of social choice mechanisms such as voting games shows that $E(H) \cup E(H^*)$ is typically dense in $W$. This can be a serious problem for social choice mechanisms, since it can also be shown that points in $E(H^*)$ support "local cycles" or turbulence.

**Definition 4.** If $H \in C(W)$ then the *local cycle set* of $H$, namely $\Gamma(H)$, is defined by $x \in \Gamma(H)$ iff $x \in \mathrm{dom}(H)$ and for any neighborhood $V(x)$ of $x$ there exists a finite set of alternatives $\{y_1, \ldots, y_r\}$ and a $\rho(H)$ cycle $x \rho(H) y_1, y_1 \rho(H) y_2, \ldots, y_r \rho(H) x$, where all the preference paths making up this cycle belong to the neighborhood $V(x)$.

Schofield (1984a) proved the following proposition.

**Proposition 1.** *If* $H \in C(W)$ *then* $\mathrm{Int}\, E(H^*) \subset \Gamma(H) \subset \mathrm{Clos}\, E(H^*)$. *If* $H \in S(W)$ *then* $H^* \in C(W)$ *and* $E(H^*)$ *is open.* (Here "Int" and "Clos" refer to the relative interior and closure.)

Since $\rho(H)$ cycles may be thought of as characterizing turbulence under the preference field $H$, any social preference field $H$ that exhibits a dense set $E(H^*)$ is badly behaved in some sense.

Until now we have dealt only with the properties of an abstract preference field $H$. We now wish to construct a quotient operator from $U(W)^N$ to $S(W)^N$.

**Definition 5.**  Let $u \in U(W)^N$ and define a family of preference fields $(h(u_1), \ldots, h(u_n))$ as follows:

$$h_i(u)(x) = h(u_i)(x) = \{v \in \Pi^{-1}(x): du_i(x)(v) > 0\}.$$

(Clearly each $h(u_i)(x)$ is a half-open cone, with $0 \in h(u_i)(x)$ for no $x \in W$.) For any subset $M \subset N$, $h_M(u)$ is defined by

$$h_M(u)(x) = \bigcap_{i \in M} h_i(u)(x).$$

If $\mathfrak{D} = \{M_1, \ldots, M_r\}$ is a *voting rule* – namely, a family of subsets of $N$ known as *decisive coalitions* – then define $h_{\mathfrak{D}}(u)(x) = \bigcup_{M \in \mathfrak{D}} h_M(u)(x)$.

**Proposition 2** (Schofield 1978).    *For any voting rule $\mathfrak{D}$ and each*

$$u \in U(W)^N,$$

*the correspondence defined by $h_{\mathfrak{D}}(u): W \to TW$ is an S-continuous preference field.*

Note that we have defined a function

$$h_{\mathfrak{D}}: U(W)^N \to S(W).$$

We call $h_{\mathfrak{D}}$ a *smooth voting rule*. Because this construction is well-defined for any $\mathfrak{D}$, Proposition 2 is valid when $\mathfrak{D} = \{i\}$. We have now constructed a *commutative diagram* (see Diagram 2).

In Diagram 2 we use the notation $h^N(u_1, \ldots, u_n) = (h_1, \ldots, h_n)$, while $\sigma_{\mathfrak{D}}$ is the social choice function mapping profiles of preference fields or local preference relations to a social preference field or local social preference relation. Thus $\sigma_{\mathfrak{D}}(h_1, \ldots, h_n) = \bigcup_{M \in \mathfrak{D}} \bigcap_{i \in M} h_i$, where this has the obvious interpretation. (Throughout this analysis $\sigma_{\mathfrak{D}}$ operates on a profile $R_1, \ldots, R_n$ of "preferences" by the combinatorial rule $\sigma_{\mathfrak{D}}(R_1, \ldots, R_n) = \bigcup_{\mathfrak{D}} \bigcap_M R_i$.) Notice that $h_{\mathfrak{D}}(u) = \sigma_{\mathfrak{D}}(h^N(u))$. Define

$$\sigma_{\mathfrak{D}}: L(W)^N \to L(W)$$

by taking local preference relations; that is, $\rho \circ \sigma_{\mathfrak{D}} = \sigma_{\mathfrak{D}} \circ \rho^N: S(W)^N \to L(W)$. Finally, $E: L(W) \to 2(W)$, where $2(W)$ is the class of subsets of $W$, induces $E: S(W) \to 2(W)$ by $E \circ \rho = E$. From Definition 2, $E(\rho) =$

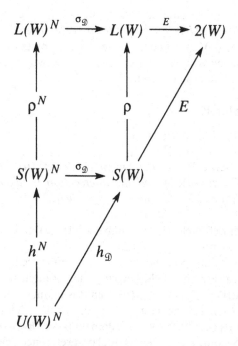

Diagram 2

$\{x \in W : y \rho x$ for no $y \in W\} = E(h_{\mathfrak{D}}(u))$ is the choice set defined by the social preference field $h_{\mathfrak{D}}(u)$, and $\rho = \rho(h_{\mathfrak{D}}(u))$ is the local preference relation defined by this field. With these definitions the diagram commutes. Since this commutative diagram is defined for any smooth manifold $W$, Diagram 2 can be regarded as a *functor diagram* (see Spanier 1966), where each map in the diagram is a functor. Thus we may write $h_{\mathfrak{D}} : U^N \to S, \ldots,$ when regarding $h_{\mathfrak{D}}$ as a functor. In later commutative diagrams of this form, we often delete reference to the manifold $W$.

A fundamental property of a smooth voting rule $h_{\mathfrak{D}}$ is the *Pareto property*, namely that $h_N \subset h_{\mathfrak{D}}$ in the sense that $h_N(u)(x) \subset h_{\mathfrak{D}}(u)(x)$ for all $x \in W$ and all $u \in U(W)^N$. Here $h_N(u)$ is the Pareto preference field defined by the profile $u$ for the society $N$. A second attractive property is *efficiency*, namely that all points in the choice set $E(h_{\mathfrak{D}}(u))$ are Pareto optimal. In the smooth context analyzed here, the *critical Pareto set* is the set $E(h_N(u)) = \{x \in W : h_N(u)(x) = \emptyset\}$. Hence the efficiency property in this context can be written as $E(h_{\mathfrak{D}}) \subset E(h_N)$, meaning that $E(h_{\mathfrak{D}}(u)) \subset E(h_N(u))$ for all $u \in U(W)^N$. Unfortunately, the results from voting theory to be presented here show that $E(h_{\mathfrak{D}}(u))$ will be empty for nearly all $u \in U(W)^N$.

Before discussing these results, we shall introduce the notion of a co-preference field. Given a profile $u \in U(W)^N$ define the *co-preference cone* of coalition $M$ at $x$, namely $p_M(u)(x)$, to be the cone obtained by taking semipositive combinations of the vectors $\{du_i(x): i \in M\}$. The two cones $h_M(u)(x)$ and $p_M(u)(x)$ are related by the following result.

**Proposition 3.**  *Suppose* $x \in \text{Int } W$.

(1)  *Then* $h_M(u)(x) = \emptyset$ *iff* $0 \in p_M(u)(x)$.
(2)  *If* $h_M(u)(x) \neq \emptyset$ *then* $[h_M(u)(x)]^* = p_M(u)(x)$.
(3)  *If* $h_M(u)(x) \neq \emptyset$ *for some* $M \in \mathfrak{D}$ *then* $[h_{\mathfrak{D}}(u)(x)]^* = p_{\mathfrak{D}}(u)(x)$, *where* $p_{\mathfrak{D}}(u)(x) = \bigcap_{\mathfrak{D}} p_M(u)(x)$ *and the intersection is taken only over those coalitions* $M$ *in* $\mathfrak{D}$ *that satisfy* $h_M(u)(x) \neq \emptyset$.

Proposition 3(1) is proved in Schofield (1985, lemma 4.3.1); (2) and (3) are proved in Schofield (1978, lemmas 1.2 and 1.3).

These definitions allow us to interpret the dual of the preference field $h_{\mathfrak{D}}(u)$. Remember that each preference field $[h_M(u)]^*$ has domain $W \setminus E(h_M(u))$. If we write $[h_M(u)]^* = h_M^*(u) = p_M(u)$ then this defines a co-preference field on $W \setminus E(h_M(u))$. Taking intersections allows us to define a co-preference field $h_{\mathfrak{D}}^*(u) = p_{\mathfrak{D}}(u): W \to TW$ with domain $W \setminus E(h_{\mathfrak{D}}(u))$.

Note also that if $h_{\mathfrak{D}}(u)$ is $S$-continuous then its dual co-preference field $h_{\mathfrak{D}}^*(u)$ is continuous, while $h_i^*(u)(x) = [h_i(u)(x)]^* = p_i(u)(x)$ is continuous on the appropriate domain $W \setminus (h_i(u))$. Thus Diagram 2 can be augmented to a functor diagram as shown in Diagram 3.

In the obvious way, $p^N(u)$ is the family of continuous fields $(p_1(u), ..., p_n(u))$ each of which maps $W \to TW$; $\sigma_{\mathfrak{D}}^*$ is the operation, dual to $\sigma_{\mathfrak{D}}$, defined by $\sigma_{\mathfrak{D}}^*(p_1(u), ..., p_n(u)) = p_{\mathfrak{D}}(u)(x)$, as in Proposition 3. Notice that in Diagram 3 we have written $E: L \to 2$ and $E: C \to 2, ...$ for the choice correspondences $E: L(W) \to 2(W)$ and $E: C(W) \to 2(W), ...$ defined as in Diagram 2 for the manifold $W$.

The double dual operation $**: C(W) \to C(W)$ can be identified with the convexification operator on continuous preference fields. That is, $(h_{\mathfrak{D}}(u)(x))^{**} = \text{Convex hull}(h_{\mathfrak{D}}(u)(x))$, where this is defined.

The duality relationship implied by Definition 3 shows that, for a Fan manifold, the union operation on the right-hand side of Diagram 3 gives a non-empty set in $W$. We can express this as follows.

**Proposition 4** (Schofield 1984a).  *If* $W$ *is a Fan manifold then* $E(h_{\mathfrak{D}}(u)) \neq \emptyset$ *if* $p_{\mathfrak{D}}(u)(x) \neq \emptyset$ *for all* $x$ *in the domain* $W \setminus E(h_{\mathfrak{D}}(u))$.

To interpret this result, suppose that $E(h_{\mathfrak{D}}(u)) = \emptyset$. Then $\text{dom}(p_{\mathfrak{D}}(u)) = W$. By the Fan theorem $E(h_{\mathfrak{D}}^*(u)) \neq \emptyset$, so $p_{\mathfrak{D}}(u)(x) = \emptyset$ for some $x \in W$.

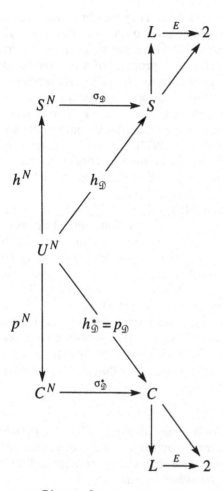

Diagram 3

Notice that by Proposition 1, if $E(h_{\mathfrak{D}}^*(u)) = \emptyset$ then the local cycle set $\Gamma(h_{\mathfrak{D}}(u))$ must be empty. On the other hand, if $\Gamma(h_{\mathfrak{D}}(u))$ is empty for the Fan manifold $W$, then – by the $S$-continuity of $h_{\mathfrak{D}}(u)$ and Proposition 1 – $E(h_{\mathfrak{D}}^*(u))$ is empty and so $E(h_{\mathfrak{D}}(u)) \neq \emptyset$. This latter result is a smooth analogue of Walker's theorem (1977) on the relationship between the lack of cycles on a compact set and the existence of an equilibrium. Note also that Propositions 3 and 4 give two techniques for characterizing $E(h_{\mathfrak{D}}(u))$.

Suppose that $x \in E(h_M(u))$ for some coalition $M$. By Proposition 3, if $x$ also belongs to the interior of $W$, then $0 \in p_M(u)(x)$. Then the vectors

$\{du_i(x): i \in M\}$ must be linearly dependent. Transversality theory (Golubitsky and Guillemin 1973) can then be used to show that "generically" $x$ must belong to a "stratified manifold" with dimension determined by $\dim(W)$ and $|M|$. *Generic* here refers to a property of a residual set in $U(W)^N$. A residual set in $U(W)^N$ is a countable intersection of open dense sets in $U(W)^N$. When $W$ is compact then "generic" implies "open dense."

A *stratified manifold* $S$ of dimension $s$ is a union of smooth manifolds $S = \bigcup_{r=1}^s S_r$, where (for $r < s$) the $r$-dimensional components are embedded in the "corners" of $S$. Smale (1973) first used transversality theory to show that, generically, the equilibrium or critical Pareto set $E(h_N(u))$ is a subset of a stratified manifold of dimension $n-1$ (in the case $w \geq n$). We use this result to analyze $E(h_{\mathfrak{D}}(u))$.

Now $E(h_{\mathfrak{D}}(u)) = \bigcap_{M \in \mathfrak{D}} \{x: h_M(u)(x) = \emptyset\} = \bigcap_{M \in \mathfrak{D}} E(h_M(u))$. Call this the *equilibrium condition* for $\mathfrak{D}$. Thus, if $N$ is finite and $x$ belongs to the equilibrium set $E(h_{\mathfrak{D}}(u))$, then $x$ must belong to the intersection of a finite number of stratified manifolds. Under some conditions on $\mathfrak{D}$, an integer $w(\mathfrak{D})$ can be calculated which characterizes $h_{\mathfrak{D}}(u)$ in the sense that if $\dim(W) \geq w(\mathfrak{D})$ then $E(h_{\mathfrak{D}}(u))$ will be generically empty. To indicate the structure of this argument, observe that McKelvey and Schofield (1987) have shown that, at any point $x$ satisfying the equilibrium condition, the gradients $\{du_i(x): i \in N\}$ must satisfy certain generalized Plott (1967) symmetry conditions. These conditions imply that there exists a family of coalitions $\{C_1, \dots, C_r\}$ with $|C_j| \leq w(\mathfrak{D})$, $j = 1, \dots, r$, such that

$$x \in \bigcap_{j=1}^r E(h_{C_j}(u)).$$

Call this the *symmetry condition* in terms of $\{C_1, \dots, C_r\}$. The generic properties of $E(h_{\mathfrak{D}}(u))$ are determined by the symmetry condition just displayed. In the proof of Theorem 2 we shall use this concept and refer to the sets $\{E(h_{C_j}(u))\}$ as *singularity submanifolds*.

To apply Proposition 4, consider the condition $p_{\mathfrak{D}}(u)(x) = \emptyset$ for all $x \in \mathrm{dom}(p_{\mathfrak{D}}(u))$. Use of Helly's theorem (Berge 1963) shows that for each $\mathfrak{D}$ there exists an integer $v(\mathfrak{D})$ such that $\dim(W) \leq v(\mathfrak{D})$ implies that $p_{\mathfrak{D}}(u)(x) = \bigcap_{\mathfrak{D}} p_M(u)(x)$ is non-empty for all $x$ in $\mathrm{dom}(p_{\mathfrak{D}}(u))$. By Proposition 4, the choice set $E(h_{\mathfrak{D}}(u))$ will exist if $W$ is a Fan manifold.

To compute $v(\mathfrak{D})$ we need the following definition.

**Definition 6.**  For any voting rule $\mathfrak{D}$:

(1)  the collegium $K(\mathfrak{D}) = \bigcap_{M \in \mathfrak{D}} M$;

(2)  if $K(\mathfrak{D}) \neq \emptyset$, call $\mathfrak{D}$ *collegial* and define the Nakamura number $k(\mathfrak{D})$ to be $\infty$;

(3)  if $K(\mathfrak{D}) = \emptyset$, say $\mathfrak{D}$ is *noncollegial* and define the *Nakamura number* by

$$k(\mathfrak{D}) = \min\{|\mathfrak{D}'| : \mathfrak{D}' \subset \mathfrak{D} : K(\mathfrak{D}') = \emptyset\}.$$

Thus any subfamily $\mathfrak{D}'$ of $\mathfrak{D}$ with $|\mathfrak{D}'| < k(\mathfrak{D})$ has a non-empty collegium. Nakamura (1979) introduced the concept of $k(\mathfrak{D})$.

It is relatively easy to show that, if $W$ is a smooth manifold of dimension at most $k(\mathfrak{D}) - 2$, then $E(p_{\mathfrak{D}}(u)) = \emptyset$. Note in particular that if $\mathfrak{D}$ is collegial then there is no dimension constraint necessary for the existence of a choice.

Proposition 4 and the transversality arguments give the following result on any smooth voting rule $h_{\mathfrak{D}}$, defined for arbitrary $\mathfrak{D}$ on a manifold $W$. (See Schofield 1983, 1989 for further details.)

**Classification result for voting rules.**

1. If $\mathfrak{D}$ is collegial then, for all $u \in U(W)^N$, $\Gamma(h_{\mathfrak{D}}(u)) = \emptyset$. If $W$ is a Fan manifold, then $E(h_{\mathfrak{D}}(u)) \neq \emptyset$.

2. Suppose $\mathfrak{D}$ is noncollegial, with $k(\mathfrak{D}) < \infty$. Then $h_{\mathfrak{D}}$ is *classified* by two integers $v(\mathfrak{D})$ and $w(\mathfrak{D})$, where $v(\mathfrak{D}) = k(\mathfrak{D}) - 2$, $w(\mathfrak{D}) \leq n - 1$, and $v(\mathfrak{D}) < w(\mathfrak{D})$. The classification has the following form:

(a)  If $\dim(W) \leq v(\mathfrak{D})$ then $\Gamma(h_{\mathfrak{D}}(u)) = \emptyset$, and if $W$ is a Fan manifold then $E(h_{\mathfrak{D}}(u)) \neq \emptyset$.

(b)  If $\dim(W) \geq v(\mathfrak{D}) + 1$ then there exists $u \in U(W)^N$ such that $\Gamma(h_{\mathfrak{D}}(u)) \neq \emptyset$ and $E(h_{\mathfrak{D}}(u)) = \emptyset$. However, if $\dim(W) = v(\mathfrak{D}) + 1$ then, for all $u \in U(W)^N$, $\Gamma(h_{\mathfrak{D}}(u)) \subset E(h_N(u))$, the critical Pareto set.

(c)  If $\dim(W) \geq w(\mathfrak{D}) + 1$, then $\{u \in U(W)^N : E(h_{\mathfrak{D}}(u)) = \emptyset\}^1$ and $\{u \in U(W)^N : \Gamma(h_{\mathfrak{D}}(u))$ is open dense$\}$ are both residual sets.[2]

To illustrate these results, suppose $\mathfrak{D}$ is the *q rule* $\mathfrak{D} = \{M : |M| \geq q\}$ for some fixed $q \leq n - 1$. Clearly $\mathfrak{D}$ is noncollegial. It is easy to show that $v(\mathfrak{D})$ is the largest integer strictly less than $q/(n - q)$ (see Greenberg 1979 and Strnad 1985).

For a general noncollegial voting rule $\mathfrak{D}$, it can be very difficult indeed to compute $w(\mathfrak{D})$ precisely.[3] However, for majority rule with $n$ odd,

---

[1]  In fact, if $W$ has empty boundary, then in dimension at least $w(\mathfrak{D})$ this property is true on a residual set.

[2]  This property will often be termed the *generic voting paradox*.

[3]  For a $q$-rule $\mathfrak{D}$, McKelvey and Schofield (1986) argued that $w(\mathfrak{D}) = 2q - n + 1$. However, see Banks (1994) for some comments on this work.

it is easy to show that the symmetry condition involves coalitions of size 2 and so $w(\mathfrak{D}) = 2$. For majority rule with $n$ even, $w(\mathfrak{D}) = 3$. Indeed, a typical weighted majority rule $\mathfrak{D}$ also has $w(\mathfrak{D}) = 3$. A rule requiring a supramajority $n/2 + k(n)$ for some $k(n) > 0$ has $w(\mathfrak{D}) \simeq 2k(n) + 1$. For example, Schofield and Tovey (1992) have studied the behavior of rules of this form when $k(n) \simeq \epsilon n$ for $\epsilon > 0$ but small, and obtained characterization results for the limiting case as $n$ approaches infinity.

Earlier it was suggested that, for an arbitrary preference field $H$, an appropriate choice model could be $E(H) \cup E(H^*)$ since this union is typically non-empty. However, the result just mentioned shows that the equilibrium set $E(h_{\mathfrak{D}}(u)) \cup E(h_{\mathfrak{D}}^*(u))$ can be dense for all $u$ in a residual set. Let us write $E(h_{\mathfrak{D}}, h_{\mathfrak{D}}^*)(u) = E(h_{\mathfrak{D}}(u), h_{\mathfrak{D}}^*(u)) = E(h_{\mathfrak{D}}(u)) \cup E(h_{\mathfrak{D}}^*(u))$. Then the classification result immediately shows that the equilibrium model $E(h_{\mathfrak{D}}, h_{\mathfrak{D}}^*)$ generically violates efficiency. That is,

$$E(h_{\mathfrak{D}}, h_{\mathfrak{D}}^*)(u) \not\subset E(h_N(u))$$

for $u$ in a residual set.

In Section 4 we show that this classification result is generically valid not just for utilities but for preferences as well. Under certain conditions, then, the choice set $E_\sigma(P_1, \ldots, P_n)$ will nearly always be empty. In an effort to solve this problem, we show in the next section how efficiency can be imposed on $E(h_{\mathfrak{D}}, h_{\mathfrak{D}}^*)$. The resulting efficient choice model is called the *heart*. We show the heart has an attractive continuity property when regarded as a correspondence from utility profiles to outcomes.

## 3    The heart of a voting rule

The propositions of Section 2 show that, for any coalition $M \subset N$ and any smooth profile $u$, the preference field $h_M(u)$ is $S$-continuous and so its dual $h_M^*(u) = p_M(u)$ is continuous. We can combine these to form a continuous preference field $hp_{\mathfrak{D}}(u)$ and a choice set called the *heart*. The heart exists and is Pareto optimal, under appropriate conditions. When the voting equilibrium $E(P_{\mathfrak{D}})$ is non-empty then, as we shall see, this set also belongs to the heart.

**Definition 7.**    Let $u \in U(W)^N$ with $\mathfrak{D}$ fixed.
    1. The *efficient preference field* for coalition $M$ is $hp_M(u): W \to TW$, where

$$hp_M(u)(x) = \begin{cases} h_M(u)(x) \cap p_M(u)(x) & \text{if } h_M(u)(x) \neq \emptyset, \\ \emptyset & \text{if } h_M(u)(x) = \emptyset, \end{cases}$$

and $\mathrm{dom}(hp_M(u)) = W$.

2. The *efficient preference field* for $\mathfrak{D}$ is

$$hp_{\mathfrak{D}}(u)(x) = \bigcup \{hp_M(u)(x): M \in \mathfrak{D}\}$$

with $\mathrm{dom}(hp_{\mathfrak{D}}(u)) = W$.

3. The *heart* of $\mathfrak{D}$ at $u$ is

$$\mathfrak{K}_{\mathfrak{D}}(u) = E(hp_{\mathfrak{D}}(u)) \cup \mathrm{Clos}(E(hp_{\mathfrak{D}}^*(u))),$$

where $hp_{\mathfrak{D}}^*(u) = [hp_{\mathfrak{D}}(u)]^*$ is the dual field with domain $W \setminus E(hp_{\mathfrak{D}}(u))$.

It is necessary to remark on the domains of these fields. As we have observed, $\mathrm{dom}(p_M(u)(x)) = W \setminus E(h_M(u))$. By defining $hp_M(u)(x) = \emptyset$ on $E(h_M(u))$, we have constructed $hp_M(u)$ so that it has domain equal to $W$; the same is true for $hp_{\mathfrak{D}}(u)$. We can define $hp_{\mathfrak{D}}^*(u)(x)$ at any point $x \notin E(hp_{\mathfrak{D}}(w))$. The principal result on $\mathfrak{K}_{\mathfrak{D}}$ follows directly from the definitions and the Fan theorem.

**Theorem 1.** *For $W$ a smooth manifold and $\mathfrak{D}$ fixed, the preference field $hp_{\mathfrak{D}}$ maps $U(W)^N$ to $C(W)$. Moreover:*

(1) *for any $u \in U(W)^N$, the heart of $\mathfrak{D}$ at $u$ satisfies the efficiency property $\mathfrak{K}_{\mathfrak{D}}(u) \subset E(h_N(u))$;*

(2) *$E(h_{\mathfrak{D}}(u)) = E(hp_{\mathfrak{D}}(u))$, so that $\mathfrak{K}_{\mathfrak{D}}(u)$ is closed in $W$;*

(3) *if $W$ is a Fan manifold then $\mathfrak{K}_{\mathfrak{D}}(u) \neq \emptyset$ for all $u \in U(W)^N$.*

*Proof:* By Propositions 1 and 2, if $u \in U(W)^N$ then each preference field $h_M(u)$ is $S$-continuous, so that its dual is continuous. The intersection $h_M(u) \cap h_M^*(u)$ is thus continuous. Since the union of continuous fields is also continuous, $h_{\mathfrak{D}}(u) \in C(W)$ for all $u \in U(W)^N$. Part (3) follows directly from the Fan theorem, as in Proposition 4. To prove part (2), if $x \in E(h_{\mathfrak{D}}(u))$ then $h_M(u)(x) = \emptyset$ for all $M \in \mathfrak{D}$. Thus $hp_{\mathfrak{D}}(u)(x) = \emptyset$ and so $x \in E(hp_{\mathfrak{D}}(u))$. On the other hand, if $x \notin E(h_{\mathfrak{D}}(u))$ then $h_M(u)(x) \neq \emptyset$ for some $M \in \mathfrak{D}$. Hence there exists $v \in \Pi^{-1}(x)$ such that $du_i(x)(v) > 0$ for all $i \in M$. A necessary condition for existence of such a $v$ is that $0 \notin p_M(u)(x)$. Thus there exists a family $\{v_i: v_i \in \mathbb{R}^w, i \in M\}$ of vectors, all lying in an open half-space in $V_+ \subset \mathbb{R}^w$, such that $v_i \in p_i(u)(x)$ for each $i \in M$.

We seek to show that some $v \in h_M(u)(x)$ can be written as the semipositive combination $v = \sum_{p_i \in M} \lambda_i v_i$. Suppose there exists some vector $v \in \mathbb{R}^w$ such that $p_M(u)(x) \subset (v)^* = V_+$ and $h_M(u)(x) \subset (v)^* = V_+$. Taking duals, it then follows that $v^{**} = v \in p_M(u)(x) \cap h_M(u)(x)$. No such vector exists iff there exists $i \in M$ such that $p_i(u)(x)$ belongs to the negative cone generated by $h_M(u)(x)$, that is, the cone $(-p_i(u)(x)) \in h_M(u)(x)$.

But then $[p_M(u)(x)] \cap h_i(u)(x) = \emptyset$, which contradicts the assumption that $h_M(u)(x) \neq \emptyset$ and $h_i(u)(x) \subset h_M(u)(x)$. This contradiction establishes the existence of the required vector $v \in h_M(u)(x) \cap p_M(u)(x)$. Thus $hp_M(u)(x) \neq \emptyset$ and so $x \notin E(hp_{\mathfrak{D}}(u))$.

We have shown that $E(h_{\mathfrak{D}}(u)) = E(hp_{\mathfrak{D}}(u))$ for all $u \in U(W)^N$. To show that $\mathcal{K}_{\mathfrak{D}}(u)$ is closed, it suffices to show that $E(h_{\mathfrak{D}}(u))$ is closed. If $x \notin E(h_{\mathfrak{D}}(u))$ then there exists $M \in \mathfrak{D}$ such that $x \notin E(h_M(u))$. By $S$ continuity there is a neighborhood $V$ of $x$ in $W$ such that $h_M(u)(x') \neq \emptyset$ for all $x' \in V$. Thus $W \setminus E(h_M(u))$ is open, and $\mathcal{K}_{\mathfrak{D}}(u)$ is closed.

To prove (1), consider $x \in E(h_{\mathfrak{D}}(u))$. Then $h_M(u)(x) = \emptyset$ for some $M \subset N$. But $h_N(u)(x) = h_M(u)(x) \cap h_{N-M}(u)(x) = \emptyset$. Thus $E(h_{\mathfrak{D}}(u)) \subset E(h_N(u))$.

Suppose now that $x \notin E(h_N(u))$. A necessary condition is that $0 \notin p_N(u)(x)$. As in part (2), there exists a family $\{v_i \in \mathbb{R}^w : i \in N\}$, belonging to an open half-space $V_+$ in $\mathbb{R}^w$, with $v_i \in p_i(u)(x)$ for all $i \in N$. Hence $p_M(u)(x) \subset V_+$ for all $M \subset N$. Thus $hp_M(u)(x) \subset V_+$, and so $hp_{\mathfrak{D}}^*(u)(x) \neq \emptyset$ for all $M \subset N$. Since $h_N(u)(x) \neq \emptyset$, it must be the case that $x \notin E(h_{\mathfrak{D}}(u))$. Thus $x \notin E(hp_{\mathfrak{D}}(u))$ and so $x$ must belong to the domain of $hp_{\mathfrak{D}}^*(u)$. Thus $x \notin E(hp_{\mathfrak{D}}^*(u))$, and hence $E(hp_{\mathfrak{D}}^*(u)) \subset E(h_N(u))$.    $\square$

Theorem 1 gives some insight into the relationship between the preference fields $h_{\mathfrak{D}}(u)$ and $hp_{\mathfrak{D}}(u)$. Essentially, $hp_{\mathfrak{D}}(u)$ is a subpreference field of $h_{\mathfrak{D}}(u)$ in the sense that

$$hp_{\mathfrak{D}}(u)(x) \subset h_{\mathfrak{D}}(u)(x) \quad \forall x \in W,$$

and, moreover, $h_{\mathfrak{D}}(u)(x) \neq \emptyset$ iff $hp_{\mathfrak{D}}(u)(x) \neq \emptyset$. Note in particular that the cycle set $\Gamma(hp_{\mathfrak{D}}(u))$ is constrained to belong to the critical Pareto set.

As we shall now show, the heart correspondence satisfies a useful continuity property. It also appears that the heart is the "attractor" for the efficient preference field that we have constructed. An interesting question is whether a subpreference field of $hp_{\mathfrak{D}}(u)$ can be constructed which preserves the continuity property (see Austen-Smith 1993).

We now give definitions of the continuity properties that we shall use.

**Definition 8.**    A correspondence $\mathcal{K}$ between topological spaces $X, Y$ is:

(1) *lower hemicontinuous* (lhc) if and only if, for any open set $V \subset Y$, the set $\{z \in X : \mathcal{K}(z) \cap V \neq \emptyset\}$ is open;
(2) *upper hemicontinuous* (uhc) if and only if, for any open set $V \subset Y$, the set $\{z \in X : \mathcal{K}(z) \subset V\}$ is open;
(3) *continuous* if and only if it is both lhc and uhc.

Note also that if $\mathfrak{JC} = \bigcup \mathfrak{JC}_i$ is a union of lhc correspondences then $\mathfrak{JC}$ itself will be lhc. We now show that the correspondence $\mathfrak{JC}_{\mathfrak{D}}: U(W)^N \to W$ is lhc when restricted to an open domain $X(W)^N$ in $U(W)^N$. To prove this, it suffices to show that $\mathfrak{JC}_{\mathfrak{D}}$ is componentwise lhc on any open set $V \subset X(W)^N$. We need to define $X(W)^N$.

It is usual, in the case where $W$ is an affine manifold with a global linear structure, to assume that preferences satisfy some appropriate convexity property. For $W$ affine, say that the utility function $u_i: W \to \mathbb{R}$ gives a *semiconvex preference* iff for no $x \in W$ does $x$ belong to the convex hull of the set $\{y \in W : u_i(y) > u_i(x)\}$. Let $\mathrm{Con}(W)$ be the set of such utility functions. Write $\mathrm{Con}(W)^N$ for the subset of $U(W)^N$ of such utilities, endowed with the induced topology. Of course, for $W$ a manifold $\mathrm{Con}(W)^N$ need not be defined. However, if $u \in \mathrm{Con}(W)^N$ then the induced preference fields do satisfy a more general property that can be defined in the case where $W$ is a manifold.

**Definition 9.**

1. Given a continuous preference field $H \in C(W)$, a preference curve $c$ for $H$, commencing at $x \in W$ and terminating at $y \in W$, is an integral curve $c$ of $H$ from $x = c(0)$ to $y = \lim_{c \to 1} c(t)$ with $c(t) \rho(H) c(t')$ for all $0 \le t' < t < 1$.

2. If $c_1, c_2$ are both preference curves for $H$, write $c_1 \subset_H c_2$ iff $c_1(0) = c_2(0)$ and $\mathrm{Im}(c_1) \subset \mathrm{Im}(c_2)$. A *maximal* preference curve $c$ for $H$ is maximal under this inclusion relation. That is, there exists no preference curve $c'$ for $H$ such that $c \subset_H c'$.

3. The preference field $H \subset C(W)$ is *locally stable* iff, for any point $z \in E(H)$ and any neighborhood $V$ of $z$ in $W$, there exists a neighborhood $V'$ of $z$ (with $V'$ a proper subset of $V$) such that any maximal preference curve for $H$ which commences at $x \in V'$ will terminate at some point $y$ in $V \cap E(H)$.

4. A profile $u \in U(W)^N$ is *locally stable* iff each field in the family

$$\{h_i(u): i \in N\} \cup \{h_M(u): M \subset N\}$$

of preference fields is locally stable. The set of locally stable utility profiles with the induced topology is written $X(W)^N$. Write $X(W)$ in the obvious way for the case $|N| = 1$.

To illustrate, suppose that $W$ is affine. If $u_i \in \mathrm{Con}(W)$ then maximal preference curves defined by $u_i$ approach the equilibrium (or critical) set

$$E(h(u_i)) = \{x \in W : du_i(x) = 0\}.$$

Thus $Con(W) \subset X(W)$. For $W$ affine and $u_i \notin Con(W)$, it is possible to define a Hessian for $u_i$ to determine the stability properties of critical points. For $W$ a manifold, Smale (1982) has shown that it is possible to define a generalized Hessian for $\{u_i : i \in M\}$ for each coalition at points in the choice or singularity set $E(h_M(u))$. Just as in the affine case, imposing the required restrictions on the generalized Hessians defines the open subspace $X(W)^N$.

**Theorem 2.** *The correspondence* $\mathcal{K}_\mathfrak{D} : U(W)^N \to W$ *is lhc on the subspace* $X(W)^N \subset U(W)^N$.

To prove this theorem we demonstrate a number of lemmas. First of all, we introduce the notion of structural stability (see McKelvey and Schofield 1986).

In general, the equilibrium set $\mathcal{K}_\mathfrak{D}(u)$ may consist of a number of disconnected components. If $W$ is affine and $u \in Con(W)^N$ then there will be only one component. However, in the general case we shall refer to components of $\mathcal{K}_\mathfrak{D}(u)$, $E(hp_\mathfrak{D}(u))$, et cetera. In particular, in light of Proposition 1 we refer to $E(hp_\mathfrak{D}^*(u))$ as the *cyclic component* of the heart.

**Definition 10.** A component $E_1(u)$ of the choice set $E(hp_\mathfrak{D}(u))$ is *structurally stable* at $u$ iff, for any open set $Y \subset W$ such that $E_1(u) \cap Y \neq \emptyset$, there exists an open set $X$ of $u$ in $U(W)^N$ such that $E_1(u') \cap Y \neq \emptyset$ for all $u' \in X$. A non-empty component $E_1(u)$ of $E(hp_\mathfrak{D}(u))$ is called *structurally unstable* otherwise.

Notice that, from the voting result, if $\dim(W) > w(\mathfrak{D})$ then $E(h_\mathfrak{D}(u)) = \emptyset$ for all $u$ in a residual set. Consequently any component $E_1(u) \subset E(h_\mathfrak{D}(u))$ must be structurally unstable. This follows because $\{u : E_1(u) = \emptyset\}$ is open dense and so there is no open set $X$ such that $E_1(u) \neq \emptyset$ for all $u \in X$.

However, if $\dim(W) \leq w(\mathfrak{D})$ then there may exist a profile $u$ and a component $E_1(u)$ of $E(hp_\mathfrak{D}(u))$ that is structurally stable at $u$. If $E_1(u)$ is in fact structurally stable, then the correspondence $E_1 : U(W)^N \to W$ will be lhc on some neighborhood $X$ of $u$ in $U(W)^N$. Consequently, Theorem 2 follows by proving lower hemicontinuity of the subcorrespondence of $\mathcal{K}_\mathfrak{D}$ obtained by taking the union of the cyclic component $E(hp_\mathfrak{D}^*(u))$ together with structurally unstable components.

**Lemma 1.** *Suppose that* $E(hp_\mathfrak{D}^*(u)) \neq \emptyset$ *for some* $u \in U$. *Then each component* $E_1(u)$ *of* $E(hp_\mathfrak{D}^*(u))$ *is lhc on some neighborhood* $X$ *of* $u$ *in* $U(W)^N$.

*Proof:* Suppose that at $u$, and with $x \in W$, $hp_\mathfrak{D}^*(u)(x) = \emptyset$. Then the intersection of cones, $\bigcap_\mathfrak{D} [hp_M(u)(x)]^*$, is empty. Project each of these cones onto the sphere $S^{w-1} \subset \mathbb{R}^w$ centered at zero. Since $S^{w-1}$ is a normal topological space, there exists a family of non-empty open sets $\{Y_M \subset S^{w-1}:$ $M \in \mathfrak{D}\}$ with $[hp_M(u)(x)]^* \subset Y_M$ and $\bigcap_{\mathfrak{D}} Y_M = \emptyset$. By Theorem 3.1 of Schofield (1978), each $hp_M^*: U(W)^N \to C(W)$ is *upper hemicontinuous*,[4] so for each $M \in \mathfrak{D}$ there exists a neighborhood $X_M$ of $u$ in $U(W)^N$ such that $[hp_M(u')(x)]^* \subset Y_M$ for all $M \in \mathfrak{D}$ and all $u' \in X_M$. Let $X = \bigcap_M X_M$. Then $u' \in X$ implies that $x \in E(hp_{\mathfrak{D}}^*(u'))$. Thus each component is lhc on an open set $X$ of $u$ in $U(W)^N$. $\qquad\Box$

The proof of Theorem 2 is completed by proving the following lemma.

**Lemma 2.** *Let $W$ be a Fan manifold. Suppose that $u \in X(W)^N$ and $E_1(u)$ is a structurally unstable component of $E(hp_{\mathfrak{D}}(u))$. Then if $Y \subset W$ is open and $Y \cap E_1(u) \neq \emptyset$, there exists an open set $X \subset X(W)^N$ with $u \in X$ such that*

$$[E_1(u') \cup \mathrm{Clos}(E(hp_{\mathfrak{D}}^*(u')))] \cap Y \neq \emptyset \quad \forall u' \in X.$$

*Proof:* By structural instability, and without loss of generality, we may assume that for any neighborhood $X'$ of $u$ in $U(W)^N$ there exists some $u' \in X'$ such that $E_1(u') = \emptyset$. We may also assume that $E(hp_{\mathfrak{D}}^*(u)) \cap Y = \emptyset$. Since $u \in X(W)^N$, each maximal preference curve approaches $E_1(u)$. Hence there exists an open set $V' \subset Y$ such that $hp_M(u)(x')$ "point into" $E_1(u)$ for all $x' \in V'$.

Thus there exists a compact set $V'' \subset V'$ such that the preference field $hp_{\mathfrak{D}}(u)$, when restricted to $V''$, has choice set $E(hp_{\mathfrak{D}}(u)/V'')$ exactly equal to $E_1(u)$. It is possible to choose an open neighborhood $X$ of $u$ in $X(W)^N$ such that – for each $M \in \mathfrak{D}$, each point $x$ on the boundary $\partial V''$ of $V''$, and each $u' \in X$ – there exists a preference curve for $hp_M(u')$ from $x$ which leads into the interior of $V''$. By this construction, we have demonstrated the existence of a compact set $V''$ and an open set $X$ of $u$ in $X(W)^N$ such that

$$E_1(u') = E(hp_{\mathfrak{D}}(u'/V'')) \quad \forall u' \in X \text{ such that } E_1(u') \neq \emptyset.$$

Suppose that $E_1(u') = \emptyset$ at some $u' \in X$. Now, $V''$ can be chosen so that it is diffeomorphic to a compact convex subset of $\mathbb{R}^w$ and hence contractible. By the Fan theorem (Schofield 1984a), $E(hp_{\mathfrak{D}}^*(u')/V'') \neq \emptyset$. Then

$$E_1(u') \cup \mathrm{Clos}(E(hp_{\mathfrak{D}}^*(u'))) \cap Y \neq \emptyset \quad \forall u' \in X. \qquad\Box$$

To illustrate Lemma 2, consider Figure 1. At the profile $u$, suppose $x \in E_1(u)$. From McKelvey and Schofield (1987) it is known that $x$ belongs to

[4] Here we implicitly impose a topology on $C(W)$ based on the projection of cones in $\mathbb{R}^w$ onto $S^{w-1}$. See Schofield (1993c).

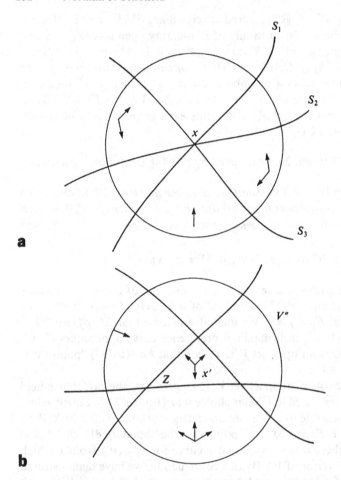

a

b

Figure 1. (a) $E_1(u) \neq \emptyset$ for profile $u$. (b) $E_1(u') = \emptyset$ for profile $u'$.

the intersection of certain singularity submanifolds. In Figure 1(a) three of these submanifolds, labeled $\{S_i: i = 1, 2, 3\}$, are shown intersecting at $x$. Vectors in the field $hp_{\mathfrak{D}}(u)(x')$ for $x'$ near to $x$ are also shown, together with the compact set $V''$. Now consider $u'$ near to $u$ with $E_1(u) = \emptyset$, so that the singularity submanifolds do not intersect. The singularity submanifolds now "bound a volume" $Z \subset W$, say. At any point $x' \in Z$, it is possible to find three vectors $\{v_i: i = 1, 2, 3\}$ such that $v_i \in hp_{\mathfrak{D}}(u')(x')$ with $\sum \lambda_i v_i = 0$ for semipositive coefficients $\{\lambda_i: i = 1, 2, 3\}$. Clearly $x' \in E(hp^*_{\mathfrak{D}}(u'))$.

It is obvious that the behavior of the heart at a structurally unstable component is difficult to analyze. Above the instability dimension $w(\mathfrak{D})$, a structurally unstable component at $u$ can "vanish" for some perturbation of $u$. If the perturbation of $u$ is within $U(W)^N$ rather than $X(U)^N$, then a cyclic component can appear as a result of the perturbation, but it may not intersect the open set $Y$. As a consequence, lower hemicontinuity may be violated. This phenomenon may be nongeneric, however.

In this section we have shown that $\mathcal{H}_{\mathfrak{D}}$ is well-behaved on a subspace $X(U)^N$ of *utility* profiles. We show in the next section that $\mathcal{H}_{\mathfrak{D}}$ can be defined on *preference* profiles in such a way that the properties we have analyzed are inherited.

## 4    The heart of a social choice rule

As mentioned in Section 2, the classical social choice problem examines the existence of a social welfare function

$$P(W)^N \xrightarrow{\ \sigma\ } P(W) \xrightarrow{\ E\ } 2(W),$$

where $E: P(W) \to 2(W)$ is the choice correspondence given by $E(P) = \{x \in W: P(x) = \emptyset\}$. Here $P(W)^N$ is the set of strict preference profiles on $W$. A social preference $P \in P(W)$ is a correspondence $P: W \to 2(W)$ that specifies the set $P(x)$ of alternatives preferred to $x$.

In the case of a voting rule $\mathfrak{D}$, $\sigma$ has the form $\sigma_{\mathfrak{D}}$ defined by

$$\sigma_{\mathfrak{D}}(P_1, \ldots, P_n) = \bigcup_{M \in \mathfrak{D}} \bigcap_{i \in M} P_i = P_{\mathfrak{D}},$$

where $\{P_i: i \in N\}$ is the profile of strict preferences on $W$, while $E(P_{\mathfrak{D}}) = \{x \in W: y \in P_{\mathfrak{D}}(x)$ for no $y \in W\}$.[5] In this notation, $P_i: W \to 2(W)$ is the correspondence defining the set $P_i(x)$ of alternatives preferred by $i$ to $x$. In general, of course, $E(P_{\mathfrak{D}})$ will be empty. More precisely, it is known that if the "Hausdorff" topology (Le Breton 1987) is put on $P(W)^N$ then under certain conditions $E(P_{\mathfrak{D}})$ will be empty for a dense set of profiles in $P(W)^N$. This result and the classification result are not quite comparable, since they are valid in different categories. However, consider the case when the preference profile is derived from smooth utility functions under the operator $q^N$ given in Section 1. Consider the commutative functor Diagram 4.

Diagram 2 showed that the function $h_{\mathfrak{D}}: U(W)^N \to S(W)$ can be factored through $S(W)^N$. That is to say, there exists a functor $\sigma_{\mathfrak{D}}: S^N \to S$ such that $h_{\mathfrak{D}} = \sigma_{\mathfrak{D}} \circ h^N$. Here $\sigma_{\mathfrak{D}}$ is defined as before by $\sigma_{\mathfrak{D}}(h_1, \ldots, h_n) = \bigcup_{\mathfrak{D}} \bigcap_M h_i$ for any profile of $S$-continuous preference fields; $E$ is the choice correspondence. In the lower, preference part of the diagram, the definition $q_{\mathfrak{D}} = \sigma_{\mathfrak{D}} \circ q^N$ gives commutativity. A natural question concerns

[5] This set has traditionally been called the *core,* or for majority rule the *Condorcet set.*

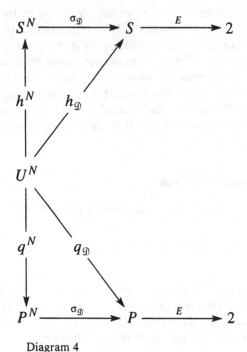

Diagram 4

the difference between $\sigma_{\mathfrak{D}}$ defined on $S(W)^N$ or $P(W)^N$. It is obvious that, in general, the equilibrium sets $E(h_{\mathfrak{D}}(u))$ and $E(q_{\mathfrak{D}}(u))$ may be different, essentially because preference is treated differently in the two models.

In the classical model two utility profiles $u, u'$ are identified if $q^N(u) = q^N(u')$, where $q$ is the quotient operation defined earlier. On the other hand, in the smooth social choice model considered here, $h^N(u) = h^N(u')$ iff at every point $x$, and for each $i \in N$, there exists a number $\lambda_i(x) > 0$ such that $du_i(x) = \lambda_i(x) du_i'(x)$. Clearly it is possible to find $u', u$ such that $q(u) = q(u')$ yet $h(u) \neq h(u')$. For example, this may be the case if the utility function $u_i$ has a critical point $x$ where $du_i^2(x) = 0$. On the other hand, if $W$ is affine and the induced preferences are strongly convex in some sense, then the equivalence classes defined by $h^N$ and $q^N$ can be identified. In this case the equilibrium sets $E(h_{\mathfrak{D}}(u))$ and $E(P_{\mathfrak{D}})$ (if they exist) will also be identical. (See Schofield 1984b.)

The previous results on the heart for a voting rule suggest that this concept can be used to give a solution to existence of a "continuous" social choice, at least in the case where preferences have a natural convexity property.

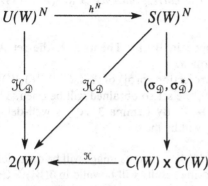

$$U(W)^N \xrightarrow{\quad h^N \quad} S(W)^N$$

$\mathcal{K}_{\mathfrak{D}} \qquad \mathcal{K}_{\mathfrak{D}} \qquad (\sigma_{\mathfrak{D}}, \sigma_{\mathfrak{D}}^*)$

$$2(W) \xleftarrow{\quad \mathcal{K} \quad} C(W) \times C(W)$$

Diagram 5

**Lemma 3.** *If $W$ is a Fan manifold then there is a well-defined functor diagram, Diagram 5, with $\mathcal{K}_{\mathfrak{D}}(h) \neq \emptyset$ for all $h \in S(W)^N$.*

*Proof:* Suppose $h = (h_1, \ldots, h_n)$ is a profile of $S$-continuous preference fields. As in Section 3, define the two continuous preference fields $hp_{\mathfrak{D}}$ and $hp_{\mathfrak{D}}^*$ by the operations $hp_{\mathfrak{D}} = \bigcup_{\mathfrak{D}}(hp_M)$ and $[hp_{\mathfrak{D}}]^* = \bigcap_{\mathfrak{D}}(hp_M)^*$. Let $(\sigma_{\mathfrak{D}}, \sigma_{\mathfrak{D}}^*)(h) = (hp_{\mathfrak{D}}, hp_{\mathfrak{D}}^*) \in C(W) \times C(W)$ and

$$\mathcal{K}(\sigma_{\mathfrak{D}}, \sigma_{\mathfrak{D}}^*)(h) = E(hp_{\mathfrak{D}}) \cup \mathrm{Clos}\, E(hp_{\mathfrak{D}}^*).$$

Clearly the diagram commutes if we define $\mathcal{K}_{\mathfrak{D}}(h) = \mathcal{K}(\sigma_{\mathfrak{D}}, \sigma_{\mathfrak{D}}^*)(h)$. As in Theorem 1, $\mathcal{K}_{\mathfrak{D}}(h) \neq \emptyset$ for all $h \in S(W)^N$.   $\square$

This lemma shows that the equilibrium notion $\mathcal{K}_{\mathfrak{D}}$ is well-defined on the space $S(W)^N$ of smooth preferences.

Let $S(W)^N$ have the quotient topology induced from the quotient map

$$h^N : U(W)^N \to S(W)^N,$$

and let $\mathfrak{I}(W)^N$ be the largest subspace of $h^N(X(W)^N)$ such that the quotient map is open on its co-image. That is, if $X$ is open in $U(W)^N$ and $\mathrm{proj}(X) = Y \subset (h^N)^{-1}(\mathfrak{I}(W)^N)$, then $h^N(Y)$ will be an open set in $\mathfrak{I}(W)^N$. Here "proj" is the natural projection mapping from $U(W)^N$, inverse to the inclusion $X(W)^N \subset U(W)^N$. Clearly the inclusion is continuous with respect to the induced topology on $X(W)^N$, so proj will be an open map.[6]

[6] It is important to note that the topology implicitly defined on $\mathfrak{I}(W)^N$ makes use of gradient information. For this reason, we shall call this the $C^1$ topology on preferences. To give an indication of the nature of this preference topology, suppose that $h_a \in S(W)$ is an $S$-continuous preference field induced from the utility function $u_a$. Then $h_a$ is characterized by the set of critical points of $u_a$ and the normalized direction gradient $du_a(x)/\|du_a(x)\|$

**Theorem 3** (Schofield 1993c).    *The correspondence* $\mathcal{H}_{\mathfrak{D}}: \mathfrak{I}(W)^N \to W$ *is well-defined and lhc.*

*Proof:*   Consider any set $V$ open in $W$. By Theorem 2, the set $X = \{u \in X(W)^N : \mathcal{H}_{\mathfrak{D}}(u) \cap V \neq \emptyset\}$ is open.

By definition, if we take the projection (proj) of $X$ in $(h^N)^{-1}(\mathfrak{I}(W)^N)$, and then map by $h^N$ into $\mathfrak{I}(W)^N$, the set so obtained will be open. Thus $h^N \circ \text{proj}(X)$ will be open in $\mathfrak{I}(W)^N$. By Lemma 3, $\mathcal{H}_{\mathfrak{D}}$ is well-defined under this operation and so $\mathcal{H}_{\mathfrak{D}}$ will be lhc on $\mathfrak{I}(W)^N$.      $\square$

Notice that if $X$ is open dense in $U(W)^N$ then its image will be open dense in $\mathfrak{I}(W)^N$. Thus the genericity voting results will be valid in $\mathfrak{I}(W)^N$. Consequently, even when a voting rule $h_{\mathfrak{D}}$ is generically badly behaved on $\mathfrak{I}(W)^N$, the heart operating on $\mathfrak{I}(W)^N$ will be lower hemicontinuous and efficient. For this reason we call $\mathfrak{I}(W)^N$ a *model space* for $U(W)^N$. Note that appropriate subspaces of $\mathfrak{I}(W)^N$ can also be used as a model space. For example, let $M(W)^N$ be the space of "Morse" preference profiles. A preference $P_i$ in $M(W)$ has a unique critical point $x_i$ called the *bliss point*, where $P_i(x_i) = \emptyset$. It can be shown that the voting paradox is generic in $M(W)^N$, and that the heart is lhc on $M(W)^N$ (Schofield 1993c). Incidentally, this proof shows $\mathfrak{I}(W)^N$ is non-empty. (We also show in the next section that a class of Euclidean preferences can also be used as a model for $U(W)^N$.)

To solve the general social choice problem, suppose that a social choice mechanism $\sigma: P(W)^N \to P(W)$ is viewed as desirable for various normative reasons. The description of $\sigma$ in general will define certain capabilities to specific coalitions at each point in $W$. For example, in the exchange model of an economy, any coalition $M$ has the capability, at a state $x$ of the world, to exchange those commodities controlled by its members. This implies that at $x$ there exists a cone of feasible acts $f_M(x)$ for this coalition. More abstractly, it is possible to define the cone $f_M(x)$ at $x$ to be the set of vectors in $\Pi^{-1}(x)$ that the rule $\sigma$ defines as feasible for coalition $M$.

As a generalization of the earlier construction, we may define the feasible and preference field for $M$ by $hf_M: W \to TW$, where $hf_M(x) = h_M(x) \cap f_M(x)$. Then the *social choice functor* gives a map $\sigma: S(W)^N \to C(W)$ defined by $\sigma(h) = h_\sigma = \bigcup hf_M$. This gives a "smooth" social choice map

$$U(W)^N \xrightarrow{h^N} S(W)^N \xrightarrow{\sigma} C(W) \xrightarrow{E} 2(W),$$

at each noncritical point $x$. Loosely speaking, a second field $h_b$ induced from $u_b$ is close to $h_a$ if the critical points and nearly all the normalized direction gradients of $h_a, h_b$ are close. Details can be found in Schofield (1993c).

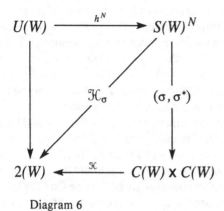

$$U(W) \xrightarrow{\ h^N\ } S(W)^N$$

$$\mathcal{H}_\sigma \qquad (\sigma, \sigma^*)$$

$$2(W) \xleftarrow{\ \mathcal{H}\ } C(W) \times C(W)$$

Diagram 6

which "approximates" the normative social choice map

$$U(W)^N \xrightarrow{q^N} P(W)^N \xrightarrow{\sigma} P(W) \xrightarrow{E} 2(W).$$

Results on the smooth social choice map can then give information on the map $\sigma: P(W)^N \to P(W)$.

In situations such as voting rules or public-goods economies, the choice sets $E(\sigma(P))$ and $E(\sigma(h))$ will often be empty, so we can define the heart correspondence, as before, by a diagram such as Diagram 6, where $\mathcal{H}_\sigma$ is non-empty for all profiles in some subdomain of $S(W)^N$.

It is even possible to construct a diagram of this sort when the active social agents are individuals, rather than coalitions. It is interesting to note that Chichilnisky (1992) has recently shown that a dual condition of the form $E(h_\sigma^*) = \emptyset$ is necessary for the existence of a competitive equilibrium, $E(h_\sigma) = E(\sigma(h))$.

Even when $E(\sigma(h))$ is empty, the heart $\mathcal{H}_\sigma(h)$ will generally be non-empty and lhc (as we have seen). Under some conditions, Michael's selection theorem (Michael 1956, 1970) can be used to give a continuous selection $g_\sigma: \mathfrak{Z}(W)^N \to W$ satisfying $g_\sigma(h) \in \mathcal{H}_\sigma(h)$. Indeed, under certain conditions it will be possible to choose $g_\sigma$ such that $g_\sigma(h) \in E(\sigma(h))$ for all $h$ such that the choice set is non-empty. This possibility is explored in the next section. In a sense, therefore, the heart $\mathcal{H}_\sigma: S(W)^N \to 2(W)$ may be viewed as a general equilibrium concept appropriate for smooth social choice, defined on a particular domain of preferences.

## 5    Spatial voting theory and Euclidean preferences

We now relate the heart to the equilibrium notions of classical social choice theory. The fact that $E(P_{\mathfrak{D}}) = \emptyset$ for a typical noncollegial voting rule has led to the examination of a set known as the *uncovered set* (Miller 1980; McKelvey 1986). For example, suppose $(P_1, ..., P_n)$ is a preference profile and $P = \sigma(P_1, ..., P_n)$ is a social preference correspondence. Define the covering correspondence $\bar{P}: W \to 2(W)$ by $y \in \bar{P}(x)$ iff $y \in P(x)$ and $z \in P(y)$ implies $z \in P(x)$. The uncovered set is $E(\bar{P}) = \{x: y \in \bar{P}(x)$ for no $x \in W\}$. Since $\bar{P}$ is acyclic, if $W$ is finite then $E(\bar{P})$ must be non-empty. If $W$ is a compact topological space and each $P_i$ is continuous in some sense, then $E(\bar{P})$ will again be non-empty (Bordes, Le Breton, and Salles 1992). In particular, if $\mathfrak{D}$ is a voting rule then $E(\bar{P})$ will belong to the Pareto set. Moreover, if $E(P) \neq \emptyset$ then $E(\bar{P}) = E(P)$. If $(P_1, ..., P_n)$ is a convex profile that converges in some sense to a profile $(P_1', ..., P_n')$ such that $E(P') \neq \emptyset$, then $E(\bar{P})$ will also converge to $E(P')$ (see Cox 1987). An interesting question is the relationship between the heart and the uncovered set, which we shall discuss in Section 6. A particularly relevant context in which to compare these two notions is in a spatial voting game where preferences are Euclidean. In this case the heart has very similar properties to the uncovered set.

**Definition 11.**    Let $W$ be a Fan space. A utility function $u_i$ is *Euclidean* iff there exists some (bliss) point $x_i \in W$ and a constant $a_i > 0$ such that

$$u_i(x) = -a_i \|x - x_i\|^2.$$

A profile $u \in U(W)^N = (u_1, ..., u_n)$ is Euclidean iff each $u_i$ is Euclidean. Let $\text{Euc}(W)^N$ be the class of such profiles. A preference $P_i$ is Euclidean iff there exists $x_i \in W$ such that $x \in P_i(y)$ iff $\|x - x_i\| < \|y - x_i\|$. A profile $(P_1, ..., P_n)$ is Euclidean iff each $P_i$ is Euclidean. Call $x_i$ the $i$th *bliss point*.

Euclidean utilities and preferences are frequently used in voting theory because $\text{Euc}(W)^N$ has very nice properties. If $u_i \in \text{Euc}(W)$ then clearly $du_i(x) = 2a_i(x_i - x)$. Hence, if $\|x_i - x_i'\| < \epsilon$ then $\|du_i(x) - du_i'(x)\| < 2a_i\epsilon$.[7] Consequently, the space of Euclidean preferences can be identified with $W$, with the usual topology induced from the Euclidean metric. Note also that $h^N$ maps $\text{Euc}(W)^N$ into a subspace of $\mathfrak{I}(W)^N$. Indeed, $h^N(\text{Euc}(W)^N)$ is homeomorphic to $W^N$ under the obvious identification (Schofield 1993c).

Since Diagram 4 shows that $h_{\mathfrak{D}}$ can be factored through $\sigma_{\mathfrak{D}}$, for any profile $u = (u_1, ..., u_n) \in \text{Euc}(W)^N$ we may simply write

$$h^N(u) = x = (x_1, ..., x_n) \in W^N$$

(where $\{x_i: i \in N\}$ are the bliss points) and identify $\sigma_{\mathfrak{D}}(x_1, ..., x_n)$ with $h_{\mathfrak{D}}(u)$. If $(P_1, ..., P_n)$ is the underlying preference profile then it is obvious

---

[7]  Note that for Euclidean preferences the $C^0$ topology and $C^1$ topology are identical, since bliss points define gradients.

that there is an identification between $P_\mathfrak{D}$ and $\sigma_\mathfrak{D}(x_1, \ldots, x_n)$. In particular, the Pareto set $E(P_N)$ is identical to the choice set $E(h_N(u))$. A relevant question is whether the voting results of Section 2 are valid in this category.

Results on the Nakamura number have been proven in the category of preferences that are convex and lower hemicontinuous (see Greenberg 1979; Schofield 1984b; Strnad 1985). Since Euclidean preferences satisfy these conditions, the results on the Nakamura number are valid in the category of Euclidean preferences. To verify the genericity results remember that the results are valid on a residual (and thus open dense) set $V$ in $U(W)^N$. To show they are valid on an open dense set of Euclidean preferences, consider the operation

$$ U(W)^N \xrightarrow{\text{proj}} \text{Euc}(W)^N \xrightarrow{h^N} W^N \subset \mathfrak{I}(W)^N. $$

Just as in the proof of Theorem 3, it is evident that this map is open; indeed, it is clear that it maps an open dense set in $U(W)^N$ to an open dense set in $W^N$. Consequently, the generic voting results are valid in the category of Euclidean preferences.[8]

The validity of the voting result on the space $W^N$ of Euclidean preference profiles implies that $W^N$ can be regarded as a *model* for the space $U(W)^N$. For a voting rule, any phenomenon that characterizes the voting rule on $U(W)^N$ can also be observed for the voting rule on $W^N$. But this also means that $\mathfrak{IC}_\mathfrak{D}$ can be used to resolve the problem of voting instability on $W^N$.

Because the composite map $h^N \circ \text{proj}: U(W)^N \to W^N$ is open, an immediate implication is that

$$ h^N \circ \text{proj}: U(W)^N \longrightarrow X(W)^N \longrightarrow \text{Euc}(W)^N \longrightarrow W^N $$

is also open. As we have noted, if $P$ is a Euclidean preference profile and $u$ is any utility profile such that $(h^N)^{-1}(P) = u$, then the critical Pareto set $E(h_N(u))$ is identical to the Pareto set $E(P_N)$. Thus the efficiency property of Theorem 1(1) can be read as $\mathfrak{IC}_\mathfrak{D} \subset E(P_N)$. That is to say, the heart is *Paretian*. We thus obtain immediately, as a corollary of Theorems 1, 2, and 3, the following result (proved first in Schofield 1993a).

**Corollary 1.** *For Euclidean preferences on a Fan space $W$, the correspondence $\mathfrak{IC}_\mathfrak{D}: W^N \to W$ is non-empty, lhc, and Paretian.*

Although cycles will be generic for any noncollegial voting rule, even when preferences are assumed to be Euclidean, it is still possible to define the

---

[8] Note that Le Breton's (1987) result on the generic voting paradox is not valid for Euclidean preferences without the dimension constraint involving $w(\mathfrak{D})$. This is because the open sets of preferences required of his construction contain nonconvex preference.

heart as an equilibrium notion that satisfies the existence, continuity, and Pareto properties. From earlier discussion it is also evident that, for any social choice rule $\sigma$, it is possible to define a parallel equilibrium notion $\mathcal{K}_\sigma$ satisfying the same existence, continuity, and Pareto properties.

In a number of papers, Chichilnisky (1980, 1982) considered the existence of a social preference functor $\sigma$, defined on a domain of smooth preferences and satisfying a Pareto-like unanimity condition. Chichilnisky and Heal (1983) showed that a necessary and sufficient condition for $\sigma$ to be continuous is that its domain be contractible. In general, of course, the space of preference profiles will not be contractible; however, the space of Euclidean preferences on a Fan space is contractible. In this case, by Corollary 1, it is possible to use a continuous selection of the heart correspondence, using Michael's (1956) selection theorem to solve the social choice problem: to obtain a social choice which continuously depends on the smooth preference profile $(u_1, \ldots, u_n)$.

**Corollary 2.** *Let $W^N$ be the space of Euclidean profiles on a Fan space $W$. For any voting rule $\mathfrak{D}$, there is an efficient, continuous social choice function $g_{\mathfrak{D}}: W^N \to W$ which approximates the social choice defined by $\sigma_{\mathfrak{D}}$, in the sense that if $E(\sigma_{\mathfrak{D}}(x)) \neq \emptyset$ then $g_{\mathfrak{D}}(x) \in E(\sigma_{\mathfrak{D}}(x))$. Moreover, if $\{x_j : j = 1, \ldots\}$ is a sequence of Euclidean profiles converging to a profile $x$ such that $E(\sigma_{\mathfrak{D}}(x)) \neq \emptyset$, then $\mathcal{K}_{\mathfrak{D}}(x_j)$ converges to $E(\sigma_{\mathfrak{D}}(x))$.*

*Proof:* We have shown that $\mathcal{K}_{\mathfrak{D}}$ exists and is lhc on $W^N$. Moreover, $\mathcal{K}_{\mathfrak{D}}$ is Paretian in the sense that, for all $x \in W^N$, $\mathcal{K}_{\mathfrak{D}}(x)$ is a subset of the Pareto set. By Michael's selection theorem, there exists a continuous selection $g_{\mathfrak{D}}$ of $\mathrm{Con}(\mathcal{K}_{\mathfrak{D}})$; that is, $g_{\mathfrak{D}}(x)$ belongs to the convex hull of $\mathcal{K}_{\mathfrak{D}}(x)$. But the Pareto set is convex, so $\mathrm{Con}(\mathcal{K}_{\mathfrak{D}}(x))$ is a subset of the Pareto set.

It is an easy matter to show that, for Euclidean preferences, $E(\sigma_{\mathfrak{D}}(x)) \neq \emptyset$ iff $E(\sigma_{\mathfrak{D}}^*(x)) = \emptyset$. When $E(\sigma_{\mathfrak{D}}(x))$ is non-empty it is also convex and so $\mathcal{K}_{\mathfrak{D}}(x) = E(\sigma_{\mathfrak{D}}(x))$. Thus $g_{\mathfrak{D}}(x)$ can be chosen so that $g_{\mathfrak{D}}(x) \in E(\sigma_{\mathfrak{D}}(x))$ when this is non-empty. The last statement follows from lhc of the heart and because $\mathcal{K}_{\mathfrak{D}}(x) = E(\sigma_{\mathfrak{D}}(x))$ when $E(\sigma_{\mathfrak{D}}(x))$ is non-empty.    $\square$

These two corollaries show that the heart satisfies the two characteristic properties of the uncovered set – namely, Pareto optimality and convergence to the core.[9] Some suggestions for using Corollary 2 are presented

---

[9]  We have proved these results for Euclidean preferences, though they are also true for Morse preferences. Notice, however, that for Morse preferences the $C^1$ topology that we employ is finer than the $C^0$ topology. It is not obvious that Cox's (1987) proof of $C^0$ convergence for the uncovered set implies $C^1$ convergence. It is possible that the convergence property for the uncovered set is strictly weaker than the $C^1$ convergence obtained for the heart. See Schofield (1993c).

in Section 7. First, however, in Section 6 we discuss an application of the concept of the heart in the case of an infinite electorate, in order to compare this notion with that of the uncovered set.

## 6  The heart of an electorate

In the previous sections the heart has been constructed for a finite set $N$ of voters. It is possible to extend the analysis to the case of a continuum society, where each voter has Euclidean preferences and the distribution of voters is described by a density function $f$, say, on the Fan space $W$. In this case a coalition $M$ is identified with a subset of $W$. Plurality rule means that any coalition with weight $\mu(M) = \int_M x\, df > \frac{1}{2}$ is winning (that is, belongs to $\mathfrak{D}$). The choice for plurality rule can be written

$$E_{1/2}(f) = \{x \in W: x \in M \ \forall M \text{ with } \mu(M) > \tfrac{1}{2} \text{ and } M \text{ a convex set}\}.$$

For example, if $W = B^w$, the $w$-dimensional ball centered on a point $0 \in W$, and if $f$ is the uniform distribution on $W$, then $E_{1/2}(f) = \{0\}$ (Arrow 1969). A useful criterion for existence of $E_{1/2}(f)$ is in terms of median hyperplanes. Here $M$ is a median hyperplane if $M$ is a subset of $\mathbb{R}^{w-1} \subset W$, and $M$ divides $W$ into two closed half-spaces $M_+$ and $M_-$ such that $\mu(M_+) = \mu(M_-) = \frac{1}{2}$. Then $x \in E_{1/2}(f)$ iff $x \in M$ for every median hyperplane. See Schofield and Tovey (1992) for fuller discussion.

To illustrate, suppose that $W = \Delta$ is the equilateral triangle in $\mathbb{R}^2$ and that $f$ is the uniform distribution on the boundary of $W$ (see Figure 2). In Figure 2, three median hyperplanes (lines in this case) are drawn parallel to the three sides of the triangles. These are labeled $M_1, M_2, M_3$. It is evident that each of these median lines divides two of the sides of $\Delta$ in the ratio $1:3$, so the relative area of the small interior triangle $\Delta'$ (bounded by these medians) to that of $\Delta$ is $1:16$, or $0.0625:1$. To see that any point in $\Delta'$ belongs to the heart, notice that for any $x$ in $\Delta'$ it is possible to choose three vectors $\{v_i: i = 1, 2, 3\}$ such that the equations $x + \lambda_i v_i \in M_i$, $i = 1, 2, 3$, have a semipositive solution $\lambda_1, \lambda_2, \lambda_3 \geq 0$, not all zero. In essence this means that $x \in \mathcal{K}_{1/2}(f)$, where $\mathcal{K}_{1/2}(f)$ is the heart under plurality rule for the distribution $f$.

In analyzing the uncovered set for such a game, McKelvey (1986) introduced the notion of the *yolk*. The yolk is the smallest ball $B(z, l)$ centered at $z \in W$, with radius $l$, such that $B(z, l) \cap M \neq \emptyset$ for every median line $M$. Notice that the ball $B$ inscribed in $\Delta'$ is a candidate for the yolk. In fact, Tovey (1992) has shown that the yolk can always be characterized in dimension $w$ as the smallest ball inscribed in a simplex formed by $w+1$ median hyperplanes. To see that $B$ is indeed the yolk, it is necessary to characterize in some way the family of all median lines in Figure 2. Consider the vertical line $M_4$ from the top vertex $a$ to the midpoint $b$ of the

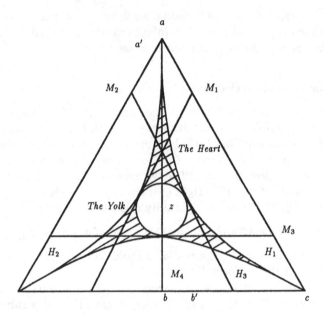

Figure 2. The yolk and heart for the uniform population on the boundary of the triangle.

base. Clearly, $M_4$ is median. Now let $a'$ be a point on the perimeter of $\Delta$ a distance $\epsilon$ from $a$, and let $b'$ be a point of distance $\epsilon'$ to the right of $b$, so that the line through $a'$ and $b'$ is a median. Increasing $\epsilon$ from 0 creates a family of median lines. Tangency points of this family inscribe a curve from $a$ to $c$, labeled $H_1$ in the diagram. In particular, every point on $H_1$ is a point of tangency between $H_1$ and some median line. Thus $H_1$ is the envelope of a family of median lines. By symmetry we may also draw the envelopes $H_2$ and $H_3$. Notice that $\{H_i: i = 1, 2, 3\}$ all touch the ball $B$; thus $B$ is the yolk. It is easy to show that the closed star-shaped object bounded by $\{H_i: i = 1, 2, 3\}$ is the heart $\mathcal{H}_{1/2}(f)$. Note the relationship of the triangle $\Delta'$ to the heart. Further observe that the choice set $E_{1/2}(f)$ in Figure 2 is empty, since the median lines $\{M_i: i = 1, 2, 3\}$ do not intersect. Now, by symmetry, the center $z$ of the yolk is at the barycenter (the intersection of the perpendicular bisectors). The barycenter divides the perpendicular bisectors in the ratio $1:2$. Consider the choice set

$$E_{5/9}(f) = \{x \in W : x \in M \ \forall M \text{ with } \mu(M) \geq \tfrac{5}{9} \text{ and } M \text{ convex}\}$$

under $\alpha$-plurality rule, with $\alpha = \tfrac{5}{9}$. Clearly $E_{5/9}(t) = \{z\}$. This is consistent with the Caplin–Nalebuff (1988) result on the existence of a $1 - (w/(w+1))^w$-supramajority rule in dimension $w$. Consequently, the family of $\alpha$-plurality rules as $\alpha$ varies from $\frac{1}{2}$ to $\frac{5}{9}$ generates a family $\mathcal{K}_\alpha(f)$ which "smoothly" collapses to the singularity point $z$.

To consider plurality rule again, at any point $y$ outside $\mathcal{K}_{1/2}(f)$, the integral curves of the preference fields point into $\mathcal{K}_{1/2}(f)$. Thus $\mathcal{K}_{1/2}(f)$ is, in some sense, an *attractor* for the preference field generated by the voting process.

Finally, consider the relationship between the heart and the uncovered set, described in the previous section. From McKelvey (1986) it is known that the uncovered set lies within a ball $B(z, l')$ centered on the yolk, but with radius $l'$ greater than the yolk radius. In general it is difficult to compute the uncovered set (Epstein 1993). In the case considered here, it will have some symmetry properties induced from the symmetry of $f$. The relationship between the heart and the uncovered set is as yet unclear, but Figure 2 is suggestive. Since it appears that the yolk intersects both the heart and the uncovered set, it is plausible that the latter two equilibrium sets always intersect. Recent analyses of the computational and asymptotic features of the yolk (Tovey 1990, 1993) may shed light on this relationship.

## 7     Conclusion: the heart of a polity

One of the most difficult problems in democratic theory concerns the appropriate way to model multiparty competition in representative democracies (see e.g. Baron 1993).

Two recent papers (Schofield 1993a,b) have suggested basing the model on the concept of the heart. Let $N = \{1, ..., n\}$ be a list of political parties competing to enter government. Let us suppose that each party $i$ may transmit a message $z_i$ in some message space $Z_i$, where $z_i$ specifies the characteristics of the utility function $u_i$ to be used by $i$. Based on the profile $z = (z_1, ..., z_n)$ of messages, the electorate allocates seats to the parties as described by a function $e$ where $e(z) \in \Delta_n$. Here $\Delta_n$ is the $(n-1)$ dimensional simplex and $e_i(z)$ is party $i$'s share of the vote. Under parliamentary rules, the vector $e(z)$ defines a family of parliamentary decisive coalitions $\mathcal{D}(z)$. The information coded in the message $z$, together with $\mathcal{D}(z)$, defines a heart – now written $\mathcal{K}\mathcal{D}(z)$ in the policy space $W$. The outcome of coalition negotiations is a finite lottery across different possible coalition outcomes, where each possible outcome belongs to the heart $\mathcal{K}\mathcal{D}(z)$.

Let $\tilde{W}$ be the space of finite lotteries on $W$, with the topology induced from the topology on $W$. We have therefore constructed a correspondence

$$\tilde{\mathcal{K}\mathcal{D}}: \textstyle\prod_i Z_i \longrightarrow \tilde{W},$$

where $\tilde{\mathcal{K}\mathcal{D}}(z)$ is the set of all possible lotteries across the set $\mathcal{K}\mathcal{D}(z)$ in $W$.

From the previous results, the heart correspondence will be lhc on an appropriate domain. It is plausible therefore that the generalized heart correspondence $\mathfrak{IC}\mathfrak{D}$ into $\tilde{W}$ will also be lhc.

By Michael's selection theorem, any convex-valued lhc correspondence admits a continuous selection. Therefore there will exist a continuous selection $g$, say, of the convex valued correspondence $\text{Con}(\mathfrak{IC}\mathfrak{D})$. Let us suppose that $g: \prod Z_i \to \tilde{W}$ is a continuous selection satisfying $g(z) \in \text{Con}(\mathfrak{IC}\mathfrak{D}(z))$ which specifies the rules of the political game. Under typical conditions, there will exist a mixed strategy Nash equilibrium $\tilde{z} \in \prod_i \tilde{Z}_i$ given by the fixed point of the best reaction correspondence induced by the true party preference profile $(u)$, the selection $g$, and the electoral response $e$. Assuming that each $u \in \text{Con}(W)^N$ gives a mixed strategy Nash equilibrium $E(u)$, we obtain the political equilibrium correspondence

$$\text{Con}(W)^N \xrightarrow{E} \prod \tilde{Z}_i \xrightarrow{g} \tilde{W}.$$

See Schofield and Parks (1993) for a first attempt at analyzing such a political model. From this point of view, the underlying theoretical question concerns the relationship between the political equilibrium obtained in such a model and the distribution of preferences in the electorate.

## REFERENCES

Arrow, K. (1969), "Tullock and an Existence Theorem," *Public Choice* 6: 105–11.
Austen-Smith, D. (1993), "Refinements of the Heart," typescript, Department of Political Science, University of Rochester, New York.
Banks, J. S. (1994), "Singularity Theory and Core Existence in the Spatial Model," typescript, Rochester Center for Economic Research, University of Rochester, New York.
Baron, D. (1993), "Government Formation and Endogenous Parties," *American Political Science Review* 87: 34–47.
Berge, C. (1963), *Topological Spaces*. London: Oliver and Boyd.
Bergstrom, T. (1975), "The Existence of Maximal Elements and Equilibria in the Absence of Transitivity," typescript, Department of Economics, University of Michigan, Ann Arbor.
   (1992), "When Non-Transitive Relations Take Maxima and Competitive Equilibrium Can't Be Beat," in W. Neuefeind and R. Riezman (eds.), *Economic Theory and International Trade: Essays in Memorium of J. Trout Rader*. Heidelberg: Springer.
Bordes, G., M. Le Breton, and M. Salles (1992), "Gillies' and Miller's Subrelations of a Relation over an Infinite Set of Alternatives: General Results and Applications to Voting Games," *Mathematics of Operations Research* 17: 508–18.
Caplin, A., and B. Nalebuff (1988), "On 64% Majority Rule," *Econometrica* 56: 787–814.
Chichilnisky, G. (1980), "Social Choice and the Topology of Spaces of Preference," *Advances in Mathematics* 37: 165–76.

(1982), "Social Aggregation Rules and Continuity," *Quarterly Journal of Economics* 87: 337–52.

(1992), "Limited Arbitrage Is Necessary and Sufficient for the Existence of a Competitive Equilibrium," typescript, Department of Economics, Columbia University, New York.

Chichilnisky, G., and G. Heal (1983), "Necessary and Sufficient Conditions for a Resolution of the Social Choice Paradox," *Journal of Economic Theory* 31: 68–87.

Cox, Gary (1987), "The Uncovered Set and the Core," *American Journal of Political Science* 31: 408–22.

Epstein, D. (1993), "Uncovering Some Subtleties of the Uncovered Set," typescript, Department of Political Science, Columbia University, New York.

Fan, K. (1961), "A Generalization of Tychonoff's Fixed Point Theorem," *Mathematische Annalen* 42: 305–10.

Golubitsky, M., and V. Guillemin (1973), *Stable Mappings and Their Singularities*. New York: Springer.

Greenberg, Joseph (1979), "Consistent Majority Rules over Compact Sets of Alternatives," *Econometrica* 41: 285–97.

Hirsch, M. (1976), *Differential Topology*. New York: Springer.

Le Breton, M. (1987), "On the Core of Voting Games," *Social Choice and Welfare* 4: 295–305.

McKelvey, R. (1986), "Covering, Dominance, and Institution-Free Properties of Social Choice," *American Journal of Political Science* 30: 283–314.

McKelvey, R., and N. Schofield (1986), "Structural Instability of the Core," *Journal of Mathematical Economics* 15: 179–98.

(1987), "Generalized Symmetry Conditions at a Core Point," *Econometrica* 55: 923–33.

Michael, E. (1956), "Continuous Selections I," *Annals of Mathematics* 63: 361–82.

(1970), "A Survey of Continuous Selections," in W. M. Fleischman (ed.), *Set-Valued Mappings, Selections and Topological Properties*. Heidelberg: Springer.

Miller, N. (1980), "A Non Solution Set for Tournaments and Majority Voting," *American Journal of Political Science* 24: 68–96.

Nakamura, K. (1979), "The Vetoers in a Simple Game with Ordinal Preference," *International Journal of Game Theory* 8: 55–61 (reprinted in K. Nakamura, *Game Theory and Social Choice*, Tokyo: Keiso Shobo and Tokyo Institute of Technology).

Plott, C. (1967), "A Notion of Equilibrium and Its Possibility under Majority Rule," *American Economic Review* 57: 787–806.

Schofield, N. (1978), "Instability of Simple Dynamic Games," *Review of Economic Studies* 45: 575–94.

(1983), "Equilibria in Simple Dynamic Games," in P. K. Pattanaik and M. Salles (eds.), *Social Choice and Welfare*. Amsterdam: North-Holland.

(1984a), "Existence of Equilibrium on a Manifold," *Mathematics of Operations Research* 9: 545–57.

(1984b), "Social Equilibrium and Cycles on Compact Sets," *Journal of Economic Theory* 33: 59–71.

(1985), *Social Choice and Democracy*. Heidelberg: Springer.

(1989), "Smooth Social Choice," *Mathematical and Computer Modelling* 12: 417–35.

(1993a), "Party Competition in a Spatial Model of Coalition Formation," in W. Barnett, M. Hinich, and N. Schofield (eds.), *Political Economy: Institutions, Competition, and Representation.* Cambridge: Cambridge University Press.

(1993b), "Political Competition in Multiparty Coalition Governments," *European Journal of Political Research* 23: 1-33.

(1993c), "General Equilibrium in a Political Economy," typescript, Center in Political Economy, Washington University in St. Louis, MO.

Schofield, N., and R. Parks (1993), "Existence of Nash Equilibrium in a Spatial Model of *n*-Party Competition," typescript, Center in Political Economy, Washington University in St. Louis, MO.

Schofield, N., and C. Tovey (1992), "Probability and Convergence for Supra-Majority Rule with Euclidean Preferences," *Mathematical and Computer Modelling* 16: 41-58.

Smale, S. (1973), "Global Analysis and Economics I: Pareto Optimum and a Generalization of Morse Theory," in M. Peixoto (ed.), *Dynamical Systems.* New York: Academic Press.

(1982), "Global Analysis and Economics," in K. J. Arrow and M. D. Intriligator (eds.), *Handbook of Mathematical Economics.* Amsterdam: North-Holland.

Spanier, E. H. (1966), *Algebraic Topology.* New York: McGraw-Hill.

Strnad, J. (1985), "The Structure of Continuous-Valued Neutral Monotonic Social Functions," *Social Choice and Welfare* 2: 181-95.

Tovey, C. (1990), "The Almost Surely Shrinking Yolk," typescript, School of Industrial and Systems Engineering, Georgia Institute of Technology, Atlanta.

(1992), "A Polynomial-Time Algorithm for Computing the Yolk in Fixed Dimension," *Mathematical Programming* 57: 259-77.

(1993), "Some Foundations for Empirical Study in the Euclidean Spatial Model of Social Choice," in W. Barnett, M. Hinich, and N. Schofield (eds.), *Political Economy: Institutions, Competition, and Representation.* Cambridge: Cambridge University Press.

Walker, M. (1977), "On the Existence of Maximal Elements," *Journal of Economic Theory* 16: 470-4.

CHAPTER 10

# Dynamical convergence in the Euclidean spatial model

*Craig A. Tovey*

## 1    Introduction

A classic result of Kramer (1977) for the Euclidean spatial model shows that repeated proposals by competing vote-maximizing parties will produce sequences converging to the minmax (Simpson–Kramer) set. This "dynamical convergence" helps establish the importance of the minmax set: The solution set possesses not only attractive normative properties (Simpson 1969; Kramer 1977; Slutsky 1979) but also dynamically attractive properties in that natural forces of majority voting tend to drive a group decision toward it.

Similarly, Miller (1980, 1983) has shown that under a variety of agenda settings, the outcome of (strategic) majority voting will lie in the uncovered set, and this dynamical property is crucial to this solution set's importance. Ferejohn, McKelvey, and Packel (1984) found a dynamical property for another solution set, the yolk. They showed, roughly speaking, that if proposals are made at random with majority voting, then the incumbent proposal will frequently be contained in the yolk.

All these results are of the same type: they demonstrate that some voting process, taking place over time, leads the group decision toward a particular solution set. The aim of this paper is to derive a dynamical result of this type for a new solution set, the $\epsilon$-*core*. This solution set has been proposed recently by Salant and Goodstein (1990) to better fit empirical data, and by Tovey (1991b) to incorporate some "friction" into the spatial model. The idea is that the incumbent or status quo has some amount, $\epsilon > 0$, of advantage versus the alternatives. Voters will vote for an alternative only if it is at least $\epsilon$ better (closer) than the incumbent.

Research supported by a Presidential Young Investigator Award from the National Science Foundation (ECS-8451032), and a Senior Research Associateship from the National Research Council at the Naval Postgraduate School, Monterey.

The parameter $\epsilon$ can be interpreted as a measure of friction, resistance to change, or incumbency advantage. This solution set is equivalent to the concept of an $\epsilon$-equilibrium or an $\epsilon$-core in game theory (Shubik and Wooders 1983; Wooders 1983), and shares much of the same motivation.

In this paper, the yolk is used not as a solution set but as an asymmetry measure for configurations of voter ideal points. The larger the yolk radius, the more skewed is the configuration. Our main result (Theorem 1) states that if $\epsilon$ is sufficiently large compared with the yolk radius, then there are no global intransitivities. Moreover, any sequence of proposals starting from $x$ will reach the $\epsilon$-core in some number of steps that is a function of $\epsilon$, the yolk radius, and the distance from $x$ to the yolk center. This result holds for any number of voters in any number of dimensions.

A crucial feature of Theorem 1 is its linkage between the "skewness" of the configuration of voter ideal points (as measured by the yolk radius) and the degree of stability enjoyed by the voting process. From Theorem 1 we may infer a plausible qualitative prediction that if the frictions or resistance to change represented by $\epsilon$ increase, then the likelihood of stability and speed of convergence will both increase. On the other hand, the more skewed the voter configuration, the slower and less likely is convergence. If we are to construct an effective predictive theory of social choice, our models should accommodate this range of observed group behavior (from rapid convergence to equilibrium, to instability), and should link these outcomes with measurable characteristics of the group (such as distributional characteristics of individual preferences).

It is worth emphasizing that Theorem 1 gives an explicit upper bound on the number of steps needed to reach equilibrium. This aspect of the result is unusually strong. As the examples in Section 3 illustrate, the absence of global intransitivities is not in itself sufficient to assure finite or even infinite convergence. On the other hand, a significant weakness of the results in this paper lies in the assumption of sincere voting. It would be very interesting to see if the results could be carried through in some form if strategic behavior were incorporated into the model.

In Section 2, we formally state the definitions and assumptions, and prove the main convergence result for the $\epsilon$-core. In Section 3, we reexamine Kramer's result. The convergence there is not fully satisfactory in two ways. First, if two parties were to follow the vote-maximizing strategy, then each could make arbitrarily small steps and there might be no appreciable movement away from the initial position. Second, if a point in the minmax set ever were reached, the process would jump out of the minmax set on the next step.

The aim of Section 3 is to develop an alternative dynamical convergence result for the minmax set that does not suffer from these two problems. We attempt to find an analogous version of Theorem 1 for supramajority voting that guarantees that any sequence of proposals will reach a super-majority core point in a finite number of steps, determined a priori. We show by several examples that this is not possible without making several more constraining assumptions. The main result of the section is Theorem 5: If we assume supermajority voting at a level a bit higher than the minmax level, require a minimum distance between proposals, and make one additional regularity assumption, then any sequence of proposals must reach the core within a certain number of steps.

## 2     Paths to the $\epsilon$-core

First we give the necessary definitions.

The set $V$ is any finite collection of (not necessarily distinct) points in $\mathbb{R}^m$. These are the ideal or bliss points of the voters. The proposal space is assumed to be all of $\mathbb{R}^m$. Throughout we will let $\|y\|$ denote the length or Euclidean norm of a vector $y \in \mathbb{R}^m$.

We suppose that there is some *voting rule,* such as simple majority, by which the voters can decide between two alternatives. The voting rule must be decisive, but it need not be neutral: one of the alternatives is designated the *incumbent,* the other is the proposed alternative, and the voting rule need not treat the two alike. For example, if the two alternatives receive exactly the same number of votes, then under simple majority voting the incumbent is the winner.

Next comes the crucial definition of a sequence of proposals. Imagine any iterative process where the initial incumbent proposal is $x$; an alternative $y$ is proposed and the voters decide between $y$ and $x$. If $y$ defeats $x$ then $y$ becomes the new incumbent proposal, and the process has completed a step or iteration. If an incumbent that cannot be defeated is reached, the process terminates. Regardless of the means by which alternatives are proposed, the history of the process is summarized by the sequence of proposals $\{x, y, \ldots\}$, where each point in the sequence defeats its predecessor.

Thus, we define a *sequence of proposals* as any sequence of points $\{x^1, x^2, \ldots\}$ such that alternative $x^{i+1}$ would defeat incumbent $x^i$ for all $i > 1$. We say that the sequence *starts at* $x^1$. If for some $j$ the point $x^j$ cannot be defeated then the sequence *terminates* at $x^j$. The point $x^j$ is called a *core point* (with respect to the operant voting rule) because it cannot be dislodged. For example, if voting is according to simple majority rule, then a proposal sequence, if it terminates, does so at a Condorcet point.

Our assumption regarding the actions of the voters is stated next.

**Assumption I.**    A voter with ideal point $v \in \mathbb{R}^m$ will vote for a proposal $y \in \mathbb{R}^m$ if and only if the incumbent proposal $x^i$ satisfies $\|x^i - v\| > \|y - v\| + \epsilon$.

The $\epsilon$-core is the set of $x \in \mathbb{R}^m$ such that, if $x$ is the incumbent, then $x$ cannot be defeated by simple majority rule when voting is according to Assumption I. When $\epsilon = 0$, a point in the $\epsilon$-core would be a Condorcet point with respect to majority voting in the classic Euclidean model. Usually there are no such points (Plott 1967). For any $V$, however, the $\epsilon$-core is non-empty for sufficiently large $\epsilon$.

Non-emptiness is perhaps the very least one would desire of a solution concept. An additional desirable property is global transitivity, which essentially means the absence of cycles (intransitivities). We define it formally in terms of a proposal sequence: A voting rule has no global intransitivities if and only if (hereafter "iff") there does not exist a sequence of proposals $\{x^i : i = 1, \ldots\}$ and an integer $j > 1$ such that $x^j = x^1$. In other words, it is not possible for a sequence of proposals to return to a point. This property is important because if it fails to hold then a voting process could cycle indefinitely even if the core were non-empty. As we will see in Section 3, however, global transitivity is not sufficient to guarantee even infinite convergence to the core.

We also need to define the yolk of the configuration $V$. Let $h$ denote any (full-dimensional) hyperplane in $\mathbb{R}^m$, and let $h^+$ and $h^-$ denote the two closed half-spaces into which $h$ divides $\mathbb{R}^m$. Then $h$ is a *median* hyperplane of $V$ iff $|V \cap h^+| \geq |V|/2$ and $|V \cap h^-| \geq |V|/2$. That is, each closed half-space must contain at least half the voter ideal points.

A yolk of $V$ is a ball in $\mathbb{R}^m$ of smallest radius that intersects every median hyperplane of $V$. The yolk was originally developed by McKelvey (1986) for $|V|$ odd and is unique in that case. Following Koehler (1990) and Stone and Tovey (1992), we permit an even number of voters as well. In this case (see Tovey 1992) the yolk may not be unique, although its radius is unique. In the theorem that follows the statement is true for any yolk. The only property that we use is that the yolk intersects all median hyperplanes of $V$. As indicated in Section 1, the yolk radius $r$ is a measure of how skewed $V$ is. If $r = 0$ then $V$ is symmetric in the sense of Plott (1967) or McKelvey and Schofield (1987). The greater is $r$, the more skewed is $V$.

We can now state the main result of the paper.

**Theorem 1.**  *Let $V$ be any set of voter ideal points in $\mathbb{R}^m$, with yolk center and radius $c$ and $r$, respectively. Suppose voting occurs according to Assumption I.*

(i)   *If $\epsilon > r$ then the $(\epsilon)$-core is non-empty.*

(ii)  *If $\epsilon > 2r$ then there are no global intransitivities and moreover, for all $x \in \mathbb{R}^m$, any sequence of proposals starting at $x$ must reach a core point in at most*

$$\left\lceil \frac{\|x-c\|-r}{\epsilon-2r} \right\rceil$$

*steps, where $\lceil a \rceil$ denotes the least integer greater than or equal to $a$.*

*Proof:* If the dimension $m = 1$ the proof is trivial. Hereafter we take $m \ge 2$.

(i) If $\epsilon > r$ then $c$ is in the $\epsilon$-core. For consider any alternative $y$ to the incumbent yolk center $c$. Let

$$\bar{y} = c + r\left( \frac{y-c}{\|y-c\|} \right).$$

The point $\bar{y}$ lies on the surface of the yolk and is collinear with $y$ and $c$. Note that $\bar{y}$ may lie between $y$ and $c$, or $y$ may lie between $\bar{y}$ and $c$, but $c$ is not between $y$ and $\bar{y}$.

The half-plane $h$ tangent to the yolk at $\bar{y}$ defines a closed half-space $h^+$ containing the yolk. On the one hand, all voters whose ideal points are in $h^+$ will vote for $c$. But, on the other hand, the half-space $h^+$ contains the yolk and therefore contains at least $|V|/2$ ideal points. (If $h^+$ contains the yolk of $V$ then $h^+$ contains the median hyperplane of $V$ that is parallel to $h$.) Thus no proposal $y$ brought against $c$ can muster more than $|V|/2$ votes, whence $c$ is undefeated.

(ii) Now suppose that incumbent proposal $x$ is defeated by proposal $y$ and that $\epsilon > 2r$. Our principal claim is that $y$ must be at least $\epsilon - 2r$ closer to the yolk center $c$ than $x$ is. That is, we claim $\|y-c\| \le \|x-c\| - \epsilon + 2r$. For readability we let $d(x, y)$ denote the distance $\|x-y\|$ between $x$ and $y$.

Let $S$ denote the hyperboloid defined as

$$S \equiv \{x \in \mathbb{R}^m \mid d(x, s) = d(y, s) + \epsilon\}.$$

The hyperboloid $S$ separates $\mathbb{R}^m \setminus S$ into two open regions; let $S^+$ denote that open region containing the point $y$. Note that, by Assumption I, the voters who vote for $y$ over $x$ are precisely those whose ideal points are located in $S^+$. If $c \in S^+$ or $c \in S$ then $d(y, c) \le d(x, c) - \epsilon \le d(x, c) - \epsilon + 2r$ and our claim would be proved. So suppose $c$ is on the other side of $S$.

At any point in $S$ there is a supporting hyperplane of $S$ and an associated unit-length normal vector. Let $z$ be the point in $S$ whose unit normal vector points to the yolk center $c$. That is, its normal vector is $(c-z)/\|c-z\|$. Let $h$ denote the supporting hyperplane of $S$ at $z$ and let $h^+$ denote the closed half-space defined by $h$ containing $y$.

Since $h^+$ contains $S^+$ and $y$ defeats $x$, we have $|V \cap h^+| \ge |V \cap S^+| > |V|/2$. Therefore, either $h$ or some hyperplane parallel to $h$ that intersects $S^+$ is a median of $V$. This fact, together with the property that $c-z$ is normal to $h$, implies that $d(z, c) \le r$.

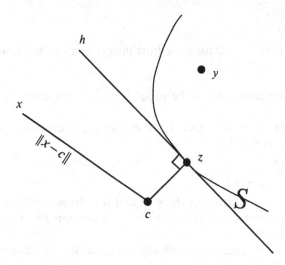

Figure 1. The plane containing $x$, $y$, $c$, and $z$.

We now restrict our attention to the 2-dimensional plane generated (as the affine hull) by $x$, $y$, and $c$. It is clear that $z$ lies on this plane as well. See Figure 1.

We have shown that $d(c, z) \leq r$. Also, by the definition of $S$, we have $d(z, y) = d(z, x) - \epsilon$. By the triangle inequality and the preceding,

$$d(c, y) \leq d(c, z) + d(z, y) \leq d(z, x) - \epsilon + r.$$

Also by the triangle inequality,

$$d(z, x) \leq d(z, c) + d(c, x) \leq d(c, x) + r \;\Rightarrow\; d(y, c) \leq d(x, c) - \epsilon + 2r.$$

This proves the claim. Every step in the sequence of proposals brings us at least $\epsilon - 2r$ closer to the yolk center $c$.

Since $\epsilon - 2r > 0$, we have immediately from the claim that there are no global intransitivities. It also follows that the process will terminate in $\lceil d(x, c)/(\epsilon - 2r) \rceil$ or fewer steps.

To improve the bound to the statement of the theorem, we notice that when $\epsilon > 2r$, the entire yolk is contained in the $\epsilon$-core. This follows from an argument almost exactly the same as in the proof of (i). As a consequence, the voting process is sure to terminate once the incumbent is within distance $r$ of $c$. If $K$ is the necessary number of steps, then $K$ integer and

$$d(x, c) - K(\epsilon - 2r) \leq r$$

implies that we may take

$$K = \left\lceil \frac{\|x - c\| - r}{\epsilon - 2r} \right\rceil$$

as desired.                                                                                      □

## 3        On Kramer's result and paths to supramajority cores

One of the attractive features of Theorem 1 is the convergence to the core in a finite number of steps. In contrast, Kramer's dynamical process does not necessarily converge. In that process, two parties alternate making proposals. Each party proposes that $y \in \mathbb{R}^m$, which maximizes the number of votes $y$ would get against incumbent proposal $x$. It is easy to see that if $y$ is such a point with respect to $x$ then so is their midpoint $(y + x)/2$. Indeed, the latter point is a more conservative choice if, for example, there is any uncertainty about $V$. Therefore, the distance between successive proposals can be arbitrarily small and convergence may fail even in the limit (see Theorem 3). Kramer's process is also not fully satisfactory because if the incumbent were the minmax set, then the succeeding proposal would not be. That is, if the process does get into the minmax set, it may pop back out in the next step.

In this section we explore the possibility of an alternative minmax-set dynamical convergence result that is more satisfactory in these respects. We will eventually succeed, but only by losing much of what was desirable in Kramer's model.

The first condition we examine is intended to prohibit arbitrarily small steps. We consider convergence properties of simple majority voting under a simple condition related to Assumption I.

**Assumption II.**    Voters vote sincerely. Any proposal $x^{i+1}$ offered against incumbent proposal $x^i$ must satisfy $\|x^i - x^{i+1}\| > \delta$. If a voter is indifferent between $x^{i+1}$ and $x^i$ then the vote is cast for the incumbent.

This assumption enforces a minimum distance between proposals. It is suggested informally at least as early as Tullock (1967). It can be thought of as an institutional restriction; see also Tovey (1991b) for a formal treatment.

Any point $x$ that would be undominated under Assumption II would be in the $\epsilon$-core with $\epsilon = \delta/2$. Clearly the converse is false in general. From the standpoint of core existence, Assumption II is thus weaker than Assumption I when $\epsilon = \delta/2$. The dynamical convergence properties that follow from Assumption II are unfortunately much weaker, as Theorem 2 shows.

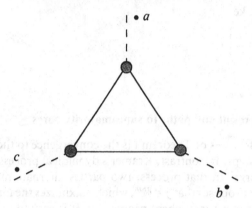

Figure 2. Cycle with large steps.

**Theorem 2.**  *Let V be any set of voter ideal points in $\mathbb{R}^m$, $m \geq 2$, with yolk center and radius c and r, respectively. Suppose voting occurs according to Assumption II, with the winner determined by simple majority.*

(i)   *If $\delta > 2r$ then the core is non-empty.*

(ii)  *For all $\delta > 0$ there may be global intransitivities. Indeed, for all $r > 0$ there exists V with yolk radius r such that, for all $\delta > 0$, transitivity fails.*

*Proof:*   (i) This follows by exactly the same argument of part (i) of Theorem 1.

(ii) Let $V$ contain three points at the vertices of an equilateral triangle (note $m \geq 2$) with center 0. In particular, $V$ consists of the points $(0, 2)$, $(\sqrt{3}, -1)$, and $(-\sqrt{3}, -1)$. See Figure 2. Let $M > 1$ be arbitrary. Situate the three points $a$, $b$, and $c$ just off the rays emanating from the origin through the triangle vertices. In particular, $a = \{1, 2M\}$; $b = \{(M - 1/2)\sqrt{3}, -(M + 1/2)\}$; $c = \{-M\sqrt{3} - 1/2, \sqrt{3}/2 - M\}$.

Obviously $a$ defeats $c$ defeats $b$ defeats $a$, and these points can be made arbitrarily distant from each other by increasing $M$. Moreover, the set $V$ can be scaled down to have arbitrarily small yolk radius without affecting the outcomes.     □

Theorem 2 shows that while Assumption II may be strong enough to assure a non-empty core, it is too weak to eliminate global intransitivities. Hence we have no assurance that a sequence of proposals will ever reach or even approach the core. We next consider supermajority voting. Theorem 3 shows that supermajority voting is a little stronger than

Assumption II: it assures a non-empty core and eliminates global intransitivities. However, it is not sufficient to guarantee infinite convergence.

**Assumption III.**  Voters vote sincerely. Any proposal $x^{i+1}$ offered against incumbent proposal $x^i$ must receive more than $\alpha|V|$ votes to defeat $x^i$. If a voter is indifferent between $x^{i+1}$ and $x^i$ then the vote is cast for the incumbent.

The set of points which cannot be defeated when voting takes place under Assumption III is called the $\alpha$-core. The smallest value $\alpha^*$ for which the $\alpha$-core is non-empty is known as the *minmax number.*

**Theorem 3.**  *Suppose voting takes place according to Assumption III with $\alpha \geq \alpha^*$. Then there are no global intransitivities, but a sequence of proposals may fail to reach the $\alpha$-core, even in the limit.*

*Proof:*  By assumption there exists at least one core point $w \in \mathbb{R}^m$. Suppose $y$ defeats $x$. Let $h$ denote the hyperplane normal to and bisecting the segment $\overline{xy}$, and let $h^+$ denote the open half-space defined by $h$ which contains $y$. According to Assumption III, there must be more than $\alpha|V|$ ideal points in $h^+$. That is, $|V \cap h^+| > \alpha|V|$.

We claim that $w \in h^+$. For if not, the point $w + \tau(y-x)$, for sufficiently small $\tau > 0$, would defeat $w$ just as $y$ defeats $x$. Therefore, as in Theorem 1, $d(y, w) < d(x, w)$ and there can be no global intransitivities.

The last part of the theorem is trivial. Place all the ideal points at 0 and let the proposal sequence be a set of points collinear with 0 such that $\|x^i\| = 1 + 2^{-i}$. $\quad\square$

The example that frustrates hopes of convergence in Theorem 3 violates the minimum interproposal distance property of Assumption II. This suggests using both Assumptions II and III in the hope of achieving a "nice" convergence property as in Theorem 1. Unfortunately, combining Assumptions II and III is still not quite enough.

**Theorem 4.**  *Suppose voting takes place according to both Assumption II and Assumption III with $\alpha \geq \alpha^*$. Then there are no global intransitivities, but for all $\delta > 0$ a sequence of proposals may fail to reach the $\alpha$-core, even in the limit.*

*Proof:*  By Theorem 3, there are no intransitivities. We modify the construction of Theorem 2 to show the failure of convergence. Place a single voter ideal point at 0, and place two ideal points at each of the three triangle vertices of $V$ in Figure 2. Let $\alpha = 4/7$, so that a proposal needs 5 votes to defeat an incumbent. The point at 0 is undefeated. The cycle $a$ beats $c$ beats $b$ beats $a$ is no longer intact, because the voter at 0 is indifferent among $a$, $b$, and $c$.

For sufficiently large $M$ let $x^0 = a(M+1)/M$; $x^1 = b(M+1/2)/M$; $x^2 = c(M+1/4)/M$; $x^3 = a(M+1/8)/M$; .... Then $\|x^{i+1}\| < \|x^i\|$ and so $x^i$ is defeated by $x^{i+1}$, but every point in the sequence is arbitrarily far from the $\alpha$-core. $\qquad\qquad\qquad\qquad\qquad\qquad\qquad\qquad\qquad\qquad\qquad\quad$ $\square$

It is possible to add one more condition to those of Theorem 4 and finally achieve finite convergence. The necessary definition and condition follow.

Let $x, r \in \mathbb{R}^m$; $\|r\| = 1$; $\tau \in \mathbb{R}$; $\tau > 0$. Let $W(x, r, \tau) = \{y \in \mathbb{R}^m \mid x \cdot r \le y \cdot r \le x \cdot r + \tau\}$, which may be visualized as a wafer of width $\tau$ wedged between two parallel hyperplanes whose normal vector is $r$.

**Assumption IV.** There exist $\tau > 0$, a point $z \in \mathbb{R}^m$, and an integer $\beta$ such that $z$ is in the $(\alpha - \beta/|V|)$-core and such that, for all $\|r\| = 1$, we have $|V \cap W(z, r, \tau)| \le \beta$.

Geometrically, this assumption says that there is a point $z$ which is a core point with respect to a smaller supramajority number $\hat{\alpha} < \alpha$, and there is a width $\tau > 0$ such that none of the wafers supported by $z$ contain too many (a fraction $\alpha - \hat{\alpha}$) points of $V$.

Though Assumption IV looks awkward, it is essentially a regularity requirement. It can be easily satisfied if the ideal points $V$ are in general position by setting $\beta = m$, selecting $z$ as the minmax point, and setting $\alpha = \alpha^* + \beta/|V|$. A set of points in $\mathbb{R}^m$ is *in general position* if no $k$-dimensional hyperplane contains more than $k$ points (that is, no two points are coincident, no three points are collinear, etc.) for all $1 \le k < m$.

For example, if the U.S. Senate in two dimensions is in general position and has $\alpha^* \le 64.5$ (see Caplin and Nalebuff 1988, Schofield and Tovey 1992, and Tovey 1991a), then $\alpha = 2/3$ satisfies Assumption IV.

**Theorem 5.** *Suppose voting takes place according to Assumptions II, III, and IV. Then there are no intransitivities, and moreover, for all $x \in \mathbb{R}^m$, any sequence of proposals starting at $x$ must reach an $\alpha$-core point in $\lceil \|x - z\|^2 / 2\delta\tau \rceil$ or fewer steps.*

*Proof:* The first statement is a corollary to Theorem 3. As usual, suppose $y$ defeats $x$, and let $h$ denote the hyperplane bisecting the line segment between $x$ and $y$. Then, as proved in Theorem 3, $z$ is in the open half-space $h^+$ defined by $h$ containing $y$.

Now consider the "wafer" $W(z, r, \tau)$, where $r = (x - y)/\|x - y\|$; it contains at most $\beta$ ideal points. If the wafer intersects $h$, then $h^+ \setminus W(z, r, \tau)$ contains more than $\alpha |V| - \beta$ ideal points, contradicting Assumption IV that $z$ is in the $(\alpha - \beta/|V|)$ core. Therefore $W(z, r, \tau)$ does not intersect $h$. It follows that the distance from $z$ to $h$ is greater than $\tau$.

We now restrict our attention to the 2-dimensional triangle defined by vertices $x$, $y$, and $z$. Let $L$ denote the length of the altitude from side $\overline{xy}$ to vertex $z$. From the previous paragraph we know that this altitude intersects the side at distance $\zeta$, $\zeta > \tau$, from the midpoint of the side. Then

$$\|x - z\|^2 = L^2 + (\|x - y\|/2 + \zeta)^2;$$

$$\|y - z\|^2 = L^2 + (\|x - y\|/2 - \zeta)^2.$$

Subtracting and applying $\|x - y\| \geq \delta$ from Assumption 2, we get

$$\|x - z\|^2 - \|y - z\|^2 = 4\zeta \|x - y\|/2 \geq 2\delta\tau.$$

Thus the square of the distance from $x$ to $z$ must decrease by an amount independent of $x$. Therefore, a core point must be reached in $\|x - z\|^2/2\delta\tau$ steps as claimed. □

As with Theorem 1, the qualitative predictions of Theorem 5 are plausible. Convergence should be faster as the minimum interproposal distance $\delta$ increases, and as $\tau$, which is a kind of ill-conditioning number, increases. Also note that Theorem 5 requires $\alpha$ somewhat greater than $\alpha^*$ in order to assure the stronger convergence, which again is plausible. Overall, Theorem 5 has disappointingly strong conditions, but Theorems 2–4 imply that weaker conditions along these lines would not suffice.

As stated in the introduction, these results do not take voter sophistication (strategic voting, deciding whether to vote) into account, and such extensions would be quite interesting.

Theorem 5 applies to a heavily modified version of Kramer's model of party competition. Parties still make proposals to maximize their votes against the incumbent, but the voting rule is $\alpha$-majority rather than simple majority; proposals must be at least $\delta$ apart; and regularity condition IV must hold. And even then we get convergence only to the $\alpha$-core, not to the $\alpha^*$-core.

It would be interesting to see if finite convergence to the $\alpha^*$-core could be obtained for a model more similar to Kramer's than that given here. One would need to prove convergence only for the vote-maximizing proposal sequences, instead of for all proposal sequences. However, I do not know how to proceed. One problem is that the proposal sequence in the proof of Theorem 3 is vote-maximizing. Therefore Assumption III does not suffice. Another problem is that if the parties maximize votes then supramajority voting would not affect the actual sequence until and unless it reaches the core. Therefore it seems impossible that Assumption II would suffice to guarantee convergence, because the vote-maximizing process could begin at (or reach) a point of distance less than $\delta$ from the minmax point.

In conclusion, the $\epsilon$-core enjoys powerful convergence properties if $\epsilon$ is large enough when compared to the asymmetry of the voter configuration. Of particular interest are the explicitly bounded finite convergence and the qualitative predictions involving (possibly) measurable quantities. With supramajority voting, the core acquires a similar powerful convergence property, but only if several additional restrictions are enforced.

**Acknowledgments.** The author is greatly indebted to John Ferejohn, John Ledyard, and Norman Schofield for suggesting this topic, in particular the search for dynamic properties of $\epsilon$-cores and other solution concepts. The author also acknowledges helpful comments from members of CORE, Belgium, and from participants at the June 1992 meeting of the Society for Social Choice and Welfare (Caen, France) and from the editor and anonymous referees.

### REFERENCES

Caplin, A., and B. Nalebuff (1988), "On 64% Majority Rule," *Econometrica* 56: 787–814.
Ferejohn, J. A., R. McKelvey, and E. Packel (1984), "Limiting Distributions for Continuous State Markov Models," *Social Choice and Welfare* 1: 45–67.
Koehler, D. H. (1990), "The Size of the Yolk: Computations for Odd and Even-Numbered Committees," *Social Choice and Welfare* 7: 231–45.
Kramer, G. H. (1977), "A Dynamical Model of Political Equilibrium," *Journal of Economic Theory* 16: 310–34.
McKelvey, R. D. (1986), "Covering, Dominance, and Institution Free Properties of Social Choice," *American Journal of Political Science* 30: 283–314.
McKelvey, R. D., and N. J. Schofield (1987), "Generalized Symmetry Conditions at a Core Point," *Econometrica* 55: 923–33.
Miller, N. (1980), "A New Solution Set for Tournaments and Majority Voting," *American Journal of Political Science* 24: 68–96.
    (1983), "The Covering Relation in Tournaments: Two Corrections," *American Journal of Political Science* 27: 382–5.
Plott, C. (1967), "A Notion of Equilibrium and Its Possibility under Majority Rule," *American Economic Review* 57: 787–806.
Salant, S. W., and E. Goodstein (1990), "Predicting Committee Behavior in Majority Rule Voting Experiments," *RAND Journal of Economics* 21: 293–313.
Schofield, N., and C. Tovey (1992), "Probability and Convergence for Supra-Majority Rule with Euclidean Preferences," *Mathematical and Computer Modelling* 16: 41–58.

Shubik, M., and M. H. Wooders (1983), "Approximate Cores of Replica Games and Economies," *Mathematical Social Sciences* 6: 27-48.

Simpson, P. B. (1969), "On Defining Areas of Voter Choice," *The Quarterly Journal of Economics* 83: 478-90.

Slutsky, S. (1979), "Equilibrium under α-Majority Voting," *Econometrica* 47: 1113-25.

Stone, R. E., and C. A. Tovey (1992), "Limiting Median Lines Do Not Suffice to Determine the Yolk," *Social Choice and Welfare* 9: 33-5.

Tovey, C. A. (1991a), "A Critique of Distributional Analysis," technical report no. NPSOR-91-16, Department of Operations Research, Naval Postgraduate School, Monterey, CA (to appear in *American Political Science Review*).

(1991b), "The Instability of Instability," technical report no. NPSOR-91-15, Department of Operations Research, Naval Postgraduate School, Monterey, CA (in revision for *American Political Science Review*).

(1992), "A Polynomial Algorithm to Compute the Yolk in Fixed Dimension," *Mathematical Programming* 57: 259-77.

Tullock, G. (1967), "The General Irrelevance of the General Impossibility Theorem," *Quarterly Journal of Economics* 81: 256-70.

Wooders, M. H. (1983), "The Epsilon Core of a Large Replica Game," *Journal of Mathematical Economics* 11: 277-300.

# Social choice and cooperative games

CHAPTER 11

# Incentives in market games with asymmetric information: Approximate NTU cores in large economies

*Beth Allen*

## 1    Introduction

Incentive compatibility considerations are certainly important for economies with asymmetric information whenever the information available to coalition members is exogenously determined. One wishes to permit strategic behavior with respect to information revelation, yet the potential withholding of information or the revelation of false information are serious concerns.

The idea followed in this paper is to pursue the interface between cooperative and noncooperative game theory – or, in other terms, the concepts of games with partial commitments or institutions with incomplete contracts – by focusing on informational motivation. Players may behave strategically within coalitions and the information of coalitions need not be exogenously given. This equilibrium determination of the extent of information sharing as the (noncooperative) strategic choices of economic agents then leads to the definition of the underlying cooperative game with asymmetric information in terms of the payoffs that can be achieved via incentive compatible net trades. In this way, the underlying cooperative game is derived from an economy with asymmetric information, and this derivation takes account of incentive considerations.[1]

Most of this research was performed during my visit to Graduiertenkolleg, Institut für Mathematische Wirtschaftsforschung, Universität Bielefeld. Discussion with Myrna Wooders convinced me to consider the $\epsilon$-core. Two anonymous referees provided helpful comments regarding final revisions. Any views expressed here are mine alone.
[1] The literature on the core of an economy with asymmetric information begins with Wilson (1978) and includes quite recent work by Yannelis (1991) and Allen (1991a,b,c, 1992). Marimón (1989) has examined the core with adverse selection, while Berliant (1992) and Boyd and Prescott (1986) have considered the cores of economies with incentive compatibility constraints having special structures based (respectively) on taxation and financial

263

Yet the presence of incentive compatibility constraints can lead to non-convexities and to games that are not balanced. For the (exact) nontransferable utility (NTU) core of finite economies, these phenomena can give rise to games with empty cores. See Allen (1992) for an explicit – and complicated – example. Randomization can restore the existence of core allocations, although at the expense of resource feasibility on average rather than almost surely. The insufficiency of convexification alone (with almost sure feasibility) to restore the non-emptiness of the core suggests (but, of course, does not prove) that the effects of large numbers will not suffice to ensure non-emptiness of the core in exact replicas.

However, rather than pursuing the "exact core of a large economy with mean resource feasibility," the strategy taken here is to explore the effects of weakening the solution concept to the approximate core. Thus, I can exploit the machinery developed in Shubik and Wooders (1983) and Wooders (1983, 1991) to analyze the $\epsilon$-core of large replica economies with nontransferable utility.[2] Randomization is still used to guarantee convexity of coalitions' incentive compatible feasible payoff sets. However, this randomization features resource feasibility with probability 1.

The remainder of this paper is organized as follows. Section 2 discusses an example of nonconvex feasible payoff sets for coalitions under incentive compatibility constraints and of resulting empty NTU cores. Section 3 presents the model, while Section 4 is devoted to a discussion of incentives. Preliminaries are gathered in Section 5; Section 6 contains the initial analysis of approximate cores. Section 7 discusses randomization. Main results appear in Section 8; their discussion follows in Section 9.

## 2     An example

The purpose of this section is to display a simple example of an exchange economy with incentive compatibility constraints which induces a game having nonconvex sets of attainable utility vectors for the grand coalition. The NTU game also fails to be balanced, although it possesses core allocations. In the example, replication restores approximate convexity

---

intermediation. Myerson (1984) and Rosenmüller (1990) have studied NTU games with incentive compatibility constraints, but they focused on solution concepts other than the core. The very recent paper by Koutsourgeras and Yannelis (1991) considered a different definition of incentive compatibility and asked whether (NTU) core allocations – defined without incentive compatibility constraints – satisfy their definition.

[2] More specifically, Wooders (1983, 1991) showed that an approximate balancedness condition implies that the approximate core is non-empty and that her condition is always satisfied for replica exchange economies with sufficiently many agents provided that a hypothesis (called efficacy of small groups) is not violated.

but not balancedness. Thus, the example helps to illustrate and explain my model but, strictly speaking, rigorously demonstrates only the need to convexify the sets of attainable payoffs in the games I consider.

The example features two goods (called $x$ and $y$), three players (indicated by subscripts 1, 2, and 3), and two states of the world, heads $H$ and tails $T$, which each occur with probability $\frac{1}{2}$. Initial endowments are assigned as follows: $e_1(H) = e_1(T) = (1,1)$; $e_2(H) = (0,4)$; $e_2(T) = (0,0)$; $e_3(H) = (4,0)$; $e_3(T) = (0,0)$. Players 2 and 3 know the state of the world (perhaps by observing their own initial endowment vectors) but player 1 knows the state only if another coalition member tells him and player 1 is unable to detect lies. State-dependent utilities are given by the following expressions:

$$u_1(x,y;H)$$

$$= \min\left(\frac{x+y-1+\sqrt{(x+y-1)^2+8x}}{4}, \frac{x+y-1+\sqrt{(x+y-1)^2+8y}}{4}\right);$$

$$u_1(x,y;T) = \begin{cases} (x+y)/2 & \text{if } x+y \le 2, \\ 1+\min(x,y,(x+y)-2) & \text{if } x+y \ge 2; \end{cases}$$

$$u_2(x,y;H) = x;$$

$$u_3(x,y;H) = y;$$

$$u_2(x,y;T) = u_3(x,y;T) = 0.$$

Although initial endowments are state dependent, they are incentive compatible. Note also that, in order to simplify calculations, I take total utility (rather than expected utility) as the payoff of each player.

Consider the state-dependent incentive compatible allocation $((5,0), (1,1))$ to player 1, $((0,0), (0,0))$ to player 2, and $((0,5), (0,0))$ to player 3, which yields total utilities of $2+1 = 3$, $0+0 = 0$, and $5+0 = 5$, respectively. Similarly, the allocation $(((0,5), (1,1)), ((5,0), (0,0)), ((0,0), (0,0)))$ gives the grand coalition the total utility vector $(3,5,0)$. However, the convex combination $\frac{1}{2}(3,0,5) + \frac{1}{2}(3,5,0) = (3,2\frac{1}{2},2\frac{1}{2})$ cannot be attained via a feasible and incentive compatible allocation, because the only allocations that give 3 to player 1 either equal one of the preceding two allocations or fail to satisfy incentive compatibility. Hence, in the NTU game generated by this economy, $V(I)$ is not a convex set.

However, replication restores approximate convexity. Indeed, in the 2-fold replica, one can give the clones of player 1 the allocations $((0,5), (1,1))$ and $((5,0), (1,1))$, respectively. This permits each copy of player 2 to receive $((2\frac{1}{2},0), (0,0))$ and each player 3 to obtain $((0,2\frac{1}{2}), (0,0))$, yielding a total payoff vector of $(3,3,2\frac{1}{2},2\frac{1}{2},2\frac{1}{2},2\frac{1}{2})$, as desired.

To check that the derived NTU game is not balanced, examine the three two-player coalitions with balancing weights $\frac{1}{2}$ each. The allocations $(((0, 5), (1, 1)), ((1, 0), (0, 0)))$ and $(((5, 0), (1, 1)), ((0, 1), (0, 0)))$ show that $(3, 1) \in V(\{1, 2\})$ and $(3, 1) \in V(\{1, 3\})$. Moreover $(4, 4) \in V(\{2, 3\})$, using the allocation $(((4, 0), (0, 0)), ((0, 4), (0, 0)))$. However, $(3, 2\frac{1}{2}, 2\frac{1}{2}) \notin V(I)$ as shown previously. This game is not balanced, but its 2-fold replica is balanced.

One can check that $(3, 0, 5)$ and $(3, 5, 0)$ belong to the core because no coalition can strictly improve the payoff of each of its members. A much more complex example (with five commodities, five states, and initial endowment vectors that are not state dependent) provided in Allen (1992) illustrates that incentive compatibility constraints can lead to emptiness of the NTU core.

## 3     The model

Let $\Omega$ be a finite set of states of the world. Assume that all agents have the same (subjective) probability $\mu$ on $(\Omega, \mathfrak{F})$, where $\mathfrak{F} = 2^{\Omega}$ with $\mu(\omega) > 0$ for all $\omega \in \Omega$. (Otherwise $\Omega$ can be reduced by a null set.) Interpret $\Omega$ as a description of all of the payoff-relevant systematic risk or common uncertainty in the economy. Note that, if $\Omega$ is infinite but each agent's information is representable by a finite partition, one could redefine a finite set of states of the world by events in the pooled information partition.

Finitely many agents are present in the pure exchange economy. Let $I$ be the set of traders or players in the induced game. Write #$I$ for the cardinality of the player set and use subscripts $i$ $(i \in I)$ to indicate individual agents. Each consumer has consumption set $\mathbb{R}_+^l$ in each state of the world, so that there are $l$ goods potentially available in each state.

Initial endowments are assumed to be independent of the state of the world in order to avoid the problem that endowments may convey information or may violate incentive compatibility (in which case the worth of coalitions may not be well defined). Write $e_i \in \mathbb{R}_+^l$ or $e_i: \Omega \to \mathbb{R}_+^l$ for $i$'s initial endowment.

Preferences are state dependent and are specified by cardinal utility functions, where expected utilities define payoffs. Write $u_i: \mathbb{R}_+^l \times \Omega \to \mathbb{R}$ and assume that, for all $i \in I$ and all $\omega \in \Omega$, $u_i(\cdot; \omega)$ is continuous and concave on $\mathbb{R}_+^l$. For the version of the model with Bayesian incentive compatibility (see Section 4), assume also that $u_i(0; \omega) \le u_i(x_i; \omega)$ for all $i \in I$, all $\omega \in \Omega$, and all $x_i \in \mathbb{R}_+^l$. For the results in Section 6, assume that

$$\sum_{\omega \in \Omega} u_i(e_i(\omega); \omega)\mu(\omega) > 0 \quad \text{for all } i \in I.$$

## 4    Information and incentives

To begin, specify traders' information by $\delta_i\colon \Omega \to S_i$, where $S_i$ is a finite set for all $i \in I$. Then $\delta_i$ generates a finite partition $P_i$ of $\Omega$ and a finite sub-$\sigma$-field $\mathcal{F}_i$ of $\mathcal{F}$. Interpret $S_i$ as the set of signals that $i$ can receive about the state of the world and $P_i$ or $\mathcal{F}_i$ (equivalently) as $i$'s initial information. Think of the sets $S_i$ and the mappings $\delta_i$ as common knowledge for all agents (and the planner or mechanism designer).[3] Take $S_i$ also to be the set of messages that agents can communicate, in the sense that an agent can convey a (true or false) subset of his actual information partition. Note that the realizations $\delta_i(\omega)$ of $i$'s signal are not observable to agents $j \neq i$ or to the planner or mechanism designer. Note also that random signals are allowed in this model in that otherwise identical copies of $\omega \in \Omega$ could be mapped to different elements of $S_i$, which is equivalent to expanding $\Omega$ to a larger (but still finite) set. Set $S = S_1 \times \cdots \times S_{\#I}$ with typical element $s = (s_1, \ldots, s_{\#I})$; write $(s_i', s_{-i}) = (s_1, \ldots, s_{i-1}, s_i', s_{i+1}, \ldots, s_{\#I}) \in S$ and $s_{-i} \in S_{-i} = \prod_{j \neq i} S_j$. Define $\delta\colon \Omega \to S$ by $\delta(\omega) = (\delta_1(\omega), \ldots, \delta_{\#I}(\omega))$ and define $\delta_{-i}$ in the obvious way. Write $\mu_i(\cdot \,|\, s_i)$ and $\mu(\cdot \,|\, s)$ for the conditional probabilities on $\Omega$ given $s_i \in S_i$ or $s \in S$, respectively.

A state-dependent allocation $x_i(\cdot)\colon \Omega \to \mathbb{R}_+^l$ for trader $i$ is *strongly incentive compatible* if $x_i(\cdot)$ is $\sigma(\bigcup_{i \in I} \mathcal{F}_i)$-measurable (i.e., $x_i(\omega) = x_i(\omega')$ whenever $\delta(\omega) = \delta(\omega')$) and if $u_i(x_i(\omega); \omega) \geq u_i(x_i(\omega'); \omega)$ for all $\omega, \omega' \in \Omega$. It is *Bayesian incentive compatible* if $x_i(\cdot)$ is $\sigma(\bigcup_{i \in I} \mathcal{F}_i)$-measurable and if, for all $s_i \in S_i$ and all $\mathcal{F}_i$-measurable $\delta_i'\colon \Omega \to S_i$,

$$\sum_{\omega \in \Omega} u_i(x_i(\delta(\omega)); \omega)\mu_i(\omega\,|\,s_i) \geq \sum_{\omega \in \Omega} u_i(x_i(s_i', \delta_{-i}(\omega)); \omega)\mu_i(\omega\,|\,s_i),$$

where $x_i(\delta(\omega)) = x_i(\omega)$, $x_i(s_i', \delta_{-i}(\omega)) = x_i(\omega')$ if $\delta(\omega') = (s_i', \delta_{-i}(\omega))$, and $x_i(s_i', \delta_{-i}(\omega)) = 0$ if there is no $\omega' \in \Omega$ for which $\delta(\omega') = (s_i', \delta_{-i}(\omega))$. In both definitions, agents' state-dependent allocations must be measurable with respect to the joint information received – or reported – by all agents, so that allocations depend only on signals. In addition, both formulations have the property that no trader $i \in I$ wishes to misreport his signal (i.e., to say $s_i'$ rather than $s_i$ when the true signal is $s_i \in S_i$). Obviously, strong

---

[3] The planner or mechanism designer does not play a formal role in my model, but is mentioned here as a referee who is able to verify that (for the classical case of strong incentive compatibility) the proposed state-dependent allocations for coalitions are indeed incentive compatible or that (for the case of Bayesian incentive compatibility) the mechanism really is Bayesian incentive compatible. However, the mechanism designer/planner is unable to observe or verify individuals' realized information or signals (as opposed to the nature of their information partition structures or signal mappings from the set of states of the world to the set of signal values, which are considered to be common knowledge).

incentive compatibility is stronger than Bayesian incentive compatibility, where the difference involves whether incentive constraints apply separately to each possible realization of $\omega \in \Omega$ or whether incentive compatibility is given in terms of expected utility conditional on the player's received signal. Strong incentive compatibility is more appropriate if players do not know the probabilities affecting their opponents.[4] Either definition can be applied (consistently) in the remainder of this paper.

## 5     NTU market games with incentive compatibility constraints

This section examines the structure of NTU games in characteristic function form that arise from exchange economies with incentive compatibility constraints. All of the previous assumptions of the model are maintained. The properties demonstrated here show that these games are well behaved and permit the application in the next section of Wooders (1983).

The data of my pure exchange economy under uncertainty generate a cooperative game that depends, of course, on agents' initial information and on incentive compatibility constraints. By definition, the correspondence $V: 2^I \to \mathbb{R}^{\#I}$ constitutes a cooperative game with nontransferable utility if $V(\emptyset) = \{0\}$ and for all $S \subseteq I$, $S \neq \emptyset$, $V(S)$ is a non-empty closed comprehensive cylinder set.

The cooperative games with nontransferable utility derived from my economic model with strong or Bayesian incentive compatibility are given by $V^S: 2^I \to \mathbb{R}^{\#I}$ and $V^B: 2^I \to \mathbb{R}^{\#I}$ with $V^S(\emptyset) = V^B(\emptyset) = \{0\}$ and, for $S \subseteq I$, $S \neq \emptyset$,

$$V^S(S) = \{(w_1, \ldots, w_{\#I}) \in \mathbb{R}^{\#I} \mid \text{for } i \in S, \text{ there are } \sigma(\bigcup_{i \in I} \mathcal{F}_i)\text{-measurable}$$
$$x_i: \Omega \to \mathbb{R}^l_+ \text{ such that } u_i(x_i(\omega); \omega) \geq u_i(x_i(\omega'); \omega) \text{ for all}$$
$$\omega, \omega' \in \Omega, \Sigma_{i \in S} x_i(\omega) = \Sigma_{i \in S} e_i(\omega) \text{ for all } \omega \in \Omega, \text{ and}$$
$$w_i \leq \int u_i(x_i(\omega); \omega) \, d\mu(\omega)\}$$

and

$$V^B(S) = \{(w_1, \ldots, w_{\#I}) \in \mathbb{R}^{\#I} \mid \text{for } i \in S, \text{ there are } \sigma(\bigcup_{i \in I} \mathcal{F}_i)\text{-measurable}$$
$$x_i: \Omega \to \mathbb{R}^l_+ \text{ such that } x_i(\cdot) \text{ is Bayesian incentive compatible,}$$
$$\Sigma_{i \in S} x_i(\omega) = \Sigma_{i \in S} e_i(\omega) \text{ for all } \omega \in \Omega, \text{ and}$$
$$w_i \leq \int u_i(x_i(\omega); \omega) \, d\mu(\omega)\}.$$

For convenience, write $V: 2^I \to \mathbb{R}^{\#I}$ for either $V^S$ or $V^B$.

---

[4]  See d'Aspremont and Gerard-Varet (1979) for a further discussion and see Holmstrom and Myerson (1983) for alternative notions of efficiency (or, implicitly, the allocations that can be achieved by the grand coalition) with incentives.

By definition, the NTU game $V: 2^I \to \mathbb{R}^{\#I}$ is *superadditive* if

$$V(S) \cap V(T) \subset V(S \cup T)$$

whenever $S \cap T = \emptyset$. This means that merging of disjoint coalitions does not necessarily decrease any agent's payoff; anything that disjoint coalitions can do separately can also be done by their union. Intuitively, incentive compatibility cannot destroy superadditivity because incentive compatibility constraints apply to an individual's allocation; they do not depend on the coalition or on the allocations of other players.

**Proposition 5.1.**  *Finite NTU games derived from exchange economies with incentive compatibility constraints as in the model are superadditive.*

*Proof:*   Let $S \subseteq I$ and $T \subseteq I$ with $S \cap T = \emptyset$. Without loss of generality, re-order the players in $I$ so that $S = \{1, ..., \#S\}$ and $T = \{\#S + 1, ..., \#S + \#T\}$. Pick $(v_1, ..., v_{\#I}) \in V(S)$ and $(v_1', ..., v_{\#I}') \in V(T)$ arbitrarily. I need to show that $(v_1, ..., v_{\#S}, v_{\#S+1}', ..., v_{\#S+\#T}', w_{\#S+\#T+1}, ..., w_{\#I}) \in V(S \cup T)$ where the $w_{\#S+\#T+1}, ..., w_{\#I}$ are arbitrary. By the definition of the games in coalition form derived from my economy, there are state-dependent allocations $x_i$: $\Omega \to \mathbb{R}_+^l$ for $i \in S$ and $x_i: \Omega \to \mathbb{R}_+^l$ for $i \in T$ such that $\int_\Omega u_i(x_i(\omega); \omega) \, d\mu(\omega) \geq v_i$ if $i \in S$, $\int_\Omega u_i(x_i(\omega); \omega) \, d\mu(\omega) \geq v_i'$ if $i \in T$,

$$\sum_{i \in S} x_i(\omega) = \sum_{i \in S} e_i(\omega), \qquad \sum_{i \in T} x_i(\omega) = \sum_{i \in T} e_i(\omega),$$

and for each $i \in S \cup T$, $x_i(\cdot)$ is incentive compatible. Taking the (same) allocations $x_i: \Omega \to \mathbb{R}_+^l$ for $i \in S \cup T$ gives $\int_\Omega u_i(x_i(\omega); \omega) \, d\mu(\omega) \geq v_i$ if $i \in S$, $\int_\Omega u_i(x_i(\omega); \omega) \, d\mu(\omega) \geq v_i'$ if $i \in T$, $\sum_{i \in S \cup T} x_i(\omega) = \sum_{i \in S \cup T} e_i(\omega)$, and, for all $i \in S \cup T$, $x_i(\cdot)$ is incentive compatible. This proves that $(v_1, ..., v_{\#S}, v_{\#S+1}', ..., v_{\#S+\#T}', w_{\#S+\#T+1}, ..., w_{\#I}) \in V(S \cup T)$, as desired.   $\square$

The game $V: 2^I \to \mathbb{R}^{\#I}$ is *comprehensive* if, for any $S \subseteq I$, $v \in V(S)$ and $w \leq v$ imply that $w \in V(S)$, or, equivalently, if $V(S) \supseteq V(S) - \mathbb{R}_+^{\#I}$ for all $S \subseteq I$. Comprehensiveness of games derived from exchange economies is automatic from the definition of $V(S)$ for any coalition $S$; this is not affected by incentive compatibility.

**Proposition 5.2.**  *The NTU games generated by my model with incentives are comprehensive.*

*Proof:*   Fix $S \subseteq I$ arbitrarily. Then $V(S) = \{(v_1, ..., v_{\#I}) \in \mathbb{R}^{\#I} \mid$ for $i \in S$, there exist $x_i: \Omega \to \mathbb{R}_+^l$ satisfying incentive compatibility, $\sum_{i \in S} x_i(\omega) = \sum_{i \in S} e_i(\omega)$, and $\int_\Omega u_i(x_i(\omega); \omega) \, d\mu(\omega) \geq v_i$ if $i \in S\}$. By definition, if $v \in V(S)$ and $w \leq v$, then $w \in V(S)$.   $\square$

**Proposition 5.3.** *Any economy satisfying my assumptions induces a game* $V: 2^I \to \mathbb{R}^{\#I}$ *in which, for all* $S \subseteq I$, $V(S)$ *is closed and* $V(S) \cap \{v \in \mathbb{R}^{\#I} \mid v_i = 0$ *if* $i \notin S\}$ *is compactly generated.*

*Proof:* Fix $S \subseteq I$. Then $X(S) = \{x \in \mathbb{R}_+^{(\#S)(\#\Omega)I} \mid$ if one writes $x_i \colon \Omega \to \mathbb{R}_+^I$ for $i \in S$, $x_i$ satisfies incentive compatibility and $\sum_{i \in S} x_i(\omega) = \sum_{i \in S} e_i(\omega)\}$ is a compact set, because the set of feasible allocations is closed and bounded while the incentive compatibility constraints (for $i \in S$) define a closed subset. Hence $V(S) \cap \{v \in \mathbb{R}^{\#I} \mid v_i = 0$ if $i \notin S\}$ is closed as the sum of the closed set $-\mathbb{R}_+^{\#I} \cap \{v \in \mathbb{R}^{\#I} \mid v_i = 0$ if $i \notin S\}$ and the compact image in $\mathbb{R}^{\#I} \cap \{v \in \mathbb{R}^{\#I} \mid v_i = 0$ if $i \notin S\}$ of $X(S)$ under the continuous functions $u_i$, $i \in S$. The proof of this assertion involves a well-known argument with asymptotic cones. Taking the cylinder set $V(S)$ in $\mathbb{R}^{\#I}$ generated by this closed set does not destroy closedness.     $\Box$

## 6     Approximate cores

This section considers the possibilities for approximate core allocations in exchange economies with asymmetric information and strong or Bayesian incentive compatibility. In particular, sufficiently large replica economies with incentive constraints have weak $\epsilon$-cores. The more economically appealing approximate core notion of the strong $\epsilon$-core is non-empty for some subsequence of replica economies with incentive compatibility constraints.

**Definition 6.1.** The sequence $\{V_r\}_{r=1}^{\infty}$ of NTU *replica games* derived from the exchange economy with (strong or Bayesian) incentive compatibility constraints has $V_1(S) = V(S)$ for all $S \subseteq I$ and, for $r \geq 1$, is defined as in the preceding section except that in the underlying ($r$th replica) economy, there are exactly $r$ agents of each *type* $i \in I$. If $S \subseteq I$, write $rS$ for the set of players in the $r'$ replica, for $r' \geq r$, containing precisely $r$ copies of each player type belonging to $S$. Write $rS = \{ir'' \mid i \in S$ and $1 \leq r'' \leq r\}$. Note that $rI$ is the player set for the game $V_r$, $r = 1, 2, \ldots$.

**Definition 6.2.** Given $\epsilon > 0$, a payoff vector $w = (w_{11}, \ldots, w_{1r}, w_{21}, \ldots, w_{2r}, \ldots, w_{\#I1}, \ldots, w_{\#Ir})$ belongs to the *strong $\epsilon$-core* of $V_r$ ($r \geq 1$) if (i) the payoffs are feasible – that is, $w \in V_r(rI)$, and (ii) for all coalitions $S_r \subseteq rI$, the payoff $w$ cannot be improved upon by $\epsilon$ or more for each player in $S_r$ – that is, $w + (\epsilon, \ldots, \epsilon) \notin \text{int } V_r(S_r)$. (In (ii), the coalition $S_r$ may have different numbers of players of each type.)

**Definition 6.3.** Given $\epsilon > 0$, a feasible payoff vector $w = (w_{11}, \ldots, w_{1r}, w_{21}, \ldots, w_{2r}, \ldots, w_{\#I1}, \ldots, w_{\#Ir}) \in V_r(rI)$ belongs to the *weak $\epsilon$-core* of $V_r$ ($r \geq 1$)

if there is some payoff vector $\bar{w} = (\bar{w}_{11}, \ldots, \bar{w}_{1r}, \bar{w}_{21}, \ldots, \bar{w}_{2r}, \ldots, \bar{w}_{\#I1}, \ldots,$ $\bar{w}_{\#Ir}) \in \mathbb{R}^{\#Ir}$ such that (i) $\#\{\bar{\imath}\bar{r} \in rI \,|\, \bar{w}_{\bar{\imath}\bar{r}} \neq w_{\bar{\imath}\bar{r}}\}/r\#I < \epsilon$, and (ii) for all coalitions $S_r \subseteq rI$, the payoff $\bar{w}$ cannot be improved upon by $\epsilon$ or more for each player in $S_r$ - that is, $\bar{w} + (\epsilon, \ldots, \epsilon) \notin \text{int } V_r(S_r)$. (Again, in (ii) $S_r$ need not contain the same number of players of each type.)

**Theorem 6.4.** *For any fixed $\epsilon > 0$, there is an integer $R$ such that for all $r \geq R$, the weak $\epsilon$-core of $V_r$ is non-empty. In particular, for every $\epsilon > 0$, sufficiently large replica economies with (strong or Bayesian) incentive compatibility have weak $\epsilon$-core allocations.*

*Proof:* The games $V^S$ and $V^B$ satisfy the basic conditions (for each coalition $S$, $V(S)$ is a non-empty proper closed cylinder set containing some strictly positive vector such that $V(S) \cap \{v \in \mathbb{R}^{\#I} \,|\, v_j = 0 \text{ if } j \notin S\}$ is bounded) of Shubik and Wooders (1983). Moreover, $\{V_r\}_{r=1}^{\infty}$ is a sequence of super-additive and per-capita bounded (i.e., equal treatment payoffs in $V_r(rI)$ are uniformly bounded above for $r = 1, 2, 3, \ldots$) replica games. Hence Theorem 1 of Shubik and Wooders (1983) applies, and the weak $\epsilon$-core of $V_r$ is non-empty whenever $r$ is sufficiently large.          $\square$

**Theorem 6.5.** *For arbitrary $\epsilon > 0$ and any integer $R$, there exists $r \geq R$ for which the strong $\epsilon$-core of $V_r$ is non-empty. In particular, every sequence of replica exchange economies with (strong or Bayesian) incentive compatibility has a subsequence for which there are strong $\epsilon$-core allocations.*

*Proof:* As in the previous proof, the conditions in Shubik and Wooders (1983) are satisfied; their Theorem 2 states that, for some subsequence $V_{r'}$ of $V_r$, the strong $\epsilon$-core of $V_{r'}$ is non-empty.          $\square$

**Remark 6.6.** Recall that, by Proposition 5.2, my games $V_r$ (derived from exchange economies with incentive compatibility constraints) are comprehensive. Hence, as Shubik and Wooders (1983) observe, there exist strong $\epsilon$-core payoffs satisfying the equal treatment property for the subsequence of replicas in Theorem 6.5. (By definition, this means that all players of the same type can be assigned identical utility allocations in the strong $\epsilon$-core along the subsequence.)

## 7     Randomization

Consider the game induced by exchange economies with randomizations over allocations satisfying incentive compatibility constraints and feasibility with probability 1.[5] I claim that permitting coalitions to use such "mixed strategies" generates a game $\hat{V}: 2^I \to \mathbb{R}^{\#I}$ for which $\hat{V}(S)$ is a convex, closed, and comprehensive cylinder set for all $S$. In fact $\hat{V}(S) = \text{conv}(V(S))$, the closed convex hull of $V(S)$. Unfortunately, $\hat{V}$ is not necessarily balanced, as demonstrated by the example in Allen (1992).

Somewhat more formally, the game generated by an exchange economy with almost surely feasible randomizations and incentive compatibility constraints is given by $\hat{V}: 2^I \to \mathbb{R}^{\#I}$ where, for $S \subseteq I$, $\hat{V}(S) = \{0\}$ if $S = \emptyset$ and otherwise (for $S \neq \emptyset$)

$$\hat{V}(S) = \{(v_1, \ldots, v_{\#I}) \in \mathbb{R}^{\#I} \,|\, \text{there is a probability measure } \nu \text{ on}$$
$$\bar{x} \in \mathbb{R}_+^{(\#I)(\#\Omega)I} \text{ such that } \Sigma_{i \in S}\, \bar{x}_i(\omega) = \Sigma_{i \in S}\, e_i(\omega) \text{ for}$$
$$\nu\text{-almost all } \bar{x}(\cdot) \text{ and all } \omega \in \Omega, \; \nu\text{-almost all } \bar{x} \text{ satisfy,}$$
$$\text{for } i \in S, \text{ incentive compatibility of } \bar{x}_i \colon \Omega \to \mathbb{R}_+^l \text{ and}$$
$$v_i \leq \iint u_i(\bar{x}_i(\omega); \omega)\, d\mu(\omega)\, d\nu(\bar{x})\}.$$

**Proposition 7.1.** *The game $\hat{V}: 2^I \to \mathbb{R}^{\#I}$ with randomization over almost surely feasible and incentive compatible allocations has sets $\hat{V}(S)$ of attainable payoff vectors which are, for all $S \subseteq I$, $S \neq \emptyset$, non-empty, closed, comprehensive, and compactly generated (in $\mathbb{R}^{\#S}$) cylinder sets.*

*Proof:*  Randomization over the sets $X(S)$ in the proof of Proposition 5.3 gives a compact and convex set of probabilities for the topology of weak convergence of probability measures. The image of $X(S)$ under the continuous and concave functions $u_i$ ($i \in S$) thus is compact and convex. Taking its comprehensive hull and then the cylinder set that this generates thus gives sets $\hat{V}(S)$, which are non-empty, closed, convex, comprehensive, and compactly generated (in $\mathbb{R}^{\#S}$) cylinder sets. In fact, by definition $\hat{V}(S) = \text{conv}(V(S))$ for all $S \subseteq I$.     □

Thus, the NTU game $\hat{V}: 2^I \to \mathbb{R}^{\#I}$ satisfies all of the properties needed to show non-emptiness of its core except balancedness. The next section sidesteps this difficulty by considering large replicas and demonstrating approximate balancedness, which then yields approximate cores.

To be pedantic, I could write $\hat{V}^S: 2^I \to \mathbb{R}^{\#I}$ and $\hat{V}^B: 2^I \to \mathbb{R}^{\#I}$ where, for all $S \subseteq I$, $\hat{V}^S(S) = \text{conv}(V^S(S))$ and $\hat{V}^B(S) = \text{conv}(V^B(S))$. The core of the economy with strong or Bayesian incentive compatibility constraints equals the (strong or Bayesian incentive compatible) state-dependent al-

---

[5] This is reminiscent of the randomizations introduced in Prescott and Townsend (1984a,b) to obtain the existence of competitive equilibrium and welfare theorems in general equilibrium exchange economies under uncertainty.

locations giving rise to expected utility allocations in the core of the NTU game $V^S \colon 2^I \to \mathbb{R}^{\#I}$ or $V^B \colon 2^I \to \mathbb{R}^{\#I}$, respectively. The core of the economy with strong or Bayesian incentive compatibility constraints and almost surely resource feasible randomization equals the (strong or Bayesian incentive compatible) state-dependent allocations giving rise to expected utility allocations in the NTU core of the (convexified) game $\hat{V}^S \colon 2^I \to \mathbb{R}^{\#I}$ or $\hat{V}^B \colon 2^I \to \mathbb{R}^{\#I}$, respectively.

## 8 Approximate cores with randomization

The main result of this paper states that all sufficiently large replica economies with incentive compatibility constraints have non-empty strong $\epsilon$-cores which contain at least one equal treatment allocation. This requires convexity of the NTU game's sets of attainable payoff vectors, so that randomization is necessary.

**Definition 8.1.** The sequence $\{\hat{V}_r\}_{r=1}^\infty$ of *NTU replica games with randomization* derived from the exchange economy with incentive compatibility constraints has $\hat{V}_1(S) = \hat{V}(S)$ for all $S \subseteq I$ and, for $r \geq 1$, is defined as the NTU game induced by an economy with incentives and randomization as in the preceding section except that, in the underlying (replica) economy, there are $r$ agents of each type $i \in I$. If $S \subseteq I$, write $rS$ for the set of players in the $r'$ replica, for $r' \geq r$, consisting of exactly $r$ copies of each player type belonging to $S$. Write $rS = \{ir'' \mid i \in S \text{ and } 1 \leq r'' \leq r\}$.

**Definition 8.2.** Given $\epsilon > 0$, a payoff vector $w = (w_{11}, \ldots, w_{1r}, w_{21}, \ldots, w_{2r}, \ldots, w_{\#I1}, \ldots, w_{\#Ir})$ belongs to the *NTU strong $\epsilon$-core with randomization* if it belongs to the *strong $\epsilon$-core* of $\hat{V}_r$ ($r \geq 1$). This is equivalent to the following two conditions: (i) the payoffs are feasible – that is, $w \in \hat{V}_r(rI)$, and (ii) for all coalitions $S_r \subset rI$, the payoff $w$ cannot be improved upon by $\epsilon$ or more for each player in $S_r$ – that is, $w + (\epsilon, \ldots, \epsilon) \notin \text{int } \hat{V}_r(S_r)$. (Note that in (ii), the coalition $S_r$ may have different numbers of clones of each type.)

**Definition 8.3.** The (feasible) payoff vector $w \in \hat{V}_r(rI)$ for $r \geq 1$ has the *equal treatment property* (ETP) if all players of the same type receive the same utility allocation or payoff in $w$. In symbols, $w \in \hat{V}_r(rI)$ satisfies ETP if $w_{ir'} = w_{ir''}$ for all $i \in I$ and all $r', r'' \leq r$. (If $r = 1$, this requirement is vacuous but true.)

**Theorem 8.4.** *Fix $\epsilon > 0$ arbitrarily. Then, if $r$ is sufficiently large, the NTU strong $\epsilon$-core with randomization in the $r$th replica economy or the* *strong ε-core of $\hat{V}_r$ is non-empty and, moreover, contains a payoff satisfying the equal treatment property.*

*Proof:* Because the sequence $\{\hat{V}_r\}_r$ of replica games (generated by my model with incentive compatibility and randomization) is a sequence of replica games in the sense of Wooders (1983) satisfying superadditivity, per-capita boundedness, and comprehensiveness, Theorems 1 and 2 of Wooders (1983) can be applied.  □

Although Theorem 8.4 is stated in terms of payoffs in the NTU core, such payoffs give rise to state-dependent core allocations for which the corresponding (expected) utility allocations satisfy the equal treatment property.

## 9    Remarks

This paper analyzes replica economies rather than more general sequences of large but finite economies (with incentives and almost surely feasible randomization), because the interpretation of the ε-core for the latter is problematic. The analog of the first part of Theorem 8.4 for nonreplicas (see Wooders 1991) would give existence of the ε-core at the expense of the possibility that the fraction ε of players receive payoffs $w$ that may fail to satisfy $w + (\epsilon, ..., \epsilon) \notin \text{int}(\hat{V}_r(S_r))$ or, in other words, a small group $S_r$ (of size at most ε) receives allocations that could be blocked so as to gain more than an ε improvement in their payoffs. Such use of the weak ε-core is troublesome here because in this framework with asymmetric information, the information of such small groups may nevertheless be essential to the achievement of state-dependent allocations for other players. If the small group could receive large gains from its participation in blocking, these players may not be willing to reveal their information (truthfully) to others. Recall that the possibility for endogenous strategic information sharing is the primary economic question addressed here by incentive compatibility.

Similarly, I focus on games with nontransferable utility instead of the more tractable case of transferable utility because I believe that the transferable utility assumption contradicts the basic premise underlying incentive compatibility. If utility were transferable, so that all coalition members maximize the coalition's total utility as their sole objective function, then they should naturally share all of their information fully and correctly. Yet, when this happens, incentive compatibility constraints are unnecessary.

Needless to say, this paper leaves unanswered the natural question of whether large economies necessarily have non-empty incentive compatible cores. In all of the examples I have analyzed with empty incentive compatible cores, replication restores the existence of state-dependent allocations in the incentive compatible (exact) core. Unfortunately, I have been unable to show that replication guarantees the existence of such a core because, in particular, I see no intuitive reason for all sufficiently large replicas to be (exactly) balanced. On the other hand, I conjecture that exchange economies with asymmetric information and an atomless continuum of agents must have non-empty incentive compatible cores.

## REFERENCES

Allen, Beth (1991a), "Market Games with Asymmetric Information and Nontransferable Utility: Representation Results and the Core," working paper no. 91-09, Center for Analytic Research in Economics and the Social Sciences, Department of Economics, University of Pennsylvania, Philadelphia.

(1991b), "Transferable Utility Market Games with Asymmetric Information: Representation Results and the Core," working paper no. 91-16, Center for Analytic Research in Economics and the Social Sciences, Department of Economics, University of Pennsylvania, Philadelphia.

(1991c), "Market Games with Asymmetric Information: Verification and the Publicly Predictable Information Core," working paper no. 91-18, Center for Analytic Research in Economics and the Social Sciences, Department of Economics, University of Pennsylvania, Philadelphia.

(1992), "Incentives in Market Games with Asymmetric Information: The Core," working paper no. 91-38, Center for Analytic Research in Economics and the Social Sciences, Department of Economics, University of Pennsylvania, Philadelphia (also discussion paper no. 9221, CORE, Université Catholiqué de Louvain, Louvain-la-Neuve, Belgium).

Berliant, Marcus (1992), "On Income Taxation and the Core," *Journal of Economic Theory* 56: 121-41.

Boyd, John H., and Edward C. Prescott (1986), "Financial Intermediary-Coalitions," *Journal of Economic Theory* 38: 211-32.

d'Aspremont, C., and L.-A. Gerard-Varet (1979), "Incentives and Incomplete Information," *Journal of Public Economics* 11: 25-45.

Holmstrom, Bengt, and Roger Myerson (1983), "Efficient and Durable Decision Rules with Incomplete Information," *Econometrica* 51: 1799-1819.

Koutsourgeras, Leonidas, and Nicholas C. Yannelis (1991), "Incentive Compatibility and Information Superiority of the Core of an Economy with Differential Information," mimeo, Department of Economics, University of Illinois, Champaign-Urbana.

Marimón, Ramón (1989), "The Core of Private Information Economies," working paper no. 131.90, UAB/IAE Discussion Papers, Universitat Autònoma de Barcelona, Spain.

Myerson, R. B. (1984), "Cooperative Games with Imcomplete [sic] Information," *International Journal of Game Theory* 13: 69-96.

Prescott, Edward C., and Robert M. Townsend (1984a), "Pareto Optima and Competitive Equilibria with Adverse Selection and Moral Hazard," *Econometrica* 52: 21-45.

(1984b), "General Competitive Analysis in an Economy with Private Information," *International Economic Review* 25: 1-20.

Rosenmüller, Joachim (1990), "Fee Games: (N)TU Games with Incomplete Information," working paper no. 190, Institut für Mathematische Wirtschaftsforschung, Universität Bielefeld, Germany.

Shubik, Martin, and Myrna Holtz Wooders (1983), "Approximate Cores of Replica Games and Economies, Part I: Replica Games, Externalities and Approximate Cores," *Mathematical Social Sciences* 6: 27-48.

Wilson, Robert (1978), "Information, Efficiency and the Core of an Economy," *Econometrica* 46: 807-16.

Wooders, Myrna Holtz (1983), "The Epsilon Core of a Large Replica Game," *Journal of Mathematical Economics* 11: 277-300.

(1991), "The Efficaciousness of Small Groups and the Approximate Core Property in Games without Side Payments: Some First Results," discussion paper no. B-179, Sonderforschungsbereich 303, Universität Bonn, Germany.

Yannelis, Nicholas C. (1991), "The Core of an Economy with Differential Information," *Economic Theory* 1: 183-98.

CHAPTER 12

# A note on implementation and strong dominance

*Tilman Börgers*

## 1    Introduction

This paper is concerned with the implementation problem, which can be described as follows: Consider a group of individuals who must make a collective decision. Assume that there is a given set of feasible alternatives. Suppose also that there is a given social choice function that specifies, for every relevant profile of individuals' preferences, the desired collective decision. Can we then design a procedure for collective decision making which guarantees for every relevant preference profile that the desired decision will come about – provided the agents behave "rationally" in the collective decision process?

The implementation problem has been investigated for various definitions of rational behavior. Broadly speaking, one can distinguish between studies that define rationality using *dominance* notions (e.g. Farquharson 1969; Gibbard 1973; Satterthwaite 1975; Moulin 1979, 1980) and studies that define rationality using *equilibrium* notions (e.g. Maskin 1977; Myerson 1985). Definitions of rationality that are based on dominance notions assume less coordination of agents' behavior than do those based on equilibrium notions.[1] In this paper we shall be concerned with the case in which rationality is defined using dominance notions.

Two subcases need to be distinguished. First, a strategy in a collective decision procedure may be regarded as rational if and only if (hereafter "iff") it is not dominated; second, a strategy may be regarded as rational iff it survives iterated deletion of dominated strategies. The first notion of

A first version of the result described in this note appeared in my paper "Undominated Strategies and Coordination in Normalform Games" (Basel, 1989). I would like to thank an anonymous referee for detailed comments. I am grateful to the Swiss National Science Foundation for financial support.
[1]  This issue is discussed in Pearce (1984).

277

278    Tilman Börgers

rationality is appropriate if no assumption is made regarding the agents' information about each other. The second notion is appropriate if it is common knowledge among the agents which preferences they have, and that all agents are "rational."[2]

This note presents a simple impossibility result on implementation in undominated and iteratively undominated strategies. I assume that the domain of the social choice function under consideration includes all "unanimous" preference profiles, that is, all preference profiles in which all agents have identical preferences. I then show that such a social choice function can be implemented in undominated strategies if and only if it is dictatorial. The same is true if one considers iteratively undominated strategies.

My result is, of course, not interesting if one considers a domain that contains only unanimous preference profiles. In that case dictatorial social choice functions are the only reasonable (e.g. Pareto efficient) ones. The interesting case is domains that contain all unanimous profiles and also some others. With such domains in mind, one can read my result as saying that no implementable social choice function can accommodate the case that agents are unanimous and simultaneously resolve conflicts in a nondictatorial manner.

After presenting my result I shall compare it to several related results in the literature. Implementation in undominated strategies has previously been considered most prominently by Gibbard (1973) and Satterthwaite (1975).[3] Well-known contributions to the problem of implementation in iteratively undominated strategies are Farquharson (1969) and Moulin (1979, 1980). The framework in this paper differs from that in the references just mentioned in that I employ the concept of strong rather than weak dominance.

Formal definitions of these concepts will be provided in the next section. Intuitively, the difference is that elimination of strongly dominated strategies follows from Bayesian rationality only, without any restrictions on players' beliefs. Weakly dominated strategies can be eliminated if it is assumed that players have "cautious" beliefs, that is, beliefs that do not attach zero probability to any of the other players' strategies.[4]

Rationality notions based on strong dominance are thus less restrictive than rationality notions based on weak dominance. Therefore, impossibility results using weak dominance immediately imply corresponding

[2] See e.g. Pearce (1984).
[3] Gibbard and Satterthwaite formulate their theorem as a result concerning implementation in dominant strategies. Note 10 explains why it can be interpreted as a result on implementation in undominated strategies.
[4] See Lemmas 3 and 4 in Pearce (1984).

impossibility results using strong dominance. The result of this paper is, however, not obtained in this way. In fact, it will become clear that my result is *not* true for weak dominance. The impossibilities that arise if strong dominance is used are much more severe than the impossibilities that result if weak dominance is used.

In this paper it is excluded that the collective decision takes the form of a lottery rather than a "pure" outcome. In the literature, some authors have permitted lotteries (see e.g. Gibbard 1978 and Abreu and Matsushima 1992). I shall compare my results to those obtained in these papers, and this comparison will suggest several questions for further research.

## 2    The result

I consider a society consisting of a finite set of individuals $i \in I = \{1, 2, ..., n\}$ ($n \geq 2$). The society has to choose one alternative out of a given finite set of possible alternatives $a \in A$. To exclude trivialities I assume that $A$ has at least two elements. Each individual $i$ has a *preference relation* $R_i$ over $A$. The expression "$a R_i b$" will be interpreted as: "$i$ finds outcome $a$ at least as good as outcome $b$." For every $i$, $R_i$ is assumed to be complete and transitive. For every $i$ we can derive from $R_i$ two other relations: first, the *strict preference relation* $P_i$ - $a P_i b$ iff $a R_i b$ and not $b R_i a$; second, the *indifference relation* $I_i$ - $a I_i b$ iff $a R_i b$ and $b R_i a$. I shall assume that $a I_i b$ implies $a = b$ for every $i \in I$ and $a, b \in A$; hence no agent is indifferent between two different alternatives. For every $i \in I$ I shall denote by $\mathfrak{R}_i$ the set of all preference relations that satisfy this restriction. (Of course, $\mathfrak{R}_i$ is the same for all $i$.) By $R$ I denote the $n$-tuple $(R_1, R_2, ..., R_n)$; $R$ is contained in $\mathfrak{R} \equiv \prod_{i \in I} \mathfrak{R}_i$. I shall call a preference profile $R \in \mathfrak{R}$ *unanimous* iff $R_1 = R_2 = \cdots = R_n$.

To choose an outcome, the society will play a game. Formally, a *game form $G$* is an $(n+1)$-tuple $(S_1, S_2, ..., S_n; g)$, where $S_1, S_2, ..., S_n$ are arbitrary finite[5] and non-empty sets and where $g$ is a mapping $g: S_1 \times S_2 \times \cdots \times S_n \to A$. For every $i$, $S_i$ denotes individual $i$'s choice set. The function $g$ associates with each possible choice of all players some outcome. If $G = (S_1, S_2, ..., S_n; g)$ is a game form then I shall write $S$ for the Cartesian product $\prod_{i \in I} S_i$. Elements of $S$ are denoted by $s$. Moreover, for $i \in I$ I

[5] It seems plausible that the results of this paper also hold if infinite strategy sets are admitted. However, to deal with infinite strategy sets I would need a somewhat more sophisticated definition of iterated deletion of dominated strategies than currently given in Definition 2. This is because with infinite strategy sets it is no longer clear that a finite (or, indeed, a countably infinite) number of iterations would be enough to delete all dominated strategies.

280    **Tilman Börgers**

denote by $S_{-i}$ the Cartesian product $\prod_{j \neq i} S_j$. Elements of $S_{-i}$ are denoted by $s_{-i}$.

Next I define the two solution concepts that will be considered in this section.

**Definition 1.** Let $G$ be a game form, let $R \in \mathfrak{R}$, and let $i \in I$. Then a strategy $s_i \in S_i$ is *undominated* iff there is no strategy $\bar{s}_i \in S_i$ such that $g(\bar{s}_i, s_{-i}) P_i g(s_i, s_{-i})$ for all $s_{-i} \in S_{-i}$. The set of all undominated strategies of player $i$ will be denoted by $D_i(G, R_i)$. Moreover, I shall write $D(G, R)$ for $\prod_{i \in I} D_i(G, R_i)$.[6]

Observe that dominance in this definition requires strict preference for all $s_{-i} \in S_{-i}$; it is therefore usually called "strong dominance." "Weak dominance," by contrast, requires strict preference only for some $s_{-i} \in S_{-i}$, and weak preference for all other $s_{-i} \in S_{-i}$. To simplify the terminology in this section, in Definition 1 the expression "undominated" is used without any further qualification.

**Definition 2.** Let $G$ be a game form and let $R \in \mathfrak{R}$. Let

$$(G^t)_{t \in \mathbb{N}} = (S_1^t, S_2^t, ..., S_n^t; g^t)_{t \in \mathbb{N}}$$

be a sequence of game forms such that:

(i)  $G^1 = G$; and
(ii) for every $t \in \mathbb{N}$ and $i \in I$, $S_i^{t+1} = D_i(G^t, R_i)$ and $g^{t+1}$ is the restriction of $g$ to $S_1^{t+1} \times S_2^{t+1} \times \cdots \times S_n^{t+1}$.

---

[6] A formal justification of the notion of "strong dominance" is provided by Lemma 3 in Pearce (1984). This lemma states that a player's strategy is not strongly dominated if and only if it maximizes expected utility given some arbitrary subjective probability measure that is defined on the other players' strategy sets. Pearce's result requires that mixed strategies also be considered. In the current section, however, mixed strategies are excluded from consideration. Pearce's framework differs from mine also in that he models agents' preferences using von Neumann–Morgenstern utility functions, thus describing their preferences over lotteries, whereas I describe only their (ordinal) preferences over pure outcomes.

In Börgers (1993) I have shown that an analog of Pearce's results that does not require mixed strategies can be obtained if only the players' preferences over pure strategy outcomes, rather than their von Neumann–Morgenstern utility functions, are taken as exogenously given and fixed. For this I had to introduce a slight modification in the definition of strong dominance. Thus the formally correct way of proceeding would be to adopt in this section the modified definition of strong dominance. I refrain from this to simplify the presentation. The result of this paper continues to hold if one replaces strong dominance by modified strong dominance.

A strategy $s_i \in S_i$ will be called *iteratively undominated* iff it is contained in $\bigcap_{t \in \mathbb{N}} S_i^t$. The set of all iteratively undominated strategies of player $i$ will be denoted by $\bar{D}_i(G, R)$. Moreover, I shall write $\bar{D}(G, R)$ for $\prod_{i \in I} \bar{D}_i(G, R)$.[7]

A *social choice function* is a function $f: \hat{\mathfrak{R}} \to A$ such that $\hat{\mathfrak{R}}$ is any nonempty subset of $\mathfrak{R}$, and such that the range of $f$ is $A$. Here $\hat{\mathfrak{R}}$ is the set of preference profiles regarded as "relevant" and, for every $R \in \hat{\mathfrak{R}}$, $f(R)$ is the "desired" collective decision. The condition that $f$ must have range $A$ is an innocuous restriction, for I shall consider domains on which it is eminently reasonable that $f$ should have range $A$. Moreover, my results would remain true even without this condition; I would only have to replace throughout the set $A$ by the range of $f$.

I am interested in social choice functions that can be implemented in undominated or iteratively undominated strategies. Formally, these properties are defined as follows.

**Definition 3.** A social choice function $f$ can be *implemented in undominated strategies* iff there is a game form $G$ such that $g[D(G, R)] = \{f(R)\}$ for all $R \in \hat{\mathfrak{R}}$.[8]

**Definition 4.** A social choice function $f$ can be *implemented in iteratively undominated strategies* iff there is a game form $G$ such that $g[\bar{D}(G, R)] = \{f(R)\}$ for all $R \in \hat{\mathfrak{R}}$.

In order to characterize implementable social choice functions, the next definition is needed.

**Definition 5.** A social choice function $f$ is *dictatorial* iff there is some $i \in I$ such that $f(R) = \text{argmax } R_i$ for all $R \in \hat{\mathfrak{R}}$.[9]

We then have the following result.

**Proposition.** *Let $f$ be a social choice function. Suppose that the domain $\hat{\mathfrak{R}}$ of $f$ includes all unanimous preference profiles in $\mathfrak{R}$. Then the following three statements are equivalent:*

[7] In this definition the sequence $G^t$ is the sequence of game forms obtained through successive elimination of strongly dominated strategies. Observe that for all $i$ and $t$ the sets $S_i^t$ are non-empty, and that, because of the finiteness of $G$, for some $t^*$ we shall have $S_i^t = S_i^{t+1}$ for all $t \geq t^*$ and all $i$. Thus $\bar{D}_i(G, R) = S_i^{t^*}$ for all $i$.

[8] Here I use the notation: $g[D(G, R)] \equiv \{a \in A \mid g(s) = a \text{ for some } s \in D(G, R)\}$.

[9] Here "argmax $R_i$" stands for the alternative in $A$ that maximizes $R_i$.

(i)   $f$ is implementable in undominated strategies;
(ii)  $f$ is implementable in iteratively undominated strategies;
(iii) $f$ is dictatorial.

*Proof:*  It is obvious that (i) implies (ii), and that (iii) implies (i). Therefore it suffices to show that (ii) implies (iii). So let $G = (S_1, S_2, \ldots, S_n; g)$ be a game form that implements $f$ in iteratively undominated strategies. Observe that $f$ having range $A$ implies that also $g$ has range $A$.

Denote by $a$ some given and fixed alternative in $A$. Define, for every $i \in I$, $S_i^a = \{s_i \in S_i \mid g(s_i, s_{-i}) = a$ for some $s_{-i} \in S_{-i}\}$ and $S_i^{\neg a} = S_i \setminus S_i^a$. Hence $S_i^a$ is the set of all those strategies of agent $i$ that do *not* exclude the possibility that outcome $a$ is realized, whereas $S_i^{\neg a}$ denotes the set of all those strategies of agent $i$ that *do* exclude the possibility that outcome $a$ is realized.

Consider a unanimous $R \in \mathfrak{R}$ such that $a = \arg\max R_i$ for all $i$. Observe that for every $i \in I$ a strategy in $S_i^a$ cannot be strongly dominated given $R_i$, since the dominating strategy would have to yield (for some $s_{-i} \in S_{-i}$) an outcome that is strictly preferred to $a$, which (by assumption) does not exist. By the same argument, neither can the second round of elimination of strongly dominated strategies eliminate any of the strategies in the sets $S_i^a$. The argument can be iterated, leading to the conclusion that $S_1^a \times S_2^a \times \cdots \times S_n^a \subseteq \bar{D}(G, R)$.

Therefore,

$$\{a\} \subseteq g(S_1^a \times S_2^a \times \cdots \times S_n^a) \subseteq g[\bar{D}(G, R)].$$

Since $G$ implements $f$, and since $R \in \hat{\mathfrak{R}}$, I may conclude that $g[\bar{D}(G, R)] = \{a\}$ and $f(R) = a$. This must be true for every unanimous $R$ for which $a = \arg\max R_i$ (for all $i$).

I shall show next that this implies that $S_i^a \neq S_i$ holds only for exactly one agent. To see that this follows, observe first that we obviously cannot have that $S_i^a \neq S_i$ holds for *no* agent $i$ because then $g[\bar{D}(G, R)] \supseteq g(S_1^a \times S_2^a \times \cdots \times S_n^a) = g(S) = A$, which contradicts the preceding paragraph.

Suppose next there were $i, j \in I$ with $i \neq j$, $S_i^a \neq S_i$ and $S_j^a \neq S_j$. Let $s$ be any strategy combination in $S$ such that $s_i \in S_i^{\neg a}$ and $s_j \in S_j^{\neg a}$. Define $b \equiv g(s)$. By construction, $b \neq a$. Let $R \in \mathfrak{R}$ be a unanimous profile that satisfies $a P_k b P_k c$ for all $k \in I$ and all $c \in A \setminus \{a, b\}$. Then $s \in \bar{D}(G, R)$. This is because, for every agent $k \in I$, a strategy can strongly dominate $s_k$ only if it yields $a$ against $s_{-k}$. However, for no agent $k \in I$ can such a strategy exist, because for every agent $k$ there is some other agent – namely, either $i$ or $j$ or both – who chooses in $s$ a strategy that excludes the possibility that $a$ is realized. This argument can again be iterated, yielding the desired conclusion $s \in \bar{D}(G, R)$. But this implies $b \in g[\bar{D}(G, R)]$, which contradicts the result derived earlier that $g[\bar{D}(G, R)] = \{a\}$.

Hence there will be exactly one agent with $S_i^a \neq S_i$. Denote this agent by $i(a)$. Combining what I have shown so far leads to the conclusion that, for every unanimous profile $R \in \mathfrak{R}$ with $a = \arg\max R_i$ for all $i \in I$, $\bar{D}_i(G, R) = S_i$ for all $i \neq i(a)$ and $\bar{D}_{i(a)}(G, R_{i(a)}) \supseteq S_{i(a)}^a$. Since $g[\bar{D}(G, R)] = \{a\}$ we may conclude that $s_{i(a)} \in S_{i(a)}^a$ implies $g(s_{i(a)}, s_{-i(a)}) = a$ for all $s_{-i(a)} \in S_{-i(a)}$. Moreover, by definition $s_{i(a)} \in S_{i(a)}^{\neg a}$ implies $g(s_{i(a)}, s_{-i(a)}) \neq a$ for all $s_{-i(a)} \in S_{-i(a)}$.

Thus, if $i(a)$ chooses a strategy from $S_{i(a)}^a$ then the resulting outcome will be $a$, regardless of what the other agents do. If agent $i(a)$ chooses a strategy from $S_{i(a)}^{\neg a}$ the resulting outcome will not be $a$, regardless (again) of what the other agents do. Agent $i(a)$ can either enforce or exclude outcome $a$.

The argument developed so far holds true for any alternative $a$. Hence for every alternative there must be an agent who, through his strategy choice, either enforces or excludes this alternative. But note that this must be the same agent for all alternatives; otherwise, the outcome would not be well-defined if one agent enforced one alternative and another agent enforced a different alternative.

Hence the game form $G$ must be such that there is one agent who can enforce or exclude any alternative. For this agent, $\{S_i^a\}_{a \in A}$ partitions $S_i$. But then the social choice function implemented by $G$ must clearly be dictatorial, whereby the agent who can enforce or exclude any alternative is the dictator. $\qquad\square$

For the case in which a full domain with at least three alternatives is considered, the result here has also been obtained by Jackson and Srivastava (1991). Their proof is built on the theorem of Gibbard and Satterthwaite. The relation between my result and this theorem will be discussed in the next section.

## 3    Discussion

In Section 2, "dominance" was defined as "strong dominance." An alternative notion of "dominance" is "weak dominance." For this latter notion of dominance, a fundamental result of Gibbard (1973) and Satterthwaite (1975) says that if $\#A \geq 3$ then a social choice function $f$ with unrestricted domain (i.e. with $\hat{\mathfrak{R}} = \mathfrak{R}$) can be implemented in undominated strategies if and only if it is dictatorial.[10] Gibbard and Satterthwaite's theorem holds

---

[10] This formulation of Gibbard and Satterthwaite's theorem is somewhat unconventional. The traditional formulation refers to implementation in weakly dominant strategies,

284    Tilman Börgers

also on some restricted domains; see for example Kalai and Muller (1977) and Muller and Satterthwaite (1985).[11]

"Undominated strategies" is a less restrictive solution concept if dominance is defined as strong dominance rather than weak dominance. It is therefore immediate that, in all contexts in which Gibbard and Satterthwaite's theorem holds, the result will remain true if one replaces the notion of weak dominance by the notion of strong dominance. However, the Proposition of Section 2 covers several cases in which the Gibbard-Satterthwaite theorem is not true.

In particular, Gibbard and Satterthwaite's theorem does not hold if there are only two alternatives. For example, simple majority voting over these two alternatives, augmented by a suitable tie-breaking rule, yields an implementable social choice function. By contrast, the Proposition applies also to the case of only two alternatives.[12]

Moreover, if there are three or more alternatives, there are domains to which Gibbard and Satterthwaite's theorem does not apply, and which nevertheless are covered by the Proposition. To show this I shall provide an example. Assume that there are two agents and three alternatives $a$, $b$, and $c$.[13] Let the domain $\hat{\Re}$ consist of all unanimous preference profiles and, in addition, of the preference profile $(\tilde{R}_1, \tilde{R}_2)$ defined by $a \tilde{P}_1 b \tilde{P}_1 c$ and $c \tilde{P}_2 b \tilde{P}_2 a$. Suppose that the social choice function $f$ assigns to unanimous preference profiles the unanimously preferred outcome, and that it assigns to $(\tilde{R}_1, \tilde{R}_2)$ the outcome $b$. By the Proposition this social choice function cannot be implemented in strategies that are not strongly dominated, but it can be implemented in strategies that are not weakly dominated. I prove the latter assertion by showing in Figure 1 a game form that implements $f$. In this figure, agent 1 chooses rows and agent 2 chooses columns. I leave it to the reader to verify that this game form does indeed implement $f$ in strategies that are not weakly dominated.

rather than implementation in strategies that are not weakly dominated. The equivalence between the formulation in the text and this traditional formulation is shown in Jackson (1992, cor. 1). Jackson's result requires that attention be restricted to the class of "bounded" game forms ("boundedness" is defined in his paper). Finite game forms are trivially bounded. In this paper I restrict attention throughout to finite game forms.

[11] Interesting restricted domains on which Gibbard and Satterthwaite's theorem is *not* valid are described in Barberà, Sonnenschein, and Zhou (1991) and, implicitly, in Sen and Pattanaik (1969). Muller and Satterthwaite (1985, n. 9) explain why Sen and Pattanaik's (1969) paper can be interpreted in this way.

[12] Observe that in the majority voting game with two alternatives, sincere voting is a weakly but not strongly dominant strategy, since the collective decision may be independent of any single agent's vote. Therefore this game does not provide a counterexample to the Proposition.

[13] The example can trivially be adapted to the general case with $\#A \geq 3$ and $n \geq 2$.

$$l \quad r$$

| | $l$ | $r$ |
|---|---|---|
| $s_1$ | $a$ | $b$ |
| $s_2$ | $a$ | $c$ |
| $s_3$ | $b$ | $b$ |
| $s_4$ | $c$ | $c$ |

Figure 1

Consider next the case of iteratively undominated strategies. Suppose that "dominance" is defined to be "weak dominance," so that the solution concept is iterated deletion of weakly dominated strategies. For this case Farquharson (1969) and Moulin (1979, 1980) have shown that nondictatorial social choice functions can be implemented, even on unrestricted domains. By contrast, the Proposition shows that this is impossible in the case of strong dominance.[14]

Another change of the framework of Section 2 that one might wish to consider is permitting the collective decision to be a lottery rather than a ("pure") outcome. It then suggests itself to introduce the restriction that agents' preferences take the form of von Neumann–Morgenstern utility functions. Hence, consider the case where the set $\Re_i$ is the set of all real-valued functions with domain $A$. Moreover, the function $f$ maps a subset of $\Re$ into the set of all probability measures on $A$. A game form is defined as before, with the exception that the codomain of $g$ is the set of all probability measures on $A$.[15] Assume again that the range of $f$ includes $A$. Finally, define dominance (as before) as "strong dominance."

Notice that the proof given in the previous section cannot be used to obtain an analogous result with lotteries. The argument of the previous section relied on the fact that for any given alternatives $a, b$ there always exists a preference relation according to which $a$ is the unique best alternative and $b$ is the unique second best alternative. This is no longer true if lotteries are considered, and if agents' preferences take the form

---

[14] Iterated deletion of weakly dominated strategies is a somewhat controversial solution procedure for which the foundations are problematic. In Börgers (1994) I have shown that a modified procedure can be justified within a formal common knowledge framework. In an earlier version of the current paper an example was used to show that also this modified procedure allows implementation of nondictatorial social choice functions on the full domain.

[15] It might, however, appear natural to allow for the possibility that the strategy sets are infinite. See in this context note 5.

of von Neumann–Morgenstern utility functions. Consider for example a lottery $\alpha$ that places all probability on the (pure) alternative $a$, and a lottery $\beta$ that places probability 0.5 on the (pure) alternative $a$ and probability 0.5 on the (pure) alternative $b$. Then there is no von Neumann–Morgenstern utility function that makes $\alpha$ the unique best outcome and $\beta$ the unique second-best outcome. If $a$ is uniquely best, then a lottery that places a probability of more than 0.5 on $a$ will always be preferred to $\beta$. It is this type of preference restriction that makes the argument of Section 2 impossible.

However, a result of Gibbard (1978) implies that, on the full domain, a function $f$ can be implemented in undominated strategies only if it is a probability mixture of a random dictatorship and of social choice functions that place all probability on only two alternatives.[16] The question arises whether this result can be strengthened and, for example, be proven also for restricted domains of the type considered in the previous section. To my knowledge, this question remains open.

Next suppose that lotteries were permitted and that the solution concept were iterated deletion of strongly dominated strategies. For this case also it is, to my knowledge, an open question which social choice functions can be implemented on the full domain.

A recent paper of Abreu and Matsushima (1992) is concerned with this implementation problem on a restricted domain. Specifically, they introduce two assumptions for the domain. The first is that the domain consists of a finite number of preference profiles only. The second is that, for every agent $i$, there exist two lotteries, $\alpha$ and $\beta$, such that agent $i$ is the only agent who always strictly prefers $\alpha$ to $\beta$. This domain restriction amounts to assuming the existence of some degree of conflict among agents. Abreu and Matsushima point out that their assumption is satisfied if, for example, the description of a collective alternative includes the allocation of a private good (say, money) and if all agents' preferences are monotonically increasing in the quantity of this good that they possess.

Abreu and Matsushima show that, with these domain restrictions, a large class of social choice functions can be implemented in strategies that survive iterated deletion of strongly dominated strategies. In fact, the implementable social choice functions are, in a sense, dense within the class of *all* social choice functions. Investigating how this result changes if Abreu and Matsushima's domain restrictions are removed might lead to an improved understanding of their result.

---

[16] Gibbard's result refers to implementation in weakly dominant strategies. The stated result follows as a corollary, using similar arguments as in the nonstochastic case.

REFERENCES

Abreu, D., and H. Matsushima (1992), "Virtual Implementation in Iteratively Un-dominated Strategies: Complete Information," *Econometrica* 60: 993-1008.
Barberà, S., H. Sonnenschein, and L. Zhou (1991), "Voting by Committees," *Econometrica* 59: 595-609.
Börgers, T. (1993), "Pure Strategy Dominance," *Econometrica* 61: 423-30.
(1994), "Weak Dominance and Approximate Common Knowledge," *Journal of Economic Theory* 64: 265-76.
Farquharson, R. (1969), *Theory of Voting*. New Haven, CT: Yale University Press.
Gibbard, A. (1973), "Manipulation of Voting Schemes: A General Result," *Econometrica* 41: 587-602.
(1978), "Straightforwardness of Game Forms with Lotteries as Outcomes," *Econometrica* 46: 595-614.
Jackson, M. O. (1992), "Implementation in Undominated Strategies: A Look at Bounded Mechanisms," *Review of Economic Studies* 59: 757-75.
Jackson, M. O., and S. Srivastava (1991), "Implementing Social Choice Functions: A New Look at Some Impossibility Results," Mimeo, Kellogg Graduate School of Management, Northwestern University, Evanston, IL.
Kalai, E., and E. Muller (1977), "Characterization of Domains Admitting Nondictatorial Social Welfare Functions and Nonmanipulable Voting Procedures," *Journal of Economic Theory* 16: 457-69.
Maskin, E. (1977), "Nash Equilibrium and Welfare Optimality," mimeo, Department of Economics, Massachusetts Institute of Technology, Cambridge.
Moulin, H. (1979), "Dominance Solvable Voting Schemes," *Econometrica* 47: 1337-51.
(1980), "Implementing Efficient, Anonymous, and Neutral Social Choice Functions," *Journal of Mathematical Economics* 7: 249-69.
Muller, E., and M. A. Satterthwaite (1985), "Strategy-proofness: The Existence of Dominant-Strategy Mechanisms," in L. Hurwicz et al. (eds.), *Social Goals and Social Organization*. Cambridge: Cambridge University Press, pp. 131-71.
Myerson, R. B. (1985), "Bayesian Equilibrium and Incentive-Compatibility: An Introduction," in L. Hurwicz et al. (eds.), *Social Goals and Social Organization*. Cambridge: Cambridge University Press, pp. 229-59.
Pearce, D. (1984), "Rationalizable Strategic Behavior and the Problem of Perfection," *Econometrica* 52: 1029-50.
Satterthwaite, M. A. (1975), "Strategy-Proofness and Arrow's Conditions: Existence and Correspondence Theorems for Voting Procedures and Social Welfare Functions," *Journal of Economic Theory* 10: 187-217.
Sen, A., and P. Pattanaik (1969), "Necessary and Sufficient Conditions for Rational Choice under Majority Decision," *Journal of Economic Theory* 1: 178-202.

CHAPTER 13

# Coalition-proof communication equilibria

*Ezra Einy & Bezalel Peleg*

## 1    Introduction

Correlated equilibria were introduced in Aumann (1974). Since then they
have been extensively investigated by many game theorists (see e.g. Forges
1986, 1993b; Myerson 1991). Several attempts to define coalition-proof
correlated equilibria have already been made (see e.g. Sinha 1991). We
offer in this paper a new definition. In our model, deviations of coalitions
are introduced *after* their players are informed of the actions they should
follow. This leads to "reduced games" with incomplete information: Improvements by coalitions on a given correlated strategy should always be
made when their players have private information.

  We now review briefly the contents of the paper. In Section 2 we define
reduced games of games with incomplete information, which we call *revised games*. Section 3 contains the definitions of coalition-proof communication equilibria and strong communication equilibria. A new kind
of efficiency – informational efficiency – is introduced in Section 4; it is
used to characterize the coalition-proof communication equilibria of two-
person Bayesian games. Section 5 is devoted to an analysis of the voting
paradox. We prove that for every choice of cardinal utilities for the three
players, the resulting game in strategic form has a coalition-proof communication equilibrium. Finally, in Section 6 we compare coalition-proof
communication equilibria with coalition-proof Nash equilibria. In particular, we describe a game with no coalition-proof Nash equilibrium that
nevertheless has a strong communication equilibrium.

## 2    Extended and revised Bayesian games

Let $S$ be a set and let $B^i$ be a set for each $i \in S$. We denote $B^S = \times_{i \in S} B^i$.
If $i \in S$ then $-i = S \backslash \{i\}$ and $B^{-i} = \times_{k \neq i} B^k$. Thus, if $i \in S$ and $b \in B^S$ then

We are grateful to F. Forges, J.-F. Mertens, and Benny Moldovanu for helpful remarks.

$b = (b^i, b^{-i})$, where $b^i \in B^i$ and $b^{-i} \in B^{-i}$. If $Q \subset S$ and $b \in B^S$ then $b^Q = (b^i)_{i \in Q}$. Also, if $B$ is a finite set then we denote by $\Delta(B)$ the set of all probability distributions over $B$.

**Definition 2.1.**  An *extended* Bayesian game is a system

$$G = (A^1, ..., A^m; T^1, ..., T^m, T^{m+1}, ..., T^n; p^1, ..., p^m; u^1, ..., u^m),$$

where

(i)   $M = \{1, ..., m\}$ is the set of *players*;

(ii)  $L = \{m+1, ..., n\}$ is the set of *outside* players ($L = \emptyset$ is possible);

(iii) $A^i$ is the (finite) set of *actions* of $i \in M$;

(iv)  $T^i$ is the (finite) set of possible *types* of $i \in N = M \cup L$;

(v)   $p^i$, $i$'s prior, is a member of $\Delta(T)$ where $T = T^N$, which represents the *beliefs* of $i \in M$; and

(vi)  $u^i : A \times T \to \mathbb{R}$ is the utility function of $i \in M$ (here $A = A^M$ and $\mathbb{R}$ is the set of real numbers).

Intuitively, the reader may consider the members of $L$ as past participants in some Bayesian game $G^*$ with the set of players $N$, who have already chosen their strategies. Thus, $G$ is a "reduced game" that the remaining players – namely, the members of $M$ – must play (see Definition 2.2). If $L = \emptyset$ then $G$ is an ordinary Bayesian game.

Let $G = (A^1, ..., A^m; T^1, ..., T^m, ..., T^n; p^1, ..., p^m; u^1, ..., u^m)$ be an extended Bayesian game. A correlated strategy for $G$ is a function $\mu : A \times T^M \to [0, 1]$ such that $\sum_{a \in A} \mu(a \mid t^M) = 1$ for every $t^M \in T^M$. For $i \in M$ we denote

$$T_+^i = \{t^i \in T^i \mid p^i(t^i) > 0\}, \tag{2.1}$$

where $p^i(t^i) = \sum_{\tau^{-i} \in T^{-i}} p^i(\tau^{-1}, t^i)$. Let $\mu$ be a correlated strategy, let $i \in M$, and let $t^i \in T_+^i$. The expected utility of $t^i$ is given by

$$U^i(\mu \mid t^i) = \sum_{t^{-i} \in T^{-i}} p^i(t^{-i} \mid t^i) \sum_{a \in A} \mu(a \mid t^M) u^i(a, t). \tag{2.2}$$

A strategy $\mu$ is a *communication equilibrium* (CE) if, for every $i \in M$, $t^i \in T_+^i$, $s^i \in T^i$, and $g^i : A^i \to A^i$, the following inequality holds:

$$U^i(\mu \mid t^i) \geq \sum_{t^{-i} \in T^{-i}} p^i(t^{-i} \mid t^i) \sum_{a \in A} \mu(a \mid (t^{M \setminus \{i\}}, s^i)) u^i((a^{-i}, g^i(a^i)), t). \tag{2.3}$$

Let $G = (A^1, ..., A^m; T^1, ..., T^m, ..., T^n; p^1, ..., p^m; u^1, ..., u^m)$ be an extended Bayesian game. Let $\mu$ be a correlated strategy, and let $\emptyset \neq S \subset M$.

**Definition 2.2.**  The *revised game* $G_{\mu, S}$ is the extended Bayesian game

$$((A^i)_{i \in S}; T^1 \times A^1, ..., T^m \times A^m, T^{m+1}, ..., T^n; (\hat{p}^i)_{i \in S}; (\hat{u}^i)_{i \in S}),$$

where
$$\hat{p}^i(t^1, a^1, \ldots, t^m, a^m, t^{m+1}, \ldots, t^n) = \hat{p}^i(t, a) = p^i(t)\mu(a \mid t^M)$$
for all $i \in S$, $t \in T$, and $a \in A$; and where
$$\hat{u}^i((b^j)_{j \in S}, (t, a)) = \hat{u}^i(b^S, (t, a)) = u^i((b^S, a^{M \setminus S}), t)$$
for all $i \in S$, $t \in T$, $b^S \in A^S$, and $a \in A$.

Let $i \in M$ and $t^i \in T_+^i$. The probability that $a^i \in A^i$ is played by $t^i$ is
$$\pi^i(a^i \mid t^i) = \sum_{t^{-i} \in T^{-i}} p^i(t^{-i} \mid t^i) \sum_{a^{-i} \in A^{-i}} \mu((a^{-i}, a^i) \mid t^M). \qquad (2.4)$$
Thus, if $i \in S$, $t^i \in T^i$, and $a^i \in A^i$, then $\hat{p}^i(t^i, a^i) > 0$ if and only if (hereafter "iff") $t^i \in T_+^i$ and $\pi^i(a^i \mid t^i) > 0$. Hence, for $i \in S$,
$$(T^i \times A^i)_+ = \{(t^i, a^i) \mid t^i \in T_+^i, a^i \in A^i, \text{ and } \pi^i(a^i \mid t^i) > 0\}. \qquad (2.5)$$
Now let $i \in S$, $(t^i, a^i) \in (T^i \times A^i)_+$, $t^{-i} \in T^{-i}$, and $a^{-i} \in A^{-i}$. Then
$$\hat{p}^i((t^{-i}, a^{-i}) \mid (t^i, a^i)) = \frac{p^i(t^{-i} \mid t^i)\mu(a \mid t^M)}{\pi^i(a^i \mid t^i)}. \qquad (2.6)$$
So, if $\eta$ is a correlated strategy for $G_{\mu, S}$, $i \in S$, and $(t^i, a^i) \in (T^i \times A^i)_+$, then the expected utility of $(t^i, a^i)$ is
$$U^i(\eta \mid (t^i, a^i))$$
$$= \sum_{t^{-i} \in T^{-i}} \sum_{a^{-i} \in A^{-i}} \hat{p}^i((t^{-i}, a^{-i}) \mid (t^i, a^i)) \sum_{b^S \in A^S} \eta(b^S \mid (t^S, a^S))\hat{u}^i(b^S, (t, a)).$$
$$(2.7)$$

**Example 2.3.** Consider the (ordinary) game in strategic form,

MATRIX 2.1

$$G: \quad \begin{array}{c c} & \begin{array}{cc} L & R \end{array} \\ \begin{array}{c} T \\ B \end{array} & \begin{array}{|c|c|} \hline 6,6 & 2,7 \\ \hline 7,2 & 0,0 \\ \hline \end{array} \end{array} \quad ;$$

this is the game of "chicken." The strategy

MATRIX 2.2

$$\mu = \begin{array}{|c|c|} \hline 0 & 2/5 \\ \hline 2/5 & 1/5 \\ \hline \end{array}$$

is a CE.

The revised game $G_{\mu,\{1,2\}}$ is $(A^1, A^2; A^1, A^2; \mu, \mu; \hat{u}^1, \hat{u}^2)$, where $A^1 = \{T, B\}$ and $A^2 = \{L, R\}$; $G_{\mu,\{1,2\}}$ is a genuine game with incomplete information. Indeed, the question of whether the players want to improve upon $\mu$ becomes meaningful only *after* the players are (privately) told which pure strategies to play in $G$. The reason for this is that $\mu$ has no "equilibrium power" before the players get their private information (as a result of implementing $\mu$). In particular, the two marginals of $\mu$ do not form a Nash equilibrium.

**Remark 2.4.** We use priors in Definition 2.1 in order to simplify the notations in Definition 2.2. The priors can be easily replaced by conditional probabilities.

## 3     Coalition-proof communication equilibria

Let $G = (A^1, ..., A^m; T^1, ..., T^m, ..., T^n; p^1, ..., p^m; u^1, ..., u^m)$ be an extended Bayesian game and let $\mu$ be a correlated strategy. If $i \in M$, $t^i \in T_+^i$, $a^i \in A^i$, and $\pi^i(a^i | t^i) > 0$ (see (2.1) and 2.4)), then the expected payoff for $t^i$ when playing $a^i$ is

$$U^i(\mu | (t^i, a^i)) = \sum_{t^{-i} \in T^{-i}} p^i(t^{-i} | t^i) \sum_{a^{-i} \in A^{-i}} \mu((a^{-i}, a^i) | t^M) \frac{u^i(a, t)}{\pi^i(a^i | t^i)}. \quad (3.1)$$

Thus, $U^i(\mu | (t^i, a^i))$ is well-defined for all $(t^i, a^i) \in (T^i \times A^i)_+$ (see (2.5)) and $i \in M$. Let $\emptyset \neq S \subset M$.

**Definition 3.1.** The strategy $\eta$ is an *improvement* of $S$ upon $\mu$ in $G$ if:

   (i)   $\eta$ is a communication equilibrium for the revised game $G_{\mu, S}$; and
  (ii)  for every $i \in S$ and $(t^i, a^i) \in (T^i \times A^i)_+$, we have $U^i(\eta | (t^i, a^i)) > U^i(\mu | (t^i, a^i))$ (see (2.7) and (3.1)).

**Remark 3.2.** The definition of coalition-proof Nash equilibrium in Bernheim, Peleg, and Whinston (1987, p. 6) cannot be directly generalized to correlated strategies, because the restriction of a correlated strategy to a proper subset of the set of players is not well-defined. However, Definition 2.9 in Peleg (1984) can be easily adapted to the present model.

**Definition 3.3.** Let $G = (A^1, ..., A^m; T^1, ..., T^m, ..., T^n; p^1, ..., p^m; \mu^1, ..., \mu^m)$ be an extended Bayesian game, let $\mu$ be a correlated strategy, and let $S \subset M$, $S \neq \emptyset$. An *internally consistent improvement* (ICI) of $S$ upon $\mu$ in $G$ is defined by induction on $|S|$, the number of members in $S$, as follows: (i) If $|S| = 1$ then $\eta$ is an ICI if it is an improvement of $S$ upon $\mu$; (ii) if $|S| > 1$ then $\eta$ is an ICI of $S$ upon $\mu$ in $G$ if (a) $\eta$ is an improvement of $S$ upon $\mu$ in $G$, and (b) if $T \subset S$ and $T \neq \emptyset$, $S$ then $T$ has no ICI upon $\eta$ in the game $G_{\mu, S}$.

**Definition 3.4.** Let $G$ be an extended Bayesian game and let $\mu$ be a communication equilibrium. Strategy $\mu$ is a *coalition-proof communication equilibrium* (CPCE) if no coalition of players has an ICI upon $\mu$.

The notation introduced here enables us to define strong communication equilibrium.

**Definition 3.5.** Let $G = (A^1, \ldots, A^m; T^1, \ldots, T^m, \ldots, T^n; p^1, \ldots, p^m; u^1, \ldots, u^m)$ be an extended Bayesian game, let $\mu$ be a correlated strategy, and let $S \subset M$, $S \neq \emptyset$. Strategy $\eta$ is a *semi-improvement* of $S$ upon $\mu$ in $G$ if:

    (i)   $\eta$ is a correlated strategy for the revised game $G_{\mu, S}$; and

    (ii)  for every $i \in S$ and $(t^i, a^i) \in (T^i \times A^i)_+$,

$$U^i(\eta \,|\, (t^i, a^i)) > U^i(\mu \,|\, (t^i, a^i)).$$

**Definition 3.6.** A communication equilibrium $\mu$ is a *strong communication equilibrium* (SCE) if no $S \subset M$, $S \neq \emptyset$, has a semi-improvement upon $\mu$.

For a definition of strong Nash equilibrium see Aumann (1967, p. 23).


## 4     Informational efficiency

Let $G = (A^1, \ldots, A^m; T^1, \ldots, T^m, \ldots, T^n; p^1, \ldots, p^m; u^1, \ldots, u^m)$ be an extended Bayesian game.

**Definition 4.1.** A communication equilibrium $\mu$ is *weakly interim efficient* (WIE) if there is no communication equilibrium $\eta$ such that $U^i(\eta \,|\, t^i) > U^i(\mu \,|\, t^i)$ for all $i \in M$ and all $t^i \in T^i_+$.

The reader is referred to Holmstrom and Myerson (1983) for the definition of interim efficiency. See also Forges (1993a, 1994) on efficiency in Bayesian games.

**Definition 4.2.** A communication equilibrium $\mu$ is *informationally efficient* (IE) if there is no improvement $\eta$ by $M$ upon $\mu$.

**Remark 4.3.** If a communication equilibrium $\mu$ is not IE then there exists a communication equilibrium $\eta$ in $G_{\mu, M}$ such that $U^i(\eta \,|\, (t^i, a^i)) > U^i(\mu \,|\, (t^i, a^i))$ for every $i \in M$ and $(t^i, a^i) \in (T^i \times A^i)_+$. Thus, for each $i \in M$, $\eta$ *is more profitable than* $\mu$, given $i$'s private information $(t^i, a^i)$. So, we may call $\mu$ "informationally inefficient."

**Remark 4.4.** Let $G = (A^1, A^2; T^1, T^2; p^1, p^2; u^1, u^2)$ be a two-person Bayesian game. A communication equilibrium $\mu$ is a CPCE iff it is IE.

**Proposition 4.5.** *Let* $G = (A^1, ..., A^m; u^1, ..., u^m)$ *be a game in strategic form. If* $\mu$ *is a weakly efficient correlated equilibrium of* $G$, *then* $\mu$ *is informationally efficient.*

*Proof:* Assume, on the contrary, that $M = \{1, ..., m\}$ has an improvement $\eta$ upon $\mu$ in $G_{\mu, M}$. Now

$$G_{\mu, M} = (A^1, ..., A^m; A^1, ..., A^m; \mu, ..., \mu; u^1, ..., u^m)$$

and $\eta : A \times A \to [0, 1]$ satisfies $\sum_{a \in A} \eta(a \,|\, b) = 1$ for all $b \in A$. Let $\xi$ be the distribution on $A$ which is induced by $\eta$: $\xi(a) = \sum_{b \in A} \mu(b)\eta(a \,|\, b)$ for all $a \in A$. Then $U^i(\xi) = U^i(\eta) > U^i(\mu)$, $i = 1, ..., m$. We shall now show that $\xi$ is a correlated equilibrium in $G$. Let $i \in M$ and let $g^i : A^i \to A^i$. Because $\eta$ is a communication equilibrium in $G_{\mu, M}$,

$$\sum_{b^{-i} \in A^{-i}} \mu(b^{-i}, b^i) \sum_{a \in A} \eta(a \,|\, b) u^i(a^{-i}, g^i(a^i))$$

$$\leq \sum_{b^{-i} \in A^{-i}} \mu(b^i, b^{-i}) \sum_{a \in A} \eta(a \,|\, b) u^i(a)$$

for all $b^i \in A^i$. Hence

$$\sum_{b^i \in A^i} \sum_{b^{-i} \in A^{-i}} \mu(b^{-i}, b^i) \sum_{a \in A} \eta(a \,|\, b) u^i(a^{-i}, g^i(a^i))$$

$$= \sum_{a \in A} \left[ \sum_{b \in A} \mu(b)\eta(a \,|\, b) \right] u^i(a^{-i}, g^i(a^i))$$

$$= \sum_{a \in A} \xi(a) u^i(a^{-i}, g^i(a^i))$$

$$\leq \sum_{b^i \in A^i} \sum_{b^{-i} \in A^{-i}} \mu(b^i, b^{-i}) \sum_{a \in A} \eta(a \,|\, b) u^i(a)$$

$$= \sum_{a \in A} \left[ \sum_{b \in A} \mu(b)\eta(a \,|\, b) \right] u^i(a) = \sum_{a \in A} \xi(a) u^i(a).$$

Thus, $\xi$ is a correlated equilibrium that strongly dominates $\mu$. Because $\mu$ is weakly efficient, the desired contradiction has been obtained.    □

We do not know whether Proposition 4.5 can be extended to games with incomplete information. We now give an example of a CPCE which is not WIE.

**Example 4.6.** Consider again the game of "chicken" $G$ of Example 2.3. Let

MATRIX 4.1

$$
\xi = \begin{array}{|c|c|}
\hline
1/3 & 1/3 \\
\hline
1/3 & 0 \\
\hline
\end{array} \; .
$$

Then $\xi$ is correlated equilibrium. Now, $U^1(\xi \mid B) = 7$; hence, $\{1, 2\}$ has no improvement upon $\xi$ in $G_{\xi, \{1, 2\}}$. Thus, $\xi$ is IE. However,

MATRIX 4.2

$$
\eta = \begin{array}{|c|c|}
\hline
1/2 & 1/4 \\
\hline
1/4 & 0 \\
\hline
\end{array}
$$

is a correlated equilibrium and $U^i(\eta) = 21/4 > 5 = U^i(\xi)$ for $i = 1, 2$. Thus, $\xi$ is not WIE. We notice that for $\epsilon > 0$ sufficiently small, $\theta = \epsilon\mu + (1-\epsilon)\eta$ (see Matrix 2.2) satisfies $U^1(\theta \mid B) < 7 = U^1(\xi \mid B)$ and $U^i(\theta) > U^i(\xi)$ for $i = 1, 2$.

## 5    An analysis of the voting paradox

We consider the following voting game. There are three voters and three alternatives; we denote by $M = \{1, 2, 3\}$ the set of voters and by $K = \{a, b, c\}$ the set of alternatives. The set of actions of voter $i$ is $A^i = K$, $i = 1, 2, 3$. Thus, each voter can cast a vote for one alternative. An alternative that receives two or three votes wins. If each alternative receives one vote, then the winner is chosen by an even-chance lottery. The utility functions of the players are assumed to satisfy: $u_\alpha^1(a) = 1$, $u_\alpha^1(b) = \alpha$ $(0 < \alpha < 1)$, and $u_\alpha^1(c) = 0$; $u_\beta^2(c) = 1$, $u_\beta^2(a) = \beta$ $(0 < \beta < 1)$, and $u_\beta^2(b) = 0$; $u_\gamma^3(b) = 1$, $u_\gamma^3(c) = \gamma$ $(0 < \gamma < 1)$, and $u_\gamma^3(a) = 0$.

Let $G(\alpha, \beta, \gamma)$ be the game $(A^1, A^2, A^3; u_\alpha^1, u_\beta^2, u_\gamma^3)$, where $0 < \alpha, \beta, \gamma < 1$. Then the ordinal preferences of the voters are those of the well-known voting paradox. We shall now prove the existence of CPCEs for $G(\alpha, \beta, \gamma)$ that do not use weakly dominated strategies. We distinguish the following cases:

$$\alpha \geq (1+\alpha)/3, \quad \beta \geq (1+\beta)/3, \quad \text{and} \quad \gamma \geq (1+\gamma)/3. \tag{5.1}$$

As the reader may easily verify, $a$ and $b$ weakly dominate $c$ w.r.t. (with respect to) $u_\alpha^1$; $c$ and $a$ weakly dominate $b$ w.r.t. $u_\beta^2$; and $b$ and $c$ weakly dominate $a$ w.r.t. $u_\gamma^3$. The strategic form of the game, which is obtained after the deletion of weakly dominated strategies, is given by:

MATRIX 5.1

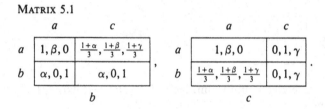

Consider the correlated strategy $\mu_1$, given by

MATRIX 5.2

$$
\begin{array}{cc}
 & \begin{array}{cc} a & c \end{array} \\
\begin{array}{c} a \\ b \end{array} & \begin{array}{|c|c|} \hline 1/3 & 0 \\ \hline 0 & 1/3 \\ \hline \end{array} \\
 & b
\end{array}
\qquad
\begin{array}{cc}
 & \begin{array}{cc} a & c \end{array} \\
\begin{array}{c} a \\ b \end{array} & \begin{array}{|c|c|} \hline 0 & 1/3 \\ \hline 0 & 0 \\ \hline \end{array} \\
 & c
\end{array}
\;.
$$

Strategy $\mu_1$ is a convex combination of Nash equilibria; hence, it is a CE. Also, it can be shown that $\mu_1$ is Pareto optimal. Therefore, $N$ has no improvement upon $\mu_1$. Consider now the coalition $\{1, 2\}$, where $U^2(\mu_1 \mid a) = \beta$. Now, if $a$ is the type of 2 in $G_{\mu_1, \{1,2\}} = (A^1, A^2; A^1, A^2, A^3; \mu_1, \mu_1; \hat{u}_\alpha^1, \hat{u}_\beta^2)$, then the type of 3 must be $b$ (see Matrix 5.2). Hence, for every communication equilibrium $\eta_{\{1,2\}}$ in $G_{\mu_1, \{1,2\}}$, we have $U^2(\eta_{\{1,2\}} \mid a) \leq \beta$ (see Matrix 5.1). Thus $\{1, 2\}$ has no improvement upon $\mu_1$. Similarly, $\{1, 3\}$ and $\{2, 3\}$ have no improvement upon $\mu_1$, and so $\mu_1$ is a CPCE:

$$\alpha < (1+\alpha)/3, \quad \beta \geq (1+\beta)/3, \quad \text{and} \quad \gamma \geq (1+\gamma)/3. \tag{5.2}$$

Consider the triple $\mu_2 = (a, c, c)$. Only $\{1, 3\}$ might improve upon $(a, c, c)$. However, if $\eta_{\{1, 3\}}$ satisfies

$$U^1(\eta_{\{1,3\}}) > 0 \text{ and } U^3(\eta_{\{1,3\}}) > \gamma,$$

then $\eta_{\{1,3\}}(b,b) > 0$. When $\alpha < (1+\alpha)/3$, $a$ weakly dominates $b$ w.r.t. $u_\alpha^1$. Therefore, if $\eta_{\{1,3\}}(b,b) > 0$ then $\eta_{\{1,3\}}$ is not a CE in $G_{\mu_2,\{1,3\}}$. Thus, $\mu_2$ is a CPCE:

$$\alpha < (1+\alpha)/3, \quad \beta < (1+\beta)/3, \quad \text{and} \quad \gamma \ge (1+\gamma)/3. \tag{5.3}$$

Again, $\mu_2 = (a,c,c)$ is a CPCE:

$$\alpha < (1+\alpha)/3, \quad \beta < (1+\beta)/3, \quad \text{and} \quad \gamma < (1+\gamma)/3. \tag{5.4}$$

Let $\mu_3 = (a,c,b)$; $\mu_3$ is Pareto optimal. Moreover, if $\eta_{\{1,2\}}$ satisfies

$$U^1(\eta_{\{1,2\}}) > (1+\alpha)/3 \quad \text{and} \quad U^2(\eta_{\{1,2\}}) > (1+\beta)/3,$$

then we must have $\eta_{\{1,2\}}(a,a) > 0$. Because $c$ weakly dominates $a$ w.r.t. $u_\alpha^2$, $\eta_{\{1,2\}}$ is not a CE. Similarly, we may prove that $\{1,3\}$ and $\{2,3\}$ cannot improve upon $\mu_3$. Thus, $\mu_3$ is a CPCE. All other possible cases are obtained by permutations of the players.

It seems to us that our solution of the voting paradox is very reasonable.

## 6    A comparison of coalition-proof communication equilibria with coalition-proof Nash equilibria

First we recall the definition of coalition-proof Nash equilibria (see Bernheim et al. 1987). Let $G = (A^1, ..., A^m; u^1, ..., u^m)$ be a game in strategic form. Here $A^1, ..., A^m$ are the (finite) sets of actions and $u^1, ..., u^m$ are the utility functions of the players. Set $\Delta(A^i) = \Sigma^i$, the set of mixed strategies of player $i$ ($i = 1, ..., m$). Let $\sigma = (\sigma^1, ..., \sigma^m) \in \Sigma$, where $\Sigma = \Sigma^1 \times \cdots \times \Sigma^m$, and for $M = \{1, ..., m\}$ let $S \subset M$, $S \ne \emptyset$. An *internally consistent improvement* (ICI) of $S$ upon $\sigma$ is defined by induction on $|S|$. If $|S| = 1$ (i.e., $S = \{i\}$ for some $i \in M$), then $\tau^i$ is an ICI of $i$ upon $\sigma$ if it is an improvement upon $\sigma$; that is, if $u^i(\tau^i, \sigma^{-i}) > u^i(\sigma)$. If $|S| > 1$ then $\tau^S$ is an ICI of $S$ upon $\sigma$ if (i) $u^i(\tau^S, \sigma^{M\setminus S}) > u^i(\sigma)$ for all $i \in S$, and (ii) no $T \subset S$ ($T \ne \emptyset, S$) has an ICI upon $(\tau^S, \sigma^{M\setminus S})$.

**Definition 6.1.**    The strategy $\sigma \in \Sigma$ is a *coalition-proof Nash equilibrium* (CPNE) if no $S \subset M$, $S \ne \emptyset$, has an ICI upon $\sigma$.

Clearly, a CPNE is a Nash equilibrium.

**Example 6.2.**    Let $G = (A^1, A^2, A^3; u^1, u^2, u^3)$, where $A^1 = \{a_1, a_2\}$, $A^2 = \{b_1, b_2\}$, $A^3 = \{c_1, c_2\}$, and $u^i$ ($i = 1, 2, 3$) are given by the following:

MATRIX 6.1

| | $b_1$ | $b_2$ | | | $b_1$ | $b_2$ |
|---|---|---|---|---|---|---|
| $a_1$ | 3, 2, 0 | 0, 0, 0 | | $a_1$ | 3, 2, 0 | 0, 3, 2 |
| $a_2$ | 2, 0, 3 | 2, 0, 3 | | $a_2$ | 0, 0, 0 | 0, 3, 2 |
| | $c_1$ | | | | $c_2$ | |

It is easy to see that $G$ does not have a coalition-proof Nash equilibrium in mixed strategies.

We show that

MATRIX 6.2

$$\mu_0 = \begin{array}{|c|c|} \hline 1/3 & 0 \\ \hline 0 & 1/3 \\ \hline \end{array} \ , \quad \begin{array}{|c|c|} \hline 0 & 1/3 \\ \hline 0 & 0 \\ \hline \end{array}$$

is a strong communication equilibrium of $G$ (and is therefore also a CPCE). Since the payoff vector for the players at $\mu_0$ is efficient within the set of payoffs for the correlated strategies in $G$, $\{1, 2, 3\}$ does not have a semi-improvement upon $\mu_0$ in the game $G$. It remains to be shown that if $S$ is a coalition with $|S| = 2$ then $|S|$ does not have a semi-improvement upon $\mu_0$. If $S = \{1, 2\}$ and $\eta$ is a correlated strategy in $G_{\mu_0, S}$, then $U^2(\eta | b_1) = 2\eta((a_1, b_1) | (a_1, b_1)) \leq 2 = U^2(\mu_0 | b_1)$. If $S = \{2, 3\}$ and $\eta$ is a correlated strategy in $G_{\mu_0, S}$, then $U^3(\eta | c_2) = 2\eta((b_2, c_2) | (b_2, c_2)) \leq 2 = U^3(\mu_0 | c_2)$. If $S = \{1, 3\}$ and $\eta$ is a correlated strategy in $G_{\mu_0, S}$, then $U^1(\eta | a^2) = 2\eta((a_2, c_1) | (a_2, c_1)) \leq 2 = U^1(\mu_0 | a_2)$. Thus, in each case, $\eta$ cannot be a semi-improvement of $S$ upon $\mu_0$ in $G_{\mu_0, S}$.

The following example is due to Aumann, and appears in Nau and Mc-Cardle (1990).

**Example 6.3.** Consider the two-person game $G$, which has the following payoff matrix:

MATRIX 6.3

| | $b_1$ | $b_2$ | $b_3$ | $b_4$ |
|---|---|---|---|---|
| $a_1$ | 0, 0 | 10, 5 | 5, 10 | 6, 6 |
| $a_2$ | 5, 10 | 0, 0 | 10, 5 | 6, 6 |
| $a_3$ | 10, 5 | 5, 10 | 0, 0 | 6, 6 |
| $a_4$ | 6, 6 | 6, 6 | 6, 6 | 7, 7 |

This game has a unique Nash equilibrium of $(a_4, b_4)$. This is also the unique coalition-proof Nash equilibrium in $G$. Let

MATRIX 6.4

$$\mu = \begin{array}{|c|c|c|c|}
\hline
0 & 1/6 & 1/6 & 0 \\
\hline
1/6 & 0 & 1/6 & 0 \\
\hline
1/6 & 1/6 & 0 & 0 \\
\hline
0 & 0 & 0 & 0 \\
\hline
\end{array}.$$

It is easy to see that $\mu$ is a correlated equilibrium of $G$. It is also easy to see that $\mu$ is an improvement of $\{1, 2\}$ upon $(a_4, b_4)$ in the game $G_{(a_4, b_4), \{1, 2\}}$. Therefore $(a_4, b_4)$ is not a CPCE.

We have not dealt with the problem of the existence of CPCEs in games with more than two players. This will be postponed to a forthcoming paper.

REFERENCES

Aumann, R. J. (1967), "A Survey of Cooperative Games without Side Payments," in M. Shubik (ed.), *Essays in Mathematical Economics in Honor of Oskar Morgenstern*. Princeton, NJ: Princeton University Press, pp. 3–27.
(1974), "Subjectivity and Correlation in Randomized Strategies," *Journal of Mathematical Economics* 1: 67–96.
Bernheim, B. D., B. Peleg, and M. D. Whinston (1987), "Coalition-Proof Nash Equilibria. I. Concepts," *Journal of Economic Theory* 42: 1–12.
Forges, F. (1986), "An Approach to Communication Equilibria," *Econometrica* 54: 1375–85.
(1993a), "Some Thoughts on Efficiency and Information," in K. Binmore et al. (eds.), *Frontiers of Game Theory*. Cambridge, MA: MIT Press.
(1993b), "Five Legitimate Definitions of Correlated Equilibrium in Games with Incomplete Information," *Theory and Decision* 35: 277–310.
(1994), "Posterior Efficiency," *Games and Economic Behavior* 6: 238–61.
Holmstrom, B., and R. B. Myerson (1983), "Efficient and Durable Decision Rules with Incomplete Information," *Econometrica* 53: 1799–1819.
Myerson, R. B. (1982), "Optimal Coordination Mechanisms in Generalized Principal–Agent Problems," *Journal of Mathematical Economics* 10: 67–81.
(1991), *Game Theory: Analysis of Conflict*. Cambridge, MA: Harvard University Press.
Nau, R., and K. McCardle (1990), "Coherent Behavior in Noncooperative Games," *Journal of Economic Theory* 50: 424–44.

300     Ezra Einy & Bezalel Peleg

Peleg, B. (1984), "Quasi-Coalitional Equilibria, Part I: Definitions and Preliminary Results," Center for Research in Game Theory and Mathematical Economics, mimeo, The Hebrew University of Jerusalem.

Sinha, S. (1991), "On Existence of Coalition-Proof Correlated Equilibrium," mimeo, Indian Statistical Institute, New Delhi.

# CHAPTER 14

# Stability of coalition structures and the principle of optimal partitioning

*Michel Le Breton & Shlomo Weber*

## 1 Introduction

Most of the conclusions of microeconomic theory are derived from the postulates about the behavior of individual consumers and producers. But in fact, individual producers are firms that represent large coalitions of different factors of production, and a whole industry may be viewed as an endogenous structure of such coalitions. Moreover, a growing number of theoretical and empirical studies reflect the fact that individual consumers are households or families. These studies[1] reject the single-utility hypothesis and instead treat a household as a *collective* decision unit.

The model of coalition formation studied in this paper belongs to the general class of environments examined by Greenberg and Weber (1993; hereafter "GW"): There is the set of individuals $N$ and the set of all possible alternatives $\Omega$, where each individual in $N$ has a utility function over $\Omega$. The feasibility constraints are given by the correspondence $\phi$ which assigns to each group of individuals (coalition) $C$ a subset of $\Omega$, denoted by $\phi(C)$, which consists of alternatives available to members of $C$, if and when $C$ forms. It is assumed that the correspondence $\phi$ is (weakly) monotone; that is, if an alternative is feasible for a coalition $C$, then it is also feasible for all coalitions that contain $C$.

Greenberg and Weber then introduce a notion of equilibrium, which borrows from both Nash equilibrium and the core, by imposing *free mobility* – each individual is free to join the coalition that adopts the alternative she likes best among those offered by the existing coalitions – and *free entry* – each coalition is free to form. In equilibrium, individuals form a partition $P$ of $N$, where each coalition $C \in P$ chooses an alternative

We wish to thank Hervé Moulin, Norman Schofield, and an anonymous referee for their valuable comments, which helped to improve the exposition of this paper.
[1] See survey in Chiappori (1992).

in $\phi(C)$ in such a way that each individual belongs to the coalition whose alternative she likes best among the *offered* alternatives. Moreover, there is no coalition $T$ and an alternative in $\phi(T)$ which makes all members of $T$ better off than they currently are. This equilibrium notion borrows from two important solution concepts: The Nash equilibrium (reflected by free mobility) and the core (reflected by free entry). It is, however, stronger than both the core of a coalition structure (Aumann and Dreze 1974), which requires only free entry, and different variants of a Nash equilibrium – for example, voting equilibrium (Epple, Filimon, and Romer 1984) or position-based institutional equilibrium (Caplin and Nalebuff 1992). The main result of the GW paper is that, if the set of alternatives available to each coalition is a compact subset of the unidimensional Euclidean space, and if the individuals' utility functions are quasiconcave, then there exists a stable coalition structure.

The main purpose of this paper is to relax the assumption of unidimensionality of the set of alternatives imposed in GW, and to consider societies in which a choice set is given by the Euclidean space of any given dimension. However, in order to obtain some meaningful results in the multidimensional setting, we impose two quite restrictive assumptions. First, we assume that all individuals have Euclidean preferences. Second, we consider models that can be represented by *simple games,* characterized by a set of *effective coalitions* $W$, so that the set $\phi(C)$ of feasible alternatives available to coalition $C$ is given by:

$$\phi(C) = \begin{cases} \Omega & \text{if } C \in W, \\ \emptyset & \text{if } C \notin W. \end{cases}$$

Thus, an effective coalition can choose, for its members, any alternative in $\Omega$ it desires, whereas a coalition that is not effective "has no say" whatsoever. We moreover require that the set $W$ consist of all coalitions that contain at least two members. It is intuitively clear, however, that in equilibrium only two-person coalitions will emerge (see Proposition 2.2).

The situation analyzed in this paper may be illustrated by the following example. Suppose that a public authority provides financial support to build schools in a region containing $n$ villages. The school budget allows for the building of $n/2$ schools only. The authority, therefore, imposes the rule that each school will absorb the children from at least two villages, but leaves the choice of school location to the villages. It seems fair on these grounds to require the cooperation of two villages as a condition to receiving the public money. Formally, each village $i \in N$ is represented by a point $p^i$ in the plane, and we denote by $d_{ij}$ the Euclidean distance between villages $i$ and $j$. We assume that the only objective of each village is to have the school be located as close as possible. We assume that $n$ is an

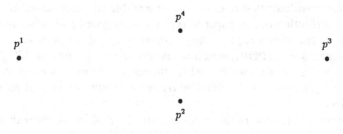

Figure 1. Example presented in Section 1.

even number; otherwise, the public rule just presented would be unfair because at least one set of three villages would be forced to cooperate.

The basic question is whether there exists a stable cooperation pattern $\pi$ between pairs of villages, resulting in the set of $n/2$ proposed school locations with the assignment of each school to two villages, that would be immune against counter-proposals. There are two stability requirements on $\pi$ that are relevant in this context. The first is free entry, which yields veto power for each pair of villages: There is no pair of villages that could find an alternative school location closer to them than those assigned by $\pi$. The second is free mobility: Among all locations in $\pi$, each village is assigned to the closest one; that is, no village will find a school closer than that assigned to it by $\pi$.

Naturally, the existence of a stable cooperation pattern depends on the geometry of the problem captured by the symmetric matrix $(d_{ij})_{i,j=1,...,n}$. Consider, for instance, the example of four villages represented by Figure 1. It is easy to see that there are two possibilities:

($\alpha$)   1 cooperates with 2, and 3 cooperates with 4; or
($\beta$)   2 cooperates with 3, and 1 cooperates with 4.

If (say) the structure $\alpha$ emerges, then the school for villages 1 and 2 should be located on the segment $[p^2, A]$, while the school for villages 3 and 4 should be located on the segment $[p^4, D]$. If the structure $\beta$ emerges, the school for villages 2 and 3 should be located on the segment $[p^2, B]$, while the school for villages 3 and 4 should be located on the segment $[p^4, C]$. One can show that such structures are, indeed, stable in our sense. It is interesting to note that villages 2 and 4 have strong bargaining power, as $d_{24}$ is small relative to $d_{13}$. But even if $d_{24}$ is close to zero, no stable cooperation involves villages 2 and 4 together. Instead, 2 and 4 will use their bargaining power to negotiate a better location from their corresponding partners.

One could easily imagine that, in general, such analysis may become quite involved. In fact, in Section 3 we provide an example of a society with six individuals that does not admit a stable coalition structure. The main contribution of this paper is to provide necessary and sufficient conditions on the matrix $(d_{ij})$ for any number $n$, called the *principle of optimal partitioning* (POP), which would guarantee not only stability but also *total stability* of a society, where the total stability of a given society containing the set of individuals $N$ requires stability of each of its even subsocieties.

The technique used in the proof is instructive, since we show that the existence of a stable structure is equivalent to the existence of core outcomes in the associated TU (transferable utility) game, even though there is no transferable money in our model.

In this paper we impose the quite restrictive assumption that any two individuals can form an effective coalition. This is, however, the simplest situation where some form of cooperation is suitable for analysis – and one that Gale and Shapley (1962) have called the "roommates problem," where individuals must form pairs of roommates in the student dormitory. Which pairs will form? It is well known that, in general, existence of a stable configuration is not guaranteed. Our paper can be considered as a contribution to the analysis of the roommates problem in a situation where individuals' utilities depend on the outcome (here, the location of school) and not on the partner. Observe also that since in our model any two-person coalition can form, this model does not belong to the class of two-sided matching games that examine markets with two types of heterogeneous agents (e.g., firms and workers, men and women, free agents and teams in professional sport), each of whom has personal preferences over potential matches with agents of the opposite type.[2]

Another restrictive assumption employed in this paper is that the schools are "provided" to pairs of villages by the central authority. A different problem could arise when the issue of cooperation is studied in a model where the cost of building a new school is financed by the coalition of villages that will use its services. Burden of financing would provide an incentive for formation of large coalitions. In general, there is a variety of different reasons to form large coalitions: increasing returns to scale, sharing of fixed cost of production, and larger power or resources. However, the power and resources of large coalitions, inciting the larger degree of conglomeration, may conflict with heterogeneity of agents' preferences and characteristics.[3] Indeed, in large coalitions the contribution of

[2] See Roth/Sotomayor (1990) for a survey of results on matching games.
[3] Feinstein (1992) indicated an important empirical implication of the trade-off between increasing returns to scale in large coalitions and heterogeneity of agents. He studied a model of the European Community whose basis is the shifting balance between EC membership, which enhances a faster growth of GNP, and the heterogeneity of the countries' preferences over commonly produced public goods.

each village toward financing the school may decline but the difficulty in reaching an agreement on location may increase.[4]

The trade-off between heterogeneity of individual preferences and the power of large coalitions is different from the question analyzed in this paper, where the nature of coalitions that will form is given by the rules of the game and is therefore not completely endogenous. In order to focus exclusively on the consequences of heterogeneity in a multidimensional set of alternatives, we ignore the dimension of increasing returns to scale. We believe that our model may still provide some insights at this stage of research, when the grounds of a general theory of coalition formation with multidimensional issue spaces are yet to be established.

The paper is organized as follows: in the next section we present the model and formally introduce the notions of stability and total stability. In Section 3 we define the principle of optimal partitioning and state our results, the proof of which is exhibited in Section 4.

## 2    The model

Let $\Omega$ denote the set of potential alternatives. Since the purpose of this paper is to study the multidimensional sets of alternatives, we assume that $\Omega = \mathbb{R}^g$ is a Euclidean space whose dimension $g$ exceeds 1. There are $n$ individuals, given by the set $N = \{1, 2, ..., n\}$. The non-empty subsets of $N$ are called *coalitions*. Each individual $i \in N$ has a preference ordering over $\Omega$ represented by the utility function $u^i : \Omega \to \mathbb{R}$. There is an a priori given set $W$ of *effective* coalitions, where each effective coalition has a power to choose any alternative in $\Omega$ for its members; an ineffective coalition has no such power. Taking into account their own preferences, individuals form coalitions in such a way that each individual $i \in N$ belongs to one and only one coalition, where each formed coalition chooses an alternative from $\Omega$. In equilibrium, the partition of society $N$ into effective coalitions and the corresponding coalitions' choice of alternatives guarantee that no individual would find it beneficial to move to another existing coalition and to adopt its chosen alternative. We require, moreover, that no effective coalition can choose an alternative that makes all its members better off than they are in equilibrium.

Let us introduce some notation and definitions. For any $C \subset N$, a collection $P$ of pairwise disjoint coalitions $C_1, C_2, ..., C_J$ is called a *partition* of $C$ if $\bigcup_{j=1}^{J} C_j = C$. The set of all partitions of $C$ is denoted by $\mathcal{P}(C)$; let $\mathcal{P} \equiv P(N)$. A partition $P$ consisting of effective coalitions is called an

---

[4] There is an immediate analogy with the type of situation in economies with local public goods analyzed by Guesnerie/Oddou (1981) and Greenberg/Weber (1986).

*effective partition,* and the set of all effective partitions of $C$ is denoted by $\mathcal{P}^W(C)$. Similarly, let $\mathcal{P}^W \equiv \mathcal{P}^W(N)$.

**Definition 2.1.**  Let the society $S$ be represented by the quadruple $(N, \Omega, U, W)$, where $U = (u^i)_{i \in N}$ is the profile of individuals' preferences. Society $S$ is called *stable* if there exists a pair $(P, \Lambda)$, where $P = (C_1, C_2, ..., C_J) \in \mathcal{P}$ and $\Lambda = \{a_1, a_2, ..., a_J\} \subset \Omega$, such that

(a)  for all $j = 1, 2, ..., J$ and all $h = 1, 2, ..., J$, $u_i(a_j) \geq u_i(a_h)$ whenever $i \in C_j$; and

(b)  there exist no $C \in W$ and $\omega \in \Omega$ such that $u_i(a) > u_i(a_h)$ for all $i \in C$ and all $a_h \in \Lambda$.

The pair $(P, \Lambda)$, satisfying 2.1(a) and 2.1(b), is called an $S$ *equilibrium.*

Condition 2.1(a) – "free mobility" – yields the best response of each individual to the existing coalition structure; that is, no individual can be made better off by migrating to another (existing) coalition.[5] Condition 2.1(b) – "free entry" – rules out any group deviations; there is no group of individuals who can form an effective coalition and choose an alternative that makes each of its members better off than they currently are.

In their paper GW considered the case where the set of alternatives is unidimensional and the set of effective coalitions $W$ satisfies the "no-exclusion" property: If a coalition $C$ is effective, then so is every $C'$ that contains $C$. They showed that under these assumptions, the single-peakedness of individuals' preferences yields the stability of society $S$. In our paper we examine this notion of stability under different assumptions. First, we consider societies whose choice set is multidimensional; this allows for a wider class of economic applications. Second, we derive conditions that guarantee not only stability but also total stability of a society, where the "total stability" of a given society requires stability of each of its subsocieties. This hereditary[6] property of total stability is reminiscent of "total balancedness" in Shapley and Shubik (1969), who, in their study of market games, distinguished between the "balancedness" of a game $V$ and its "total balancedness" – which amounts to balancedness of each of the subgames of $V$. In order to guarantee the stability of a society with a multidimensional set of alternatives, one needs to impose the following quite

[5]  A similar condition is used by Epple et al. (1984) in their model of majority voting over local public goods and by Caplin/Nalebuff (1992) to define the notion of a position-based institutional equilibrium in their model of political process, where – after the institutions' choice of positions – no individual wishes to switch to another institution.

[6]  In topology, a property of a topological space $\Im$ is called *hereditary* if it is satisfied for all subspaces of $\Im$; see e.g. Kolmogorov/Fomin (1957).

restrictive assumptions on individual preferences and the set of effective coalitions.

**Assumption A.**   For each $i \in N$, the utility function $u^i$ represents the spherical preferences. That is, for each $i \in N$ there exists an alternative $p^i \in \Omega$, called $i$'s *ideal point*, such that $u^i(\omega) = -|p^i - \omega|$ for each $\omega \in \Omega$. The set satisfying Assumption A of all profiles of preferences of individuals in $N$ is denoted by $\mathfrak{U} \equiv \mathfrak{U}^N$.

**Assumption B.**   For any three different individuals $i, j, k$, the affine space spanned by their ideal points $p^i, p^j, p^k$ is of the full dimension.

**Assumption C.**   The set of effective coalitions $W$ consists of all coalitions with at least two members; that is,

$$W = \{C \subset N \mid |C| \geq 2\},$$

where $|C|$ denotes the cardinality of coalition $C$.

Assumption C implies that only societies with an even number of individuals can be stable and, moreover, that in equilibrium the set of all individuals is partitioned into two-person coalitions.

**Proposition 2.2.**   *Let society $S$ satisfy Assumptions A and B. If a pair $(P, \Lambda)$ constitutes an $S$ equilibrium then each coalition $C$ in $P$ contains exactly two individuals.*

*Proof:*   Let society $S$ satisfy Assumptions A–C and let the pair $(P, \Lambda)$ constitute an $S$ equilibrium. By Assumption B, no one-person coalition is effective. Therefore, suppose by negation that there exists a coalition $C \in P$ consisting of more than two players. Let $a(C)$ denote the alternative adopted by $C$ in equilibrium. By Assumption A, there exist two different players $i$ and $j$, both in $C$, such that $a(C)$ does not lie on the straight line $L$ connecting the ideal points $p^i$ and $p^j$. Denote by $a_L(C)$ the projection of $a(C)$ on $L$. Then $|a_L(C) - p^i| < |a(C) - p^i|$ and $|a_L(C) - p^j| < |a(C) - p^j|$, implying that $a_L(C)$ is closer than $a(C)$ to both $p^i$ and $p^j$. That is, both players $i$ and $j$ would prefer $a_L(C)$ over $a(C)$, a contradiction to 2.1(b). Hence all coalitions in $P$ consist of two individuals, and thus all society consists of an even number of individuals.          □

Let us now extend the notion of society to subsets of $N$. Toward this end, for each $M \subset N$ define by $W^M$ the set of all effective subsets of $M$; that is, $W^M = \{C \in W \mid C \subset M\}$. Define by $\mathfrak{U}^M$ the set satisfying Assumption A of profiles of preferences of individuals in $M$.

**Definition 2.3.**   Let the society $S = (N, \Omega, U, W)$ where $U = \{u_i\}_{i \in N}$, and let the non-empty subset $M$ of $N$ be given. Then the quadruple $S^M = (M, \Omega, U^M, W^M)$, where $U^M = \{u_i\}_{i \in M}$, is called a *subsociety* of $N$.

To introduce the notion of total stability, consider subsocieties of society $S$ obtained from $S$ by truncating it by a given subgroup of individuals. Proposition 2.2 allows us to restrict our analysis to those societies and subsocieties with an even number of individuals.

**Definition 2.4.**   The society $S = (N, \Omega, U, W)$ is called *totally stable* if, for each even subset $M$ of $N$, the subsociety $S^M = (M, \Omega, U^M, W^M)$ is stable.

In the next section we introduce and discuss the principle of optimal partitioning, which constitutes the necessary and sufficient condition for the total stability of a class of societies satisfying Assumptions A and B.

## 3    Principle of optimal partitioning

In order to illuminate the nature of conditions that yield the existence of an equilibrium, we begin this section by presenting two examples. The first shows that there is a society with an even number of individuals which fails to admit an equilibrium, even though it satisfies Assumptions A and B. We then modify this example in such a way that ensures the set of equilibria is non-empty. The discussion of reasons for non-existence of an equilibrium in Example 3.1 – and for its existence in Example 3.2 – could be helpful in providing an intuition of our main result, stated in Proposition 3.6.

**Example 3.1.**   *Let $S = (N, \Omega, U, W)$ be the society satisfying Assumptions A and B, where $\Omega = \mathbb{R}^2$ is the set of alternatives and $N = \{1, 2, 3, 4, 5, 6\}$ is the set of players whose ideal points are given by $p^1 = (-R - r, r)$, $p^2 = (-R - r, -r)$, $p^3 = (-R, 0)$, $p^4 = (R, 0)$, $p^5 = (R + r, r)$, and $p^6 = (R + r, -r)$, where $R > 2r > 0$.* (See Figure 2.) *Then $S$ does not admit an equilibrium.*

*Proof:*   We shall here give only an intuitive argument for non-existence of an equilibrium for the society $S$, and present the formal proof in Section 4. The location of individuals' peaks in $S$ would suggest partitioning the set $N$ into two triples $C = \{1, 2, 3\}$ and $C' = \{4, 5, 6\}$. However, this partition is not "optimal" and is inconsistent with the structure of effective coalitions. That is, individuals 1, 2, 3 cannot agree on the one alternative, since any alternative would be rejected by at least two of them.

Figure 2. Location of individuals' ideal points in society $S$ of Example 3.1.

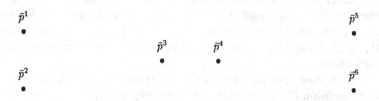

Figure 3. Location of individuals' ideal points in society $\bar{S}$ of Example 3.2.

Since the same is true for the triple 4, 5, 6, an equilibrium (if one exists) should contain a pair $\bar{C}$ consisting of one individual from $C$ and one individual from $C'$. However, given the choices of the two remaining individuals in $C$ and the two in $C'$ - say, $a$ and $a'$, respectively - it is impossible to "please" both partners in $\bar{C}$, since at least one member of $\bar{C}$ would prefer either $a$ or $a'$ to the alternative offered in $\bar{C}$.

Let us modify the society $S$ presented in Example 3.1 in such a way that would yield the existence of an equilibrium.

**Example 3.2.**   *Let $\bar{S} = (N, \Omega, \bar{U}, W)$ be a society no different from society $S$ of Example 3.1 save that the ideal points of individuals 3 and 4 are now given by $\bar{p}^3 = (-r, 0)$ and $\bar{p}^4 = (r, 0)$. (See Figure 3.) Then the set of $\bar{S}$ equilibria is non-empty and, moreover, a pair $(P, \Lambda)$ is an $\bar{S}$ equilibrium if and only if $P = \{D, E, F\}$, where $D = \{1, 2\}$, $E = \{3, 4\}$, $F = \{5, 6\}$, and $\Lambda = \{d, e, f\}$ for $d \in [p^1, p^2]$, $e \in [p^3, p^4]$, and $f \in [p^5, p^6]$. Thus, in equilibrium, the society is partitioned into three pairs $D, E, F$, each pair choosing an alternative located on the straight line connecting the ideal points of its members.*

*Proof:*   Note that the distance between the ideal points of any two individuals constituting a coalition in $P$ is equal to $2r$. Because each coalition in $P$ can adopt an alternative coinciding with the peak of one of its members, it follows that, in equilibrium, no individual $l$ supports an alternative more than $2r$ distant from $l$'s peak. Let $\{j, k\} \in P$ and $l \neq j, k$. Since the distance from the ideal point $p^l$ of individual $l$ to the interval connecting the peaks of $j$ and $k$ is at least $R > 4r$, it follows that only the partition $P$ can emerge in $\bar{S}$ equilibrium. To complete the proof, it remains to observe that each pair in $P$ would reject an alternative that does not belong to the interval connecting the peaks of its members.     □

The difference between the societies $S$ and $\bar{S}$ (of Examples 3.1 and 3.2, respectively) is that, unlike in society $S$, the peaks of individuals in society $\bar{S}$ are partitioned in an optimal way to allow the formation of coalitions (1, 2), (3, 4), and (5, 6) consisting of individuals whose peaks are close to each other.

Let us now formalize the notion of optimal partitioning. First, for each coalition $C$ we denote *degree of heterogeneity*,[7] $h(C)$, as the length of the shortest path passing through the ideal points of all members of $C$. Obviously, the degree of heterogeneity of coalition $C$ is low if the peaks of all members of $C$ are close to each other. Formally, denote by $\Pi(C)$ the set of all possible orderings of members of $C$. For each $\pi = \{i_1^\pi, i_2^\pi, \ldots, i_{|C|}^\pi\} \in \Pi(C)$, define by $h^\pi(C)$ the sum of the distances between consecutive (with respect to $\pi$) players in $C$:[8]

$$h^\pi(C) \equiv r(i_1^\pi, i_2^\pi) + r(i_2^\pi, i_3^\pi) + \cdots + r(i_{|C|-1}^\pi, i_{|C|}^\pi) + r(i_{|C|}^\pi, i_1^\pi)$$

where, for each two players $i$ and $j$, $r(i, j)$ denotes the distance between their ideal points. We thus have the following.

**Definition 3.3.** The *degree of heterogeneity of coalition* $C$, $h(C)$, is given by

$$h(C) = \min_{\pi \in \Pi(C)} h^\pi(C).$$

Obviously, if $C = \{i, j\}$ is a two-person coalition then $h(C) = 2r(i, j)$ is the double distance between $i$'s and $j$'s peaks. If $C = \{i, j, k\}$ is a three-person coalition then $h(C) = r(i, j) + r(j, k) + r(k, i)$ is the perimeter of the triangle created by the ideal points $p^i$, $p^j$, and $p^k$.

Let $C$ be an effective coalition. For each partition $P$ of $C$ into effective coalitions with $P \in \mathcal{P}^W(C)$, denote by $H(C)$ the sum of degrees of heterogeneity of members of $P$; that is,

---

[7]  This notion is similar to that used by Bénabou (1992) for an economy with the unidimensional space of agents' characteristics.

[8]  The so-created collection of coalitions $\{(i_1^\pi, i_2^\pi), (i_2^\pi, i_3^\pi), \ldots, (i_{|C|-1}^\pi, i_{|C|}^\pi), (i_{|C|}^\pi, i_1^\pi)\}$ is called a *full cycle* (on $C$).

$$H^P(C) = \sum_{D \in P} h(D).$$

**Definition 3.4.** Define the *partitioned degree of heterogeneity of coalition C, H(C),* by

$$H(C) = \min_{P \in \mathcal{P}^H(C)} H^P(C).$$

Because the partition $\{C\}$ is trivially effective for each effective coalition $C$, it follows that $h(C) \geq H(C)$; that is, the partitioned degree of heterogeneity of $C$ does not exceed its degree of heterogeneity. But since, for all two- and three-person coalitions, the only effective partition of $C$ is $C$ itself, it follows that $h(C) = H(C)$ whenever the cardinality of $C$ does not exceed 3.

For each effective coalition $C$, denote by $\mathcal{P}^2(C)$ the set of partitions of $C$ into two-person coalitions.

**Definition 3.5.** Define the *restricted partitioned degree of heterogeneity of coalition C, H²(C),* by

$$H^2(C) = \min_{P \in \mathcal{P}^2(C)} H^P(C).$$

Because the set $\mathcal{P}^2(C)$ is non-empty if and only if $C$ is even,[9] we put $H^2(C) = \infty$ for all odd coalitions $C$. Observe also that, since $\mathcal{P}^2(C) \subset \mathcal{P}^W(C)$, it follows that

$$H^2(C) \geq H(C) \quad \text{for all } C \in W. \tag{1}$$

We are now in position to define the *principle of optimal partitioning* (POP), which plays the central role in this paper. The inequality (1) indicates that, in general, the restricted partitioned value of heterogeneity $H$ and the partitioned value of heterogeneity $H^2$ do not coincide; and, in particular, Definition 3.5 implies that the inequality (1) is strict for all odd coalitions. If these two values do coincide for a given even coalition $C$, this means that the optimal partition of $C$ into effective coalitions could be obtained by partitioning $C$ into two-person coalitions only. We say that POP holds (for $N$) if this is the case for all even subsets $C$ of $N$.

**Principle of optimal partitioning** (POP). For all even subsets $C$ of $N$, $H(C) = H^2(C)$. A partition $P \in P^2(C)$ for which $H^P(C) = H^2(C) = H(C)$ is called an *optimal partition* of $C$.

[9] We call a coalition *even* if it contains an even number of players and *odd* if it contains an odd number of individuals.

312     Michel Le Breton & Shlomo Weber

It is easy to verify that POP is violated for the society $S$ constructed in Example 3.1, but holds for the society $\bar{S}$ examined in Example 3.2.

The main result of this paper is that POP is a necessary and sufficient condition for total stability, and that an equilibrium for the entire society can be obtained only via optimal partitioning of the set of individuals.

**Proposition 3.6.** *Let* $S = (N, \Omega, U, W)$ *be a society satisfying Assumptions $A$ and $B$. Then $S$ is totally stable if and only if POP holds. (In particular, POP is a sufficient condition for the stability of the society $S$.) Moreover, if a pair $(P, \Lambda)$ constitutes an $S$ equilibrium then $P$ is an optimal partition of $N$.*

For societies with a small number of individuals we can state even sharper results.

**Proposition 3.7.** *Let a society $S$ satisfy Assumptions $A$ and $B$. If $S$ consists of either two or four individuals, it is always totally stable. If $S$ consists of six individuals it is totally stable if and only if it is stable.*

The proofs of Propositions 3.6 and 3.7 are presented in the next section.

## 4     Proofs of the results

*Proof of Example 3.1*

We shall prove here that the society $S$ defined in Example 3.1 does not admit an equilibrium. Assume, to the contrary, that the pair $(P, \Lambda)$ is an $S$ equilibrium. Then there is an alternative $a \in \Lambda$ that lies inside the triangle generated by the points $p^1, p^2, p^3$, and there is a (different) alternative $a' \in \Lambda$ that lies inside the triangle generated by the points $p^4, p^5, p^6$. Note that the set $\Lambda$ contains at least three alternatives; otherwise, either $a$ or $a'$ is supported in equilibrium by at least three players. However, the result of Greenberg (1979) implies that, in a three-individual society with a two-dimensional set of alternatives, every alternative is rejected by at least one two-person coalition, contradicting 2.1(a). Since no one-person coalition is effective, it follows that $\Lambda$ consists of three different alternatives, $\Lambda = \{a, a', b\}$. Let $b = (b^1, b^2) \in \mathbb{R}^2$ and consider first the case where $b^1 \geq 0$. Since $R > 4r$, it follows that each of the players $1, 2, 3$, would prefer $a$ to $b$. Thus, in equilibrium two different alternatives, $a'$ and $b$, are supported by three individuals $4, 5, 6$, implying that either $a'$ or $b$ is supported by only one individual, contradicting the ineffectiveness of one-person coalitions. Obviously, the case $b^1 \leq 0$ would lead to a similar conclusion. Thus, the set of $S$ equilibria is empty.                    $\square$

*Proof of Proposition 3.6*

Let $S$ be a society satisfying Assumptions A–C with even number of individuals, and let $M$ be an even coalition that generates the subsociety $S^M$. Choose a positive number $T$ such that

$$T \geq n \max_{i \neq j} r(i, j). \tag{2}$$

Define the following side-payment game in characteristic form $(M, V)$, with the value $v(C)$ of a coalition $C \subset M$ given by

$$v(C) = \begin{cases} 0 & \text{if } C = \{i\}, \\ 2T - r(i, j) & \text{if } C = \{i, j\}, \\ \max_{P \in \mathcal{P}^{12}(C)} \sum_{C \in P} v(C) & \text{if } |C| > 2, \end{cases}$$

where $\mathcal{P}^{12}(C)$ is the set of partitions of coalition $C$ into one- and two-person coalitions. Note also that this definition implies that

$$v(M) = Tm - H^2(M). \tag{3}$$

The proof of Proposition 3.6 is carried out in two steps. First, we shall show that the core of the game $(M, V)$, denoted Core$(M, V)$ and defined by

$$\text{Core}(M, V) \equiv \left\{ x \in \mathbb{R}^n \,\middle|\, \sum_{i \in M} x^i = v(M) \text{ with } \sum_{i \in C} x^i \geq v(C) \text{ for all } C \subset M \right\},$$

is non-empty if and only if the set of $S^M$ equilibria is non-empty. Second, we shall prove that Core$(M, V)$ is non-empty if and only if POP holds for $M$.

**Claim 4.1.**  Core$(M, V)$ *is non-empty if and only if the set of* $S^M$ *equilibria is non-empty.*

**Claim 4.2.**  Core$(M, V)$ *is non-empty if and only if POP holds (for $M$).*

Before proceeding with the proof of the claims, for each two-person coalition $C = (i, j)$ define the subset of the 2-dimensional Euclidean space $X^C$ by

$$X(C) = \{ x^C = (x^i, x^j) \in [T - r(i, j), T]^2 \mid x^i + x^j = 2T - r(i, j) \}.$$

Set

$$X(P) = \{ x \in \mathbb{R}^m_+ \mid x^C \in X(C) \,\forall C \in P \}.$$

First we shall prove the following lemmata.

**Lemma 4.3.**  *Let $P \in \mathcal{P}^2(M)$ and $x \in X(P)$. If $x \notin$ Core$(M, V)$ then there exists a coalition $C = (i, j)$ and $(z^i, z^j) \in X(C)$ such that $z^i > x^i$ and $z^j > x^j$.*

**Lemma 4.4.** *If* Core$(M,V)$ *is non-empty then there exists a partition* $P \in \mathcal{P}^2(M)$ *and a vector* $X \in$ Core$(M,V)$ *such that* $x^C \in X(C)$ *for each* $C \in P$.

To prove these two lemmata, note that Assumption A implies the "triangle inequality"; that is, for any triple of different players $i, j, k$ we have

$$r(i,j) < r(i,k) + r(j,k). \tag{4}$$

*Proof of Lemma 4.3:* Let $P \in \mathcal{P}^2(M)$ and $x \in X(P)$. Assume that $x$ is not in the core. Then there exists a coalition $C = (i,j) \notin P$ with $v(C) > x^i + x^j$. If $\max[x^i, x^j] < T$, we are done. So suppose, without loss of generality, that $x^i \geq T$ and, consequently, $x^j < T - r(i,j)$. Take $(i,k) \in P$ (note that $j \neq k$). Thus $x^k \leq T - r(i,k)$ and, moreover, $x^j + x^k < 2T - r(i,j) - r(i,k)$, which by (4) is less than $2T - r(j,k)$. Since both values $x^j$ and $x^k$ are less than $T$, there is a vector $(z^j, z^k) \in X((j,k))$ such that $z^j > x^j$ and $z^k > x^k$. □

*Proof of Lemma 4.4:* Let $X \in$ Core$(M,V)$. By definition of the game $(M,V)$, there exists a partition $P \in \mathcal{P}^2(M)$ such that $\sum_{i=1}^n x^i = \sum_{C \in P} v(C)$. Hence $\sum_{i \in C} x^i = v(C)$ for each $C \in P$. If $x^i \leq T$ for each $i \in M$, we are done. Suppose, therefore, that there exists $x^k > T$. Then there is a player $l \in M$ such that $C = (k,l) \in P$. Consider a vector $Y = (y^i)_{i \in M}$ given by

$$y^i = \begin{cases} x^i & \text{if } i \neq k,l, \\ T & \text{if } i = k, \\ T - r(k,l) & \text{if } i = l. \end{cases}$$

We wish to show that $Y$ also belongs to Core$(V,M)$. Suppose, by way of contradiction, that there is a (two-person) coalition $D$ which blocks $Y$. Since $X$ is in the core and $y^i \geq x^i$ for all $i \neq k$, $D$ must contain $k$ - say, $D = (k,m)$. Then $v(D) > T + y^m$. It follows that $y^m < T - r(k,m)$, which together with $y^l = T - r(k,l)$ implies that

$$y^m + y^l < 2T - (r(k,l) + r(k,m)) < 2T - r(l,m).$$

Thus the coalition $(l,m)$ blocks $Y$. But then it would also block $X$, a contradiction, showing that $Y$ belongs to Core$(M,V)$. □

*Proof of Claim 4.1:* Suppose that $(P, \Lambda)$ is an $S^M$ equilibrium, where $P = \{C_1, ..., C_L\}$. Clearly, for each $l = 1, 2, ..., L$ the alternative $a(C_l) \in \Lambda$ adopted by a coalition $C_l$, $l = 1, 2, ..., L$, lies on the straight line between the ideal points of members of $C_l$. Consider a vector $X \in \mathbb{R}_+^m$ where for each $i \in C_l \in P$ the coordinate $x^i$ is defined by

$$x^i = T - d(p^i, a(C_l)).$$

Let us show that $X$ belongs to Core $(M, V)$. Suppose, to the contrary, that $X$ is not in the core. Then, by Lemma 4.3, there is a two-person coalition $C = (k, t)$ with $(z^k, z^t) \in X(C)$, $z^k > x^k$, and $z^t > x^t$. Define $r = z^k - (T - r(k, t))$. Choose an alternative $\omega$ that lies on the straight line between the peaks $p^k$ and $p^t$ and is located at distance $r$ from $p^k$. (Note that $z^k \leq T$ implies that $0 \leq r \leq r(k, t)$.) Then both $k$ and $t$ are better off by choosing $\omega$ than at $(P, \Lambda)$, a contradiction to $(P, \Lambda)$ being an $S$ equilibrium.

Suppose now that Core$(M, V)$ is non-empty. Then, by Lemma 4.4, there exist a partition $P \in \mathcal{P}^2(M)$ and a vector $X \in \text{Core}(M, V)$ such that $x^C \in X(C)$ for each $C \in P$. For any $C = (i, j) \in P$, denote $d^i = T - x^i$ and define an alternative $a(C)$ to be on the straight line between the peaks $p^i$ and $p^j$ and located at distance $d^i$ from $p^i$ and distance $r(i, j) - d^i$ from $p^j$. (Again note that $0 \leq r^i \leq r(i, j)$ for each $(i, j) \in P$.) Consider the pair $(P, \Lambda)$, where $\Lambda = \{a(C)\}_{C \in P}$. We shall show that this pair constitutes an $S^M$ equilibrium. To verify 2.1(a), assume, in negation, that there exist $i \in C \in P$ and $D = (k, t) \in P$ such that $|p^i - a(C)| > |p^i - a(D)|$. Then there exists a number $\epsilon$ such that the alternative $a^\epsilon(D) \equiv a(D) + \epsilon(p^k - p^t)$ belongs to the interval $[p^k, p^t]$ and, moreover, $p^i$ is closer to $a^\epsilon(D)$ than to $a(C)$; that is, $|p^i - a^\epsilon(D)| < |p^i - a(C)|$. Thus, either $k$ or $t$, say $k$, prefers $a^\epsilon(D)$ over $a(D)$ and therefore, by choosing the alternative $a^\epsilon(D)$, the coalition $(i, k)$ makes both its members better off relative to $x^i$ and $x^k$ (respectively), a contradiction to $X$ being in the core.

To verify 2.1(b), assume, in negation, that there is a coalition $B = (k, t)$ with $k \in C_1 \in P$ and $t \in C_2 \in P$, and an alternative $\omega$ such that $|p^k - \omega| < |p^k - a(C_1)|$ and $|p^t - \omega| < |p^t - a(C_2)|$. Then the value of coalition $B$, $v(kl) = 2T - r(k, l)$, satisfies

$$v(kl) \geq 2T - (|p^k - a| + |p^t - a|) > T - |p^k - a(C_1)| + T - |p^t - a(C_2)|.$$

But the last term is equal $x^k + x^t$, yielding a contradiction to $X$ being in the core.   □

To prove Claim 4.2, we need the following definition and lemmata.

**Definition 4.5.**   A collection of subsets $\delta = \{B_1, B_2, ..., B_K\}$ of $M$ is called *balanced* if there exist positive numbers $\gamma_1, \gamma_2, ..., \gamma_K$, called *balancing weights,* such that

$$\sum_{B_k \in \delta(i)} \gamma_k = 1 \quad \text{for all } i \in M,$$

where $\delta(i) = \{C \in \delta \mid i \in C\}$. A balanced collection of coalitions is called *minimal* if none of its proper subcollections is balanced.

The following lemma could be easily obtained from the result of Bondareva (1962) and Shapley (1967).

**Lemma 4.6.**   Core$(M, V)$ *is non-empty if and only if*

$$\max(M) \sum_{\delta \in \Delta_2^*} \sum_{C \in \delta} \gamma(C) v(C) \le v(M),$$

*where $\Delta_2^*(M)$ denotes the set of all minimal balanced collections that consist of coalitions with no more than two players.*

The next lemma is a special case of the result due to Balinski (1970):

**Lemma 4.7.**   *Let $\delta \in \Delta_2^*(M)$ be a balanced collection. There exists a partition of $M$ into pairwise disjoint sets (not necessarily all non-empty) $M_l$, $l = 0, 1, \ldots, L$, where each non-empty $M_l$, $l = 1, 2, \ldots, l$, is an odd coalition with at least three players such that $\delta$ consists of full cycles on each $M_l$ (each coalition with the balancing weight of $\frac{1}{2}$) and a partition of $M_0$ (each coalition with the balancing weight of 1).*

*Proof of Claim 4.2:*   Suppose first that POP holds for $N$; that is, suppose $H^2(D) = H(D)$ for each even (and effective) coalition $D \subset N$. Consider an even subset $M$ of $N$. We shall show that Core$(V, M)$ is non-empty. By Lemma 4.6, it would be sufficient to prove that for any $\delta \in \Delta_2^*(M)$,

$$\sum_{C \in \delta} \gamma(C) v(C) \le v(M). \tag{5}$$

Take any $\delta \in \Delta_2^*(M)$. By Lemma 4.7, there exists a partition of $M$ into $L + 1$ pairwise disjoint sets (not necessarily all non-empty) $M_l$, $l = 0, 1, \ldots, L$, where the cardinality of $M_l$ is an odd number exceeding 1 for $l = 1, 2, \ldots, L$, so that $\delta$ consists of full cycles on all $M_l$ (each coalition with the balancing weight of $\frac{1}{2}$) and a partition of $M_0$ (each coalition with the balancing weight of 1).

Assume first that $\delta$ contains at least one singleton. Since the value of any two-person coalition is less than $2T$, it follows that the left side of (5) can be evaluated as

$$\sum_{C \in \delta} \gamma(C) v(C) \le T(m - |M_0|) + T(|M_0| - 1) = T(m - 1). \tag{6}$$

The right side of (6), however, is the sum of $m/2$ values of two-person coalitions. Then, by (2) we have

$$v(M) \ge Tm - (m/2) \max_{i \ne j} r(i, j) > T(m - 1). \tag{7}$$

Obviously, (6) and (7) imply (5) in this case. Consider now the case where $\delta$ contains no singletons. Then the set $F = \bigcup_{l=1}^{L} M_l$ and its complement $M_0 = M \setminus F$ each consists of an even number of players. Observe that

$$\sum_{C \subset F, C \in \delta} \gamma(C) v(C) \leq Tf - \frac{1}{2} \sum_{l=1}^{L} h(M_l) = Tf - \frac{1}{2} H^P(F) \leq Tf - \frac{1}{2} H(F),$$
(8)

where $P$ is the partition of $E$ into the sets $M_1, M_2, \ldots, M_L$ and $f = |F|$. A similar argument applies to the set $M_0$:

$$\sum_{C \subset M_0, C \in \delta} \gamma(C) v(C) = T(m-f) - \frac{1}{2} \sum_{c \subset M_0, C \in \delta} h(C)$$

$$= T(m-f) - \frac{1}{2} H^{P^*}(M_0) \leq T(m-f) - \frac{1}{2} H^2(M_0),$$
(9)

where $P^*$ is the partition of $M_0$ generated by the balanced collection $\delta$. Because POP implies that $H(F) = H^2(F)$, the inequality

$$H^2(F) + H^2(M_0) \leq H^2(M)$$

together with (8) and (9) yields

$$\sum_{C \in \delta} \gamma(C) v(C) \leq Tm - H^2(M).$$
(10)

But, by (4), the right side of (10) is equal to $v(M)$, which finally proves that (5) holds.

To complete the proof of Claim 4.2, assume now that POP does not hold for the even set $D \subset N$ with $d$ individuals. Then $H(D) < H^2(D)$. However, $Td - H(D)$ represents the value $\sum_{C \in \delta} \gamma(C) v(C)$, where $\delta$ is a balanced collection on $D$ that contains odd cycles. By (4), this value exceeds $v(D)$. Thus, Lemma 4.6 implies that $\mathrm{Core}(D, V)$ is empty. $\qquad \square$

To complete the proof of Proposition 3.6, it remains to show that if a pair $(P, \Lambda)$ constitutes an $S^M$ equilibrium then $P$ is an optimal partition of $M$, that is, $H^P(M) = H^2(M) = H(M)$. Suppose that the pair $(P, \Lambda)$ is an $S^M$ equilibrium, where the partition $P = \{C_1, \ldots, C_L\}$ consists of two-person coalitions and $\Lambda = \{a(C_1), \ldots, a(C_L)\} \subset \Omega$, where each $a(C_l)$ lies on the straight line between the peaks of the members of $C_l$, $l = 1, \ldots, L$. By Claim 4.1, the vector $X \in \mathbb{R}_+^m$, where for each $i \in C_l \in P$ the coordinate $x^i$ is defined by

$$x^i = T - d(p^i, a(C_l)),$$
(11)

belongs to Core$(M, V)$. By summing up the expressions in (11), we obtain $\sum_{i \in M} x^i = Tm - H^P(M)$, which together with (1) and (3) yields $H^P(M) = H^2(M) = H(M)$. $\square$

*Proof of Proposition 3.7*

Let $S$ be a society satisfying Assumptions A and B. The case of two individuals is straightforward. Consider, therefore, a society $S$ consisting of four individuals. Consider an ordering $\pi \in \Pi(N)$ such that $H(N) = h^\pi(N)$ Suppose, without loss of generality, that $\pi = \{1, 2, 3, 4\}$. Then

$$H(N) = r(1, 2) + r(2, 3) + r(3, 4) + r(4, 1). \tag{12}$$

However,

$$r(1, 2) + r(3, 4) = \tfrac{1}{2} H^{P'}(N), \tag{13}$$

$$r(2, 3) + r(1, 4) = \tfrac{1}{2} H^{P''}(N), \tag{14}$$

where $P' = \{(1, 2), (3, 4)\}$ and $P'' = \{(2, 3), (1, 4)\}$ are two different partitions of the set $N$ into two pairs of two-person coalitions. Combining (12)–(14), we obtain

$$H(N) = \tfrac{1}{2} H^{P'}(N) + \tfrac{1}{2} H^{P''}(N) \geq H^2(N),$$

which, together with (1), yields $H(N) = H^2(N)$. Then Proposition 3.6 implies the existence of an equilibrium for society with four individuals.

Since Assumptions A–C guarantee the existence of an equilibrium for societies with either two or four individuals, it follows that total stability of the society with six individuals is equivalent to its stability. $\square$

REFERENCES

Aumann, R. J., and J. Dreze (1974), "Cooperative Games with Coalition Structures," *International Journal of Game Theory* 3: 217-37.
Balinski, M. (1970), "On the Maximum Matching, Minimal Covering," in H. W. Kuhn (ed.), *Proceedings of the Princeton Symposium on Mathematical Programming*. Princeton, NJ: Princeton University Press.
Bénabou, R. (1992), "Heterogeneity, Stratification and Growth," discussion paper, Department of Economics, Massachusetts Institute of Technology, Cambridge.
Bondareva, O. N. (1962), "Theory of the Core of the *n*-person Game" (in Russian), *Vestnik Leningradskogo Universiteta* 13: 141-2.
Caplin, A., and B. Nalebuff (1992), "Individuals and Institutions," *American Economic Review (Papers and Proceedings)* 82: 317-22.
Chiappori, P.-A. (1992), "'Collective Models of Household Behavior: The Sharing Rule Approach," discussion paper, DELTA EHESS, Paris.

Epple, D., R. Filimon, and T. Romer (1984), "Equilibrium among Local Jurisdictions: Toward an Integrated Treatment of Voting and Residential Choice," *Journal of Public Economics* 24: 281–308.

Feinstein, J. S. (1992), "Public-Good Provision and Political Stability in Europe," *American Economic Review (Papers and Proceedings)* 82: 323–9.

Gale, D., and L. S. Shapley (1962), "College Admissions and the Stability of Marriage," *American Mathematical Monthly* 69: 9–15.

Greenberg, J. (1979), "Consistent Majority Rules over Compact Sets of Alternatives," *Econometrica* 47: 627–36.

Greenberg, J., and S. Weber (1986), "Strong Tiebout Equilibrium under Restricted Preferences Domain," *Journal of Economic Theory* 38: 101–17.

(1993), "Stable Coalition Structures with Unidimensional Set of Alternatives," *Journal of Economic Theory* 60: 62–82.

Guesnerie, R., and C. Oddou (1981), "Second Best Taxation as a Game," *Journal of Economic Theory* 25: 67–91.

Kolmogorov, A. N., and C. V. Fomin (1957), *Elements of the Theory of Functions and Functional Analysis.* Rochester, NY: Graylock Press.

Roth, A. E., and M. Sotomayor (1990), *Two-Sided Matching: A Study in Game-Theoretic Modeling and Analysis.* Cambridge: Cambridge University Press.

Shapley, L. S. (1967), "On Balanced Sets and Cores," *Naval Research Logistics Quarterly* 14: 453–60.

Shapley, L. S., and M. Shubik (1969), "On Market Games," *Journal of Economic Theory* 1: 9–25.

CHAPTER 15

# The holdout game: An experimental study of an infinitely repeated game with two-sided incomplete information

*Richard D. McKelvey & Thomas R. Palfrey*

## 1    Introduction

This paper investigates a two-person infinitely repeated game of incomplete information in which both players have private information on their individual type before the first game is played; this initial private information is followed by an infinite sequence of identical simultaneous-move stage games. Players observe their own payoff and the other player's move after each stage game has been played. Payoffs in the game are given by the discounted sum of payoffs in all the stage games.

The information structure is that each player knows his or her own type, but only the distribution from which the other player's type was drawn. The types of the two players are drawn independently, and each player's payoff function in the stage game is determined solely by that player's own type. This information structure is thus sometimes referred to as one of *independent private values.*

Games of this sort fall in a class of games that have been studied in a recent collection of papers by Kalai and Lehrer (1993), Jordan (1991a,b, 1992), and McKelvey and Palfrey (1992a). Jordan (1991b) established the existence of a Bayesian Nash equilibrium of the infinitely repeated game, and Kalai and Lehrer (1993) and Jordan (1991b) proved that, in every Bayesian Nash equilibrium, the sequence of play along the equilibrium path will eventually be empirically indistinguishable from play that could

This research was supported in part by National Science Foundation grant no. SES-9011828 to the California Institute of Technology. We wish to thank Mark Fey, Daniel Kim, Janice Lau, Jessie McReynolds, and Jeff Prisbrey for research assistance. Comments by participants in the June 1992 meeting of the Society for Social Choice and Welfare (Caen, France) are gratefully acknowledged. The data for the experiment are available from the authors on request.

have arisen at some Nash equilibrium of the infinitely repeated game in which the actual draws of the two players were common knowledge. In other words, enough information is leaked in the early rounds of play so that play eventually mimics an equilibrium as if the players' types have been perfectly revealed. The "as if" caveat is relevant; the theorems do not imply that players' beliefs about each other's type converge to complete information (i.e., to a degenerate posterior at the true type).

As interesting as these theorems are, other results from the folk theorem literature suggest that they place few restrictions on the possible patterns of equilibrium play. McKelvey and Palfrey (1992a) proposed a stationarity requirement that imposes very strong restrictions on the equilibrium play. This requirement, called *belief stationarity*, means that the behavioral strategies at a given stage can depend on history only to the extent that different histories lead to different common knowledge beliefs about player types. In other words, if players have common knowledge beliefs $\pi$ at stage $t$ and $\pi$ at stage $t'$, then each player must be mixing over his or her actions with the same probability distribution at stage $t'$ as at stage $t$. The authors also showed that, even with such a stationarity restriction, equilibrium play along some paths may be very complicated, exhibiting a rich nonlinear dynamic in which the trajectory of beliefs along such a path is chaotic.

Nonetheless, belief stationarity leads in some games to the selection of a unique subgame perfect equilibrium. Thus, the motivation for this refinement is in much the same spirit as the restrictions on equilibrium imposed in most of the bargaining literature with complete information, following Rubinstein (1982). There one also finds that stationarity (of a different sort) selects a unique equilibrium among an otherwise indeterminate set of possible equilibria.

This raises some obvious questions: As an empirical matter, how does play proceed in these games? Is there evidence that players are playing some Bayesian Nash equilibrium? Does the belief stationary equilibrium provide an accurate prediction for play? Does the sequence of play eventually converge to "complete information play"? What empirical regularities or anomalies can be identified?

We investigate these questions experimentally in the context of a simple bargaining game that we call the *holdout* game, which is related to a simultaneous-move version of the bargaining game studied by Chatterjee and Samuelson (1987). At each point in time, a player may either hold out ($H$) or give in ($G$). Each player may be either of two types. One type is a "tough" player, who has a dominant strategy in the stage game of holding out. The other "flexible" type's best response in the stage game depends on the probability that the opponent will give in; if that probability is sufficiently high (low), then the flexible type of player will give in (hold out). One can think of the game as a simple caricature of a bargaining game, where agreement hinges on at least one of the sides making a concession on a particular feature of the contract being negotiated. The two types then index some combination of the costs associated with making the concession and the value of the other terms of the contract. Section 2 solves for a symmetric belief stationary equilibrium of the game. Section 3 describes the experimental procedures and the specific parameters of the games that were conducted in the laboratory. Section 4 presents the results of the experiment.

## 2 The holdout game

The holdout game is a two-person, infinitely repeated game of incomplete information whose stage game is given in the following matrix.

|   | $G$ | | $H$ | |
|---|---|---|---|---|
| $G$ | $1-c_1$ | $1-c_2$ | $1-c_1$ | $1$ |
| $H$ | $1$ | $1-c_2$ | $0$ | $0$ |

In each round, either player can either give in ($G$) or hold out ($H$). If neither player gives in, then both players receive a payoff of 0. The basic value of agreement is equal to 1, and both players receive this if at least one player gives in. The cost to player $i$ of giving in equals $c_i$.

In the analysis that follows, we make the following assumptions. Each player has two possible types (values of $c_i$), $c_L$ and $c_H$. We assume $c_L < 1 < c_H$. To save on notation we write $c = c_L$. Thus, in a one-shot game, a $c_H$ type (or "high-cost" type) has a dominant strategy of holding out, and a $c$ type (or "low-cost" type) does not have a dominant strategy. Types are independently drawn with the probability that $c_i = c$ equal to $q_1$ for player 1 and $q_2$ for player 2, which is common knowledge.

### 2.1 One-shot Bayesian equilibrium

Before analyzing the infinitely repeated version of the holdout game, we characterize the solution to the one-shot game.

There are three classes of equilibria to the one-shot game, depending on the relative values of $c$ and $q = (q_1, q_2)$. In one kind of equilibrium, one player adopts a separating strategy (i.e., chooses $H$ if $c_i = c_H$ and $G$ if $c_i = c$) and the other player always holds out, regardless of type. These equilibria exist if $q_i$ is sufficiently large for at least one of the players. A second kind of equilibrium arises in which both players adopt separating strategies. These arise if $q_i$ is low for both players.

The third kind of equilibrium is one in which both players adopt semi-pooling strategies (i.e., player $i$ chooses $H$ if $c_i = c_H$ and chooses $G$ with probability $p_i > 0$ if $c_i = c$). Routine calculation shows that the equilibrium $p_i$ depends on $q_i$ and $c$ in the following way:

$$p_i(q) = (1-c)/q_i.$$

In this equilibrium, both players obtain an expected utility of $1-c$ (this feature of the equilibrium will simplify later calculations). This kind of equilibrium only arises if $q_i > 1-c$ for both players. Except for knife-edge cases, there are no other kinds of equilibrium.

## 2.2     The infinitely repeated game

In the infinitely repeated version of the holdout game, we assume that both players discount future payoffs using the same discount factor $\delta$, and we solve for a symmetric belief stationary perfect Bayesian equilibrium. We also conjecture that the equilibrium is unique if $c + \delta > 1$.

A belief stationary strategy profile is a collection of four functions – $p_{H1}(q_1, q_2)$, $p_1(q_1, q_2)$, $p_{H2}(q_1, q_2)$, and $p_2(q_1, q_2)$ – denoting, for each possible type of each player, the probability of giving in as a function of the currently held beliefs of both players about the type of the other player. Thus, $q_1$ denotes the current belief held by player 2 that player 1 is a low type, and $q_2$ denotes the current belief held by player 1 that player 2 is a low type. Symmetry requires that $p_{H2}(q, q') = p_{H1}(q', q)$ and $p_2(q, q') = p_1(q', q)$ for all $(q', q)$ in the unit square. To reduce notation, we drop the player subscripts, and simply look at the strategies of player 1, denoted $p_H(q_1, q_2)$ and $p(q_1, q_2)$.

Characterization of a symmetric belief stationary equilibrium is done by first solving the game at the boundary of the unit square of beliefs (i.e., for one-sided incomplete information), which then pins down the equilibrium mixing probabilities for interior values of $q$ (i.e., before either player's type has been revealed). This latter task is nontrivial, but in our case it is simplified since there is an equilibrium in which high-cost types always hold out. We conjecture that $p_H$ must identically equal zero for all beliefs in any belief stationary equilibrium. The reason is that belief stationarity rules out the kind of history-dependent strategies used in folk theorem constructions. Without such punishment schemes, it would not seem possible to provide intertemporal threats and incentives to induce high-cost types to violate their one-shot dominant strategies. Although this is not formally proved, we nonetheless restrict attention in the remainder of the paper to the equilibrium with $p_H = 0$.

We proceed in two steps. First, we show that if beliefs begin on the diagonal ($q_1 = q_2$) then the unique equilibrium path implies a trajectory of beliefs that remain on the diagonal until, after some point, they jump to the boundary. We then characterize the symmetric belief stationary equilibrium on the diagonal and on the boundary of the belief space. A solution off the diagonal is given in McKelvey and Palfrey (1993).

For any $\mathbf{q} = (q_1, q_2)$ we define $V(\mathbf{q} : \sigma)$ to equal the value to player 1 of the continuation game under the strategy profile $\sigma$. We suppress the dependence on $\sigma$ and simply write this as $V(\mathbf{q})$. Similarly, we define $V^G(\mathbf{q})$ (or $V^H(\mathbf{q})$) to be the value to player 1 in the continuation game if $G$ (or $H$, respectively) is chosen in the current period. We denote by $V_{GG}$ the future continuation value (starting next period) to player 1 if both players choose $G$ in the current period; $V_{GH}$, $V_{GH}$, and $V_{HG}$ are defined analogously. Finally, we make the following assumption throughout.

**Assumption 1.**  $c + \delta > 1$.

We first prove that if beliefs are on the diagonal then, in any symmetric belief stationary equilibrium, the beliefs in the continuation game of the next period are either on the diagonal or on the boundary of the belief space. At the boundary, at least one player's type is common knowledge. Therefore, once beliefs reach a boundary, they stay on the boundary forever.

**Proposition 1.**  *If* $\mathbf{q} = (q_1, q_2)$ *satisfies* $q_1 = q_2 = q$ *then, along any symmetric belief stationary equilibrium path, the updated beliefs at the beginning of the next period,* $\hat{\mathbf{q}} = (\hat{q}_1, \hat{q}_2)$, *must satisfy either* $\hat{q}_1 = \hat{q}_2 < q$ *or* $\hat{q}_1 = 1$ *or* $\hat{q}_2 = 1$.

*Proof:*  We first show that $q_1 = q_2 = q$ implies $p(\mathbf{q}) > 0$. If $p(\mathbf{q}) = 0$, then $\hat{\mathbf{q}} = \mathbf{q}$ since both types hold out. This implies $V(\mathbf{q}) = 0$, by stationary and symmetry, but player 1 can guarantee $(1 - c)/(1 - \delta) > 0$ by giving in forever - a contradiction. Since $p(\mathbf{q}) > 0$, there are four possible histories: $(GG, GH, HG, HH)$. The updated beliefs are, respectively:

$$(1,1), \left(1, \frac{(1-p)q}{1-pq}\right), \left(\frac{(1-p)q}{1-pq}, 1\right), \left(\frac{(1-p)q}{1-pq}, \frac{(1-p)q}{1-pq}\right). \qquad \square$$

**Proposition 2.**  *If* $q_1 = 1$ *then* $V(\mathbf{q}) = (1 - c)/(1 - \delta)$.

*Proof:*  If also $q_2 = 1$, then the unique symmetric belief stationary equilibrium is an infinite repetition of the unique one-shot symmetric Nash equilibrium where $p = 1 - c$. This yields a value of $(1 - c)/(1 - \delta)$. The remainder of the proof consists of showing that when $q_1 = 1$ and $q_2 < 1$, the unique equilibrium has $p(\mathbf{q}) = 1$; this implies the result directly. To prove this, first observe that for low values of $q_2$ ($q_2 < 1 - c$) the revealed player will always choose $G$, because

$$V^H \leq q_2\left(\frac{1}{1-\delta}\right) < \frac{1-c}{1-\delta} = V^G.$$

(Recall that $1/(1-\delta)$ is the highest feasible continuation payoff.) Accordingly, player 2 will hold out, so $\hat{q}_2 = q_2$.

Next, consider $q_2 \geq 1 - c$ and observe that, for the revealed player to have $p_1 < 1$, we must also have $p_2 q_2 \geq 1 - c$ because the value of continuation to player 1 does not depend on player 1's move (by belief stationarity). This requires $p_2 \geq (1-c)/q_2$. Therefore, following $H$ by player 2, Bayes's rule implies:

$$\hat{q}_2 < \frac{q_2 + c - 1}{c}.$$

So, for values of $q_2$ between $1 - c$ and $1 - c^2$, this implies $\hat{q}_2 < 1 - c$. The continuation game following $H$ by player 2 will therefore have player 1 choosing $G$ forever and player 2 choosing $H$ forever. This gives

$$V_2^H(\mathbf{q}) = p_1 + \frac{\delta}{1-\delta} \quad \text{and} \quad V_2^G(\mathbf{q}) = \frac{1-c}{1-\delta}.$$

Hence $V_2^G(\mathbf{q}) \geq V_2^H(\mathbf{q})$ requires $c + \delta \leq 1$, a contradiction. Therefore, $V_2(\mathbf{q}) = 1/(1-\delta)$ for $q_1 = 1$ and $q_2 < 1 - c^2$.

The argument is now completed by induction. Suppose that the equilibrium must always satisfy $p_1 = 1$ and $p_2 = 0$ for all $q_1$ and $q_2 < 1 - c^{n-1}$. Then it must also be true for $q_2 < 1 - c^n$. □

**Proposition 3.** *For all* $\mathbf{q} = (q_1, q_2)$ *such that* $q_1 > 0$,

$$p(\mathbf{q}) > 0 \Rightarrow V(\mathbf{q}) = \frac{1-c}{1-\delta}.$$

*Proof:* If $p(\mathbf{q}) > 0$ then $V^G(\mathbf{q}) = V(\mathbf{q})$. But $V^G(\mathbf{q}) = (1-c)/(1-\delta)$, since $\hat{q}_1 = 1$ if player 1 chooses $G$ and $V(1, \cdot) = (1-c)/(1-\delta)$. □

**Proposition 4.** *If* $\mathbf{q} = (q_1, q_2)$, *with*

$$q_1 = q_2 = q > P = \frac{(1-c)(1-\delta)}{1-\delta(1-c)},$$

*then* $p(\mathbf{q}) = P/q$.

*Proof:*   It is easily verified that $p(\mathbf{q}) < 1$ in the region of $\mathbf{q}$. By the proof of Proposition 1, $p(\mathbf{q}) > 0$. We must therefore have $V^G(\mathbf{q}) = V^H(\mathbf{q}) = (1-c)/(1-\delta)$, and thus

$$V^G(\mathbf{q}) = \frac{1-c}{1-\delta} = V^H(\mathbf{q}) = pq\frac{1}{1-\delta} + (1-pq)\delta\frac{1-c}{1-\delta} \;\Rightarrow\; p = \frac{P}{q}. \qquad \Box$$

**Proposition 5.**   *If $\mathbf{q} = (q_1, q_2)$ satisfies $q_1 = q_2 = q \le P$, then $p(q) = 1$.*

*Proof:*   From the preceding, there is no mixed strategy equilibrium when $p < q$. From Proposition 1, $p(\mathbf{q}) > 0$. Thus, $p(\mathbf{q}) = 1$ is the only possibility. Routine calculations verify this. $\qquad \Box$

## 3    Experimental design and procedures

We conducted six laboratory sessions using a total of 80 subjects who were undergraduate students at California Institute of Technology and Pasadena Community College. The sessions were carried out on a system of networked computers at the Caltech Laboratory for Experimental Economics and Political Science. Subjects were seated at terminals that were separated by partitions. Communication between subjects was prohibited.

At the beginning of each session, the subjects were randomly divided into equal-sized sets of red players (the row players) and blue players (the column players). Instructions were read aloud to the subjects and the rules and information structure of the games they were about to play were publicly announced and explained.

The subjects then played a sequence of between 12 and 15 (depending on how long each game lasted) "stochastic horizon" repeated games, called *matches*. In each match, each red subject was matched with a blue subject, each player was randomly assigned a cost type, and each pair repeatedly played the game until the termination rule was satisfied. A stochastic horizon was induced by using a random stopping rule, which was implemented by publicly rolling a 10-sided die after each play of the game. The "infinite game" terminated when a 1 was rolled, in order to induce a constant discount factor of $\delta = 0.9$.

After a match, the draw of the opponent's type was revealed to each player. Except after the last match, subjects were then anonymously rematched with a different player of the other color, and everyone was reassigned a new type. Participants were never told the identity of the players they were matched with, nor were they told the sequence in which their opponents were assigned (except that it was "a new opponent" in the next match). Subjects were informed that their type and the type (and identity) of their opponent remained the same in every period of any given match. The complete instructions are in the appendix (pp. 343–8).

At the conclusion of the experiment, subjects were paid in lottery tickets, following a standard procedure for inducing risk-neutral preferences over risky outcomes. We felt that such a control was important to rule out risk aversion as a possible explanation for any deviations from the theoretical predictions that might be observed.

The payoff tables used in the experiment consisted of the following four payoff matrices, corresponding to the four possible pairs of cost types.

MATRIX 1

|   | A | B |
|---|---|---|
| A | 4, 4 | 4, 6 |
| B | 6, 4 | 2, 2 |

MATRIX 2

|   | A | B |
|---|---|---|
| A | 4, 1 | 4, 5 |
| B | 6, 1 | 2, 4 |

MATRIX 3

|   | A | B |
|---|---|---|
| A | 1, 4 | 1, 6 |
| B | 5, 4 | 4, 2 |

MATRIX 4

|   | A | B |
|---|---|---|
| A | 1, 1 | 1, 5 |
| B | 5, 1 | 4, 4 |

At the beginning of each match, one of the four states (matrices) was randomly selected. The row player (Red) was told which row the selected matrix was in, and the column player (Blue) was told which column the selected matrix was in. For example, if matrix 2 was selected, Red was told it was either 1 or 2, and Blue was told it was either 2 or 4. The payoffs were presented arbitrarily, with no reference to "cost type," "holdout," or "give in," et cetera. Strategies were labeled $A$ and $B$, where $A$ corresponds to giving in and $B$ corresponds to holding out.

The payoffs were chosen to produce a game equivalent to the holdout game with parameters $c = 0.5$ and $c_H = 4$, with the probability of a low-cost type equal to 0.75. The top (left) two payoff tables correspond to a low-cost type for Red (Blue), and the bottom (right) two matrices correspond to a high-cost type for Red (Blue). The payoff tables differ cosmetically from the game studied in the previous section, but the experimental game is equivalent to that game. This is because the utility function of each type is a positive linear transformation[1] of the utility for the corresponding type in the matrix of Section 2.

[1] To obtain the payoff function of Section 2, subtract 2 units from the payoffs of the low types and then divide by four, and subtract 4 units from the payoffs of the high types.

Table 1. *Frequency of information states in experimental matches*

|          | Player 2 | | |
| -------- | --- | ---- | ----- |
| Player 1 | Low | High | Total |
| Low      | 141 | 48   | 189   |
| High     | 40  | 10   | 50    |
| Total    | 181 | 58   | 239   |

The information structure in all matches (except the first four) followed exactly the information structure described in the theoretical model of Section 2. The first four matches were conducted as repeated games of complete information in order for the subjects to gain some experience with the screen display and keyboard, the record-keeping tasks, and the way lottery tickets converted into money. This also afforded them an opportunity to become familiar with the basic strategic elements of the four component games, corresponding to the four possible type profiles, of $(c, c)$, $(c, c_H)$, $(c_H, c)$, and $(c_H, c_H)$. These four matches were conducted in that exact sequence. A discount factor of $\delta = 0.75$ was induced in these complete information games to reduce their elapsed time. In these matches, each subject was told the opponent's type – before the first period of the match – by publicly announcing exactly which one of the four payoff matrices was being used.

After approximately two hours, the experimental session was ended following the termination of a match. Subjects were then paid their earnings privately in cash, one at a time, in an adjoining room.

## 4    Data analysis

The data analysis addresses three questions. First, how well does the symmetric belief stationary equilibrium account for the data in our experiment? Second, is there evidence that subjects eventually play an equilibrium strategy for the true state? Third, does behavior change across matches as subjects become more experienced?

Our data consisted of a total of 239 matches of varying length, which yielded a total of 370 low-type subjects and 108 high-type subjects. The matches were distributed among the four information states as in Table 1. The actual and expected distributions of match lengths are given in Figure 1 and Table 2.

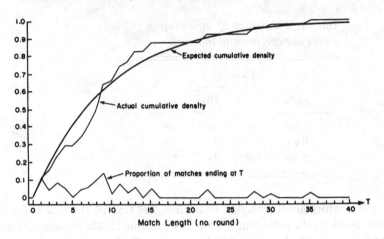

Figure 1. Actual and predicted frequency distribution of match lengths.

Table 2. *Frequency distribution of match lengths*

| $T$ | $f(T)$ |
|-----|--------|
| 1 | 28 |
| 2 | 10 |
| 3 | 20 |
| 4 | 12 |
| 6 | 11 |
| 7 | 14 |
| 8 | 24 |
| 9 | 34 |
| 10 | 5 |
| 11 | 19 |
| 12 | 6 |
| 13 | 14 |
| 15 | 12 |
| 22 | 11 |
| 28 | 8 |
| 30 | 5 |
| 35 | 6 |
| Total | 239 |

Table 3. *Proportion of high
types giving in by round*

| Round | Percent | $n$ |
|-------|---------|-----|
| 1 | .0926 | 108 |
| 2-5 | .0242 | 330 |
| 6-10 | .0277 | 325 |
| 11-20 | .0251 | 239 |
| 21-30 | .0362 | 138 |
| 31-36 | .0000 | 25 |
| Total | .0326 | 1165 |

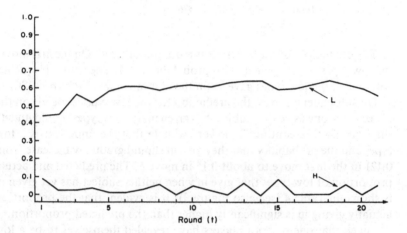

Figure 2. Proportion giving in by type of subject ($H$ or $L$) and round ($t$).

### 4.1    *Belief stationarity*

The first question is addressed by comparing the data to the predictions
of Propositions 1-5 in Section 2. We separate out the predictions for the
high and low types.

The prediction for the high types is that they should never give in. Table
3 displays the data relevant to this hypothesis (see also Figure 2). On the
first move, 9% ($n = 108$) of the high types choose to give in. This drops
to an average of about 2%-3%, after the first round. The average probability of giving in, across all rounds, is about 3% ($n = 1165$). The data in
Table 3 are aggregated across all incomplete information matches.

Table 4. *Predicted (p\*) and actual (p) proportion of low types giving in when neither subject has revealed*

| Round | $p^*$ | $p$ | $n$ |
|-------|-------|-------|-----|
| 1 | .121 | .441 | 370 |
| 2 | .125 | .454 | 119 |
| 3 | .130 | .435 | 46 |
| 4 | .136 | .353 | 17 |
| 5 | .143 | .182 | 11 |
| 6 | .152 | .444 | 9 |
| 7 | .163 | .667 | 3 |
| 8 | .177 | .000 | 1 |
| Total | .124 | .436 | 576 |

The prediction for the low types is more complicated. On the first move, the low types should give in with probability 0.121. The actual frequency with which the low types gave in on the first move was 44% ($n = 370$).

On subsequent moves, the prediction for the low types depends on the history. As long as neither subject has given in, the low types should update their beliefs to a continually lower estimate that the opponent is a low type, and the probability that they give in should gradually increase from 0.121 in the first move to about 0.15 in move 5. The predicted and actual proportion of low types that give in when neither subject has yet given in is shown in Table 4 (see also Figure 3). It is evident that the proportion actually giving in is significantly higher than the predicted proportion.

Given that one or both players have revealed themselves to be a low type (by choosing to give in), the equilibrium strategy for the low type is as follows: If both subjects simultaneously revealed themselves to be low, then both players should subsequently choose to give in with probability 0.5 in each round. If only the opponent has given in, then the player should give in with probability 0. If the player in question has given in, but the opponent has not, then the player should give in with probability 1. Table 5 shows the data for the low types for the case where at least one subject has revealed (see also Figure 3). In the early rounds, there are occasional attempts by the subject who has revealed to refrain from continuing to give in. Also, about 10% of the time, the subject who has not revealed will reveal even after the other subject has already revealed. After about the fifth round, Figure 3 shows that – at least at a highly aggregated level – behavior is fairly consistent with the equilibrium predictions.

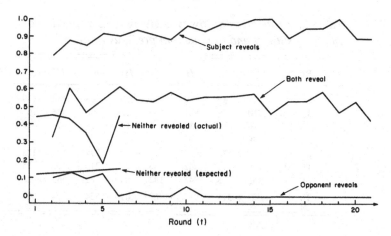

Figure 3. Proportion of low types giving in by whether subject and opponent have revealed or not.

Table 5. *Proportion of low types giving in by whether subject and opponent have revealed or not*

|  | Player that has revealed | | | | | |
|---|---|---|---|---|---|---|
|  | Both | $n$ | Self | $n$ | Other | $n$ |
| Predicted | .500 | | 1.00 | | 0.00 | |
| *Round* | | | | | | |
| 2 | .327 | 55 | .789 | 90 | .103 | 68 |
| 3 | .605 | 81 | .877 | 114 | .132 | 76 |
| 4 | .465 | 99 | .848 | 105 | .095 | 63 |
| 5 | .533 | 105 | .917 | 96 | .122 | 49 |
| 6–10 | .561 | 472 | .913 | 381 | .012 | 163 |
| 11–20 | .541 | 290 | .955 | 242 | .000 | 95 |
| 21–35 | .462 | 121 | .955 | 134 | .029 | 34 |
| Total | .529 | 1223 | .908 | 1162 | .058 | 548 |
| First revelation | .500 | 80 | .826 | 149 | .100 | 90 |

In addition to giving round-by-round data, Table 5 also gives the frequency of giving in on the first move after at least one subject has revealed: see the row labeled "First revelation." Here also, 10% of the time, the subject who has not yet revealed reveals after the opponent has revealed.

Table 6. *Probability of low type giving in as a function of move of subject and opponent in previous round*

| Round | GG | n | GH | n | HG | n | HH | n |
|-------|------|-----|------|------|------|-----|------|-----|
| 2     | .327 | 55  | .789 | 90   | .103 | 68  | .454 | 119 |
| 3     | .710 | 38  | .887 | 106  | .129 | 70  | .476 | 103 |
| 4     | .546 | 44  | .838 | 117  | .103 | 78  | .378 | 45  |
| 5     | .478 | 23  | .893 | 112  | .119 | 67  | .559 | 59  |
| 6–10  | .566 | 122 | .913 | 496  | .100 | 279 | .538 | 132 |
| 11–20 | .539 | 26  | .962 | 366  | .033 | 210 | .600 | 25  |
| 21–35 | .333 | 3   | .945 | 182  | .000 | 82  | .545 | 22  |
| Total | .527 | 311 | .912 | 1469 | .079 | 854 | .497 | 505 |

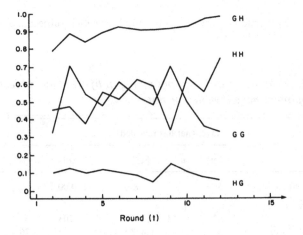

Figure 4. Proportion of low types giving in by actions in previous round.

Although Table 5 shows that, when both subjects have revealed their type, they give in approximately 50% of the time (as predicted), this masks what is really going on in the data. If we look at data at the individual level we find that, in most of these cases, one of the subjects is giving in every round while the opponent is holding out every round. Thus, at the aggregate level, 50% of the subjects in this category are giving in, but in fact all pairs are playing a pure strategy equilibrium. Table 6 illustrates this phenomenon (see also Figure 4). This table displays the probability of giving in as a function of the previous-period move. We see that if both subjects have given in (or if both subjects have held out), then there is about a 50% chance of giving in (or holding out) on the next move.

Table 7. *Percent correct guess of state by player type, opponent type, and length (T) of match*

| | Player type | | | | |
| | High | | Low | | |
| | Opponent | | Opponent | | |
| | H | L | H | L | Total |
|---|---|---|---|---|---|
| $T > 0$ | .737 (19) | .786 (84) | .560 (84) | .685 (257) | .682 (444) |
| $T > 5$ | .714 (14) | .814 (59) | .576 (59) | .664 (176) | .679 (308) |
| $T > 10$ | .600 (10) | .769 (26) | .539 (26) | .667 (84) | .657 (146) |

Thus these two categories tend to empty out, and become smaller over time. On the other hand, once one subject gives in and the other holds out, that pattern persists with a probability of at least 0.9 (by move 5) into the next move. Eventually, each pair thus settles into a pure strategy equilibrium where one player holds out and the other mixes. We do not see mixing or alternation schemes. This pure strategy equilibrium occurs even when both subjects have revealed their type.

Our second question concerns whether there is any evidence for the theorems of Kalai and Lehrer and of Jordan (KLJ). Do subjects eventually play an equilibrium for the correct state? We should emphasize that there is no way we could present evidence that would refute this assertion. First, the theorems say nothing about how long it should take for convergence. Second, folk theorems may apply once we drop the assumption of belief stationarity, and we must consider the possibility that nearly any pattern of play apparent in the first $K$ periods might be part of an equilibrium to the infinitely repeated game that could be enforced by sufficiently severe punishments off the equilibrium path. Thus, the most we can do is present any obvious evidence supporting the KLJ hypothesis, if such evidence exists.

A first question relevant to the KLJ hypothesis is whether subjects were able to figure out the correct state. In our experiments, after each match was over, we asked subjects to guess the true state before it was revealed to them. We did not pay subjects anything to reveal this information to us, since we did not want to contaminate their incentives for choosing optimal strategies. Nevertheless, they had no obvious reason to intentionally misreport this information, which is summarized in Table 7. Table 7 shows that subjects were only able to guess the state correctly about 68% of the time.[2] Players who were high types did better than low types, and all subjects did somewhat better when their opponent was a low type than when their opponent was a high type. This is what one would expect at the predicted equilibrium. There does not seem to be any increase in the success rate as the length of the match increases. In fact, if anything, the accuracy of the prediction goes down as the length of the match increases, indicating that the early periods reveal most (if not all) of the information that is revealed.

Of course, the KLJ hypothesis does not require that subjects learn the correct state, only that they play an equilibrium of the correct state. To address this question, we will select some salient equilibria for each state, and find out how frequently in our experiments the subjects eventually select one of the equilibria of the correct state.

Once we drop the condition of belief stationarity, a *strategy* is a function that determines, for each possible history $h$, a probability $p(h) = (p_1(h), p_2(h))$ that each player will give in. Consider the following equilibria for each state:

$$\text{Both 1 and 2 High} \quad p(h) = (0,0) = p_{HH} \text{ for all } h;$$
$$\text{1 High and 2 Low} \quad p(h) = (0,1) = p_{HL} \text{ for all } h;$$
$$\text{1 Low and 2 High} \quad p(h) = (1,0) = p_{LH} \text{ for all } h;$$
$$\text{Both 1 and 2 Low} \quad p(h) = (1,0) = p_{LL1} \text{ for all } h, \text{ or}$$
$$p(h) = (0,1) = p_{LL2} \text{ for all } h.$$

We cannot, of course, observe behavior for histories that do not occur in the data. Instead, we simply check whether the data in our experiments converge to the equilibrium play predicted by the strategies just listed. For each match, each round $t$, and each player $i$, we compute the cumulative average $\bar{p}_i(t)$ up to time $t$ that player $i$ has given in. Write $\bar{p}(t) = (\bar{p}_1(t), \bar{p}_2(t))$. Convergence to equilibrium entails that, for each true state $s$, $\lim_t \bar{p}(t) \to p_s^*$, where $p_s^*$ is one of the selected equilibria for the true state. Figures 5–8 show the results of these calculations, with one figure for each true state. These figures show the time path of the difference $\bar{p}_2(t) - \bar{p}_1(t)$ for each match; thus, each match corresponds to a line on the figure. For state 1, convergence is equivalent to the difference going to +1 or −1. For states 2 and 3, convergence is equivalent to the difference going to +1 and −1 respectively. For state 4, convergence implies that the difference goes to 0. The figures are roughly consistent with convergence.

---

[2] Note that this is worse than one would expect by chance, since by always guessing Low they would achieve 75%.

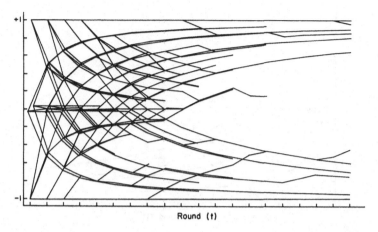

Round (t)

Figure 5. Differences in cumulative holdout probabilities by round, state 1: both players low cost. In order to distinguish data points where both players hold out from those where neither does, data points are plotted at $(x_t, y_t)$, where $t$ is the period, $x_t = t + D$, $y_t = (F_{2t} - F_{1t} + \Delta)$, $\Delta = 0.05(F_{2t} + F_{1t} - 1)$, and $F_{it}$ is the cumulative probability, to round $t$, that player $i$ has chosen to hold out.

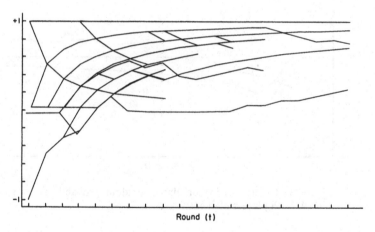

Round (t)

Figure 6. Differences in cumulative holdout probabilities by round, state 2: player 1 low cost, player 2 high cost.

## 4.2 Experience

The analysis has so far been at a highly aggregated level. In this section we break down the analysis according to how much experience a subject

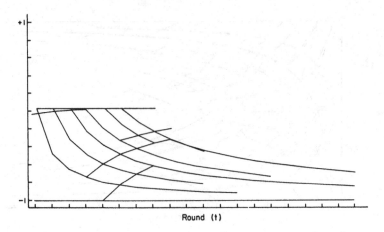

Figure 7. Differences in cumulative holdout probabilities by round, state 3: player 1 high cost, player 2 low cost.

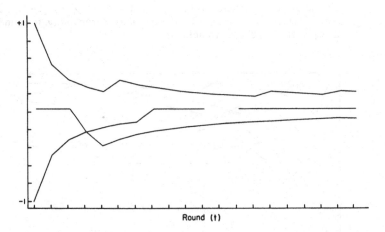

Figure 8. Differences in cumulative holdout probabilities by round, state 4: both players high cost.

has had. Recall that in each session, subjects play up to 14 matches, each one of which is an "infinitely" repeated game. Because of the combined presence of asymmetric information and dynamics, one might expect systematic changes in the behavior of subjects across matches, as they become more experienced in the task and become more familiar with the strategic subtleties of the environment. That subjects adjust their behavior in predictable ways has been well documented in most experimental environments.

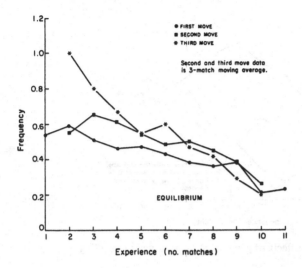

Figure 9. Give-in frequencies for low types as a function of experience.

We first examine behavior by high-cost types. We find that there is no significant change in behavior for these types (see Table 2) between the first five matches and the remaining matches. Although there is more giving in by inexperienced low types, this percentage is based on very small numbers (a total of 10 observations of giving in out of 108 chances).

In contrast, the behavior of low-cost types changes a lot with experience. Figure 9 displays the give-in frequencies in the first, second, and third moves as a function of experience, conditional on both players in the match having held out in previous moves. Here we use a finer breakdown of the experience variable. There are sufficient first-move data to enable a breakdown by match number. That is, data from "match number 1" are pooled data of all low-cost type moves from the first match played during the session.[3] There were insufficient second-move data to do this, since cases are excluded if either player gave in on move 1. We therefore report three-match moving averages for the second-move data. That is, data reported as "match number 2" data in the figure are averaged over matches 1, 2, and 3. In general, the data reported as "match number $t$" are averaged over matches $t-1$, $t$, and $t+1$. The same is true for the third-move data.

The results are striking. Experience leads low-cost players to hold out more frequently in the early stages of a match, when neither player has

---

[3] More precisely, it is the first incomplete information match. Recall that there were four complete information matches that preceded the incomplete information matches.

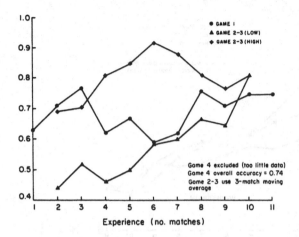

Figure 10. Effects of experience on accuracy of guessing.

given in yet. This leads to giving-in frequencies more in line with theoretical predictions. Recall (Table 3) that the prediction is for give-in frequencies below 20% in the early rounds of a match, with virtually no difference in the give-in probabilities between moves 1, 2, and 3. Inexperienced subjects systematically violate both of these predictions; for example, in match 2, subjects give in 40% of the time in the first move, 55% of the time on the second (conditional) move, and 100% of the time on the third (conditional) move. Although the order is consistent with the theory (give-in frequencies increase with the move number), the magnitudes of the give-in frequencies – and the magnitude of the cross-move differences in the give-in probabilities – are much too large. By the end of a session (match 10), give-in probabilities have dropped to around 20% in all three moves, with no significant cross-move differences.

Finally, we examine the effect of experience on the ex post guessing accuracy of the players. Here the theoretical predictions differ depending on the state, and depending on whether the guess is made by a high- or a low-cost type. We break down the data by match number, taking three-match moving averages as before for states 2 and 3 (owing to small sample sizes). State 4 (High, High) occurred only ten times and so was excluded entirely. The results are displayed in Figure 10. In all cases, experience leads to more accurate guessing. Recall that this differs from the result obtained for "within-match" experience. That is, subjects did not guess better in longer matches than they did in shorter matches (Table 7). Thus we conclude that it is experience across matches that matters. The improvement in guessing accuracy is particularly strong for low types in states 2 and 3, where accuracy improves from 42% to 80%. Pooling across all states and types, overall accuracy begins under 60% and ends up just over 75%. Since the probability of playing a low opponent is 75%, this is almost exactly the accuracy that would occur by making the best guess at the beginning of the game, conditioning only on one's own assigned type (i.e., guess the other player is a low type). One surprising feature of these data is that there is very little difference in the guessing accuracy of experienced high types and low types in games 2 and 3. Theoretically there should be a difference, with high-type accuracies near 1 and low-type accuracies between 0.5 and 0.75.

### 4.3  Summary

In summary, we see significant deviations from the symmetric belief stationary equilibrium. Most significantly, we have the following results.

(1)  The probability of giving in before either subject has revealed is consistently too high (0.45 vs. 0.12), but converges toward the equilibrium with experience.

(2)  The low types will occasionally (about 10% of the time) give in and reveal themselves to be low, even after their opponent has done so.

(3)  There is no evidence of a mixed equilibrium once both subjects have revealed. Rather, one subject gets stuck giving in forever.

(4)  The high types, especially on their first move, do not always adopt their dominant strategy of always holding out (10% error rate on the first move.)

(5)  Experience leads to more accurate inferences by subjects about the type of opponents they are facing.

### 5  Conclusions

The theoretical model based on the Bayesian equilibrium of an infinitely repeated game generates predictions that are not well supported by data from inexperienced subjects, but are much better supported by data from experienced subjects. The give-in probabilities of low-cost types are significantly higher than theory would predict, but steadily decline and approach theoretical predictions as subjects gain experience. The ability of subjects to make accurate inferences about which game they are engaged in (i.e., ability to identify opponent type from observed histories) also shows a steady improvement with experience. The two qualitative predictions that seem to hold up regardless of experience are: (1) high types rarely give in (rare violation of dominated strategies); and (2) if a low-type player $i$ gives in before $i$'s opponent gives in, then $i$ gives in in almost all subsequent moves of the match. One qualitative prediction completely fails, with experienced as well as inexperienced subjects: we did *not* observe mixing behavior by low types in matches where both players gave in for the first time on the same move. Rather, following such histories, one of the two players eventually ends up contributing in (almost) all later moves, while the other player (almost) exclusively holds out.

We believe this last observation arises because, in the game of complete information played by two low-cost types (which is simply a version of the game of "chicken"), the mixed strategy equilibrium is unstable under many definitions of stability of a Nash equilibrium (e.g., Cournot stability, fictitious play, replicator dynamic, etc.). The only stable equilibria of such a game are the two asymmetric pure strategy equilibria in which one player gives in and the other holds out. We conjecture that there is an alternative model, related to stability, that is well suited to the incomplete information environment of our experiments and that also can explain why the play of these games inevitably reduces to exactly one of the low types giving in. The model is based on "imperfect play" of the sort studied in McKelvey and Palfrey (1992b), El-Gamal and Palfrey (1994), El-Gamal, McKelvey, and Palfrey (1993), and Schmidt (1992). These models are similar in spirit to ideas developed by Harsanyi (1973) and Selten (1975), both of whom introduce the possibility of "noisy play" in a rigorous (but different) way. Suppose that players cannot perfectly implement a behavioral strategy but may instead accidentally choose some other (nonequilibrium) behavioral strategy with some probability, and suppose further that these "trembling" probabilities are commonly known by all the players. This produces a more complicated game of incomplete information in which the inferences by players about their opponent's type can never rule out either type. That is, if a player observes an opponent give in, there is still some possibility that the opponent is a high-cost type who erred. This means, for example, that even when both players are low types who both give in first at the same move, the continuation stage game is not the complete information game of chicken but simply a game of incomplete information in which both players are more likely to be low-cost types than in the previous move. More importantly, if in the continuation game one of the players happens to give in before the other, that player then becomes the more likely one to be a low-cost type. We conjecture that the equilibrium to this "error" version of the game will have the property that, as the probability of errors becomes small, later moves of a match (with at least one low-cost type) will necessarily see one player giving in with probability close to 1 and the other player holding out with probability close to 1. Moreover, in the equilibrium of this perturbed game, there would always be some small probability (increasing with the probability of error) that two low-cost players will at some point appear to reverse roles, with the player who had been holding out giving in and the player who had been giving in holding out.

## Appendix: Instructions for the experiments

This is an experiment in group decision making, and you will be paid for your participation *in cash,* at the end of the experiment. Different subjects may earn different amounts. What *you* earn depends partly on your decisions, partly on the decisions of others, and partly on chance.

The entire experiment will take place through computer terminals, and all interaction between you will take place through the computers. It is important that you not talk or in any way try to communicate with other subjects during the experiments. If you disobey the rules, we will have to ask you to leave the experiment.

We will start with a brief instruction period. During the instruction period, you will be given a complete description of the experiment and will be shown how to use the computers. If you have any questions during the instruction period, raise your hand and your question will be answered so everyone can hear.

The subjects will be divided into two groups, containing equal numbers of subjects. The groups will be labeled the RED group and the BLUE group. To determine which color you are, will you each please select an envelope as the experimenter passes by you.

[EXPERIMENTER: PASS OUT ENVELOPES]

If you chose BLUE, you will be BLUE for the entire experiment. If you chose RED, you will be RED for the entire experiment. Please remember your color, because the instructions are slightly different for the BLUE and the RED subjects.

[DISPLAY PAYOFF TABLES USING AN OVERHEAD]

| | 1 | | | 2 | |
|---|---|---|---|---|---|
| | A | B | | A | B |
| A | 4, 4 | 4, 6 | A | 4, 1 | 4, 5 |
| B | 6, 4 | 2, 2 | B | 6, 1 | 2, 4 |

| | 3 | | | 4 | |
|---|---|---|---|---|---|
| | A | B | | A | B |
| A | 1, 4 | 1, 6 | A | 1, 1 | 1, 5 |
| B | 5, 4 | 4, 2 | B | 5, 1 | 4, 4 |

[*Note:* The row payoffs were written in Red, and the column payoffs were written in Blue. This was also done on the subjects' computer screens.]

The four tables in this figure represent the four possible payoff tables that will be used in this experiment. They are indicated as table 1, table 2, table 3, and table 4. The experiment will consist of a number of matches. In each match, you will first be matched with another subject of the opposite color. The experimenter will then select one of the four payoff matrices. Whichever one is selected will be the one that you use for the entire match. Each match will consist of a number of rounds. In each round, you and the subject you are matched with will simultaneously choose actions (RED chooses U or D, BLUE chooses L or R). The payoff matrix that is selected gives the payoff, in points, to you and the subject that you are matched with for a single round of the match. You will repeat this for each round.

In each match, after each round, we will roll a four-sided die. If it comes up with a 1, then the match will end. Otherwise, we continue with another round. Thus, in each match, we will continue to run additional rounds until the first time the die lands with a 1. For example, if the first time the die comes up with a 1 is on the third round, then this means that the match will consist of three rounds.

To compute your payoff for a match, we will first compute the match value. This is the value per round multiplied by the number of rounds. Each round is worth 15¢. Thus, the match is worth 15¢ multiplied by the number of rounds in the match. In each match, you will earn either the match value or 0. To determine whether you earn the match value or 0, we compute the number of points you earned in the match and divide it by the maximum possible number of points you could have made. This value is multiplied by 1000 to determine your *score* for the match. (In this case, the maximum possible number of points is 6 times the number of rounds.) Your score represents the number of lottery tickets you own out of a total of 1000. Thus, if your score is 437, you own all the numbers from 0 up to, but not including, 437. To determine your payoff, we will draw a lottery ticket for you between 0 and 999. If the ticket is one of the tickets you own, you win the value of the match. Otherwise, you get nothing for the match.

The experiment consists of several matches. In each match, you are matched with a different player of the opposite color from yours. Thus, if you are a BLUE player, in each game, you will be matched with a RED player. If you are a RED player, in each game you are matched with a BLUE player.

[BEGIN COMPUTER INSTRUCTION]

We will now begin the computer instruction session. During the instruction session, we will teach you how to use the computer by going through a few practice games. During the instruction session, *do not hit any keys until you are told to do so,* and when you are told to enter information, *type exactly what you are told to type.* You are not paid for these practice games.

Please turn on your computer now by pushing the button labeled "MASTER" on the right-hand side of the panel underneath the screen.

[WAIT FOR SUBJECTS TO TURN ON COMPUTERS]

When the computer prompts you for your name, type your full name. Then hit the ENTER key.

[WAIT FOR SUBJECTS TO ENTER NAMES]

When you are asked to enter your color, type R if your color is RED, and B if your color is BLUE. Then hit ENTER.

[WAIT FOR SUBJECTS TO ENTER COLORS]

You now see the experiment screen. Throughout the experiment, the bottom of the screen will tell you what is currently happening, and the top will show you the payoff table.

The top line of the upper part of the screen tells you your subject number and your color. Please record your color and subject number on the top left-hand corner of your record sheet.

Each of the four possible payoff tables is shown on the upper screen. In this match, the first table has been selected. This is indicated by the fact that the first payoff table is highlighted in gray. This means table 1 will be used for the entire first match.

The bottom part of the screen prompts you for your input and records the moves that have been made by you and the other subject. The subject that you are matched with is indicated on the second row of the bottom screen. It is important to note that you will be matched with a new subject for each match.

We will now start the first practice game. Remember, do not hit any keys until you are told to do so. If you are a RED subject, you are prompted to enter a choice of the row (U or D). If you are a BLUE subject, you are prompted to enter a choice of a column (L or R). Will all the RED subjects please choose U and all the BLUE subjects please choose L on your terminals now. After you enter your choice, you must confirm it by pressing Y.

[WAIT FOR SUBJECTS TO CHOOSE]

Since RED chose U and BLUE chose L, this means that the outcome is in the upper left-hand cell of the highlighted table, so that the BLUE subject gets a payoff of 4, and the RED subject gets a payoff of 4. The move that was chosen by each subject, as well as your payoff, is recorded on the bottom of the screen.

In the actual experiment, at this point, we would throw a four-sided die to determine whether to stop the match or continue with another round. For the practice session, we will not actually throw the die, but we will show you what your payoff would be if we threw the first 1 on the fourth round.

The match now proceeds to the second round. The second round is just like the first. This time, will the RED subject please choose U, and the BLUE subject choose R, and then confirm your choice.

[WAIT FOR SUBJECTS TO CHOOSE]

Since RED chose U and BLUE chose R, this means that the outcome is in the upper right-hand cell, so that the RED subject gets a payoff of 4, and the BLUE subject gets a payoff of 6. The move that was chosen by each subject, as well as your payoff, is again recorded on the bottom of the screen. The match now proceeds to the third round.

[HAVE SUBJECTS DO 2 MORE ROUNDS (DL AND DR)]

In the practice match, we are assuming that the match ends after the fourth round. This means that you will be paid for 4 rounds in this match. Enter this number in column (1) of your record sheet. [Note: See Figure 11.] Each round is worth 15¢, so the total value of this match is $V = 60$¢. Enter this in column (2). The total number of points you could have earned is 4 times 6, or 24. Enter this in column (3). Now, add up your own payoffs for the first 4 rounds, and enter this in column (4). Divide this number by 24, and multiply by 1000 to get your score. Enter this number in column (5). Your score is the number of lottery tickets you have earned. You have all of the lottery tickets numbered from 0 up to (but not including) $s$. To determine your lottery number, we will throw three ten-sided dice to determine a number between 0 and 999. You will then add 100 times your player number to this number to determine your lottery ticket, $L$, the last three digits of this number. If your lottery ticket is a number below $s$, then you earn $V$. If it is above or equal to $s$, you earn $0.00 for this match.

[THROW DICE TO GET $L$]

We have thrown a number $L$. Enter this number in column (6). If $L$ is below $s$ (your entry in column 6), then enter $V$ into the final column (column 7). If $L$ is above or equal to $s$, then enter $0.00 into the final column. You are not being paid for the practice session, but if this were the real experiment, then the payoff you have recorded in column 7 would be

Record Sheet

Your Color:_____      Your Subject #_____

| | (1) | (2) | (3) | (4) | (5) | (6) | (7) |
|---|---|---|---|---|---|---|---|
| | # of rounds | Match Value | Possible Total | Your Total | Your Score | Lottery number | Your Payoff |
| | $n$ | $V = n \times v$ | $T = n \times m$ | $t$ | $s = 1000 \times \frac{t}{T}$ | $L$ | $V$ if $L < s$<br>$0$ if $L \geq s$ |
| Practice | ____ | ____ | ____ | ____ | ____ | ____ | $ ____ |
| ( )( ) 1 | ____ | ____ | ____ | ____ | ____ | ____ | $ ____ |
| ( )( ) 2 | ____ | ____ | ____ | ____ | ____ | ____ | $ ____ |
| ( )( ) 3 | ____ | ____ | ____ | ____ | ____ | ____ | $ ____ |
| ( )( ) 4 | ____ | ____ | ____ | ____ | ____ | ____ | $ ____ |
| ( )( ) 5 | ____ | ____ | ____ | ____ | ____ | ____ | $ ____ |
| ( )( ) 6 | ____ | ____ | ____ | ____ | ____ | ____ | $ ____ |
| ( )( ) 7 | ____ | ____ | ____ | ____ | ____ | ____ | $ ____ |
| ( )( ) 8 | ____ | ____ | ____ | ____ | ____ | ____ | $ ____ |
| ( )( ) 9 | ____ | ____ | ____ | ____ | ____ | ____ | $ ____ |
| ( )( ) 10 | ____ | ____ | ____ | ____ | ____ | ____ | $ ____ |
| ( )( ) 11 | ____ | ____ | ____ | ____ | ____ | ____ | $ ____ |
| ( )( ) 12 | ____ | ____ | ____ | ____ | ____ | ____ | $ ____ |
| ( )( ) 13 | ____ | ____ | ____ | ____ | ____ | ____ | $ ____ |
| ( )( ) 14 | ____ | ____ | ____ | ____ | ____ | ____ | $ ____ |
| ( )( ) 15 | ____ | ____ | ____ | ____ | ____ | ____ | $ ____ |
| | | | | | Participation Fee | | $ ____ |
| | | | | | TOTAL | | $ ____ |

DATE _____      EXPERIMENT # _____

YOUR NAME (Print)_____    SOC SEC # _____

SIGNATURE_____    RECIEVED $ _____

Figure 11. Record sheet for decision-making experiment.

money you have earned from the first match, and you would be paid this amount for that game at the end of the experiment. The total you earn over all of the matches is what you will be paid for your participation in the experiment.

[WAIT FOR SUBJECTS TO RECORD PAYOFFS]

This concludes the practice session. In the actual experiment there will be several matches, and, of course, it will be up to you to make your own decisions. After the last match, the experiment ends and we will pay each of you privately, in cash, the total amount you have accumulated during all ten games, plus your guaranteed five-dollar participation fee. No other person will be told how much cash you earned in the experiment. You need not tell any other participants how much you earned.

Are there any questions before we begin?

[ANSWER QUESTIONS]

We will now begin with the actual experiment. If there are any problems from this point on, raise your hand and an experimenter will come and assist you.

[START EXPERIMENT]

[SECOND PART OF EXPERIMENT]

At this point, we are going to change the rules. You will now be using the same payoff tables as before, and will be paid in exactly the same manner. The only difference will be the information that you have. As before, prior to a match, we will draw one of the four payoff tables to be the one that you will use. However, this time, you will not be told which payoff table is being used. If you are a RED player, you will only be told whether the payoff table is one of the top two or one of the bottom two. If you are the BLUE player you will only be told that it is one of the two on the left or one of the two on the right. The information will be indicated on your screen by highlighting two of the possible payoff matrices. You will only know that the correct payoff matrix is one of the highlighted ones.

[*Note:* In the original script, "BLUE" and "RED" were inadvertently reversed in the preceding paragraph. However, we believe there was no confusion because the information conditions were illustrated using color-coded overhead, where the experimenter explicitly showed which payoff tables would be highlighted for each color of player, and the computer screens were also color-coded.]

We will determine which payoff table to use by rolling two four-sided dice. We will roll the first four-sided die. If it comes up with a 1, we will choose one of the bottom two tables, otherwise we choose one of the top two. We then roll a second four-sided die. If it comes up with a 1, we choose the right-hand table. Otherwise, we choose the left-hand table.

## REFERENCES

Chatterjee, K., and L. Samuelson (1987), "Bargaining with Two-Sided Incomplete Information: An Infinite Horizon Model with Alternating Offers," *Review of Economic Studies* 54: 175–92.

El-Gamal, M. A., R. D. McKelvey, and T. R. Palfrey (1993), "A Bayesian Sequential Experimental Study of Learning in Games," *Journal of the American Statistical Association* 88: 428–35.

El-Gamal, M. A., and T. R. Palfrey (1994), "Vertigo: Comparing Structural Models of Imperfect Behavior in Experimental Games," *Games and Economic Behavior* (to appear).

Harsanyi, J. C. (1973), "Games with Randomly Disturbed Payoffs: A New Rationale for Mixed Strategies," *International Journal of Game Theory* 2: 1–23.

Jordan, J. S. (1991a), "Bayesian Learning in Normal Form Games," *Games and Economic Behavior* 3: 60–81.

(1991b), "Bayesian Learning in Repeated Games," *Games and Economic Behavior* (to appear).

(1992), "The Exponential Convergence of Bayesian Learning in Normal Form Games," *Games and Economic Behavior* 4: 202–17.

Kalai, E., and E. Lehrer (1993), "Bayesian Learning Leads to Nash Equilibrium," *Econometrica* 61: 1019–45.

McKelvey, R. D., and T. R. Palfrey (1992a), "Stationarity and Chaos in Infinitely Repeated Games of Incomplete Information," working paper no. 803, Department of Social Science, California Institute of Technology, Pasadena.

(1992b), "An Experimental Study of the Centipede Game," *Econometrica* 60: 803–36.

(1993), "Endogeneity of Alternating Offers in a Bargaining Game," working paper no. 876, Department of Social Science, California Institute of Technology, Pasadena.

Rubinstein, A. (1982), "Perfect Equilibrium in a Bargaining Model," *Econometrica* 50: 97–109.

Schmidt, David R. (1992), "Reputation Building by Error-Prone Agents," working paper, Department of Social Science, California Institute of Technology, Pasadena.

Selten, R. (1975), "A Re-Examination of the Perfectness Concept for Equilibrium Points of Extensive Form Games," *International Journal of Game Theory* 4: 25–55.

# Other applications

CHAPTER 16

# Exact aggregation under risk

*William A. Barnett*

## 1    Introduction

Virtually the entire literature on exact aggregation over goods and on duality theory requires perfect certainty or risk neutrality. It is widely believed that these theorems do not hold under risk aversion. This paper proves that much of the existing perfect certainty theory is immediately applicable when risk aversion applies only to future variables and not to any contemporaneous variables. Although the perfect certainty theory does not apply when there is risk aversion relative to current variables, an exact aggregation theorem is proved that is applicable under those conditions.

## 2    Microfoundations of consumer demand for money

### 2.1    *Introduction*

To illustrate our results, we use a model of a consumer who consumes goods and the services of monetary assets. In this section we formulate the consumer's stochastic decision problem over consumer goods and monetary assets. The consumer's decisions are made in discrete time over a finite planning horizon for the time intervals $t, t+1, ..., s, ..., t+T$, where $t$ is the current time period and $t+T$ is the terminal planning period. The variables used in defining the consumer's decision are as follows:

$\mathbf{x}_s = n$-dimensional vector of planned real consumption of goods and services during period $s$;

$\mathbf{p}_s = n$-dimensional vector of goods and services' expected prices and of durable goods' expected rental prices during period $s$;

Research on this project was partially supported by NSF grant SES 9223557.

$\mathbf{a}_s = k$-dimensional vector of planned real balances of monetary assets during period $s$;

$\rho_s = k$-dimensional vector of expected nominal holding-period yields of monetary assets;

$A_s =$ planned holdings of the benchmark asset during period $s$;

$R_s =$ expected one-period holding yield on the benchmark asset during period $s$;

$\mathbf{I}_s =$ sum of all other sources of income during period $s$;

$p_s^* = p_s^*(\mathbf{p}_s) =$ true cost-of-living index.

Define $Y$ to be a compact subset of the $(n+k+2)$-dimensional nonnegative orthant. The consumer's consumption possibility set $S(s)$ for $s \in \{t, \ldots, t+T\}$ is:

$$S(s) = \left\{ (\mathbf{a}_s, \mathbf{x}_s, A_s) \in Y : \right.$$

$$\sum_{i=1}^{n} p_{is} x_{is} = \sum_{i=1}^{k} [(1+\rho_{i,s-1})p_{s-1}^* a_{i,s-1} - p_s^* a_{is}]$$

$$\left. + (1+R_{s-1})p_{s-1}^* A_{s-1} - p_s^* A_s + \mathbf{I}_s \right\}. \quad (2.1)$$

Under the assumption of rational expectations, the distribution of random variables is known to the consumer. Since current-period interest rates are not paid until the end of the period, they may be contemporaneously unknown to the consumer. Nevertheless, observe that during period $t$ the only interest rates that enter into $S(t)$ are those paid during period $t-1$, which are known at the start of period $t$. Similarly, $\mathbf{p}_t$ and $p_t^*$ are determined and known to the consumer at the start of period $t$. Hence $(\mathbf{a}_t, \mathbf{x}_t, A_t)$ can be chosen deterministically in a manner that assures that $(\mathbf{a}_t, \mathbf{x}_t, A_t) \in S(t)$ with certainty. However, this is not possible for $s > t$ because – at the beginning of time period $t$, when the intertemporal decision is solved – the constraint sets $S(s)$ for $s > t$ are random sets. Hence, for $s > t$ the values of $(\mathbf{a}_s, \mathbf{x}_s, A_s)$ must be selected as a stochastic process.

The benchmark asset $A_s$ provides no services other than its yield $R_s$. As a result, the benchmark asset does not enter the consumer's intertemporal utility function except in the last instant of the planning horizon.[1] The asset is held only as a means of accumulating wealth to endow subsequent planning horizons. The consumer's intertemporal utility function is

[1] A nonzero probability must exist that $R_s$, the holding-period return on the benchmark asset, will exceed that of any other asset during period $s$, since no other motivation for holding the benchmark asset exists within Problem 2 at any $s$. In fact, since the variance of the distribution of $R_s$ is likely to be high relative to that of $r_{is}$ for any $i$, we should expect the mean of $R_s$ to exceed that of any element of $\mathbf{r}_s$.

$$U = U(\mathbf{a}_t, ..., \mathbf{a}_s, ..., \mathbf{a}_{t+T}; \mathbf{x}_t, ..., \mathbf{x}_s, ..., \mathbf{x}_{t+T}; A_{t+T}),$$

where $U$ is assumed to be intertemporally additively (strongly) separable, such that

$$U = u(\mathbf{a}_t, \mathbf{x}_t) + \left(\frac{1}{1+\xi}\right) u(\mathbf{a}_{t+1}, \mathbf{x}_{t+1}) + \cdots$$

$$+ \left(\frac{1}{1+\xi}\right)^{T-1} u(\mathbf{a}_{t+T-1}, \mathbf{x}_{t+T-1}) + \left(\frac{1}{1+\xi}\right)^T u(\mathbf{a}_{t+T}, \mathbf{x}_{t+T}, A_{t+T})$$

$$= \sum_{s=t}^{t+T-1} \left(\frac{1}{1+\xi}\right)^{s-t} u(\mathbf{a}_s, \mathbf{x}_s) + \left(\frac{1}{1+\xi}\right)^T u_T(\mathbf{a}_{t+T}, \mathbf{x}_{t+T}, A_{t+T}), \quad (2.2)$$

and the consumer's subjective rate of time preference, $\xi$, is assumed to be constant.[2] The single-period utility functions, $u$ and $u_T$, are assumed to be increasing and strictly quasiconcave.

Given the price and interest-rate processes, the consumer selects the deterministic point $(\mathbf{a}_t, \mathbf{x}_t, A_t)$ and the stochastic processes $(\mathbf{a}_s, \mathbf{x}_s, A_s)$, $s = t+1, ..., t+T$, to maximize the expected value of $U$ over the planning horizon, subject to the sequence of choice-set constraints. Formally, the consumer's decision problem is as follows.

**Problem 1.** Choose the deterministic point $(\mathbf{a}_t, \mathbf{x}_t, A_t)$ and the stochastic process $(\mathbf{a}_s, \mathbf{x}_s, A_s)$, $s = t+1, ..., t+T$, to maximize

$$u(\mathbf{a}_t, \mathbf{x}_t) + E_t \left[ \sum_{s=t+1}^{t+T-1} \left(\frac{1}{1+\xi}\right)^{s-t} u(\mathbf{a}_s, \mathbf{x}_s) + \left(\frac{1}{1+\xi}\right)^T u_T(\mathbf{a}_{t+T}, \mathbf{x}_{t+T}, A_{t+T}) \right]$$

$$(2.3)$$

subject to $(\mathbf{a}_s, \mathbf{x}_s, A_s) \in S(s)$ for $s = t, ..., t+T$.

We use $E_t$ to designate the expectations operator conditional upon the information that exists at time $t$.

In the case of an infinite planning horizon, the decision problem becomes the following.

**Problem 2.** Choose the deterministic point $(\mathbf{a}_t, \mathbf{x}_t, A_t)$ and the stochastic process $(\mathbf{a}_s, \mathbf{x}_s, A_s)$, $s = t+1, ..., \infty$, to maximize

$$u(\mathbf{a}_t, \mathbf{x}_t) + E_t \left[ \sum_{s=t+1}^{\infty} \left(\frac{1}{1+\xi}\right)^{s-t} u(\mathbf{a}_s, \mathbf{x}_s) \right] \quad (2.4)$$

---

[2] Although money may not exist in the elementary utility function, there does exist a derived utility function that contains money, so long as money has positive value in equilibrium. See e.g. Arrow and Hahn (1971), Phlips and Spinnewyn (1982), and Feenstra (1986). We implicitly are using that derived utility function.

subject to $(\mathbf{a}_s, \mathbf{x}_s, A_s) \in S(s)$ for $s \geq t$, and also subject to

$$\lim_{s \to \infty} E_t \left( \frac{1}{1+\xi} \right)^{s-t} A_s = 0.$$

The latter constraint rules out perpetual borrowing at the benchmark rate of return, $R_t$.[3]

## 2.2    Existence of a monetary aggregate for the consumer

In order to assure the existence of a monetary aggregate for the consumer, we partition the vector $\mathbf{a}_s$ of monetary asset quantities so that $\mathbf{a}_s = (\mathbf{m}_s, \bar{\mathbf{m}}_s)$. We correspondingly partition the vector $\rho_s$ of those assets' interest rates so that $\rho_s = (\mathbf{r}_s, \bar{\mathbf{r}}_s)$. We then assume that the utility function $u$ is blockwise weakly separable in $\mathbf{m}_s$ and in $\mathbf{x}_s$ for some such partition of $\mathbf{a}_s$. Hence there exists a monetary aggregator ("category utility") function $M$, consumer-goods aggregator function $X$, and a utility function $u^*$ such that

$$u(\mathbf{a}_s, \mathbf{x}_s) = u^*(M(\mathbf{m}_s), \bar{\mathbf{m}}_s, X(\mathbf{x}_s)). \tag{2.5}$$

We assume that the terminal-period utility function in the case of a finite planning horizon is correspondingly weakly separable, so that

$$u_T(\mathbf{a}_s, \mathbf{x}_s, A_s) = u_T^*(M(\mathbf{m}_s), \bar{\mathbf{m}}_s, X(\mathbf{x}_s), A_s).$$

Then it follows that the exact monetary aggregate, measuring the welfare acquired from consuming the services of $\mathbf{m}_s$, is

$$M_s = M(\mathbf{m}_s). \tag{2.6}$$

We define the dimension of $\mathbf{m}_s$ to be $k_1$ and the dimension of $\bar{\mathbf{m}}_s$ to be $k_2$, so that $k = k_1 + k_2$.

It is clear that equation (2.6) does define the exact monetary aggregate in the welfare sense, since $M_s$ measures the consumer's subjective evaluation of the services received from holding $\mathbf{m}_s$. However, it also can be shown that (2.6) defines the exact monetary aggregate in the aggregation-theoretic sense. In particular, the stochastic process $M_s$, $s \geq t$, contains all the information about $\mathbf{m}_s$ needed by the consumer in order optimally to solve the rest of his or her decision problem. This conclusion is based upon the next theorem, which we will call the consumer's aggregation theorem.

---

[3] This constraint is common in infinite-horizon stochastic control problems. See e.g. Sargent (1987, pp. 31, 33).

Let

$$I'_s = I_s + \sum_{i=1}^{k_1} [(1+r_{i,s-1})p^*_{s-1}m_{i,s-1} - p^*_s m_{is}],$$

and let

$$S'(s) = \Big\{ (\bar{m}_s, \mathbf{x}_s, A_s) \in Y:$$

$$\sum_{i=1}^{n} p_{is}x_{is} = \sum_{i=1}^{k_2}[(1+\bar{r}_{i,s-1})p^*_{s-1}\bar{m}_{i,s-1} - p^*_s \bar{m}_{is}]$$

$$+ (1+R_{s-1})p^*_{s-1}A_{s-1} - p^*_s A_s + I'_s \Big\}, \qquad (2.7)$$

where $Y'$ is the projection of $Y$ onto the $(n+k_2+2)$-dimensional subspace having $(\bar{m}_s, \mathbf{x}_s, A_s)$ as components. Let the deterministic point $(\mathbf{a}^*_t, \mathbf{x}^*_t, A^*_t)$ and the stochastic process $(\mathbf{a}^*_s, \mathbf{x}^*_s, A^*_s)$, $s \geq t+1$, solve Problem 1 (or Problem 2, if $T = \infty$). Consider the following decision problems, which are conditional upon prior knowledge of the aggregate process $M^*_s = M(\mathbf{m}^*_s)$, although not upon the component processes $\mathbf{m}^*_s$.

**Problem 1a.** Choose the deterministic point $(\bar{m}_t, \mathbf{x}_t, A_t)$ and the stochastic process $(\bar{m}_s, \mathbf{x}_s, A_s)$, $s = t+1, \ldots, t+T$, to maximize

$$u^*(M^*_t, \bar{m}_t, \mathbf{x}_t) + E_t \Bigg[ \sum_{s=t+1}^{t+T-1} \Big(\frac{1}{1+\xi}\Big)^{s-t} u^*(M^*_s, \bar{m}_s, \mathbf{x}_s)$$

$$+ \Big(\frac{1}{1+\xi}\Big)^T u^*_T(M^*_T, \bar{m}_s, \mathbf{x}_s, A_s) \Bigg] \qquad (2.8)$$

subject to $(\bar{m}_s, \mathbf{x}_s, A_s) \in S'(s)$ for $s = t, \ldots, t+T$, with the process $M^*_s$ given for $s \geq t$.

**Problem 2a.** Choose the deterministic point $(\bar{m}_t, \mathbf{x}_t, A_t)$ and the stochastic process $(\bar{m}_s, \mathbf{x}_s, A_s)$, $s = t+1, \ldots, \infty$, to maximize

$$u^*(M^*_t, \bar{m}_t, \mathbf{x}_t) + E_t \Bigg[ \sum_{s=t+1}^{\infty} \Big(\frac{1}{1+\xi}\Big)^{s-t} u^*(M^*_s, \bar{m}_s, \mathbf{x}_s) \Bigg] \qquad (2.9)$$

subject to $(\bar{m}_s, \mathbf{x}_s, A_s) \in S'(s)$ for $s \geq t$, and also subject to

$$\lim_{s \to \infty} E_t \Big(\frac{1}{1+\xi}\Big)^{s-t} A_s = 0,$$

with the process $M^*_s$ given for $s \geq t$.

**Theorem 1** (consumer's aggregation theorem). *Let the deterministic point* $(\mathbf{m}_t, \bar{m}_t, \mathbf{x}_t, A_t)$ *and the stochastic process* $(\mathbf{m}_s, \bar{m}_s, \mathbf{x}_s, A_s)$, $s = t+1, \ldots,$

$t+T$, solve Problem 1. Then the deterministic point $(\bar{\mathbf{m}}_t, \mathbf{x}_t, A_t)$ and the stochastic process $(\bar{\mathbf{m}}_s, \mathbf{x}_s, A_s)$, $s = t+1, \ldots, t+T$, will solve Problem 1a conditional upon $M_s^* = M(\mathbf{m}_s)$ for $s = t, \ldots, t+T$. Similarly, let the deterministic point $(\mathbf{m}_t, \bar{\mathbf{m}}_t, \mathbf{x}_t, A_t)$ and the stochastic process $(\mathbf{m}_s, \bar{\mathbf{m}}_s, \mathbf{x}_s, A_s)$, $s \geq t+1$, solve Problem 2. Then the deterministic point $(\bar{\mathbf{m}}_t, \mathbf{x}_t, A_t)$ and the stochastic process $(\bar{\mathbf{m}}_s, \mathbf{x}_s, A_s)$, $s \geq t+1$, will solve Problem 2a conditional upon $M_s^* = M(\mathbf{m}_s)$ for $s \geq t$.

Clearly this aggregation theorem, proved in the appendix, applies not only when $M_s$ is produced by voluntary behavior but also when the $M_s$ process is exogenously imposed upon the consumer, as through a perfectly inelastic supply function for $M_s$ imposed by central-bank policy. In that case, Problems 1a and 2a describe optimal behavior by the consumer in the remaining variables. Since $(\bar{\mathbf{m}}_s, \mathbf{x}_s, A_s)$ are not assumed to be weakly separable from $M_s$, the information about $M_s$ is needed in the solution of Problems 1a and 2a for the processes $(\bar{\mathbf{m}}_s, \mathbf{x}_s, A_s)$. For example, the marginal rate of substitution between labor and goods may depend upon the value of $M_s$. Alternatively, information about the simple-sum aggregate over the components of $\mathbf{m}_s$ is of no use in solving either Problem 1a or 2a unless the monetary aggregator function $M$ happens to be a simple sum. In other words, the simple-sum aggregate contains useful information about behavior only if the components of $\mathbf{m}_s$ are perfect substitutes in identical ratios (linear aggregation with *equal* coefficients).

The implications of Theorem 1 for monetary policy are most clearly indicated by the recursive Bellman solution of Problem 2a. Since we introduce the Bellman solution in Section 2.3, we leave further discussion of policy to Section 2.4.

## 2.3    The solution procedure

Using Bellman's principle, we can derive the first-order conditions for solving Problems 1 and 2.

We concentrate on the infinite–planning horizon Problem 2, rather than on the finite–planning horizon Problem 2, because the contingency-plan functions ("feedback rules") that solve Problem 1 are time-dependent, whereas – in the case of an infinite planning horizon – those solution functions are independent of time. Time enters only through the variables that enter those equations as arguments, rather than through time shifting of the functions themselves.

We begin by solving the budget constraint in equation (2.1) for the quantity of an arbitrary consumer good, $x_{js}$. We then use the resulting rearranged constraint to eliminate $x_{js}$ from the intertemporal utility function in Problem 2 for all $s \geq t$. For notational simplicity, we let $j = 1$. Let $\mathbf{z}_{1s} = (\mathbf{a}_s, A_s)$. To apply Bellman's method, we must define the control and state variables. Define the control variables during period $s$ to be $\mathbf{z}_s = (\mathbf{z}_{1s}, \hat{\mathbf{x}}_s)$, where $\hat{\mathbf{x}}_s = (x_{2s}, ..., x_{ns})$; similarly define $\hat{\mathbf{p}}_s = (p_{2s}, ..., p_{ns})$. We define the state variables during period $s$ to be $\sigma_s = (\sigma_{1s}, \phi_s)$, where the price and income state variables are $\phi_s = (\hat{\mathbf{p}}_s, p_s^*, p_{s-1}^*, R_{s-1}, \rho_{s-1}, \mathbf{I}_s)/p_{1s}$, and where $\sigma_{1s} = (\mathbf{a}_{s-1}, A_{s-1})$.

Having eliminated the budget constraint by substitution as just described, Problem 2 can be rewritten as follows.

**Problem 2b.** Choose the deterministic point $\mathbf{z}_t$ and the stochastic process $\mathbf{z}_s$, $s = t+1, ..., \infty$, to maximize

$$u(\mathbf{z}_t, \sigma_t) + E_t \left[ \sum_{s=t+1}^{\infty} \left( \frac{1}{1+\xi} \right)^{s-t} u(\mathbf{z}_s, \sigma_s) \right], \tag{2.10}$$

subject to

$$\sigma_{1,s+1} = \mathbf{z}_{1s} \tag{2.11}$$

and

$$\lim_{s \to \infty} E_t \left( \frac{1}{1+\xi} \right)^{s-t} A_s = 0, \tag{2.12}$$

with $\sigma_t$ given.

Equations (2.11) are the transition equations, $\sigma_{s+1} = \mathbf{g}(\mathbf{z}_s, \sigma_s)$, providing the evolution of future state variables as functions of the controls and the current state. That the current state $\sigma_s$ does not appear on the right-hand side of the transition equations permits a simplification in the derivation of the Euler equations. The stochastic evolution of the remaining state variables is treated as given by the price-taking consumer. We assume that the $\phi_s$ process is Markovian. We define $F(\phi_{s+1}|\phi_s)$ to be the transition function of the $\phi_s$ process, where the transition function of a Markov process is the conditional distribution of the value of the process at $t$, conditional upon its lagged value at $t-1$.

The recursive Bellman structure of the problem is clear, and hence we can write down the Bellman equation directly. To that end, we define the value function $V(\sigma_t)$ to be the maximized value of intertemporal utility, (2.10), subject to (2.11) and (2.12), with $\sigma_t$ given; hence $V(\sigma_t)$ is the optimized value of the objective function in decision Problem 2b. The Bellman recursion equation is then

$$V(\sigma_s) = \max_{z_s}\left\{u(z_s, \sigma_s) + E_t\left[\left(\frac{1}{1+\xi}\right)V(\sigma_{s+1}) \mid \sigma_s\right] : \sigma_{1,s+1} = z_{1s}\right\}$$

$$= \max_{z_s}\left\{u(z_s, \sigma_s) + E_t\left[\left(\frac{1}{1+\xi}\right)V(\phi_{s+1}, \sigma_{1,s+1}) \mid \sigma_s\right] : \sigma_{1,s+1} = z_{1s}\right\}$$

$$= \max_{z_s}\left\{u(z_s, \sigma_s) + E_t\left[\left(\frac{1}{1+\xi}\right)V(\phi_{s+1}, z_{1s}) \mid \sigma_s\right]\right\}$$

$$= \max_{z_s}\left\{u(z_s, \sigma_s) + \int\left[\left(\frac{1}{1+\xi}\right)V(\phi_{s+1}, z_{1s})\right]dF(\phi_{s+1} \mid \phi_s)\right\} \qquad (2.13)$$

with $\sigma_s$ given (see e.g. Sargent 1987, p. 30).

To solve Problem 2b by Bellman's method, equation (2.13) would be solved subject to (2.12) recursively starting at $s = t$ with $\sigma_t$ given. The solution at each iteration determines the state for the next iteration. The result is the following system of contingency plans ("feedback rules") that solve Problem 2b for the control variables $(a_s, A_s, \hat{x}_s)$ for all $s \geq t$:

$$(a_s, A_s, \hat{x}_s) = h(a_{s-1}, A_{s-1}, \phi_s). \qquad (2.14)$$

That is, $z_s = h(\sigma_s)$.

Since we do not know the form of the value function $V$, we cannot solve Bellman's recursion in closed form for the optimal contingency plans. Instead we use Bellman's equation to solve for the first-order conditions. The method is straightforward. Let

$$\tilde{V}(z_s, \sigma_s) = u(z_s, \sigma_s) + E_t\left[\left(\frac{1}{1+\xi}\right)V(\phi_{s+1}, z_{1s}) \mid \sigma_s\right]. \qquad (2.15)$$

Then the Bellman recursion equation (2.13) can be written as

$$V(\sigma_s) = \max_{z_s}\{\tilde{V}(z_s, \sigma_s) : \sigma_s \text{ given}\}. \qquad (2.16)$$

Hence it follows that, for interior solutions, the solution contingency plans (2.14) must satisfy the following first-order conditions

$$\frac{\partial \tilde{V}(z_s, \sigma_s)}{\partial z_s} = 0. \qquad (2.17)$$

From equations (2.15) and (2.17), it follows that

$$\frac{\partial u(z_s, \sigma_s)}{\partial z_s} + E_t\left[\left(\frac{1}{1+\xi}\right)\frac{\partial V(\phi_{s+1}, z_{1s})}{\partial z_{1s}}\bigg| \sigma_s\right] = 0. \qquad (2.18)$$

However, observe that the unknown function $V$ is in equation (2.18). The following procedure can be used to eliminate that unknown function. First, observe from the transition equations (2.11) that $\sigma_{1,s+1} = z_{1s}$, so that

$$\frac{\partial V(\phi_{s+1}, \mathbf{z}_{1s})}{\partial \mathbf{z}_{1s}} = \frac{\partial V(\phi_{s+1}, \sigma_{1,s+1})}{\partial \sigma_{1,s+1}}. \tag{2.19}$$

To evaluate the right-hand side of equation (2.19), we substitute the solution contingency plans, $\mathbf{z}_s = \mathbf{h}(\sigma_s)$, into equation (2.13) to eliminate the control variables, and then differentiate (2.13) with respect to $\sigma_s$ to acquire the Benveniste and Scheinkman equations. As is well known, the Benveniste and Scheinkman equations do not contain the unknown function $V$ when $\partial \mathbf{g}/\partial \sigma_s = \mathbf{0}$, as is the case with our very simple transition equations $\sigma_{1,s+1} = \mathbf{z}_{1s}$.[4] Hence equations (2.19) can be substituted into (2.18) to acquire the Euler equations for the control variables.

The Euler equations that will be of most use to us are those for monetary assets. Replacing $X(\mathbf{x}_t)$ by $c_t$ in $u$, those Euler equations become:

$$E_t\left[\frac{\partial u}{\partial m_{it}} - \rho \frac{p_t^*(R_t - r_{it})}{p_{t+1}^*} \frac{\partial u}{\partial c_{t+1}}\right] = 0 \tag{2.20}$$

for $i = 1, \ldots, k_1$, where $c_t = X(\mathbf{x}_t)$ is the exact quantity aggregate over $\mathbf{x}_t$, and $p_t^*$ is its dual exact price aggregate.[5] Similarly, we can acquire the Euler equation for the consumer goods aggregate $c_t$, rather than for each of its components. The resulting Euler equation for $c_t$ is

$$E_t\left[\frac{\partial u}{\partial c_t} - \rho \frac{p_t^*(1+R_t)}{p_{t+1}^*} \frac{\partial u}{\partial c_{t+1}}\right] = 0. \tag{2.21}$$

## 2.4 Deceptive simplifications

After inspection of the expected utility function in either Problem 1 or 2, one is tempted to conclude that an easy way may exist of dealing with the challenging quantity aggregation problems posed by the model. In particular, the fact that the level of current-period utility, $u(\mathbf{a}_t, \mathbf{x}_t) = u^*(M(\mathbf{m}_s), \bar{\mathbf{m}}_s, \mathbf{x}_s)$, is known with certainty suggests that a method may exist for using perfect certainty methods for tracking $M = M(\mathbf{m}_s)$ without any approximation error at all, as perhaps by a Divisia index line integral in continuous time. But that appearance is deceiving.

There would appear to be two easy ways out of the risk-aversion complication. The first would be the approach derived by Barnett (1980) in the perfect certainty case. By that means, the sequence of constraints in

[4] See Sargent (1987, pp. 21, 31) regarding the Benveniste and Scheinkman equations when $\partial \mathbf{g}/\partial \sigma_s = \mathbf{0}$. See Sargent (1987, p. 31) for the general form of the resulting Euler equations. Alternatively, the Euler equations could be derived by variational methods; see e.g. Stokey and Lucas (1989, sec. 4.5).

[5] Assuming that $X$ is linearly homogeneous, the exact-price aggregator function is the unit cost function.

Problem 1 is collapsed into a single intertemporal wealth constraint containing discounted prices and user costs. The intertemporal decision is then solved in two stages. The second stage is maximization of $u(\mathbf{a}_t, \mathbf{x}_t)$ subject to a current-period expenditure constraint, in which monetary services flows are valued by their current-period user costs. That second-stage decision is in the standard form used in the literature on index number theory. Hence it would appear that we have access to the existing literature on index number theory under perfect certainty.

While this procedure works in the perfect certainty case, it is not applicable under risk aversion. The reason is that the current-period user costs derived by Barnett (1978) for the services of monetary asset $a_{it}$ are $p_t^*(R_t - \rho_{it})/(1 + R_t)$. In Problem 1, however, $R_t$ and $\rho_{it}$ are not known during period $i$ because interest is paid at the end of the period. Hence the second-stage budget constraints are random constraints containing random user costs. But the objective function in the second-stage decision is utility, not expected utility. Since it is impossible for binding deterministic choices of current monetary asset and goods purchases to satisfy a random constraint, Barnett's (1980) method of decomposing the intertemporal decision into a two-stage budgeting procedure does not apply to our current model.

Another particularly enticing simplification is as follows. Recall that constraint (2.1) is entirely deterministic when $s = t$. Hence it may appear that we can maximize $u(\mathbf{a}_t, \mathbf{x}_t)$ subject to (2.1) with $s = t$, conditional upon optimal values of any variables not selected within that decision. In this manner, all aspects of the decision are deterministic. The utility function is deterministic and the constraint is deterministic. Again it may appear that we could find a means of producing a Divisia index that will track $M = M(\mathbf{m}_s)$ without any error due to risk aversion.

To see that this will not work, consider the last stage of a Bellman recursive solution to the decision problem. That final stage will indeed contain equation (2.1) with $s = t$ as its sole constraint. However, the objective function will not be $u(\mathbf{a}_t, \mathbf{x}_t)$ alone but rather the sum of $u(\mathbf{a}_t, \mathbf{x}_t)$ and the Bellman recursion function. In the final stage of the Bellman solution, that recursion function will include $(\mathbf{a}_t, A_t)$ as arguments. Hence the choice of $\mathbf{a}_t$ will affect both terms of the objective function, and not just the initial $u(\mathbf{a}_t, \mathbf{x}_t)$ term. As a result, blockwise weak separability of $\mathbf{a}_t$ within $u(\mathbf{a}_t, \mathbf{x}_t)$ would not be sufficient to permit us to use the conventional derivation of the Divisia index as a means of tracking the economic monetary aggregate.

## 2.5    Monetary policy

With the Bellman solution at hand, we are in a position to give further consideration to the policy implications of monetary aggregation in light of $M(\mathbf{m}_s)$, the *Theoretical aggregate*. Hence we now return to Theorem 1 and Problem 2a. Clearly, the Bellman equation can be written in a manner analogous to that done for Problem 2. The only changes are that the controls now are $(\bar{\mathbf{m}}_s, \hat{\mathbf{x}}_s, A_s)$, $s = t, \ldots, \infty$, and the state variables are $(\bar{\mathbf{m}}_{s-1}, A_{s-1}, \phi_s, M_s^*)$, where $\phi_s = (\hat{\mathbf{p}}_s, p_s^*, p_{s-1}^*, R_{s-1}, \bar{\mathbf{r}}_{s-1}, \mathbf{I}_s')/p_{1s}$. Hence the solution contingency plans solving Problem 2a are of the form

$$(\bar{\mathbf{m}}_s, \hat{\mathbf{x}}_s, A_s) = \mathbf{h}(\bar{\mathbf{m}}_{s-1}, A_{s-1}, \phi_s, M_s^*), \qquad (2.22)$$

where all controls and state variables are deterministic for $s = t$.

The appearance of $M_s^*$ as a state variable has interesting policy implications. If $M_s^*$ is used as an indicator in the conduct of monetary policy then clearly the monetary aggregate will indeed contain information about $(\bar{\mathbf{m}}_s, \hat{\mathbf{x}}_s, A_s)$, and thereby about the final targets of monetary policy both in goods and labor markets. Alternatively, suppose that such policy instruments as the monetary base are used to target the equilibrium path of $M_s^*$ as an intermediate target of policy. Assuming that the instruments are used in a manner not subject to the Lucas critique, as for example through an open loop policy, the equilibrium stochastic process for $M_s^*$ can be influenced by policy. Under our assumption of rational expectations, economic agents will know about the policy rule and hence about the targeted equilibrium process for $M_s^*$. The consumer then can solve Problem 2a to acquire the optimal solution for the remaining variables conditional upon the targeted process for $M_s^*$.

We see that only $M_s^*$ can play these roles if policy operates through a monetary target or indicator. The simple-sum aggregate, which does not appear as a control in $\mathbf{h}$, can serve neither role. In fact the only information from the portfolio $\mathbf{m}_s^*$ that is useful in solving Problem 2a is $M_s^* = M(\mathbf{m}_s^*)$, since $\mathbf{m}_s^*$ enters the contingency plans $\mathbf{h}$ only through $M$. Analogous results for firm demand for monetary services are derived in the appendix.

## 3    The risk-neutral case

Under risk neutrality, the decision of each of the agents modeled in this section can be solved in two stages. In the first stage, expenditure is budgeted to aggregates. In the second stage, the budgeted expenditure on each aggregate is allocated over its components. For details of the two-stage budgeting solutions, see Barnett (1987). Only the contemporaneous second-stage decision is relevant to our purposes. For each of our economic agents, the contemporaneous second-stage decision is to maximize the current-period service flow produced from the components of the aggregate, subject to the budgeted constraint on current-period expenditure on those components. The service-flow objective function is the agent's separable aggregator function over the components. Because that second-stage decision has the same form for firms and consumers (aside from a change in notation for variables and functions), we present it only for one economic agent, the consumer.

In the perfect certainty case, Barnett (1978, 1980) proved that the nominal user cost of the services of $m_{it}$ is $\pi_{it}$, where

$$\pi_{it} = p^* \frac{R_t - r_{it}}{1 + R_t}. \tag{3.1}$$

The correspondingly real user cost is $\pi_{it}/p^*$. In the risk-neutral case, the user cost formulas are the same as in the perfect certainty case, but with the interest rates replaced by their expected values. The second-stage decision may be summarized as follows.

**Problem 3.** Choose $\mathbf{m}_t \geq 0$ to maximize $M(\mathbf{m}_t)$ subject to $\mathbf{m}_t' \pi_t = E_t$, where $E_t$ is total expenditure budgeted to $\mathbf{m}_t$ in the first stage.

It can be shown that the solution value of the exact monetary aggregate $M(\mathbf{m}_t)$ can be tracked without error (see e.g. Barnett 1983) by the Divisia index:

$$d \log M_t = \sum_{i=1}^{k_1} s_{it} d \log m_{it}, \tag{3.2}$$

where the flawless tracking ability of the index in the risk-neutral case holds regardless of the form of the unknown aggregator function $M$. However, under risk aversion the ability of equation (3.2) to track $M(\mathbf{m}_t)$ is compromised, and the rate at which that tracking ability deteriorates is unknown as the degree of risk aversion increases above zero. We can investigate the magnitude of that error by econometrically estimating $M(\mathbf{m}_t)$.

## 4    A generalization

That the Divisia index tracks exactly under perfect certainty is well known. However, we show in this section that neither perfect certainty nor risk neutrality are needed for exact tracking of the Divisia index; only contemporaneous prices and interest rates need be known. Future interest rates and prices need not be known, and risk-averse behavior need not be excluded. The proof is as follows.

Assume that $R_t$, $p_t^*$, and $\mathbf{r}_t$ are known at time $t$, although their future values are stochastic. Then the Euler equations (2.20) for $\mathbf{m}_t$ are

$$\frac{\partial u}{\partial m_{it}} - \rho p_t^* (R_t - r_{it}) E_t \left[ \frac{1}{p_{t+1}^*} \frac{\partial u}{\partial c_{t+1}} \right] = 0 \tag{4.1}$$

for $i = 1, ..., k_1$. Similarly, the Euler equation (2.21) for aggregate consumption $c_t$ of goods becomes

$$\frac{\partial u}{\partial c_t} - \rho p_t^*(1+R_t)E_t\left[\frac{1}{p_{t+1}^*}\frac{\partial u}{\partial c_{t+1}}\right] = 0. \tag{4.2}$$

Eliminating $E_t[(1/p_{t+1}^*)(\partial u/\partial c_{t+1})]$ between (4.1) and (4.2), we acquire

$$\frac{\partial u}{\partial m_{it}} = \frac{(R_t - r_{it})}{1+R_t}\frac{\partial u}{\partial c_t}. \tag{4.3}$$

However, by the assumption of weak separability of $u$ in $\mathbf{m}_t$ we have

$$\frac{\partial u}{\partial m_{it}} = \frac{\partial u}{\partial M_t}\frac{\partial M}{\partial m_{it}}, \tag{4.4}$$

where $M_t = M(\mathbf{m}_t)$ is the exact monetary aggregate that we seek to track. Substituting (4.3) into (4.4) and using (3.10), we find that

$$\frac{\partial M}{\partial m_{it}} = \pi_{it}\frac{\partial u/\partial c_t}{\partial u/\partial M_t}. \tag{4.5}$$

Now substitute (4.5) into the total differential of $M$ to acquire

$$dM(\mathbf{m}_t) = \frac{\partial u/\partial c_t}{\partial u/\partial M_t}\sum_{i=1}^{k_1}\pi_{it}dm_{it}. \tag{4.6}$$

But since $M$ is assumed to be linearly homogeneous, we have Euler's equation for linearly homogeneous functions. Substituting (4.5) into Euler's equation yields

$$M(\mathbf{m}_t) = \frac{\partial u/\partial c_t}{\partial u/\partial M_t}\sum_{j=1}^{k_1}\pi_{jt}m_{jt}. \tag{4.7}$$

Dividing (4.6) by (4.7) we acquire (3.2), which is the Divisia index. Hence the exact tracking property of the Divisia index is compromised neither by uncertainty regarding future interest rates and prices nor by risk aversion. Nevertheless, this assumption is not trivial, since current-period interest rates are not paid until the *end* of the current period.

Furthermore, all of the usual theorems regarding the Divisia index remain valid under uncertainty with respect to future interest rates and prices. This can be seen by dividing (4.3) by itself for two different values of $i$ to acquire the marginal rate of substitution between $m_{it}$ and $m_{jt}$:

$$\frac{\partial M/\partial m_{it}}{\partial M/\partial m_{jt}} = \frac{\pi_{it}}{\pi_{jt}}.$$

It immediately follows that the first-order conditions for solving Prob-3 are satisfied, and hence the usual properties and theorems regarding the Divisia index are relevant.

## 5     Strong separability in currency

Strong separability in currency produces an interesting special case of the Divisia index. In particular, that special case produces the CE ("currency equivalence") index advocated by Hutt (1963, p. 92, footnote), Rotemberg (1991), and Rotemberg, Driscoll, and Poterba (1991). In this section, we prove that the CE index is a fully nested special case of the Divisia index.

As demonstrated in Section 2.2, the derivation of the Divisia monetary index requires the assumption of blockwise weak separability of monetary assets from other goods and assets in the utility function, so that an exact monetary aggregate exists. In addition to that fundamental existence condition, we also need perfect certainty (or risk neutrality) with respect to contemporaneous current-period prices and interest rates, but not necessarily with respect to future prices and interest rates. Although for convenience we have assumed linear homogeneity of the monetary asset category utility function $M$, that assumption is not required. If $M$ is not linearly homogeneous, then $M$ is not the monetary asset aggregator function; rather, the distance function is, and the Divisia index then tracks the distance function. See Barnett (1987, sects. 7, 8).

As we now show, the derivation of the CE index requires the category utility function $M$ to be linearly homogeneous itself and also to be strongly separable in currency. Both of those assumptions are empirically implausible, but the CE index does produce a potentially useful special case under certain circumstances. In particular, the CE index is completely linear and hence can be aggregated over economic agents more easily than the Divisia index. The CE index also can be used to measure the stock of money, rather than the flow of monetary services, as has been shown by Barnett (1991).

Under these assumptions of linear homogeneity and strong separability, the monetary asset category utility function over $m_t$ can be written $M(\mathbf{m}_t) = \phi m_{1t} + h(m_{2t}, \ldots, m_{k_1 t})$, where $\phi$ is an unknown constant positive parameter and $h$ is the aggregator function over noncurrency monetary assets. Setting $\phi = 1$ is a harmless positive linear transformation of the category utility function $M$, and hence we shall follow Rotemberg et al. (1991) by normalizing $\phi$ at 1 so that $M(\mathbf{m}_t) = m_{1t} + h(m_{2t}, \ldots, m_{k_1 t})$. Observe that the marginal utility $\partial M / \partial m_{jt}$ is independent of currency holding $m_{1t}$, and that $\partial M / \partial m_{1t} = 1$ independent of the holding of other assets $m_{2t}, \ldots, m_{k_1 t}$. These implications of the CE assumptions are empirically most unappealing, but the implied form of $M(\mathbf{m}_t)$ – as a simple sum of $m_{1t}$ and of the exact aggregate over other monetary assets $h(m_{2t}, \ldots, m_{k_1 t})$ – clearly produces the currency equivalent interpretation. In particular, the exact aggregate over other monetary assets is required by the assumed form of $M$ to be a perfect substitute for currency, so that $M(\mathbf{m}_t)$ is the sum of currency and a perfect substitute for currency.

We now further explore the implications of the condition $\partial M/\partial m_{1t} = 1$. In particular, we multiply through by $m_{1t}/M(\mathbf{m}_t)$ to derive

$$\frac{\partial \log M_t}{\partial \log m_{1t}} = \frac{m_{1t}}{M_t}. \tag{5.1}$$

We shall now see what happens to the Divisia monetary index under the CE restriction (5.1). From the Divisia index formula (3.2), we know that

$$\frac{\partial \log M_t}{\partial \log m_{1t}} = s_{1t}. \tag{5.2}$$

From (5.1) and (5.2) we have that $M_t = m_{1t}/s_{1t} = (\mathbf{m}'_t\boldsymbol{\pi}_t/m_{1t}\pi_{1t})m_{1t}$, so that

$$M_t = \sum_{i=1}^{k_1} \frac{(R_t - r_{it})}{R_t} m_{it}, \tag{5.3}$$

which is the CE index.

Clearly, the CE index is acquired as a special case by imposing two very strong and entirely unnecessary assumptions upon the Divisia index. Furthermore, the CE index possesses a very undesirable property, which to my knowledge is not possessed by any reputable index number: it is not locally linearly homogeneous. In other words, even if all components are growing at exactly the same rate, the CE index itself may not be growing at that rate. In fact, the growth rate of this index could even have a different sign from the sign of the growth rate of all its components!

This can be seen by taking the total differential of (5.3) and dividing through by (5.3) to obtain

$$d \log M_t = \sum_{i=1}^{k_1} s_{it} d \log m_{it} + \sum_{i=1}^{k_1} s_{it} d \log \pi_{it}. \tag{5.4}$$

The problem is evident by comparing (5.4) with the Divisia index (3.2). In the Divisia index, if $d \log m_{it} = \lambda$ for all $i$, then $d \log M_t = \lambda$, since

$$\sum_{i=1}^{k_1} s_{it} = 1.$$

Hence the Divisia index gets the right answer in the one case in which everyone would agree on the right answer. In contrast, the CE index will get the wrong answer in that case, unless the second term of (5.4) is exactly equal to zero, where that second term is the Divisia user cost aggregate for monetary services. It is small consolation that (5.4) would exactly track linearly homogeneous $M(\mathbf{m}_t) = m_{1t} + h(m_{2t}, ..., m_{k_1t})$, if that were exactly the utility function over $\mathbf{m}_t$ and if the Euler equations were exactly satisfied by the data.

Nevertheless, the CE index – unlike the Divisia index – is linear in the levels of the component monetary assets. Hence aggregation over economic agents is simple.[6] In addition, Barnett (1991) has shown that the CE index is the discounted present value of expenditure on the services of the Divisia aggregate under stationary expectations. This result permits the CE index to be interpreted as the stock aggregate implied by the Divisia flow aggregate under stationary expectations. In fact, such an interpretation provides a resolution of the troublesome issue raised by the non-homogeneity of equation (5.4), since (5.4) can be written as

$$d \log Q_t = d \log[M(\mathbf{m}_t)\Pi(\pi_t)],$$

where $Q_t$ is the CE index, $M(\mathbf{m}_t)$ is the Divisia quantity index, and $\Pi(\pi_t)$ is the Divisia user cost index. The result is Barnett's (1991) interpretation as user cost–evaluated expenditure on the services of $\mathbf{m}_t$. Under stationary expectations, the same result is evaluated after discounting the future stream of such expenditures over an infinite horizon to produce a stock aggregate.

If the CE aggregate is thereby interpreted as $M(\mathbf{m}_t)\Pi(\pi_t)$ then we should not expect the aggregate to have the same properties that we require for an index measuring $M(\mathbf{m}_t)$, and hence (5.4) should not bother us. Furthermore, the ease of aggregation over consumers should not surprise us, since CE index values are given in units of expenditure, rather than units of quantity demanded.

## 6    Conclusions

In recent years, there has been much progress in the development of aggregation and index number theory. The two theories have become unified by the availability of theorems proving the order of approximation of certain index numbers to the exact aggregator functions of economic aggregation theory. In addition, the relevance of that literature to monetary aggregation has been established since the derivation of the user cost formula for monetary services has been available. However, virtually the entire literature on index number theory, and most of the theory on aggregation over goods, was produced under the assumption of perfect certainty. Much research is needed on duality theory and functional structure

---

[6] With the Divisia index, formal aggregation usually requires subaggregation over similar demographic groups followed by Divisia aggregation over the groups. See Barnett (1987, sect. 9) and Barnett and Serletis (1990). Hence data is required for asset holdings by those demographic groups, unless the assumptions of Gorman or Muellbauer (see Barnett 1981, apx. B1.2) for the existence of a representative economic agent are satisfied.

and on nonparametric statistical approximations to aggregator functions under risk. We provide one such new aggregation theorem for consumers and for firms under risk. Our theorem demonstrates the role in aggregation theory of the Theoretical aggregate, and hence captures the potential usefulness of the Theoretical aggregate in modeling and in policy. We produce the theorem in a form that is immediately applicable to monetary aggregation.

The aggregation theory developed in this paper demonstrates that under rational expectations the Theoretical aggregate can be used either as an indicator or as an intermediate target. If used as an intermediate target, the Theoretical monetary aggregate becomes a state variable in the contingency plans ("feedback rules") solving the economic agent's decision problem, which we formulate as a recursive Bellman iteration. Hence if the Theoretical monetary aggregate is used as an intermediate target, its solution process will predictably influence behavior in other markets through the role of the intermediate target as a state variable in economic agents' contingency plans. The simple-sum aggregate, on the other hand, cannot be used as an intermediate target or as an indicator, since it plays no role in the behavior of any economic agent regardless of whether or not the aggregate is targeted. Without information on the Theoretical monetary aggregate, economic behavior remains conditional upon information regarding every disaggregated monetary asset's market. That dependency is not altered by the availability of information on any simple-sum monetary aggregate.

Having proved those theorems, we investigate nonparametric statistical index numbers as approximations to the exact Theoretical aggregate. We prove that the Divisia index tracks the exact aggregate without error when the only risk is relative to future prices and interest rates. However, if there is uncertainty and non–risk neutrality relative to contemporaneous interest rates, the Divisia index's exact tracking property is compromised.

### Appendix A: Proof of consumer's aggregation theorem

*Proof of Theorem 1:* Let the deterministic point $(\mathbf{m}_t, \bar{\mathbf{m}}_t, \mathbf{x}_t, A_t)$ and the stochastic process $(\mathbf{m}_s, \bar{\mathbf{m}}_s, \mathbf{x}_s, A_s)$, $s = t+1, \ldots, t+T$, solve Problem 1; but let the deterministic point $(\bar{\mathbf{m}}_t, \mathbf{x}_t, A_t)$ and the stochastic process $(\bar{\mathbf{m}}_s, \mathbf{x}_s, A_s)$, $s = t+1, \ldots, t+T$, *not* solve Problem 1a conditional upon the process $M_s^* = M(\mathbf{m}_s)$ given for $s = t, \ldots, t+T$. Then there exists $(\bar{\bar{\mathbf{m}}}_s, \tilde{\mathbf{x}}_s, \tilde{A}_s) \in S'(s)$, $s = t, \ldots, t+T$, such that (2.8) evaluated at $(\bar{\bar{\mathbf{m}}}_t, \ldots, \bar{\bar{\mathbf{m}}}_{t+T}; \tilde{\mathbf{x}}_t, \ldots, \tilde{\mathbf{x}}_{t+T}; \tilde{A}_{t+T})$ is strictly greater than (2.8) evaluated at $(\bar{\mathbf{m}}_t, \ldots, \bar{\mathbf{m}}_{t+T}; \mathbf{x}_t, \ldots, \mathbf{x}_{t+T}; A_{t+T})$ conditional upon $M_s^* = M(\mathbf{m}_s)$.

Hence (2.3) evaluated at $(\mathbf{m}_t, \ldots, \mathbf{m}_{t+T}; \bar{\bar{\mathbf{m}}}_t, \ldots, \bar{\bar{\mathbf{m}}}_{t+T}; \tilde{\mathbf{x}}_t, \ldots, \tilde{\mathbf{x}}_{t+T}; \tilde{A}_{t+T})$ is strictly greater than (2.3) evaluated at $(\mathbf{m}_t, \ldots, \mathbf{m}_{t+T}; \bar{\mathbf{m}}_t, \ldots, \bar{\mathbf{m}}_{t+T};$

$\mathbf{x}_t, \ldots, \mathbf{x}_{t+T}; A_{t+T})$. But since $(\bar{\bar{\mathbf{m}}}_s, \tilde{\mathbf{x}}_s, \tilde{A}_s)$, $s = t+1, \ldots, t+T$, is feasible for Problem 1a conditional upon $M_s = M(\mathbf{m}_s)$, it follows that $(\mathbf{m}_s, \bar{\bar{\mathbf{m}}}_s, \tilde{\mathbf{x}}_s, \tilde{A}_s)$ is feasible for Problem 1; hence our assumption that $(\mathbf{m}_s, \bar{\bar{\mathbf{m}}}_s, \mathbf{x}_s, A_s)$, $s = t, \ldots, t+t$, solves Problem 1 is contradicted. The analogous proof by contradiction applies to Problem 2a.                                    $\square$

### Appendix B: Demand for monetary assets by manufacturing firms

### B.1    *The model*

Manufacturing firms also hold portfolios of monetary assets. The firm is assumed to maximize the expected present value of its profit flow subject to its technology. Although monetary services may enter the elementary decision only through constraints, there does exist a derived production function that contains monetary assets; see Barnett (1987) and Fischer (1974). We begin with that derived technology. The firm's intertemporal technology over the $T$-period planning horizon can be described by the transformation function

$$W(\delta_t, \ldots, \delta_{t+T}; \epsilon_t, \ldots, \epsilon_{t+T}; \kappa_t, \ldots, \kappa_{t+T}; \lambda_t, \ldots, \lambda_{t+T}) = 0,$$

where

$\delta_s$ = vector of planned production of $n$ outputs during period $s$;

$\epsilon_s$ = vector of planned real balances of $k$ monetary assets held during period $s$;

$\kappa_s$ = vector of planned use of $\bar{k}$ other factors during period $s$.

The transformation function $W$ is assumed to be strictly quasiconvex in $\delta_t, \ldots, \delta_{t+T}; \epsilon_t, \ldots, \epsilon_{t+T}; \kappa_t, \ldots, \kappa_{t+T}$, increasing in $\delta_s$, and decreasing in $\epsilon_s$ and in $\kappa_s$. As indicated, we can incorporate $(\lambda_t, \ldots, \lambda_{t+T})$ as stochastic Markov shocks. As with the consumer, we assume that current interest rates and future prices are random.

The production possibility set of the firm is the closed random set

$$Y = \{(\delta_t, \ldots, \delta_{t+T}; \epsilon_t, \ldots, \epsilon_{t+T}; \kappa_t, \ldots, \kappa_{t+T}) \in Z:$$

$$W(\delta_t, \ldots, \delta_{t+T}; \epsilon_t, \ldots, \epsilon_{t+T}; \kappa_t, \ldots, \kappa_{t+T}; \lambda_t, \ldots, \lambda_{t+T}) = 0\}, \qquad \text{(B.1)}$$

where $Z$ is a compact subset of the $(n+k+\bar{k})T$-dimensional nonnegative orthant. The decision problem for the firm is to select the sequences of factor inputs and produced outputs over the planning horizon to maximize the expected present value of profits subject to the firm's technology constraint $Y$.

The firm's single-period profits during period $s$ are

$$\psi_s = \delta_s' \nu_s - \kappa_s' \zeta_s + \sum_{i=1}^{k}[(1+r_{i,s-1})p_{s-1}^* \epsilon_{i,s-1} - p^* \epsilon_{is}], \qquad (B.2)$$

where

$\nu_s$ = vector of output prices, and

$\zeta_s$ = vector of prices of the factors $\kappa_s$.

The discounted present value of the firm's profit flow during the $T+1$ periods, plus the discounted present value of the firm's monetary asset portfolio at the end of the planning horizon, is

$$\psi^* = \sum_{s=t}^{t+T} \frac{\psi_s}{\theta_s} + \frac{1}{\theta_{t+T+1}} \sum_{i=1}^{k} p_{t+T}^* \epsilon_{i,t+T}(1+r_{i,t+T}),$$

where the discount factor $\theta_s = 1.0$ for $s = t$ and

$$\theta_s = \prod_{a=t}^{s-1}(1+R_a) \quad \text{for } t+1 \le s \le t+T+1.$$

Hence the firm's decision problem is as follows.

**Problem B1.**   Choose $(\delta_t, ..., \delta_{t+T}; \epsilon_t, ..., \epsilon_{t+T}; \kappa_t, ..., \kappa_{t+T})$ to maximize the expectation $E_t(\psi^*)$ subject to $(\delta_t, ..., \delta_{t+T}; \epsilon_t, ..., \epsilon_{t+T}; \kappa_t, ..., \kappa_{t+T}) \in Y$.

In this solution, $(\delta_t, \epsilon_t, \kappa_t)$ are deterministic, since current purchases are binding. The firm's solution (B.2) for optimized current profits also is deterministic, since it contains only lagged interest rates along with current and lagged prices, each of which is known with certainty during period $t$. However, the choices of $(\delta_{t+1}, ..., \delta_{t+T}; \epsilon_{t+1}, ..., \epsilon_{t+T}; \kappa_{t+1}, ..., \kappa_{t+T})$ are random. As a result, $\psi_s$ for $s \ge t+1$ are random. We see that

$$E_t(\psi^*) = \psi_t + E_t\left[\sum_{s=t+1}^{t+T} \frac{\psi_s}{\theta_s} + \frac{1}{\theta_{t+T+1}} \sum_{i=1}^{k} p_{t+T}^* \epsilon_{i,t+T}(1+r_{i,t+T})\right]. \qquad (B.3)$$

## B.2   *Existence of a monetary aggregate for the firm*

To assure the existence of a monetary aggregate for the firm, we partition the vector $\epsilon_s$ of monetary asset quantities so that $\epsilon_s = (\epsilon_{1s}, \bar{\epsilon}_s)$, where $\epsilon_{1s}$ has $k_1$ elements and $\bar{\epsilon}_s$ has $k_2 = k - k_1$ elements. We then assume that the transformation function $W$ is blockwise weakly separable in $\epsilon_{1s}$. Hence there exists a monetary aggregator function $M^f$ and a transformation function $W^*$ such that

$$W(\delta_t, \ldots, \delta_{t+T}; \epsilon_t, \ldots, \epsilon_{t+T}; \kappa_t, \ldots, \kappa_{t+T}; \lambda_t, \ldots, \lambda_{t+T})$$
$$= W^*(\delta_t, \ldots, \delta_{t+T}; M^f(\epsilon_{1t}), \ldots, M^f(\epsilon_{1,t+T});$$
$$\bar{\epsilon}_t, \ldots, \bar{\epsilon}_{t+T}; \kappa_t, \ldots, \kappa_{t+T}; \lambda_t, \ldots, \lambda_{t+T}). \tag{B.4}$$

It follows that the firm's exact monetary aggregate, measuring the service flow received by the firm from the monetary asset portfolio $\epsilon_{1s}$, is

$$M_t^f = M^f(\epsilon_{1s}). \tag{B.5}$$

Note that we assume only that there exists some partition, $\epsilon_s = (\epsilon_{1s}, \bar{\epsilon}_s)$, such that (B.4) holds. Testing for which partition satisfies the weak separability assumption (B.4) is the subject of a growing literature.

As in the consumer case, the fact that equation (B.4) defines the monetary aggregate in the welfare sense is clear. By its definition, $M_t^f$ is the productive service flow perceived to be received by the firm from the portfolio $\epsilon_{1s}$. The following theorem demonstrates that $M_t^f$ is the monetary aggregate in the aggregation-theoretic sense also – that is, in the sense of containing the information needed to permit conditional solution of the rest of the firm's decision problem.

Let $(\delta_t^*, \ldots, \delta_{t+T}^*; \epsilon_t^*, \ldots, \epsilon_{t+T}^*; \kappa_t^*, \ldots, \kappa_{t+T}^*)$ solve Problem B1, and let $M_s^{f*} = M^f(\epsilon_{1s}^*)$. Define

$$Y'(M_t^{f*}, \ldots, M_{t+T}^{f*}) = \{(\delta_t, \ldots, \delta_{t+T}; \bar{\epsilon}_t, \ldots, \bar{\epsilon}_{t+T}; \kappa_t, \ldots, \kappa_{t+T}) \in Z':$$
$$W^*(\delta_t, \ldots, \delta_{t+T}; M_t^{f*}, \ldots, M_{t+T}^{f*}; \bar{\epsilon}_t, \ldots, \bar{\epsilon}_{t+T};$$
$$\kappa_t, \ldots, \kappa_{t+T}; \lambda_t, \ldots, \lambda_{t+T}) = 0\},$$

where $Z'$ is the projection of $Z$ onto the $(n + k_2 + \bar{k})T$-dimensional subspace having $(\delta_t, \ldots, \delta_{t+T}; \bar{\epsilon}_t, \ldots, \bar{\epsilon}_{t+T}; \kappa_t, \ldots, \kappa_{t+T})$ as components. Let

$$\bar{\psi}_s = \delta_s' \nu_s - \kappa_s' \zeta_s + \sum_{i=1}^{k_2} [(1 + r_{i,s-1}) p_{s-1}^* \bar{\epsilon}_{i,s-1} - p^* \bar{\epsilon}_{is}],$$

and let

$$\bar{\psi}^* = \sum_{s=t}^{t+T} \frac{\psi_s}{\theta_s} + \frac{1}{\theta_{t+T+1}} \sum_{i=1}^{k} p_{t+T}^* \bar{\epsilon}_{i,t+T} (1 + r_{i,t+T}).$$

Consider the following decision problem, which is conditional upon prior knowledge of the stochastic process $M_s^{f*}$ for $s = t, \ldots, t+T$.

**Problem B2.** Choose $(\delta_t, \ldots, \delta_{t+T}; \epsilon_{2t}, \ldots, \epsilon_{2,t+T}; \kappa_t, \ldots, \kappa_{t+T})$ to maximize the expectation $E_t(\bar{\psi}^*)$ subject to $(\delta_t, \ldots, \delta_{t+T}; \epsilon_{2t}, \ldots, \epsilon_{2,t+T}; \kappa_t, \ldots, \kappa_{t+T}) \in Y'(M_t^{f*}, \ldots, M_{t+T}^{f*})$.

Our aggregation theorem for the manufacturing firm can now be written as follows.

**Theorem B1** (manufacturing firm's aggregation theorem). *Let the process* $(\delta_t, ..., \delta_{t+T}; \epsilon_t, ..., \epsilon_{t+T}; \kappa_t, ..., \kappa_{t+T})$ *solve Problem B1. Then* $(\delta_t, ..., \delta_{t+T};$ $\bar{\epsilon}_t, ..., \bar{\epsilon}_{t+T}; \kappa_t, ..., \kappa_{t+T})$ *solves Problem B2 conditional upon the process* $M_s^{f*} = M^f(\epsilon_{1s})$ *given for* $s = t, ..., t+T$.

*Proof:* Let the process $(\delta_t, ..., \delta_{t+T}; \epsilon_{1t}, ..., \epsilon_{1,t+T}; \bar{\epsilon}_t, ..., \bar{\epsilon}_{t+T}; \kappa_t, ...,$ $\kappa_{t+T})$ solve Problem B1; but let $(\delta_t, ..., \delta_{t+T}; \bar{\epsilon}_t, ..., \bar{\epsilon}_{t+T}; \kappa_t, ..., \kappa_{t+T})$ *not* solve Problem B2 conditional upon the given process $M_s^{f*} = M^f(\epsilon_{1s})$ for $s = t, ..., t+T$. Then there exists $(\tilde{\delta}_t, ..., \tilde{\delta}_{t+T}; \tilde{\bar{\epsilon}}_t, ..., \tilde{\bar{\epsilon}}_{t+T}; \tilde{\kappa}_t, ..., \tilde{\kappa}_{t+T}) \in$ $Y'(M_t^{f*}, ..., M_{t+T}^{f*})$ such that $E_t(\bar{\psi}^*)$ evaluated at $(\tilde{\delta}_t, ..., \tilde{\delta}_{t+T}; \tilde{\bar{\epsilon}}_t, ..., \tilde{\bar{\epsilon}}_{t+T};$ $\tilde{\kappa}_t, ..., \tilde{\kappa}_{t+T})$ is strictly greater than $E_t(\bar{\psi}^*)$ evaluated at $(\delta_t, ..., \delta_{t+T}; \bar{\epsilon}_t, ...,$ $\bar{\epsilon}_{t+T}; \kappa_t, ..., \kappa_{t+T})$.

Hence $E_t(\psi^*)$ evaluated at $(\tilde{\delta}_t, ..., \tilde{\delta}_{t+T}; \epsilon_{1t}, ..., \epsilon_{1,t+T}; \tilde{\bar{\epsilon}}_t, ..., \tilde{\bar{\epsilon}}_{t+T}; \tilde{\kappa}_t, ...,$ $\tilde{\kappa}_{t+T})$ is strictly greater than $E_t(\psi^*)$ evaluated at $(\delta_t, ..., \delta_{t+T}; \epsilon_{1t}, ..., \epsilon_{1,t+T};$ $\bar{\epsilon}_t, ..., \bar{\epsilon}_{t+T}; \kappa_t, ..., \kappa_{t+T})$. But since $(\tilde{\delta}_t, ..., \tilde{\delta}_{t+T}; \tilde{\bar{\epsilon}}_t, ..., \tilde{\bar{\epsilon}}_{t+T}; \tilde{\kappa}_t, ..., \tilde{\kappa}_{t+T})$ is feasible for Problem B2 conditional upon $M_s^{f*} = M^f(\epsilon_{1s})$, it follows that $(\tilde{\delta}_t, ..., \tilde{\delta}_{t+T}; \epsilon_{1t}, ..., \epsilon_{1,t+T}; \tilde{\bar{\epsilon}}_t, ..., \tilde{\bar{\epsilon}}_{t+T}; \tilde{\kappa}_t, ..., \tilde{\kappa}_{t+T})$ is feasible for Problem B1. Thus our assumption that $(\delta_t, ..., \delta_{t+T}; \epsilon_{1t}, ..., \epsilon_{1,t+T}; \bar{\epsilon}_t, ...,$ $\bar{\epsilon}_{t+T}; \kappa_t, ..., \kappa_{t+T})$ solves Problem B1 is contradicted, proving the theorem. $\square$

Hence, as with the consumer, knowledge of the monetary aggregate $M_s^{f*}$ process is sufficient for optimal solution for the remaining variables in the economic agent's decision. Knowledge of the component process $\epsilon_{1s}$ is not needed. The same cannot be said for the simple-sum aggregate over the components of $\epsilon_{1s}$ unless the aggregator function $M_f$ happens to be a simple sum. In other words, the components of $\epsilon_{1s}$ must be indistinguishable perfect substitutes in order for the simple-sum aggregate to have information relevant to the firm's behavior in other markets.

## REFERENCES

Arrow, K. J., and F. Hahn (1971), *General Competition Analysis*. San Francisco: Holden-Day.
Barnett, William A. (1978), "The User Cost of Money," *Economics Letters* 1: 145-9.
(1980), "Economic Monetary Aggregates: An Application of Index Number and Aggregation Theory," *Journal of Econometrics* 14: 11-48.
(1981), *Consumer Demand and Labor Supply: Goods, Monetary Assets and Time*. Amsterdam: North-Holland.
(1983), "New Indices of Money Supply and the Flexible Laurent Demand System," *Journal of Business and Economic Statistics* 1: 7-23.
(1987), "The Microeconomic Theory of Monetary Aggregation," in William A. Barnett and Kenneth J. Singleton (eds.), *New Approaches to Monetary Economics* (Proceedings of the Second International Symposium in Economic

374     **William A. Barnett**

Theory and Econometrics). Cambridge: Cambridge University Press, pp. 115–68.

(1991), "Reply," in Michael T. Belongia (ed.), *Monetary Policy on the 75th Anniversary of the Federal Reserve System* (Proceedings of the Fourteenth Annual Economic Policy Conference of the Federal Reserve Bank of St. Louis). Dordrecht: Kluwer, pp. 223–31.

Barnett, William, and Apostolos Serletis (1990), "A Dispersion-Dependency Diagnostic Test for Aggregation Error: With Applications to Monetary Economics and Income Distribution," *Journal of Econometrics* 43: 5–34.

Feenstra, Robert C. (1986), "Functional Equivalence between Liquidity Costs and the Utility of Money," *Journal of Monetary Economics* 17: 271–91.

Fischer, Stanley (1974), "Money and the Production Function," *Economic Inquiry* 12: 517–33.

Hutt, W. H. (1963), *Keynesianism – Retrospect and Prospect.* Chicago: Henry Regnery.

Phlips, Louis, and Frans Spinnewyn (1982), "Rationality versus Myopia in Dynamic Demand Systems," in R. L. Basmann and G. F. Rhodes (eds.), *Advances in Econometrics.* Greenwich, CT: JAI Press, pp. 3–33.

Rotemberg, Julio (1991), "Commentary: Monetary Aggregates and Their Uses," in Michael T. Belongia (ed.), *Monetary Policy on the 75th Anniversary of the Federal Reserve System* (Proceedings of the Fourteenth Annual Economic Policy Conference of the Federal Reserve Bank of St. Louis). Dordrecht: Kluwer, pp. 223–31.

Rotemberg, Julio J., John C. Driscoll, and James M. Poterba (1991), "Money, Output, and Prices: Evidence from a New Monetary Aggregate," *Journal of Business and Economic Statistics* (to appear).

Sargent, Thomas J. (1987), *Dynamic Macroeconomic Theory.* Cambridge, MA: Harvard University Press.

Stokey, Nancy L., and Robert E. Lucas, Jr. (1989), *Recursive Methods in Economic Dynamics.* Cambridge, MA: Harvard University Press.

CHAPTER 17

# The stochastic dominance ordering of income distributions over time: The discounted sum of the expected utilities of incomes

*Thierry Karcher, Patrick Moyes, & Alain Trannoy*

## 1    Introduction

There is a large amount of work dealing with the measurement of welfare and inequality in a society (Atkinson 1970; Dasgupta, Sen, and Starrett 1973; Rothschild and Stiglitz 1973; Shorrocks 1983). Given the diversity of value judgments regarding inequality and welfare, it is now a well-established tradition to look for unambiguous criteria in order to rank income distributions. In the case of welfare measurement, which is what we are interested in, *stochastic dominance orderings* have been shown to be suitable candidates (see Fishburn and Vickson 1978 for a presentation). For practical reasons, it is sometimes more convenient to use *inverse stochastic dominance orderings,* which have been shown to generate the same ranking of distributions up to the second order (see e.g. Foster and Shorrocks 1988). Inverse stochastic dominance orderings have been used by Bishop, Formby, and Thistle (1991) to compare the standard of living of different countries, and by Jenkins (1991) to depict the pattern of inequality over time in the United Kingdom.

   Although the stochastic dominance orderings provide unambiguous rankings of *snapshot* income distributions, it is not clear that they constitute appropriate measures of social welfare. A major motivation for the approach we develop in this paper is the strong belief that a static description of income measured over a short period does not provide sufficient information and may therefore lead to unwarranted conclusions. Indeed, it is often necessary to describe directly the way incomes change

A preliminary version of this paper was presented at the first Social Choice and Welfare Conference, June 1992 (Caen, France). We would like to thank A. Nizard, P. Picard, and an anonymous referee for helpful comments. Needless to say, the authors bear sole responsibility for any remaining deficiency.

over time, as well as to assess the effect of such movements on inequality and welfare when incomes are measured over a longer period. Attempts are often made to assess whether or not inequality has increased or decreased over time by using a simple comparative static analysis (see e.g. Jenkins 1991). However, since the individuals' positions on the cardinal income scale rarely remain unchanged over time, an increase in a snapshot measure of inequality is clearly consistent with there having been a significant amount of equalizing mobility over time. Only if all individuals' earnings remain constant from period to period will a measure of inequality or welfare give the same result irrespective of the length of the accounting period. In addition, policy makers as well as individuals are often involved in making comparisons among projects in terms of income prospects. (See e.g. Karcher and Trannoy 1992 and Trannoy and Karcher 1991 for a comparison of education careers in France.) Since there are systematic variations in earnings with age, and as age distributions generally differ between occupations, a simple comparison of average earnings measured over a short period will be of little value. Though the general importance of the life cycle in economics has often been emphasized, very little attention has actually been given to the process of earnings changes with age. Analysis of the distributional impact of government activities on social insurance – such as pensions, unemployment benefits, and health insurance – clearly provides another example where a longer-term perspective is needed. Indeed, each policy involves redistribution between individuals as well as redistribution between stages of the life cycle: from work to retirement, or from periods of work to periods of unemployment and sickness. Quite surprisingly, there are relatively few studies concerned with the evaluation of intertemporal distributions of income.

In this study, we are interested in the measurement of the standard of living or social welfare a society derives from a given distribution of individual incomes over time. To keep things simple, we traditionally assume a *utilitarian social welfare function* such that the social welfare in a given situation is simply the sum of individual utilities; we will further assume the same utility function across individuals. Given a utilitarian social welfare function, there are two possible ways of introducing the time dimension into the analysis. A first possibility is to discount individual snapshot incomes and then compute mean utility over the population: social welfare is thus the *expected utility of the discounted sum of incomes*. As a second possibility, we can compute the average utility at any given time and then take the discounted sum of the snapshot mean utilities: social welfare then becomes the *discounted sum of the expected utilities of incomes*. Taking this latter definition as the true measure of social welfare amounts to implicitly assuming that mobility has no impact on social welfare. This claim arises because snapshot expected utilities are symmetrical functions of incomes, and so a permutation of incomes at any given time period leaves snapshot social welfare unchanged. On the contrary, social welfare is generally not invariant with respect to such permutations when social welfare is viewed as the sum of the utilities of discounted streams of individual incomes. This explains why the latter view is taken in studies concerned especially with the measurement of the extent of mobility (e.g. Maasoumi and Zandvakili 1990). In this paper we will admit that mobility does not matter and will therefore define social welfare as the discounted sum of the expected utilities of incomes.[1]

We introduce in Section 2 the general notation employed in the paper, and recall some basic definitions and results concerning stochastic dominance for snapshot distributions. We examine in Section 3 the orderings of intertemporal distributions generated by the principle of unanimity applied to some general classes of utilitarian social welfare functions. Defining social welfare as the discounted sum of the expected utilities of income in each period results in two degrees of freedom in the measurement of welfare: the utility function for the snapshot income distribution, and the $(T+1)$-tuple of discounting functions. With respect to the former, we consider efficiency-regarding utility functions, efficiency- and equality-loving functions, and functions with decreasing inequality aversion. For discounting, we admit four types of functions: those that react positively to increments, those that reflect time impatience and declining time impatience, and those that use a constant discount rate. Finally, Section 4 concludes by pointing to directions for further research. Unless stated in the text, proofs of the propositions will be relegated to the Appendix.

## 2     Preliminary definitions and notation

We consider a society (or, more precisely, a generation) $N := \{1, 2, ..., n\}$ with $n \geq 2$ such that each individual $i \in N$ lives $T+1$ periods of time labeled $t = 0, 1, ..., T$. Typically, an *intertemporal income structure* is represented by an $n \times (T+1)$ matrix $X \equiv [x_i^t]$, where $x_i^t$ is the income that individual $i$ receives at time $t$. We assume that incomes are bounded, so that $\underline{z} < x_i^t \leq \bar{z}$ for all $i \in N$ and all $t = 0, 1, ..., T$, where $-\infty < \underline{z} < \bar{z} < +\infty$. We therefore allow for possibly negative incomes at some time periods, which is not unrealistic within an intertemporal framework. We denote as $\mathfrak{X} := \{X \equiv [x_i^t] \mid \underline{z} < x_i^t \leq \bar{z} \; \forall i \in N \text{ and } \forall t = 0, 1, ..., T\}$ the set of intertemporal

---

[1]  The analysis of the former definition is slightly more complicated; see Karcher, Moyes, and Trannoy (1993) for preliminary investigations.

income structures. Given $X \in \mathfrak{X}$, we denote as $x^t := (x_1^t, \ldots, x_n^t)$ the snapshot or within-time distribution at time $t$; hence we can write equivalently $X = [x^0; x^1; \ldots; x^T]$. Similarly, we let $x_i := (x_i^0, x_i^1, \ldots, x_i^T)$ represent the lifetime income distribution (equivalently, the income profile or income stream) of individual $i$ in situation $X$.

We let $x_{()}^t := (x_{(1)}^t, \ldots, x_{(n)}^t)$ stand for the ordered version of the snapshot distribution $x^t := (x_1^t, \ldots, x_n^t)$. That is, $x_{()}^t := \Pi x^t$ for some permutation matrix $\Pi$ such that $x_{(1)}^t \leq x_{(2)}^t \leq \cdots \leq x_{(n)}^t$. We denote as $F_t^1 : [\underline{z}, \bar{z}] \to [0, 1]$ the *cumulative distribution function* (CDF) corresponding to $x^t$, and we define $F_t^r : [\underline{z}, \bar{z}] \to \mathbb{R}$ by the recursive rule

$$F_t^{r+1}(z) = \int_{\underline{z}}^{z} F_t^r(s)\, ds \quad \text{for all } z \in [\underline{z}, \bar{z}] \tag{2.1}$$

with $r = 1, 2$. Given $x^t := (x_1^t, \ldots, x_n^t)$, it is well known that $F_t^r(z)$ can be equivalently written as

$$F_t^r(z) = \frac{1}{(r-1)!} \sum_{j=1}^{q(z; x^t)} \left( \frac{z - x_{(j)}^t}{n} \right)^{r-1} \quad (r = 1, 2, 3), \tag{2.2}$$

where $q(z; x^t) := \#\{j \in \{1, 2, \ldots, n\} \mid x_{(j)}^t \leq z\}$. We therefore obtain

$$F_t^1(z) = \frac{q(z; x^t)}{n} =: P_1(z; x^t), \tag{2.3a}$$

$$F_t^2(z) = \frac{1}{n} \sum_{j=1}^{q(z; x^t)} (z - x_{(j)}^t) =: P_2(z; x^t), \tag{2.3b}$$

$$F_t^3(z) = \frac{1}{2n^2} \sum_{j=1}^{q(z; x^t)} (z - x_{(j)}^t)^2 =: P_3(z; x^t), \tag{2.3c}$$

for all $z \in [\underline{z}, \bar{z}]$ (see e.g. Foster and Shorrocks 1988). In addition, it is convenient to define the means of distributions $x^t$ in terms of their CDFs:

$$\mu_{F_t^1} = \int_{\underline{z}}^{\bar{z}} z\, dF_t^1(z) \quad \text{for all } t = 0, 1, \ldots, T. \tag{2.4}$$

Given the income structure $Y := [y_i^t]$, we denote as $G_t^1 : [\underline{z}, \bar{z}] \to [0, 1]$ the CDF corresponding to $y^t$; we similarly define $\mu_{G_t^1}$, $G_t^r : [\underline{z}, \bar{z}] \to \mathbb{R}$, and $P_r(z; y^t)$ for $r = 1, 2, 3$.

We use $H_t^1 : [0, 1] \to [\underline{z}, \bar{z}]$ to represent the *inverse cumulative distribution function* (ICDF) corresponding to distribution $x^t$, defined by

$$H_t^1(p) := \inf\{\underline{z} \leq z \mid F_t^1(z) \geq p\} \ \forall p \in (0, 1] \quad \text{and} \quad H_t^1(0) := x_{(1)}^t. \tag{2.5}$$

We define recursively the functions $H_t^r : [0, 1] \to \mathbb{R}$ by the rule

$$H_t^{r+1}() = \int_0^p H_t^r(q)\, dq \ \forall p \in [0, 1] \quad (r = 1, 2). \tag{2.6}$$

Using Lemma 1 in Muliere and Scarsini (1989), for any given $x^t := (x_1^t, ..., x_n^t)$ we deduce that

$$H_t^r(p) = \frac{1}{(r-1)!} \sum_{j=1}^{k(p)} \left(p - \frac{j-1}{n}\right)^{r-1} (x_{(j)}^t - x_{(j-1)}^t) \quad (r = 1, 2, 3), \qquad (2.7)$$

for all $p \in [0, 1]$, where $x_{(0)} = 0$ and $k(p) := \min\{k \in \{1, 2, ..., n\} \mid p \le k/n\}$. We therefore obtain

$$H_t^1(p) = x_{(k)}^t =: \text{RO}(p; x^t) \quad \text{and} \qquad (2.8a)$$

$$H_t^2(p) = \frac{1}{n} \sum_{j=1}^{k-1} x_{(j)}^t + \left(p - \frac{k-1}{n}\right) x_{(k)}^t =: \text{GL}(p; x^t) \qquad (2.8b)$$

for all $(k-1)/n < p \le k/n$ $(k = 1, 2, ..., n)$. Given the income structure $Y := [y_i^t]$, we denote as $K_t^1 \colon [0, 1] \to [\underline{z}, \bar{z}]$ the inverse distribution function corresponding to $y^t$, and we similarly define $K_t^r \colon [0, 1] \to \mathbb{R}$ for $r = 2, 3$. The terms $\text{RO}(p; x^t)$ and $\text{GL}(p; x^t)$ represent (respectively) the rank-order statistic and the generalized Lorenz curve for distribution $x^t$ (see Shorrocks 1983). We will say that $x^t$ *rank-order dominates* $y^t$, written $x^t \ge_{\text{RO}} y^t$, if and only if $\text{RO}(p; x^t) \ge \text{RO}(p; y^t)$ for all $p \in [0, 1]$. Similarly, $x^t$ *generalized Lorenz dominates* $y^t$, written $x^t \ge_{\text{GL}} y^t$, if and only if $\text{GL}(p; x^t) \ge \text{GL}(p; y^t)$ for all $p \in [0, 1]$. The following equivalences are well known (see e.g. Foster and Shorrocks 1988).

**Lemma 2.1.** *Let $x^t, y^t \in [\underline{z}, \bar{z}]^n$. We then have the two following equivalences:*

(a)   $P_1(z; x^t) \le P_1(z; y^t)$ *for all* $z \in [\underline{z}, \bar{z}]$ *if and only if* $x^t \ge_{\text{RO}} y^t$.
(b)   $P_2(z; x^t) \le P_2(z; y^t)$ *for all* $z \in [\underline{z}, \bar{z}]$ *if and only if* $x^t \ge_{\text{GL}} y^t$.

Given $X \in \mathfrak{X}$ and $t = 0, 1, ..., T$, we find it convenient to denote as $x^{(t)} := (x^0; x^1; ...; x^t)$ the distribution consisting of the first $t + 1$ snapshot distributions. Similarly, we let $\bar{x}^{(t)} := (x^{(0)}; x^{(1)}; ...; x^{(t)})$ for all $t = 0, 1, ..., T$. Then, given the income structure $X \in \mathfrak{X}$, it is worthy to note that

$$P_r(z; x^{(t)}) = \sum_{\tau=0}^{t} P_r(z; x^\tau) \quad \forall z \in [\underline{z}, \bar{z}] \ \forall t = 0, 1, ..., T, \qquad (2.9)$$

with $r = 1, 2, 3$. *Mutatis mutandis,* a similar relation holds for distributions $\bar{x}^{(t)}$ $(t = 0, 1, ..., T)$.

## 3    The stochastic dominance ordering of intertemporal income structures

We traditionally assume a social welfare function $W \colon \mathfrak{X} \to \mathbb{R}$ such that $W(X)$ represents the welfare of the society in state $X$. As stated in Section 1, at this preliminary stage we focus on utilitarian social welfare functions that define social welfare as the discounted sum of the expected utilities of incomes; we further assume the same utility function across individuals. Therefore, the welfare of the society in state $X$ may be written as

$$W_{V,U}(X) = \sum_{t=0}^{T} V_t\left(\frac{1}{n}\sum_{i=1}^{n} U(x_i^t)\right) = \sum_{t=0}^{T} V_t\left(\int_{\underline{z}}^{\bar{z}} U(z)\,dF_t^1(z)\right), \quad (3.1)$$

where $U \in \mathcal{U} := \{U : \mathbb{R} \to \mathbb{R}\}$ is the common snapshot utility function and $V := (V_0, V_1, \ldots, V_T)$ is a $(T+1)$-tuple of discounting functions. We let $\mathcal{V} := \{V := (V_0, V_1, \ldots, V_T) \mid V_t : \mathbb{R} \to \mathbb{R}$ for all $t = 0, 1, \ldots, T\}$ represent the set of admissible $(T+1)$-tuples of discounting functions. To shorten notation, we denote as $\mathrm{EU}(F_t^1)$ (resp. $\mathrm{EU}(G_t^1)$) the expected utility or snapshot welfare of society in state $X$ (resp. $Y$) at time $t$. Without loss of generality, we restrict attention to comparisons of income structures for a given society. Indeed, within a utilitarian framework, the case of such comparisons across societies of different sizes poses no additional difficulty provided one subscribes to the *principle of population*.[2] Definition (3.1) incorporates the two dimensions of the income distribution process over time. The first dimension concerns the distribution of *income between individuals at a given period of time*; this has been extensively studied in the literature. (See e.g. Atkinson 1970; Dasgupta et al. 1973; Fields and Fei 1978; Foster and Shorrocks 1988; Kolm 1976; Rothschild and Stiglitz 1973; Sen 1973). The second dimension involves the distribution of *society welfare over time*, and is closely related to the literature on the comparison of income prospects (see e.g. Bohren and Hansen 1980; Ekern 1981; Trannoy and Karcher 1991). Quite clearly, the ordering of the income distributions will depend on the choice of a particular utility function and a particular sequence of income discounting functions. Because there is some uncertainty about the appropriate utility function as well as the correct sequence of discounting functions to be used, the current practice is to require unanimity of value judgments. We will follow this general practice, and examine several different sets of utility functions and income discounting functions that may be considered reasonable candidates within our framework. Given these unambiguous welfare orderings, the next step is to identify those elementary transformations of incomes by which – if distribution $X$ results from distribution $Y$ by means of a finite sequence of such transformations – one may conclude that $X$ is preferred to $Y$ according to (3.1). Because the classes of utility functions and discounting functions are generally too large to be of empirical relevance, one must devise

---

[2] The principle of population (see e.g. Dalton 1920) would require that $W(X) = W(Y)$ whenever $X$ is the $q$-replication of $Y$: $X = \underbrace{(Y; \ldots; Y)}_{q \text{ times}}$.

informationally less demanding rules in order to implement the corresponding welfare orderings. Since our social welfare functions are symmetric with respect to the distribution of snapshot incomes, we will assume henceforth that individual incomes in each period are arranged in a nondecreasing order; that is, $x_1^t \le x_2^t \le \cdots \le x_n^t$ for all $t = 0, 1, \ldots, T$ and all $X \in \mathfrak{X}$.

## 3.1  *Preference for more efficiently distributed incomes*

In this section we assume that, at each time, higher incomes are always preferred to lower incomes. Hence the utility function must be nondecreasing, and we define $U_1 := \{U \in U \mid U'(z)$ is continuous, bounded, and nonnegative over $(\underline{z}, \bar{z})\}$. We find it convenient to introduce an example to help illustrate the forthcoming definitions.

**Example 3.1.** Consider the following income structures, which involve two individuals ($i = 1, 2$) and three periods ($t = 0, 1, 2$):

$$X^{(1)} = \begin{bmatrix} 2 & 4 & 2 \\ 2 & 4 & 6 \end{bmatrix}; \quad X^{(2)} = \begin{bmatrix} 2 & 4 & 2 \\ 4 & 4 & 6 \end{bmatrix}; \quad X^{(3)} = \begin{bmatrix} 2 & 2 & 2 \\ 4 & 4 & 6 \end{bmatrix};$$

$$X^{(4)} = \begin{bmatrix} 2 & 2 & 4 \\ 4 & 2 & 6 \end{bmatrix}; \quad X^{(5)} = \begin{bmatrix} 2 & 2 & 4 \\ 4 & 2 & 6 \end{bmatrix}.$$

We first assume that overall social welfare increases with snapshot welfare, which amounts to requiring that the discounting functions $V_t$ be nondecreasing. We let $V_1 := \{V := (V_0, V_1, \ldots, V_T) \in V \mid V_t'(u) \ge 0 \ \forall u \in \mathbb{R}$ and $\forall t = 0, 1, \ldots, T\}$.

**Definition 3.1.1.** Given two income structures $X, Y \in \mathfrak{X}$, we will say that $X$ is obtained from $Y$ by an *increment* if there exists a couple $(i, t)$ such that (i) $x_i^t - y_i^t = \Delta > 0$ and (ii) $x_j^\tau = y_j^\tau$ for all $(j, \tau) \ne (i, t)$. Equivalently, we will say that $Y$ is obtained from $X$ by means of a *decrement*.

An increment is the simplest transformation one may think of: it consists of giving more income at a given time to one individual. A short glance at the five income structures of Example 3.1 indicates that $X^2$ and $X^5$ follow (respectively) from $X^1$ and $X^4$ through an increment of two units of income, whereas a decrement of two units is needed in order to obtain $X^3$ from $X^2$ and $X^4$ from $X^3$. Suppose that $X$ results from $Y$ by means of a single increment; that is, $y_i^t = z^\circ < z^* = x_i^t$ for some couple $(i, t)$, and $x_j^\tau = y_j^\tau$ for all $(j, \tau) \ne (i, t)$. Using the mean value theorem, $W_{V,U}(X) \ge W_{V,U}(Y)$ simplifies to

$$V_t'(\xi')[U(z^*) - U(z^\circ)] \geq 0, \tag{3.2}$$

where $\xi' \in (\mathrm{EU}(F_t^1), \mathrm{EU}(G_t^1))$. Letting $\Delta := z^* - z^\circ$ and integrating, we obtain

$$V_t'(\xi') \int_0^\Delta U'(z^\circ + s) \, ds \geq 0, \tag{3.3}$$

from which we may conclude the following.

**Remark 3.1.1.** A sufficient condition for $W_{V,U}(X) \geq W_{V,U}(Y)$, for all $(V, U) \in V_1 \times U_1$, is that $X$ be obtained from $Y$ by means of a finite sequence of increments.

When the utility functions are nondecreasing with income, a sufficient condition for overall welfare to increase as a result of an increment is that the derivatives of the discounting functions be nonnegative. Regarding the implementation of unanimity over $V_1 \times U_1$, we obtain the following proposition.

**Proposition 3.1.1.** *Let $X, Y \in \mathfrak{X}$. Then the two following statements are equivalent:*

    (a)  $W_{V,U}(X) \geq W_{V,U}(Y)$ *for all* $(V, U) \in V_1 \times U_1$;

    (b)  $F_t^1(z) \leq G_t^1(z)$ *for all* $z \in [\underline{z}, \bar{z}]$ *and all* $t = 0, 1, \ldots, T$.

A necessary and sufficient condition for income structure $X$ to be preferred to income structure $Y$ by an efficiency-minded observer is that the snapshot CDFs in situation $X$ be nowhere below the corresponding snapshot CDFs in situation $Y$. Appealing to Lemma 2.1, this condition turns out to be equivalent to rank-order dominance at each time period. The following corollary makes this precise.

**Corollary 3.1.1.** *Let $X, Y \in \mathfrak{X}$. Then the two following statements are equivalent:*

    (a)  $W_{V,U}(X) \geq W_{V,U}(Y)$ *for all* $(V, U) \in V_1 \times U_1$;

    (b)  $x^t \geq_{\mathrm{RO}} y^t$ *for all* $t = 0, 1, \ldots, T$.

These two results provide, in a sense, a test of consistency: other things being equal, an increase in welfare at a given time period results in an overall welfare improvement. However, this is a highly restrictive condition that is unlikely to be met in practical situations. In particular, regarding our five income structures, unanimity over $V_1 \times U_1$ appears to be decisive in only half of the cases.

We next assume that an extra amount of expected utility is socially more valuable at time $t$ than at time $t+1$, which amounts to requiring that $V_t'(u) \geq V_{t+1}'(v)$ for all $u, v \in \mathbb{R}$ and all $t = 0, 1, \ldots, T-1$. This generalizes the usual assumption of *time impatience* in the case of a single individual: if society is to be given an extra unit of snapshot welfare, then it is preferable to receive it at time $t$ rather than at time $t+1$. We denote as $V_2 := \{V := (V_0, V_1, \ldots, V_T) \in V_1 \mid V_t'(u) \geq V_{t+1}'(v) \; \forall u, v \in \mathbb{R} \text{ and } \forall t = 0, 1, \ldots, T-1\}$ the class of $(T+1)$-tuples of discounting functions verifying time impatience.

**Definition 3.1.2.** Given two income structures $X, Y \in \mathfrak{X}$, we will say that $X$ is obtained from $Y$ by a $\Pi_+$ *transformation* if there exist two couples $(i_1, t_1)$ and $(i_2, t_2)$ with $t_1 < t_2$ such that: (i) $y_{i_1}^{t_1} = x_{i_2}^{t_2}$; (ii) $x_{i_1}^{t_1} = y_{i_2}^{t_2}$; (iii) $y_{i_1}^{t_1} < y_{i_2}^{t_2}$; and (iv) $x_j^\tau = y_j^\tau$ for all $(j, \tau) \neq (i_1, t_1), (i_2, t_2)$. Equivalently, we will say that $Y$ is obtained from $X$ by means of a $\Pi_-$ transformation.

Less formally, a $\Pi_+$ transformation corresponds to the situation where the richer individual $i_2$ is given at time $t_2$ the income the poorer individual $i_1$ receives at time $t_1$ and vice versa. Inspecting the income structures defined in Example 3.1 reveals that $X^3$ results from $X^1$ by means of a $\Pi_+$ transformation whereas a $\Pi_-$ transformation is needed in order to obtain $X^5$ from $X^3$. Suppose that $X$ obtains from $Y$ by means of a single $\Pi_+$ transformation; that is, suppose $y_{i_1}^{t_1} = x_{i_2}^{t_2} = z^\circ < z^* = x_{i_1}^{t_1} = y_{i_2}^{t_2}$ for some $(i_1, t_1), (i_2, t_2)$ with $t_1 < t_2$, and that $x_j^\tau = y_j^\tau$ for all $(j, \tau) \neq (i_1, t_1), (i_2, t_2)$. Appealing again to the mean value theorem and integrating, it can be shown that $W_{V,U}(X) \geq W_{V,U}(Y)$ is equivalent to

$$[V_{t_1}'(\xi^{t_1}) - V_{t_2}'(\xi^{t_2})] \int_0^\Delta U'(z^\circ + s) \, ds \geq 0, \tag{3.4}$$

where $\xi^{t_1}, \xi^{t_2} \in (\mathrm{EU}(F_t^1), \mathrm{EU}(G_t^1))$ and $\Delta := z^* - z^\circ$. We can therefore conclude as follows.

**Remark 3.1.2.** A sufficient condition for $W_{V,U}(X) \geq W_{V,U}(Y)$, for all $(V, U) \in V_2 \times U_1$, is that $X$ be obtained from $Y$ by means of a finite sequence of $\Pi_+$ transformations.

Requiring the derivatives of the discounting functions to be nonincreasing with time guarantees that overall welfare will increase as a result of a $\Pi_+$ transformation. We turn next to the implementation procedure.

**Proposition 3.1.2.** *Let $X, Y \in \mathfrak{X}$. Then the two following statements are equivalent:*

   (a)  $W_{V,U}(X) \geq W_{V,U}(Y)$ *for all* $(V,U) \in V_2 \times U_1$;
   (b)  $\sum_{s=0}^{t} F_s^1(z) \leq \sum_{s=0}^{t} G_s^1(z)$ *for all* $z \in [\underline{z}, \bar{z}]$ *and all* $t = 0, 1, ..., T$.

A necessary and sufficient condition for income structure $X$ to be preferred to income structure $Y$ by any efficiency-minded and time-impatient observer is that the sum of the CDFs over the first $t$ periods of time in situation $X$ be nowhere above the corresponding sum of CDFs in situation $Y$. Appealing to Lemma 2.1, this condition turns out to be equivalent to applying rank-order dominance over the first $t$ distributions in succession, as the next corollary indicates.

**Corollary 3.1.2.** *Let* $X, Y \in \mathfrak{X}$. *Then the two following statements are equivalent:*

   (a)  $W_{V,U}(X) \geq W_{V,U}(Y)$ *for all* $(V,U) \in V_2 \times U_1$;
   (b)  $x^{(t)} \geq_{RO} y^{(t)}$ *for all* $t = 0, 1, ..., T$.

Turning back to our five income structures, the introduction of time impatience results in a less partial ordering of the income structures: only 2 out of 10 pairs are not comparable.

We now assume that, the earlier a transfer of snapshot utility takes place, the more valuable it is for the society. More precisely: Transferring an amount $\Delta u$ of utility from time $s+1$ to time $s$ is always preferable to transferring the same amount from time $t+1$ to time $t$, provided that $s < t$. This corresponds to the assumption of *declining time impatience*, which amounts to requiring that $V_s'(u_s) - V_{s+1}'(v_s) \geq V_t'(u_t) - V_{t+1}'(v_t)$ for all $u_s$, $v_s, u_t, v_t \in \mathbb{R}$ and all $s < t$. We denote as $V_3 := \{V := (V_0, V_1, ..., V_T) \in V_2 \mid V_t'(u_0) - V_{t+1}'(u_1) \geq V_{t+1}'(v_0) - V_{t+2}'(v_1) \; \forall u_0, u_1, v_0, v_1 \in \mathbb{R} \text{ and } \forall t = 0, 1, ..., T-2\}$ the class of $(T+1)$-tuples of discounting functions verifying time impatience at a declining rate.

**Definition 3.1.3.** Given two income structures $X, Y \in \mathfrak{X}$, we will say that $X$ is obtained from $Y$ by a $\Pi_{+-}$ *transformation* if there exist four couples $(i_1, t_1), (i_2, t_2), (i_3, t_3),$ and $(i_4, t_4)$ with $t_1 < t_2 < t_4$, $t_1 < t_3 < t_4$, and $t_2 - t_1 = t_4 - t_3$ such that: (i) $y_{i_1}^{t_1} = x_{i_2}^{t_2}$; (ii) $x_{i_1}^{t_1} = y_{i_2}^{t_2}$; (iii) $x_{i_3}^{t_3} = y_{i_4}^{t_4}$; (iv) $y_{i_3}^{t_3} = x_{i_4}^{t_4}$; (v) $y_{i_1}^{t_1} = y_{i_4}^{t_4} < y_{i_2}^{t_2} = y_{i_3}^{t_3}$; and (vi) $x_j^\tau = y_j^\tau$ for all $(j, \tau) \neq (i_1, t_1), (i_2, t_2), (i_3, t_3),$ $(i_4, t_4)$. Equivalently, we will say that $Y$ is obtained from $X$ by means of a $\Pi_{-+}$ transformation.

Less formally, a $\Pi_{+-}$ transformation combines a $\Pi_+$ transformation and a $\Pi_-$ transformation of the same extent, the latter taking place some distance away from the former in the future. A careful examination of

Example 3.1 indicates that $X^5$ results from $X^1$ by means of a $\Pi_{+-}$ transformation. Suppose that $X$ results from $Y$ by means of a single $\Pi_{+-}$ transformation; that is, suppose

$$y_{i_1}^{t_1} = x_{i_2}^{t_2} = x_{i_3}^{t_3} = y_{i_4}^{t_4} = z^\circ < z^* = x_{i_1}^{t_1} = y_{i_2}^{t_2} = y_{i_3}^{t_3} = x_{i_4}^{t_4}$$

for some $(i_1, t_1)$, $(i_2, t_2)$, $(i_3, t_3)$, $(i_4, t_4)$ with $t_1 < t_2 < t_4$, $t_1 < t_3 < t_4$ and $t_2 - t_1 = t_4 - t_3$, and suppose $x_j^\tau = y_j^\tau$ for all $(j, \tau) \neq (i_1, t_1), (i_2, t_2), (i_3, t_3), (i_4, t_4)$. Appealing to a similar argument as before, it can be shown that $W_{V,U}(X) \geq W_{V,U}(Y)$ is equivalent to

$$[(V_{t_1}'(\xi^{t_1}) - V_{t_2}'(\xi^{t_2})) - (V_{t_3}'(\xi^{t_3}) - V_{t_4}'(\xi^{t_4}))] \int_0^\Delta U'(z^\circ + s)\, ds \geq 0, \qquad (3.5)$$

where $\xi^{t_r} \in (\text{EU}(F_t^1), \text{EU}(G_t^1))$, for $r = 1, 2, 3, 4$ and $\Delta := z^* - z^\circ$. We therefore have the following conclusion.

**Remark 3.1.3.** A sufficient condition for $W_{V,U}(X) \geq W_{V,U}(Y)$, for all $(V, U) \in V_3 \times U_1$, is that $X$ be obtained from $Y$ by means of a finite sequence of $\Pi_{+-}$ transformations.

Actually, imposing time impatience at a declining rate will guarantee that overall welfare increases as a result of $\Pi_{+-}$ transformation. Turning to the implementation procedure, we have our next proposition.

**Proposition 3.1.3.** *Let $X, Y \in \mathfrak{X}$. Then the two following statements are equivalent:*

(a) $W_{V,U}(X) \geq W_{V,U}(Y)$ *for all* $(V, U) \in V_3 \times U_1$;

(b1) $\sum_{s=0}^t \sum_{r=0}^s F_r^1(z) \leq \sum_{s=0}^t \sum_{r=0}^s G_r^1(z)$ *for all* $t = 0, 1, ..., T-1$ *and all* $z \in [\underline{z}, \bar{z}]$, *and*

(b2) $\sum_{s=0}^T F_s^1(z) \leq \sum_{s=0}^T G_s^1(z)$ *for all* $z \in [\underline{z}, \bar{z}]$.

Consider an efficiency-minded observer endowed with impatience but at a declining rate. Then a necessary and sufficient condition for income structure $X$ to be preferred to income structure $Y$ by any such observer is that: (i) the double sum of the CDFs in situation $X$ over the first $T-1$ periods be nowhere above the corresponding double sum of CDFs in situation $Y$; and (ii) over the whole period, the sum of the CDFs in $X$ be nowhere above the sum of the CDFs in $Y$. Appealing to Lemma 2.1, these conditions turn out to be equivalent to applying rank-order dominance over suitable replications of the first $t$ distributions in succession, as the next corollary shows.

**Corollary 3.1.3.**   *Let* $X, Y \in \mathfrak{X}$. *Then the two following statements are equivalent:*

   (a)   $W_{V,U}(X) \geq W_{V,U}(Y)$ *for all* $(V, U) \in V_3 \times U_1$;
   (b)   $\bar{x}^{(t)} \geq_{RO} \bar{y}^{(t)}$ *for all* $t = 0, 1, \ldots, T-1$, *and* $x^{(T)} \geq_{RO} y^{(T)}$.

Considering the pairwise comparisons of income structures of Example 2.1, only one case of incomparability survives the introduction of declining time impatience – namely, $X^1$ versus $X^4$.

We could continue to narrow down the set of discounting functions by requiring that the second differences of the derivatives of the discounting functions be nonincreasing. However, the significance of this assumption is far from clear and so we will not continue in this direction. In most practical situations, the current procedure is to use a constant discount rate when comparing intertemporal projects. Suppose there are two projects that generate income structures $X$ and $Y$, respectively. Given a constant discount rate $\rho \in [0, 1]$ and a utility function $U$, we will say that the former project is preferable to the later project if

$$\sum_{t=0}^{T} \rho^t \left( \frac{1}{n} \sum_{i=1}^{n} U(x_i^t) \right) \geq \sum_{t=0}^{T} \rho^t \left( \frac{1}{n} \sum_{i=1}^{n} U(y_i^t) \right). \tag{3.6}$$

We will follow for now this well-established tradition, but allow for possibly different views regarding the particular value of the constant discount rate. Therefore, we will require that $\rho$ belong to some closed subinterval $\Omega$ of $[0, 1]$ and denote as $V_\Omega := \{V := (V_0, V_1, \ldots, V_T) \in V \mid \exists \rho \in \Omega,$ $\forall u \in \mathbb{R}, V_t(u) := \rho^t u\}$ the class of $(T+1)$-tuples of discounting functions with a constant discount rate $\rho \in \Omega$. Clearly, for all $V \in V_\Omega$, $V_t'(u)$ is nonnegative, decreasing, and convex with $t$; hence, $V_\Omega \subseteq V_3$. We thus have the following result.

**Proposition 3.1.4.**   *Let* $X, Y \in \mathfrak{X}$ *and* $\Omega \subseteq [0, 1]$. *Then the two following statements are equivalent:*

   (a)   $W_{V,U}(X) \geq W_{V,U}(Y)$ *for all* $(V, U) \in V_\Omega \times U_1$;
   (b)   $\sum_{t=0}^{T} \rho^t F_t^1(z) \leq \sum_{t=0}^{T} \rho^t G_t^1(z)$ *for all* $\rho \in \Omega$ *and all* $z \in [\underline{z}, \bar{z}]$.

We omit the proof of this result, which is in all respects similar to the proofs of Propositions 3.1.1–3.1.3. Though it is fairly obvious, Proposition 3.1.4 raises the question of how condition (b) can be implemented. The following lemma provides a means of checking whether Proposition 3.1.4(b) holds.

**Lemma 3.1** (Trannoy and Karcher 1991). *Let* $Q((u_0, \ldots, u_T); \rho) := \rho^0 u_0 + \rho^1 u_1 + \cdots + \rho^T u_T$ *and* $Q((v_0, \ldots, v_T); \rho) := \rho^0 v_0 + \rho^1 v_1 + \cdots + \rho^T v_T$, *and define* $\Delta u_t := v_t - u_t$ *for all* $t = 0, 1, \ldots, T$. *Then the two following statements are equivalent:*

(a) $Q((v_0, \ldots, v_T); \rho) \geq Q((u_0, \ldots, u_T); \rho)$ *for all* $\rho \in [0, 1]$;

(b) *there exists an integer* $m \geq T$ *such that*
$\sum_{s=0}^{t} C_{m-t}^{m-s} \Delta u_s \geq 0$ *for all* $t = 0, 1, \ldots, T$ *and*
$\sum_{s=0}^{T} C_{m-t}^{m-s} \Delta u_s \geq 0$ *for all* $t = T+1, \ldots, m$.

This lemma can be adapted to the case where one considers dominance over a subinterval $\Omega \subseteq [0, 1]$. We note that the implementation of unanimity over $V_\Omega \times U_1$ involves a finite number of steps. Indeed, let $\mathcal{Z}(X; Y)$ represent the set of all distinct values taken by individual incomes in situations $X$ and $Y$:

$$\mathcal{Z}(X; Y) := \{z_k \in [\underline{z}, \bar{z}] \mid$$
$$\exists (i, t) \in N \times \{0, 1, \ldots, T\}; z_k = x_i^t \text{ or } z_k = y_i^t\}. \quad (3.7)$$

Now arrange the elements of $\mathcal{Z}(X; Y)$ in ascending order so that $\underline{z} = z_0 < z_1 < \cdots < z_q < z_{q+1} = \bar{z}$, where $q := \#\mathcal{Z}(X; Y)$. Given these conventions, we have $[\underline{z}, \bar{z}] = \bigcup_{k=0}^{q} I_k$, where $I_k := [z_k, z_{k+1}]$ for all $k = 0, 1, \ldots, q$. Because $F_t^1(z)$ and $G_t^1(z)$ are constant over every subinterval $I_k$, a necessary and sufficient condition for $\sum_{t=0}^{T} \rho^t [F_t^1(z) - G_t^1(z)] \leq 0$, for all $z \in [\underline{z}, \bar{z}]$, is that $\sum_{t=0}^{T} \rho^t [F_t^1(z_k) - G_t^1(z_k)] \leq 0$ for all $k = 0, 1, \ldots, q$. Therefore, letting $\Delta u_t = G_t^1(s) - F_t^1(s)$, we must check that condition (b) of Lemma 3.1 holds for all $s \in \mathcal{Z}(X; Y)$.

## 3.2 *Preference for more efficiently and equally distributed incomes*

The dominance criteria examined so far have a common feature – higher incomes are preferred to lower incomes – that is captured by the condition that the common within-time utility function is nondecreasing. Here, we go a step further and introduce a concern for more equally distributed incomes across individuals. Therefore, we assume a nondecreasing, concave utility function and define $U_2 := \{U \in U_1 \mid U''(z) \text{ is continuous, bounded, and nonpositive over } (\underline{z}, \bar{z})\}$. The next example will help illustrate the forthcoming definitions.

**Example 3.2.** Consider the following income structures, which involve four individuals ($i = 1, 2, 3, 4$) and three periods ($t = 0, 1, 2$):

$$Y^{(1)} = \begin{bmatrix} 2 & 3 & 2 \\ 6 & 3 & 2 \\ 6 & 5 & 2 \\ 6 & 5 & 6 \end{bmatrix}; \quad Y^{(2)} = \begin{bmatrix} 3 & 3 & 2 \\ 5 & 3 & 2 \\ 6 & 5 & 2 \\ 6 & 5 & 6 \end{bmatrix}; \quad Y^{(3)} = \begin{bmatrix} 3 & 2 & 2 \\ 5 & 3 & 2 \\ 6 & 5 & 2 \\ 6 & 6 & 6 \end{bmatrix};$$

$$Y^{(4)} = \begin{bmatrix} 3 & 2 & 2 \\ 5 & 2 & 2 \\ 6 & 6 & 2 \\ 6 & 6 & 6 \end{bmatrix}; \quad Y^{(5)} = \begin{bmatrix} 3 & 2 & 2 \\ 5 & 2 & 2 \\ 6 & 6 & 3 \\ 6 & 6 & 5 \end{bmatrix}.$$

We examine successively the cases of (i) nondecreasing discounting functions, (ii) time impatience, (iii) time impatience at a declining rate, and (iv) a constant discount rate.

First we consider the case where the discounting functions $V_t$ are nondecreasing with average utility, that is, $V \in V_1$.

**Definition 3.2.1.** Given two income structures $X, Y \in \mathfrak{X}$, we will say that $X$ is obtained from $Y$ by a *progressive transfer* if there exists a triple $(i, j, t)$ such that: (i) $x_i^t - y_i^t = y_j^t - x_j^t > 0$; (ii) $y_i^t < x_i^t \le y_j^t$; (iii) $y_i^t \le x_j^t < y_j^t$; and (iv) $x_k^\tau = y_k^\tau$ for all $(k, \tau) \ne (i, t), (j, t)$. Equivalently, we will say that $Y$ is obtained from $X$ by means of a *regressive* transfer.

The notion of a progressive transfer was introduced in the static framework by Dalton (1920) in order to capture the basic idea of inequality reduction. Examination of Example 3.2 reveals that a transfer of one unit of income from individual 2 to individual 1 at time $t = 0$ is needed in order to obtain $Y^2$ from $Y^1$, so that $Y^2$ follows from $Y^1$ by means of a progressive transfer. A similar situation arises between individuals 3 and 4 at time $t = 2$ when moving from $Y^4$ to $Y^5$. Conversely, income structures $Y^3$ and $Y^5$ obtain from income structures $Y^2$ and $Y^4$ (respectively) through a regressive transfer of the same amount. Suppose that $X$ results from $Y$ by means of a single progressive transfer; that is, there exists $(i, j, t)$ with $i < j$ such that (i) $y_i^t = z^\circ < z^* = y_j^t$, (ii) $x_i^t = z^\circ + \Delta \le z^* - \Delta = x_j^t$, and (iii) $x_k^\tau = y_k^\tau$ for all $(k, \tau) \ne (i, t), (j, t)$. It is not restrictive to suppose that the individuals' positions have been preserved during the transfer, since by definition the snapshot welfare functions are symmetric. Using the mean value theorem, $W_{V, U}(X) \ge W_{V, U}(Y)$ can be equivalently rewritten as

$$V_t'(\xi')[(U(z^\circ + \Delta) - U(z^\circ)) - (U(z^*) - U(z^* - \Delta))] \ge 0, \quad (3.8)$$

where $\xi' \in (\mathrm{EU}(F_t^1), \mathrm{EU}(G_t^1))$. By setting $\gamma := z^* - z^\circ - \Delta$ and integrating twice, we obtain

$$-V_i'(\xi') \int_0^\gamma \int_0^\Delta U''(z^\circ + t + s)\, dt\, ds \geq 0, \qquad (3.9)$$

and we therefore conclude as follows.

**Remark 3.2.1.** A sufficient condition for $W_{V,U}(X) \geq W_{V,U}(Y)$, for all $(V,U) \in V_1 \times U_2$, is that $X$ be obtained from $Y$ by means of a finite sequence of progressive transfers.

Because the utility functions are concave, for overall welfare to increase as a result of progressive transfer it is sufficient that the derivatives of the discounting functions be nonnegative. Turning to the implementation procedure, we have the next proposition.

**Proposition 3.2.1.** *Let $X, Y \in \mathfrak{X}$. Then the two following statements are equivalent:*

   (a)   $W_{V,U}(X) \geq W_{V,U}(Y)$ *for all* $(V,U) \in V_1 \times U_2$;
   (b)   $F_t^2(z) \leq G_t^2(z)$ *for all* $z \in [\underline{z}, \bar{z}]$ *and all* $t = 0, 1, ..., T$.

A necessary and sufficient condition for income structure $X$ to be preferred to income structure $Y$, by an efficiency- and equality-minded observer, is that the integrals of the snapshot CDFs in situation $X$ be nowhere below the integrals of the corresponding snapshot CDFs in situation $Y$. Appealing to Lemma 2.1, this condition turns out to be equivalent to generalized Lorenz dominance at each time period. Precisely, we have the following.

**Corollary 3.2.1.** *Let $X, Y \in \mathfrak{X}$. Then the two following statements are equivalent:*

   (a)   $W_{V,U}(X) \geq W_{V,U}(Y)$ *for all* $(V,U) \in V_1 \times U_2$;
   (b)   $x^t \geq_{GL} y^t$ *for all* $t = 0, 1, ..., T$.

Other things being equal, an increase of welfare – as measured by any nondecreasing and concave utilitarian social welfare function at a given time period – results in an overall welfare improvement. Although generalized Lorenz dominance is more powerful than rank-order dominance, there is still little hope that condition (b) of Proposition 3.2.1 could be fulfilled in practice. In the case of our example, unanimity over $V_1 \times U_2$ appears to be decisive as long as progressive transfers are involved (i.e., in 50% of cases).

We next assume time impatience, and assume that the derivatives of the discounting functions are nonincreasing with time.

390     Thierry Karcher, Patrick Moyes, & Alain Trannoy

**Definition 3.2.2.** Given two income structures $X, Y \in \mathfrak{X}$, we will say that $X$ is obtained from $Y$ by a $PT_+$ *transformation* if there exist two triples $(i_1, j_1, t_1)$, $(i_2, j_2, t_2)$ with $t_1 < t_2$, $i_1 < j_1$, and $i_2 < j_2$ such that: (i) $x_{i_1}^{t_1} - y_{i_1}^{t_1} = y_{j_1}^{t_1} - x_{j_1}^{t_1} = \Delta > 0$; (ii) $y_{i_1}^{t_1} < x_{i_1}^{t_1} \leq y_{j_1}^{t_1}$; (iii) $y_{i_1}^{t_1} \leq x_{j_1}^{t_1} < y_{j_1}^{t_1}$; (iv) $y_{i_2}^{t_2} - x_{i_2}^{t_2} = x_{j_2}^{t_2} - y_{j_2}^{t_2} = \Delta > 0$; (v) $x_{i_2}^{t_2} < y_{i_2}^{t_2} \leq x_{j_2}^{t_2}$; (vi) $x_{i_2}^{t_2} \leq y_{j_2}^{t_2} < x_{j_2}^{t_2}$; and (vii) $x_k^\tau = y_k^\tau$ for all $(k, \tau) \neq (i_1, t_1), (j_1, t_1), (i_2, t_2)$, and $(j_2, t_2)$. Equivalently, we will say that $Y$ is obtained from $X$ by means of a $PT_-$ transformation.

Less formally, a $PT_+$ transformation combines a progressive transfer at time $t_1$ with a regressive transfer at time $t_2$, both transfers being of the same amount. Inspecting the income structures defined in Example 3.2, we note that $Y^3$ results from $Y^1$ by means of a $PT_+$ transformation, while a $PT_-$ transformation is needed in order to obtain $Y^5$ from $Y^3$. Suppose, without loss of generality, that $X$ obtains from $Y$ by means of a single $PT_+$ transformation; that is, suppose $y_{i_1}^{t_1} = x_{i_2}^{t_2} = z^\circ < z^* = x_{j_2}^{t_2} = y_{j_1}^{t_1}$ and

$$x_{i_1}^{t_1} = y_{i_2}^{t_2} = z^\circ + \Delta \leq z^* - \Delta = y_{j_2}^{t_2} = x_{j_1}^{t_1}$$

for some $(i_1, j_1, t_1)$, $(i_2, j_2, t_2)$, and that $x_k^\tau = y_k^\tau$ for all $(k, \tau) \neq (i_1, t_1), (j_1, t_1)$, $(i_2, t_2)$, and $(j_2, t_2)$. Here we have assumed that, at each time period, the individuals' positions have not been modified by the transfer. Using the mean value theorem and integrating, it can be shown that $W_{V,U}(X) \geq W_{V,U}(Y)$ is equivalent to

$$-[V_{i_1}'(\xi^{t_1}) - V_{i_2}'(\xi^{t_2})] \int_0^\gamma \int_0^\Delta U''(z^\circ + t + s) \, dt \, ds \geq 0, \qquad (3.10)$$

where $\xi^{t_1}, \xi^{t_2} \in (\mathrm{EU}(F_t^1), \mathrm{EU}(G_t^1))$ and $\gamma := z^* - z^\circ - \Delta$. Thus, we deduce the following.

**Remark 3.2.2.** A sufficient condition for $W_{V,U}(X) \geq W_{V,U}(Y)$, for all $(V, U) \in V_2 \times U_2$, is that $X$ be obtained from $Y$ by means of a finite sequence of $PT_+$ transformations.

Actually, requiring that the derivatives of the discounting functions be nonincreasing with time guarantees that overall welfare will increase as a result of $PT_+$ transformation. Regarding the implementation of unanimity over $V_2 \times U_2$, we have our next proposition.

**Proposition 3.2.2.** *Let $X, Y \in \mathfrak{X}$. Then the two following statements are equivalent:*

  (a)  $W_{V,U}(X) \geq W_{V,U}(Y)$ *for all* $(V, U) \in V_2 \times U_2$;
  (b)  $\sum_{s=0}^t F_s^2(z) \leq \sum_{s=0}^t G_s^2(z)$ *for all* $z \in [\underline{z}, \bar{z}]$ *and all* $t = 0, 1, ..., T$.

A necessary and sufficient condition for income structure $X$ to be preferred to income structure $Y$, by any efficiency- and equality-minded observer endowed with time impatience, is that the sum of the integrals of the CDFs over the first $t$ periods of time in situation $X$ be nowhere above the corresponding integrals in situation $Y$. Appealing to Lemma 2.1, this condition turns out to be equivalent to applying generalized Lorenz dominance over the first $t$ distributions in succession.

**Corollary 3.2.2.** *Let $X, Y \in \mathfrak{X}$. Then the two following statements are equivalent:*

(a) $W_{V,U}(X) \geq W_{V,U}(Y)$ *for all* $(V, U) \in V_2 \times U_2$;

(b) $x^{(t)} \geq_{\mathrm{GL}} y^{(t)}$ *for all* $t = 0, 1, \ldots, T$.

As expected, the introduction of time impatience results in a less partial ordering of the income structures: only 2 among 10 pairs of income structures are not comparable.

Now let us assume time impatience at a declining rate, and require the derivatives of the discounting functions to be concave with time.

**Definition 3.2.3.** Given two income structures $X, Y \in \mathfrak{X}$, we will say that $X$ is obtained from $Y$ by a *$PT_{+-}$ transformation* if there exist four triples $(i_1, j_1, t_1)$, $(i_2, j_2, t_2)$, $(i_3, j_3, t_3)$, and $(i_4, j_4, t_4)$ with $i_r < j_r$ for all $r = 1, 2, 3, 4$, $t_1 < t_2 < t_4$, $t_1 < t_3 < t_4$, and $t_2 - t_1 = t_4 - t_3$ such that: (i) $x_{i_1}^{t_1} - y_{i_1}^{t_1} = y_{j_1}^{t_1} - x_{j_1}^{t_1} = \Delta > 0$; (ii) $y_{i_1}^{t_1} < x_{i_1}^{t_1} \leq y_{j_1}^{t_1}$; (iii) $y_{i_1}^{t_1} \leq x_{j_1}^{t_1} < y_{j_1}^{t_1}$; (iv) $y_{i_2}^{t_2} - x_{i_2}^{t_2} = x_{j_2}^{t_2} - y_{j_2}^{t_2} = \Delta > 0$; (v) $x_{i_2}^{t_2} < y_{i_2}^{t_2} \leq x_{j_2}^{t_2}$; (vi) $x_{i_2}^{t_2} \leq y_{j_2}^{t_2} < x_{j_2}^{t_2}$; (vii) $y_{i_3}^{t_3} - x_{i_3}^{t_3} = x_{j_3}^{t_3} - y_{j_3}^{t_3} = \Delta > 0$; (viii) $x_{i_3}^{t_3} < y_{i_3}^{t_3} \leq x_{j_3}^{t_3}$; (ix) $x_{i_3}^{t_3} \leq y_{j_3}^{t_3} < x_{j_3}^{t_3}$; (x) $x_{i_4}^{t_4} - y_{i_4}^{t_4} = y_{j_4}^{t_4} - x_{j_4}^{t_4} = \Delta > 0$; (xi) $y_{i_4}^{t_4} < x_{i_4}^{t_4} \leq y_{j_4}^{t_4}$; (xii) $y_{i_4}^{t_4} \leq x_{j_4}^{t_4} < y_{j_4}^{t_4}$; and (xiii) $x_k^\tau = y_k^\tau$ for all $(k, \tau) \neq (i_r, t_r), (j_r, t_r)$ $(r = 1, 2, 3, 4)$. Equivalently, we will say that $Y$ is obtained from $X$ by means of a $PT_{-+}$ transformation.

As is clear from the definition, a $PT_{+-}$ transformation combines a $PT_+$ transformation at time $t_1$ with a $PT_-$ transformation at time $t_2$. A careful examination of Example 3.2 reveals that $Y^5$ results from $Y^1$ by means of a $PT_{+-}$ transformation. Suppose that $X$ obtains from $Y$ by means of a single $PT_{+-}$ transformation; that is, suppose

$$y_{i_1}^{t_1} = x_{i_2}^{t_2} = x_{i_3}^{t_3} = y_{i_4}^{t_4} = z^\circ < z^* = y_{j_1}^{t_1} = x_{j_2}^{t_2} = x_{j_3}^{t_3} = y_{j_4}^{t_4} \quad \text{and}$$

$$x_{i_1}^{t_1} = y_{i_2}^{t_2} = y_{i_3}^{t_3} = x_{i_4}^{t_4} = z^\circ + \Delta \leq z^* - \Delta = x_{j_1}^{t_1} = y_{j_2}^{t_2} = y_{j_3}^{t_3} = x_{j_4}^{t_4}$$

for some $(i_r, j_r, t_r)$, and that $x_k^\tau = y_k^\tau$ for all $(k, \tau) \neq (i_r, t_r), (j_r, t_r)$ with $r = 1, 2, 3, 4$. We have assumed that, at each period, the individuals' positions have not been modified by the transfer. Appealing to the mean value theorem and integrating, $W_{V,U}(X) \ge W_{V,U}(Y)$ is shown to be equivalent to

$$-[(V'_{t_1}(\xi^{t_1}) - V'_{t_2}(\xi^{t_2})) - (V'_{t_3}(\xi^{t_3}) - V'_{t_4}(\xi^{t_4}))]$$

$$\int_0^\gamma \int_0^\Delta U''(z^\circ + t + s)\, dt\, ds \ge 0, \quad (3.11)$$

where $\xi^{t_r} \in (\mathrm{EU}(F_t^1), \mathrm{EU}(G_t^1))$ for all $r = 1, 2, 3, 4$ and $\gamma := z^* - z^\circ - \Delta$. We can therefore conclude as follows.

**Remark 3.2.3.** A sufficient condition for $W_{V,U}(X) \ge W_{V,U}(Y)$, for all $(V, U) \in V_3 \times U_2$, is that $X$ be obtained from $Y$ by means of a finite sequence of $\mathrm{PT}_{+-}$ transformations.

Requiring the derivatives of the discounting functions to be nonincreasing and concave with time guarantees that overall welfare will increase as a result of $\mathrm{PT}_{+-}$ transformation. Regarding the implementation of unanimity over $V_3 \times U_2$, we have the following proposition.

**Proposition 3.2.3.** *Let $X, Y \in \mathfrak{X}$. Then the two following statements are equivalent:*

(a)   $W_{V,U}(X) \ge W_{V,U}(Y)$ *for all* $(V, U) \in V_3 \times U_2$;

(b1)   $\sum_{s=0}^t \sum_{r=0}^s F_r^2(z) \le \sum_{s=0}^t \sum_{t=0}^s G_r^2(z)$ *for all* $t = 0, 1, ..., T-1$ *and all* $z \in [\underline{z}, \overline{z}]$; *and*

(b2)   $\sum_{s=0}^T F_s^2(z) \le \sum_{s=0}^T G_s^2(z)$ *for all* $z \in [\underline{z}, \overline{z}]$.

Consider an efficiency- and equality-minded observer endowed with impatience but at a declining rate. Then a necessary and sufficient condition for income structure $X$ to be preferred to income structure $Y$ by any such observer is that: (i) the double sums of the integrals of the CDFs over the first $T-1$ periods of time in situation $X$ be nowhere above the corresponding integrals in situation $Y$; and (ii) for the whole period, the sum of the integrals of the CDFs in $X$ be nowhere above the corresponding integrals in $Y$. Appealing to Lemma 2.1, these conditions turn out to be equivalent to applying generalized Lorenz dominance over suitable replications of the first $t$ distributions in succession.

**Corollary 3.2.3.** *Let $X, Y \in \mathfrak{X}$. Then the two following statements are equivalent:*

(a)   $W_{V,U}(X) \ge W_{V,U}(Y)$ *for all* $(V, U) \in V_3 \times U_2$;

(b)   $\tilde{x}^{(t)} \ge_{\mathrm{GL}} \tilde{y}^{(t)}$ *for all* $t = 0, 1, ..., T-1$, *and* $x^{(T)} \ge_{\mathrm{GL}} y^{(T)}$.

Regarding our example, only one case of incomparability survives the introduction of declining time impatience – namely, $Y^1$ versus $Y^4$.

Finally, we direct our attention to intertemporal social welfare functions with a constant discount rate, that is, $V \in V_\Omega$ where $\Omega \subseteq [0,1]$. Making use of arguments similar to those in the proofs of Propositions 3.2.1–3.2.3, we obtain the following equivalence.

**Proposition 3.2.4.** *Let $X, Y \in \mathfrak{X}$ and $\Omega \subseteq [0,1]$. Then the two following statements are equivalent:*

   (a)  $W_{V,U}(X) \geq W_{V,U}(Y)$ *for all* $(V, U) \in V_\Omega \times U_2$;

   (b)  $\sum_{t=0}^{T} \rho^t F_t^2(z) \leq \sum_{t=k/0}^{T} \rho^t G_t^2(z)$ *for all* $\rho \in \Omega$ *and all* $z \in [\underline{z}, \bar{z}]$.

Condition (b) of this proposition is easily implemented using Lemma 3.1 and the method sketched at the end of Section 3.1. Indeed, since $F_t^2(z)$ and $G_t^2(z)$ are affine over every subinterval $I_k$, we need only check that condition (b) of Lemma 3.1 holds for all $s \in Z(X; Y)$ with $\Delta u_t = F_t^2(s) - G_t^2(s)$. This provides us with the most powerful ordering of income structures when one restricts attention to nondecreasing and concave snapshot utility functions.

## 3.3   *Preference for more efficiently and equally distributed incomes with decreasing inequality aversion*

In our process of narrowing down the set of social welfare functions, we will now restrict attention to nondecreasing and concave within-time utility functions that exhibit, in addition, decreasing inequality aversion. This further restriction is captured by the condition that the second derivatives of the utility function be nondecreasing. Therefore, we consider snapshot utility functions whose first three derivatives alternate in sign, and we define $U_3 := \{U \in U_2 \mid U'''(z)$ is continuous, bounded, and nonnegative over $(\underline{z}, \bar{z})\}$. Again we introduce an example in order to illustrate the forthcoming definitions.

**Example 3.3.** Consider the following income structures, which involve six individuals ($i = 1, 2, \ldots, 6$) and three periods ($t = 0, 1, 2$):

$$
Z^{(1)} = \begin{bmatrix} 2 & 3 & 2 \\ 5 & 3 & 2 \\ 5 & 3 & 2 \\ 5 & 3 & 2 \\ 5 & 6 & 5 \\ 5 & 6 & 5 \end{bmatrix}; \quad
Z^{(2)} = \begin{bmatrix} 3 & 3 & 2 \\ 3 & 3 & 2 \\ 5 & 3 & 2 \\ 5 & 3 & 2 \\ 5 & 6 & 5 \\ 6 & 6 & 5 \end{bmatrix}; \quad
Z^{(3)} = \begin{bmatrix} 3 & 2 & 2 \\ 3 & 3 & 2 \\ 5 & 3 & 2 \\ 5 & 5 & 2 \\ 5 & 5 & 5 \\ 6 & 6 & 5 \end{bmatrix};
$$

$$Z^{(4)} = \begin{bmatrix} 3 & 2 & 2 \\ 3 & 2 & 2 \\ 5 & 5 & 2 \\ 5 & 5 & 2 \\ 5 & 5 & 5 \\ 6 & 5 & 5 \end{bmatrix}; \quad Z^{(5)} = \begin{bmatrix} 3 & 2 & 2 \\ 3 & 2 & 2 \\ 5 & 5 & 2 \\ 5 & 5 & 3 \\ 5 & 5 & 3 \\ 6 & 5 & 6 \end{bmatrix}.$$

As in the preceding paragraphs, we examine successively the cases of (i) nondecreasing discounting functions, (ii) time impatience, (iii) time impatience at a declining rate, and (iv) a constant discount rate.

We first consider the case where the discounting functions $V_t$ are nondecreasing with average utility, that is, $V \in V_1$.

**Definition 3.3.1.** Given two income structures $X, Y \in \mathfrak{X}$, we will say that $X$ is obtained from $Y$ by a *progressive composite transfer* if there exist a 5-tuple $(i, j, k, l, t)$ with $i < j < l$ and $i < k < l$, two couples $(z_1, z_2), (z_3, z_4)$, and a real $\Delta > 0$ such that: (i) $y_i^t = z_1 < z_2 = y_j^t$; (ii) $x_i^t = z_1 + \Delta \le z_2 - \Delta = x_j^t$; (iii) $x_k^t = z_3 - \Delta < z_4 + \Delta = x_l^t$; (iv) $y_k^t = z_3 \le z_4 = y_l^t$; and (v) $x_h^\tau = y_h^\tau$ for all $(h, \tau) \ne (i, t), (j, t), (k, t), (l, t)$. Equivalently, we will say that $Y$ is obtained from $X$ by means of a *regressive* composite transfer.

As is clear from the definition, a progressive composite transfer combines a progressive transfer and a regressive transfer, the progressive transfer taking place somehow lower down in the income distribution.[3] Examination of Example 3.3 reveals that $Z^2$ is obtained from $Z^1$ by distributing evenly between individuals 1 and 6 the two units of income taken from individual 2 at time $t = 0$; according to Definition 3.3.1, $Z^2$ follows from $Z^1$ by means of a progressive composite transfer. Similarly, $Z^4$ obtains from $Z^5$ through a progressive composite transfer, whereas a regressive composite transfer is needed in order to obtain $Z^3$ from $Z^2$ and $Z^5$ from $Z^4$. Suppose that $X$ results from $Y$ by means of a single progressive composite transfer as just defined, and assume that the individuals' positions have not been modified by the transfer. Using the mean value theorem, $W_{V,U}(X) \ge W_{V,U}(Y)$ can be equivalently rewritten as

$$V_t'(\xi')[(U(z_1 + \Delta) - U(z_1)) - (U(z_2) - U(z_2 - \Delta))]$$
$$\ge V_t'(\xi')[(U(z_3) - U(z_3 - \Delta)) - (U(z_4 + \Delta) - U(z_4))], \quad (3.12)$$

[3] The notion of a progressive composite transfer is due to Kolm (1976), who referred to it as *transfer sensitivity*. Later on, Shorrocks and Foster (1987) proposed a stronger version of transfer sensitivity they called *favorable composite transfer* (FACT). However, as they pointed out, both types of transfers yield equivalent results when one restricts attention to additive social welfare functions (which is typically our case).

where $\xi' \in (\text{EU}(F_t^1), \text{EU}(G_t^1))$. Letting $\eta := z_3 - z_1 - \Delta = z_2 - z_1 - \Delta$, $\gamma := z_4 - z_3 + \Delta = z_2 - z_1 - \Delta$, and integrating three times, we obtain

$$V_t'(\xi') \int_0^\eta \int_0^\gamma \int_0^\Delta U'''(z_1 + s + t + v) \, ds \, dt \, dv \geq 0. \qquad (3.13)$$

We therefore conclude as follows.

**Remark 3.3.1.** A sufficient condition for $W_{V,U}(X) \geq W_{V,U}(Y)$, for all $(V, U) \in V_1 \times U_3$, is that $X$ be obtained from $Y$ by means of a finite sequence of progressive composite transfers.

In the case of utility functions with nondecreasing second derivatives, for overall welfare to increase as a result of a progressive composite transfer it is sufficient that the derivatives of the discounting functions be nonnegative. Regarding the implementation of unanimity over $V_1 \times U_3$, we have the next proposition.

**Proposition 3.3.1.** *Let $X, Y \in \mathfrak{X}$. Then the two following statements are equivalent:*

   (a)  $W_{V,U}(X) \geq W_{V,U}(Y)$ *for all* $(V, U) \in V_1 \times U_3$;
   (b1)  $\mu_{F_t^1} \geq \mu_{G_t^1}$ *for all* $t = 0, 1, \ldots, T$, *and*
   (b2)  $F_t^3(z) \leq G_t^3(z)$ *for all* $t = 0, 1, \ldots, T$ *and all* $z \in [\underline{z}, \bar{z}]$.

A necessary and sufficient condition for income structure $X$ to be preferred to income structure $Y$, by any efficiency- and equality-minded observer with decreasing inequality aversion, is that: (i) the mean income in $X$ be no less than the mean income in $Y$ at each time period; and (ii) the double integrals corresponding to every snapshot CDF in $X$ be less than the corresponding double integrals in situation $Y$, at each time period. We note here that no simple equivalence exists in terms of ICDFs (see, however, Shorrocks and Foster 1987 and Davies and Hoy 1991 in the case of snapshot distributions). Other things being equal, an increase of welfare – as measured by any nondecreasing and concave (with decreasing inequality aversion) utilitarian social welfare function at a given time period – results in an overall welfare improvement. Condition (b) of Proposition 3.3.1 is conclusive in half the cases introduced in Example 3.3.

We next consider the case of time impatience; that is, we assume that the derivatives of the discounting functions are nonincreasing with time.

**Definition 3.3.2.** Given two income structures $X, Y \in \mathfrak{X}$, we will say that $X$ is obtained from $Y$ by a *$PCT_+$ transformation* if there exist two 5-tuples

$(i_1, j_1, k_1, l_1, t_1)$, $(i_2, j_2, k_2, l_2, t_2)$ with $i_r < j_r < l_r$ and $i_r < k_r < l_r$ $(r = 1, 2)$, two couples $(z_1, z_2)$, $(z_3, z_4)$, and a real $\Delta > 0$ such that: (i) $y_{i_1}^{t_1} = x_{i_2}^{t_2} = z_1 < z_2 = x_{j_2}^{t_2} = y_{j_1}^{t_1}$; (ii) $x_{i_1}^{t_1} = y_{i_2}^{t_2} = z_1 + \Delta \le z_2 - \Delta = y_{i_2}^{t_2} = x_{j_1}^{t_1}$; (iii) $x_{k_1}^{t_1} = y_{k_2}^{t_2} = z_3 - \Delta < z_4 + \Delta = y_{l_2}^{t_2} = x_{l_1}^{t_1}$; (iv) $y_{k_1}^{t_1} = x_{k_2}^{t_2} = z_3 \le z_4 = x_{l_2}^{t_2} = y_{l_1}^{t_1}$; and (v) $x_h^\tau = y_h^\tau$ for all $(h, \tau) \neq (i_r, t_r)$, $(j_r, t_r)$, $(k_r, t_r)$, $(l_r, t_r)$ with $r = 1, 2$. Equivalently, we will say that $Y$ is obtained from $X$ by means of a PCT$_-$ transformation.

Less formally, a PCT$_+$ transformation combines a progressive composite transfer at time $t_1$ with a regressive composite transfer at time $t_2$, both transfers being of the same amount. Inspecting the income structures defined in Example 3.3 reveals that $Z^3$ results from $Z^1$ by means of a PCT$_+$ transformation, whereas a PCT$_-$ transformation is needed in order to obtain $Z^5$ from $Z^3$. Suppose that $X$ results from $Y$ by means of a single PCT$_+$ transformation as given in Definition 3.3.2. Appealing again to the mean value theorem and integrating, it can be shown that $W_{V, U}(X) \ge W_{V, U}(Y)$ is equivalent to

$$[V_{t_1}'(\xi^{t_1}) - V_{t_2}'(\xi^{t_2})] \int_0^\eta \int_0^\gamma \int_0^\Delta U'''(z_1 + s + t + v)\, ds\, dt\, dv \ge 0, \qquad (3.14)$$

where $\xi^{t_1}, \xi^{t_2} \in (EU(F_t^1), EU(G_t^1))$, $\eta := z_3 - z_1 - \Delta = z_2 - z_1 - \Delta$, and $\gamma := z_4 - z_3 + \Delta = z_2 - z_1 - \Delta$. We therefore conclude as follows.

**Remark 3.3.2.** A sufficient condition for $W_{V, U}(X) \ge W_{V, U}(Y)$, for all $(V, U) \in V_2 \times U_3$, is that $X$ be obtained from $Y$ by means of a finite sequence of PCT$_+$ transformations.

Requiring that the derivatives of the discounting functions be nonincreasing with time guarantees that overall welfare will increase as a result of PCT$_+$ transformation, as we shall show. The next result suggests a procedure for implementing unanimity over $V_2 \times U_3$.

**Proposition 3.3.2.** Let $X, Y \in \mathfrak{X}$. Then the two following statements are equivalent:

   (a)   $W_{V, U}(X) \ge W_{V, U}(Y)$ for all $(V, U) \in V_2 \times U_3$;

   (b1)   $\sum_{s=0}^t \mu_{F_s^1} \ge \sum_{s=0}^t \mu_{G_s^1}$ for all $t = 0, 1, \ldots, T$; and

   (b2)   $\sum_{s=0}^t F_s^3(z) \le \sum_{s=0}^t G_s^3(z)$ for all $t = 0, 1, \ldots, T$ and all $z \in [\underline{z}, \bar{z}]$.

A necessary and sufficient condition for income structure $X$ to be preferred to income structure $Y$ – by any efficiency- and equality-minded (but with decreasing inequality aversion) observer endowed with time impatience – considering the $T$ periods in succession, is that: (i) the sum of the mean incomes over the first $t$ periods in situation $X$ be no less than the corresponding mean incomes in $Y$; and (ii) the sum of the double integrals of the CDFs in situation $X$ over the first $t$ periods be nowhere above the corresponding integrals in situation $Y$. As expected, application of this procedure results in a less partial ordering of the income structures: only 2 out of 10 pairs of the income structures introduced in Example 3.3 remain not comparable.

Now let us assume time impatience at a declining rate, which amounts to requiring that $V \in V_3$.

**Definition 3.3.3.**  Given two income structures $X, Y \in \mathfrak{X}$, we will say that $X$ is obtained from $Y$ by a *$PCT_{+-}$ transformation* if there exist four 5-tuples $(i_1, j_1, k_1, l_1, t_1)$, $(i_2, j_2, k_2, l_2, t_2)$, $(i_3, j_3, k_3, l_3, t_3)$, $(i_4, j_4, k_4, l_4, t_4)$ with $i_r < j_r < l_r$ and $i_r < k_r < l_r$ for $r = 1, 2, 3, 4$, two couples $(z_1, z_2)$ and $(z_3, z_4)$, and a real $\Delta > 0$ such that: (i) $y_{i_1}^{t_1} = x_{i_2}^{t_2} = z_1 < z_2 = x_{j_2}^{t_2} = y_{j_1}^{t_1}$; (ii) $x_{i_1}^{t_1} = y_{i_2}^{t_2} = z_1 + \Delta \leq z_2 - \Delta = y_{j_2}^{t_2} = x_{j_1}^{t_1}$; (iii) $x_{k_1}^{t_1} = y_{k_2}^{t_2} = z_3 - \Delta < z_4 + \Delta = y_{l_2}^{t_2} = x_{l_1}^{t_1}$; (iv) $y_{k_1}^{t_1} = x_{k_2}^{t_2} = z_3 \leq z_4 = x_{l_2}^{t_2} = y_{l_1}^{t_1}$; (v) $x_{i_3}^{t_3} = y_{i_4}^{t_4} = z_1 < z_2 = y_{j_4}^{t_4} = x_{j_3}^{t_3}$; (vi) $y_{i_3}^{t_3} = x_{i_4}^{t_4} = z_1 + \Delta \leq z_2 - \Delta = x_{j_4}^{t_4} = y_{j_3}^{t_3}$; (vii) $y_{k_3}^{t_3} = x_{k_4}^{t_4} = z_3 - \Delta < z_4 + \Delta = x_{l_4}^{t_4} = y_{l_3}^{t_3}$; (vii) $x_{k_3}^{t_3} = y_{k_4}^{t_4} = z_3 \leq z_4 = y_{l_4}^{t_4} = x_{l_3}^{t_3}$; and (viii) $x_h^\tau = y_h^\tau$ for all $(h, \tau) \neq (i_r, t_r), (j_r, t_r), (k_r, t_r), (l_r, t_r)$ with $r = 1, 2, 3, 4$. Equivalently, we will say that $Y$ is obtained from $X$ by means of a $PCT_{-+}$ transformation.

Therefore, a $PCT_{+-}$ transformation involves a $PCT_+$ transformation at time $t_1$ and a $PCT_-$ transformation at time $t_2$. A careful examination of Example 3.3 indicates that $Y^5$ results from $Y^1$ by means of a $PCT_{+-}$ transformation. Suppose that $X$ results from $Y$ by means of a single $PCT_{+-}$ transformation as just defined. Appealing once again to the mean value theorem and letting $\eta := z_3 - z_1 - \Delta = z_2 - z_1 - \Delta$ and $\gamma := z_4 - z_3 + \Delta = z_2 - z_1 - \Delta$, it can be shown that $W_{V,U}(X) \geq W_{V,U}(Y)$ is equivalent to

$$[(V_{t_1}'(\xi^{t_1}) - V_{t_2}'(\xi^{t_2})) - (V_{t_3}'(\xi^{t_3}) - V_{t_4}'(\xi^{t_4}))]$$

$$\int_0^\eta \int_0^\gamma \int_0^\Delta U'''(z_1 + s + t + v)\, ds\, dt\, dv \geq 0, \quad (3.15)$$

where $\xi^{t_r} \in (EU(F_t^1), EU(G_t^1))$ for $r = 1, 2, 3, 4$. We therefore conclude as follows.

**Remark 3.3.3.**  A sufficient condition for $W_{V,U}(X) \geq W_{V,U}(Y)$, for all $(V, U) \in V_3 \times U_3$, is that $X$ be obtained from $Y$ by means of a finite sequence of $PCT_{+-}$ transformations.

For a $\text{PCT}_{+-}$ transformation to result in an overall welfare increase, it is sufficient that the derivatives of the discounting functions be nonincreasing and concave with time. The implementation of unanimity over $V_2 \times U_3$ becomes slightly more complicated, as is shown in the next proposition.

**Proposition 3.3.3.** *Let $X, Y \in \mathfrak{X}$. Then the two following statements are equivalent:*

(a)  $W_{V,U}(X) \geq W_{V,U}(Y)$ *for all* $(V,U) \in V_3 \times U_3$;

(b1) $\sum_{s=0}^{t} \sum_{r=0}^{s} \mu_{F_r^1} \geq \sum_{s=0}^{t} \sum_{r=0}^{s} \mu_{G_r^1}$ *for all* $t = 0, 1, ..., T-1$,

(b2) $\sum_{s=0}^{T} \mu_{F_s^1} \geq \sum_{s=0}^{T} \mu_{G_s^1}$,

(b3) $\sum_{s=0}^{t} \sum_{r=0}^{s} F_r^3(z) \leq \sum_{s=0}^{t} \sum_{t=0}^{s} G_r^3(z)$ *for all* $t = 0, 1, ..., T-1$
*and for all* $z \in [\underline{z}, \bar{z}]$, *and*

(b4) $\sum_{s=0}^{T} F_s^3(z) \leq \sum_{s=0}^{t} G_s^3(z)$ *for all* $z \in [\underline{z}, \bar{z}]$.

For income structure $X$ to be preferred to income structure $Y$ – by any efficiency- and equality-minded (but with decreasing inequality aversion) observer endowed with time impatience at a declining rate – the four following conditions must hold: (i) the double sum of the mean incomes in situation $X$ over the first $T-1$ periods of time is no less than the corresponding sum in situation $Y$; (ii) the sum of the mean incomes in $X$ over the whole period is no less than the corresponding sum in $Y$; (iii) the double sum of the double integrals of the CDFs in situation $X$ over the first $T-1$ periods of time is nowhere above the corresponding integrals in situation $Y$; and (iv) the sum of the double integrals of the CDFs in $X$ over the whole period are nowhere above the corresponding integrals of the CDFs in $Y$. Only one case of incomparability – namely, $Z^1$ versus $Z^4$ – survives this sequential procedure.

Finally, by restricting attention to intertemporal social welfare functions with a constant discount rate (i.e., $V \in V_\Omega$ where $\Omega \subseteq [0,1]$), we obtain the following equivalence.

**Proposition 3.3.4.** *Let $X, Y \in \mathfrak{X}$ and $\Omega \subseteq [0,1]$. Then the two following statements are equivalent:*

(a)  $W_{V,U}(X) \geq W_{V,U}(Y)$ *for all* $(V,U) \in V_\Omega \times U_3$;

(b1) $\sum_{t=0}^{T} \rho^t F_t^3(z) \leq \sum_{t=0}^{T} \rho^t G_t^3(z)$ *for all* $\rho \in \Omega$ *and all* $z \in [\underline{z}, \bar{z}]$, *and*

(b2) $\sum_{s=0}^{T} \rho^t \mu_{F_s^1} \geq \sum_{s=0}^{T} \rho^t \mu_{G_s^1}$ *for all* $\rho \in \Omega$.

This provides us with the most powerful ordering of income structures of this paper. Here, the procedure (sketched in Section 3.1) to implement the ranking of income structures using constant discount rates must be amended, because $F_t^3(z)$ and $G_t^3(z)$ are no longer linear over every sub-interval $I_k$, $k = 0, 1, ..., q$. Consider any interval $I_k := [z_k, z_{k+1}]$. It is well known that necessary and sufficient conditions for $F_t^3(z) - G_t^3(z) \leq 0$, for all $z \in [z_k, z_{k+1}]$, are (i) $F_t^3(z_k) - G_t^3(z_k) \leq 0$, (ii) $F_t^3(z_{k+1}) - G_t^3(z_{k+1}) \leq 0$, and (iii) $F_t^3(u_k^*) - G_t^3(u_k^*) \leq 0$, where

$$u_k^* \in (z_k, z_{k+1}) \text{ is defined by } F_t^2(u_k^*) - G_t^2(u_k^*) = 0$$

(see e.g. Fishburn and Vickson 1978, p. 79). Denote as $\mathcal{Y}(X; Y)$ the set of points $u_k^*$ (there are at most $T+1$ such points), and let

$$\mathcal{Z}^*(X; Y) := \mathcal{Z}(X; Y) \cup \mathcal{Y}(X; Y).$$

Since any positive linear combination of quadratic functions is quadratic, a necessary and sufficient condition for $\sum_{t=0}^{T} \rho^t [F_t^3(z) - G_t^3(z)] \leq 0$, for all $z \in [\underline{z}, \bar{z}]$, is that $\sum_{t=0}^{T} \rho^t [F_t^3(u) - G_t^3(u)] \leq 0$ for all $u \in \mathcal{Z}^*(X; Y)$. Therefore, we must check that condition (b) of Lemma 3.1 holds, letting successively (i) $\Delta u_t = G_t^3(s) - F_t^3(s)$ for all $s \in \mathcal{Z}^*(X; Y)$, and (ii) $\Delta u_t = \mu_{F_s^1} - \mu_{G_s^1}$.

One might derive even stronger orderings by narrowing still further the class of snapshot utility functions. Exploiting the formal similarity between the treatment of risk and welfare measurement suggests an appeal to the class of utility functions with *decreasing absolute risk aversion,* denoted $U_D$. Because this class is a proper subset of the class of nondecreasing and concave utility functions with decreasing inequality aversion, it is clear that $V_\Omega \times U_D$ would imply a more powerful ordering of income structures than would $V_\Omega \times U_3$. However, though the assumption that $-U''/U'$ is decreasing with wealth seems plausible when choosing among risky prospects, we remark that most of the commonly used measures of welfare and inequality do violate the condition of *decreasing absolute inequality aversion.*[4] Furthermore, we note that there exists no simple procedure to implement stochastic dominance with decreasing absolute risk aversion unless one restricts attention to very specific cases (see the discussion in Fishburn and Vickson 1978).

## 4    Summary and suggestions for further research

To conclude, we would stress that this work represents only a preliminary incursion into the fields of intertemporal welfare measurement, and insist that our analysis calls for further investigation. Given the different families of snapshot utility functions and discounted functions considered

---

[4] Indeed, it is generally assumed that inequality is not modified when all incomes increase in the same *proportion* (constant relative inequality aversion), though the view that equal *additions* to incomes do not affect inequality (constant absolute inequality aversion) has also been proposed; see Kolm (1976).

Table 1. *Stochastic dominance orderings of income structures for different classes of utility and discounting functions*

---

$U_1 := \{U \in U \mid U'(z) \text{ is nonnegative over } (\underline{z}, \bar{z})\}$

$V_1$: $\quad F_t^1(z) \le G_t^1(z) \; \forall z \in [\underline{z}, \bar{z}] \; \& \; \forall t = 0, 1, \ldots, T$

$V_2$: $\quad \sum_{s=0}^t F_s^1(z) \le \sum_{s=0}^t G_s^1(z) \; \forall z \in [\underline{z}, \bar{z}] \; \& \; \forall t = 0, 1, \ldots, T$

$V_3$: $\quad \sum_{s=0}^t \sum_{r=0}^s F_r^1(z) \le \sum_{s=0}^t \sum_{r=0}^s G_r^1(z) \; \forall z \in [\underline{z}, \bar{z}] \; \& \; \forall t = 0, 1, \ldots, T$
$\quad \sum_{s=0}^T F_s^1(z) \le \sum_{s=0}^T G_s^1(z) \; \forall z \in [\underline{z}, \bar{z}]$

$V_\Omega$: $\quad \sum_{t=0}^T \rho^t F_t^1(z) \le \sum_{t=0}^T \rho^t G_t^1(z) \; \forall \rho \in \Omega \; \& \; \forall z \in [\underline{z}, \bar{z}]$

$U_2 := \{U \in U_1 \mid U''(z) \text{ is nonpositive over } (\underline{z}, \bar{z})\}$

$V_1$: $\quad F_t^2(z) \le G_t^2(z) \; \forall z \in [\underline{z}, \bar{z}] \; \& \; \forall t = 0, 1, \ldots, T$

$V_2$: $\quad \sum_{s=0}^t F_s^2(z) \le \sum_{s=0}^t G_s^2(z) \; \forall z \in [\underline{z}, \bar{z}] \; \& \; \forall t = 0, 1, \ldots, T$

$V_3$: $\quad \sum_{s=0}^t \sum_{r=0}^s F_r^2(z) \le \sum_{s=0}^t \sum_{r=0}^s G_r^2(z) \; \forall z \in [\underline{z}, \bar{z}] \; \& \; \forall t = 0, 1, \ldots, T$
$\quad \sum_{s=0}^T F_s^2(z) \le \sum_{s=0}^T G_s^2(z) \; \forall z \in [\underline{z}, \bar{z}]$

$V_\Omega$: $\quad \sum_{t=0}^T \rho^t F_t^2(z) \le \sum_{t=0}^T \rho^t G_t^2(z) \; \forall \rho \in \Omega \; \& \; \forall z \in [\underline{z}, \bar{z}]$

$U_3 := \{U \in U_2 \mid U'''(z) \text{ is nonnegative over } (\underline{z}, \bar{z})\}$

$V_1$: $\quad \mu_{F_t^1} \ge \mu_{G_t^1} \; \forall t = 0, 1, \ldots, T$
$\quad F_t^3(z) \le G_t^3(z) \; \forall z \in [\underline{z}, \bar{z}] \; \& \; \forall t = 0, 1, \ldots, T$

$V_2$: $\quad \sum_{s=0}^t \mu_{F_s^1} \ge \sum_{s=0}^t \mu_{G_s^1} \; \forall t = 0, 1, \ldots, T$
$\quad \sum_{s=0}^t F_s^3(z) \le \sum_{s=0}^t G_s^3(z) \; \forall z \in [\underline{z}, \bar{z}] \; \& \; \forall t = 0, 1, \ldots, T$

$V_3$: $\quad \sum_{s=0}^t \sum_{r=0}^s \mu_{F_r^1} \ge \sum_{s=0}^t \sum_{r=0}^s \mu_{G_r^1} \; \forall t = 0, 1, \ldots, T-1$
$\quad \sum_{s=0}^T \mu_{F_s^1} \ge \sum_{s=0}^T \mu_{G_s^1}$
$\quad \sum_{s=0}^t \sum_{r=0}^s F_r^3(z) \le \sum_{s=0}^t \sum_{r=0}^s G_r^3(z) \; \forall t = 0, 1, \ldots, T-1 \; \& \; \forall z \in [\underline{z}, \bar{z}]$
$\quad \sum_{s=0}^T F_s^3(z) \le \sum_{s=0}^t G_s^3(z) \; \forall z \in [\underline{z}, \bar{z}]$

$V_\Omega$: $\quad \sum_{t=0}^T \rho^t F_t^3(z) \le \sum_{t=0}^T \rho^t G_t^3(z) \; \forall \rho \in \Omega \; \& \; \forall z \in [\underline{z}, \bar{z}]$

---

here, the application of the general principle of unanimity has led us to 12 dominance criteria. Table 1 emphasizes the parallels that can be drawn in Sections 3.1–3.3. In the case of discrete distributions, it is generally more efficient to use implementation procedures based on the ICDFs (see Corollaries 3.1.1–3.3.3) rather than the CDFs; this typically arises when working with highly disaggregated data or percentiles.

Regarding the chosen social welfare function, one may legitimately feel that focusing on model (3.1) is far too restrictive. First, we concede that the restrictions we placed on the classes of utility functions and discounting functions are extremely demanding, particularly so for the discounting functions. This can be illustrated with the concept of time impatience. According to our definition, society is impatient if it prefers to be given an extra amount of welfare at time $t$ rather than at time $t+1$ *irrespective* of the welfare levels attained in periods $t$ and $t+1$, although the traditional definition of impatience would require the same welfare levels in both periods (see e.g. Malinvaud 1977, p. 246). As a second point, we note that the assumption of additive discounting over time can be easily dispensed with. The adoption of a social welfare function such as $W_{V,U}(X) = V(\text{EU}(F_0^1), \ldots, \text{EU}(F_T^1))$, where $V: \mathbb{R}_+^{T+1} \to \mathbb{R}$ is not necessarily additively separable, would lead to similar results by suitably restricting the set of discounting functions. It is also interesting to note that essentially the same results can be obtained by choosing

$$W_\phi(X) = \sum_{t=0}^{T} \left( \frac{1}{n} \sum_{i=1}^{n} \phi_t(x_i^t) \right), \tag{4.1}$$

where $\phi_t$ is the snapshot utility function at time $t$. The exercise then consists of narrowing down the set of admissible $(T+1)$-tuples of utility functions $\Phi := \{\phi := (\phi_0, \phi_1, \ldots, \phi_T) \,|\, \phi_t: \mathbb{R}_+ \to \mathbb{R} \text{ for all } t = 0, 1, \ldots, T\}$.[5] The equivalence is worth noting, since Atkinson and Bourguignon (1987) seem to impose weaker restrictions on the social welfare function. A challenging question is to know if our results still hold when one does not assume any form of additive separability. This issue is of crucial importance for the theory of inequality measurement in an intertemporal framework, and it deserves further investigation.

On the other hand, it would certainly be fruitful to seek more powerful criteria for ranking income distributions over time. This can only be done by further narrowing down the classes of social welfare functions through the introduction of more specific value judgments. One possibility would be to restrict attention to particular families of utility functions such as (i) the *constant relative inequality aversion* (CRIA) family defined by $U(z) := (1/(1-\epsilon))z^{1-\epsilon}$ for $0 \le \epsilon \le \infty$ ($\epsilon \ne 1$) and $U(z) := \ln z$ for $\epsilon = 1$ (Atkinson 1970), or (ii) the *constant absolute inequality aversion* (CAIA) family defined by $U(z) := 1 - e^{-\eta z}$ for $0 < \eta \le \infty$ and $U(z) := z$ for $\eta = 0$ (Kolm 1976). In the manner of our treatment of constant discount rates, another idea would be to search for dominance over a given interval of the range of all the possible values of the inequality aversion parameter.

As long as one thinks that mobility does not matter, the dominance criteria presented in this paper are potential candidates for welfare measurement within an intertemporal framework. Mobility is widely expected to reduce inequality when incomes are measured over a sufficiently long period. To illustrate this, consider the two following income structures:

---

[5] This is essentially the model adopted by Atkinson and Bourguignon (1987) when dealing with welfare comparisons across families of different sizes.

$$X = \begin{bmatrix} 1 & 4 \\ 5 & 2 \end{bmatrix}; \quad Y = \begin{bmatrix} 1 & 2 \\ 5 & 4 \end{bmatrix}.$$

According to any of our dominance criteria, situations $X$ and $Y$ are judged as being equivalent, though $X$ is in some obvious sense intertemporally more equal than $Y$. Indeed, cumulating incomes up to the second period for each individual, it can be observed that the cumulated distribution in situation $X$ obtains from the cumulated distribution in situation $Y$ by means of a progressive transfer. Our next task will be to investigate the possibility of devising new dominance criteria that react positively to such equalizing movements of incomes along time by suitably restricting the classes of social welfare functions.

## Appendix

### A.1   *Proof of Propositions 3.1.1–3.1.3*

*Sufficiency*

Suppose that $W_{V,U}(X) \geq W_{V,U}(Y)$, and let $\Delta G_t^1(z) := F_t^1(z) - G_t^1(z)$ for all $z \in [\underline{z}, \bar{z}]$ and all $t = 0, 1, \ldots, T$. Using the mean value theorem and integrating by parts, we obtain equivalently

$$-\int_{\underline{z}}^{\bar{z}} U'(z) \left[ \sum_{t=0}^{T} V_t'(\xi^t) \Delta G_t^1(z) \right] dz \geq 0 \tag{A.1}$$

for some $\xi^t \in (\mathrm{EU}(F_t^1), \mathrm{EU}(G_t^1))$ $(t = 0, 1, \ldots, T)$. Since by assumption $U'(z) \geq 0$, we are looking for conditions which guarantee that the term within brackets in (A.1) is nonpositive. We consider successively three cases.

*Case 1:* $(U, V) \in V_1 \times U_1$. Clearly, $F_t^1(z) \leq G_t^1(z)$, for all $z \in [\underline{z}, \bar{z}]$ and all $t = 0, 1, \ldots, T$, will guarantee that (A.1) is verified.

*Case 2:* $(U, V) \in V_2 \times U_1$. Appealing to the partial summation formula of Abel, the term within brackets in (A.1) can be rewritten as

$$\sum_{t=0}^{T-1} (V_t'(\xi^t) - V_{t+1}'(\xi^{t+1})) \left[ \sum_{s=0}^{t} \Delta G_s^1(z) \right] + V_T'(\xi^T) \left[ \sum_{s=0}^{T} \Delta G_s^1(z) \right] \geq 0. \tag{A.2}$$

We deduce that a sufficient condition for (A.1) to hold is that

$$\sum_{s=0}^{t} F_s^1(z) \leq \sum_{s=0}^{t} G_s^1(z)$$

for all $z \in [\underline{z}, \bar{z}]$ and all $t = 0, 1, \ldots, T$.

*Case 3:* $(U, V) \in V_3 \times U_1$. Appealing once again to the partial summation formula of Abel, (A.2) can be rewritten as

$$\sum_{t=0}^{T-2} ((V_t'(\xi^t) - V_{t+1}'(\xi^{t+1})) - (V_{t+1}'(\xi^{t+1}) - V_{t+2}'(\xi^{t+2}))) \left[ \sum_{s=0}^{t} \sum_{r=0}^{s} \Delta G_r^1(z) \right]$$

$$+ (V_{T-1}'(\xi^{T-1}) - V_T'(\xi^T)) \left[ \sum_{s=0}^{T-1} \sum_{r=0}^{s} \Delta G_r^1(z) \right]$$

$$+ V_T'(\xi^T) \left[ \sum_{s=0}^{T} \Delta G_s^1(z) \right] \geq 0, \tag{A.3}$$

which shows that conditions (b1) and (b2) of Proposition 3.1.3 are sufficient for (A.1) to hold.

### *Necessity*

We examine successively Propositions 3.1.1, 3.1.2, and 3.1.3 to show that, if condition (b) is not satisfied, then we can find an admissible couple $(U^*, V^*)$ such that $\Delta W_{V^* U^*} := W_{V^* U^*}(X) - W_{V^* U^*}(Y) < 0$.

*Case 1:* $(U, V) \in V_1 \times U_1$. Let $(t^*, z^*)$ be the smallest (in the lexicographic sense) couple $(t, z)$ such that $P_1(z; x^t) > P_1(z; y^t)$. Choose $V^* := (V_0^*, V_1^*, \ldots, V_T^*)$, defined by $V_s^*(u) = 0$ for all $s \neq t^*$ and by $V_{t^*}^*(u) = u$ for all $u \in \mathbb{R}$; clearly, $V^* \in V_1$. Furthermore, define

$$\phi^*(z) := \begin{cases} 0 & \text{for } \underline{z} \leq z < z^*, \\ z^* & \text{for } z^* \leq z \leq \bar{z}, \end{cases} \tag{A.4}$$

and let $U^* \in U_1$ be a suitable approximation of $\phi^*$ (see Fishburn and Vickson 1978, p. 75). We obtain $\Delta W_{V^* U^*} = [P_1(z^*; y^t) - P_1(z^*; x^t)]z^* < 0$ and hence a contradiction.

*Case 2:* $(U, V) \in V_2 \times U_1$. Let $(t^*, z^*)$ be the smallest couple $(t, z)$ such that $P_1(z; x^{(t)}) > P_1(z; y^{(t)})$. Then the proof goes as in case 1, taking $V^* := (V_0^*, V_1^*, \ldots, V_T^*)$ such that $V_s^*(u) = u$ for all $s = 0, 1, \ldots, t^*$ and $V_s^*(u) = 0$ for all $s = t^*+1, \ldots, T$.

*Case 3:* $(U, V) \in V_3 \times U_1$. We suppose first that condition (b2) of Proposition 3.1.3 is false, and let $z^*$ be the smallest $z$ such that $P_1(z; x^{(T)}) > P_1(z; y^{(T)})$. Taking $V^* := (V_0^*, V_1^*, \ldots, V_T^*)$ such that $V_t^*(u) = u$, for all $t = 0, 1, \ldots, T$, yields a contradiction. Suppose next that (b1) is false, and let $(t^*, z^*)$ be the smallest couple $(t, z)$ such that $P_1(z; \tilde{x}^{(t)}) > P_1(z; \tilde{y}^{(t)})$. Choosing $V^* := (V_0^*, V_1^*, \ldots, V_T^*)$ defined by $V_s^*(u) = (t^*-s+1)u$ for all $s = 0, 1, \ldots, t^*$ and $V_s^*(u) = 0$ for all $s = t^*+1, \ldots, T$, we arrive once again at a contradiction. $\square$

404    Thierry Karcher, Patrick Moyes, & Alain Trannoy

## A.2    Proof of Propositions 3.2.1–3.2.3

### Sufficiency
Integrating (A.1) by parts, we obtain

$$-U'(\bar{z})\left[\sum_{t=0}^{T} V_t'(\xi^t)\Delta G_t^2(\bar{z})\right] + \int_{\underline{z}}^{\bar{z}} U''(z)\left[\sum_{t=0}^{T} V_t'(\xi^t)\Delta G_t^2(z)\right]dz \geq 0. \quad (A.5)$$

Since by assumption $U'(z) \geq 0$ and $U''(z) \leq 0$, we are looking for conditions which guarantee that the two terms within brackets in (A.5) are nonpositive.

*Case 1:* $(U, V) \in V_1 \times U_2$. Clearly $F_t^2 \leq G_t^2(z)$, for all $z \in [\underline{z}, \bar{z}]$ and all $t = 0, 1, ..., T$, is sufficient for (A.5) to hold.

*Case 2:* $(U, V) \in V_2 \times U_2$. Appealing to the partial summation formula of Abel, the second term within brackets in (A.5) will be nonpositive if and only if

$$\sum_{t=0}^{T-1} (V_t'(\xi^t) - V_{t+1}'(\xi^{t+1}))\left[\sum_{s=0}^{t} \Delta G_s^2(z)\right] + V_T'(\xi^T)\left[\sum_{s=0}^{T} \Delta G_s^2(z)\right] \geq 0. \quad (A.6)$$

Therefore $\sum_{s=0}^{t} F_s^2(z) \leq \sum_{s=0}^{t} G_s^2(z)$, for all $z \in [\underline{z}, \bar{z}]$ and all $t = 0, 1, ..., T$, is clearly sufficient for (A.5) to hold.

*Case 3:* $(U, V) \in V_3 \times U_2$. Appealing once again to the partial summation formula of Abel, (A.6) can be rewritten as

$$\sum_{t=0}^{T-2} ((V_t'(\xi^t) - V_{t+1}'(\xi^{t+1})) - (V_{t+1}'(\xi^{t+1}) - V_{t+2}'(\xi^{t+2})))\left[\sum_{s=0}^{t}\sum_{r=0}^{s} \Delta G_r^2(z)\right]$$

$$+ (V_{T-1}'(\xi^{T-1}) - V_T'(\xi^T))\left[\sum_{s=0}^{T-1}\sum_{r=0}^{s} \Delta G_r^2(z)\right]$$

$$+ V_T'(\xi^T)\left[\sum_{s=0}^{T} \Delta G_s^2(z)\right] \geq 0, \quad (A.7)$$

which proves that conditions (b1) and (b2) of Proposition 3.2.3 are sufficient for (A.5) to hold.

### Necessity
Consider the nondecreasing and concave utility function defined by

$$\phi^*(z) := \begin{cases} z - z^* & \text{for } \underline{z} \leq z < z^*, \\ 0 & \text{for } z^* \leq z \leq \bar{z}, \end{cases} \quad (A.8)$$

and let $U^* \in U_2$ be a suitable approximation of $\phi^*$. The proofs of necessity for Propositions 3.2.1–3.2.3 are similar to the proofs of necessity for Propositions 3.1.1–3.1.3, and are therefore omitted. □

## A.3   Proof of Propositions 3.3.1–3.3.3

### Sufficiency

Integrating (A.5) by parts, we obtain

$$U'(\bar{z})\left[\sum_{t=0}^{T} V_t'(\xi^t)(\mu_{F_t^1} - \mu_{G_t^1})\right] + U''(\bar{z})\left[\sum_{t=0}^{T} V_t'(\xi^t)(F_t^3(\bar{z}) - G_t^3(\bar{z}))\right]$$

$$- \int_{\underline{z}}^{\bar{z}} U'''(z)\left[\sum_{t=0}^{T} V_t'(\xi^t)(F_t^3(z) - G_t^3(z))\right]dz \geq 0. \qquad (A.9)$$

Since by assumption $U'(z) \geq 0$, $U''(z) \leq 0$, and $U'''(z) \geq 0$, we are looking for conditions which guarantee that the three terms within brackets in (A.9) are nonpositive.

*Case 1:* $(U, V) \in V_1 \times U_3$. Clearly, $\mu_{F_t^1} \geq \mu_{G_t^1}$ (for all $t = 0, 1, ..., T$) and $F_t^3(z) \leq G_t^3(z)$ (for all $t = 0, 1, ..., T$ and all $z \in [\underline{z}, \bar{z}]$) are sufficient for (A.9) to hold.

*Case 2:* $(U, V) \in V_2 \times U_3$. Appealing to the partial summation formula of Abel, the first term within brackets in (A.9) will be nonpositive if and only if

$$\sum_{t=0}^{T-1} (V_t'(\xi^t) - V_{t+1}'(\xi^{t+1}))\left[\sum_{s=0}^{t} \Delta\mu_{G_s^1}\right] + V_T'(\xi^T)\left[\sum_{s=0}^{T} \Delta\mu_{G_s^1}\right] \geq 0. \qquad (A.10)$$

Performing a similar exercise with the third bracketed term in (A.9), we obtain

$$\sum_{t=0}^{T-1} (V_t'(\xi^t) - V_{t+1}'(\xi^{t+1}))\left[\sum_{s=0}^{t} \Delta G_s^3(z)\right] + V_T'(\xi^T)\left[\sum_{s=0}^{T} \Delta G_s^3(z)\right] \geq 0. \qquad (A.11)$$

Therefore $\sum_{s=0}^{t} \mu_{F_s^1} \geq \sum_{s=0}^{t} \mu_{G_s^1}$ (for all $t = 0, 1, ..., T$) and $\sum_{s=0}^{t} F_s^3(z) \leq \sum_{s=0}^{t} G_s^3(z)$ (for all $t = 0, 1, ..., T$ and all $z \in [\underline{z}, \bar{z}]$) are clearly sufficient for (A.9) to hold.

*Case 3:* $(U, V) \in V_3 \times U_3$. Appealing once again to the partial summation formula of Abel, (A.10) can be rewritten as follows:

$$\sum_{t=0}^{T-2} ((V_t'(\xi^t) - V_{t+1}'(\xi^{t+1})) - (V_{t+1}'(\xi^{t+1}) + V_{t+2}'(\xi^{t+2})))\left[\sum_{s=0}^{t} \sum_{r=0}^{s} \Delta\mu_{G_r^1}\right]$$

$$+ (V_{T-1}'(\xi^{T-1}) - V_T'(\xi^T))\left[\sum_{s=0}^{T-1} \sum_{r=0}^{s} \Delta\mu_{G_r^1}\right]$$

$$+ V_T'(\xi^T)\left[\sum_{s=0}^{T} \Delta\mu_{G_s^1}\right] \geq 0. \qquad (A.12)$$

Similarly, an analogous manipulation within (A.11) yields

$$\sum_{t=0}^{T-2}((V_t'(\xi^t)-V_{t+1}'(\xi^{t+1}))-(V_{t+1}'(\xi^{t+1})-V_{t+2}''(\xi^{t+2})))\left[\sum_{s=0}^{t}\sum_{r=0}^{s}\Delta G_r^3(z)\right]$$

$$+(V_{T-1}'(\xi^{T-1})-V_T'(\xi^T))\left[\sum_{s=0}^{T-1}\sum_{r=0}^{s}\Delta G_r^3(z)\right]$$

$$+V_T'(\xi^T)\left[\sum_{s=0}^{T}\Delta G_s^3(z)\right]\ge 0. \tag{A.13}$$

We conclude that conditions (b1) and (b2) (resp. (b3) and (b4)) are sufficient for (A.12) (resp. (A.13)) to hold.

### Necessity

We argue by way of contradiction, and consider successively the cases
where condition (b) of Propositions 3.3.1–3.3.3 is not satisfied.

*Case 1:* $(U,V)\in V_1\times U_3$. Suppose first that condition (b2) of Proposition
3.3.1 is false, and let $z^*$ be the smallest $z$ such that $P_3(z;x^{(T)})>P_3(z;y^{(T)})$.
Choose $V^*:=(V_0^*,V_1^*,...,V_T^*)$ defined by $V_s^*(u)=0$ for all $s\neq t^*$ and by
$V_{t^*}^*(u)=u$ for all $u\in\mathbb{R}$; clearly, $V^*\in V_1$. Furthermore, define

$$\phi^*(z):=\begin{cases}-\frac{1}{2}(z-z^*)^2 & \text{if } \underline{z}\le z<z^*,\\ 0 & \text{if } z^*\le z\le\bar{z},\end{cases} \tag{A.14}$$

and let $U^*\in U_3$ be a suitable approximation of $\phi^*$. We obtain $\Delta W_{V\cdot U^*}=$
$[P_3(z^*;y')-P_3(z^*;x')]z^*<0$ and hence a contradiction. Suppose next
that condition (b1) of Proposition 3.3.1 is false and let $t^*$ be the smallest
$t$ such that $\mu_{F_t'}<\mu_{G_t'}$. Choosing $V^*:=(V_0^*,V_1^*,...,V_T^*)$ as before and taking $U^*(z):=z$, we obtain $\Delta W^*=\mu_{F_{t^*}'}-\mu_{G_{t^*}'}<0$.

*Case 2:* $(U,V)\in V_2\times U_3$. Suppose first that condition (b2) of Proposition 3.3.2 is false, and let $(t^*,z^*)$ be the smallest couple $(t,z)$ such that
$P_3(z;x^{(t)})>P_3(z;y^{(t)})$. Then we arrive at a contradiction taking $V^*:=$
$(V_0^*,V_1^*,...,V_T^*)$ such that $V_s^*(u)=u$ for all $s=0,1,...,t^*$ and $V_s^*(u)=0$
for all $s=t^*+1,...,T$. Suppose next that condition (b1) of Proposition
3.3.2 is false, and let $t^*$ be the smallest $t$ such that $\sum_{s=0}^{t}\mu_{F_s'}<\sum_{s=0}^{t}\mu_{G_s'}$.
Choosing $V^*:=(V_0^*,V_1^*,...,V_T^*)$ as before and taking $U^*(z):=z$, we ar-
rive once again at a contradiction.

*Case 3:* $(U,V)\in V_3\times U_3$. We consider successively the four necessary
conditions of Proposition 3.3.3. Suppose that (b1) is false and let $(t^*,z^*)$
be the smallest couple $(t,z)$ such that $\sum_{s=0}^{t}\sum_{r=0}^{s}\mu_{F'_{(r)}}>\sum_{s=0}^{t}\sum_{r=0}^{s}\mu_{G'_{(r)}}$.
We arrive at a contradiction by choosing $U^*(z):=z$ and $V^*:=(V_0^*,V_1^*,...,$
$V_T^*)$ such that $V_s^*(u)=(t^*-s+1)u$ for all $s=0,1,...,t^*$ and $V_s^*(u)=0$ for
all $s=t^*+1,...,T$. In the case where (b2) is not fulfilled, a contradiction is
reached by choosing $U^*$ as before and taking $V^*:=(V_0^*,V_1^*,...,V_T^*)$ such

that $V_s^*(u) = u$ for all $s = 0, 1, ..., T$. Suppose next that (b3) is false, and let $(t^*, z^*)$ be the smallest couple $(t, z)$ such that $P_3(z; \bar{x}^{(t)}) > P_3(z; \bar{y}^{(t)})$. Choosing $U^*$ as defined in (A.14) and taking $V^* := (V_0^*, V_1^*, ..., V_T^*)$ such that $V_s^*(u) = (t^* - s + 1)u$ for all $s = 0, 1, ..., t^*$ and $V_s^*(u) = 0$ for all $s = t^* + 1, ..., T$, we arrive at a contradiction. Finally, in the case where (b4) is false, we arrive at a contradiction by choosing $U^*$ as just defined and letting $V_s^*(u) = u$ for all $s = 0, 1, ..., T$. $\square$

## REFERENCES

Atkinson, A. B. (1970), "On the Measurement of Inequality," *Journal of Economic Theory* 2: 244-63.

Atkinson, A. B., and F. Bourguignon (1987), "Income Distributions and Differences in Needs," in G. R. Feiwel (ed.), *Arrow and the Foundation of the Theory of Economic Policy*. New York: Macmillan.

Bishop, J. A., J. P. Formby, and P. D. Thistle (1991), "Rank Dominance and International Comparisons of Income Distributions," *European Economic Review* 35: 1399-1409.

Bohren, O., and T. Hansen (1980), "Capital Budgeting with Unspecified Discount Rates," *Scandinavian Journal of Economics* 82: 45-58.

Dalton, H. (1920), "The Measurement of the Inequality of Incomes," *Economic Journal* 30: 348-61.

Dasgupta, P., A. K. Sen, and D. Starrett (1973), "Notes on the Measurement of Inequality," *Journal of Economic Theory* 6: 180-7.

Davies, J., and M. Hoy (1991), "Making Inequality Comparisons when Lorenz Curves Intersect," discussion paper no. 1991-12, Department of Economics, University of Guelph, Ontario.

Ekern, S. (1981), "Time Dominance Efficiency Analysis," *Journal of Finance* 36: 1023-34.

Fields, G. S., and J. C. H. Fei (1978), "On Inequality Comparisons," *Econometrica* 46: 305-16.

Fishburn, P. C., and R. G. Vickson (1978), "Theoretical Foundations of Stochastic Dominance," in G. A. Whitmore and M. C. Findlay (eds.), *Stochastic Dominance*. Lexington, MA: Lexington Books.

Foster, J. E., and A. F. Shorrocks (1988), "Poverty Orderings and Welfare Dominance," *Social Choice and Welfare* 5: 179-98 (reprinted in W. Gaertner and P. K. Pattanaik (eds.), *Distributive Justice and Inequality*, Berlin: Springer).

Jenkins, S. P. (1991), "Income Inequality and Living Standards: Changes in the 1970s and 1980s," *Fiscal Studies* 12: 1-28.

Karcher, T., P. Moyes, and A. Trannoy (1993), "The Stochastic Dominance Ordering of Income Distributions over Time: II - The Expected Utility of the Discounted Sum of Incomes," discussion paper, Faculté des Sciences Economiques et de Gestion, Laboratoire d'Analyse et de Recherche Economiques, Pessac.

Karcher, T., and A. Trannoy (1992), "Criteria of Stochastic and Temporal Dominance with Application to the Comparison of Career Profiles in National Education" (in French), discussion paper, Faculté des Sciences Economique, Centre de Recherche en Economie Mathématique et Économétrie, Rennes.

Kolm, S.-C. (1976), "Unequal Inequalities I," *Journal of Economic Theory* 12: 416-42.

Maasoumi, E., and S. Zandvakili (1990), "Generalized Entropy Measures of Mobility for Different Sexes and Income Levels," *Journal of Econometrics* 43: 121-33.

Malinvaud, E. (1977), *Leçons de Théorie Microéconomique,* 4th ed. Paris: Dunod.

Muliere, P., and M. Scarsini (1989), "A Note on Stochastic Dominance and Inequality Measurement," *Journal of Economic Theory* 49: 314-23.

Rothschild, M., and J. E. Stiglitz (1973), "Some Further Results on the Measurement of Inequality," *Journal of Economic Theory* 6: 188-204.

Sen, A. K. (1973), *On Economic Inequality.* Oxford: Clarendon Press.

Shorrocks, A. F. (1983), "Ranking Income Distributions," *Economica* 50: 3-17.

Shorrocks, A. F., and J. E. Foster (1987), "Transfer Sensitive Inequality Measures," *Review of Economic Studies* 54: 485-97.

Trannoy, A., and T. Karcher (1991), "Temporal Dominance Criteria with Application to the Comparison of Career Profiles in National Education" (in French), discussion paper, Faculté des Sciences Economique, Centre de Recherche en Economie Mathématique et Économétrie, Rennes.

# Social choice and welfare
## *Conference program*

*Caen, June 9–12, 1992*

### Plenary sessions

AMARTYA SEN   Harvard University
"Rationality and Social Choice"
KENNETH ARROW   Stanford University
"The Political Basis of Economic Reform in Eastern Europe"

### Regular sessions

*Theme 1: Equity*

*Session 1: Equality of opportunity*
RICHARD ARNESON   University of California, San Diego
"Equality"
JOHN E. ROEMER   University of California, Davis
"Implementing a Social Policy of Equality of Opportunity for Welfare"
MARC FLEURBAEY   University of California, Davis
"Equal Opportunity or Equal Social Outcome"
JOHN HARSANYI   University of California, Berkeley
"Utilities, Preferences, and Substantive Goods"

*Session 2: Equity as no-envy*
SERGE-CHRISTOPHE KOLM
Ecole Nationale Superieure des Ponts et Chaussées, Paris
"Super-Equity"
RAJIV VOHRA   Brown University
"Equity and Efficiency in Nonconvex Economies"

*Session 3: Fair division*
WILLIAM THOMSON   University of Rochester
"Population Monotonicity"
BHASKAR DUTTA   Indian Statistical Institute, Dehli
"A Characterization of Egalitarian Equivalence"
YVES SPRUMONT   Université de Montréal
"Axiomatizing Ordinal Welfare Egalitarianism"

*Session 4: Fair division*
ENRIQUETA ARAGONES   Northwestern University
"A Solution to the Envy-Free Selection Problem in Economies
with Indivisible Goods"
JORGE NIETO   Universidad Pública de Navarra
"Stable and Consistent Solutions on Economic Environments"
HONORATA SOSNOWSKA   Warsaw School of Economics
"Some Further Remarks on the Voluntary Exchange of
Libertarian Rights"

*Session 5: Axiomatic cooperative games*
HERVÉ MOULIN   Duke University
"Axiomatic Comparison of Cost Sharing Methods"
WALTER BOSSERT   University of Waterloo
"Generalized Ginis and Cooperative Bargaining Solutions"
KOICHI TADENUMA   Hitotsubashi University
"Reduced Games, Consistency, and the Core"

*Session 6: Axiomatic cooperative games*
MYRNA HOLTZ WOODERS   University of Toronto
"An Axiomatization of the Core for Finite and Continuum
Games"
EYAL WINTER   The Hebrew University of Jerusalem
"On Bargaining Position Descriptions in Non-Transferable
Utility Games: Symmetry versus Asymmetry"

*Session 7: Axiomatic bargaining and cooperative games*
JOHANN K. BRUNNER   University of Linz
"Bargaining with Reasonable Aspirations"
HANNU SALONEN   University of Oulu
"A Note on Continuity of Bargaining Solutions"
ANDREAS PFINGSTEN   Universität-Gesamthochschule-Siegen
"Profit-Based Payment Schemes in the Banking Sector"

ELENA YANOWSKAYA
St. Petersburg Institute for Economics and Mathematics
"A Connection between Social Choice Functions and
Solutions of Cooperative Game Theory"

*Session 8: Measurement of inequality*
JAMES E. FOSTER  Vanderbilt University
"Polarization and the Decline of the Middle Class:
Canada and the United States"
UDO EBERT  University of Oldenburg
"Income Inequality and Differences in Household Size"
THIERRY KARCHER, PATRICK MOYES, & ALAIN TRANNOY
Université de Bordeaux
"The Welfare Ranking of Income Distributions over
Time"
ELCHANAN BEN PORATH  Northwestern University
"Linear Measures, the Gini Index, and the Income–Equality
Trade-off"

*Session 9: Measurement of inequality*
C. R. BARRETT  University of Birmingham
"Measures of Inequality and Poverty, and Fuzzy
Comparisons"
VALENTINO DARDANONI  University of California, San Diego
"Measuring Social Mobility"
MANIMAY SENGUPTA  University of Canterbury, New Zealand  and
PRASANTA PATTANAIK  University of California, Riverside
"On an Index of Poverty"

*Session 10: Inequality measures*
PETER J. LAMBERT  University of York
"Taxes and the Level of the Playing Field"
FRANCOIS MANIQUET  University of Namur
"Surplus-Value and Inequality Measurement"
JOLANDA VAN LEEUWEN  Erasmus University, Rotterdam
"Ranking Welfare Distributions, Does It Make Sense?"
DULCE CONTRERAS  Universitat de Valéncia
"Simulating and Comparing Income's Distributions"
TOMAS PHILIPSON  University of Chicago
"Inequality Measurement in Segregation and Individual
Preferences"

*Theme 2: Individual and collective choice*

*Session 11: Individual choices*
WILLIAM BARNETT    Washington University in St. Louis
"Exact Aggregation under Risk"
JOHN BROOME    University of Bristol
"Causes of Preference Are Not Objects of Preference"
DAVID SCHMEIDLER    Tel Aviv University and Ohio State University
"On the Uniqueness of Subjective Probabilities"

*Session 12: Orders and utilities*
ITZHAK GILBOA    Northwestern University
"Additive Representations of Non-Additive Measures"
CARMEN HERRERO    University of Alicante
"Numerical Representation of Acyclic Preferences on a
Countable Set"
TON STORCKEN    Tilburg University
"Towards an Axiomatization of Orderings"
MARLIES KLEMISCH-AHLERT    University of Osnabrück
"Freedom of Choice: A Comparison of Different Rankings of
Opportunity Sets"
JUAN-ENRIQUE MARTINEZ-LEGAZ    University of Barcelona
"Compatible Preorders and Linear Operators on $\mathbb{R}^n$"

*Session 13: Aggregation of preferences*
IAIN MCLEAN    University of Warwick
"The First Golden Age of Social Choice, 1784–1803"
DONALD E. CAMPBELL    William and Mary    and
JERRY KELLY    Syracuse University
"$T$ or $1 - T$? That Is the Trade-off"
BERNARD LECLERC & BERNARD MONJARDET
Ecoles des Hautes Etudes, Paris
"Ordinal Theory of Consensus"
JOHN A. WEYMARK    University of British Columbia
"Generalized Median Social Welfare Functions"
FRANCIS BLOCH    Brown University
"Nondictatorial Social Welfare Functions with Different
Discrimination Structures"
JAMES REDEKOP    University of Waterloo
"Arrow Theorems in Nonstandard Economic Environments"

*Session 14: Aggregation of preferences*
MARCIN MALAWSKI
Institute of Computer Science, Polish Academy of Sciences
"Social Choice Theory without the Pareto Principle: A
Simple Proof of Wilson's Theorem"
ESTEBAN INDURAIN   Universidad Publica de Navarra
"Aggregation of Preferences: An Algebraic Overview"
OLIVIER HUDRY
Ecole Nationale Supérieure des Télécommunications, Paris
"Complexity of Aggregation Problems"
NICOLAS ANDJIGA   Université de Yaoundé
"A Note on the Dominance of a Constitution"

*Session 15: Choice functions and tournaments*
TARADAS BANDYOPADHYAY   University of California, Riverside
"Path Independence, Rational Choice, and von Neumann–
Morgenstern Rationalization"
MARK JOHNSON   University of Alabama
"A Computational Approach to the Problem of Collective
Choice"
JEAN-FRANCOIS LASLIER
Conservatoire National des Arts et Metiers, Paris
"Choosing from a Tournament: A Progress Report"
JEAN LAINÉ   Keele University
"On Regular Contractible Tournaments"
GILBERT LAFFOND   Conservatoire National des Arts et Metiers, Paris
"The Mixed Strategy Equilibrium of a Tournament Zero-Sum
Game"

*Session 16: Information pooling*
SVEN BERG   University of Lund
"Condorcet's Jury Theorem, Dependency among Jurors"
V. L. KREPS & N. N. VOROB'EV
St. Petersburg Institute for Economics and Mathematics
"On the Probability of Combined Outcome for Independent
Choices"

*Session 17: Formal models of rights*
PRASANTA K. PATTANAIK   University of California, Riverside   and
KOTARO SUZUMURA   Hitotsubashi University
"Individual Rights and Social Evaluations: A Conceptual
Framework"

EDWARD J. GREEN   University of Minnesota
"On the Origins of Limited Government"
PETER J. HAMMOND   Stanford University
"A Third Formulation of Rights"
RAJ DEB   Southern Methodist University
"Waiver, Effectivity, and Rights as Game Forms"

*Session 18: Strategy-proofness*
SALVADOR BARBERA   Universitat Autonoma de Barcelona
"Strategy-proof Exchange"
SCOTT SHENKER   Palo Alto Research Center, Xerox Corporation
"On the Strategy-proof and Smooth Allocation of Private
Goods in Production Economies"
JORDI MASSO   Universitat Autonoma de Barcelona
"Voting under Constraints"
MICHEL LE BRETON   Université d'Aix-Marseille II
"Strategy-proof Social Choice Functions over Product
Domains with Unconditional Preferences"

*Session 19: Strategy-proofness*
DIEGO MORENO   University of Arizona
"Nonmanipulable Decision Mechanisms for Economic
Environments"
HANS PETERS   Rijksuniversiteit Limburg
"On Uncompromisingness and Strategy-proofness"
JOSÉ ALCALDE   Universitat Autonoma de Barcelona
"Top Dominance and the Possibility of Strategy-proof Stable
Solutions to the Marriage Problem"
DOMINIQUE LEPELLEY & BONIFACE MBIH   Université de Caen
"The Vulnerability of Four Social Choice Functions to
Coalitional Manipulation of Preferences"
NICK BAIGENT   Tulane University
"Strategy-proofness and Aggregations of Choice Functions"

*Session 20: Implementation under complete information*
MATTHEW JACKSON   Northwestern University
"Implementing Social Choice Functions: A New Look at
Some Impossibility Results"
SANJAY STRIVASTAVA   Carnegie–Mellon University
"Sophisticated Voting Rules: The Case of Two Tournaments"
TILMAN BÖRGERS   University College London
"A Note on Implementation and Strong Dominance"

*Session 21: Implementation under incomplete information*
JACQUES CRÉMER   Université des Sciences Sociales, Toulouse   and
CLAUDE D'ASPREMONT   Université Catholique de Louvain
"New Results on the Existence of Bayesian Incentive
Compatible Mechanisms"
CLAUDIO MEZZETTI   University of North Carolina, Chapel Hill
"Bayesian and Weakly Robust First-Best Mechanisms:
Characterizations"
ARUNAVA SEN   Indian Statistical Institute, New Delhi
"Implementation in Bayesian Equilibrium"

*Session 22: Implementation*
STEF TIJS   Tilburg University
"Effectivity Functions and Associated Claim Game
Correspondences"
LUIS CORCHÓN   Universitat D'Alacant
"Robust Implementation under Alternative Information
Structures"
TAKEHIKO YAMATO   Tokyo University
"Nash Implementation and Double Implementation: An
Equivalence Theorem"
FRANK PAGE, JR.   University of Alabama
"Bayesian Incentive Compatible Mechanisms"


*Theme 3: Political economy*

*Session 23: Voting systems*
ROGER B. MYERSON   Northwestern University
"Effectiveness of Electoral Systems for Reducing Government
Corruption: A Game-Theoretic Analysis"
ROBERT J. WEBER   Northwestern University
"Polls, Election History, and Coordination in Three-way
Elections: Some Experimental Evidence"
WILLIAM V. GEHRLEIN   University of Delaware
"Condorcet Efficiency and Social Homogeneity"
DONALD G. SAARI   Northwestern University
"Symmetry Extensions of 'Neutrality': Advantage to the
Condorcet Loser"

*Session 24: Voting systems*
LEWIS A. KORNHAUSER & JEAN PIERRE BENOIT   New York University
"Voting Simply in the Election of Assemblies"

ALAN TAYLOR   Union College
   "Quasi-Weightings, Trading, and Desirability Relations in
   Simple Games, I"
WILLIAM S. ZWICKER   Union College
   "Quasi-Weightings, Trading, and Desirability Relations in
   Simple Games, II"
ANDRANIK TANGUIANE   Institut National Polytechnique de Grenoble
   "Inefficiency of Democratic Decision Making in Unstable
   Society"
BURT L. MONROE   Lincoln College, University of Oxford
   "Paired Comparisons and the Theory of Social Choice"

*Session 25: Political games*
DAVID AUSTEN-SMITH   University of Rochester
   "Strategic Transmission of Costly Information"
JEFFREY BANKS   University of Rochester
   "Repeated Elections with Candidate Uncertainty"
REBECCA MORTON   Texas A & M University
   "Special Interests, Parties, and Platform Divergence"
NORMAN SCHOFIELD   Washington University in St. Louis
   "Probability and Convergence of the Core"
CRAIG TOVEY   Georgia Institute of Technology
   "Instability, Stability, and Dynamical Convergence of the Core"

*Session 26: Political games*
ARTHUR LUPIA   University of California, San Diego
   "Direct Legislation and the Paradox of Competition"
SAMUEL MERRILL III   Wilkes University
   "An Empirical Test of the Proximity and Directional Models
   of Spatial Competition: Voting in Norway and Sweden"
BERNARD GAUTHIER   Hautes Etudes Commerciales, Montreal
   "Hierarchies and Delegation of Contracts"
SUZANNE LOHMANN   Stanford University
   "Delegation and the Regulation of Risk"
JAMES SNYDER   University of Chicago
   "The Dimensions of Constituency Preferences: Voting on
   California Ballot Propositions, 1974–1990"

*Session 27: Ethics, law, and social choice*
JOHN DROBAK   Washington University
   "The Constitutional Requirements of 'Government by Purchase'
   in a Democratic State"

JOHN FEREJOHN   Stanford University
   "Interpretative Conventions and the Construction of Statutes"
JAMES JOHNSON   Northwestern University   and
JACK KNIGHT   University of Chicago
   "Jurisprudence and the Strategic Behavior of Courts"
ANDREW RUTTEN   Cornell University
   "The Neglected Politics of Constitutional Reform"


*Session 28: Public goods*
RICHARD CORNES   The Australian National University
   "Dyke Maintenance and Other Stories: Some Neglected Types
   of Public Goods"
ALAIN TRANNOY   C.R.E.M.E. University of Cergy-Pontoise
   "The Private Provision of Public Good in the Case of Satiation
   Points: The Case of a Quasi-Linear Economy"
HANS WIESMETH   Universität Bonn
   "The Equivalence of Core and Lindahl Equilibria in an
   Economy with Semi-Public Goods"


*Session 29: Public finance*
LOUIS GEVERS   Facultés Notre-Dame De La Paix, Namur
   "Private Information and Redistribution"
JONATHAN HAMILTON
   University of Florida and Universitat Autonoma de Barcelona
   "The Separation of Allocation and Distribution in
   Second-Best Economies"
ALISON WATTS   Duke University
   "Insolvency and the Division of Cleanup Costs"


*Theme 4: Markets and games*


*Session 30: Market equilibrium*
STEVEN BRAMS   New York University
   "Two-Stage Auctions"
GRACIELA CHICHILNISKY   Columbia University
   "Markets and Social Choices"
PHILIPPE MICHEL   Université de Paris 1
   "Economic Growth from a Normative Point of View:
   Historical Background and New Considerations"
ANTONIA VILLAR   University of Alicante
   "Positive Profits, Increasing Returns, and Social Equilibrium"

ALEXANDER VASIN   Moscow University
"The Convergence to Competitive Equilibrium and the
Conditions of Pure Competition"

*Session 31: Noncooperative games*
JOHN O. LEDYARD   California Institute of Technology
"Characterization of Interim Efficiency in a Public Goods
Problem"
THOMAS PALFREY   California Institute of Technology
"Learning in Repeated Games of Incomplete Information"

*Session 32: Bargaining*
IVAN MENSHIKOV
Computing Center of the Russian Academy of Science, Moscow
"A Model of Negotiation in an Extensive-Form Game"
BENNY MOLDOVANU   Universität Bonn
"Delay and Other Effects of Externalities on Negotiation"
CLARA PONSATI OBIOLS   Universitat Autonoma de Barcelona
"Unique Equilibrium in a Model of Bargaining over Many
Issues"
JOSEPH ABDOU   Université de Paris
"Solvability of Game Forms: The Infinite Case"

*Session 33: Strategic cooperative games*
BEZALEL PELEG   The Hebrew University of Jerusalem
"Coalition-proof Correlated Equilibria"
SHLOMO WEBER   University of York, Toronto
"Stable Coalition Structures with Unidimensional Set of
Alternatives"
BETH ALLEN   University of Pennsylvania
"Incentives in Market Games with Asymmetric Information:
The Core"

*Session 34: Strategic cooperative games*
KAUSHIK BASU   Dehli School of Economics
"Group Rationality, Utilitarianism, and Escher's Waterfall"
LIN ZHOU   Yale University
"A Refined Bargaining Set of an N-Person Game and
Endogenous Coalition Formation"
MICHEL TRUCHON   Université de Laval
"Voting Games and Acyclic Collective Choice Rules"

JUNE PARKER   The University of Hull
"Extreme Points of the Core of a Convex Game"
HANS HALLER   Virginia Polytechnic Institute and State University
"Collusion Properties of Values"

*Session 35: Evolutionary models of cooperation*
PEYTON YOUNG   University of Maryland
"An Evolutionary Model of Bargaining"
DAVID CANNING   Columbia University
"The Evolution of Language Conventions in Common Interest:
Signaling Games"

*Session 36: Experiments*
WULF GAERTNER   Universität Osnabrück
"Evaluation via Extended Orderings: Some Empirical Findings"
OLGA MENSHIKOVA   Laboratory of Experimental Economics, Moscow
"Laboratory Market in Moscow"
MARK OLSON   University of Amsterdam
"An Experimental Examination of the Assignment Problem:
Nontransfer Mechanisms"
CHRISTIAN SEIDL   Universität Kiel
"An Empirical Rejection of the Dependency of Distributional
Attitudes on Subjective Income Evaluation and Work
Participation"